Lecture Notes in Computer Science 10514

Commenced Publication in 1973
Founding and Former Series Editors:
Gerhard Goos, Juris Hartmanis, and Jan van Leeuwen

More information about this series at http://www.springer.com/series/7409

Regina Bernhaupt · Girish Dalvi
Anirudha Joshi · Devanuj K. Balkrishan
Jacki O'Neill · Marco Winckler (Eds.)

Human-Computer Interaction – INTERACT 2017

16th IFIP TC 13 International Conference
Mumbai, India, September 25–29, 2017
Proceedings, Part II

 Springer

Editors
Regina Bernhaupt
Ruwido Austria GmbH
Neumarkt am Wallersee
Austria

Devanuj K. Balkrishan
Indian Institute of Technology Bombay
Mumbai
India

Girish Dalvi
Indian Institute of Technology Bombay
Mumbai
India

Jacki O'Neill
Microsoft Research Centre India
Bangalore
India

Anirudha Joshi
Indian Institute of Technology Bombay
Mumbai
India

Marco Winckler 🔘
Université Paul Sabatier
Toulouse
France

ISSN 0302-9743   ISSN 1611-3349 (electronic)
Lecture Notes in Computer Science
ISBN 978-3-319-67683-8   ISBN 978-3-319-67684-5 (eBook)
DOI 10.1007/978-3-319-67684-5

Library of Congress Control Number: 2017953425

LNCS Sublibrary: SL3 – Information Systems and Applications, incl. Internet/Web, and HCI

Printed on acid-free paper

This Springer imprint is published by Springer Nature
The registered company is Springer International Publishing AG
The registered company address is: Gewerbestrasse 11, 6330 Cham, Switzerland

Foreword

The 16th IFIP TC13 International Conference on Human–Computer Interaction, INTERACT 2017, took place during September 25–29, 2017, in Mumbai, India. This conference was held on the beautiful campus of the Indian Institute of Technology, Bombay (IIT Bombay) and the Industrial Design Centre (IDC) was the principal host. The conference was co-sponsored by the HCI Professionals Association of India and the Computer Society of India, in cooperation with ACM and ACM SIGCHI. The financial responsibility of INTERACT 2017 was taken up by the HCI Professionals Association of India.

The International Federation for Information Processing (IFIP) was created in 1960 under the auspices of UNESCO. The Technical Committee 13 (TC13) of the IFIP aims at developing the science and technology of human–computer interaction (HCI). TC13 has representatives from 36 countries, apart from 16 expert members and observers. TC13 started the series of INTERACT conferences in 1984. These conferences have been an important showcase for researchers and practitioners in the field of HCI. Situated under the open, inclusive umbrella of the IFIP, INTERACT has been truly international in its spirit and has attracted researchers from several countries and cultures. The venues of the INTERACT conferences over the years bear a testimony to this inclusiveness.

In 2017, the venue was Mumbai. Located in western India, the city of Mumbai is the capital of the state of Maharashtra. It is the financial, entertainment, and commercial capital of the country and is the most populous city in India. *Mumbaikars* might add that it is also the most hardworking.

The theme of INTERACT 2017 was "Global Thoughts, Local Designs." The theme was designed to let HCI researchers respond to challenges emerging in the new age of global connectivity where they often design products for users who are beyond their borders belonging to distinctly different cultures. As organizers of the conference, we focused our attention on four areas: *India, developing countries, students,* and *research.*

As the first INTERACT in the subcontinent, the conference offered a distinctly Indian experience to its participants. The span of known history of India covers more than 5,000 years. Today, India is the world's largest democracy and a land of diversity. Modern technology co-exists with ancient traditions within the same city, often within the same family. Indians speak 22 official languages and hundreds of dialects. India is also a hub of the information technology industry and a living laboratory of experiments with technology for developing countries.

INTERACT 2017 made a conscious effort to lower barriers that prevent people from developing countries from participating in conferences. Thinkers and optimists believe that all regions of the world can achieve human development goals. Information and communication technologies (ICTs) can support this process and empower people to achieve their full potential. Today ICT products have many new users and many new uses, but also present new challenges and provide new opportunities. It is no surprise that HCI researchers are showing great interest in these emergent users. INTERACT 2017 provided a platform to explore these challenges and opportunities but also made it easier for people from developing countries to participate. We also introduced a new track called Field Trips, which allowed participants to directly engage with stakeholders within the context of a developing country.

Students represent the future of our community. They bring in new energy, enthusiasm, and fresh ideas. But it is often hard for students to participate in international conferences. INTERACT 2017 made special efforts to bring students to the conference. The conference had low registration costs and several volunteering opportunities. Thanks to our sponsors, we could provide several travel grants. Most importantly, INTERACT 2017 had special tracks such as Installations, a Student Design Consortium, and a Student Research Consortium that gave students the opportunity to showcase their work.

Finally, great research is the heart of a good conference. Like its predecessors, INTERACT 2017 aimed to bring together high-quality research. As a multidisciplinary field, HCI requires interaction and discussion among diverse people with different interest and background. The beginners and the experienced, theoreticians and practitioners, and people from diverse disciplines and different countries gathered together in Mumbai to learn from each other and to contribute to each other's growth. We thank all the authors who chose INTERACT 2017 as the venue to publish their research.

We received a total of 571 submissions distributed in two peer-reviewed tracks, five curated tracks, and seven juried tracks. Of these, the following contributions were accepted:

- 68 Full Papers (peer reviewed)
- 51 Short Papers (peer reviewed)
- 13 Case Studies (curated)
- 20 Industry Presentations (curated)
- 7 Courses (curated)
- 5 Demonstrations (curated)
- 3 Panels (curated)
- 9 Workshops (juried)
- 7 Field Trips (juried)
- 11 Interactive Posters (juried)
- 9 Installations (juried)
- 6 Doctoral Consortium (juried)
- 15 Student Research Consortium (juried)
- 6 Student Design Consortium (juried)

The acceptance rate for contributions received in the peer-reviewed tracks was 30.7% for full papers and 29.1% for short papers. In addition to full papers and short papers, the present proceedings feature contributions accepted in the form of case studies, courses, demonstrations, interactive posters, field trips, and workshops.

The final decision on acceptance or rejection of full papers was taken in a Program Committee meeting held in Paris, France, in March 2017. The full-paper chairs, the associate chairs, and the TC13 members participated in this meeting. The meeting discussed a consistent set of criteria to deal with inevitable differences among the large number of reviewers. The final decisions on other tracks were made by the corresponding track chairs and reviewers, often after additional electronic meetings and discussions.

INTERACT 2017 was made possible by the persistent efforts over several months by 49 chairs, 39 associate chairs, 55 student volunteers, and 499 reviewers. We thank them all. Finally, we wish to express a special thank you to the proceedings publication co-chairs, Marco Winckler and Devanuj Balkrishan, who did extraordinary work to put together four volumes of the main proceedings and one volume of adjunct proceedings.

September 2017   Anirudha Joshi
                                                         Girish Dalvi
                                                      Marco Winckler

IFIP TC13 (http://ifip-tc13.org/)

Established in 1989, the International Federation for Information Processing Technical Committee on Human–Computer Interaction (IFIP TC 13) is an international committee of 37 member national societies and 10 Working Groups, representing specialists of the various disciplines contributing to the field of human–computer interaction (HCI). This includes (among others) human factors, ergonomics, cognitive science, computer science, and design. INTERACT is its flagship conference of IFIP TC 13, staged biennially in different countries in the world. The first INTERACT conference was held in 1984 running triennially and became a biennial event in 1993.

IFIP TC 13 aims to develop the science, technology, and societal aspects of HCI by: encouraging empirical research; promoting the use of knowledge and methods from the human sciences in design and evaluation of computer systems; promoting better understanding of the relation between formal design methods and system usability and acceptability; developing guidelines, models, and methods by which designers may provide better human-oriented computer systems; and, cooperating with other groups, inside and outside IFIP, to promote user-orientation and humanization in system design. Thus, TC 13 seeks to improve interactions between people and computers, to encourage the growth of HCI research and its practice in industry and to disseminate these benefits worldwide.

The main focus is to place the users at the center of the development process. Areas of study include: the problems people face when interacting with computers; the impact of technology deployment on people in individual and organizational contexts; the determinants of utility, usability, acceptability, and user experience; the appropriate allocation of tasks between computers and users especially in the case of automation; modeling the user, their tasks, and the interactive system to aid better system design; and harmonizing the computer to user characteristics and needs.

While the scope is thus set wide, with a tendency toward general principles rather than particular systems, it is recognized that progress will only be achieved through both general studies to advance theoretical understanding and specific studies on practical issues (e.g., interface design standards, software system resilience, documentation, training material, appropriateness of alternative interaction technologies, guidelines, the problems of integrating multimedia systems to match system needs, and organizational practices, etc.).

In 2015, TC 13 approved the creation of a Steering Committee (SC) for the INTERACT conference. The SC is now in place, chaired by Jan Gulliksen and is responsible for:

- Promoting and maintaining the INTERACT conference as the premiere venue for researchers and practitioners interested in the topics of the conference (this requires a refinement of the aforementioned topics)
- Ensuring the highest quality for the contents of the event

- Setting up the bidding process to handle the future INTERACT conferences; decision is made up at TC 13 level
- Providing advice to the current and future chairs and organizers of the INTERACT conference
- Providing data, tools and documents about previous conferences to the future conference organizers
- Selecting the reviewing system to be used throughout the conference (as this impacts the entire set of reviewers)
- Resolving general issues involved with the INTERACT conference
- Capitalizing history (good and bad practices)

In 1999, TC 13 initiated a special IFIP Award, the Brian Shackel Award, for the most outstanding contribution in the form of a refereed paper submitted to and delivered at each INTERACT. The award draws attention to the need for a comprehensive human-centered approach in the design and use of information technology in which the human and social implications have been taken into account. In 2007, IFIP TC 13 also launched an Accessibility Award to recognize an outstanding contribution in HCI with international impact dedicated to the field of accessibility for disabled users. In 2013 IFIP TC 13 launched the Interaction Design for International Development (IDID) Award that recognizes the most outstanding contribution to the application of inter-active systems for social and economic development of people in developing countries. Since the process to decide the award takes place after papers are sent to the publisher for publication, the awards are not identified in the proceedings.

IFIP TC 13 also recognizes pioneers in the area of HCI. An IFIP TC 13 pioneer is one who, through active participation in IFIP Technical Committees or related IFIP groups, has made outstanding contributions to the educational, theoretical, technical, commercial, or professional aspects of analysis, design, construction, evaluation, and use of interactive systems. IFIP TC 13 pioneers are appointed annually and awards are handed over at the INTERACT conference.

IFIP TC 13 stimulates working events and activities through its Working Groups (WGs). Working Groups consist of HCI experts from many countries, who seek to expand knowledge and find solutions to HCI issues and concerns within their domains. The list of Working Groups and their area of interest is given here.

WG13.1 (Education in HCI and HCI Curricula) aims to improve HCI education at all levels of higher education, coordinate and unite efforts to develop HCI curricula and promote HCI teaching.

WG13.2 (Methodology for User-Centered System Design) aims to foster research, dissemination of information and good practice in the methodical application of HCI to software engineering.

WG13.3 (HCI and Disability) aims to make HCI designers aware of the needs of people with disabilities and encourage the development of information systems and tools permitting adaptation of interfaces to specific users.

WG13.4 (also WG2.7) (User Interface Engineering) investigates the nature, con-cepts, and construction of user interfaces for software systems, using a framework for reasoning about interactive systems and an engineering model for developing user interfaces.

WG 13.5 (Resilience, Reliability, Safety and Human Error in System Development) seeks a frame-work for studying human factors relating to systems failure, develops leading-edge techniques in hazard analysis and safety engineering of computer-based systems, and guides international accreditation activities for safety-critical systems.

WG13.6 (Human-Work Interaction Design) aims at establishing relationships between extensive empirical work-domain studies and HCI design. It promotes the use of knowledge, concepts, methods, and techniques that enable user studies to procure a better apprehension of the complex interplay between individual, social, and organizational contexts and thereby a better understanding of how and why people work in the ways that they do.

WG13.7 (Human–Computer Interaction and Visualization) aims to establish a study and research program that will combine both scientific work and practical applications in the fields of HCI and visualization. It integrates several additional aspects of further research areas, such as scientific visualization, data mining, information design, computer graphics, cognition sciences, perception theory, or psychology, into this approach.

WG13.8 (Interaction Design and International Development) is currently working to reformulate its aims and scope.

WG13.9 (Interaction Design and Children) aims to support practitioners, regulators, and researchers to develop the study of interaction design and children across international contexts.

WG13.10 (Human-Centered Technology for Sustainability) aims to promote research, design, development, evaluation, and deployment of human-centered technology to encourage sustainable use of resources in various domains.

New Working Groups are formed as areas of significance in HCI arise. Further information is available on the IFIP TC13 website at: http://ifip-tc13.org/

IFIP TC13 Members

Officers

Chair

Philippe Palanque, France

Vice-chair for Growth and Reach Out INTERACT Steering Committee Chair

Jan Gulliksen, Sweden

Vice-chair for Working Groups

Simone D.J. Barbosa, Brazil

Vice-chair for Awards

Paula Kotze, South Africa

Treasurer

Virpi Roto, Finland

Secretary

Marco Winckler, France

Webmaster

Helen Petrie, UK

Country Representatives

Australia
Henry B.L. Duh
Australian Computer Society

Austria
Geraldine Fitzpatrick
Austrian Computer Society

Brazil
Raquel Oliveira Prates
Brazilian Computer Society (SBC)

Bulgaria
Kamelia Stefanova
Bulgarian Academy of Sciences

Canada
Lu Xiao
Canadian Information Processing Society

Chile
Jaime Sánchez
Chilean Society of Computer Science

Croatia
Andrina Granic
Croatian Information Technology Association (CITA)

Cyprus
Panayiotis Zaphiris
Cyprus Computer Society

Czech Republic
Zdeněk Míkovec
Czech Society for Cybernetics and Informatics

Denmark
Torkil Clemmensen
Danish Federation for Information
    Processing

Finland
Virpi Roto
Finnish Information Processing
    Association

France
Philippe Palanque
Société informatique de France (SIF)

Germany
Tom Gross
Gesellschaft für Informatik e.V.

Hungary
Cecilia Sik Lanyi
John V. Neumann Computer Society

India
Anirudha Joshi
Computer Society of India (CSI)

Ireland
Liam J. Bannon
Irish Computer Society

Italy
Fabio Paternò
Italian Computer Society

Japan
Yoshifumi Kitamura
Information Processing Society of Japan

Korea
Gerry Kim
KIISE

The Netherlands
Vanessa Evers
Nederlands Genootschap voor
    Informatica

New Zealand
Mark Apperley
New Zealand Computer Society

Nigeria
Chris C. Nwannenna
Nigeria Computer Society

Norway
Dag Svanes
Norwegian Computer Society

Poland
Marcin Sikorski
Poland Academy of Sciences

Portugal
Pedro Campos
Associacão Portuguesa para o Desen-
volvimento da Sociedade da Informaçåo
    (APDSI)

Singapore
Shengdong Zhao
Singapore Computer Society

Slovakia
Wanda Benešová
The Slovak Society for Computer
    Science

Slovenia
Matjaž Debevc
The Slovenian Computer Society
    INFORMATIKA

South Africa
Janet L. Wesson
The Computer Society of South Africa

Spain
Julio Abascal
Asociación de Técnicos de Informática
    (ATI)

Sweden
Jan Gulliksen
Swedish Interdisciplinary Society
  for Human–Computer Interaction
Swedish Computer Society

Switzerland
Denis Lalanne
Swiss Federation for Information
  Processing

Tunisia
Mona Laroussi
Ecole Supérieure des Communications
  De Tunis (SUP'COM)

UK
José Abdelnour Nocera
British Computer Society (BCS)

United Arab Emirates
Ghassan Al-Qaimari
UAE Computer Society

USA
Gerrit van der Veer
Association for Computing Machinery
  (ACM)

Expert Members

Dan Orwa	University of Nairobi, Kenya
David Lamas	Tallinn University, Estonia
Dorian Gorgan	Technical University of Cluj-Napoca, Romania
Eunice Sari	University of Western Australia, Australia and UX Indonesia, Indonesia
Fernando Loizides	Cardiff University, UK and Cyprus University of Technology, Cyprus
Frank Vetere	University of Melbourne, Australia
Ivan Burmistrov	Moscow State University, Russia
Joaquim Jorge	INESC-ID, Portugal
Marta Kristin Larusdottir	Reykjavik University, Iceland
Nikolaos Avouris	University of Patras, Greece
Paula Kotze	CSIR Meraka Institute, South Africa
Peter Forbrig	University of Rostock, Germany
Simone D.J. Barbosa	PUC-Rio, Brazil
Vu Nguyen	Vietnam
Zhengjie Liu	Dalian Maritime University, China

Observer

Masaaki Kurosu, Japan

Working Group Chairs

**WG 13.1 (Education in HCI
and HCI Curricula)**

Konrad Baumann, Austria

**WG 13.2 (Methodologies
for User-Centered System Design)**

Marco Winckler, France

WG 13.3 (HCI and Disability)

Helen Petrie, UK

WG 13.4/2.7 (User Interface Engineering)

José Creissac Campos, Portugal

WG 13.5 (Resilience, Reliability, Safety, and Human Error in System Development)

Chris Johnson, UK

WG 13.6 (Human-Work Interaction Design)

Pedro Campos, Portugal

WG 13.7 (HCI and Visualization)

Peter Dannenmann, Germany

WG 13.8 (Interaction Design and International Development)

José Adbelnour Nocera, UK

WG 13.9 (Interaction Design and Children)

Janet Read, UK

WG 13.10 (Human-Centered Technology for Sustainability)

Masood Masoodian, Finland

Conference Organizing Committee

General Conference Chairs

Anirudha Joshi, India
Girish Dalvi, India

Technical Program Chair

Marco Winckler, France

Full-Paper Chairs

Regina Bernhaupt, France
Jacki O'Neill, India

Short-Paper Chairs

Peter Forbrig, Germany
Sriganesh Madhvanath, USA

Case Studies Chairs

Ravi Poovaiah, India
Elizabeth Churchill, USA

Courses Chairs

Gerrit van der Veer, The Netherlands
Dhaval Vyas, Australia

Demonstrations Chairs

Takahiro Miura, Japan
Shengdong Zhao, Singapore
Manjiri Joshi, India

Doctoral Consortium Chairs

Paula Kotze, South Africa
Pedro Campos, Portugal

Field Trips Chairs

Nimmi Rangaswamy, India
José Abdelnour Nocera, UK
Debjani Roy, India

Industry Presentations Chairs

Suresh Chande, Finland
Fernando Loizides, UK

Installations Chairs

Ishneet Grover, India
Jayesh Pillai, India
Nagraj Emmadi, India

Keynotes and Invited Talks Chair

Philippe Palanque, France

Panels Chairs

Antonella De Angeli, Italy
Rosa Arriaga, USA

Posters Chairs

Girish Prabhu, India
Zhengjie Liu, China

Student Research Consortium Chairs

Indrani Medhi, India
Naveen Bagalkot, India
Janet Wesson, South Africa

Student Design Consortium Chairs

Abhishek Shrivastava, India
Prashant Sachan, India
Arnab Chakravarty, India

Workshops Chairs

Torkil Clemmensen, Denmark
Venkatesh Rajamanickam, India

Accessibility Chairs

Prachi Sakhardande, India
Sonali Joshi, India

Childcare Club Chairs

Atish Patel, India
Susmita Sharma, India

Food and Social Events Chair

Rucha Tulaskar, India

Local Organizing Chairs

Manjiri Joshi, India
Nagraj Emmadi, India

Proceedings Chairs

Marco Winckler, France
Devanuj Balkrishan, India

Sponsorship Chair

Atul Manohar, India

Student Volunteers Chairs

Rasagy Sharma, India
Jayati Bandyopadhyay, India

Venue Arrangements Chair

Sugandh Malhotra, India

Web and Social Media Chair

Naveed Ahmed, India

Program Committee

Associated Chairs

Simone Barbosa, Brazil
Nicola Bidwell, Namibia
Pernille Bjorn, Denmark
Birgit Bomsdorf, Germany
Torkil Clemmensen, Denmark
José Creissac Campos, Portugal
Peter Forbrig, Germany
Tom Gross, Germany
Jan Gulliksen, Sweden
Nathalie Henry Riche, USA
Abhijit Karnik, UK
Dave Kirk, UK
Denis Lalanne, Switzerland
Airi Lampinen, Sweden
Effie Law, UK
Eric Lecolinet, France
Zhengjie Liu, China
Fernando Loizides, UK
Célia Martinie, France
Laurence Nigay, France

Monique Noirhomme, Belgium
Philippe Palanque, France
Fabio Paterno, Italy
Helen Petrie, UK
Antonio Piccinno, Italy
Kari-Jouko Raiha, Finland
Dave Randall, Germany
Nimmi Rangaswamy, India
John Rooksby, UK
Virpi Roto, Finland
Jan Stage, Denmark
Frank Steinicke, Germany
Simone Stumpf, UK
Gerrit van der Veer, The Netherlands
Dhaval Vyas, India
Gerhard Weber, Germany
Janet Wesson, South Africa
Marco Winckler, France
Panayiotis Zaphiris, Cyprus

Reviewers

Julio Abascal, Spain
José Abdelnour Nocera, UK
Silvia Abrahão, Spain
Abiodun Afolayan Ogunyemi, Estonia
Ana Paula Afonso, Portugal
David Ahlström, Austria
Muneeb Ahmad, Australia
Deepak Akkil, Finland
Sarah Alaoui, France
Komathi Ale, Singapore
Jan Alexandersson, Germany
Dzmitry Aliakseyeu, The Netherlands
Hend S. Al-Khalifa, Saudi Arabia
Fereshteh Amini, Canada
Junia Anacleto, Brazil
Mads Schaarup Andersen, Denmark
Leonardo Angelini, Switzerland
Huckauf Anke, Germany
Craig Anslow, New Zealand
Nathalie Aquino, Paraguay
Oscar Javier Ariza Núñez, Germany
Parvin Asadzadeh, UK
Uday Athavankar, India
David Auber, France
Nikolaos Avouris, Greece
Sohaib Ayub, Pakistan
Chris Baber, UK
Cedric Bach, France
Naveen Bagalkot, India
Jan Balata, Czech Republic
Emilia Barakova, The Netherlands
Pippin Barr, Denmark
Oswald Barral, Finland
Barbara Rita Barricelli, Italy
Michel Beaudouin-Lafon, France
Astrid Beck, Germany
Jordan Beck, USA
Roman Bednarik, Finland
Ben Bedwell, UK
Marios Belk, Germany
Yacine Bellik, France
David Benyon, UK
François Bérard, France

Arne Berger, Germany
Nigel Bevan, UK
Anastasia Bezerianos, France
Sudhir Bhatia, India
Dorrit Billman, USA
Pradipta Biswas, India
Edwin Blake, South Africa
Renaud Blanch, France
Mads Bødker, Denmark
Cristian Bogdan, Sweden
Rodrigo Bonacin, Brazil
Claus Bossen, Denmark
Paolo Bottoni, Italy
Nadia Boukhelifa, France
Nina Boulus-Rødje, Denmark
Judy Bowen, New Zealand
Margot Brereton, Australia
Roberto Bresin, Sweden
Barry Brown, Sweden
Emeline Brulé, France
Nick Bryan-Kinns, UK
Sabin-Corneliu Buraga, Romania
Ineke Buskens, South Africa
Adrian Bussone, UK
Maria Claudia Buzzi, Italy
Marina Buzzi, Italy
Federico Cabitza, Italy
Diogo Cabral, Portugal
Åsa Cajander, Sweden
Eduardo Calvillo Gamez, Mexico
Erik Cambria, Singapore
Pedro Campos, Portugal
Tara Capel, Australia
Cinzia Cappiello, Italy
Stefan Carmien, Spain
Maria Beatriz Carmo, Portugal
Luis Carriço, Portugal
Stefano Carrino, Switzerland
Géry Casiez, France
Fabio Cassano, Italy
Thais Castro, Brazil
Vanessa Cesário, Portugal
Arnab Chakravarty, India

Matthew Chalmers, UK
Teresa Chambel, Portugal
Chunlei Chang, Australia
Olivier Chapuis, France
Weiqin Chen, Norway
Mauro Cherubini, Switzerland
Fanny Chevalier, France
Yoram Chisik, Portugal
Eun Kyoung Choe, USA
Mabrouka Chouchane, Tunisia
Elizabeth Churchill, USA
Gilbert Cockton, UK
Ashley Colley, Finland
Christopher Collins, Canada
Tayana Conte, Brazil
Nuno Correia, Portugal
Joelle Coutaz, France
Rui Couto, Portugal
Céline Coutrix, France
Nadine Couture, France
Lynne Coventry, UK
Benjamin Cowan, Ireland
Paul Curzon, UK
Edward Cutrell, India
Florian Daiber, Germany
Nick Dalton, UK
Girish Dalvi, India
Jose Danado, USA
Chi Tai Dang, Germany
Ticianne Darin, Brazil
Jenny Darzentas, Greece
Giorgio De Michelis, Italy
Clarisse de Souza, Brazil
Ralf de Wolf, Belgium
Andy Dearden, UK
Dmitry Dereshev, UK
Giuseppe Desolda, Italy
Heather Desurvire, USA
Amira Dhouib, Tunisia
Ines Di Loreto, Italy
Paulo Dias, Portugal
Shalaka Dighe, India
Tawanna Dillahunt, USA
Anke Dittmar, Germany
Andre Doucette, Canada
Pierre Dragicevic, France

Steven Drucker, USA
Carlos Duarte, Portugal
Julie Ducasse, France
Andreas Duenser, Australia
Bruno Dumas, Belgium
Paul Dunphy, UK
Sophie Dupuy-Chessa, France
Sourav Dutta, India
James Eagan, France
Grace Eden, Switzerland
Brian Ekdale, USA
Linda Elliott, USA
Chris Elsden, UK
Morten Esbensen, Denmark
Florian Evéquoz, Switzerland
Shamal Faily, UK
Carla Faria Leitao, Brazil
Ava Fatah gen. Schieck, UK
Camille Fayollas, France
Tom Feltwell, UK
Xavier Ferre, Spain
Pedro Ferreira, Denmark
Sebastian Feuerstack, Brazil
Patrick Tobias Fischer, Germany
Geraldine Fitzpatrick, Austria
Rowanne Fleck, UK
Daniela Fogli, Italy
Asbjørn Følstad, Norway
Manuel J. Fonseca, Portugal
Renata Fortes, Brazil
André Freire, UK
Parseihian Gaëtan, France
Radhika Gajalla, USA
Teresa Galvão, Portugal
Nestor Garay-Vitoria, Spain
Roberto García, Spain
Jose Luis Garrido, Spain
Franca Garzotto, Italy
Isabela Gasparini, Brazil
Cally Gatehouse, UK
Sven Gehring, Germany
Stuart Geiger, USA
Helene Gelderblom, South Africa
Cristina Gena, Ireland
Cristina Gena, Italy
Vivian Genaro Motti, USA

Manfred Tscheligi, Austria
Truna Turner, Australia
Markku Turunen, Finland
Pankaj Upadhyay, India
Heli Väätäjä, Finland
Pedro Valderas, Spain
Stefano Valtolina, Italy
Jan van den Bergh, Belgium
Thea van der Geest, The Netherlands
Davy Vanacken, Belgium
Jean Vanderdonckt, Belgium
Christina Vasiliou, Cyprus
Radu-Daniel Vatavu, Romania
Shriram Venkatraman, India
Nervo Xavier Verdezoto, UK
Himanshu Verma, Switzerland
Arnold P.O.S. Vermeeren,
   The Netherlands
Jo Vermeulen, Belgium
Chi Thanh Vi, UK
Nadine Vigouroux, France
Jean-Luc Vinot, France
Dong Bach Vo, UK
Lin Wan, Germany

Xiying Wang, USA
Yi Wang, USA
Ingolf Waßmann, Germany
Jenny Waycott, Australia
Gerald Weber, New Zealand
Kurtis Weir, UK
Benjamin Weyers, Germany
Jerome White, USA
Graham Wilson, UK
Heike Winshiers-Theophilus, Namibia
Wolfgang Woerndl, Germany
Katrin Wolf, Germany
Andrea Wong, USA
Nelson Wong, Canada
Gavin Wood, UK
Adam Worrallo, UK
Volker Wulf, Germany
Naomi Yamashita, Japan
Pradeep Yammiyavar, India
Tariq Zaman, Malaysia
Massimo Zancanaro, Italy
Juergen Ziegler, Germany
Gottfried Zimmermann, Germany

Sponsors and Partners

Silver Sponsors

Adobe

A NASSCOM INITIATIVE

LEAD PARTNERS

facebook

Gala Dinner Sponsor

Design Competition Sponsor

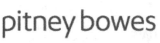

Pitney Bowes

Education Partners

Interaction Design Foundation (IDF)

Friends of INTERACT

Ruwido GmBH, Austria   Oxford University Press   Converge by CauseCode Technologies

Exhibitors

balsamiq®

Partners

International Federation for Information Processing

SIGCHI

In-cooperation with ACM   In-cooperation with SIGCHI

IDC
IIT Bombay

HCI Professionals'
Association of India

Industrial Design Centre, IIT Bombay   HCI Professionals' Association of India

Computer Society of India   IIT Bombay

Contents

Human Perception, Cognition and Behaviour

Information on Demand, on the Move, and Gesture Interaction

Interaction at the Workplace

Interaction with Children

Digital Inclusion

Contextualizing ICT Based Vocational Education for Rural Communities: Addressing Ethnographic Issues and Assessing Design Principles

K.P. Sachith[✉], Aiswarya Gopal, Alexander Muir,
and Rao R. Bhavani

AMMACHI Labs, Amrita School of Engineering, Amritapuri, Amrita Vishwa
Vidyapeetham, Amrita University, Coimbatore, India
{sachith.kp, aiswarya.madhu, alexander.muir}
@ammachilabs.org, bhavani@amrita.edu

Abstract. Recently, combining Information and Communication Technologies (ICT) with Technical Vocational Education and Training (TVET) for a low literate population is gaining interest, as this can lead to more effective socio-economic development. This strategy can more easily provide employment and bring community wide change because of the improved quality and relevance of education materialQuery. Although TVET providers are present throughout India that uses some ICT, challenges remain for prospective students including illiteracy, language, resource limits and gender boundaries. Providing TVET that is accessible to low-literate people in rural village communities requires a shift in the design of ICT so that it is universally useable, even for communities like tribal India that has a largely oral culture. In this article, we detail the design and development of an ICT driven TVET model for a mostly illiterate audience in rural India and measure its efficacy. Through our ethnographic and usability study with 60 low-literate oral and novice village users, we present the issues faced and the solutions we incorporated into our new model. The results show that users performed better in the vocational course units with the solutions incorporated.

Keywords: ICT4D · TVET

1 Introduction

Today, Information and Communication Technology (ICT) is becoming increasingly available to people around the globe, especially in developing countries. Smaller devices such as tablets and smart phones are available for increasingly cheaper rates, and are reaching all groups of people. There is increasing interest by researchers and NGOs in applying computers, mobile phones, and tablets for serving economically poor populations in the field of Information and Communication Technology for Development (ICT4D). Technology has proven to be an effective tool in alleviating poverty, in areas such as education, networking, and employment.

R. Bernhaupt et al. (Eds.): INTERACT 2017, Part II, LNCS 10514, pp. 3–12, 2017.
DOI: 10.1007/978-3-319-67684-5_1

Vocational training and skill development are connected to both economic productivity and social wellbeing [1]. TVET helps people to gain employment, especially those with limited formal education [2]. However, it is difficult to make TVET readily accessible to economically and educationally challenged communities, at first simply for its novelty, but more importantly because most technology has been designed for formally education, literate, and urban populations [3]. ICT driven TVET is a promising solution to accelerate learning for people with low literacy, as compared to conventional models because it is more easily adapted to multimedia instruction, but should be designed with the end user in mind. ICT elements like multimedia textbooks were found to be advantageous in reducing average learning time and in enhancing understanding of a subject matter when presented properly [4].

The User Interface (UI) of the ICT devices for TVET, need to be designed with the level of literacy of the target users in mind. The design process needs to be re-thought for the ICT4D context, where many of the basic assumptions that underpin the methods may not always hold true for low literate community. For example, many illiterate users are unfamiliar with the concepts of lists and the hierarchy used in modern UIs [5]. This paper shall discuss orality and its roots, as well as abstract versus operational thinking and its implications for ICT4D [6].

This paper will present the observations and results of a series of usability studies on low-literate, rural audiences using two units from a vocational training course for toilet construction in five villages in India. The tests were conducted to measure the efficacy of the package which included "pre-training" activity, contextual videos, and a supporting game module. Five tests[1] were conducted at different villages across the country from 2016 to 2017, with 60 illiterate and semiliterate participants. In the consecutive tests, problems were observed and analyzed at two different levels: user and the system level. Some solutions for these problems were included in the next trial of the test. The study discovered various issues related with the package we tested, and refinements were made iteratively on the instructional video, and design changes were incorporated into the UI of the game module. The paper also presents a pre-training module as a solution that empowers low literate rural audiences to more easily take up ICT for using vocational training. The module enables low literate users to physically use the devices, trains the user to listen to and answer questions, and introduces and familiarizes the user with the UIs and its components from the start.

2   Related Works

Introducing ICT into TVET has accelerated learning in populations with low- or semi-literacy. Bhavani et al. has demonstrated that using ICT in vocational education for rural populations is more flexible, accessible, and provides a high amount of scalability [2]. From the same study, it has been observed and analyzed that there are advantages to using interactive multimedia textbooks over standard formal school

---

[1] The first 5 tests were conducted from date to date, by staff at [Anonymous], in the following locations: Byse, Karnataka; 2 tests at Ettimadai, Coimbatore, Tamil Nadu; Kondalgavu, Chattisgarh; Gudipadichervu, Andhra.

textbooks. ICT becomes a powerful medium for providing TVET, especially for the rural sector, when compared with the traditional classroom setup designed for urban areas.

The target audience for ICT4D includes illiterate or semi-literate populations. For this reason, ICT4D researchers have proposed doing away with text-based instruction, and have instead recommended non-textual designs [7]. In this section, we shall discuss the various modalities available or introduced to overcome the issues faced by low-literate or semi-literate users, especially understanding and using abstract symbols and following navigation procedures. UIs that use voice, graphics, and video have been proposed to better meet the requirements of the target population. Audio-output as a means of instruction (as opposed to text) has become primary topic for research, as it is a more natural means of expression well suited to learners who may struggle with literacy (ibid). Multimodal interfaces such as the VideoKhethi, introduced by Cuendet et al., a mobile system, helps farmers to find and watch agricultural extension videos in their own language and dialect, have been developed for use on smart phones with graphics and touch interfaces including speech recognition. This was designed to help improve agricultural practices among rural groups [8]. Exploration of touch gestures to enable a better and natural experience for first-time; low-literate users have been conducted. Research has demonstrated that soft-key mapping on devices with keypads is more challenging for low-literate users [9]. According to the same study, ICT devices, like tablets, exploit the advantages of touch gestures, and needs no or comparatively less training for first time users, when compared with text driven devices like laptops or mini-computers.

Oral users are not necessarily acquainted with the system of abstract learning from books or other formal systems. Rather, learning often happens in the original environment, in concrete situations, and through practical experience. This means that learning and teaching happens in an informal, yet very immersive way where oral and visual transmission of knowledge is the primary mode of delivery. With this in mind, it is important to properly characterize the target audience. Sherwani et al. tries to better understand ICT4D users in terms of their thinking, communication and culture [10]. In their work, the illiterate community is not considered as less privileged, but referred as "oral users." Orality talks about how people think, communicate, and learn in a culture where writing has not become prevalent. Orality theory claims that writing has so fundamentally transformed consciousness in literate cultures that we—literate researchers—are unable to grasp how oral cultures and people function. When one develops a user centered design for oral users, consideration should be given to cultural practices of community knowledge building and transmission which includes: (a) organization and transmission of information, (b) learning information, and (c) remembering information.

3 Our Work

Our team is a South India-based organization, concentrating on developing technology enhanced vocational and skill development courses for empowering women, especially in villages and rural areas across the country [3]. We provide vocational courses using ICT devices, such as tablets and laptops, reinforced by expert trainers and post-training support. The educational model we use is a virtual media enhanced vocational course, which has been developed end to end by the team at AMMACHI Labs. The vocational training model follows a multimodal learning approach in which the user learns through verbal and nonverbal (audio, visual and textual) representations of the material. In order to test the efficacy of our approach, we took two units from our Rural Toilet Builder vocational course, focusing on training rural women in India to build toilets for their community.

3.1 Target Community

Usability tests were conducted at 5 different villages across the country from 2016 to 2017, with illiterate and semiliterate women participants (see Table 1). All of the women were from families that are financially supported by men and/or women working for daily wages, and in unskilled, manual work. Over 50% of our participants had little or no literacy, and less than 15% could read complex sentences. To test the level of literacy, participants were given a sheet of paper with some sentences on it in their mother tongue, and requested to read out what they could. As for the participants' familiarity with technology, mobile phones are the most common technology that these women may have seen or handled. None of them had previous experience in using tablet or a computer. The primary language for communication was Kannada, Tamil, and Hindi (depending on the location). Low-literate users think, communicate, and learn in a culture where writing has not become internalized. In order to make them eligible for a TVET model, the user were first introduced to the material through a physical training where they used physical gestures to answer questions. The training was taken to the next level by asking question through images and answering through picking the correct image. After this the same set of questions were asked through tablet devices and answered by touch-gestures, slowly equipping them to use technology-enhanced models for learning.

Table 1. Overview of the series of user studies

Study number, location and participant count	Study focus
1. Karnataka: 10	Get the toilet building training status of the program happening in Byse
2. Tamil Nadu: 12	Educational usability of the plum bob and site selection videos and interactive quizzes. Need for pretraining identified
3. Chhattisgarh: 8	Educational usability of the plum bob and site selection videos and interactive quizzes Pilot test of pretraining
4. Andhra Pradesh: 8	Educational usability of the plum bob and site selection videos and interactive quizzes. Pilot test of pretraining
5. Tamil Nadu: 10	Educational usability of the plum bob and site selection videos and interactive quizzes. Evaluation of pretraining

3.2 Experimental Setup – Application

The teaching application was driven by an animated character that is similar to a "traditional" village lady. This means she was wearing clothing similar to what our target population wears (sari), has a similar skin, hair, and eye color, wore common accessories (no fancy gold ornaments, etc.), and behaved in ways that were familiar to them. The language of instruction was also their mother tongue. A character narrator was introduced to the users so that they could more easily connect to the application in a grounded way, rather listening to instructions through a disembodied voice. The interface was designed with minimal text elements, and supported by graphics, animation and audio intelligible to a person who cannot read [11].

3.2.1 Classroom and Interactive Games

The classroom provides the theoretical knowledge of the vocational trade the student is learning, and the necessary concepts for the eventual occupation they are training for. Each classroom contains multimedia content: videos displaying recorded demonstrations and explanations by experts in the field, accompanied by animations, images, and some text. It gives theoretical knowledge on a specific component in the course through video footage, accompanied by text, audio, 2D and 3D illustrations and animations. In the toilet building course, the video included real women from a village in Tamil Nadu recorded in handling the different elements of construction. This is an important part of our training videos, as it boosts the confidence of the target students to see people they can identify with doing these new, sometimes difficult skills. The course also includes simple, interactive games in between classroom chapters that use 2D illustrations and animations to create interactive exercises where users navigate through practical, real-world scenarios and apply the theoretical knowledge gained through the classroom. This module requires the user to answer questions, played by audio, on the content provided in the instructional video. The response is given through a touch gesture, and is succeeded by a feedback screen which shows the correct response. This exercise is repeated to re-emphasize the concepts to the user. The user interface does not provide negative reinforcement for wrong responses from the user, in order to avoid reducing the student's enthusiasm; rather, it guides the user to the correct answer in case they make an error.

3.2.2 Practical Assessment

Following the classroom and intervening games, the user's understanding is assessed. The units we selected for the usability tests required both cognitive and operational skills, and the assessments reflect both. The student was assessed in an environment that allowed them to use the skills they were learning, and which was conducive for assessing cognitive skills. Cognitive skills were assessed with oral questions by the field staff on concepts taught in the training. Operational skills were assessed by asking the student to physically demonstrate the proper use of the tools explained in the classroom in the real world, where they are observed using the tools.

3.3   Experimental Setup – System Setup

The vocational training courses, and our usability tests, require a classroom set up to deliver the educational content to the participant. In terms of location, both urban areas and rural communities in India frequently lack both steady electricity and quiet, undisturbed spaces for maintaining a classroom environment. Rural areas are frequently difficult to reach and face a lack of facilities including secure rooms and poor internet connectivity. Our TVET design already addresses some of the environmental and social challenges that working in a rural, remote area bring, such as limited electricity, etc., through our innovative deployment model discussed at length in our other publications [3]. However, even after building local trust, providing training in low-infrastructure environments and encouraging enthusiasm from users, we still faced the issue of the users not fully understanding the original UI.

3.4   Iterations on Design Principles, Ethnographic Issues and Solutions Incorporated

The first and second usability study came up with issues which we have classified as:

3.4.1   Educational
The participants were mostly illiterate, first-time users of technology. The teaching methodology and the UI which was initially used were not effective enough with the target population. Many students failed to understand the concepts in the training or even how to use the UI. The primary challenge faced by participants was to think and consider concepts in abstract terms. This could be due a lack of formal schooling and exposure to abstract ideas in a formal setting. This is reflected in popular learning and development theories which argue that abstract thinking is learned mostly through formal, modern education models [12]. For example, user was able to understand the usage of the tool, i.e., a plum bob to check the level of the surface. But their knowledge was only restricted to checking the level of the bricks which was introduced to them, not to other materials. The users were also not familiar with a model of education where they needed to pay attention to a video, process the knowledge, and then apply it in the successive sections. Even for games, which were slightly easier to grasp, the participants struggled to understand that the games were meant to test concepts from the associated video classroom. The participants typically answered from their existing knowledge and life experience, even if it contradicted what was just taught in the classroom.

3.4.2   Interface Related Issues

3.4.2.1. Classroom
In the original classroom, the animations and the video footage used abstract symbols like a tick mark, crosses, and concentric circles to indicate correct or wrong procedures and to bring attention to a particular portion in the visual. This was initially not understood by the users, as it was the first time they were introduced to illustrations and animations using these abstract symbols. The video was narrated in the regional

language, but followed a more formal style that did not include some the regional terms or slang they were comfortable with. This caused the participants to misunderstand some topics discussed in the video. Following the initial user tests, the animations in the video were redesigned to be more contextual, and less abstract for better understanding in the successive tests. The operational skills were re-emphasized by repeating the instruction on proper usage of tool in the video. Some of the important changes in the iteration we made included changing the camera angles for the user so that they felt they were a part of the process, using close and tight shots for validation scenarios, using expressions and hand gestures to convey correct and wrong procedures, and included some consequences of doing a step in the wrong manner (see Fig. 1a and b).

(a)   **(b)**

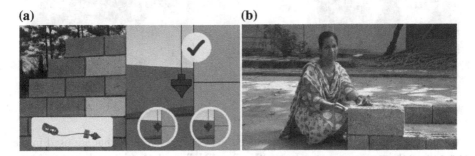

Fig. 1. (a, b) Comparing the initial version and final version of Plumbob video

3.4.2.2. User Interface

The original interface tested used buttons and abstract symbols to operate and navigate through the application. The concept of "navigation" was new to them. The application was navigated using buttons which used minimum text in the regional language. Abstract symbols such as ticks or cross marks were used as icons to give feedback to the user on a particular question. The game modules in this initial test introduced help videos in the introduction screen of each unit. This did not help the users much because this population is not familiar with the concept of "help videos". The user played the games with touch gestures, and each answer was followed by a feedback screen which showed the correct response. This was repeated to re-emphasize the concept to the user. A correct response was appreciated by the animation character by gestures to motivate and increase the engagement of the user.

3.4.2.3. Adjusting the UI and Introducing a Pre-training Module

In addition to adjusting the symbols used and perspective of the games and videos based on the first usability study, we designed and tested a "pre-training" module in the latter half of the usability studies. This was meant to help acquaint the students with the user interface and components of the training so that they would be more comfortable, and therefore successful in the training. The pre-training module includes a set of educational activities to develop the students' ability to understand different question templates and to understand and become familiar with the common elements used in the training. The pre-training session was mainly divided into: (a) Physical representation, (b) Paper prototype, and (c) Tablet interface. Each of the three sessions had all of the variations of questions in the interactive game module. The templates included: True or false, identify the parts of a particular object, sequencing steps, and answering by listening to a context and choosing the correct option from a set of options. In the first session, we demonstrated the symbols using our arms and hands, and asked the participants to reproduce the gesture, as shown in Figs. 2 and 3. All of the participants responded correctly with the new gestures. This equipped them to gain the knowledge of abstract symbols like right and wrong for answering a yes or no question.

Fig. 2. Physical tick gesture

Fig. 3. Paper prototype

In the paper prototype session, we introduced the abstract symbols that are used in the course through images on paper. Large "Yes" or "No" symbols (tick and cross) and the user interface were first introduced on paper. The participants were asked to touch the icon on the paper as their response to the set of questions. The same set of questions which was asked in the first and the second phase of the pre-training were reproduced on the tablets. While the participants seemed to grasp the abstract symbols and progression of the activity, there were still some issues in using the technology itself. Specifically, it was difficult for the participant to correctly understand the touch and the drag gesture, often applying too much pressure, not understanding the consequence of using too many fingers, or not touching for the appropriate length of time.

3.5 Quantitative and Qualitative Results

The above graphs (Figs. 4a and b) show the results of Study 2 and Study 5, which are two comparable user studies. Study 2 was the first time the challenges by students were

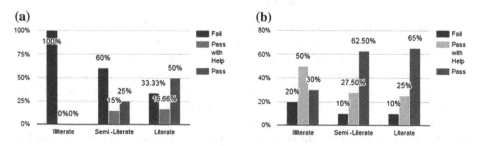

Fig. 4. (a, b) Rate of successfully answering questions

fully documented, and by Study 5 all of the improvements to the UI, including the pre-training, were tested. The results from studies 3 and 4 were helpful and provided more insight to us on what we could improve, however results are not usable for comparison cases in this analysis. The results are shown in terms of the participant's literacy levels: For the non-literate group, there is a dramatic change from 0% of questions being successfully answered, to 80% successfully answered. 30% of the questions were answered without help from the moderator. For the low-literacy and literate groups, there is also a notable shift. For low literacy participants, the percentage of questions answered without any help goes from 25% to 63%. During later studies the participants were noticeably more confident and less reluctant to use the system. These results are encouraging for future studies that can assess the learning of populations in other areas and in other contexts. The limitations of this study, including a limited population, on testing a single course (toilet building), and short time duration could be addressed in future work.

4   Conclusions

The results of comparing Study 2 and Study 5 (our two comparison cases) show a strong increase in the ease with which the non-literate students could engage with the tablet-based training. Contextualizing the content and introducing pre-training module helps students succeed because it gives them practice in using the interface to answer quiz-style questions. This approach demonstrates an initially effective strategy to address the challenges faced by illiterate and first time technology users in accessing vocational training. To date and using this model, we have successfully trained over 250 women who have collectively built over 250 toilets in 21 states across the country[2].

References

1. Work, D.: 2006 ILO Asia-Pacific Working Paper Series Subregional Office for South Asia, New Delhi Employment Challenge and Strategies in India an Assessment in the Framework of ILO's Global Employment Agenda (2008)
2. Bhavani, B., Sheshadri, S., Unnikrishnan. R.: Vocational education technology: rural India. In: Proceedings of the 1st Amrita ACM-W Celebration on Women in Computing in India. ACM (2010)
3. Coley, C., Sheshadri, S., Bhavani, R.R.: Ensuring training-transfer and personal performance after TVET: a strategy within the rural, Indian context for post-training engagement of TVET students for long-term success, pp. 1–14 (n.d.)
4. Ng, K.H., Komiya, R.: Multimedia textbook for virtual education environment. Eng. Sci. Educ. J. **11**(2), 73–79 (2002)
5. Medhi, I., Toyama, K., Joshi, A., Athavankar, U., Cutrell, E.: A comparison of list vs. hierarchical UIs on mobile phones for non-literate users. In: Kotzé, P., Marsden, G., Lindgaard, G., Wesson, J., Winckler, Marco (eds.) INTERACT 2013. LNCS, vol. 8118, pp. 497–504. Springer, Heidelberg (2013). doi:10.1007/978-3-642-40480-1_33

---

[2] For more information, please see our website: www.ammachilabs.org.

6. Price, P.: Multimedia technologies and solutions for educational applications: opportunities, trends and challenges. In: Proceedings of the 2007 IEEE 9th International Workshop on Multimedia Signal Processing, MMSP 2007 (0326214), pp. 3–8 (2007). doi:10.1109/MMSP.2007.4412804

7. Medhi, I., Toyama, K.: Full-context videos for first-time, non-literate PC users. In: 2007 International Conference on Information and Communication Technologies and Development, 2007 ICTD (2007). https://doi.org/10.1109/ICTD.2007.4937400

8. Cuendet, S., Medhi, I., Bali, K., Cutrell, E.: VideoKheti: making video content accessible to low-literate and novice users. In: CHI 2013, pp. 1–10 (2013)

9. Medhi I., Patnaik, S., Brunskill, E., Gautama, S.N.N., Thies, W., Toyama, K.: Designing mobile interfaces for novice and low-literacy users. ACM Trans. Comput.-Hum. Interact., **18**(1) (2011)

10. Sherwani, J., Ali, N., Rosé, C.P., Rosenfeld, R.: Orality-grounded HCID: understanding the oral user. Inf. Technol. Int. Dev. **5**(4), 37–50 (2009)

11. Manly, J., Touradji, P., Tang, M., Stern, Y.: Literacy and memory decline among ethnically diverse elders. J. Clin. Exp. Neuropsychol. **25**(5), 680–690 (2003). doi:10.1076/jcen.25.5.680.14579

12. Strauss, S.: Theories of cognitive development and their implications for curriculum development and teaching. In: Moon, B., Ben-Peretz, M., Brown, S. (eds.) Routledge International Companion to Education, pp. 33–50. Routledge, London (2000)

Enhancing Access to eLearning for People with Intellectual Disability: Integrating Usability with Learning

Theja Kuruppu Arachchi[1,2(✉)], Laurianne Sitbon[1],
and Jinglan Zhang[1]

[1] Science and Engineering Faculty, Queensland University of Technology,
Brisbane, QLD, Australia
theja.kuruppuarachchi@hdr.qut.edu.au,
{laurianne.sitbon, jinglan.zhang}@qut.edu.au
[2] Main Library, University of Ruhuna, Matara, Sri Lanka
tka@lib.ruh.ac.lk

Abstract. eLearning can provide people with Intellectual Disability (ID) extended learning opportunities in using information technology, thus potentially increasing digital inclusion. In order to make this a motivating experience, designs of eLearning are required to be compatible with their cognitive abilities. It is as yet unclear how to design an engaging eLearning environment that integrates usability with learning. This paper aims to explore the applicability of learning theories along with usability guidelines in designing an eLearning environment for people with ID. We discuss psychological theories on teaching and learning, and literature on challenges and opportunities of eLearning for people with ID. Based on that understanding, we present guidelines that integrate different learning theories with eLearning, for learner centered interaction design of eLearning modules for people with ID. We present a case study of applying these inclusive design considerations to an eLearning module about health information access.

Keywords: Accessibility and usability · Inclusive design · People with intellectual disability · eLearning · Human computer interaction (HCI)

1 Introduction and Background

Working with the Internet has been identified as a motivating involvement in digital participation among people with Intellectual Disability (ID). The Internet supports its user to be independent. Hence, as noted by Harrysson et al., the opportunity to use the Internet creates a "smart and awesome" episode for people with ID [1]. However many still experience difficulties when interacting with the Internet and accessing information. Rocha et al. reported that people with ID are able to increase their ability to navigate the Internet, provided that they receive continuous training [2]. Hence, the introduction of training programs on Internet access, for people with ID, is set to support them to improve and maintain their ability to engage with the Internet [3]. According to Sitbon et al., "satisfying an information need may act as a motivator to encourage users to

© IFIP International Federation for Information Processing 2017
Published by Springer International Publishing AG 2017. All Rights Reserved
R. Bernhaupt et al. (Eds.): INTERACT 2017, Part II, LNCS 10514, pp. 13–32, 2017.
DOI: 10.1007/978-3-319-67684-5_2

develop skills they may not otherwise be interested in developing" [4]. We aim to develop an accessible eLearning module that teaches people with ID to access online health information. This provides the opportunity to learn skills to use the Internet in an eLearning platform, while interacting with a computer and the Internet, in a motivating, learning environment [5].

eLearning also has the potential to support a learner to practice skills to use the Internet in context. eLearning, as the term itself denotes, is learning facilitated with technology [6]. eLearning delivers instruction using a web-based medium, for the learner to access remotely. In an eLearning platform, the learner uses the Internet to navigate through learning materials. eLearning allows the learner to practise at their own pace with adequate support [7]. The opportunity to learn skills to use the Internet, in an eLearning platform provides the learner with an appropriate environment for practising such skills. According to Kolb's experiential learning theory, which emphasises learning from experience, learning is a process "whereby knowledge is created through transformation of experience" [8]. Knowledge results from the combination of grasping and transforming experience. Hence, we posit that eLearning platforms best fit with such learning situations as improving skills to use the Internet.

Designing an eLearning module for people with ID needs to consider the learner's specific abilities and context. Version No. 031 of The Victorian Intellectually Disabled Persons Services Act 1986 defines intellectual disability thus:

"intellectual disability in relation to a person over the age of five years, means the concurrent existence of - (a) significant sub-average general intellectual functioning; and - (b) significant deficits in adaptive behaviour -each of which became manifest before the age of 18 years" [9].

Intellectual disability is different from "Learning Disability". According to official definition adopted by the Learning Disabilities Association of Canada January 30, 2002, learning disability is generally referred to as "a group of disorders, presumed due to central nervous system" [10]. In this paper, we investigate how to address the conceptual needs of people with ID, beyond the needs of people with learning disability. The main focus of the process of designing eLearning modules for people with ID should be guided by minimising the cognitive capacity required by the learner to interact with the system and the content in order to maximise the cognitive resources available for the learning process [11]. The eLearning designs should be usable and accessible to them.

eLearning designs should address the cognitive capacity, different abilities and needs of people with ID. Web accessibility has been outlined to ensure that "people with disabilities can perceive, understand, navigate, and interact with the web" [12]. Learning theories have suggestions on designing learning materials, considering the learner situation. The literature suggests that it is important to consider existing usability guidelines and learning theories together, in order to increase the accessibility, usability, and pedagogical values of eLearning designs [13], and offer the learner a motivating learning environment [14]. Learners with ID have not been included in most of the designs and the online collaborations present in the typical eLearning designs presently available. eLearning designs should allow people with ID to learn at their own pace. Most of the currently available eLearning approaches are knowledge driven. They aim to teach subject knowledge such as mathematics [15], languages and communication. Practice driven eLearning aims to support the learner to improve abilities through continued practical activities, such as practising skills to use computers and the Internet. Having on-site support persons, such as tutors, presents additional opportunities to develop the learner's education potential in eLearning [7]. The availability of such support people is often critical, and should be embedded in the design. The paucity of research on designing these types of eLearning for the people with ID, led us to investigate designing a motivating, rich eLearning experience for learners with ID. Addressing the gap in the literature, around eLearning design guidelines that integrate existing usability principles with strategies from learning and pedagogical psychology, this paper contributes a set of new guidelines that can be applied to a learner-centered interaction design of eLearning modules for people with ID.

In the forthcoming section, Sect. 2 of this article, we review studies on challenges and opportunities of eLearning for people with ID. In Sect. 3, we discuss psychological theories on teaching and learning, which will be used to understand design considerations for an eLearning module for people with ID. Then, we present a theoretical view of the interactions in an eLearning environment for people with ID in Sect. 4. In Sect. 5, these are incorporated in a functional model for eLearning design that integrates learning theories. Then we further integrate the identified learning theories into a theoretical framework of design guidelines for learner centered interaction design of eLearning environments for people with ID. Section 5 ends with a presentation of new design guidelines, which reflect the usability requirements as well as the pedagogical requirements of an eLearning environment for people with ID. In Sect. 6, we present an application of these guidelines in a case study that develops a prototype of an eLearning module for people with ID.

2   eLearning for People with Intellectual Disability

Information and communication technology (ICT) empowers people with ID. Although people with ID experience difficulties in meeting demands of day-to-day life compared to others [16], they can be supported to increase their capacity to be included in society by adjusting the environment, allowing them to experience, acquire and improve their abilities.

Renblad explored the views of people with ID on their experience with ICT and empowerment [17]. The study employed qualitative methods of data collection; study of original sources of groups' reports from a conference, participant observation and interviews. The study reports that information and communication technology increases the opportunities for people with ID to be involved in social relationships and make decisions. Opportunity to use technology in eLearning adds motivational value to the learning environment that leads to a better learning experience [14]. Hence, the eLearning module we design aims to empower people with ID to be included with the Internet and use online health information, which will be a support for them to look at their health issues with confidence.

Wong et al. explored ICT training needs among people with ID, with reference to their competency of using human computer interfaces [3]. A total of 57 people with mild or moderate intellectual disability, aged between 14 and 17 years participated in the study. Researchers identified that Microsoft's Internet Explorer (IE) was the most popular web browser among the participants, and that the most popular activities were exploring websites, searching with Yahoo, and working with bookmarks, as well as using the print and save functions. They defined three task categories: general, hardware related, and software related. Software-related tasks were to "start web browser, close web browser, explore websites, respond to dialog box, use customised bookmarks, add book marks, take printouts, save website, open saved website and use search engine". According to the performance of participants in the assigned tasks, the researchers concluded that the training programs for people with ID should be twofold: basic training associated with improving basic computer skills among low-performance groups, and advanced training on essential functions, including "orientation and attention" on the Internet. As Wong et al. noted, learning programs on computer skills designed for people with ID should be ability-specific.

Ogunbase designed a Web-Based Learning Environment (WBLE) model, and studied the effect of the learner's culture on their engagement with the learning environment [18]. According to the study, Ogunbase reported that the use of WBLE among African and European learners had been affected by different learning cultures shaped by their cultural background. Ogunbase highlights the need to consider cultural issues, in order to design WBLEs effectively. Hence, eLearning environments for people with ID should incorporate their cultural values.

For strengthening the interactions of people with ID with the learning environment, eLearning modules should be designed in conference with learning theories. Seo and Woo developed 'Math Explorer', a multimedia computer assisted instruction program for teaching mathematics for elementary level students with learning disabilities [15]. In the test for acceptance of the interface features, they identified three types of critical user interface design features: "instruction driven, manifest structure and adaptive interaction interfaces". One of the instruction driven features they identified was to introduce the subject content in small amounts. The other instruction-driven feature was to use visual representations, animations and graphics to provide an attractive and motivating experience. Manifest structure interface features were to "maintain simplicity and consistency", use "appropriate fonts and colours", and to highlight and colour-code the current tasks. Researchers utilised adaptive interaction interface features to provide feedback adaptive to student performance, and to support them with adaptive multimedia. According to the user study, Seo and Woo concluded that specific interface design guidelines should be incorporated in designs of computer assisted teaching programs, considering the capacity of the short-term memory of the students with learning difficulties.

Following a "community based ICT training program" for people with ID, Li-Tsang et al. conducted a study to identify additional support needed [19]. The interview with the participants of the training program and their caregivers showed that while the training program had increased the participants' interest in using computers, there remained the need for continued training on Internet use, with close support. Bunning et al. investigated the teachers' interaction with students with ID during eLearning [20]. They studied five single cases with severe intellectual disability, aged 11–18 years, using video ethnography. The study showed that teacher interaction supported the learner to increase their motivation to learn. Heath et al. reported that it was encouraging for the learner to have closer interaction with the teacher, who encouraged them with signposts "you do it, you have a go", with nonverbal behaviours, looking at the child and pointing at the screen, and then with movements prompting initiation of action. The study concluded that, on-site teacher interaction, as a mediator of eLearning, was a support for students with ID to execute learning activities better.

Together these studies indicated that eLearning environments for people with ID could create a motivating learning experience, when designed according to the learning theories attending to their specific needs.

3 Pedagogical Approaches for Learner Centered Design

Designing eLearning environments for people with ID is a complex process. eLearning design should devote attention to well-defined learning tasks as well as the usability of learning interfaces [21] that address leaners' needs and learning patterns [18]. Learning theories guide the design of motivating learning environments. eLearning modules need to be developed referring to the learning theories, so the contents and the presentation are psychologically appropriate to the learner' status quo.

The learning and teaching principles reported from decades of research and practice belong to three commonly accepted learning theories: behavioural theory, social cognitive theory and constructivist learning theory [22]. Different theorists describe different points relevant to teaching and learning situations. One single theory cannot address everything to be considered in a particular educational setting. Schunk states that it is necessary to "be eclectic" and use a blend of theories to address a learning situation [23]. Similarly, the American Psychological Association's Board of Educational Affairs used psychological principles belonging to these three theories, to define fourteen learner-centered psychological principles that provide a learner-centered approach for educational designs at schools [24]. Our contribution in this article is selecting the principles that are relevant and integrating them with eLearning design guidelines.

3.1 Behavioral Learning Theory

Behavioural theory explains the effect of external stimulators and inhibitors on the individual's behaviour. Skinner's theory, operant conditioning, clarifies learning as a behaviour to obtain or avoid the consequences that follow [25]. Accordingly, positive reinforcements can be incorporated in eLearning designs to encourage the learner to be engaged. Skinner's approach to achieve this is to define clear goals of instruction, sequence the subject content logically, allow learner's pace of learning, and provide immediate feedback for the learner's performance. Each phase is designed to be appropriately small enough and to include subject content that prepares the learner for the next phase, and supports the learner to complete the tasks at optimal speed [26].

3.2 Social Cognitive Theory

Social cognitive theory focuses on interactions of behavioural and personal factors with social settings. It explains that learning behaviours could be inspired through observing and imitating a model [22]. Hence, cognitive theory describes learning as an internal process in which the learner uses his memory, thinking reflection, abstraction and metacognition skills. Bandura described learning behaviour as a result of interactions among these three factors; personal characteristics, behavioural patterns and social environment [27]. According to Bandura, personal characteristics relate to beliefs about the ability to carry out learning tasks. Hence, clear goals and reduced anxiety support a better learning experience. Considering the learners' working memory capacity, subject content should be presented in appropriate amounts, and in sequence. Learning tasks should not overload the learners' working memory [28]. The learner must be supported to make memory links between new experiences and some related information from long-term memory. Hence, designs for eLearning should accommodate functions with familiar examples that increase the learners' ability to complete given tasks.

According to social cognitive theory, personal and behavioural factors dominate the environmental factors, in determining the learning behaviour. Bandura describes this concept as personal agency, which relates to the habit of self-controlled and self-regulated learning. The learner's preference for self-regulation suggests the need of endowing eLearning modules with choices for the learner according to their learning needs.

Online learning designs should include information in small amounts, and provide opportunity to link new knowledge with existing knowledge, and apply it in real life. Allowing for learner choice creates positive thinking to engage with learning activities.

3.3 Constructivist Learning Theory

Constructivism describes the nature of learning; how people develop as meaningful learners. It involves the learner' process of understanding how to perform a task according to a previous experience. Bruner described this type of learning as discovery learning [29]. According to Schunk, constructivist learning environments are designed for "meaningful learning" [23]. Teacher's involvement supports the learner to experience the topics in multiple perspectives.

Brooks and Brooks described five principles with reference to constructivist learning environments [30]. The first principle is to incorporate teaching lessons that "seek and value learners' points of view". It suggests the importance of considering the learners' perspectives when designing learning environments. Constructivist learning environments not only identify the learner, but also address them. Hence, a constructivist learning environment acknowledges relativity, talks to and with the learner, gives opportunity to express the learners' point of view, follows up with the learner's elaboration, and accounts for "interesting ideas" instead of grouping into "right" and "wrong" [30].

The second principle puts forward that constructivist learning environments are developed around primary concepts and "big ideas". Instead of presenting the curriculum in separate subtopics, the use of a holistic approach supports the learner to understand how the concepts relate as a whole [30]. Subject concepts for the eLearning module needs to be integrated with the holistic aim of supporting the learner. Structuring eLearning about online information seeking around "big ideas" and broad concepts supports the learner to understand multiple access points to the subject content.

According to the third principle, constructivist learning environments are designed to address the learners' suppositions. Learning activities are designed so that they support the learner to develop their skills, either consistent with, or counter to, the learners' beliefs. Cognitive, social and emotional demands of the learning materials are matched with the learner's abilities [30]. Brooks and Brooks' functional principles; "posing problems emerging relevance, structuring learning around primary concepts, and seeking and valuing students' points of view", assist curriculum designs that value student suppositions.

The fourth principle mentions that constructivist learning environments pose problems in emerging relevance. Relevant subject content is identified by probing pre-existing learning needs. An alternative strategy is to stimulate the learner's interest by allowing them to recognise the value for life [30].

The fifth principle deals with assessments, and declares that constructivist learning environments "assess student learning in the context of daily teaching". Instead of the true - false and multiple choice questions, constructivist learning environments conduct assessments by providing the learner the opportunity to demonstrate acquired skills, or to describe or discuss the learned topics in terms of value for their life [23]. This is used as a nonjudgmental feedback process between learners themselves and the instructor [30]. This type of assessment focusses on the next step after student feedback, that encourages teacher to consider redesigns for learning activities [23].

These learning theories, that are defined in three contexts: the learner behaviour (Behavioural learning theory), the learner's cognitive process (Social cognitive theory), and learning as an experience and learner development (Constructivist learning theory), can collectively be considered when designing eLearning environments.

4 Interaction Design and eLearning

Anderson describes six forms of educational interactions in online learning: student-student interactions, student-content interactions, student-teacher interactions, teacher-content interactions, teacher-teacher interactions, and content-content interactions [28]. Garrison states that the interactions among learners, subject content and the teacher, in online learning provide a connective and collaborative learning environment [31]. The theory of online learning interaction presented by Anderson suggests the possibility of substituting various forms of student interactions for each other, depending on the situations that matter ("costs, content, learning objectives, convenience, technology used and time availability"), without affecting the quality of learning. According to Anderson, maintaining an extensive mastery of one of the three forms of interactions is sufficient for successful learning [32]. However, in learner-centered design of eLearning, the value of learner-interface interaction cannot be discounted [11, 15, 33–35].

4.1 Interactions in eLearning

In an eLearning environment, the learner interacts directly with the interface to maintain the other interactions: with the teacher, with the content and with other students. Hence, we propose that interaction design of eLearning should consider four additional interactions: content-interface, learner-interface, teacher-interface, and interface- interface (Fig. 1).

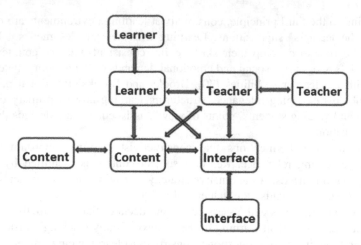

Fig. 1. A generic model of interactions in eLearning

Learner-Interface Interaction. The learner interacts with the interface to access learning material, to submit completed activities, discuss with peers and the teacher. The learners can read each others' discussion threads and post replies. Interface supports the learner to save and print the subject content as well as discussion pages.

Content-Interface Interaction. Content-interface interaction creates an opportunity to present the subject content in appropriate formats and in accessible amounts. It acts as the medium for instruction display. The content can be presented with readable font size, acceptable colours, relevant visual images, and concept maps. The presentation of content can be facilitated with audio and video descriptions.

Interface-Interface Interaction. Interface-interface interaction focuses on organisation of the eLearning module. It allows the learner to navigate between the subject content list, discussion threads, assessments and personal account from any page. The presentation of repetitive functions consistently in appropriate places of each page, supports the learner to navigate between pages and perform functions using a reduced amount of working memory.

Teacher-Interface Interaction. Teacher-interface interaction provides space for the teacher to introduce the module, present subject content, give announcements, introduce links to further reading, and clarify technical issues and assessment procedures.

A major factor that needs to be considered when designing an eLearning module that encourages these types of interactions is how to increase the learner's motivation. As pointed out by Li-Tsang et al., [19], people with ID need close support when learning digital skills. We propose that such context can include a tutor, who supports the leaner on-site. The tutor interacts with the learner and the eLearning interface, thus adding the following interactions to the model.

Tutor-Interface Interaction. The eLearning module for people with ID should include an additional tutor interface, with which the tutor directly interacts to support the learner by personalising the interface according to the learner preferences: font size, colours, level of challenge etc. Furthermore, the tutor may clarify welcome messages as well as help pages.

Tutor-Learner Interaction. The tutor interacts with the learner to support them to perform learning tasks, provide additional concrete examples from their day-to-day life, and clarify wording of the module where appropriate.

5 Integrating Usability with Learning

An eLearning module that maintains the above mentioned interactions performs four main functions: delivering subject content, sharing feedback and support, performing assessments, and providing the platform/interface. Instructional strategies should be carefully chosen to design these functions to motivate the learner and to make them relevant to the learner. We developed a functional model for better understanding of the applicability of learning theories in eLearning designs (Fig. 2).

According to this functional model, the subject content of the eLearning module needs to be designed considering learning theories, in order to make the subject content relevant to the learner context as well as to make it accessible.

According to the learning theories, the subject content should be designed considering pre-existing learning needs (need to learn internet functions as identified by Wong et al. [3]), student suppositions (need more clarifications to content with on-site support and/or videos) and organised with well-defined goals. Social cognitive theory describes that subject content in online learning should be described in small amounts with examples linked to existing memory, to support the learner with limited capacity of working memory [28]. Redesigns for the subject content should be considered according to emerging educational needs with introduction of new technologies, levels of challenge, and how to stimulate the learner's interests.

eLearning designs should follow assessment strategies described in learning theories referring to the learner's context. Constructivist learning theory mentions that assessments should be non-judgemental parallel to teaching and learning, and allow the learner to demonstrate skills learnt and discuss applications in life. Social cognitive theory that emphasises the need of preventing working memory overload during learning, suggests that assessments should occur while the learner practises or applies the skills in real life. In a typical eLearning environment, the learner can be assessed considering the contribution in the form of their posts on activities given, and discussions with peers. Assessment strategies need to be selected according to the learner's background.

In an eLearning environment for people with ID, assessment should be defined as a role of the on-site tutor. Parallel to learning, the on-site tutor observes the learner demonstrating skills, discusses applications of skills, encourages the learner with non-judgmental feedback on the learner's performance, and identifies redesign needs as a continuous user evaluation of the module. The tutor needs to keep notes on redesign needs according to the learner's performance.

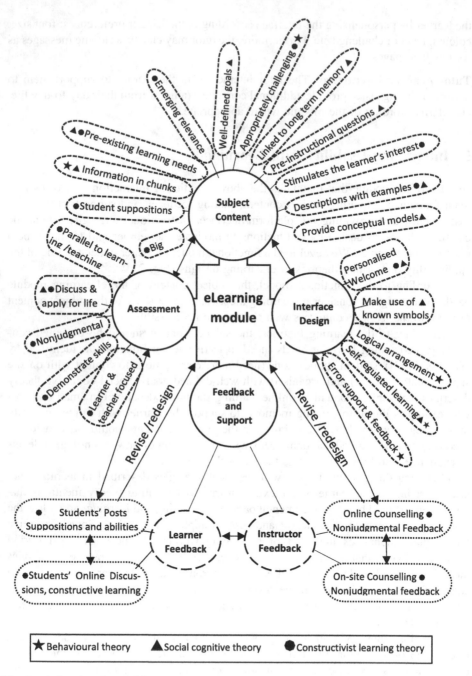

Fig. 2. A functional model for eLearning design that integrate learning theories: a guide for the designer

Learning theories that have recommendations on interface design should be followed to make the designs relevant to the learner abilities and to create motivating learning environments. Personalised welcome, as suggested in social cognitive theory and constructivist theory, can be incorporated in eLearning interface design, by providing an introduction to the learning module, referring to the needs of the expected learner, for encouraging them to be engaged with learning. eLearning environments should be designed to be supportive to perform learning activities at the learner's pace, considering the learner's cognitive level.

According to Schunk, some developmental limitations can cause slower responses in self-regulated learning [36]. Hence, social cognitive theory suggests that designs for eLearning modules for people with ID need to include well described content. Multimedia presentations that display skills can be incorporated for the learner to observe, imitate, and improve the self-regulatory skills for a given task. The interface should be designed with the use of known symbols to represent known actions. Such eLearning environments support the learner with limited cognitive skills. Interface designs should provide immediate feedback on the learner's performance, by acknowledging errors that have occurred and facilitating corrections to offer an engaging learning environment. Furthermore, these interface designs need to be iteratively redesigned referring to revisions introduced to the content, and suggestions from student and instructor assessments and feedback.

The proposed functional model integrates the learning theories with relevant functions of an eLearning module. It can be used as a guide by designers, as well as by teachers, to identify applicable strategies, including the modifications described to develop eLearning environments appropriate to the learner context.

5.1 Guidelines for eLearning Designs for People with Intellectual Disability

People with ID, having limited cognitive and functional abilities experience difficulties in accessing eLearning environments designed for the general population. Our aim is to describe the applicability of pedagogical theories in designing eLearning environments for increasing accessibility to people with ID. For motivating people with ID to be engaged with eLearning, designs should follow guidelines that strengthen the interactions in an eLearning environment, referring to the learner context.

While learning in an eLearning environment, the learner interacts with subject content, instructor, peers and the interface. The learner should initially learn how to use the interface. Usability deals with presenting the interface in a format that is "easy to learn and remember, effective, and pleasant to use" [37]. Nielsen presents nine heuristics for evaluating user interfaces [38, 39]. Nielsen's heuristics emphasise real conversation, user friendliness, consistent format, instant feedback, effective navigation, expertise benefit, efficient feedback, minimising errors, documented guidance.

Referring to existing literature on usability and instructional approaches, Mehlenbacher et al. presented a heuristic tool for evaluating eLearning environments [40]. Their usability heuristics focussed on the challenges of designing and evaluating eLearning environments. They discuss five dimensions in eLearning design: "the learner's background, knowledge and social dynamics, instructional context, instruction display, instructor activities, and environment and tools". Costabile et al. presents usability criteria and guidelines for eLearning platforms, considering the effectiveness and efficiency of the platform for learning. These guidelines are applicable in eLearning designs. Still, there is a need for eLearning design guidelines that address the context of the learner with ID who needs additional attention on cognitive accessibility and approaches to increase motivation and engagement. As literature suggests, eLearning design guidelines should integrate learning theories with usability criteria for guiding accessible eLearning designs.

Accessibility refers to inclusive design that strengthens interactions between the user and web-based design. Our aim is to present design guidelines that integrate usability principles with theories from learning and pedagogical psychology, and which can be used in inclusive designs of eLearning modules accessible to people with ID. For achieving that aim, we outline a theoretical framework of guidelines for learner centered design of eLearning environments for the learners with ID (Fig. 3). The framework models a set of guidelines for interaction design from a learner-centered perspective which accounts for the learner's individuality as well as their interactions.

At this point, we describe design guidelines about the subject content and the interface.

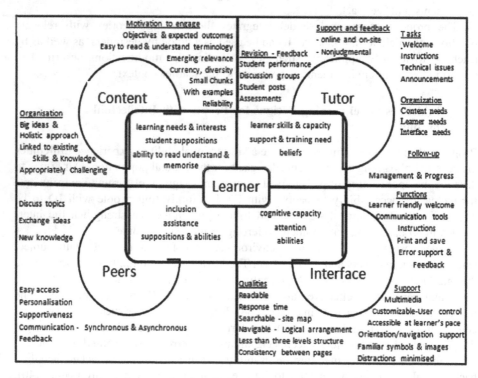

Fig. 3. A theoretical framework of guidelines for learner centered interaction design of eLearning environments for people with intellectual disability

Implications for Designing Subject Content. Learner-centered design of subject content should reflect the learner context: their learning needs and interests, their suppositions about learning the proposed content, and ability to read, understand and memorise the content presented in one page. Design guidelines that integrate both usability criteria and learning theories guide this type of design to develop motivating and engaging learning experiences.

The study of the problem situation, needing new eLearning design, creates an understanding of the learner context to be incorporated with the design. This problem analysis should aim to understand the accessibility requirements to make the content learner friendly, easy to understand and relevant. To achieve the identified accessibility requirements in content design, design guidelines should take on board relevant psychological principles about teaching and learning. This suggests that to make eLearning accessible to the learner with intellectual disability, design guidelines should include the following principles: make the topics and content appropriately challenging; organise the content around big ideas with a holistic approach; introduce topics with emerging relevance; use content, examples and images linked to existing knowledge and experiences. Emerging relevance can be connected with topics already discussed in the content, learner interests and abilities, new developments in technology and/or in the discussed subject, and current topics in discussion.

Implications for Designing the Interface. Learner-centered design for the eLearning interface should understand and address the learner context: learner's abilities, cognitive capacity and level of attention. For making eLearning accessible to people with ID, the design should consider the accessibility requirements representing the learner's context.

The eLearning interface design should minimise distractions, maintain consistency, and be easy to operate, read, and navigate. The interface should be supportive, providing quick (response time) and feedback, as well as with personalisation features. Design guidelines regarding accessible eLearning designs for people with ID should include prospects from both learning theories and usability criteria. Referring to learning theories, the eLearning interface should appropriately use known symbols, logical arrangement with a course map and less than three levels structure to enhance navigability. Personalisation by allowing learning at learner's pace, providing options to save the content, make bookmarks, customise fonts, font size, colours and graphics is important to motivate the learner with personalised welcome. eLearning interface should be helpful with immediate and understandable feedback. Usability criteria can be incorporated to guide the eLearning interface design to be accessible by means of minimising distractions. They include avoiding too many graphics, blinking, and animations, four different colours or less, giving priority to the learner's preference about font type and colour, avoiding capital letters, using colours to highlight, and minimising hyperlinks (with acknowledgements that the learner will be directed to a website outside the eLearning module). Considering the learner's capacity to use the mouse to move around, icons and menus should be appropriately large, clues as pop-ups or written words close to the icon should be used to help the learner as necessary. In order to increase the readability and visualisation, suitable font size

Table 1. Guidelines for learner-centered design of an eLearning environment for learners with intellectual disability

Interaction	Learner context	Accessibility requirement	Guidelines
Learner - interface	Attention	Minimised distractions	Without too many graphics, blinking, and animations
			Small number of colours (<4)
			Font type and colours appropriate to the learner preference
			Highlighting with colour codes instead of capitalisation of letters
			Minimum Hyperlinks in the content pages
	Mobility	Easy to operate	Icons and menus large enough to be pointed
			Prompts and cues to help the learner
	Cognitive capacity	Readability & visualisation	Font size according to the user preference (>14 point)
			Short sentences (<7 words)
			Minimum number of sentences in one screen (<4)
			Leave space between lines
			Use white background
			Multimedia, graphics, and images to make the contents familiar and descriptive
		Consistency	Every screen designed maintaining same format
			Consistent positioning of title, menus, forward, backward, print, and save buttons
			Consistency in use of font size and colours
		Feedback	Feedback with error messages and support
	Learner abilities	Navigability	Less than three levels structure
			Orientation support by means of logical arrangement, course map and menus
			Use known symbols
			Highlight and colour-code the current tasks
		Personalisation	Possibility to personalise font size, colours and graphics
			Possibility to save pages and make bookmarks
			Allows learning at the learner's pace; self-regulated learning
Learner - content	Learning needs and interests, student suppositions	Easy to understand, relevant	Content appropriately challenging
			Content organised around big ideas with holistic approach
			Topics introduced in immerging relevance
			Content, examples and images linked to existing skills and knowledge
	Ability to read and memorise	Learner friendly	Content in easy to read and easy to understand terminology
			Content presented on small chunks
			Explained with examples including images and or multimedia

(>14 point), sentence length (<7 words), and number of sentences per screen (<4) should be decided during an iterative design process. A white background and space between the lines can increase visibility. Each page of the eLearning module should follow a consistent format to help the learner's orientation within the page, minimising the use of cognitive capacity for positioning, and reducing the possibilities for misleads and distractions.

Designing an eLearning module for People with ID needs considerations on their cognitive capacities and abilities. The guidelines we suggest here use learning theories and usability criteria in combination to address the accessibility needs of People with ID, as an approach to guide learner-centered interaction design of eLearning. Table 1 presents the guidelines from a practical standpoint.

6   A Design for an eLearning Module for People with Intellectual Disability: A Case Study

We apply these guidelines in designing an eLearning module to increase the abilities of people with ID to be included in online information. The eLearning module describes and teaches how to access health information. It offers the user an opportunity to improve skills needed to use the Internet while learning in the practical environment, navigating between pages and the units of the module.

One unit of that module is about describing for the learner, how to find a Medical Centre close by, and then identifying the link for making an appointment. In the meantime, the learner becomes familiar with two other types of information: location and the opening hours of the Medical Centre. The two screens of the prototype we designed are presented in Figs. 4 and 5 respectively. This eLearning module does not include an assessment. Instead, a tutor, who gives on-site support to the learner, observes the learner's behaviour during learning and gives non-judgemental feedback, to encourage engagement with learning.

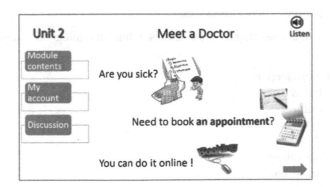

Fig. 4. eLearning module screen

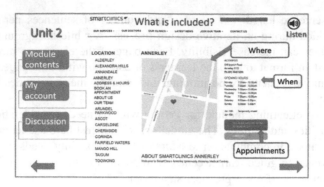

Fig. 5. eLearning module screen

We adopted the following key guidelines while designing the content of our prototype.

- Content in small chunks/units
- Outline in the first screen
- Easy to read terminology
- One point in one screen
- Relevant learning tasks
- Few examples to familiarise
- Questions to ask from peers
- Big ideas for teaching skills to use internet
  - Online searching
    Web search engine can be used to find a website
  - Navigation and orientation
    Menu helps to navigate in a website
    Links direct to a new website
    Forward and backward buttons to go to next and previous pages
  - Communication
    The Internet delivers messages

We adopted the following key guidelines while designing the interface of our prototype.

- Video with introduction
- Content to be printed
- Make icons large
- Menu in every page
- Instant feedback
- Minimise distractions
- Simple and understandable
- Sitemap help orientation
- Audio descriptions to content

We have divided the module into small units. For example, one of them, which we describe here, includes eight screens. Each screen includes a small amount of information, and can be viewed without scrolling. The screen in Fig. 4 includes only three sentences, which comprise thirteen words. The content is described in simple language. Referring to the learners' cognitive capacity, contents have been further clarified with examples and images. Use of several examples for clarifying one term aims at making it familiar to most. Furthermore, the content is arranged in logical order. The first page of our prototype (Fig. 4) includes a topic that describes the goal of the unit, "Meet a doctor". Then it describes the background, and extends to the objective of the unit; learn how to make an appointment online, instead of mentioning it as a single sentence "This unit aims to teach you, how to make an appointment for meeting a doctor when you are sick".

We have used different screens to discuss different sub topics: entering key words to search, using the search results page etc. Each of these subtopics has been described with two examples that search for two different Medical Centre websites and familiarise with links to online appointments, opening hours and the location of each Medical Centre (Fig. 5). Each unit introduces questions that support them to discuss what they learnt from the unit. For example, the unit we describe here gives a question to find a Medical Centre close to them, and find the link to make online appointments, the location of the Medical Centre, and opening hours.

Learning tasks have been selected for the learner to develop navigation and online searching skills as well as the ability to communicate with others using Internet, referring to their existing skills and preferences. This module helps them to experience how a menu and the forward and backward buttons work, as they use the module to learn how to access online health information. They also experience how the link from the search results directs them to a website. The opportunity to make an appointment online explains to them that the Internet can deliver their request to the Medical Centre.

In each page, we presented large icons for better and improved visibility. We included menu buttons, back and forward buttons, and an icon to access audio, which are large enough as well. The menu and the other icons have been included in every page in the same position. We have not included animations and blinking pictures to minimise distractions. We have made the screen designs simple and understandable, consistently using the same format. The menu guides the learner to navigate through the module. Furthermore, we have used a known symbol, with a description word "Listen" to encourage its use. Font size and colours have been selected to personalise the interface to the learner. Each screen of the unit prepares the learner to learn the next screen.

7 Conclusion

Designing accessible eLearning modules requires careful attention to technological usability as well as the psychological appropriateness of the teaching material presented. This article suggests eLearning design guidelines that consider principles of teaching and learning along with usability criteria to address the learner's needs. First, we have presented learning theories that relate to the four elements of an eLearning environment: content, interface, assessments, and feedback. We incorporated the learning and teaching strategies into a theoretical framework of guidelines for learner-centered interaction design of eLearning modules for people with ID. Then, we used that framework to establish the guidelines for eLearning module design. Finally, we presented a concrete example of the application of the guidelines through a case study.

This paper focuses on the content and interface design. That is, we have not addressed the learner-teacher interactions and the learner-peers interactions. In future work, we will further explore these interactions, and the role of on-site support people to determine how universal designs of eLearning platforms should account for their contributions and requirements.

Acknowledgements. The authors would like to thank the anonymous reviewers and editors from INTERACT 2017 for their very much helpful comments on the previous version of this paper. The authors wish to acknowledge the University Grant Commission, Sri Lanka, University of Colombo and Queensland University of Technology for their support for this research study.

References

1. Harrysson, B., Svensk, A., Johansson, G.I.: How people with developmental disabilities navigate the Internet. Br. J. Spec. Educ. **31**(3), 138–142 (2004)
2. Rocha, T., et al.: Accessibility and usability in the internet for people with intellectual disabilities. In: Proceedings of 2nd International Conference on Software Development for Enhancing Accessibility and Fighting Info-exclusion-DSAI (2009)
3. Wong, A.W.K., et al.: Competence of people with intellectual disabilities on using human–computer interface. Res. Dev. Disabil. **30**(1), 107–123 (2009)
4. Sitbon, L., et al.: Towards universal search design. In: Proceedings of the 2014 Australasian Document Computing Symposium. ACM (2014)
5. Standen, P., Brown, D.: Using virtual environments with pupils with learning difficulties. In: Hegarty, L.F.A.J. (ed.) ICT and Special Educational Needs: A Tool for Inclusion. pp. 96–108. Open University Press, Berkshire (2004)
6. Mayes, T., de Freitas, S.: Learning and e-learning. Rethinking Pedagogy Digital Age, 13 (2007)
7. Standen, P.J., Brown, D.J., Cromby, J.J.: The effective use of virtual environments in the education and rehabilitation of students with intellectual disabilities. Br. J. Educ. Technol. **32** (3), 289–299 (2001)
8. Kolb, D.A.: Experiential learning: experience as the source of learning and development. Prentice-Hall Inc., New Jersey (1984)
9. Victoria: Intellectually Disabled Persons Services Act 1986. Melbourne, Vic (1987)
10. National Definition of Learning Disabilities Adopted by the Learning Disabilities Association of Canada (2015). http://www.ldac-acta.ca/learn-more/ld-defined/official-definition-of-learning-disabilities
11. Melis, E., Weber, M., Andrès, E.: Lessons for (pedagogic) usability of eLearning systems. In: Rosset, A.T. (ed.) Proceedings of World Conference on e-Learning in Corporate, Government, Healthcare, and Higher Education, Chesapeake, VA, USA. AACE (2003)
12. Henry, S.L.: Introduction to Web Accessibility: Web Accessibility Initiative (WAI) W3C (2005). https://www.w3.org/WAI/intro/accessibility.php

13. Squires, D.: Usability and educational software design: special issue of interacting with computers. Interact. Comput. **11**(5), 463–466 (1999)
14. Maldonado, U.P.T., et al.: E-learning motivation, students' acceptance/use of educational portal in developing countries: a case study of Peru. In: 2009 Fourth International Conference on Computer Sciences and Convergence Information Technology (2009)
15. Seo, Y.-J., Woo, H.: The identification, implementation, and evaluation of critical user interface design features of computer-assisted instruction programs in mathematics for students with learning disabilities. Comput. Educ. **55**(1), 363–377 (2010)
16. Harris, J.C.: Intellectual Disability: Understanding its Development, Causes, Classification, Evaluation, and Treatment. Oxford University Press, Oxford (2006)
17. Renblad, K.: How do people with intellectual disabilities think about empowerment and information and communication technology (ICT)? Int. J. Rehabil. Res. **26**(3), 175–182 (2003)
18. Ogunbase, A.O.: Pedagogical Design and Pedagogical Usability of Web-based Learning Environments: Comparative Cultural Implications between Africa and Europe. In: School of Information Sciences. University of Tampere, Tampere (2016)
19. Li-Tsang, C.W.P., et al.: A 6-month follow-up of the effects of an information and communication technology (ICT) training programme on people with intellectual disabilities. Res. Dev. Disabil. **28**(6), 559–566 (2007)
20. Bunning, K., Heath, B., Minnion, A.: Interaction between teachers and students with intellectual disability during computer-based activities: the role of human mediation. Technol. Disabil. **22**(1,2), 61–71 (2010)
21. Mayes, J.T., Fowler, C.J.: Learning technology and usability: a framework for understanding courseware. Interact. Comput. **11**(5), 485–497 (1999)
22. Snowman, J., Biehler, R.: Psychology Applied to Teaching. Houghton Mifflin Company, Boston (2006)
23. Schunk, D.H.: Learning theories. Printice Hall Inc., New Jersey (1996)
24. APA. Learner-Centered Psychological Principles: A Framework for School Reform & Redesign (1997). https://www.apa.org/ed/governance/bea/learner-centered.pdf
25. Skinner, B.F.: Operant behavior. Am. Psychol. **18**(8), 503 (1963)
26. Skinner, B.F.: The shame of American education. Am. Psychol. **39**(9), 947 (1984)
27. Bandura, A.: Social Foundations of Thought and Action: A Social Cognitive Theory. Prentice-Hall, Inc, New Jersey (1986)
28. Anderson, T.: The Theory and Practice of Online Learning. Athabasca University Press, Edmonton (2008)
29. Bruner, J.S.: The act of discovery. Harvard Educ. Rev. **31**, 21–32 (1961)
30. Brooks, J.G., Brooks, M.G.: Search of Understanding: The Case for Constructivist Classrooms. ASCD (1999)
31. Garrison, R.: Implications of online learning for the conceptual development and practice of distance education. REVUE DE L'ÉDUCATION À DISTANCE **23**(2), 93–104 (2009)
32. Anderson, T.: Getting the mix right again: an updated and theoretical rationale for interaction. Int. Rev. Res. Open Distrib. Learn. **4**(2) (2003)
33. Metros, S.E., Hedberg, J.G.: More than just a pretty (inter) face: the role of the graphical user interface in engaging eLearners. Q. Rev. Dis. Educ. **3**(2), 191 (2002)
34. Fryia, G.D., Wachowiak-Smolikova, R., Wachowiak, M.P.: Human-computer interface design in an e-Learning system for individuals with cognitive and learning disabilities. In: 4th International Conference on Digital Information Management, ICDIM 2009. IEEE (2009)

35. Hillman, D.C., Willis, D.J., Gunawardena, C.N.: Learner-interface interaction in distance education: an extension of contemporary models and strategies for practitioners. Am. J. Distance Educ. **8**(2), 30–42 (1994)

36. Zimmerman, B.J., Schunk, D.H.: Self-regulated Learning and Academic Achievement: Theoretical Perspectives. Routledge, Abingdon (2001)

37. Molich, R., Nielsen, J.: Improving a human-computer dialogue. Commun. ACM **33**(3), 338–348 (1990)

38. Nielsen, J.: Enhancing the explanatory power of usability heuristics. In: Proceedings of the SIGCHI Conference on Human Factors in Computing Systems, pp. 152–158. ACM, Boston, Massachusetts, USA (1994)

39. Nielsen, J., Molich, R.: Heuristic evaluation of user interfaces. In: Proceedings of the SIGCHI Conference on Human Factors in Computing Systems, pp. 249–256. ACM, Seattle, Washington, USA (1990)

40. Mehlenbacher, B., et al.: Usable e-learning: a conceptual model for evaluation and design. In: 11th International Conference on Human-Computer Interaction 2005 Proceedings of HCI International (2005)

Identifying Support Opportunities for Foreign Students: Disentangling Language and Non-language Problems Among a Unique Population

Jack Jamieson[1,2(✉)], Naomi Yamashita[2], and Jeffrey Boase[1,3]

[1] Faculty of Information, University of Toronto, Toronto, Ontario, Canada
jack.jamieson@mail.utoronto.ca, j.boase@utoronto.ca
[2] NTT Communication Science Laboratories, Kyoto, Japan
naomiy@acm.org
[3] Institute of Communication, Culture, Information and Technology,
University of Toronto, Toronto, Ontario, Canada

Abstract. This study investigates how foreign students address language-related and other problems as a means of identifying opportunities to support them with language and social technologies. We identify support opportunities by distinguishing between different types of problems – e.g. whether they are language-related and whether they involve essential activities in their lives or at school – and the extent to which support already exists. Our unique sample of 15 foreign graduate students who live in Japan but study in English helped us disentangle problems relating to language skills versus those relating to other challenges. We examine these issues using a multi-method approach where students used a mobile app to record experiences and interactions over five weeks, and then discussed this data during an in-depth interview. We use our results to identify specific support opportunities that can be addressed through the development of social and language technologies.

Keywords: Foreign students · Cultural differences · Intercultural communication · Non-native speakers

1 Introduction

The experience of studying in a foreign country involves many challenges, and international students often experience difficulties such as acculturative stress [1], loneliness [2], and language difficulty [3, 4]. These problems can have a detrimental effect on students' motivation and performance at school, as well as their overall well-being [5, 6]. Success at overcoming these difficulties is related to a variety of factors including students' backgrounds and coping styles [1], their relationships with people who can provide support [7–10], and access to supportive technologies [11]. We study different types of problems experienced by foreign students as a means of identifying opportunities to support them with language and social technologies.

© IFIP International Federation for Information Processing 2017
Published by Springer International Publishing AG 2017. All Rights Reserved
R. Bernhaupt et al. (Eds.): INTERACT 2017, Part II, LNCS 10514, pp. 33–53, 2017.
DOI: 10.1007/978-3-319-67684-5_3

We investigate sources of stress and support experienced by 15 foreign graduate students in Japan. We identified problems discussed by each participant, and found they could be categorized along two dimensions. First, we distinguish between functional problems—those that have a direct consequence related to essential tasks such as academic work or accessing basic needs—and non-functional problems, which are related to non-essential activities but nonetheless contribute to acculturative stress. Second, we distinguish between problems caused primarily by language difficulty and those for which language difficulty is not a major factor. Most problems that were not caused by language-difficulty were related to cultural differences, but this was not by definition. The level of provided support varied substantially between categories. Based on our analysis, we discuss reasons for shortfalls in support for some types of problems, which sources of support were most effective for addressing those problems, and how to improve access those support opportunities.

This article focuses on an understudied population with a different arrangement of language difficulties than represented in most previous studies. Much research in this area describes non-English students studying in countries where English is the dominant language inside and outside of school [e.g. 10, 12, 18]. Students in those studies tend to use two languages: the host-country language (usually English) for most activities and their native language for communicating with co-nationals and with people back home. By contrast, participants in our study use three languages in their everyday lives: the host-country language (Japanese) and a common language (English) for various communication with host-country people and other foreigners, and their native language for communicating with co-nationals and people back home. Most academic activities are conducted using English, though conversations with Japanese lab mates and administrative staff often involve speaking Japanese. Although all but one of the participants are non-native speakers of English, they all reported high English proficiency and almost never attributed difficulties to their own English limitations. Their Japanese proficiency was far lower, so Japanese communications were more difficult. This allowed us to identify non-language problems that may have been masked by language difficulties in other contexts. Had language been a larger obstacle in many situations, it would have been more difficult to identify the non-linguistic components of those problems. When language difficulty was significant, it helped us identify types of communication that are especially difficult to support, such as informal communications.

In addition, many studies emphasize the value of integration for long-term adjustment to the host country. However, as Maundeni [12] pointed out, long-term acculturation is not a universal goal for international students. Most participants in this study indicated they plan to return to their home country after completing school or to look for work outside of Japan. Studying students who plan to return to their home country allowed us to focus on support from relationships that did not necessarily assist long-term integration to Japan, but helped with more immediate coping. For example, 6 of this study's 15 participants were Muslim, and for these students other Muslims were extremely important for supporting challenges related to their religious practices.

Another contribution of this study is its multi-method approach that draws on a combination of data sources. Participants used a mobile phone application, *Study Abroad Scrapbook*, to record their experiences over the course of five weeks. Then, the data collected using this app was discussed and expanded upon during an in-depth interview. Daily reporting to the mobile app provided a longitudinal account including persistent or evolving problems, and helped identify problems that may not have surfaced through interviews alone. Interview designs were informed by results from the mobile app, providing a means to follow up, clarify, and gather details in great depth. Combining interviews and daily questionnaires helped draw on the strengths of both approaches while mitigating their respective limitations.

The results of this study contribute to a better understanding of (1) the kinds of problems experienced by international students and which of those problems are most lacking in support; (2) how international students draw on various relationships and technologies to overcome these problems; and (3) opportunities for designers of social and language technologies to facilitate access to support that can improve the wellbeing and performance of international students.

2 Background

Previous research has studied many challenges faced by international students as well as ways these challenges can be supported by various relationships and technological aids. Adapting to life in a new country involves many challenges, which can contribute to acculturative stress, "the psychological and physical discomfort experienced when the adaptation to a new cultural environment seems to be overly demanding" [1]. Foreign students may experience difficulties with necessary tasks such as schoolwork and meeting basic needs, and these problems may be compounded by social and emotional challenges. Loneliness is a particularly evident difficulty, including personal loneliness (loss of contact with families and close friends), social loneliness (loss of networks of like-minded people), and cultural loneliness, "triggered by the absence of the preferred cultural and/or linguistic environment" [2].

2.1 Social Support

Social support is important for overcoming these kinds of stresses. Cohen and Ashby Wills [13] described a *buffering model* of social support, finding evidence that integration into a social network could reduce the effects of stressful experiences. Foreign students' social networks tend to consist of distinct groups with different functions: Friendships with co-nationals from the same home country; friendships with other sojourners; and friendships with host-nationals [7].

Relationships with co-nationals are often close friendships, providing emotional support and opportunities to express one's cultural values with like-minded peers [9]. In contrast, friendships with sojourners from different countries provide companionship for "recreational, 'non-cultural' and non-task oriented activities" [9]. Strong relationships with host-nationals are associated with reduced loneliness [14] and better adaptation and longer-term integration [2, 8, 15–17]. This finding is relatively consistent for students in Western countries (America, Britain, Germany, Australia) and in China [8], Taiwan [18] and Japan [10, 19, 20]. Strong relationships, regardless of source, have been found to have a positive effect early in sojourners' adaptation, but too much contact with co-nationals can hinder long-term adjustment to the host country [21].

Many studies of international students' social networks have focused on friendship networks and excluded other relationships [12]. Likely related to this narrow scope, some studies have overlooked ways in which social networks can cause stress as well as provide support [10]. To build upon this work, we asked participants to report on communications with all types of people, and interviews yielded many comments about relationships that caused stress as well as those that provided support.

Much of the work about international students' support networks has been inattentive to how communication technologies can facilitate relationships. Past research not involving international students, but college students more generally has investigated the role of social media for facilitating social support [22, 23]. Ellison et al. [24] found that Facebook use was positively related to the maintenance and creation of social capital, and that Facebook was typically used to maintain or strengthen relationships that also involved offline connections. Additionally, contemporary communication technologies have increased opportunities for college students living away from home to maintain relationships with friends and family [25]. However, too much communication with parents has been associated with lower autonomy [26].

Studies of international students [27] and immigrant communities [28] have found these groups use social media both to build connections to their host country and to reinforce their identities related to their home country culture. Both Facebook and home country social media sites are important for international students [29, 30], but a desire to connect with other cultural groups has been found to be negatively associated with the number of friends on home country sites [30].

2.2 Language Support

Language difficulties are a key challenge for foreign students [31]. They can complicate formal activities such as understanding academic work [32] and contribute to barriers for informal communication [33]. In environments that use a common language for intercultural communication, non-native speakers may perceive themselves to lack language proficiency and experience anxiety that lowers their willingness to communicate [34]. Furthermore, barriers between intercultural speakers can encourage language-based cliques where intercultural communication is avoided [33, 35]. Finally, language difficulties can cause misunderstandings that deteriorate trust [36] and interpersonal relationships in multilingual workplaces [37]. Because previous research demonstrates that language difficulties have diverse impacts, we designed this study to be attentive to language-related problems and sources of support in a variety of situations.

The literature cited here focuses on English language environments. In our study the situation is slightly different because foreign students are more skilled at English than host-nationals. And, while English is the main language of study for our participants, informal conversations occur using both English and Japanese. Previous work has explored methods for improving intercultural communication between native and non-native speakers. This includes efforts to reduce cognitive burden [38] and improve comprehension [39, 40] for non-native speakers, and to establish conversational grounding in multilingual conversations [41–43]. For the most part, evaluations of these kinds of tools are based on how participants perform communication tasks in lab settings. Yuan et al. [33] is a notable exception, investigating real-world organizational communication and using that as a basis for design recommendations.

3 Research Questions

Studies about social support have described how relationships with different groups of people facilitate different kinds of support for foreign students [7, 9, 10] and how social media technologies are used to build and maintain relationships [22–24]. These studies have tended to examine problems and support independently from one another. We build upon this work by studying how specific types of problems are supported and why others are not. By doing so, we identify opportunities for improving access to support where it is lacking. We investigate these issues through the following questions, *RQ1: What types of problems do foreign students identify?* and *RQ2: To what extent are these problems adequately supported, and what reasons can be identified for varying levels of support?*

Previous research regarding language support has been proactive about designing technologies to improve intercultural communication, but these efforts have mostly focused on instrumental, task-oriented communication [42, 44, 45]. We contribute to research about language support by considering how current technologies are used in a real-world setting and ways they fall short in supporting foreign students. Based on this study, we identify ways in which social and language technologies could be improved to better support international students' lives—*RQ3: How can inadequately supported problems be addressed using language and social technologies?*

4 Method

4.1 Recruitment

We recruited 15 foreign graduate students from Kyoto University (8 males, 3 females) and Nara Institute for Science and Technology (3 males). Participants were screened through a brief survey, and only respondents who reported a high level of English proficiency were considered. Because more than 15 people applied, we selected the 15 most suitable respondents by preferring students with little previous experience in Japan and who planned to stay in Japan for more than one year. These participants were most suitable because we were interested in students who were in the process of acculturating to a country where they intend to live for an extended period. At the time of recruitment, 12 participants had been in Japan for less than six months, and three had been in Japan a longer time. It was the first time in Japan for nine participants, four had visited Japan once before, and two had visited more often. In regards to Japanese language proficiency, 4 participants reported they did not speak Japanese, 9 reported low ability, and 2 reported medium ability. The median time participants planned to stay in Japan was three years. Participants studied a variety of fields, including electrical engineering, agricultural engineering, robotics, public health, and social informatics.

Twelve participants were between 20–29 years of age, and 3 were between 30–39. Participants' countries of origin were: Bangladesh (N = 2), China (N = 3), France, (N = 1), Germany (N = 1), Indonesia (N = 4), Malaysia (N = 1), Paraguay (N = 1), Thailand (N = 2).

4.2 Data Collection

The researchers designed an application called *Study Abroad Scrapbook*, and each participant was provided an Android smartphone with this software installed. For five weeks, participants were asked to complete a brief questionnaire each day. Three types of data were collected through these questionnaires.

Communication Logs: Participants were asked to indicate who they had communicated with each day, and whether the communication was weak or strong (see Fig. 1). Before participants began using the software, we provided them with a definition of "weak communications" as including brief email exchanges, small-talk, or similar communications, and "strong communications" as a longer conversation or more substantial communication. By collecting this log data, we could identify which relationships were associated with particular problems and support. Previous studies of foreign students' social support networks have used similar self-reports of communication in a cross-sectional design [7–9, 15]. By asking participants to report who they communicate with each day we adapt these approaches to a longitudinal model. Participants' logs do not specify medium (e.g. face-to-face, social media, phone call), so it is not possible to address the effects of different media affordances [46] based on these logs, however we did discuss this issue during the interviews described below.

Fig. 1. Screenshots of *Study Abroad Scrapbook*. Left: daily questionnaire screen. Right: screen used to log strong and weak communications.

Emotions and Experiences: Each day, participants were asked to rate how they experienced homesickness, language difficulty, and culture shock, as well as how comfortable, excited and content they felt about their lives in Japan. Each item was rated on a scale from 1 (not at all) to 5 (strongly). Questions about homesickness and culture shock were included because they have been identified by Akhtar and Kröner-Herwig as significant dimensions of acculturative stress [1]. We also wanted to assess positive aspects of participants' experiences, which is why we asked about excitement, comfort, and contentment. Lastly, we asked about language difficulty because it is a major obstacle for sojourners across numerous studies [2, 4, 47]. This data was mainly used during follow-up interviews with participants, where we probed about how trends and changes in their emotions and experiences related to problems and support opportunities.

Diary Entries: At the end of each questionnaire, participants were invited to write a brief text post about their day, focusing on their communication and adding context to the previous questions. These entries were a source of rich qualitative data in which participants described their problems and strategies, if any, for overcoming them.

Since the *Study Abroad Scrapbook* was installed on a mobile phone, participants could choose where, when, and how to answer the daily questions. This encouraged participants to write about issues that were personally meaningful to them, and granted them the freedom to make posts at whatever times were convenient for them.

Semi-structured Interviews: After five weeks using the app, a semi-structured interview was conducted with each participant. These interviews lasted approximately 1 h and were audio-recorded and transcribed for analysis. These interviews were used to investigate and add context to themes that emerged in data collected using *Study Abroad Scrapbook*. Additionally, during interviews we collected information about the people participants had logged communication with, including how they know each other, what language(s) they use together, whether each person lived in Japan, and whether they were Japanese, from the same home country as the participant, or from somewhere else.

While daily entries in *Study Abroad Scrapbook* encouraged participants to note even minor events from each day, during the interviews participants were more likely to talk about significant problems they'd experienced. Accordingly, the app helped identify issues that may have been fleeting and not been raised by participants in an interview, and the interviews provided context about which issues raised in the diaries were significant and which were minor. Interview questions were informed by patterns and specific events described in the data. This allowed the interviewer to hone in on specific instances that may not have been evident in an interview alone. As well as informing the interview questions, data collected using the app allowed researchers to identify where observations expressed in interviews by one or two participants were evident across a broader segment of the participants. For example, when a few participants discussed that a community of fellow sojourners from their home country provided comfort and support, it was possible to use communication logs and comfort ratings from the app to investigate the role of such communities more broadly.

4.3　Data Analysis

Participants' diary entries and interview transcripts were analyzed using a qualitative open coding approach [48] in which categories were developed through immersion in the data. After meaningful categories were developed, two researchers coded 141 salient excerpts from the data. A first pass coding revealed greater clarity regarding definitions was required for some of the categories. After better defining these codes the data was again coded. The coding included three dimensions whose Kappa scores for an inter-coder reliability test were 0.84, 0.95. and 0.86. Remaining inconsistencies were resolved through discussion among the two coders. Additionally, quantitative analysis was used to identify trends and relationships among the communication logs and ratings of emotions and experiences collected through the app.

5　Results

RQ1 asked *what type of problems do foreign students identify?* Through the course of reading participants' diary entries and interviewing them, two distinct types of problems became apparent. The first were functional problems, which must be overcome to carry out essential tasks for everyday life or school. Failure to address such problems has a direct effect, such as academic penalty or not being able to meet a basic need (like food or shelter). Were such problems not addressed, it could pose a direct threat to participants' abilities to live in Japan and complete their studies. In contrast, non-functional problems are related to things that are not required, but nonetheless contribute to acculturative stress. Non-functional problems might include feeling excluded from social situations, inconveniences when travelling for leisure, or difficulty participating in optional activities that would be easy in one's home country. Although the particular composition of functional and non-functional problems in this study was unique to our participants' situation, anyone undergoing a transition into a new culture experiences both types of challenges to some extent. Distinguishing problems in this way helped to identify how problems with direct, functional consequences may be supported differently from problems whose consequences are less direct, though just as significant.

Problems were further distinguished by whether participants noted that they were caused by a language breakdown. Although language was a persistent challenge in many aspects of participants' lives, we classify "language-related" problems as those where language was the clear and immediate cause of a problem. Using these two axes, we propose a typology of foreign students' problems, presented in Table 1.

Based on this typology, 65% of excerpts coded from participants' diary entries and interview transcripts concerned functional problems (N = 92) and 35% were about non-functional problems (N = 49). 59% (N = 54) of the functional problems were language-related and 41% (N = 38) were not. In contrast, only 35% (N = 17) of the non-functional problems were language-related, while 65% (N = 32) were not language-related.

Table 1. Typology of foreign students' problems by functionality and language-relatedness.

Language-relatedness	Functionality	
	Functional *Problems with direct impact on essential tasks*	Non-functional *Related to non-essential activities, but still cause stress if unaddressed*
Language-related Language is the clear and direct cause of the problem	E.g. using Japanese language to open a bank account; communicating with professors about work-related matters	E.g. feeling excluded from Japanese colleagues' small talk; not being able to communicate during a social occasion
Not language-related Language is not the primary cause of the problem	E.g. adapting to Japanese pedagogical styles; accommodating religious needs that are uncommon in Japan	E.g. feeling discriminated against; adapting to Japanese socializing styles

5.1   Sources and Levels of Support

Having formulated a typology of the problems identified by our participants, we address the first part of RQ2—*to what extent are problems adequately supported?*—by coding participants' diaries and interview transcripts for three levels of support: No support, where participants did not identify receiving any support for a problem; inadequate support, where some support was provided but the problem persisted or continued to cause stress; and adequate support that helped the participant overcome the problem without lingering stress. Support was considered adequate if the participant indicated satisfaction with how it helped him or her overcome the problem in the end; this includes cases where a problem was described as challenging but had no evidence of dissatisfaction or lingering stress (Fig. 3).

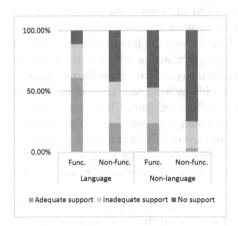

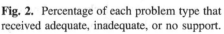

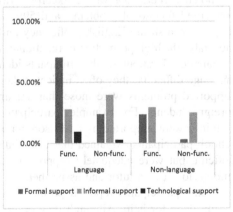

Fig. 2. Percentage of each problem type that received adequate, inadequate, or no support.

Fig. 3. Percentage of each type of problem associated with formal, informal, and technological support.

Figure 2 shows what percentage of each type of problem was associated with each support level. Functional, language-related problems were by far the most likely to be associated with adequate support (61%), and by far the least likely to be associated with no support (11%). In contrast, non-functional, not language-related problems were often associated with no support (75%) and only one item from this category was associated with adequate support (3%). Functional, not language-related problems and non-functional, language-related problems had similar levels of support to each other.

When some kind of support was identified by participants, we identified sources of support among three categories: *Formal support* provided as part of a formal relationship such as by professors, tutors who were formally assigned to support a particular student, and staff at businesses and train stations; *informal support* provided by friends, strangers, and classmates who have no formal obligation to help; and *technological support* provided by tools such as Google translate or electronic dictionary software. In some cases, participants identified multiple sources of support for the same problem, in which case all of the identified categories were included.

5.2 Types of Problems and Support

Given the significant variations in the types and levels of support that participants identified for each type of problem, this section presents examples of problems and their support in each category. By doing so, we address the second part of RQ2, *what reasons can be identified for varying levels of support?* Participants' descriptions of problems and explanations for varying levels of support are quoted from their diary entries and interview transcripts; the source of each quotation is indicated in brackets (e.g.: [#7.69, interview] refers to excerpt #69, which was taken from participant 7's interview).

Functional, Language-Related

As noted earlier, 65% of the excerpts drawn from the interviews and diary entries concerned functional problems, and 59% of these were language-related. Since participants had strong English proficiency and English was the lingua franca in most of their labs, the high proportion of functional, language-related problems warrants further explanation. First, although participants identified many functional problems related to language difficulty, they often indicated these problems were well supported. The best supported problems were those that are universally experienced by the majority of foreign students. For example, participants indicated that many essential academic activities were supported by professors who could speak sufficient English. Outside of school, participants explained that essential tasks such as opening bank accounts were difficult, but were adequately supported because their laboratories assigned a senior student to act as a tutor and assist them.

Some participants reported problems when working with Japanese lab mates or asking them for help. Although they described their lab mates as generally willing to help, participants often reported that their Japanese peers were lacking in English proficiency. This caused communication breakdowns, and was viewed as causing hesitance on the part of Japanese students to communicate with foreigners. One participant explained how he improved his ability to overcome these problems by studying Japanese language and using technology:

> Our seniors will guide us directly to use the equipment. But some of the seniors [...] are not used to speaking English. So that's kind of a big problem in my first semester. But [...] I also study some basic of language. Now I'm able to communicate easily with my senior, you can say, my tutor, to use all the equipment [...] [We use] both English and Japanese. But my senpai [senior] sometimes he cannot find the English words, so I use Google Translate to translate his words to English [#7.69, interview].

Problems that were not universally experienced were unlikely to be adequately supported by professors or other Japanese colleagues and often required foreign students to communicate in Japanese. For example, a minority of participants took some courses that required understanding Japanese, and had significant difficulty. Outside of school, several participants had needs that were challenging to achieve, such as Muslim participants who described difficulty asking restaurant and store staff whether foods were halal:

> Sometimes here the food label does not contain any information about halal, haram [...] I want to ask is it halal, but they don't understand English [#10.90, interview].

Faced with this difficulty, Muslim students were likely to seek support from their Muslim peers, both in-person and using social media:

> We have a Muslim community, they have post on Facebook with foods that are halal, and we follow that [#8.82, interview].

Sharing information with other Muslims made it possible to overcome difficulties that Japanese hosts were unable to support, but required more work than had those difficulties been supported by participants' universities. It is likely that Japanese peers and university administrators were not aware of the extent of these difficulties because support was sought through Muslim communities of which they are not members.

Non-functional, Language-Related

Non-functional, language-related problems were less supported than functional ones, with only 24% being associated with adequate support. Inside of school, these typically related to non-essential laboratory activities conducted in Japanese or informal communication with Japanese lab mates. Outside of school most of these problems were related to activities such as shopping for non-essentials, travelling for leisure, and socializing with Japanese people, all of which often required communicating in Japanese. When participants indicated adequate support for these problems it was because they relied on someone who translated between Japanese and English or they encountered Japanese people who spoke English well enough to communicate.

Language barriers were difficult to overcome when socializing with Japanese peers, and many participants described a mutual reluctance to mingle between Japanese and foreigners. When participants did socialize with Japanese peers, it was common for language difficulties to persist despite efforts to surmount them:

> [T]hey try to speak English to me sometimes. [B]ut most of the conversation is in Japanese. I sometimes feel like alone with them because I have nothing to say [#5.45, diary].

One participant identified a strategy to address this problem, explaining that text chatting was a useful approach for informal conversations with Japanese people in English:

[S]ocial media or email is better option for communicating with Japanese, since they're good at writing English rather than talking in English. [E]ven sometimes I talk to them with emoji/stickers because they're cute and simple [#4.40, diary].

Finally, even though participants preferred using English when possible, several commented that English was still difficult compared to their mother tongue. One participant remarked that speaking in foreign languages consumed some of his brain's "processing abilities" [#3.27, interview] and others expressed feeling comfort when socializing with co-nationals in their native language, which is consistent with previous research [33]. Finding opportunities to communicate with co-nationals was one way to address this problem, but participants did not identify any other methods of support.

Functional, Not Language-Related
Most functional problems that were not caused by language difficulty were related to cultural differences. Several participants identified differences between Japanese academic styles and those of their home countries. In one case, this made it difficult for a student to understand her professors' expectations for her work. Informal conversations with fellow foreign students helped her cope with this difficulty:

In the beginning, I thought it's only me. But when we have a conversation we talk, useless things, we have the same experiences. I thought it was only me! [#6.65, interview].

Other problems were more related to specific needs of individual participants, and were thus less universal. As described earlier, Muslim students had language difficulties when trying to ask whether various foods were halal. Additionally, problems related to Muslim religious practices extended past language. For example, there were few halal options available on campus regardless of one's ability to ask about them. Their university addressed some needs, such as providing a prayer room for Muslim students. When support from their university was lacking, Muslim participants tended to turn to other Muslims.

Outside of campus, problems based on cultural differences were generally either supported by co-nationals and other foreigners, or not identified with any support. One participant expressed frustration with the lack of support from his Japanese colleagues:

I came here with my family [...] so I think any person who is aware that I am here with my family will know that I need to buy so many things [...] I found all of them by myself. Nobody told me. After that I realized, after getting the things, and talking to people, I realized they knew about it. But they never told me [...] Sometimes [Japanese people] are supportive, but they are not really that open [#15.131, interview].

His statement reinforces a common theme in participants' remarks, that Japanese peers were described as providing help when asked, but as not volunteering support on their own. As a result, participants identified many cases where their expectations of support were not met and this gap in expectations itself was described as a cultural difference.

Non-functional, Not Language-Related

These problems were the least likely to be supported (only 3% were associated with adequate support). Although language difficulty was a common barrier for developing social relationships, cultural differences played a further role. Participants' expectations of relationship norms in their laboratories differed from those of their Japanese peers. One participant felt Japanese members of his lab distinguished between friends and work-colleagues, which he believed constrained his ability to socialize with them:

> A person told me a phrase, if I translate in English it's "laboratory friend." For me it is friends or not friends, or something like acquaintance [...] Laboratory is some business and friends are private. So, they have a very clear boundary [#3.26, interview].

Similarly, another participant expressed unhappiness that his Japanese lab mates were not socially open with him:

> Latin American people [...] we are so open ... For example, in the morning you ride to the office. If it were Latin America, you will go and say hello to everyone. To everyone! [...] but in Japan it's kind of difficult because they always ignore you. [...] I come here and sit at my place and the guy next to me won't even look at me. So really for me that's still difficult [#15.134, interview].

Some support for these social difficulties was provided by a small minority of Japanese people with whom participants had developed friendships, but more commonly participants socialized with other foreigners, especially co-nationals, instead.

An additional problem experienced by some participants was perceived racial discrimination. During this study, we did not identify support opportunities to prevent discrimination from taking place, but we did note that participants who felt discriminated against tended to seek emotional support from family and romantic partners, who were overwhelmingly co-nationals:

> I talk with my wife, but I don't talk with Japanese people about that [#1.6, interview].

5.3   Highlighting Co-national Support for Strong Cultural Differences

The previous findings have shown that relationships with co-nationals are crucial for supporting problems related to cultural practices that are not well recognized in the host country. In this section, we discuss how Muslim participants had especially strong relationships with their co-national communities. Our results echo previous research highlighting that Muslim students' religious concerns tend to be poorly addressed by host-nationals [49], and we found evidence that co-national communities were instrumental for addressing those concerns.

Among our 15 participants, 6 were from Muslim countries and observed Muslim customs. Using participants' communication logs, we compared how many people Muslim and non-Muslim participants had logged communication with per day. We distinguished between three groups of people living in Japan: *Japanese people, co-nationals,* and *people from other countries.* Although participants logged both strong (in-depth or lengthy) and weak (brief or trivial) communications, we focused on strong communications as a clearer indication of close relationships. Muslim participants had strong communications with more people per day than non-Muslims in all categories. The largest difference was in the number of co-nationals; Muslims logged strong communications with an average of 1.40 co-national sojourners per day, compared to 0.61 for non-Muslims.

A Spearman's correlation was run to evaluate the relationship between the number of co-nationals Muslim and non-Muslim participants logged strong communications with per day, and how comfortable they reported feeling about their lives in Japan that day. For Muslims, there was a moderate but significant positive correlation between these two variables ($r_s = .4060$, $p < .001$) and for non-Muslims there was a weak but significant negative correlation ($r_s = -.2190$, $p < .001$). Neither Muslim or non-Muslim participants had a significant correlation between comfort and strong communications with other groups. This suggests that communication with many co-nationals had a comforting effect for Muslims.

A potential explanation for why Muslims seemed to have close relationships with their co-national communities is that they seemed to have strong cultural differences not only with Japanese people, but with other foreigners. A participant from China noted experiencing culture shock more with Muslims than with Japanese people:

> Such as Indonesia, mainly about the language and also their behavior, because they need to pray every day and their food has much requirements [#2.21, interview].

A Muslim student presents a similar observation from the opposite view, identifying his religious customs as a barrier for socializing with non-Muslims:

> Halal food. That's why I avoid going out with them. One of the reasons. But when I stay with my country people, what they cook I can eat everything [...] during the sunset I have prayer time. So, some people are going at that time but I can't go [#8.83, interview].

These remarks are consistent with previous research arguing that religious differences act as barriers for relationships between Muslim and non-Muslim students [50, 51], and suggest a reason that Muslim participants in this study were motivated to communicate often with other Muslims who were often co-national.

6 Discussion

Our study revealed how different types of problems experienced by foreign students were provided with differing levels of support. Many of the best supported problems were those that are commonly experienced by almost all foreign students. One explanation is that because these challenges are common to most foreign students, they are more visible to university staff who can then prepare support in advance.

The least supported language-related problems tended to involve informal communications. Informal communication is generally ad-hoc, in contrast to the scheduled, agenda-driven nature of formal communication, and is valuable for helping members of an organization learn about each other, improve social relations, and perform collaborative work [52]. There was evidence that Japanese students in particular, but also some foreign students, socialized in language cliques [33] where they grouped themselves by native language. This decreased opportunities for informal communication between Japanese and foreign students, and when they did socialize both sides had difficulty understanding each other. Foreign students who have difficulty making Japanese friends are less likely to be able to turn to those people for either practical or emotional support, so this may contribute to significant problems in the future.

Most problems that were not language-related were based around cultural differences. Participants often claimed that their Japanese professors and colleagues did not recognize or volunteer support for these kinds of problems. As a result, participants often sought support from co-nationals or sojourners from other countries who more likely to have experienced the same difficulties, and therefore were better able to provide practical and emotional support. Muslims stood out as having different problems and support strategies than other participants, and co-national relationships seemed to be particularly important for them. We considered why this could be the case. Although Muslims are well represented among international students in Japan (in 2015 there were 3,600 Indonesians studying at Japanese universities), students from other countries such as China are far more populous [53]. Therefore, the presence of co-national Muslim communities is insufficient to explain this finding. Another explanation is that Muslim participants had significant cultural differences not just with Japanese, but also with other foreigners. This is consistent with previous studies of Muslim international students in other countries [50, 51]. Despite this, Muslims logged strong communications with a greater number of people in all categories (co-national, other sojourner, and Japanese) than non-Muslims did. One explanation for Muslim participants' stronger indications of support is that, by communicating with a larger number of people they may have gained access to more diverse information and resources for solving their problems. That they could build expansive social networks in spite of cultural barriers may be key to understanding how these participants found more support for their problems.

Given the uniqueness of our study population, to what extent could we expect to see similar results in other contexts? It is likely that the general pattern of functional problems being better supported than non-functional problems could also be found among foreign students in other countries and members of other intercultural organizations. Functional problems tend to be visible because they often (1) require urgent resolution and (2) relate to commonly experienced needs. Regarding the relatively high level of support for language problems, particularly with academic tasks, one explanation is that a significant amount of communication with professors and peers was conducted in a mutual second language, distributing the burden of intercultural communication. In contexts without a common second-language, host-country people are less likely to possess awareness and ability to support sojourners in communicating.

6.1   Design Implications

The bulk of our analysis served to categorize foreign students' problems, identify which types of problems are most lacking in support, and consider why this occurs. Based on this analysis, RQ3 asks *how can inadequately supported problems be addressed using language and social technologies?* We suggest three approaches for designers to facilitate increased support where it is most needed. These approaches would support efforts for foreign students to communicate their needs and develop relationships that could provide information, resources, and emotional support.

Supporting Face to Face Intercultural Communication

For those who lacked the language ability to converse face-to-face, text-based communication could be conducted using tools like social media sites. Japanese colleagues were described as more capable at writing than speaking English, and foreign lab members could use Google Translate to understand Japanese text. However, text-based communications bear little resemblance to face-to-face conversations that are characterized by spontaneity and improvisation. Given that many technological efforts to support intercultural communication are related to online rather than in-person conversations [54], tools designed to be integrated alongside face-to-face communication may improve efforts to socialize among intercultural peers. Also, previous studies have focused almost exclusively on supporting non-native speakers' comprehension, but our study highlights the need for supporting non-native speakers' in *generating* speech.

One method could be adapting support features of written communication media to face-to-face communication. Linguistic search engines such as NetSpeak [55, 56] and Linggle [57] aim to support writers (especially non-native speakers) by suggesting how to complete phrases based on a corpus of common expressions. And, software such as SwiftKey [58] use machine learning to provide next-word suggestions based on text input. A future step may be to combine such tools with speech recognition, so non-native speakers could view suggestions when struggling to find a word or expression.

Machine translation [45] is another promising approach, but is still in an early stage of development. Future advancements may help machine translation become a viable way for people to have complex inter-linguistic conversations using their native languages, which could be a substantial boon for supporting informal communications. This may be particularly relevant for the context of this study where English was used as a lingua franca among multiple groups of non-native English speakers. Especially since, in spite of their strong English proficiency, our participants noted that their native languages were still more comfortable.

Evaluating Technologies for Informal Communication

Many evaluations of existing technologies to support intercultural communication use metrics such as the speed and accuracy at which participants can complete a task [42, 44, 45]. These metrics are effective for understanding instrumental communication that is most useful toward solving functional problems. This is consistent with our finding that technological support was identified for 9% of functional problems and only 3% of non-functional problems. However, these metrics do not seem well-suited for evaluating informal communication, which is often less instrumental. Therefore, future studies may improve our understanding of how technologies can facilitate informal communication by investigating the use of these tools in natural settings. As well as task completion, researchers could evaluate qualities such as shared knowledge, community cohesion, feelings of belonging, and spontaneity among intercultural peers.

Communicating Problems

In many cases, participants indicated that their professors, colleagues, and other Japanese people seemed unaware of the severity of certain problems. A common observation was that Japanese people provided support when asked directly, but rarely volunteered. Instead of constantly asking Japanese colleagues for help, participants often turned to other foreigners. Foreign students would benefit from tools that help them communicate their difficulties to host-nationals. With regard to language-difficulties, previous work has demonstrated that making native-speakers aware of non-native speakers' difficulties encouraged more effective communication strategies [41]. Additionally, language barriers tend to be asymmetric because, although native speakers are aware of non-native speakers' difficulties, they do not understand how this affect non-native speakers' behavior [59]. Awareness of cultural differences seems to be similarly asymmetric, and therefore difficult for institutions to effectively support.

Yuan et al. [33] pointed to the potential of systems that increase "awareness of others' linguistic and cultural backgrounds" for helping members of multicultural organizations identify peers who understand their cultural needs. When our participants turned to co-nationals for support it was often organized through Facebook groups or other communication channels outside their university. Accordingly, the problems and support discussed in those channels were not visible to administrators or faculty who could create formal support mechanisms within their institution. Universities and other organizations with multicultural populations could improve their awareness of cultural differences by providing their own platforms for foreign members to discuss their difficulties. This could be pursued through software that prompts people to make notes of their challenges, or through social networking services with matchmaking systems based on mutual problems, cultural practices, and goals. Information shared through such systems could then be communicated to other members of the organization, taking appropriate measures to preserve individuals' privacy. Applied to a university context, such approaches could improve institutional awareness of problems related to cultural difference, and encourage policies and practices to better support foreign students.

7 Conclusion and Future Work

This study focused on a five-week period in participants' first year of graduate programs in Japan. We investigated how different types of problems experienced by foreign students are met with different levels of support. We shed light on factors that influence the availability of support, and used these findings to identify opportunities for addressing poorly supported problems. The unique population of our study helped disentangle language and non-language problems. Both language and culture barriers are asymmetrical and generally higher when seen from international students' side. For our population, language barriers related to English are higher from the Japanese side, but culture barriers (adaptation to Japanese culture) are higher from the international students' side. Often, culture barriers (like Japanese habits) are invisible from the Japanese side so it causes stress to the international students. As a result, they may attribute some Japanese behaviors to negative motivations such as discrimination, but the root cause could be a lack of awareness.

Our technical recommendations about face-to-face communication address language asymmetry by focusing on non-natives generating speech. And our discussion of tools for improving institutional knowledge of foreign students' difficulties addresses barriers caused by asymmetric awareness of both language and cultural difficulties. Mutual deficits of awareness may lead foreign students to perceive certain Japanese behaviors negatively and discourage communication with Japanese people. Providing them ways to explain their own behavior may help illuminate these difficulties. Other methods for highlighting these barriers could include sensing behaviors using pervasive technologies, clustering them into groups using machine learning techniques, and visualizing/highlighting differences between Japanese and international students.

Although our study provides insight into the problems and support opportunities experienced early in their sojourns, it does not identify changes that might occur later in their studies. Future work may benefit from a longitudinal approach that could better address longer-term adjustment. Additionally, similar approaches may be valuable for studying sojourners in other contexts, such as other types of multicultural organizations.

Acknowledgements. This work is partially supported by Grant for Scientific Research (A) 17H00771 from Japan Society for the Promotion of Science (JSPS). Additionally, this research was supported by the Social Sciences and Humanities Research Council of Canada.

 Social Sciences and Humanities   Conseil de recherches en   Canadä
Research Council of Canada   sciences humaines du Canada

References

1. Akhtar, M., Kröner-Herwig, B.: Acculturative stress among international students in context of socio-demographic variables and coping styles. Curr. Psychol. **34**, 803–815 (2015)
2. Sawir, E., Marginson, S., Deumert, A., Nyland, C., Ramia, G.: Loneliness and international students: an Australian study. J. Stud. Int. Educ. **12**, 148–180 (2008)
3. Martirosyan, N.M., Hwang, E., Wanjohi, R.: Impact of English proficiency on academic performance of international students. J. Int. Stud. **5**, 60–71 (2015)
4. Sawir, E., Marginson, S., Forbes-Mewett, H., Nyland, C., Ramia, G.: International student security and English language proficiency. J. Stud. Int. Educ. **16**, 434–454 (2012)
5. Abouserie, R.: Sources and levels of stress in relation to locus of control and self esteem in university students. Educ. Psychol. **14**, 323–330 (1994)
6. Zajacova, A., Lynch, S.M., Espenshade, T.J.: Self-efficacy, stress, and academic success in college. Res. High. Educ. **46**, 677–706 (2005)
7. Bochner, S., McLeod, A., Lin, B.: Friendship patterns of overseas students: a functional model. Int. J. Psychol. **12**, 277–294 (1977)
8. Chaoping, L., Ning, Z., Qiong, Z., Zhenglin, C.: Cross-cultural adaptation of foreign students in Chinese university: based on network of social support. Cross-Cult. Commun. **10**, 16–20 (2014)
9. Furnham, A., Alibhai, N.: The friendship networks of foreign students: a replication and extension of the functional model. Int. J. Psychol. **20**, 709–722 (1985)
10. Tanaka, T., Takai, J., Kohyama, T., Fujihara, T., Minami, H.: Social networks of international students in Japan: perceived social support and relationship satisfaction. Jpn. J. Exp. Soc. Psychol. **33**, 213–223 (1994)
11. Habib, L., Johannesen, M., Øgrim, L.: Experiences and challenges of international students in technology-rich learning environments. Educ. Technol. Soc. **17**, 196–206 (2014)
12. Maundeni, T.: The role of social networks in the adjustment of African students to British society: students' perceptions. Race Ethn. Educ. **4**, 253–276 (2001)

13. Cohen, S., Wills, T.A.: Stress, social support, and the buffering hypothesis. Psychol. Bull. **98**, 310–357 (1985)
14. Church, A.T.: Sojourner adjustment. Psychol. Bull. **91**, 540–572 (1982)
15. Hendrickson, B., Rosen, D., Aune, R.K.: An analysis of friendship networks, social connectedness, homesickness, and satisfaction levels of international students. Int. J. Intercult. Relat. **35**, 281–295 (2011)
16. Rienties, B., Héliot, Y., Jindal-Snape, D.: Understanding social learning relations of international students in a large classroom using social network analysis. High. Educ. **66**, 489–504 (2013)
17. Ward, C., Kennedy, A.: Where's the "culture" in cross-cultural transition? Comparitive studies of sojourner adjustement. J. Cross-Cult. Psychol. **24**, 221–249 (1993)
18. Ma, A.S.: Social networks, cultural capital and attachment to the host city: comparing overseas Chinese students and foreign students in Taipei. Asia Pac. Viewpoint **55**, 226–241 (2014)
19. Tanaka, T., Takai, J., Kohyama, T., Fujihara, T., Minami, H.: Effects of social networks on cross-cultural adjustment. Jpn. Psychol. Res. **39**, 12–24 (1997)
20. Tanaka, T., Takai, J., Takaya, K., Fujihara, T.: Adjustment patterns of international students in Japan. Int. J. Intercult. Relat. **18**, 55–75 (1994)
21. Geeraert, N., Demoulin, S., Demes, K.A.: Choose your (international) contacts wisely: a multilevel analysis on the impact of intergroup contact while living abroad. Int. J. Intercult. Relat. **38**, 86–96 (2014)
22. Steinfield, C., Ellison, N.B., Lampe, C.: Social capital, self-esteem, and use of online social network sites: a longitudinal analysis. J. Appl. Dev. Psychol. **29**, 434–445 (2008)
23. Valenzuela, S., Park, N., Kee, K.F.: Is there social capital in a social network site?: Facebook use and college students' life satisfaction, trust, and participation. J. Comput.-Mediat. Commun. **14**, 875–901 (2009)
24. Ellison, N.B., Steinfield, C., Lampe, C.: The benefits of Facebook "friends:" social capital and college students' use of online social network sites. J. Comput.-Mediat. Commun. **12**, 1143–1168 (2007)
25. Smith, M.E., Nguyen, D.T., Lai, C., Leshed, G., Baumer, E.P.: Going to college and staying connected: communication between college freshmen and their parents. In: Proceedings of the ACM 2012 Conference on Computer Supported Cooperative Work, pp. 789–798. ACM, New York (2012)
26. Hofer, B.: The electronic tether: parental regulation, self-regulation, and the role of technology in college transitions. J. First-Year Exp. Stud. Transit. **20**, 9–24 (2008)
27. Zhang, S., Jiang, H., Carroll, J.M.: Babel or great wall: social media use among Chinese students in the United States. In: Proceedings of the 30th ACM International Conference on Design of Communication, pp. 37–46. ACM, New York (2012)
28. Rao, X., Hemphill, L.: Asian American Chicago Network: a case study of Facebook group use by immigrant groups. In: Proceedings of the 19th ACM Conference on Computer Supported Cooperative Work and Social Computing Companion, pp. 381–384. ACM, New York (2016)
29. Saw, G., Abbott, W., Donaghey, J., McDonald, C.: Social media for international students – it's not all about Facebook. Libr. Manag. **34**, 156–174 (2013)
30. Yuan, C.W., Setlock, L.D., Fussell, S.R.: International students' use of Facebook vs. a home country site. In: CHI 2014 Extended Abstracts on Human Factors in Computing Systems, pp. 2101–2106. ACM, New York (2014)
31. Morita, N.: Negotiating participation and identity in second language academic communities. TESOL Q. **38**, 573–603 (2004)

32. Hansen, M., Scholz, L., Jucks, R.: Intercultural communication in university teaching. In: Proceedings of the 3rd International Conference on Intercultural Collaboration, pp. 187–190. ACM, New York (2010)

33. Yuan, C.W., Setlock, L.D., Cosley, D., Fussell, S.R.: Understanding informal communication in multilingual contexts. In: Proceedings of the 2013 Conference on Computer Supported Cooperative Work, pp. 909–922. ACM, New York (2013)

34. Yashima, T.: Willingness to communicate in a second language: the Japanese EFL context. Mod. Lang. J. **86**, 54–66 (2002)

35. Tange, H., Lauring, J.: Language management and social interaction within the multilingual workplace. J. Commun. Manag. **13**, 218–232 (2009)

36. Henderson, J.K.: Language diversity in international management teams. Int. Stud. Manag. Org. **35**, 66–82 (2005)

37. Chevrier, S.: Cross-cultural management in multinational project groups. J. World Bus. **38**, 141–149 (2003)

38. Yamashita, N., Echenique, A., Ishida, T., Hautasaari, A.: Lost in transmittance: how transmission lag enhances and deteriorates multilingual collaboration. In: Proceedings of the 2013 Conference on Computer Supported Cooperative Work, pp. 923–934. ACM, New York (2013)

39. Gao, G., Yamashita, N., Hautasaari, A.M., Echenique, A., Fussell, S.R.: Effects of public vs. private automated transcripts on multiparty communication between native and non-native English speakers. In: Proceedings of the SIGCHI Conference on Human Factors in Computing Systems, pp. 843–852. ACM, New York (2014)

40. Pan, Y., Jiang, D., Picheny, M., Qin, Y.: Effects of real-time transcription on non-native speaker's comprehension in computer-mediated communications. In: Proceedings of the SIGCHI Conference on Human Factors in Computing Systems, pp. 2353–2356. ACM, New York (2009)

41. Gao, G., Yamashita, N., Hautasaari, A.M.J., Fussell, S.R.: Improving multilingual collaboration by displaying how non-native speakers use automated transcripts and bilingual dictionaries. In: Proceedings of the 33rd Annual ACM Conference on Human Factors in Computing Systems, pp. 3463–3472. ACM, New York (2015)

42. Yamashita, N., Inaba, R., Kuzuoka, H., Ishida, T.: Difficulties in establishing common ground in multiparty groups using machine translation. In: Proceedings of the SIGCHI Conference on Human Factors in Computing Systems, pp. 679–688. ACM, New York (2009)

43. Yamashita, N., Ishida, T.: Effects of machine translation on collaborative work. In: Proceedings of the 2006 20th Anniversary Conference on Computer Supported Cooperative Work, pp. 515–524. ACM, New York (2006)

44. Gao, G., Xu, B., Hau, D.C., Yao, Z., Cosley, D., Fussell, S.R.: Two is better than one: improving multilingual collaboration by giving two machine translation outputs. In: Proceedings of the 18th ACM Conference on Computer Supported Cooperative Work and Social Computing, pp. 852–863. ACM, New York (2015)

45. Hara, K., Iqbal, S.: Effect of machine translation in interlingual conversation: lessons from a formative study. In: CHI 2015 Proceedings of the 33rd Annual ACM Conference on Human Factors in Computing Systems, pp. 3473–3482. ACM, New York (2015)

46. Setlock, L.D., Fussell, S.R.: What's it worth to you?: the costs and affordances of CMC tools to Asian and American users. In: Proceedings of the 2010 ACM Conference on Computer Supported Cooperative Work, pp. 341–350. ACM, New York (2010)

47. Yeh, C.J., Inose, M.: International students' reported English fluency, social support satisfaction, and social connectedness as predictors of acculturative stress. Couns. Psychol. Quart. **16**, 15–28 (2003)

48. Neuman, W.L.: Social Research Methods: Qualitative and Quantitative Approaches. Allyn & Bacon, Boston (2003)
49. Sherry, M., Thomas, P., Chui, W.H.: International students: a vulnerable student population. High. Educ. **60**, 33–46 (2010)
50. Chen, Y.-L., Liu, M.-C., Tsai, T.-W., Chen, Y.-H.: Religious practices in cross-cultural contexts: Indonesian male science students' adjustment in Taiwan. J. Couns. Psychol. **62**, 464–475 (2015)
51. Tummala-Narra, P., Claudius, M.: A qualitative examination of Muslim graduate international students' experiences in the United States. Int. Perspect. Psychol. Res. Pract. Consult. **2**, 132–147 (2013)
52. Kraut, R.E., Fish, R.S., Root, R.W., Chalfonte, B.L.: Informal communication in organizations: form, function, and technology. In: Oskamp, S., Spacapan, S. (eds.) Human Reactions to Technology: Claremont Symposium on Applied Social Psychology, pp. 145–199. SAGE Publications, Beverly Hills (1990)
53. Report on 2015 Foreign Students Enrollment Survey (in Japanese) (2016). http://www.mext. go.jp/a_menu/koutou/ryugaku/__icsFiles/afieldfile/2016/04/08/1345878_2.pdf
54. He, H.A., Huang, E.M.: A qualitative study of workplace intercultural communication tensions in dyadic face-to-face and computer-mediated interactions. In: Proceedings of the 2014 Conference on Designing Interactive Systems, pp. 415–424. ACM, New York (2014)
55. Stein, B., Potthast, M., Trenkmann, M.: Retrieving customary web language to assist writers. In: Gurrin, C., He, Y., Kazai, G., Kruschwitz, U., Little, S., Roelleke, T., Rüger, S., van Rijsbergen, K. (eds.) ECIR 2010. LNCS, vol. 5993, pp. 631–635. Springer, Heidelberg (2010). doi:10.1007/978-3-642-12275-0_64
56. Potthast, M., Hagen, M., Beyer, A., Stein, B.: Improving cloze test performance of language learners using web n-grams. In: Proceedings of COLING 2014, the 25th International Conference on Computational Linguistics: Technical Papers, Dublin, Ireland, pp. 962–973 (2014)
57. Boisson, J., Kao, T.-H., Wu, J.-C., Yen, T.-H., Chang, J.S.: Linggle: a web-scale linguistic search engine for words in context. In: Proceedings of the 51st Annual Meeting of the Association for Computational Linguistics, pp. 139–144. Association for Computational Linguistics, New York (2013)
58. SwiftKey: Smart Prediction Technology for Easier Mobile Typing. https://swiftkey.com
59. He, H., Yamashita, N., Hautasaari, A., Cao, X., Huang, E.: Why did they do that? Exploring attribution mismatches between native and non-native speakers using videoconferencing. In: Proceedings of the 20th ACM Conference on Computer Supported Cooperative Work and Social Computing (CSCW 2017). ACM, New York (2017)

PersonaBrowser

Status Quo and Lessons Learned from a Persona-Based Presentation Metaphor of WCAG

Alexander Henka[✉] and Gottfried Zimmermann

Responsive Media Experience Research Group (REMEX),
Stuttgart Media University, Nobelstr. 10, 70569 Stuttgart, Germany
henka@hdm-stuttgart.de, gzimmermann@acm.org

Abstract. In this paper, we examine how personas need to be designed to transport the information of accessibility resources like the Web Content Accessibility Guidelines (WCAG) in a user-centered way, while preserving their vivid nature. We discuss the benefits and issues, e.g., that using only impairments as a tie is not sufficient and comes with side-effects. We conducted a study to state the status quo of linking WCAG to personas by measuring the user experience of a system highlighting this connection, to the WCAG Quick Reference. Furthermore, this work highlights some issues when deploying those resources in lectures for teaching accessibility, pin-points some solutions to overcome these issues and reports on our lessons learned on the usage of this user-centered presentation metaphor of WCAG.

Keywords: Personas · HCI · Accessibility · WCAG · Presentation metaphor · Meaning making · Creating tension · PersonaBrowser

1 Introduction

It was reported that accessibility resources can overwhelm web authors (i.e. all persons involved in the making process of a web application) with information [1, 2]. Also, the classification how severe reported accessibility issues are for some users, is not always evident for a web author [3, 4] and the interpretation differs even more between beginners and experts [5]. While experienced evaluators have the knowledge on how a certain WCAG success criterion should be applied and how different users can benefit from its compliance, it can be tough for beginners to make the connection between a WCAG success criterion and the benefits for users that comes with its compliance [5]. Since accessibility is considered strongly a user centered issue [3, 6], and is characterized as follows: "*[Accessibility is, when] specific users with specific disabilities can use it [the software] to achieve specific goals with the same effectiveness, safety and security as non-disabled people*" [3], it should be an obligation to feature the connection to the user, and to provide a motivation for the relevance of each success criteria. This is especially important for beginners in the application of WCAG. Therefore, the usage of automatic testing tools, checking a web applications' accommodation to WCAG, is not fully sufficient to state the accessibility of a web application [7, 8]. While WCAG

Published by Springer International Publishing AG 2017. All Rights Reserved
R. Bernhaupt et al. (Eds.): INTERACT 2017, Part II, LNCS 10514, pp. 54–63, 2017.
DOI: 10.1007/978-3-319-67684-5_4

(version 2.0) forms the technical foundation, and provides rules and instructions to solve - or avoid - defects on web applications, there is also the other side of the coin (respectively: the barrier).

Following the user centered view on barriers, as stated above, a defect on a web application only turns into a barrier if the defect hinders a specific user with specific traits from achieving their specific goals. It is this tension, i.e. seeing a barrier from the user perspective, that can actually create meaning for barriers, and for the success criteria of WCAG, and therefore help to meet the requirements of people with impairments.

From a sociology point of view, Bowker and Star [9] stated: *"We [humans] know what something is by contrast with what is not"*; e.g., light versus darkness, or in the way that silence makes musical notes perceivable. As they further explained: *"We often cannot see we take for granted - unless we encounter someone who does not take it for granted"*. Bowker and Star conclude that "tension" between contexts is necessary to create meaning and that information, generally spoken, only gains weight if it can be interpreted in multiple ways.

This provides a sociological explanation why web authors who are new to the topic of accessibility have issues to classify the severity of reported accessibly issues. It can therefore be hard for novices to see barriers and distinguish between severe and trivial accessibly issues [4], since they themselves can perform all use-cases in a web application. Hence, they take the interaction paradigm of a web application for granted – unless, they encounter someone who is actually facing barriers during the interaction, for example while observing a user test. On the other hand, the values of constructional accessibility, like ramps to bypass stairs, are easier recognized, since we encounter them almost every day. We can regularly observe people and situations in which the physical circumstances of our world impose a barrier. In contrast, interaction with software is usually a more private affair; there is no (legal) way of overseeing a product's users.

Another difference between software- and constructional accessibility is that constructional accessibility can imply meaning for everybody. If someone is facing stairs in the contextual situation of traveling with a baby buggy or carrying heavy luggage, the importance of a ramp or an elevator is highly valuated. In other situations, however, the barrier that stairs can imply may be overlooked or not be recognized. Therefore, a specific object or situation may be experienced differently in different contexts, which then creates meaning, following the argumentation of Bowker and Star.

This tension between contexts is stripped away when focusing solely on (automatic) tools, which evaluate the conformance of web application to WCAG. This could be problematic for beginners as literature suggests [3, 5]. At some point, a web author has internalized WCAG to an extent in which WCAG and its success criteria are taken "for granted". Hence, the web author can state the severity of potential accessibly issues and has in-depth knowledge on how people with disabilities interact with web applications; thus, the web author has become a web accessibility expert. This process is called: *naturalization* [9]. At this point, the web author has an intrinsic knowledge of the meaning of web barriers. Forgotten are the struggles of being new to the accessibility topic when everything was strange and odd.

Rooted in the disciplines of human centered design, *personas* [10] are a widely-used concept to transport user needs and requirements and to keep track of them during the product development process. Using walkthrough techniques to question product features and evaluating interaction paradigms, personas can be a tool to create contextual tension, thus seeing the product through the eyes of the persona.

In this paper, we present and discuss an approach for creating tension in the presentation of WCAG by using personas as a classification schema. The underlying principle is that each success criterion of a guideline should be represented as a set of personas affected by the success criterion; similar concepts have been discussed in [11, 12]. This paper provides an insight on the status quo of augmenting WCAG with personas. Hence, this work outlines some major issues when adding personas to WCAG and seeks to identify steps on how personas should be constructed and used in this context to overcome these issues. The remainder of this paper is structured as follows. Section 2 provides an overview on our persona in context concept and how it differs from the persona concept advocated by Cooper [10]. Section 3 introduces our work in this area, the PersonaBrowser, and a user experience study we conducted with students. In Sect. 4, we present the lessons that we have learned from our study and our conclusions.

2   Personas

Personas can be useful to solve some main obstacles and traps in the product development process: *the elastic user*; *the self-referential design*; and *design edge cases* [10, 13, 14], and they *limit the action space* [13, 15].

The *elastic user* refers to the issue that without having a common framing, the "user" is - metaphorically spoken - stretched to justify any decision and feature of a product. The *self-referential design* points to the common mistake of developers putting themselves "into the seat" as the later users of a product; hence, ignoring the needs and goals of the real users. Personas can also provide guidance in political disputes and discussions on *design edge cases,* helping to decide the issue of whether a certain feature should be included or excluded in a product, or on issues of the general design approach. With personas, the blurry "user" becomes tangible - with specific needs and requirements. One can refer directly to "Anna" and state: "Yes, someone might want that feature, but we are not designing for someone - we are designing for Anna" [10]. If the usage of personas is engrained into the working habits of the project team from the beginning [14, 16], personas can indeed become a *boundary object* [9] among team members and stakeholders.

Personas support the *"limitation of action space"* pattern [13, 15] since they cluster the needs and requirements of a product's end users by reducing the complexity from satisfying "the user", a vague and unknown entity, to a manageable number of personas (cf. [29]).

2.1   Personas: Vehicle and Information

Personas are, in their essence, just a different form of conveying user needs and requirements in a product development cycle, mainly advocated by the scholar of user centered design. To understand this tool, one has to distinguish between the vehicle, which is the shape or appearance, respectively, and the information, transported in said vehicle.

According to Cooper et al. [10], the important information that is conveyed in personas are the goals and motivations of end user towards the usage of certain product [17]. These are usually gathered through interviews and observations. It is the narrative framing that forms the vehicle and brings a persona to life [13]. This framing puts a mental model into the reader's head; it thus makes the behavior of that pictured personas vivid. To bolster the vividness, personas are usually accompanied by a photo, a name and other details that makes a persona an authentic character. Despite the fact that they are often called *hypothetical users*, personas are never an image or a representation of the average user-group, they are, as said, vehicles to communicate the important information – of real users – during product development in the most appropriate way for the development team.

The distinction between the information and the vehicle raises an interesting question: Can any form of information be more vivid and memorable if told by dint of personas – here, in the sense of wrapping something "bulky" up in the most delightful way for the audience? Much like one would hide a dog's medicine, a "bulky" but important piece, in a sausage slice so that a dog would eagerly swallow it. This work explores to reveal principles of how this vehicle needs to be designed to create tension and support meaning making to make WCAG more comprehensible for beginners. Following the dog's medicine analogy, WCAG is the "bulky" information and personas are the sausage.

2.2   Using Personas to Communicate the Relevance of WCAG Success Criteria

The benefits of personas as a vehicle to transport the needs and requirements of people with disabilities have been highlighted in various works, notably in tools and learning environments [18–22]. Besides [20], where personas with disabilities are used in the original fashion, these are all examples where the information that needs to be transported is the needs and preferences of the user group itself. This differs from the approach explored in our work. Here, the important information is not the needs and preferences of the user group but a set of rules. And these rules are not directly bound to the goals and motivations of a future user.

Ontologies have been developed [23, 24] to provide links between success criteria and impairments for which those criteria are considered essential. While these ontologies also make use of user entities similar to personas, they are dedicated to classifying the success criteria according to their relevance for certain impairments.

We envision to adapt the narrative persona concept to convey information outside its designated usage fashion, as introduced by Cooper [10]. The stories told by personas are tightly coupled with the information contained, or in other words, the stories are the information told in a narrative way. The information is constructed by clustering the goals and motivations of the end user towards a certain product. When using personas to communicate the relevance of WCAG success criteria, there are no goals or motivations directly involved to tell the story. People, artificial or real, are driven by motivations to reach a certain goal. When an application, for example a web shop, is compromised by defects that lead to barriers and hinders people from achieving their goals, then this application should adhere to WCAG. But, WCAG success criteria do not represent "goals" for users in any sense. This raises the question of what "items" the narrative nature of personas should be constructed of to convey the meaning for the success criteria (for details see Sect. 4).

3 The PersonaBrowser

In a web application called *PersonaBrowser*, we implemented a visualization of the connection between WCAG success criteria and personas for which the conformance of certain success criteria is essential. As a structural foundation, we used the ontology described in [23]. The *PersonaBrowser* illustrates nine personas, grouped into four categories of general impairment types: *visual, auditory, physical,* and *cognitive.* The personas are based on the "day-in-the-life" stories developed by the *MOOCA* project [27]. The term "persona" was actually avoided in *MOOCAP* to emphasize the fact, that they were created by experts and not by newly researched data. Nevertheless, the validity and the benefits of the *MOOCAP's* stories for conveying the needs and requirements of people with disabilities have been presented in [19]. For their usage in the PersonaBrowser, we added additional web links featuring further information about the impairment and used assistive technologies. A user of the *PersonaBrowser* can read about a persona, their life, needs, and essential WCAG success criteria. We also provided a mechanism to filter the WCAG success criteria for each persona according to conformance levels and (on a second view) all success criteria according to impairments and conformance levels.

3.1 User Experience Study with the PersonaBrowser

Since novices could benefit from featuring WCAG in a human-centered fashion (cf. Sect. 1), we used the *PersonaBrowser* as a teaching tool in an introductory HCI course (jointly hosted by the bachelor course programs media informatics and mobile media at the Stuttgart Media University) to field-test the PersonaBrowser over a period of three months. The study consisted of two parts with different goals. In the first part, we wanted to get insights on principles of how personas should to be constructed to serve as proper vehicles for WCAG success criteria, by identifying current issues in linking success criteria and personas based on impairments; thus, tackling the question raised in Sect. 2.2. This part consisted of observations in the class when using the *PersonaBrowser* for teaching accessibly, and informal feedback from the students (Sect. 3.2). In the second part, we wanted to quantify the effect on a user's experience with WCAG as generated by the means of personas. Therefore, we compared the user experience of the *PersonaBrowser* with that of the *WCAG Quick Reference* [25], which we used in a prior instance of the same course (with different students) as a teaching tool. The quantitative measurement of the user experience was based on the *User Experience Questionnaire* (UEQ) [26].

3.2   Results of the User Experience Study

For the quantitative comparison of the user experience between the *PersonaBrowser* and the *WCAG Quick Reference*, we included the WCAG Quick Reference in the PersonaBrowser, literally, with original colors and font styles as in the specification [25]. We surveyed 65 undergraduate students from two semesters, all novices in accessible design. One group of students (n = 38) worked solely with the *PersonaBrowser*, while the other group (n = 27) worked solely with the *WCAG Quick Reference*. We assessed the user experiences of both groups, using the *User Experience Questionnaire* (UEQ) [26] (see Fig. 1). In general, the UEQ yields the following aspects of user experience, including pragmatic and hedonic aspects: *Attractiveness*: Do users like or dislike the product? *Perspicuity*: Is it easy to learn how to use the product? (pragmatic). *Efficiency*: Can users solve their tasks without unnecessary effort? (pragmatic). *Dependability*: Does the user feel in control of the interaction? (hedonic). *Stimulation*: Is it exciting and motivating to use the product? (hedonic). *Novelty* Is the product innovative and creative? (hedonic). For each aspect, the scale ranges from −3 to +3 [28].

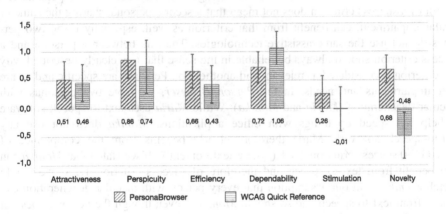

Fig. 1. Results of the UEQ. Comparison of scale means and the corresponding 5% confidence intervals.

The UEQ considers scores starting at 0.8 as positive and starting at −0.8 as negative. The overall user experience is therefore, at best, in the scale of *average*, for both systems. It should be noted that the study took place within the context of a mandatory lecture and that the results could have been influenced by a rather low motivation of some participants towards the topic of HCI and accessibility. Nevertheless, our result shows the issues of the *WCAG Quick Reference* when it comes to its usability for beginners. We did not expect any significant differences in the pragmatic values (perspicuity, efficiency), since the only thing we added in the PersonaBrowser is the connection between success criteria and personas based on their impairments, but the higher *efficiency* score can be seen as a hint for the benefits of a user-centered presentation metaphor due to its complexity reduction (cf. Sect. 4). While the average scores of *perspicuity, efficiency* and *stimulation* are higher for the *PersonaBrowser*, the pertaining T-Tests showed no significant differences ($\alpha = 0.05$). Only for *novelty*, the study reveals a significant difference between the PersonaBrowser and the *WCAG Quick Reference*. The UEQ score for novelty is still low, but this seems to be a hint that a user-centered presentation metaphor can be effective to catch the interest of web authors. While the *PersonaBrowser* has a higher *efficiency* score, the lower score for *dependability* was rather unexpected. This discrepancy can be explained under the spotlight of an issue that occurs if impairments are used as the only mean to link success criteria to the personas – the *elastic system*, see Sect. 4.

4   Discussion

We have learned some lessons from actively using the PersonaBrowser as a preparation tool for the accessibility course.

Elastic System. Using only impairments as anchors to success criteria leads to an *elastic system,* where personas can be stretched to justify almost any success criteria. Personas are never an embodiment of the average user. Just because one persona can benefit of a success criterion does not mean that a second persona, sharing the same or similar impairment, can benefit from that criterion as well; especially if the two personas do not use the same assistive technologies. The link between a persona and a success criterion should always be reliable in the sense that it is clearly described why this criterion is considered as relevant and another not. Personas are specific and so are their impairments and needs. In the *PersonaBrowser*, we have two personas with macular degeneration (*Maria* and *Monika*). While *Maria* uses text-to-speech software to help her speed up things with office applications, *Monika* does not use any text-to-speech software. Maria therefore clearly benefits from the compliance of WCAG 2.0 success criterion 1.1.1 ("None-text content"). If we stated that *Monika* can also benefit from text-to-speech and therefore of success criterion 1.1.1, we would stretch *Monika* to fit our assumption that every person with macular degeneration can benefit from text-to-speech and so should *Monika* – even though the persona does not hold for this assumption. This would blur the personas towards average users and would therefore make them less precise. But, being precise and specific is what personas make vivid and suitable for the construction of a mental model [10, 13]. Therefore, the meaning should be constructed based on the entire persona (including its context) and not only on their impairments. Issues with this elasticity can also be seen in the average score for "dependability" in the user experience test (see Fig. 1).

Action Space Shift. One exercise in the accessibility course was to examine a web application for barriers. This exercise was split up into three sessions each focusing on one WCAG principle. (Exception: Principles 3 and 4 were combined since principle 4 has only two success criteria.) The students using the *WCAG Quick Reference* had to state the conformance for all success criteria of a single principle during a session. Doing so, the complexity for the tutors was moderate, as they had to explain the success criteria of each principle once during a session. In contrast, the *PersonaBrowser* offers a more user-centered approach. A student had to pick a set of three personas for which they had to state the conformance of one principle per session. Since not every success criterion is relevant for every persona, the complexity for the students was reduced. At the same time, the complexity for the tutors increased, since they had to discuss every success criterion nine times during one session, one time for every persona. Combined with ambiguity due to the elasticity of the personas, the complexity was actually not reduced but shifted from the students to the tutors. While this might be unique for teaching scenarios, it advocates the meaning for precise personas.

WCAG as the Culprit. From our observations, the descriptions of the WCAG success criteria, including what barriers they address and what needs to be tested for their assessment, were hardly read by the students using the *PersonaBrowser*. While the personas reduced the action space, the students often tried to conclude the implications of a success criterion by the needs of the personas and the heading of a criterion. This is probably triggered by the task given to the students, namely to state the accessibility for the chosen persona set. As one students puts it: *"The vita of the fictitious people are cumbersome, if one is just interested in the impairments [hence, which criteria applies]."* We have learned from this that — when used in the context of personas – the description of WCAG needs to be adapted in order to be told from the perspective of personas and in a more application-oriented manner (cf. [1]). This would better accommodate the needs of web authors, namely being able to assess the accessibility of their applications. The low result for "stimulation" in the UEQ (see Fig. 1) can be interpreted in light of this effect.

Barriers as a Tie to Wrap the Stories Around. As described above, a mapping between a success criteria and impairments is not sufficient to establish a confident vehicle to convey the relevance and meaning of the success criterion. As in the example with ramps and stairs (Sect. 1), meaning for solutions is only created if the problem becomes obvious. Most success criteria are actually a set of solutions for which the problems are not evident. In the run-up of this study, we conducted a survey among accessibility novices. After working in accessibility and with WCAG for several months, we asked for their opinion on what would make accessibility resources more comprehensible. From 44 participants, a vast majority (86%) agreed that it would be helpful for comprehension to highlight the impact if a criterion is *not* met; hence, this empathizes the relevance of featuring barriers. This leads back to our question on how the narrative shape of a persona should be constructed to convey WCAG in a vivid way. We therefore argue that the barriers should be the center around which the stories are told.

This study provided insights into the status quo of a persona-centered presentation metaphor for WCAG, discussed the potential of such a system and outlined the issues that arise with it. We stated that using impairments as a link between personas and WCAG success criteria is not sufficient and creates an overly elastic system. Based on our experience and observations, we discussed some initial suggestions to overcome the issues. Yet, more research is needed e.g., to test if novices, using a system, built on the principles discussed here, will have a better comprehension of WCAG or the impact of said system on experts, since our initial study focused solely on novices and, as discussed in Sect. 4, there might be implications that are unique for teaching scenarios.

References

1. Swallow, D., Power, C., Petrie, H., Bramwell-Dicks, A., Buykx, L., Velasco, C.A., Parr, A., Connor, J.: Speaking the language of web developers: evaluation of a web accessibility information resource (WebAIR). In: Miesenberger, K., Fels, D., Archambault, D., Peñáz, P., Zagler, W. (eds.) ICCHP 2014. LNCS, vol. 8547, pp. 348–355. Springer, Cham (2014). doi:10.1007/978-3-319-08596-8_54
2. Petrie, H., Power, C., Swallow, D.: i2web deliverable 3.2: requirements for web developers and web commissioners in ubiquitous Web 2.0 design and development (2011)
3. Brajnik, G.: Beyond Conformance: The Role of Accessibility Evaluation Methods. Springer, Heidelberg (2008). doi:10.1007/978-3-540-85200-1_9
4. Dias, A.L., de Mattos Fortes, R.P., Masiero, P.C.: HEUA: a heuristic evaluation with usability and accessibility requirements to assess web systems. In: Proceedings of the 11th Web for all Conference, New York, NY, USA, pp. 18:1–18:4 (2014)
5. Brajnik, G., Yesilada, Y., Harper, S.: Testability and validity of WCAG 2.0: the expertise effect. In: Proceedings of the 12th International ACM SIGACCESS Conference on Computers and Accessibility, New York, NY, USA, pp. 43–50 (2010)
6. Cooper, M., Sloan, D., Kelly B., Lewthwaite, S.: A challenge to web accessibility metrics and guidelines: putting people and processes first. In: Proceedings of the International Cross-Disciplinary Conference on Web Accessibility, New York, USA, pp. 20:1–20:4 (2012)
7. Kelly, B., Sloan, D., Brown, S., Seale, J., Petrie, H., Lauke, P., Ball, S.: Accessibility 2.0: people, policies and processes. In: Proceedings of the 2007 International Cross-disciplinary Conference on Web Accessibility (W4A), New York, pp. 138–147 (2007)
8. Brajnik, G.: Web accessibility testing: when the method is the culprit. In: Miesenberger, K., Klaus, J., Zagler, W.L., Karshmer, A.I. (eds.) ICCHP 2006. LNCS, vol. 4061, pp. 156–163. Springer, Heidelberg (2006). doi:10.1007/11788713_24
9. Bowker, G.C., Star, S.L.: Sorting Things Out: Classification and Its Consequences. The MIT Press, Cambridge (1999)
10. Cooper, A.: The Inmates are Running the Asylum. Macmillan Publishing Co. Inc., Indianapolis (1999)
11. Henka, A., Zimmermann, G.: Persona based accessibility testing. In: Stephanidis, C. (ed.) HCI 2014. CCIS, vol. 435, pp. 226–231. Springer, Cham (2014). doi:10.1007/978-3-319-07854-0_40
12. Zimmermann, G., Vanderheiden, G.: Accessible design and testing in the application development process: considerations for an integrated approach. Univ. Access Inf. Soc. 7 (1-2), 117–128 (2007)
13. Adlin, T., Pruitt, J.: The Persona Lifecycle. Morgan Kaufmann, Burlington (2006)
14. Massanari, A.L.: Designing for imaginary friends: information architecture, personas and the politics of user-centered design. New Media Soc. 12(3), 401–416 (2010)
15. Stiegler, A., Zimmermann, G.: Gamification and accessibility. In: Zhou, J., Salvendy, G. (eds.) ITAP 2015. LNCS, vol. 9193, pp. 145–154. Springer, Cham (2015). doi:10.1007/978-3-319-20892-3_15
16. Blomquist, A., Arvola, M.,: Personas in action: ethnography in an interaction design team. In: Proceedings of the Second Nordic Conference on Human-Computer Interaction, pp. 197–200 (2002)
17. Cooper, A., Reimann, R., Cronin, D., Noessel, C.: About Face: The Essentials of Interaction Design. Wiley, Indianapolis (2014)

18. Bailey, C., Pearson, E.: Development and trial of an educational tool to support the accessibility evaluation process. In: Proceedings of the International Cross-Disciplinary Conference on Web Accessibility, New York, NY, USA, pp. 2:1–2:10 (2011)

19. Loitsch, C., Weber, G., Voegler, J.: Teaching accessibility with personas. In: Miesenberger, K., Bühler, C., Penaz, P. (eds.) ICCHP 2016. LNCS, vol. 9758, pp. 453–460. Springer, Cham (2016). doi:10.1007/978-3-319-41264-1_62

20. Schulz, T., Skeide Fuglerud, K.: Creating personas with disabilities. In: Miesenberger, K., Karshmer, A., Penaz, P., Zagler, W. (eds.) ICCHP 2012. LNCS, vol. 7383, pp. 145–152. Springer, Heidelberg (2012). doi:10.1007/978-3-642-31534-3_22

21. Wöckl, B., Yildizoglu, U., Buber, I., Aparicio Diaz, B., Kruijff, E., Tscheligi, M.,: Basic senior personas: a representative design tool covering the spectrum of European older adults. In: Proceedings of the 14th International ACM SIGACCESS Conference on Computers and Accessibility, New York, NY, USA, pp. 25–33 (2012)

22. Van Isacker, K., Slegers, K., Gemou, M., Bekiaris, Evangelos: A UCD approach towards the design, development and assessment of accessible applications in a large scale European integrated project. In: Stephanidis, C. (ed.) UAHCI 2009. LNCS, vol. 5614, pp. 184–192. Springer, Heidelberg (2009). doi:10.1007/978-3-642-02707-9_20

23. Lopes, R., Votis, K., Carricco, L., Tzovaras, D., Likothanassis, S.: Towards the universal semantic assessment of accessibility. In: Proceedings of the 2009 ACM Symposium on Applied Computing, pp. 147–151 (2009)

24. Ponsard, C., Beaujeant, P., Vanderdonckt, J.: Augmenting accessibility guidelines with user ability rationales. In: Kotzé, P., Marsden, G., Lindgaard, G., Wesson, J., Winckler, M. (eds.) INTERACT 2013. LNCS, vol. 8117, pp. 579–586. Springer, Heidelberg (2013). doi:10. 1007/978-3-642-40483-2_41

25. W3C. Web Content Accessibility Guidelines (WCAG) 2.0. http://www.w3.org/TR/2008/REC-WCAG20-20081211/

26. Laugwitz, B., Held, T., Schrepp, M.: Construction and evaluation of a user experience questionnaire. In: Holzinger, A. (ed.) USAB 2008. LNCS, vol. 5298, pp. 63–76. Springer, Heidelberg (2008). doi:10.1007/978-3-540-89350-9_6

27. MOOCs for Accessibility Partnership (2017). http://gpii.eu/moocap/

28. Schrepp, M.: User Experience Questionnaire Handbook (2017). http://www.ueq-online.org

29. Henka, A., Stiegler, A., Zimmermann, G.: Using video game patterns to raise the intrinsic motivation to conduct accessibility evaluations. In: Rebelo, F., Soares, M. (eds.) Advances in Ergonomics in Design. Advances in Intelligent Systems and Computing, vol. 485. Springer, Cham (2016). doi:10.1007/978-3-319-41983-1_7

Women in Crisis Situations: Empowering and Supporting Women Through ICTs

Tara Capel[✉], Dhaval Vyas, and Margot Brereton

Queensland University of Technology (QUT), Brisbane, QLD, Australia
{t.capel, d.vyas, m.brereton}@qut.edu.au

Abstract. Women are more likely to experience poverty than their male counterparts, through negative life events that can potentially place women in a crisis situation. Past studies highlight that there is a need for a better understanding of the tools that could both support and empower women in crisis situations. We respond to this with a study that illustrates how we may be able to generate ideas for designing technologies that are both empowering and supportive. In collaboration with a non-profit community care center in Australia, we undertook a qualitative study of thirteen women in crisis situations to better understand the issues they faced. We took an in-situ approach, where we provided video and disposable cameras to these participants letting them record their experiences. Through an analysis of their videos and photos followed by semi-structured interviews, we show that while each participant had different life experiences that initially appear unrelated, there are three common challenges they face. These are: their living conditions, social isolation and stigma. As our findings are from an exclusively female perspective, through this research we contribute to the HCI literature on understanding the specific issues faced by women in crisis situations and aim to inform designs for technology that can support and empower women in challenging circumstances.

Keywords: Women · Crisis situations · Life disruptions · Empowerment · ICTs

1 Introduction

An estimated 13.9% of all people within Australia live below the internationally accepted poverty line [1, 8]. Within Australia, women are overrepresented in key poverty indicators [8, 21] and are relatively more likely to experience poverty than men (14.7% for women compared to 13% for men) [1, 8].

Certain adverse life events have the potential to place women in crisis situations, making them vulnerable. In this paper, we aim to develop a better understanding about the lives of women in crisis situations and how we can design technologies to both support and empower them. We use the term 'women in crisis situations' to refer to any woman who is struggling financially and has gone through any number of adverse life events. These life events can be divorce, becoming a widow, domestic violence, homelessness, and suffering from mental health issues or disability [2, 8, 51]. Factors

© IFIP International Federation for Information Processing 2017
Published by Springer International Publishing AG 2017. All Rights Reserved
R. Bernhaupt et al. (Eds.): INTERACT 2017, Part II, LNCS 10514, pp. 64–84, 2017.
DOI: 10.1007/978-3-319-67684-5_5

such as the wage gap, and lower education and employment rates also disproportionately affect women and exacerbate their crisis situations [21].

Previous research has focused on supporting vulnerable communities of people [17, 44, 52, 53, 55], and, in particular, there have been several distinct HCI and CSCW projects that have explored how we can support women both during and after an adverse life event, which Massimi et al. [36] have termed as 'life disruptions'. Recent studies on life disruptions have contributed to a better understanding of technology use in difficult circumstances, and how women have adapted them in certain practices [9, 36]. For example, Clarke et al. [9] explored the potential of photography in rebuilding lives of victims of domestic violence.

While a majority of research in this area has focused on a singular life disruption, such as domestic violence, this paper will focus on a broad range of these adverse life events to uncover the similarities they share. Within an Australian context, we aim to understand and explore the common issues women in crisis situations face. We chose to focus our study on women specifically as this group is more likely to find themselves in low socio-economic positions, and we were interested in finding the issues specific to them. There is growing evidence that suggests that certain crisis situations such as domestic violence have triggered an increase in women's homelessness in Australia [37].

In order to do this, we carried out a qualitative study in collaboration with a non-profit community care center. Due to the services they offered, the center drew in people from all walks of life. As we were interested in recruiting participants with a diverse range of issues and backgrounds, we worked with social workers and volunteers of the community care center to be able to recruit appropriate participants. Our study involved using self-reported experiences [8] where each of our thirteen female participants were given a self-reported probe kit containing a video camera and disposable camera with a set of task cards to complete over a period of one to two weeks. We then completed a semi-structured contextual interview with each of our participants based on the videos and photos returned in the packs.

Our findings show that there are three common challenges our participants share: their living conditions, social isolation and stigma. In this paper, we will elaborate on these challenges providing empirical evidence and discuss the implications for design. Through this research we contribute to the growing understanding of the specific issues faced by women in crisis situations and aim to inform designs for technology that can support and empower them.

2 Related Work

2.1 Women in Crisis

Women experience poverty in greater numbers than their male counterparts due overall to lower education, rates of employment, and pay [21]. While gender pay gaps are not always an indication of direct discrimination, they do represent poorer outcomes for women regarding economic and personal freedom [12, 21].

Economic disadvantage and poverty place women either in, or at risk of significant housing stress, and also limit the housing options available to them [21]. While the data would suggest that men are slightly more likely to experience homelessness and housing stress than women, this may not paint a holistic picture of women's experiences of homelessness. For example, before sleeping rough, women will often seek temporary accommodation with friends or family members, or will even couch surf between places. There are also more women residing in church group accommodation or rented State or Territory housing authority accommodation.

In an effort to retain a home, women are also more likely to sustain financial or other pressures across other areas of their lives. For example, women will remain in unsafe accommodation, or enter into or continue a relationship in order to have a place to live [50]. Consequently, domestic violence places women in crisis situations and remains the most significant cause of this group becoming homeless.

As the numbers of women in the older population increase, there is also growing concern around the increasing numbers of older, single women experiencing homelessness and housing stress [13]. With longer life expectancies than men, it means that the majority of older women are widows, which can lead to unwanted and unplanned changes in social and economic circumstances [14]. In addition to the emotional toll, widows often face a decline in their financial situation due to the loss of spousal income. The consequences of these losses may force the widow to make major changes to her lifestyle, including living arrangements.

Divorce is also a key life-course risk that can have significant economic impacts on women [16]. Female-headed households are at greater risk of homelessness or housing stress due to systemic poverty and gender inequality [21]. Women are more likely than men to be living in rented households receiving Commonwealth Rent Assistance. Over one-third of those living in rented households who were receiving a form of housing assistance were under 18 years old. This reflects the high number of one parent families, which are largely headed by women, receiving such assistance.

For certain groups of women, there are additional forms of disadvantage. For example, culturally and linguistically diverse (CALD) women require access to appropriate language or cultural support services, and may also be affected by ongoing "queue jumping" stigma [21]. For Indigenous Australian women, lower levels of education and life expectancy paired with higher unemployment rates all contribute to greater social and economic disadvantage, as well as homelessness [21].

From these studies one can clearly see that there are a range of reasons that lead to women being in crisis situations.

2.2 Low Income and HCI

The field of Human Computer Interaction has seen a recent increase in the number of studies focusing on people from a low socio-economic background and the positive role technology can play in improving their lives [55]. Consequently, there is much research around the importance of technology use in these low socio-economic groups [17, 44, 52, 53].

Different socioeconomic classes can reflect and reinforce how technology is used in everyday life [3, 57]. Studies around the use of technology within the homeless youth population found that technologies such as mobile phones were used for staying connected with others and managing identity amongst friends and case workers [32]. These digital tools were also used in finding employment, creating videos to portray their lives on the street via story-telling, and constructing online identities [52, 53].

It is evident that financial resilience in low-income communities is influenced and shaped by both social networks and social skills [17]. Engaging in meaningful activities with Information and Communication Technologies (ICTs) may be related to socio-economic security, social inclusion, empowerment and increased social capital. For example, Dillahunt [17] explored how individuals within low income communities with limited social capital use technologies in order to increase social capital and achieve socioeconomic security. Similarly, Grimes et al. [25] studied the use of a system called EatWell, which allowed African Americans with low incomes to create and share nutrition related voice memories on their phones with their neighborhood.

The emergence of the peer-to-peer sharing economy has also shown potential in this area. There have been some early studies performed around these ideas of peer-to-peer interventions that could support low income communities [6, 18, 35]. Early observations of peer-to-peer sharing mechanisms to support disadvantaged communities have elicited success factors such as balanced reciprocity, collective efficacy and employment generation through vertical capital [18].

The research suggests that these community-centric ICTs can help in reducing stigma and empower low income communities in creating their own social infrastructure [45, 55]. There is much potential for creating community-centric, socially inclusive technologies to assist with alleviating the stigma associated with hardship.

2.3 Technology and Women's Empowerment

Although there is extensive research on the nature of women's use of ICTs at school and work [34], it is only recently that the HCI and CSCW communities have begun to explore the role technology plays in personal, rather than professional settings [20, 36]. Part of this work has looked at addressing certain types of adverse life events that are uncontrollable, unpredictable, and destabilizing, which have been referred to as life disruptions [36]. While each disruption is unique, Massimi et al. [36] found patterns of social and technical reconfigurations that occur in a variety of different contexts. This research contributes to understanding how women in particular use and relate to technology during these times of personal crisis [26].

Studies around the use of technology for women who have experienced domestic violence show how technology can support the rebuilding of lives [5, 9, 19]. For example, Clarke et al. [9] explored the potential of photography in rebuilding lives of victims after domestic violence, and; Conde et al. [29] focused on the safety concerns of domestic violence survivors. They presented a system which warns potential victims and law enforcement organizations about the physical proximity of the aggressor [29]. These technologies provide survivors of violence the access to social connections and public resources in a time of isolation and change [26]. However, while technologies such as mobile phones can support a sense of security, they can also be used to enable the continued control associated with abuse. These types of situations illustrate a need for designers to consider both physical and emotional safety along with functional usability.

There have been studies performed around designing technologies to foster social connection with women who are isolated [10, 33, 39, 49]. This has highlighted the rising importance of online coping. For example, Ingen et al. [54] explored how individuals use online coping strategies after experiencing a negative life event.

Fox et al. [23] studied forms of hacking in feminist hackerspaces which are workspaces that support the creative and professional pursuits of the women who utilize the spaces. They found the member bases of these spaces were typically Caucasian, well-educated and well-paid, which did not always represent the group's desired membership or set of ideals. Ethnic and socio-economic diversity within the groups was both encouraged and sought after. There remains little research into how these spaces could attract marginalized women such as those in crisis situations, and the potential of maker and hackerspaces in terms of women's economic empowerment.

The literature shows that there is an opportunity to improve worldwide economic conditions through a better understanding of women's situations and the design of tools that can empower women [4, 27, 41, 43, 45, 46].

3   The Study

We applied a bottom-up approach to investigate the everyday lived experiences and practices of women in crisis situations in a metropolitan city of Australia. We collaborated with a community care center in the city to be able to recruit a diverse range of participants. From an ethical point of view, we carefully considered our recruitment, interaction and data collection with such a vulnerable group. Due to the sensitive nature of the research, we worked closely with the community care center to mediate contact between ourselves and the women who were relying on their services. Our research processes and activities were informed by our institute's ethics guidelines and we gained approval from our institute's ethics committee prior to commencing this research.

3.1   Participants

We visited the drop-in sessions organized by the community care center twice a week in order to recruit participants for our study. At the beginning of each of these drop-in sessions an announcement was made about our research activity, with members of the research team present to informally discuss the scope of the research and the role of participants. Our study flyers were also attached to the center's noticeboards. Table 1 shows the list of participants recruited from the community care center. Over the course of three months we recruited thirteen women who relied on the center's weekly pantry, where they were able to pick up fruit, vegetables and bread free of cost. Our participants came from diverse backgrounds and represented different age ranges and levels of crisis situation. They were all struggling with severe financial hardship and eleven of the thirteen were unemployed.

Table 1. Participants involved in the study.

Age	Crisis situation
20s	P8 (Refugee)
30s	P3 (Anxiety, Depression), P10 (Recovering Addict)
40s	P4 (Divorcee, Depression), P12 (Health Issues, Disability)
50s	P1 (Homeless, Heath Issues), P5 (Bipolar Disorder, Divorcee), P6 (Unemployed), P9 (Recovering Addict, Domestic Violence), P13 (Unemployed, Caring for ill husband), P11 (Depression, Unemployed)
60s	P7 (Caring for ill husband, Depression), P2 (Widower, Ex-Offender)

3.2 Methods

In the first part of the study, we used a self-reporting probe kit [8, 47]. Each participant was given a pack that contained a disposable camera and video camera to capture certain experiences of their lives over one to two weeks (Fig. 1) [8]. The participants were asked to record a short 10–15 film about how they live well on a low income using the video camera provided. They were encouraged to share their experiences and stories, give advice to other women, show some of their favourite places to visit, as well as any other information they wanted to share.

The pack also included cards designed to prompt the participant to take certain photographs with the disposable camera [8]. These cards were used as a means to encourage them to record their everyday experiences and things that were important to them. For example: "these are my five favourite possessions" and "this is the best part of my week". They were also free to use the camera to capture anything else they wanted to share with us.

The use of photography in sensitive settings is well documented [8, 9, 22, 32, 40], however video remains relatively underutilized in comparison when researching such settings [8, 28], but has proven successful when used in other domestic settings in full control of the participant [47]. This kind of activity represents a useful means of engaging participants and encouraging creativity and honesty in their responses. Due to their vulnerabilities, they may not be comfortable discussing their issues in person with the researchers; hence this provided them a way to reflect on their lives without us being there. It also allowed us to gather longitudinal information whilst having minimal impact on their actions, as the participants were in full control of what was captured [22].

The self-reporting probe kit itself shares similarities with and is inspired by self-authored video prototypes [47] and cultural probes [24] adaptations of which have been previously reported to work well in other settings [11, 56]. As it is somewhat of a hybrid, we refer to it as a self-reporting probe kit. The task cards guided the interaction between the probe and the participant, with an intent to gather both data as well as inspiration. The video and images that resulted from the return packs were also reviewed by the researchers with a view to use the material to inform a follow-up semi-structured interview.

Fig. 1. The video and disposable camera with task cards used in the study.

Subsequently, we visited our participants in their existing accommodation for the semi-structured interview based on the understanding and insights gained from the returned content. We were mainly interested in the issues they struggled with and how they were coping with their existing situations. These interviews were recorded and later transcribed. At the conclusion of the interview, each participant was provided a $20 gift voucher for their participation. Aside from the monetary incentive, many of the participants expressed that their reason for getting involved in our study was in the hopes that by sharing their experiences they may be able to help other women in a similar situation.

3.3 Data Analysis

We analyzed our data by carefully reading field notes and interview transcripts, and reviewing the photo artefacts created by our participants. Using thematic analysis [7], we identified common challenges across all of our participants to illuminate the similarities that these life disruptions share. Once this process was completed; we discussed our findings with the social workers of the community care center to corroborate our results with their knowledge and experience.

4 Results

We gained invaluable insight from the videos and photos that the participants captured and the findings extended beyond what would have been possible from the interviews alone. Allowing them to take the camera packs away enabled the participants the space and time to think through and reflect on the things they wanted to share with the research team.

The types of photos that were captured were largely informed and influenced by the statement cards provided with the camera, as was our intention. Through these photos they shared parts of their identity and experiences, including images of their favorite possessions and other items that were important to them, places they liked to visit, and where they lived.

For example, P4 took a photo of the animal shelter where she volunteers. This was one of her favorite places to visit as she enjoys looking after and spending time with the animals. *"I love animals they give such unconditional love, they don't have the ego that humans have. They're such a joy to be around and animals have been my lifeline I think."*

The video aspect of the pack was particularly well-received. Through the videos the participants shared and emphasized aspects of their lives that we may not have been exposed to otherwise. It also enabled the participants some agency within the research, for example P11 used the video camera to interview a friend in a similar situation. As previously mentioned, many of the women involved themselves in the study in order to help other women and were eager to pass along their knowledge of living well on a low income. Some of the videos captured were a way for the participants to share their stories and experiences, but they also provided a means for imparting advice they had for other women who may be in a similar situation. For example, P5 filmed a cooking demonstration to show other women how she cooks on a budget using the items she collects from the community center's pantry. In order to be able share advice and good practices, P9 suggested a noticeboard to be implemented in a space within the community center, where bite-sized pieces of information and advice pertinent to women could be displayed and shared. Figure 2 shows some examples of the images and video clips captured.

Fig. 2. From left to right: A photo of the animal shelter P4 volunteers at, the food P5 was using to cook, and a still frame from P1's comedy sketch.

Based on the data analysis, we organized our findings into three challenges. In the following, we discuss these challenges and provide examples from the field.

4.1 Living Conditions

This challenge refers to our participant's living conditions. Many of the women involved in the study felt insecure within their current living situations. While this reflects how close many of our participants are to becoming homeless, we detail some of the existing practices they had in place to prevent this from occurring.

4.1.1 Housing Insecurity

All participants felt, or had previously felt, insecure within their living environments, where five of the thirteen participants had spent some time in a homeless shelter. P1 was living in a boarding house at the time of this study and feared being kicked out by the owner as she had seen it happen to other tenants. Consequently she kept to herself to avoid getting in any trouble. P1 believed she had been taken advantage of financially by friends as well as by boarding house type accommodation owners. This was due to her being so desperate for a place to stay as she did not think women were safe on the streets. *"Going to stay with people that took advantage of me like I've even got a girlfriend and she let me stay and I used to just pay her more and more so she wouldn't throw me out on the street, constantly giving money to her just to keep a roof over my head. She'd want this and she'd want that, so I'd have to lie and say that I didn't have any more money... One more thing I've noticed in boarding houses and similar sit-uations I've been in, sometimes you feel like the landlord and that is sort of taking advantage of people and stuff like that like, just because they know that no one wants to live on the street and so they put up the rent or conditions aren't the best or you know, I've seen traumatic situations and it's kind of scary."*

Hygiene was also a huge concern for her as part of her safety. She recalled numerous occasions where she was unable to access facilities required to keep herself and her clothes clean. While the boarding house provided a washing machine, it was coin operated and she often could not afford the money required to use it.

In order to stay off the streets, a common practice we saw was couchsurfing (practice of moving from one friend's house to another). For example, after her divorce, P5 was unable to stay in her marital home and couch surfed between friends and family members until she was able to secure a place of her own. P6 had recently moved and was living in a caravan in her mother-in-law's front yard until she could find suitable housing. P9 was forced to leave her home due to domestic violence between herself, her daughter and her daughter's partner and was staying with a friend. *"I don't have a stable place to live because of what's happening in my life, with my daughter. She has attracted a dysfunctional partner which is inevitable because she was born and bred with me and I was with a dysfunctional partner for pretty much most of my life."* One of P10's greatest fears was to do with ensuring her and her young daughter had a place to live. *"One of my biggest fears is breaching my lease and basically having housing, issues with paying for housing and that kind of thing and keeping housing, that's something that worries me a lot."* As a single mother, she expressed her desire to be able to share housing with other single mothers in order to cut down on rent and other household expenses. She mentioned this would also help alleviate some of the social isolation that comes with being a single parent.

4.1.2   Interacting with People

Nine of the thirteen participants felt unsafe due to the people they came into contact with both in their living environments and at community services. P1 found many of the community services she relied on to be *"full of junkies and other scary people"*, and was apprehensive about interacting with unsafe people at the drop-ins she goes to. She also mentioned that she finds being on the streets scary due to the people she may meet. P9 had similar feelings regarding the unsafe people at the services she relied on. *"Some of these places can be really quite difficult...because you're exposed to some serious mentally disturbed issues."*

For both P4 and P12, the biggest safety concern they had was around where they lived, due to the people they were surrounded by. P4 felt constantly on edge where she was living. *"You've got people turning up who are wanting drugs, who aren't of sound mind who could do anything and then there's people within there who are dealing and trafficking. I think that's my biggest concern, where I'm living, I don't feel safe there. And I haven't felt safe there since I moved in there. But the past six months I've felt very unsafe to the point where I want to get out."*

P4 had recently started to house sit in order to remove herself from the situation for short periods of time. *"So then I started doing house sitting, and people would let me stay there so I can take myself out of that negative environment for a couple of weeks and then go back feeling like my tank's a little bit fuller and I can handle it. You've got to come up with some really interesting strategies when you're living in circumstances you normally wouldn't choose for yourself."*

4.1.3   Protection from the Elements

Having spent much of her life as a homeless woman, P1 was also concerned for her safety from the elements and would constantly be on the lookout for cover from rain and insects. *"It's really scary with rain and insects... you look at buildings and think is that empty, where's a thing I can crawl under... is there an underneath the house, is there a veranda, who's living there? Just in case you might become homeless I find I look at buildings in that way."*

4.1.4   Ensuring Safety

All participants reported using their phones as a means of ensuring their safety. This includes being able to call for help if someone were to approach them, or if they found themselves in an unsafe situation. For example, P1 finds her phone important in case she had to call the police if someone approached her on the streets. Whereas P3 would use her phone if she was stranded somewhere and needed help with money. One example was when P3's travel card was overcharged and she had to call a family member to send her money for a bus fare so she would be able to be able to catch the bus home. P3 also mentioned that her phone helps her to know that her son is safe when at school as he can get in contact with her if something were to happen. For P9, her phone was a way for her daughter, who was in a volatile relationship, to contact her or the police if needed. *"I always hated phones but now I realize how essential they actually are in this world at the moment as a safety device."*

4.2   Social Isolation

This challenge refers to the ways our participants have felt isolated due to their situation.

4.2.1   Family and Friends

All of our participants felt isolated from friends and family due to their circumstances. For example, P1 was separated from her family at a young age and feels isolated from society. She would use her phone to ring friends, however when her phone was stolen she had no way of getting in touch with them until she was able to replace her phone. P2 lost contact with family and friends when she went to jail, and P4 feels isolated from friends as she does not believe they could understand what she is going through.

Since her divorce, P5 struggles to stay in contact with family members from her ex-husband's side of the family. *"I've got two stepsons, whom I'm still in contact with but I don't see as much because I'm not invited to the family do's obviously, so I don't see as much of them and it's a bit hard, they've got lives of their own, they're both married now so it's a bit hard to see as much of them as I would like."* Due to her isolation, P5 was used to doing activities alone. Figure 3 is a photo of the park outside her home that she would visit by herself. She would take a cup of tea and sit at one of the tables to get herself out of the house.

P8 is a refugee woman who had recently arrived in Australia. She is raising three young children and is unable to work due to her visa conditions. She relies on a few friends she has in Australia to come and visit her at her home. Many of her friends and family remained in her home country. P9 would often decline invitations from friends to go out to eat as she wasn't able to afford a meal out. *"They'll say 'let's go catch up, we'll go to so and so for a bite to eat'. I'll often decline or I'll say I ate something before I came. It's because there is no way I can put $10.90 on a panini and then $4.90 on a coffee, I just couldn't. That's the effect."*

4.2.2 Changing Communities and Networks

Over the course of their life disruptions, our participants both lost and gained different communities and networks of people. While these did have the potential to lead to negative experiences due to some of the people they would come into contact with, there were also positive aspects to finding new support systems. In one case, P3 felt like she was going through her mental health issues alone, so a friend encouraged her to join a mental health group on Facebook where members are able to share information and stories. She finds it helpful to talk with others who are going through a similar situation she is. *"You are made to feel very alone, very isolated, and to know that you're not the only one; it's a relief."*

After becoming unemployed, P4 has felt the need to reach out to community groups to help with her emotional mental state. As she is a divorced woman she often feels like she is on her own. *"It's difficult when you are on your own, because you've got to do everything on your own. There's so much responsibility on your shoulders to manage everything and so I think when I was married that was a lot easier on so many levels: financially, emotional support. If I had a choice I wouldn't be single, I would have that support, that connection and that ability to rely on someone else. I think the single person does it tough in many ways because there might not be as much support out there compared to families... I've just sort of felt over the years that it's really hard being single."*

Due to the amount she has had to move, P5 had lost many of her networks of friends and feels she doesn't have a lot of people around her that she can go out and do things with. Consequently, she stated that she goes to a lot of places by herself. However, she is trying to participate in community activities during the week which she finds through community centers and her caseworker. Figure 4 is an example from a knitting workshop organized by the community care center.

Fig. 3. A photo taken by P5 showing a park she often visits.

Fig. 4. A photo taken by P5 showing a knitting workshop she attends at a community center.

4.2.3 Learning New Technology

Our participants also felt like they were isolated from learning new technologies which left them further behind. For example, P2 lost contact with family and friends when she went to jail. Her daughter helps her use Facebook to try and find people she has lost touch with as she doesn't know how to use a computer. She also creates artistic LED lights that can be used on the outside of buildings for festivals like Christmas, and wished she was able to share and sell her work. P3 is unsure how to use a computer so she relies on word of mouth and community notice boards in order to find out about community resources.

While P4 was technologically savvy and would often use her phone and laptop, she felt isolated from having access to learning new technologies. She felt this would disadvantage her when she went to re-enter the workforce. P9 also mentioned she felt *"handicapped"* as she did not know how to access technology in order to be able to learn how to use it. *"It's daunting to me really, 'cause I'm old school, I wasn't born into it like the young people are. It is not normal to me, I don't know how to access it... I know it would benefit my life if I started to study it I'd be able to be a bit more fluent on the computer. But I do feel a bit handicapped, not knowing that knowledge."*

4.3 Stigma

Many of our participants felt stigmatized due to their circumstances and the crisis situations they were in. For example, P1 felt the stigma attached to being a homeless woman. She recalled numerous occasions when she was called derogatory names. *"For me personally it was more...the hygiene situation because of smell and dirty clothes and getting thrown out of places cause I stink and it's just been so full on. I can think of numerous occasions where I was called names and stuff and been referred to as a 'bag lady' or 'pigeon woman' is another one. It's just human dignity to have a place to stay."* However, through the videos she shared with us that she had the desire to be comedian, and provided us with video clips of her performing stand-up routines and telling jokes about her situation. This was one of the ways she coped with the nature of her situation.

In P3's case, the stigma she felt around her situation was abetted by both her mental health and her husband. She had suffered from depression and anxiety since she was a child and consequently felt like an outcast both at school and at home with her family.

Due to this she had felt stigmatized by her mental health since she was young. *"My depression was under control until I met my husband and he just had an ability to make me look and behave like when I was younger, like it was all my fault, I'm psycho, I'm crazy, there's something wrong with me, normal people don't get upset like this, normal people don't panic or worry like this, so it got worse."*

P2 felt the stigma attached to being an ex-offender, despite being wrongly convicted and having her charges dropped. Even though she was in a poor financial position, she had been prioritizing paying a lawyer in order to be able to clear her name, which was something that was very important to her. *"I just want to go back to normal, living normally like I was living before I was arrested. The whole thing has just been absurd...It's been really hard since they released me from jail."*

P4 felt stigma around being unemployed, referencing the common misconception that people who rely on unemployment benefits are *"dole bludgers"* – someone who chooses to receive welfare rather than work. *"It's not like I'm sitting there being a bludger so I think people have that stigma attached to people who aren't working, it is not fun at all living off that small amount of money."* P11 felt similar stigma attached to being unemployed. *"You don't feel part of the working community, you sort of hang out with people who are similar circumstances, which is fine but at times you start feeling like you're a loser."* Many of our participants still had issues around having to ask for help and attend community centers in order to get food. However, P6 felt the community center was one of the places where she did not feel judged. *"You don't feel like people are looking down on you, and they don't make you feel that way. They make everyone feel comfortable there, no one is judging. People get judged so much these days and people are having a hard enough time as it is."* Being a part of her community had helped P10 go back to university to study, and eventually gain employment, which had helped improve her self-esteem. This shows some of the positive sides of connecting women in crisis back into their community. While P5 had bipolar disorder, she believed that being part the community helped her gain self-esteem. *"I went to a concert at QPAC and it was just great, you were with the mainstream people and I felt like a mainstream person, 'cause when you're mixing with people with disabilities you feel like you're labelled with that so it was really nice to get out of that circle."*

5   Discussion

This paper has attempted to understand the common issues shared by women who are in crisis situations. We used a bottom-up approach to investigate the everyday lived experiences and practices of women in crisis situations.

Past studies highlight that there is a need for a better understanding of the tools that could both support and empower women in crisis [4, 27, 41, 43, 45, 46]. We respond to this with a study that illustrates how we may be able to generate ideas for designing technologies that are both empowering and supportive. We involved a highly diverse demography of women in crisis situations – representing widows/divorcees, single mothers, the homeless, ex-offenders, refugees and a range of health problems. As our findings are from an exclusively female perspective, we contribute to the understanding of the issues faced by women in crisis situations. Our findings show three common challenges shared by our participants: their living conditions, social isolation and stigma. Similar studies focused on homeless men have found nuanced differences between the issues women and men in these types of crisis situations face [38, 42]. While the men involved in the studies also faced housing insecurity, the impact this had on their physical and mental health was more of a concern. Similar to the women involved in our study, men felt socially isolated from friends and family, and would often attend community centres for social interaction.

Housing security was one of the most important issues for our participants. Due to safety concerns, women are more likely to couch surf or stay with friends or family before resorting to sleeping on the streets [1]. We found this was not just due to concern for personal safety, but also because of hygiene needs and protection from the elements. Many participants also felt unsafe due to the people they interacted with, either in their living environments or within the community services they relied on. Consequently, their interactions with the different communities and networks gained over the course of their life disruptions provided both positive and negative experiences. Many of our participants felt isolated from their family and friends, and their situations had also caused many of them to feel stigmatized due to their circumstances. Our results did highlight the role of technologies such as mobile phones in crisis situations. All of our participants owned a mobile phone and ten of our participants had access to a smart phone. During the study, only one of the participants had her phone stolen and she was able to replace it with another phone within a few days of the event occurring. This particular participant would only use her phone for text and calls, and was using pre-paid credit loaded onto her phone. Other participants owned phones they were paying off through phone plans that include calls, text and data.

We showed how mobile phones assisted women in getting appropriate help when stranded or in an unsafe situation. In P9's case, she used her phone mainly to assist and advise her daughter who was in a volatile relationship. In turn we show that there is potential to better our understanding of the issues faced by women in crisis situations and build on the existing technologies [4, 27, 41, 43, 45, 46] that can support and empower women in these challenging circumstances.

In this discussion, we compare the demographic differences across our participants and their crisis situations. We end with three design implications for future technology that might assist in supporting and empowering women in crisis.

5.1 Differences in Crisis Situations

The greatest difference in terms of our participants' demography and their crisis situations was the participant's ability to *bounce back* from their life disruption. For example, while P4 and P6 were both unemployed and living on government support, they were taking steps towards finding suitable employment. However, due to her homelessness and health issues, P1 faced many more barriers in both finding employment, as well as being accepted as a member of the community.

The women exiting from a volatile and abusive relationship came with a different set of privacy and safety concerns compared to the women who were divorced or who had become widowed. Having left a volatile relationship herself, P9 was now concerned with helping her daughter leave her abusive partner while ensuring he would not be able to locate either of them.

In terms of age, we observed that younger women tended to be in a better position when it came to overcoming their crisis situation. For example, while 35 year old P10 went through a crisis situation in her late 20's, due to her age she was able to gain both a university degree and employment. However, P10 does remain underemployed and in an insecure housing situation. Our older participants mentioned that they found it more difficult to move around from place to place.

Each crisis situation had the potential to lead directly into another. For example, in the case of P3, her mental health had led her to enter into a controlling relationship, and P9's drug addiction had led her into an abusive relationship. For P5, her mental health issues had led to her divorce. Many of our participants were also close to becoming homeless. This underlines the importance in assisting women during these initial crisis situations, for example through education, helping them to re-enter the workforce, or ensuring vulnerable women have a secure place to live.

5.2 Design Implications

Based on our findings, we discuss three implications for designing technology that might assist in supporting and empowering women in crisis situations. These are:

- Sharing accommodation
- Engaging in social and community based activities
- Participating in an online creative community hub

5.2.1 Sharing Accommodation

We found many of our participants felt insecure within their current living arrangements. Several were close to becoming homeless and many feared for their personal safety due to the people they came into contact with. To ensure they had a safe place to stay, our participants would couch surf, sleep in a caravan, or stay with family and friends. There is ongoing research into the potential of the sharing economy within vulnerable communities [6, 18, 35]. Certain peer-to-peer interventions have so far proved useful in helping individuals find temporary employment, increase social interaction, and access resources [18]. Well-known services such as AirBNB and couchsurf.com have been studied in regards to hospitality exchange [30, 31]; however, services such as these are not always a viable option for those from a low socio-economic background. An initial design opportunity would be to explore how we could build on this sharing economy in order to provide a system more accessible to disadvantaged women, where women could connect with each other to allow them to look for housing together. This system could also allow women who are living in accommodation they cannot easily afford to look for a housemate. This has the potential to allow women to share costs associated with both accommodation and household bills. As was mentioned by P10, this kind of system would be useful for single mothers looking for other single mothers to rent with. Challenges that would need to be considered include finding a place large enough to accommodate two families and supporting children who are unknown to each other in living together. As majority of our participants had access to a mobile phone, technology could play an important role in this design idea. It could enable the user to both search for and find the right place to live, and also the right housemate to share with. This type of system could also potentially be deployed amongst the women who attend the community center in order to further mitigate some potential risks involved in sharing accommodation. This would help to support and empower women by ensuring they feel safe both where they are living and who they are living with.

5.2.2 Engaging in Social and Community Based Activities

We found that many of our participants felt isolated in numerous ways due to their circumstances. Walker et al. [49] found that mobile technology could enhance interpersonal and community connectedness and there is potential to build on the existing technologies [10, 33, 39, 49] that foster social connection between women in crisis. We contend that design efforts should be spent on providing technology that better supports connecting women in the community. This could involve a match-making system in order for women to be linked with other women who visit the community center who are also looking to socialize. Once matched it could suggest free activities for them to do together, for example recommended walks around the area, and free events that they could attend. This could also be extended to allow them to organize ride sharing to different community services or activities. Another aspect to this design idea would be providing women with a platform to find out about community services and other activities that are available to them within their community that they may not know about.

Extending on this, designers could also explore how technologies could allow women in crisis situations to actively engage in activities such as volunteering. This could allow members to find and apply for volunteering opportunities in their community. For P4, volunteering at the animal shelter had been an important aspect of coping with her crisis situation. Another aspect of this design idea is allowing community members to complete tasks that help a fellow member of the community. Bellotti et al. [6] explored how the concept of time banking could be enhanced to the point of being experienced as a 'random act of kindness.' Some examples of these 'random acts of kindness,' could include helping a homeless woman with her washing, or helping someone through a crisis situation they have been through themselves. Members should then be able to share their stories and experiences of these acts with the community, as this could help with motivating other members to contribute towards helping each other. This would be within a community center environment and would therefore directly help the community involved. Both aspects of this design idea would allow otherwise marginalized groups of women to connect back to their community which may lead to alleviation of social isolation, lift self-esteem, and assist with feelings of empowerment.

5.2.3 Online Creative Community Hub

Through the self-reported experiences we found that many of the women were trying to convey both their own stories and experiences, and also advice and good practices they could pass along to other women in similar circumstances. P9 suggested a noticeboard to be displayed within a space in the community center in order for this advice to be displayed and shared with other women. Both creating and sharing stories about personal experiences can be a powerful way for people in crisis situations to build connections with others who have experienced, or are experiencing, similar difficulties [15]. Davis et al. [15] created digital stories with participants who were housebound, and developed an interactive display to share these stories at a local community event. They found that each storyteller enjoyed seeing the other stories and felt a sense of relief that they were not alone in their experiences. Clarke et al. [9] explored the role of photography in re-building the lives of women who had experienced domestic violence, where the women involved in the study would bring in photos they had taken. These photos were put in a sequence with added words and sounds from audio recordings, and a final screening of these creations was shared and discussed within the group.

Building on this previous work and the suggestion from P9, an online community platform could be designed, where women could use text, voice over, photos and videos in order to not only share their stories and experiences, but also to impart advice and good practices to other women through a fun and engaging medium. There is also potential for the videos created for this research to be shared beyond the research team to the women they were intended for, with the permission of the participants involved. Involving women in such a platform would allow them to support each other and empower them to share their experiences in order to help other women. This could be moderated through the community center. There is also potential for this to be extended to allow women to showcase their creativity and create entrepreneurial activities, similar to the feminist maker/hackerspaces [23]. However, this online platform would also enable them to earn money off items they have created, such as knitwear, furniture or art, while also creating an online community hub to enable the exchange of ideas. For example, P2 could share and sell her LED light creations. P1 could use her comedic sketches and jokes to both show her skills as a comedian, as well as discuss how she uses humor to cope with her situation. There is potential for such a platform to allow for the economic empowerment of women in crisis situations and may also attract marginalized women to the existing maker/hackerspaces. As many of our participants felt isolated from learning technology, it would also empower women to participate digitally and learn how to use the technology involved.

5.3 Challenges

Researching within a sensitive setting such as women in crisis situations comes with certain challenges. In regards to our methodology, their situations did not always afford them the time to take photos and videos, and as such some of the packs were returned half finished, and one has yet to be returned. Some of the participants took longer to complete the pack than we initially had expected and a few struggled to use the video camera and required additional assistance in learning how to use it. This required one of the research team members to work with them in taking the videos and photos and in some cases we became involved in parts of the video creation. We found the best approach in these instances was to work with them in learning how to use the cameras, then allow them to take the cameras away again and continue to use them without us being present. While this was not the intention of the self-reported probe kit, it did allow us to build more rapport with the participants that required additional help. The limitation of relying on the disposable camera was that some of the photos did not turn out well when the participant did not use the flash, especially the indoor photos. The participant would then have to remember the photo that had been taken. Another limitation of our study would be that all our participants were recruited from the same community care center. However, we believe that there is potential for this research to be extended by recruiting participants who rely on other services.

6 Conclusion

This paper focused on the issues faced by women in crisis situations and how we can design technology to both support and empower them. The self-reported photos and videos generated through the video and disposable cameras and semi-structured contextual interviews have provided us with unique insights into the issues faced by women in crisis situations. Our methods engaged participants and provoked more contextual, visual and longitudinal experiences which helped to inform our semi-structured contextual interviews. Our participants had different circumstances; however they shared three common challenges: their living conditions, social isolation and stigma. Based on our findings, we have proposed three implications for the design of a technology in this area – namely sharing accommodation, engaging in social and community based activities, and participating in an online creative community hub. We contribute to the growing understanding of the specific issues faced by women in crisis situations and how technology can be designed to support and empower women in challenging circumstances.

References

1. ACOSS: Australian Council of Social Service. Poverty in Australia Report 2014. http://www.acoss.org.au/poverty-2/
2. AMA: Australian Medical Association. Women's Heath 2014. https://ama.com.au/position-statement/womens-health-2014
3. Ames, M.G., Go, J., Kaye, J.J., Spasojevic, M.: Understanding technology choices and values through social class. In: Proceedings of the ACM 2011 Conference on Computer Supported Cooperative Work (CSCW 2011), pp. 55–64. ACM, New York (2011). http://dx.doi.org/10.1145/1958824.1958834
4. Ajjan, H., Beninger, S., Mostafa, R., Crittenden, V.L.: Empowering women entrepreneurs in emerging economies: a conceptual model. Organ. Markets Emerg. Econ. 5(1), 16–30 (2014)
5. Arief, B., Coopamootoo, K.P.L., Emms, M., van Moorsel, A.: Sensible privacy: how we can protect domestic violence survivors without facilitating misuse. In: Proceedings of the 13th Workshop on Privacy in the Electronic Society (WPES 2014), pp. 201–204. ACM, New York (2014). http://dx.doi.org/10.1145/2665943.2665965
6. Bellotti, V., Carroll, J.M., Han, K.: Random acts of kindness: the intelligent and context-aware future of reciprocal altruism and community collaboration. In: International Conference on Collaboration Technologies and Systems (CTS), pp. 1–12. IEEE (2013)
7. Braun, V., Clarke, V.: Using thematic analysis in psychology. Qual. Res. Psychol. 3(2), 77–101 (2006)

8. Capel, T., Taylor, J.L., Vyas, D.: Using self-reported experiences to explore the issues of women in crisis situations. In: Proceedings of the 28th Australian Conference on Computer-Human Interaction (OzCHI 2016), pp. 483–488. ACM, New York (2016). https://doi.org/10.1145/3010915.3010962

9. Clarke, R., Wright, P., Balaam, M., McCarthy, J.: Digital portraits: photo-sharing after domestic violence. In: Proceedings of the SIGCHI Conference on Human Factors in Computing Systems (CHI 2013), pp. 2517–2526. ACM, New York (2013). http://dx.doi.org/10.1145/2470654.2481348

10. Clarke, R., Wright, P., McCarthy, J.: Sharing narrative and experience: digital stories and portraits at a women's centre. In CHI 2012 Extended Abstracts on Human Factors in Computing Systems (CHI EA 2012), pp. 1505–1510. ACM, New York (2012)

11. Crabtree, A., Hemmings, T., Rodden, T., Cheverst, K., Clarke, K., Dewsbury, G., Rouncefield, M.: Designing with care: adapting cultural probes to inform design in sensitive settings. In: Proceedings of the 2004 Australasian Conference on Computer-Human Interaction (OZCHI2004), pp. 4–13, November 2003

12. Cassells, R., Duncan, A., Ong, R.: Gender equity insights 2016: inside Australia's gender pay gap. BCEC/WGEA Gender Equity Series, Issue 1 (2016)

13. Darab, S., Hartman, Y.: Understanding single older women's invisibility in housing issues in Australia. Hous. Theory Soc. 30(4), 348–367 (2013)

14. Davidson, P.M., DiGiacomo, M., McGrath, S.J.: The feminization of aging: how will this impact on health outcomes and services? Health Care Wom. Int. 32(12), 1031–1045 (2011)

15. Davis, H., Waycott, J., Zhou, S.: Beyond YouTube: sharing personal digital stories on a community display. In: Ploderer, B., Carter, M., Gibbs, M., Smith, W., Vetere, F. (eds.) Proceedings of the Annual Meeting of the Australian Special Interest Group for Computer Human Interaction (OzCHI 2015), pp. 579–587. ACM, New York (2015). http://dx.doi.org/10.1145/2838739.2838771

16. de Vaus, D., Gray, M., Qu, L., Stanton, D.: The economic consequences of divorce in Australia. Int. J. Law Policy Fam. 28, 26–47 (2014)

17. Dillahunt, T.R.: Fostering social capital in economically distressed communities. In: Proceedings of the SIGCHI Conference on Human Factors in Computing Systems (CHI 2014), pp. 531–540. ACM, New York (2014)

18. Dillahunt, T.R., Malone, A.R.: The promise of the sharing economy among disadvantaged communities. In: Proceedings of the 33rd Annual ACM Conference on Human Factors in Computing Systems (CHI 2015), pp. 2285–2294. ACM, New York (2015). http://dx.doi.org/10.1145/2702123.2702189

19. Dimond, J.P., Fiesler, C., Bruckman, A.S.: Domestic violence and information communication technologies. Interact. Comput. 23(5), 413–421 (2011)

20. Dimond, J.P., Poole, E.S., Yardi, S.: The effects of life disruptions on home technology routines. In: Proceedings of the 16th ACM International Conference on Supporting Group Work (GROUP 2010), pp. 85–88. ACM, New York (2010)

21. ERA: Equity Rights Alliance. Housing Fact Sheet. http://equalityrightsalliance.org.au/

22. Fox, S., Le Dantec, C.: Community historians: scaffolding community engagement through culture and heritage. In: Proceedings of the 2014 Conference on Designing Interactive Systems (DIS 2014), pp. 785–794. ACM, New York (2014). http://dx.doi.org/10.1145/2598510.2598563

23. Fox, S., Ulgado, R.R., Rosner, D.: Hacking culture, not devices: access and recognition in feminist hackerspaces. In: Proceedings of the 18th ACM Conference on Computer Supported Cooperative Work & Social Computing, pp. 56–68. ACM, February 2015

24. Gaver, B., Dunne, T., Pacenti, E.: Design: cultural probes. Interactions 6(1), 21–29 (1999). http://dx.doi.org/10.1145/291224.291235

25. Grimes, A., Bednar, M., Bolter, J.D., Grinter, R.E.: EatWell: sharing nutrition-related memories in a low-income community. In: Proceedings of the 2008 ACM Conference on Computer Supported Cooperative Work (CSCW 2008), pp. 87–96. ACM, New York (2008). http://dx.doi.org/10.1145/1460563.1460579

26. Gupta, P., Singh, P., Goyal, V.: Women safety and technology: analysis of women distress helpline for efficient technological intervention (2015). https://repository.iiitd.edu.in/jspui/handle/123456789/353

27. Huyer, S.: Women, ICT and the information society: global perspectives and initiatives. In: Morrell, C., Sanders, J. (eds.) Proceedings of the International Symposium on Women and ICT: Creating Global Transformation (CWIT 2005), Article 1. ACM, New York (2005). http://dx.doi.org/10.1145/1117417.1117418

28. Jewitt, C.: An introduction to using video for research. National Centre for Research Methods, NCRM Working Paper (2012)

29. Jordán Conde, Z., Marsh, W.E., Luse, A.W., Tao, L.-S.E.: GuardDV: a proximity detection device for homeless survivors of domestic violence. In: CHI 2008 Extended Abstracts on Human Factors in Computing Systems (CHI EA 2008), pp. 3855–3860. ACM, New York (2008). http://dx.doi.org/10.1145/1358628.1358943

30. Lampinen, A.: Hosting together via couchsurfing: privacy management in the context of network hospitality. Int. J. Commun. **10**, 20 (2016)

31. Lampinen, A., Cheshire, C.: Hosting via Airbnb: motivations and financial assurances in monetized network hospitality. In: Proceedings of the 2016 CHI Conference on Human Factors in Computing Systems, pp. 1669–1680. ACM (2016)

32. Le Dantec, C.A., Keith Edwards, W.: Designs on dignity: perceptions of technology among the homeless. In: Proceedings of the SIGCHI Conference on Human Factors in Computing Systems (CHI 2008), pp. 627–636. ACM, New York (2008)

33. Le Dantec, C.A., Farrell, R.G., Christensen, J.E., Bailey, M., Ellis, J.B., Kellogg, W.A., Keith Edwards, W.: Publics in practice: ubiquitous computing at a shelter for homeless mothers. In: Proceedings of the SIGCHI Conference on Human Factors in Computing Systems (CHI 2011), pp. 1687–1696. ACM, New York (2011)

34. Long, J.: 'There's no place like home'? Domestic life, gendered space and online access. In: Morrell, C., Sanders, J. (eds.) Proceedings of the International Symposium on Women and ICT: Creating Global Transformation (CWIT 2005), Article 12. ACM, New York (2005). http://dx.doi.org/10.1145/1117417.1117429

35. Malmborg, L., Light, A., Fitzpatrick, G., Bellotti, V., Brereton, M.: Designing for sharing in local communities. In: Proceedings of the 33rd Annual ACM Conference Extended Abstracts on Human Factors in Computing Systems (CHI EA 2015), pp. 2357–2360. ACM, New York (2015)

36. Massimi, M., Dimond, J.P., Le Dantec, C.A.: Finding a new normal: the role of technology in life disruptions. In: Proceedings of the ACM 2012 Conference on Computer Supported Cooperative Work (CSCW 2012), pp. 719–728. ACM, New York (2012). http://dx.doi.org/10.1145/2145204.2145314

37. Menih, H.: From a victim of abuse to homelessness. In: Interpersonal Crimes: A Critical Study of Systematic Bias against Men, p. 59 (2013)

38. Mission Australia: The Michael Project, 2007–2010: New perspectives and possibilities for homeless men. Sydney: Mission Australia (2012)

39. Moncur, W., Gibson, L., Herron, D.: The role of digital technologies during relationship breakdowns. In: Proceedings of the 19th ACM Conference on Computer-Supported Cooperative Work & Social Computing (CSCW 2016), pp. 371–382. ACM, New York (2016). http://dx.doi.org/10.1145/2818048.2819925

40. Noland, C.M.: Auto-photography as research practice: identity and self-esteem research. J. Res. Pract. **2**(1), Article M1 (2006)

41. Pattanaik, D.: Engendering knowledge networks: empowering women through ICT. In: Morrell, C., Sanders, J. (eds.) Proceedings of the International Symposium on Women and ICT: Creating Global Transformation (CWIT 2005), Article 8. ACM, New York (2005). http://dx.doi.org/10.1145/1117417.1117425

42. Quine, S., Kendig, H., Russell, C., Touchard, D.: Health promotion for socially disadvantaged groups: the case of homeless older men in Australia. Health Promot. Int. **19**(2), 157–165 (2004)

43. Ramos, A.M.G., Prieto, L.A.: Digital inclusion of low-income women: are users of internet able to improve their life conditions?. In: Proceedings of the XV International Conference on Human Computer Interaction (Interacción 2014), 5 p., Article 78. ACM, New York (2014)

44. Roberson, J., Nardi, B.: Survival needs and social inclusion: technology use among the homeless. In: Proceedings of the 2010 ACM Conference on Computer Supported Cooperative Work (CSCW 2010), pp. 445–448. ACM, New York (2010)

45. Rogers, Y., Marsden, G.: Does he take sugar? Moving beyond the rhetoric of compassion. Interactions **20**(4), 48–57 (2013)

46. Shroff, G., Kam, M.: Towards a design model for women's empowerment in the developing world. In: Proceedings of the SIGCHI Conference on Human Factors in Computing Systems (CHI 2011), pp. 2867–2876. ACM, New York (2011)

47. Snow, S., Rittenbruch, M., Brereton, M.: Prototyping the self-authored video interview: challenges and opportunities. In: Abascal, J., Barbosa, S., Fetter, M., Gross, T., Palanque, P., Winckler, M. (eds.) INTERACT 2015. LNCS, vol. 9297, pp. 150–158. Springer, Cham (2015). doi:10.1007/978-3-319-22668-2_13

48. Stavrositu, C., Shyam Sundar, S.: Does blogging empower women? Exploring the role of agency and community. J. Comput.-Mediated Commun. **17**(4), 369–386 (2012)

49. Walker, R., Koh, L., Wollersheim, D., Liamputtong, P.: Social connectedness and mobile phone use among refugee women in Australia. Health Soc. Care Commun. **23**(3), 325–336 (2015)

50. Watson, J.: Gender-based violence and young homeless women: femininity, embodiment and vicarious physical capital. Soc. Rev. **64**(2), 256–273 (2016)

51. WHO: World Health Organization. Women's Health. http://www.who.int/topics/womens_health/en/

52. Woelfer, J.P., Hendry, D.G.: Designing ubiquitous information systems for a community of homeless young people: precaution and a way forward. Pers. Ubiquit. Comput. **15**(6), 565–573 (2011)

53. Woelfer, J.P., Hendry, D.G.: Homeless young people's experiences with information systems: life and work in a community technology center. In: Proceedings of the SIGCHI Conference on Human Factors in Computing Systems (CHI 2010), pp. 1291–1300. ACM, New York (2010)

54. van Ingen, E., Utz, S., Toepoel, V.: Online coping after negative life events measurement, prevalence, and relation with internet activities and well-being. Soc. Sci. Comput. Rev. **34**, 511–529 (2015)

55. Vines, J., McNaney, R., Clarke, R., Lindsay, S., McCarthy, J., Howard, S., Romero, M., Wallace, J.: Designing for- and with- vulnerable people. In: CHI 2013 Extended Abstracts on Human Factors in Computing Systems (CHI EA 2013), pp. 3231–3234. ACM, New York (2013)

56. Vyas, D., Eliëns, A., van de Watering, M.R., Van Der Veer, G.C.: Organizational probes: exploring playful interactions in work environment. In: Proceedings of the 15th European conference on Cognitive ergonomics: The Ergonomics of Cool Interaction, p. 35. ACM (2008)

57. Yardi, S., Bruckman, A.: Social and technical challenges in parenting teens' social media use. In: Proceedings of the SIGCHI Conference on Human Factors in Computing Systems (CHI 2011), pp. 3237–3246. ACM, New York (2011)

Games

Effects of Image-Based Rendering and Reconstruction on Game Developers Efficiency, Game Performance, and Gaming Experience

George E. Raptis[1(✉)], Christina Katsini[1], Christos Fidas[1,2], and Nikolaos Avouris[1]

[1] HCI Group, Department of Electrical and Computer Engineering, University of Patras, Patras, Greece
{raptisg, katsinic}@upnet.gr,
{fidas, avouris}@upatras.gr
[2] Department of Cultural Heritage Management and New Technologies, University of Patras, Patras, Greece

Abstract. Image-based rendering and reconstruction (IBR) approaches minimize time and costs to develop video-game assets, aiming to assist small game studios and indie game developers survive in the competitive video-game industry. To further investigate the interplay of IBR on developers' efficiency, game performance, and players' gaming experience we conducted two evaluation studies: a comparative, ecologically valid study with professional game developers who created games with and without an IBR-based game development pipeline, and a user study, based on eye-tracking and A/B testing, with gamers who played the developed games. The analysis of the results indicates that IBR tools provide a credible solution for creating low cost video game assets in short time, sacrificing game performance though. From a player's perspective, we note that the IBR approach influenced players' preference and gaming experience within contexts of varying levels of player's visual intersections related to the IBR-created game assets.

Keywords: Evaluation study · Video games · Image-based rendering and reconstruction · Game development efficiency · Game performance · Gaming experience

1 Introduction

The video game industry is continuously growing with revenue over $90 billion worldwide [1, 2]. Thousands of people worldwide work on creating video games for entertainment, as well as for education, business and art [3]. The video game market is very competitive, with an increasing demand for sophisticated and more realistic games. Such requirements are barrier for small game studios and indie developers, as they need more resources, in terms of cost, time, expertise, and technology, to keep up with the competition. Therefore, small game studios and indie developers struggle to

© IFIP International Federation for Information Processing 2017
Published by Springer International Publishing AG 2017. All Rights Reserved
R. Bernhaupt et al. (Eds.): INTERACT 2017, Part II, LNCS 10514, pp. 87–96, 2017.
DOI: 10.1007/978-3-319-67684-5_6

survive, and this has a direct negative consequence on the video game industry and the economy, as these developers bring in creativity and innovation.

One way to overcome this, is to introduce novel cost-effective technologies which are primarily based on image [4–7] and video [8–11] reconstruction techniques. The users of such techniques can capture real-life scenes and objects with conventional apparatus (*e.g.*, smartphones, photo cameras). The captured images/videos are then used to build the 3D realistic models of assets. Image-based reconstruction (IBR) seems to produce better results [12].

Motivation and Research Question. Although it is known that IBR and photogrammetric methods provide a short-cut for creating 3D assets for video-games development [4–6, 13–15], to the authors' knowledge, there is no thorough ecological study involving different stakeholders (game developers and game players) and investigating the interplay of a state-of-the-art IBR game development pipeline on game developers' efficiency, game performance, and gaming experience. In the context of the reported study a fully integrated research-based state-of-the-art pipeline for games development bootstrapped to game developers' requirements [16] was used.

Hence, the research questions investigated in this paper are: (a) to explore the effects of games created with IBR on game developers' efficiency, in terms of time required to create video-games by also considering game performance metrics (game size, loading time, and scalability), and (b) to explore the effects of games created with IBR on gaming experience, in terms of gamers' preference and graphics quality.

2 Method of Study

2.1 Procedure

We conducted two user studies: (a) a comparative evaluation study during which video game prototypes were developed with the traditional vs. IBR methods aiming to gather quantitative and qualitative feedback related to efficiency and performance measures, and (b) an eye-tracking A/B testing study with gamers playing the game prototypes created during the comparative evaluation study.

Comparative Study of Creating Game Assets with and Without IBR. For this study, two professional game developers participated and developed two different games over a period of six months (May to October 2016). The participants developed their games within their own working conditions (*i.e.*, ecologically valid conditions), without the intervention or help of our research team. They were asked to keep track of their activities and the time needed to perform the necessary tasks, adopting an activity diary-log approach. We provided them with a diary template. Moreover, several semi-structured interviews were conducted during and after the game development phase.

Comparative Study of Playing Games Created with and Without IBR. For this in-lab study twelve gamers were recruited (5 females, 7 males), aged 20–32, and played different versions of the games created with the traditional and the IBR approach. They were recruited through email invitations, and they were undergraduate and postgraduate university students. All individuals were experienced gamers, playing video games more than twelve hours per week, and they had never played any of the games used in the study before. After the recruitment of the participants, twelve in-lab sessions were scheduled (*i.e.*, one for each participant). In each session, the participant was asked to play the four game versions, wearing the eye-tracking apparatus. To avoid bias effects, six gamers played first the one game, and the other six played the other game first. In both groups, three participants played the traditional version first, and the rest three played the IBR version first. After the play-session, each participant was asked to fill a user experience questionnaire. Finally, each participant was asked to provide feedback and comments on their gaming experience through an unstructured interview. The participants were not informed that the two versions were developed using different technologies until the end of the interview.

2.2 Instruments and Apparatus

IBR-Based Game Development Integrated Pipeline. The IBR pipeline used in our study was the CR-PLAY environment [17–21]. CR-PLAY is a state-of-the-art mixed pipeline for creating game assets and integrating them in the game development workflow, using IBR techniques [18, 22]. CR-PLAY users follow a three-step approach to build a game asset: (a) capture real-life objects (*e.g.*, a building) by taking a sequence of photos from multiple angles; (b) reconstruct them as 3D point cloud models; (c) and import them into their standard game development workflow.

The Games. Two video-games were created and played in our studies: *Survive the Weekend* and *Basketball Stars*. *Survive the Weekend* is a hidden object game in which the player is asked to find a number of items in a play-room within a given time. *Basketball Stars* is a first-person sport shooting game, and the players' goal is to shoot as many baskets as possible in a predefined amount of time against an opponent. The two games have a different intersection between the game assets and the game play in terms of visual search and visual attention, as *Survive the Weekend* requires constant visual attention of players through the whole scene, because they are searching for the hidden items; while *Basketball Stars* requires players' attention on specific game assets.

Apparatus. Game developers used their own computer systems to develop the games. Gamers played the games on a desktop computer (with Intel Core i7-4500U at 2.40 GHz, and 8 GB RAM). The screen used was the LG 22MP48D, at a screen resolution of 1920 × 1080 pixels. To investigate the participants' visual behavior, Tobii Pro Glasses 2 were used to record their eye movement patterns.

Gaming Experience Questionnaire. To measure gaming experience, we used the Immersive Experience Questionnaire (IEQ) [23]. IEQ is a credible and highly validated tool to evaluate players' experience [24, 25]. It consists of 31 questions of Likert type, including questions about graphics quality.

3 Results

3.1 Effects of IBR on Game Developers Efficiency in Creating Video-Game Assets

The development of a game prototype with IBR took approximately 12 man-hours, regardless of the complexity of the scene. However, the time needed to develop a game prototype with the traditional approach was highly dependent on the number of assets to be included in the game, their complexity, and whether they have been used in other projects or were available from third-party providers. In our case study, the game developers were free to re-use any game asset and/or use third-party assets, as they would normally do, strengthening the ecological validity of the study. To create a game based on a simple scene with few items (N = 3), approximately 26 man-hours were required, while for a game based on a complex scene with many items (N = 19), 160 man-hours were required. In both cases, the developers required less time to create the IBR version. The interviews revealed that IBR reversed the process the game developers followed to develop a game, as the IBR game scenario was based on the reconstructed scene, while traditionally they created the scenes based on the scenario.

3.2 Effects of IBR on Game Performance (Size, Loading-Time, and Scalability)

Game performance is a multidimensional variable, which can be measured on game file-size, loading-time, and scalability. In terms of file-size, the executable was bigger for the IBR versions (300 MB for a simple scene, and 330 MB for a complex scene) compared to the traditional versions (15 MB for a simple scene, 20 MB for a complex scene). The loading times were in-line with the file-size findings, and they were increased for the IBR versions (10 s for a simple scene, 20 s for a complex scene) compared to the traditional versions (2 s for both a simple and a complex scene). The aforementioned results reflect on the scene complexity and the size of point cloud models, introduced in IBR. Therefore, this has an impact on the scalability of a game, as developers could not build many levels.

3.3 Effects of IBR on Gaming Experience

Effects of IBR on Game Players' Preference. The game players were asked to state which version they preferred: IBR or traditional. Ten participants stated that they preferred the traditional version of *Survive the Weekend*, a significant difference according to binomial statistical test (p = .019). In contrary, eleven participants stated that they preferred the IBR version of *Basketball Stars*, a significant difference according to the binomial statistical test (p = .003). When playing the IBR version of *Survive the Weekend*, the participants had to explore the whole scene to find and collect the hidden items, and they stated that most of the game elements were blurry when they were navigating through the scene. They also stated that many objects were not naturally placed and lighted in the scene. On the other hand, the *Basketball Stars* scene was more static, as the players could not navigate through the scene. Therefore, no blurring objects were noticed in the IBR version, and the participants found it to be more photorealistic, with smooth transitions and nice interaction.

Graphics Quality. To measure how much the players valued the graphics quality, we conducted an independent-samples t-test for each game, with the technology factor (traditional and IBR) as the independent variable, and the graphics quality score (calculated using IEQ) as the dependent variable. In both tests, the assumptions were met. Regarding the *Survive the Weekend* game, the participants preferred the graphics of the traditional version (5.11 ± 1.48 vs. 4.01 ± 1.42, $p = .046$). Regarding the *Basketball Stars* game, the participants preferred the graphics of the IBR version (5.09 ± 1.34 vs. 4.32 ± 1.17, $p = .042$). This was also reflected on the overall immersion score, as the participants were more immersed when playing the traditional version of *Survive the Weekend* (4.72 ± 0.66 vs. 4.64 ± 0.57, $p = .061$), and the IBR version of *Basketball Stars* (5.19 ± 0.51 vs. 4.84 ± 0.59, $p = .019$).

Eye-Tracking Analysis. The eye-tracking analysis verified the aforementioned finding, as the participants fixated many times and for long time periods on the whole backdrop scene, visually scanning for the hidden objects, in both versions of *Survive the Weekend*. On the other hand, they fixated intensively in specific areas of interest (*i.e.*, basket, shooter, power bar) when playing *Basketball Stars*, as their goals was to shoot and score. The heat-maps of both versions of both games are depicted in Fig. 4.

4   Findings and Discussion

The findings of our studies are summarized into three categories: (a) efficient creation of game assets with IBR, (b) the bottleneck in performance when using IBR, and (c) effective use of IBR depends on game type (Table 1).

Table 1. The main findings of our studies on developers'efficiency, gaming performance and gaming experience

Metric	Finding
Developers' efficiency	IBR provided a faster approach for creating video-game objects, for both simple and complex scenes. However, traditional approaches can be considered for simple scenes
Gaming performance	Traditional approach outperformed IBR in terms of file size, loading times, and scalability. IBR games scenes and objects were bigger in size, had increased loading times, and were less scalable
Gaming experience	The game type plays an important role on the effective use of IBR. Gaming experience was better for traditional games which require heavy visual interaction with the game assets and the scene (*e.g.*, hidden-objects games). However, gaming experience was better for IBR games which require light visual interaction effect with the game scene (*e.g.*, point-and-click at a static target), as they provide a more photorealistic environment

Efficient Creation of Game Assets with IBR. The IBR technology provided a faster method to create photorealistic game assets in comparison to the traditional approach (Fig. 1). The main benefit for the game developers is that IBR time to delivery is independent of the assets complexity, as our study indicated that the asset creation times were similar for creating games of varying game elements complexity.

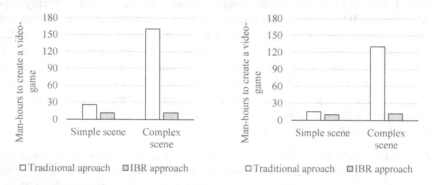

Fig. 1. Game developers created the IBR game versions in less time than the traditional game versions, in both complexity levels.

The Bottleneck in Performance when Using IBR. In the presented study, the game performance reflects on the executable file-size, the loading time, and the scalability of the game. In both games, the IBR versions were bigger in size, had longer loading periods, and were less scalable than the traditional ones (Fig. 2). Despite the fact that some of the aforementioned issues are technology-related and can be resolved (*e.g.*, reduce file-size by incorporating sophisticated image compression algorithms), the IBR game performance will remain poor since game assets are not based on polygons. Game developers can create gamers quickly when they use IBR, but the game performance (in terms of file-size, loading time, and scalability) is a bottleneck.

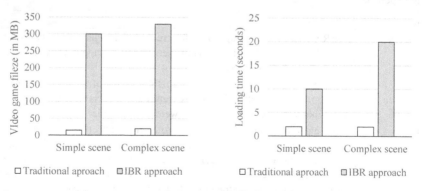

Fig. 2. IBR games were bigger in size than the traditional versions for both simple and complex scenes (left). IBR games had also longer loading times than the traditional versions for both simple and complex scenes (right).

Game Genre Affects Preference of IBR Video-Games. Game players preferred the graphics quality of traditional *Survive the Weekend* (*i.e.*, a game with heavy interaction with assets throughout the scene) than the graphics of the IBR version; and the graphics of IBR *Basketball Stars* (*i.e.*, a game with light interaction with the scene), than the graphics of the traditional version. This was also reflected on their answers when they were asked explicitly which of the two versions (traditional or IBR) they preferred. Games that require players to interact with the largest part of the scene or with most of the game assets (*e.g.*, hidden objects games) require high visual attention. Therefore, as users visually explore the game environment, they can detect IBR-related flaws (*e.g.*, bad lightning, non-normal position of an object, blurred assets), which influence their gaming experience (Fig. 3). On the other hand, when the players are engaged with a video game with more static scenes (*e.g.*, point-and-click games), visually focusing on specific areas of the scene, they typically do not detect IBR-related flaws, and they enjoy the game more, as it is more realistic and aesthetically pleasant (Fig. 3).

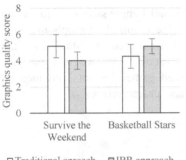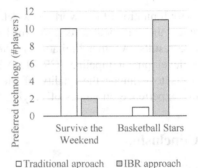

Fig. 3. Gamers liked more the graphics of the traditional version of *Survive the Weekend*, and the graphics of the IBR version of *Basketball Stars* (left); Study participants preferred the traditional version of the visual-search games (*e.g.*, *Survive the Weekend*), and the IBR version of the point-and-shoot games (*e.g.*, *Basketball Stars*).

Our eye-tracking analysis reflects on this finding (Fig. 4), as the players tend to fixate on various spots of the visual scene evenly, when playing a visual search game. On the other hand, their fixations are more intense and focused on specific areas of interest (*e.g.*, the game assets they interact with) when playing games which use the background scenes to provide a more photorealistic perception, but they are not part of the game-play or the players are not required to interact with them. Overall, the effect of IBR on gaming experience depends on the game type and the degree of the visual search activity (*e.g.*, traditional methods will be preferred for games with heavy visual search, while IBR will be preferred for games with lighter visual interaction).

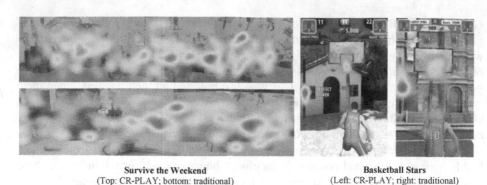

Survive the Weekend
(Top: CR-PLAY; bottom: traditional)

Basketball Stars
(Left: CR-PLAY; right: traditional)

Fig. 4. The participants visually interacted with the whole scene when playing *Survive the Weekend*; but, they visually focused on specific areas of interest when playing *Basketball Stars*.

4.1 Limitations and Future Work

The main limitation of our work is the relatively small sample sizes used in our studies. However, the statistical tests performed met all the required assumptions, providing credible results. Another limitation is the use of a research, but state-of-the-art IBR game development pipeline (CR-PLAY). As a future work, we will engage more end-users to evaluate the quality of the produced game elements and measure the gaming experience on games of varying types and characteristics.

5   Conclusion

In this paper, we investigated, through two evaluation studies, the impact of image-based rendering and reconstruction (IBR) on game developers efficiency, games performance and game players' experience. In the first study, we engaged two professional game developers who created, during a six-month period and within ecologically valid conditions, two versions (traditional and IBR) of two different games. In the second study, twelve experienced gamers played the four game versions in the context of an in-lab, A/B testing, eye-tracking approach. The analysis of the results revealed benefits of the IBR approach, such as reduced time and costs for creating photorealistic game assets. Drawbacks were also revealed, such as increased loading times, huge file sizes of deployed games and scalability issues which can be credited to the very nature of the IBR technology. Regarding, the players' gaming experience, the analysis of the results revealed mixed outcome regarding players' preference of games created with the traditional vs. IBR approach which should be further investigated.

References

1. Newzoo: Top 100 Countries by 2015 Game Revenues (2015)
2. Entertainment Software Association (ESA): Essential Facts about the Computer and Video Game Industry (2016)

3. Fuchs, M.: The video game industry: formation, present state, and future. **6**, 83–87 (2014). doi:10.1386/jgvw.6.1.83_5
4. Ackermann, J., Langguth, F., Fuhrmann, S., Goesele, M.: Photometric stereo for outdoor webcams. In: Proceedings of IEEE Computer Society Conference Computer Vision Pattern Recognition, pp. 262–269 (2012). doi:10.1109/CVPR.2012.6247684
5. Laffont, P.Y., Bousseau, A., Drettakis, G.: Rich intrinsic image decomposition of outdoor scenes from multiple views. IEEE Trans. Vis. Comput. Graph. **19**, 210–224 (2013). doi:10.1109/TVCG.2012.112
6. Chaurasia, G., Duchene, S., Sorkine-Hornung, O., Drettakis, G.: Depth synthesis and local warps for plausible image-based navigation. ACM Trans. Graph. **32**, 1–12 (2013). doi:10.1145/2487228.2487238
7. Goesele, M., Ackermann, J., Fuhrmann, S., Haubold, C., Klowsky, R., Darmstadt, T.: Ambient point clouds for view interpolation. ACM Trans. Graph. **29**, 1 (2010). doi:10.1145/1833351.1778832
8. Tompkin, J., Kim, K.I., Kautz, J., Theobalt, C.: Videoscapes: exploring sparse unstructured video collections. ACM Trans. Graph. **31**, 12 (2012). doi:10.1145/2185520.2185564
9. Lipski, C., Linz, C., Berger, K., Sellent, A., Magnor, M.: Virtual video camera: image-based viewpoint navigation through space and time. Comput. Graph. Forum. **29**, 2555–2568 (2010). doi:10.1111/j.1467-8659.2010.01824.x
10. Ballan, L., Brostow, G.J., Puwein, J., Pollefeys, M.: Unstructured video-based rendering: interactive exploration of casually captured videos. ACM Trans. Graph. **29**, 11 (2010). doi:10.1145/1778765.1778824
11. Levieux, P., Tompkin, J., Kautz, J.: Interactive viewpoint video textures. In: ACM International Conference Proceeding, pp. 11–17 (2012). doi:10.1145/2414688.2414690
12. Starck, J., Kilner, J., Hilton, A.: Objective quality assessment in free-viewpoint video production. In: 3DTV Conference True Vision - Capture, Transmission Display 3D Video, pp. 225–228 (2008). doi:10.1109/3DTV.2008.4547849
13. Capturing Reality. https://www.capturingreality.com/
14. Meerstone Archa eological Consultancy: 3D Modelling with AgiSoft PhotoScan -Tests to determine the suitability of AgiSoft PhotoScan for archaeological recording, pp. 1–4 (2010)
15. Raof, A.N.A., Setan, H., Chong, A., Majid, Z.: Three dimensional modeling of archaeological artifact using photomodeler scanner. J. Teknol. **75**, 143–153 (2015). doi:10.11113/jt.v75.5283
16. Fidas, C., Avouris, N., Orvieto, I.: Requirements elicitation for new video game development tools: a case study, pp. 1–18 (2015)
17. CR-PLAY. http://www.cr-play.eu/
18. Cayon, R.O., Djelouah, A., Drettakis, G.: A Bayesian approach for selective image-based rendering using superpixels. In: Proceedings of - 2015 International Conference on 3D Vision, 3DV 2015, pp. 469–477 (2015). doi:10.1109/3DV.2015.59
19. Fuhrmann, S., Goesele, M.: Floating scale surface reconstruction. ACM Trans. Graph. **33**, 1–11 (2014). doi:10.1145/2601097.2601163
20. Gryka, M., Terry, M., Brostow, G.J.: Learning to remove soft shadows. ACM Trans. Graph. **34**, 1–15 (2015). doi:10.1145/2732407
21. Langguth, F., Goesele, M.: Guided capturing of multi-view stereo datasets. In: Eurographics 2013 - Short Paper Proceedings, pp. 93–96 (2013). doi:10.2312/conf/EG2013/short/093-096
22. Fuhrmann, S., Langguth, F., Moehrle, N., Waechter, M., Goesele, M.: MVE—an image-based reconstruction environment. Comput. Graph. **53**, 44–53 (2015). doi:10.1016/j.cag.2015.09.003

23. Jennett, C., Cox, A.L., Cairns, P., Dhoparee, S., Epps, A., Tijs, T., Walton, A.: Measuring and defining the experience of immersion in games. Int. J. Hum Comput Stud. **66**, 641–661 (2008). doi:10.1016/j.ijhcs.2008.04.004
24. Denisova, A., Nordin, A.I., Cairns, P.: The convergence of player experience questionnaires. In: Proceedings of the 2016 Annual Symposium on Computer-Human Interaction in Play - CHI PLAY 2016, pp. 33–37. ACM Press, New York (2016). doi:10.1145/2967934.2968095
25. Nordin, A.I., Denisova, A., Cairns, P.: Too many questionnaires: measuring player experience whilst playing digital games. In: Seventh York Doctoral Symposium on Computer Science & Electronics, pp. 69–75 (2014). doi:10.1007/s11031-006-9051-8

Exploring in-the-Wild Game-Based Gesture Data Collection

Kiyoshi Oka[1(⊠)], Weiquan Lu[2], Kasım Özacar[1], Kazuki Takashima[1], and Yoshifumi Kitamura[1]

[1] Research Institute of Electrical Communication,
Tohoku University, Sendai, Japan
oka@riec.tohoku.ac.jp
[2] National University of Singapore, Singapore, Singapore
icd-office@ml.riec.tohoku.ac.jp

Abstract. This paper presents an automatic 3D gesture collection concept and architecture based on a rhythm game for public displays. The system was implemented using an off-the-shelf gesture controller, was deployed on a public vertical screen, and was used to study the effects of alternative gesture guidance conditions. In the evaluation presented, we examined how alternative gesture guidance conditions affect users' engagement. The study showed that demonstration animation (CDA) and tracking state feedback (TSI) each encourages sustained game engagement. The underlying concept and architecture presented here offer actionable UI design insight to help creating large gesture corpus from diverse populations.

1 Introduction

Gesture elicitation with off-the-shelf controllers such as Microsoft Kinect and Leap Motion has made gesture-based interfaces more accessible. Interfaces leveraging this class of controllers hold the promise for intuitive 3D interaction and provide benefits such as touch-free and remote interactions in public spaces [11]. For example, gesture-based interaction can benefit interaction in areas where touch input is not suitable. However, to develop gesture-based interfaces, UI designers may incorporate gesture recognition systems, often requiring a large corpus of training data [1–3]. In many cases, it is difficult to efficiently collect a large corpus of training data in a short period of time, representing a limitation in the use of gesture elicitation controllers.

This paper proposes and validates a low-cost concept and architecture (Fig. 1) to collect an in-the-wild gesture corpus from a large and potentially diverse user population. The proposed system is based on a rhythm game combined with a Walk-Up-and-Use Display [4, 5]. The system consists of a sensor for detecting 3D hand gestures and a computer with a large display for running a game. The system can be deployed in a public space and store gestures to an online database, and the collected data may then be used to make a large gesture corpus that would help development and evaluation of robust gesture recognition algorithms. In such systems, however, users of the system should be informed of how to use such a display as they approach it, while

R. Bernhaupt et al. (Eds.): INTERACT 2017, Part II, LNCS 10514, pp. 97–106, 2017.
DOI: 10.1007/978-3-319-67684-5_7

also being attracted to use the system, which can be a challenging task for UI designers [4]. For in-the-wild settings, the systems should (a) teach users how to interact with the system and (b) help sustaining user engagement at least of one full game session.

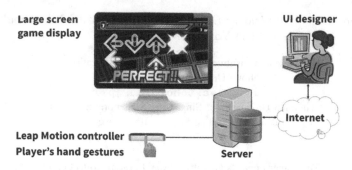

Fig. 1. Proposed concept and system architecture.

To address these challenges, we developed a gesture collection system using a rhythm game that can be deployed in-the-wild, and explored the types of guidance would result in greater sustained user engagement in opportunistic data collection. The game-based gesture collection system, Gesture Gesture Revolution (GGR), was designed for a Walk-Up-and-Use Display to serve as a platform for in-the-wild studies. We then conducted an in-the-wild study using GGR to investigate the effects of different guidance conditions on user's total engagement process. The main contributions of this paper are (a) describing design and implementation of an automatic gesture collection system using a simple rhythm game for a Walk-Up-and-Use Display and its fundamental benefits, and (b) describing a three-week user study that found that the guidance conditions with Contextualized Demonstration Animation (CDA) and Tracking State Indicator (TSI) result in more correct and sustained user gesture input.

2 Related Work

There have been successful examples of such in-the-wild gesture studies. For example, Hinrichs [10] carried out a field study at an aquarium to investigate how visitors interact with a large interactive table, and found that users' choice and use of gestures were affected by the interaction and social contexts. Walter [11] compared three strategies in revealing mid-air gestures in interactive public displays, and found that 56% of users were able to perform gestures with spatial division. Marshall [5] used a Walk-Up-and-Use tabletop in-the-wild to study social interactions around such devices, and found that these interactions were very different from those in lab settings. Most recently, Ackad [8] used an in-the-wild study to explore whether their system design supported learning, how their tutorial feedback mechanisms supported learning, and the effectiveness for browsing hierarchical information. Based on this related work, we use the in-the-wild approach as it enabled us to collect large and realistic data from diverse users if proper guidance was provided.

With respect to guidance, there were also many studies that have used the concept of "gesture guidance" [4, 7–9]. Gesture guidance systems are displays that show the gesture commands that can be used by the user to interact with the system. Rovelo et al. [4] compared a dynamic gesture guidance system with a printed traditional static gesture guidance showing snapshots of gesture sequences in a lab-based study. They found that for simple gestures, the dynamic system did not necessarily significantly improve users' ability to learn and perform the correct gestures, but for complex gestures, the dynamic guide did result in an improvement. While previous work addressed the learning of gestures in a lab-based study, we are more interested in the effects of guidance conditions on the engagement process for an in-the-wild setting.

3   Game-Based Gesture Collection

We implemented an in-house design large-display game called Gesture Gesture Revolution (GGR) and designed it as an in-the-wild study platform that enabled passers-by to interact with the game by using simple stroke gestures.

3.1   Creating Gesture Gesture Revolution (GGR)

We studied several different game genres that use body or hand movements, and decided to base our game on the rhythm and dance genre, made popular by Konami's Dance Dance Revolution [6]. This game concept is simple and offers a range of game design possibilities, while providing sufficient methods for conducting experiments by controlling the game and constraining gesture interactions.

We selected four simple hand gestures for collection: swipe up, swipe down, swipe left, and swipe right. These gestures were selected because they appeared simple to perform, but users could perform them in a wide variety of ways, thereby presenting a challenge for gesture recognition systems. Such gestures could be reliably detectable by the Leap Motion sensor, and they could be incorporated into more complex gestures.

We now describe the gameplay of GGR. When the game starts, an arrow appears at the top of the screen, and starts moving downwards (Fig. 2(a)). The arrow indicates which gesture is required for that part of the game. When the arrow reaches the bottom, the player must complete the correct gesture to score points (Fig. 2(b)). The player scores a different amount of points, depending on when s/he completes the gesture. The closer s/he is to the bottom of the screen, the more points s/he receives. However, the player receives no points if s/he performs the gesture too early (too far from the bottom of the screen), too late (the arrow moves out of the screen), or s/he performs wrong gestures (Fig. 2(c)). Depending on the scores, the players would receive different visual feedback (Bad, Good, Great, Perfect and Wrong Gesture). We focused only on visual feedback as it sufficiently shows the user the state of gesture input, and we plan to use different channels (e.g., sound) in a follow-up study.

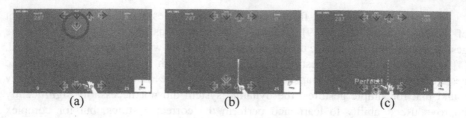

Fig. 2. Sequence of game dynamics (left to right): (a) An arrow appears at the top of the screen. (b) As the arrow moves down, the player must make the required gesture in order to score points. (c) If timed correctly, the player will receive the maximum score.

3.2 System Architecture

Our prototype of the system was implemented using a client-server architecture consisting of a database server backend, and a game client frontend (Fig. 1). A server hosted the game software (created in Unity) and MySQL database (part of the WAMP server package). We used a desktop computer with an Intel i7-6700 CPU and 8 GB RAM, running Windows Server 2012 R2. The 50-in. large plasma TV was used to display the game and visual feedback for players. The server was connected to the Internet, and therefore enabled researchers to remotely access the database, update the parameters/variables of the game, and monitor the gameplay.

4   In-the-Wild Study

We conducted an in-the-wild study to evaluate the potential of game-based opportunistic gesture data collection and the effects of the three traditional guidance types on user engagement. The in-the-wild approach was chosen in order to obtain diverse gesture data from many different users with minimal resources.

4.1 Implemented Guidance Conditions in GGR

We designed three guidance conditions, two levels and one control, based on the concept of Scaffolding Means (Instructing, Modeling and Feeding-back) [19]:

- Looping Introductory Animation (LIA). The Looping Introductory Animation (Fig. 3(a)) included detailed instructions on how, when and where all the gestures were needed in the game. The animation was played in a loop until a user interrupted the loop by placing his/her hand over the Leap Motion sensor. This was the implementation of Instructing [19], and served as a standard guidance that could quickly show all necessary steps of the game.
- Contextualized Demonstration Animation (CDA). As shown in Fig. 3(b), this animation sequence was overlaid on the game view just before a user was required to perform a specific gesture for the first time. This was a form of Modeling [19], and provided dynamic and explicit models that users could imitate when preforming required gestures.

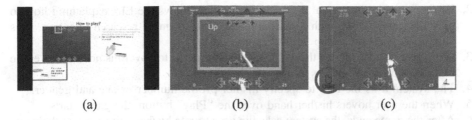

| (a) | (b) | (c) |

Fig. 3. Implemented guidance types: (a) Looping Introductory Animation (LIA), (b) Contextualized Demonstration Animation (CDA), (c) Tracking State Indicator (TSI).

- Tracking State Indicator (TSI). This indicator was shown at all times, and had two states. One state indicated that the system was detecting the user's hand gesture successfully (Fig. 3(c)), and another indicated that the system was not detecting the user's hand gesture successfully. This was a form of Feeding-back [19], and served as an implicit guidance that would give users a fundamental understanding of how fingers are tracked.

The LIA was shown at the start of the game, in every guidance condition, as it was implemented as part of core functionality of the system. The other two guidance conditions were mutually exclusive. As the experiment was conducted over a span of three weeks, Week 1 was LIA alone (LIA), Week 2 was LIA with CDA (LIA + CDA), and Week 3 was LIA with TSI (LIA + TSI).

4.2 Deployment Venue

The system was deployed as a typical Walk-Up-and-Use Display. Figure 4 shows a snapshot of the system deployment with a group of passers-by playing the game. It consisted of a Panasonic 50-in. display mounted on a high display stand. The system was configured to power on at 08:30 am and shut down at 08:30 pm every day, as per requirements from the exhibition venue sponsors. A research institute within a local university was the exhibition venue. About 400 individuals passed through this venue every day, and about 25% were female, according to our visual observation. About 80% of human traffic moving in and out of the building had to pass by the exhibit, as it was placed between the entrance and elevators.

Fig. 4. System deployment.

4.3 Experiment Protocol

We used the following protocol:

1. A potential user walks into the venue.

2. His/her attention is drawn to the display, which shows the LIA explaining how to play the game, along with a disclaimer and statement of research intention. This animation plays on a loop until the game starts.
3. If the user decides to play the game, s/he is instructed to hover his/her hand over the Leap Motion for about 2 s to activate the game.
4. The system asks the user to specify his/her profile number or age and gender.
5. When the user hovers his/her hand over the "Play" button, the game starts.
6. After the game ends, the system asks the user to rate his/her enjoyment of the game on a scale of 1 to 5.
7. Once done, the system displays the user's score on a leaderboard, generates a user profile number and shows it to the user. The user can then use the profile number when s/he plays the game next time. This allows us to track repeat users, and also allows users to keep track of their own progress.
8. Finally, the system returns to the initial LIA, awaiting the next user.

4.4 Measurements

In order to investigate which guidance conditions would result in greater user engagement, we measured five dependent variables.

1. Correctness was defined as the average number of correct gestures made by each player, over the total number of gestures required in the game session.
2. Percentage of partial quitters (Partial Quitters) was defined as the number of users who managed to perform at least one gesture successfully but decided to quit playing before completing the game, over the total number of users.
3. Percentage of successful task completions (Completions) was defined as the number of users who successfully completed the task (performing 25 gestures correctly), over the total number of users.
4. Score was defined as the total average score obtained by the users, with higher scores awarded for more challenging moves.
5. Average number of sustained successful gesture performances (Sustained) was defined as the average number of chained successful gesture performances.

5 Results

During the three-week experiment period, the system recorded a total of 171 unique users (Mean age = 26.6, SD = 9.57, 38 females). Based on the data, we conducted statistical analysis in terms of Correctness, Partial Quitters, Completions, Score and Sustained. We excluded the data from self-reported repeat user sessions, meaning that all the data was from users who only played for the first time, enabling us to conduct a between-subjects analysis.

Correctness. Figure 5(a) shows the average number of correct gestures made by each user, over the total number of gestures required in the game session. Since the data did not fit the assumption of normality, we conducted the Kruskal-Wallis test and found that different guidance types had a significant effect on correctness ($p < 0.01$).

The post-hoc Steel-Dwass test was carried out to compare the three guidance conditions and it revealed that the correctness was significantly higher in the LIA (Looping Introductory Animation) + CDA (Contextualized Demonstration Animation) condition than in the LIA-only condition ($p < 0.01$). We further conducted the Steel test that focuses on differences between the baseline (LIA) and each of the LIA+CDA and LIA +TSI (Tracking State Indicator) conditions, and found that the correctness was significantly higher in the LIA+CDA and LIA+TSI conditions, than in the LIA-only condition ($p < 0.01$, $p < 0.05$).

Partial Quitters. Figure 5(b) shows the percentage of partial quitters. We conducted a chi-square test in order to statistically compare the proportions across guidance conditions, and did not find any significant effect of different guidance conditions on partial quitters ($\chi^2 = 1.51$, $p \geq 0.05$).

Completions. Figure 5(c) shows the percentage of successful task completions. We used a chi-square test in order to statistically compare the proportions, and found that the different guidance types had a significant effect on completions ($\chi^2 = 7.60$, $p < 0.05$). Chi-square pairwise comparisons with Bonferroni corrections revealed that the number of completions were significantly higher in the LIA+CDA condition than in the LIA-only condition ($p < 0.05$).

Score. Figure 5(d) shows the average score. Kruskal-Wallis test revealed that different guidance types had a significant effect on the score ($p < 0.01$). The post-hoc Steel-Dwass test revealed that the score was significantly higher in the LIA+CDA condition than in the LIA-only condition ($p < 0.01$).

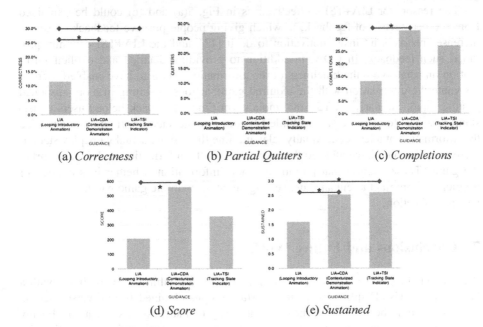

(a) *Correctness*   (b) *Partial Quitters*   (c) *Completions*

(d) *Score*   (e) *Sustained*

Fig. 5. Graphs of (a) Correctness, (b) Partial quitters, (c) Completions, (d) Score and (e) Sustained. * depicts p < 0.05.

Sustained. Figure 5(e) shows the average number of sustained successful gesture performances. Kruskal-Wallis test revealed that different guidance types had a significant effect on the number of sustained successful gesture performances ($p < 0.01$). The post-hoc Steel-Dwass test revealed that the LIA+TSI condition offered significantly more sustained successful gesture performances than the LIA-only condition ($p < 0.01$). We further conducted the Steel test that focused on differences between baseline (LIA) and each of the LIA+CDA and LIA+TSI conditions, and found that the average number of sustained successful gesture performances was significantly higher in the LIA+CDA and LIA+TSI conditions, than in the LIA-only condition ($p < 0.05$, $p < 0.01$).

6 Discussion

First of all, the system successfully encouraged many passers-by to participate in the game and collected data from various users just by deploying the system in a public place (e.g., the game was played over 100 times in the first week of the deployment), thereby suggesting the potential for low-cost and automatic gesture data collection.

In terms of user engagement, Fig. 5(a) and (e) show that LIA+CDA and LIA+TSI had significant effects on Correctness and Sustained. Furthermore, In Fig. 5(c) and (d), we see that LIA+CDA has a significantly higher percentage of Completions and Score (LIA+TSI was also trending in that direction, but the differences were not significant). These suggest that incorporating CDA and TSI resulted in more correct and sustained gesture input.

The reason for LIA+TSI's effectiveness in Fig. 5(a) and (e) could be explained from the perspective of feedback, in which giving people positive feedback on a task increases people's intrinsic motivation to do it [12], and the LIA+TSI certainly provided such feedback. In CDA, in addition to providing detailed and explicit information on what to do, the timeliness of the information seems to have enabled users to associate the information with the required game actions, resulting in more sustained gesture input. Similarly, in TSI, the implicit yet timely feedback helped users understand how best to play the game. While LIA did provide such information, it provided the information at a less contextually relevant time (before the actual gameplay started) therefore this could have affected the association of the information with its use during the game. These suggest that providing timely information, whether it is explicit or implicit, is important to enhance user engagement in rhythmic game-based, in-the-wild gesture collection.

7 Conclusions and Future Work

We presented a gesture data collection system using a rhythm game combined with a Walk-Up-and-Use Display, to create a gesture corpus obtained from diverse users at low cost. The in-the-wild study showed that the system successfully encouraged many passers-by to engage in the game and collected data from various users just by deploying the system in a public place, thereby suggesting the potential of low-cost and automatic gesture data collection. We also examined the effects of different gesture guidance conditions on user engagement in Walk-Up-and-Use displays and found that the guidance conditions with Contextualized Demonstration Animation and Tracking State Indicator resulted in sustained user engagement.

While this represents early work, the current results offer interesting insights into automatic gesture data collection, and pave the way for several future directions, such as further investigations of the venue, game design (e.g., sound effects, game genres), and conducting laboratory studies. Different gestures, applications and guidance models should also be investigated in order to generalize our proposed concept and results. Furthermore, we plan to analyze and evaluate the obtained gesture dataset by using it to train gesture recognition systems.

Acknowledgment. This research is supported by the National Research Foundation, Prime Minister's Office, Singapore under its International Research Centres in Singapore Funding Initiative. This work is also supported by JSPS Bilateral Joint Research Project, and Cooperative Research Project Program of the Research Institute of Electrical Communication, Tohoku University.

References

1. Chen, F.-S., Fu, C.-M., Huang, C.-L.: Hand gesture recognition using a real-time tracking method and hidden Markov models. Image Vis. Comput. **21**, 745–758 (2003)
2. Hoffman, M., Varcholik, P., LaViola, J.J.: Breaking the status quo: improving 3D gesture recognition with spatially convenient input devices. In: Virtual Reality Proceedings IEEE, pp. 59–66 (2010)
3. Luzhnica, G., Simon, J., Lex, E., Pammer, V.: A sliding window approach to natural hand gesture recognition using a custom data glove. In: 2016 Proceedings of the IEEE Symposium 3D User Interfaces, pp. 81–90 (2016)
4. Rovelo, G., Degraen, D., Vanacken, D., Luyten, K., Coninx, K.: Gestu-Wan - an intelligible mid-air gesture guidance system for walk-up-and-use displays. In: Abascal, J., Barbosa, S., Fetter, M., Gross, T., Palanque, P., Winckler, M. (eds.) INTERACT 2015. LNCS, vol. 9297, pp. 368–386. Springer, Cham (2015). doi:10.1007/978-3-319-22668-2_28
5. Marshall, P., Morris, R., Rogers, Y., Kreitmayer, S., Davies, M.: Rethinking "multi-user" - an in-the-wild study of how groups approach a walk-up-and-use tabletop interface. In: Proceedings of Conference Human Factors in Computer System, pp. 3033–3042 (2011)
6. Konami: DanceDanceRevolution. http://www.konami.jp/bemani/ddr/jp/
7. Delamare, W., Coutrix, C., Nigay, L.: Designing guiding systems for gesture-based interaction. In: Proceedings of the 7th ACM SIGCHI Symposium on Engineering Interactive Computer System - EICS 2015, pp. 44–53 (2015)
8. Ackad, C., Clayphan, A., Tomitsch, M., Kay, J.: An in-the-wild study of learning mid-air gestures to browse hierarchical information at a large interactive public display. In: Proceedings of the International Joint Conference on Pervasive Ubiquitous Computer, International Symposium Wearable Computer, pp. 1227–1238 (2015)
9. Delamare, W., Janssoone, T., Coutrix, C.C., Nigay, L.: Designing 3D gesture guidance: visual feedback and feedforward design options. In: Proceedings of the International Working Conference on Advanced Visual Interfaces - AVI 2016, pp. 152–159 (2016)

10. Hinrichs, U., Carpendale, S.: Gestures in the wild: studying multi-touch gesture sequences on interactive tabletop exhibits. In: Annual Conference on Human Factors Computer System, pp. 3023–3032 (2011)
11. Walter, R., Bailly, G., Müller, J.: StrikeAPose: revealing mid-air gestures on public displays. In: SIGCHI Conference on Human Factors Computer System, pp. 841–850 (2013)
12. Deci, E.E.L.: Effects of externally mediated rewards on intrinsic motivation. J. Pers. Soc. Psychol. **18**, 105–115 (1971)

From Objective to Subjective Difficulty Evaluation in Video Games

Thomas Constant[✉], Guillaume Levieux[✉], Axel Buendia,
and Stéphane Natkin

Conservatoire National des Arts et Métiers, CNAM-Cédric,
292 Rue St Martin, 75141 Paris Cedex 03, France
{thomas.constant,guillaume.levieux,axel.buendia,
stephane.natkin}@lecnam.net

Abstract. This paper describes our research investigating the perception of difficulty in video games, defined as players' estimation of their chances of failure. We discuss our approach as it relates to psychophysical studies of subjective difficulty and to cognitive psychology research into the overconfidence effect. The starting point for our study was the assumption that the strong motivational pull of video games may lead players to become overconfident, and thereby underestimate their chances of failure. We design and implement a method for an experiment using three games, each representing a different type of difficulty, wherein players bet on their capacity to succeed. Our results confirm the existence of a gap between players' actual and self-evaluated chances of failure. Specifically, players seem to underestimate high levels of difficulty. The results do not show any influence on difficulty underestimation from the players gender, feelings of self-efficacy, risk aversion or gaming habits.

Keywords: User modelling · Affective HCI · Emotion · Motivational aspects · Tools for design · Modelling · Evaluation · Fun/Aesthetic design

1 Introduction

Jesper Juul proposed defining a video game as "*a rule-based formal system with a variable and quantifiable outcome, where different outcomes are assigned different values, the player exerts effort in order to influence the outcome, the player feels attached to the outcome, and the consequences of the activity are optional and negotiable*" [1]. In this definition, the player *exerts effort* to influence the outcome, emphasizing the fact that a video game must have a certain level of difficulty to be considered as such.

Many authors acknowledge challenge as one of the most fundamental aspect of a video game's inherent appeal. Malone proposes three features of computer games that render them captivating: challenge, curiosity and fantasy [2]. In his model, challenge is directly related to game difficulty and corresponds to the

© IFIP International Federation for Information Processing 2017
Published by Springer International Publishing AG 2017. All Rights Reserved
R. Bernhaupt et al. (Eds.): INTERACT 2017, Part II, LNCS 10514, pp. 107–127, 2017.
DOI: 10.1007/978-3-319-67684-5_8

uncertainty of the player reaching the game's goals. Lazzaro proposes a four-factor model, where *Hard Fun* relates to the feeling of overcoming difficult tasks [3]. Sweetser et al. also see challenge as one of the most important parts of their Game Flow framework [4]. This work builds upon Mihaly Csikszentmihalyi's Flow Theory [5], which deals with the properties of activities that have a strong, intrinsic ability to motivate. Csikszentmihalyi's research has found that these activities provide *perceived challenges, or opportunities for action, that stretch (neither overmatching nor underutilizing) existing skills* [5]. A study of a large population of players of two commercial games confirmed that players prefer specific levels of difficulty [6]. Ryan et al. have also studied intrinsic motivation, applying their Self-Determination Theory to video games. They show how enjoyment relates to the feeling of *competence* - which relies on an optimal level of challenge - and thus to game difficulty [7]. Finally, Jesper Juul provides insight on how failure, and thus difficulty, is one of the core aspects of video game enjoyment and learning progression [8,9].

In order to foster and maintain a players' motivation, it is therefore essential to correctly set the difficulty of a video game. To do this, one can either provide different difficulty settings for the player to select or use an algorithm that adapts difficulty in real time to match the game designer's theoretical difficulty curve to the player's player skill level [10–12].

Both methods require a prior evaluation of the game's difficulty. For this the game designer might provide a heuristic which may or may not accurately express the game's difficulty. Alternatively, sensors may be used to estimate workload or affective state, but this method is currently only feasible in a lab setting and its efficacy is still being studied [13,14]. We could also try to estimate players' chances of failure [15]. Each of these approaches provide insight into a specific aspect of a game's difficulty.

Difficulty is in itself a complex notion. We can draw distinctions between *skill-based* difficulty, *effort-based* difficulty [16], and between *sensory, logical* and *motor* difficulty [15,17]. Moreover, video games are created for an aesthetic purpose, evoking specific emotions in the player [18]. Thus, we must draw a fundamental distinction between *objective difficulty* and *subjective difficulty*. Objective difficulty is estimated directly by observing gameplay variables and events, while subjective difficulty is a psychological construct of the player. When adapting a game's difficulty, especially when using a dynamic difficulty adjustment (DDA) algorithm, we are relying on an objective estimation of difficulty, which may be quite different to what the player actually feels while playing the game.

In this paper we present our work on studying the relationship between subjective and objective difficulty in the context of video games. First, we review various studies on both subjective and objective difficulty estimation, looking first at the psychophysical approach of perceived difficulty, then at cognitive psychology research on overconfidence. We then introduce our own method for measuring objective and subjective difficulty. In this method, objective difficulty is modeled using a mixed effects logistic regression to estimate the player's actual chances of failure for a given challenge. We defined subjective difficulty as the players' estimation of their chances of failure, which we gathered using an in-game betting system. This is followed by a description of the three games we developed for this study that allowed us to separate out logical, motor and sensory gameplay. Lastly, we present and discuss our results.

2 Psychophysical Approach to Subjective Difficulty

Many studies have tried to clarify the link between the subjective and objective difficulty of various tasks: Raven's progressive matrices, number memorization, visual letter search, wire labyrinth tasks [19,20], Fitts' tapping task [21,22], throwing darts at a moving target [23], rock climbing [24], reaction time, even while riding a bike [19,25]. All these experiments take a psychophysical approach, trying to estimate the link between objective difficulty as a stimulus and subjective difficulty as a perception or evaluation of this stimulus.

These studies use various techniques to estimate objective difficulty, and often tend to draw a distinction between objective difficulty and performance. For all of the Fitts' tapping tasks, authors use Fitts' law [26] as a measure of objective difficulty, and time as a measure of performance. When such a law is not available, however, they rely solely on performance, e.g. response time or success frequency [20,23], or they select a variable highly correlated with perceived difficulty such as, in the case of the rock-climbing experiment, electromyographic data from a specific muscle [24]. In addition, in these studies objective difficulty is never assessed with regard to each subject's abilities, but across all or a few subgroups of subjects. In our research, we do not rely on any specific objective difficulty estimation but follow a more generic approach that allows for cross-game comparisons. We estimate a mapping between the challenge's variables and the player's chance of failing it. We also use a mixed effect model that takes into account each player's abilities.

In the psychophysical studies, subjective difficulty is assessed using a free scale. Very often, a reference value is given to the subject, e.g. a subjective difficulty of 10 for a specific task [21]. Deligniere proposes the DPE-15 scale, a 7-point Likert scale with intermediate values, as a more convenient and comparable measure [23]. In our experiment, we integrated this measure with gameplay and used a specific 7-point scale, as described in Sect. 4. To avoid the problem of subjective interpretation of the notion of difficulty, we concentrated on the success probability, as estimated by the player.

Except in Slifkin and Grilli [21], all subjective evaluations were carried out at the end of each challenge, often after having repeated the challenge many times. We considered that to understand what the player feels during play, rather than while reflecting on a past game session, it might be useful to look at the player's evaluation of current difficulty during each challenge. As our measure of subjective difficulty is an estimation of the chance of failure, it can be integrated into the gameplay and thus be repeated more often without pulling the player out of the game (see Sect. 4).

3   Overconfidence and the Hard/Easy Effect

We define subjective difficulty as the player's own evaluation of their chance of failure. This evaluation is a complex cognitive process, often rushed, based on the interpretation of incomplete information about the game state, based on in-game performance feedback as well as assessments of the player's own knowledge and skills with respect to a specific challenge. Cognitive psychology research on judgmental heuristics looks at how this kind of reasoning can be biased, and can help us understand how players may have wrongly evaluated their chances of success.

Heuristic approaches to judgment and decision-making have opened up a vast field of research into explaining human behavior in the context of uncertainty. Kahneman and Frederick [27,28] consider that, when confronted to a complex decision, people substitute one attribute of the decision with a simpler, more accessible one, in order to reduce cognitive effort. In some cases, the use of judgmental heuristics can lead to fundamental errors, called *cognitive biases* by Kahneman and Tversky [29].

The overconfidence effect is one of these biases. Well-studied in the domain of finance, this behavior relies on a surrealistic evaluation of our own knowledge and skills, leading to an overestimation of our abilities or those of others [30–34]. Overconfidence seems particularly useful to study in relation to video games as they are essentially built with the motivation of the player in mind. The self-efficacy theory of motivation states that having a strong feeling of confidence in one's future chances of success is a key aspect of motivation [35]. Video games that feature a well-crafted difficulty curve can manipulate players' perception of their chances of success to keep them motivated.

Overconfidence has already been studied in many games. In a game of bridge, beginners or amateurs players can misjudge both their performances and play outcomes [36]. The same effect has been noticed in other games where novice players show an inferior ability to predict their odds of winning during poker tournaments [37], and games of chess [38], and in gambling games [39,40]. To summarize: the overconfidence effect appears when the players have a limited knowledge of the game. This applies to any type of game, whether it be a pure game of chance such as a slot machine, or a skill-based game like chess.

There are many situations and cognitive biases that influence a player's over-estimation or underestimation of their chances of success. These include: level of expertise [41,42], the *gambler's fallacy* [43,44], the *hot hand bias* [44,45], the *illusion of control* [46,47] and the *hard/easy effect*. While all these aspects of overconfidence are worth studying in the context of video games, for our research we chose to focus on the *hard/easy effect*. The *hard/easy effect* specifies that for low and high levels of difficulty, decision-makers fail to estimate the true difficulty of a task [48]. For low levels, they underestimate their chances of success; for high levels they overestimate [33,41].

Using the hard/easy effect as our starting point, our research focused on two main aspects. First, from a methodological point of view, we wanted our experiment to simulate as closely as possible the experience of a real video game.

For this reason we used a dynamically adjusted difficulty beginning at a low difficulty level. In addition, instead of evaluating player confidence by explicitly asking them if they felt confident on a percentage scale, we used a betting mechanism integrated into gameplay. In this way we avoided to breaking player immersion. Second, our research distinguished between three types of difficulty. We used three different games, each focusing on a specific type. We describe our experiment in the following section.

4   Experimentation

As we have previously emphasized, video games feature different types of difficulty. In our experiment we sought to assess them separately, with a view to distinguishing between the various facets of video games. Using Levieux et al.'s [15,17] approach we considered three categories of difficulty in games: sensory, logical and motor. Sensory difficulty relates to the effort needed to acquire information about the game state. Logical difficulty corresponds to the effort needed to induce or deduce, from the available information, the solution to a problem in terms of action(s) to perform. Lastly, motor difficulty relates to the physical agility needed to perform these actions. To realize an accurate analysis of the player's behavior for each of these types, the experiment was split between three custom-designed games, all played within a single program.

For this experiment, we chose a general, practical approach wherein we estimated the probability of a player failing a specific challenge relative to their current skill level [15]. Our definition of difficulty builds upon Malone's definition of challenge as a source of uncertainty in video games [2]. Uncertainty in success or failure is what Costikyan also calls *uncertainty of outcomes* [49]. We follow these authors and consider the difficulty as such. We directly ask players to evaluate their success chances, and thus avoid to use the term "difficulty" which has a less accurate meaning. Additionally, we were able to make a distinction between logical, motor and sensory tasks by separating them into three different games (described in Sect. 4.3). In order to maximize player motivation and create an experience that was as close as possible to a real game, the system dynamically adapted difficulty based on analyzing player success or failure. Many games use dynamic difficulty adaptation, including racing games (e.g.rubberbanding in *Mario Kart*), and RPGs (e.g. *Fallout*) or FPSs (e.g. *Unreal Tournament*) where the difficulty in defeating an opponent depends on the player's level. Games without dynamic difficulty adaptation may use a predetermined difficulty curve based on the mean level of the players. Few games use completely random difficulty, but even in these (e.g. *FTL*, *The Binding of Isaac*), there is a global progression. Thus, while randomness would be more convenient for statistical analysis it would be of limited use from a game design perspective.

In addition, to avoid any memory bias on the past challenge and to better monitor the actual feeling of the player, we measured subjective difficulty during the game session rather than with post-experiment questionnaires [50]. To do this without pulling the player out of the game, we used a betting system, which we describe in the following section.

4.1 Measuring Subjective Difficulty

Our proposition takes cognitive psychology tools for measuring overconfidence and integrates them into gameplay. Our goal was to avoid disrupting the game session in order to maintain a high level of engagement and motivation. The measure is taken before the player's actions, as a pre-evaluation, but after having given them all the elements necessary to make their judgment. We used a betting system based on a 7-point Likert scale, which was integrated into the game progression and in this way tied to the player's score. If the player won, the amount they bet was added to their score; if they lost the amount was subtracted. This motivated the player to think carefully about their self-evaluation. An in-game question served to instruct the player on how to bet and reminded them to take care in assessing their own performance, thus their own confidence.

Measurement of subjective difficulty was based on the player's bet, designated as D_{subj}. With b being the bet value we used the formula $D_{subj} = 1 - \frac{b-1}{6}$ to get the estimated chances of failure.

4.2 Measuring Objective Difficulty

As Levieux et al. define it [15,17], the objective difficulty of a challenge can be estimated based on players' failures and successes in completing it. In order to take into account personal differences, we estimated the objective difficulty for each challenge using a mixed effects logistic regression [51]. The time and difficulty parameters of each challenge (e.g. cursor speed, number of cells) were used as fixed effect parameters, and we added random intercepts. We used a mixed model throughout repeated evaluations of the same subject. The random intercepts gave us a coefficient for each player that we used as a global evaluation of their performance level. The gap between the players' objective difficulty and their evaluations of their odds of success is called the *difficulty estimation error*. The designs of the three games, each one based on a difficulty type - logical, motor or sensory, are detailed in the next section.

4.3 Game Descriptions

Our experiment was based on the observation of players' betting in relation to the three dimensions of difficulty. Each dimension was represented by a specific game, described below, for which all the adjustment variables for the challenges are pre-established and common for all players. An initial series of playtests was also conducted with the target audience in the same settings used during the experiments for the purpose of gameplay calibration.

A brief story was included in order to enhance player motivation and to provide a narrative justification for the betting system. In the game universe, the player must save citizens of a mysterious kingdom who have been transformed into sheep by a local sorcerer. The player challenges the sorcerer during three tests, one for each kind of difficulty. The player's sole objective is to save as many sheep as possible. In turn, each game is an opportunity for the player to save doomed citizens by betting between one and seven sheep against their odds of winning.

All three games have a common user interface except for the central frame which depends on each sub-game (Fig. 1). All important information is displayed at the bottom of this frame: the number of remaining turns, the global score, and, in the case of the logical game, the remaining number of actions. Directives are placed below the main title on a colored banner: blue for directives, red for corrective feedbacks. A rules reminder is accessible at the bottom of the screen.

Feedback is provided throughout the game, at the end of each turn. Positive (on green background) and negative (on red) feedback is displayed on both sides of the screen, allowing the player to constantly follow their number of saved and lost sheep. Sound effects accompany this bleating for a saved sheep, a sorcerer's mocking laugh for a lost one. Animations are used to provide a more stimulating in-game interface.

For each game we modified the difficulty using a *difficulty parameter*. This parameter varied from 0 to 1 and was used to interpolate gameplay parameters, which we define in the following section. The difficulty parameter started at 0.2 and increased or decreased by 0.1 after each turn, based on the player's success or failure.

Logical Difficulty. The logical task is based on a well-known sliding-puzzle game. The player must restore the numerical order of a 300-pixel-wide grid composed of 9 squares. The fifth square, originally placed on the middle of the grid, is the only one that can be moved. This square can only be moved by switching its position with an adjacent square (Fig. 1a). At the beginning of each turn, before displaying the grid, the fifth square is randomly moved several times and the mixed up grid is displayed for 20 s before disappearing. The player has all the information required to place a bet: the remaining time is visible and

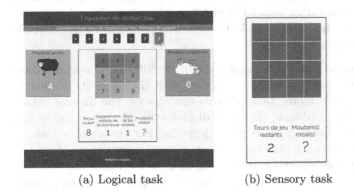

(a) Logical task   (b) Sensory task   (c) Motor task

Fig. 1. Game interface for the logical, sensory and motor tasks. The logical task is shown using the whole user interface, while for the motor and sensory task only the center frame was used. Screenshots were taken for the easiest levels of difficulty. (Color figure online)

the number of moves is specified. After betting, the grid will reappear and the player can begin to move the fifth square to restore the numerical order. The difficulty parameter allows us to adapt the difficulty by changing the number of steps during the randomization of the grid linearly from 1 to 11 steps.

Sensory Difficulty. For sensory difficulty, we designed a 300-pixel-wide grid composed of multiple squares (Fig. 1b). At the end of a countdown timer, five of them fade out during a limited time that we can approximate as follows, with t being the fade-out time and d as the difficulty parameter: $t = d^2 - 0.24d + 1.2$[1]. The player's task is to find the squares that have faded out by clicking on the grid. These squares are displayed in blue while the others remain in gray in order to avoid any color perception bias. The winning squares are shown after making a bet, over the player's squares selection. By doing this we wanted to induce a near-miss effect, allowing the player to see if they selected all, some or none of the winning squares. The countdown timer is set to 3 s. The number of squares varies with the difficulty of the task: when the player wins, the grid gains one square on each side. Meanwhile, the surface of the grid remains the same, meaning the squares become smaller after a winning round. For the maximum difficulty level the grid measures 11 by 11 squares; the minimum level grid size is 4 by 4. The difficulties in between are linearly interpolated using the difficulty parameter. Random locations are used for winning squares to avoid the most simple patterns, thus minimizing pattern-induced variations of difficulty for a specific difficulty parameter value. For example, for a 5×5 grid any adjacent winning squares are forbidden.

Motor Difficulty. The motor difficulty game is a basic and common reflex-based task. A cursor goes back and forth along a horizontal segment at a linear speed. The player must stop the cursor when it covers a black mark at the center (Fig. 1c). They can only stop the cursor by clicking on a button. Before they do this, the player must bet on their chance of success. This evaluation is not timed. Difficulty is based on the cursor's speed, which ranges linearly from 100 to 400 pixels per second. The sliding area is 320 pixels wide, the cursor is 15 pixels wide, and the black target 2 pixels wide.

Protocol Consistency. These three tasks, although different in nature, share a similar protocol and always provide the player with the elements needed to evaluate difficulty. For the motor task, players can observe the moving cursor before betting. For the logical task, the game displays the number of moves and lets the player view the problem for a fixed duration. For the sensory task, in which visual memory is crucial, the player selects tiles to solve the problem, but without any feedback before betting. Initial playtests showed that the task was very frustrating if the player had to stop focusing on the grid for betting without selecting the tiles. Each game has specific gameplay, as each one focuses on a

---

[1] This equation is a quadratic regression of the fade-out time. In the game, the color is incrementally modified during the game loop, but plotting this equation is much clearer than reading the color update code.

specific dimension of difficulty. Results can thus be compared between games while taking account of gameplay differences.

4.4   Procedures

Our experiment was conducted in Paris at the *Cité des sciences de l'industrie*, a national museum dedicated to science and critical thinking, during a school vacation period. The target audience was young volunteers, both gamers and non-gamers. Some who were invited to participate declined saying they lacked gaming experience or were not interested in taking part in a science experiment.

Nine laptops, all with the same configuration, were used in an isolated room. Each one had a mouse and a headset. The main program runs on a web browser, and was developed with JS, HTML5 and CSS. Participants were informed of the game's goal - to save as many sheep as possible - and of the duration of the experiment, approximately 40 min, questionnaire included. They were told not to communicate during the session. Before playing, the participants had to fill an online questionnaire used to create several different user profiles:

- **A gaming habits profile**, based on the amount of time that participants spent playing board games, video games (including social games) and gambling games.
- **A self-efficacy profile**, based on General Self-Efficacy scales [52,53] and adapted to video games situations. This part of the questionnaire was only accessible for the participants who answered yes to the question *"Do you consider yourself as a video game player?"* in the gaming habits section. The purpose of this was to check for any negative or positive effects of the participant's gaming ability on their self-estimation of their confidence.
- **A risk aversion profile**, based on Holt and Laury's Ten-Paired Lottery-Choices [54] in order to evaluate the impact of risk incentive on the player's confidence.

Our three games, each focusing on a different task, are all accessed and experienced within the context of a single software application (the "program"). The program's user flow is the same for all players:

- A **prologue** introduces the story before a random selection of the 3 tasks.
- A specific page presents **the rules** of the task before it starts. Players can take as much time as they want to understand them.
- Each task lasts 33 turns. The first 3 turns are used as a practice phase. At the end of this practice phase the score is reset to 0.
- The **turn progression** is identical for all the tasks. First, players have to observe the current game state in order to evaluate the difficulty. Then, they have to bet from 1 to 7 sheep on whether they will succeed. The same question is always asked of the player:*"How many sheep are you betting on your chances of winning?"*. This question allowed us to estimate the player's perception of their chances of failure. By validating the bet, the system unlocks the game and players can try to beat the challenge. The result is presented on screen

and the score is updated at the same time. Then a new turn begins with an appropriate adjustment to the difficulty level: when players win, the difficulty increases; when they lose, the difficulty decreases.
- After each task, **a game hub** allows the player to check their progression and score, and to progress to another task.
- After completing the 3 tasks a brief narrative **epilogue** announces the player final score: the total number of sheep won and lost.

To avoid any order effect, task selection is randomized. The best score of the day was written on a board, visible to the players. At the end of each turn the designed difficulty of a challenge, the player's bet and their score, were logged to CSV files.

5   Results

A total of 80 participants played the games. While some left the experiment before the end, we kept the results for all completed games, giving us a total of 6990 observations. For each task we remove outliers, such as players who did not use the betting system to perform a self-assessment, always placed the same bet, or players with outlying performance. A very low score may reflect some user experience issues, and some players took advantage of the adaptive difficulty system in order to maximize their score by deliberately losing with a low bet then by placing a high bet on the next easier challenge and so on. Nine outliers were removed: one from the motor task, three from the perceptive task, and six for logical one. We thus removed 300 observations from the dataset.

5.1   Modeling Objective Difficulty

As explained in Sect. 4.2, we performed a logit mixed effect regression to evaluate objective difficulty. For each task, we reported the conditional R^2, i.e. using both fixed and random effects [55] and evaluated the model by performing a 10-fold cross-validation, using our model as a binary predictor of the challenge outcome (Fig. 2).

As can be seen in Fig. 2, the difficulty parameter is always highly significant, and has the strongest effect on failure probability, especially for the sensory task. This means that we were indeed manipulating objective difficulty by changing this parameter.

The effect of time is always negative and significant. This means that if the difficulty parameter stays constant, objective difficulty seems to decrease overtime. This might indicate that players are actually learning as their success rate improves overtime for a given difficulty parameter value. The time effect is strongest for the logical task (-1), which is coherent with the fact that the player should learn more from a logical problem than from a purely sensory motor one (respectively, -0.46 and -0.37). Also, it may be noted that we have the highest standard deviation of random intercept for the logical task, which means that inter-individual differences are the highest for this task.

Parameters / Tasks	Logical	Motor	Sensory
Difficulty parameter	4.88 $(p < 2e - 16)$***	3.23 $(p < 2e - 16)$***	9.1 $(p < 2e - 16)$***
Time	-1 $(p = 2e - 6)$***	-0.46 $(p = 0.0051)$**	-0.37 $(p = 0.0454)$*
σ(random intercepts)	1.24	0.83	0.76
R^2	0.48	0.28	0.42
Cross Validation	0.66	0.61	0.69

Fig. 2. Modeling objective difficulty for each task: logit mixed effect regression results for difficulty and time over failures.

The link between the difficulty parameter and the objective difficulty of the game can be plotted to better understand each challenge difficulty dynamics. We chose to plot objective difficulty over the difficulty parameter at time $t = 0$. We also used the random intercept to separate the player into three groups of levels using k-means (Fig. 3).

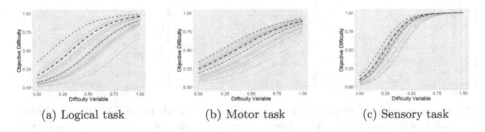

(a) Logical task   (b) Motor task   (c) Sensory task

Fig. 3. Objective difficulty for each task at $t = 0$. The blue dashed line represents median players, red dashed lines show the first and last quartiles. The least competent players are in yellow, average players in cyan and best players in green. (Color figure online)

Curves in Fig. 3 show information about our design of each task's difficulty. We can see that the logical task is the most balanced, with objective difficulty being the closest to the difficulty parameter value. The motor task is a bit too hard for low difficulty levels: objective difficulty is around 0.25 where the difficulty parameter is 0. Also, the sensory task should vary more slowly: objective difficulty reaches maximum when the difficulty parameter is only 0.5.

Figure 4 shows the progression of objective difficulty during the game. The curves confirm the balancing of each task and the efficiency of the difficulty adaptation system, as the players reach the average objective difficulty level (0.5) in all cases. The logical task starts at 0.2 for average players and goes up. The motor task is too hard at the beginning, and thus bad players see a decrease in difficulty overtime. The sensory task shows a "wavy" pattern, which may be related to the fact that the difficulty is less stable for this game. Indeed, the

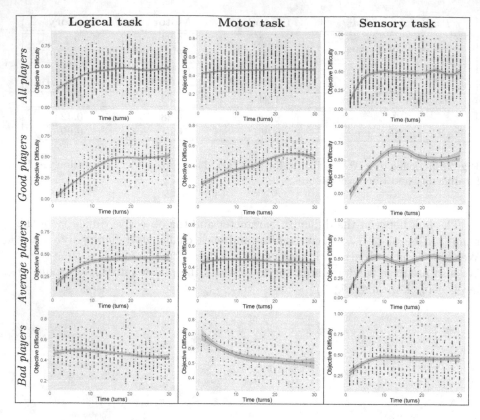

Fig. 4. Progression of objective difficulty overtime for all tasks and players during the entire play session. The blue line represents median players, dots represent the observations for each turn. (Color figure online)

difficulty parameter varies by 0.1 of a step for all tasks, but as the maximum objective difficulty is already reached at 0.5 it varies approximately twice as fast as the logical one.

Overall, the objective difficulty model is the weakest for the motor task with a low conditional R^2 (0.28) and the lowest prediction accuracy (0.61). R^2 and prediction accuracy are higher for the logical ($R^2 = 0.48$, $accuracy = 0.66$) and sensory tasks ($R^2 = 0.42$, $accuracy = 0.69$).

5.2   Differences Between Objective and Subjective Difficulty

To investigate the differences between objective and subjective difficulty, we separate the data into 16 equally sized bins using the objective difficulty as estimated by the mixed effect model. In each bin, we compute, for each player, the mean subjective difficulty. We thus have only one value by player in the bin, and each observation is thus independent from the others. Then, for each bin, we test the null hypothesis that the bin's median subjective difficulty is equal to the objective difficulty at the center of the bin's interval. We use a Wilcoxon Signed Rank Test and computed the 95% confidence interval (red bars) and pseudo median (black dot and triangles), plotted in Fig. 5. We show only the pseudo median and confidence intervals for bins with enough samples to run the Wilcoxon signed rank test. The blue line represents our null hypothesis, where objective difficulty equals subjective difficulty. These results allow us to safely reject the null hypothesis for each median represented by an empty triangle in the plots, where the Wilcoxon signed rank test p-value is lower than 0.05.

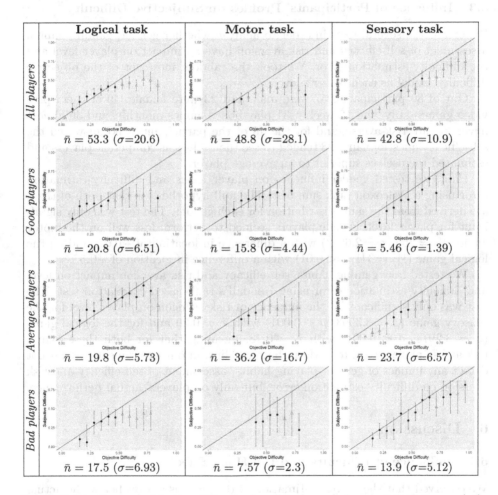

Fig. 5. Subjective and objective difficulty for all tasks and players. $\bar{n}$ is the mean (sd) number of players in each bin for each task and level. (Color figure online)

There seems to be a strong *hard effect* for both logical and motor tasks. For the sensory task, players seem to be slightly overconfident for all objective difficulties. When split by level, the effect seems stable for the motor task, but the relatively low number of bad ($\bar{n} = 7.57$) and good players ($\bar{n} = 15.8$) might mean this result is not significant. The same can be seen in the sensory task, where pseudo medians are always under the calibrated evaluation but the results lose significance with the decreased number of subjects. For the logical task, however, while bin sizes are equivalent for the three conditions, average (i.e. averagely-performing) players seem better calibrated. This result should be investigated further within a specific experiment to provide more in-depth results.

5.3 Influence of Participants' Profiles on Subjective Difficulty

We conducted several tests in order to analyze whether gender, gaming habits, assessment of self-efficacy and risk aversion have an impact on player level and the difficulty-estimation error. We took the random intercept of the objective difficulty model as each player's level.

Out of 80 participants, 57 were male and 23 were female. 49 of them play video games daily, and 12 weekly. 31 play board games monthly, and 36 almost never. 58 are risk-averse, and for the 46 of the participants who answered the self-efficacy questionnaire, 28 tended to see themselves as competent players and estimated themselves superior to an average player.

First, we tested gender influence on player levels and difficulty-estimation error using a Wilcoxon rank sum test. The null hypothesis is that both of them are derived from the same distribution for each gender. The test was only significant for player level. Female players seemed to perform less well on the motor game ($W = 255$, $p = 2.6^{e-5}$) with a difference in location of -0.67, and on the logical game ($W = 341$, $p < 0.01$) with a difference in location of -0.82.

We tested how gaming habits, self-efficacy and risk aversion impact on level and difficulty-estimation error using Kendall's rank-based correlation test. The test was only significant for the influence of risk aversion on player level for the sensory game ($z = 3.3093$, $p < 0.001$) with $\tau = 0.29$ and for the logical game ($z = 3.2974$, $p < 0.001$) with $\tau = 0.28$, meaning that for both these games risk averse players tend to perform better. Thus, in our experiment, we did not detect any impact of gender, playing habits, assessment of self-efficacy and risk aversion on difficulty-estimation error, but only on players' actual performance.

6 Discussion

6.1 Influence of Difficulty and the Hard Effect

We observed that the players estimation of difficulty is always below the actual objective difficulty, except for the logical and motor tasks on the easiest difficulty levels. More precisely, motor and logical tasks show the existence of a strong *hard effect* - that is, an overestimation of the player's chances of success at the hardest levels of difficulty (Fig. 5). Contrary to studies related to overconfidence, in addition to the *hard effect*, nothing seems to indicate any *easy effect* - that is, an underestimation of the chances of success for the easiest tasks [48,56].

The presence of a *hard effect* and absence of an *easy effect* might be explained by the players' confidence in the game designers: games are rarely impossible to finish. What makes games different from many other tasks is that difficulty is artificially created for entertainment: players know that, given enough time, they are almost always supposed to eventually win. This may lead players to feel overconfident in their chances of success.

Moreover, player overconfidence and the hard effect may be stronger in our games than in previous cognitive psychology studies due to player progression. Indeed, our games allow players to experiment and learn from their failures, thereby improving their performance. This feeling of progression and mastery may help players to become more confident in their chances of success. In cognitive psychology studies, where general knowledge questionnaires are very often used, this might not be the case.

Players' global confidence towards the game and their feelings of progression and mastery are also enhanced by the use of the DDA algorithm. By presenting players with challenges that are adapted to their current level, the game is neither too boring nor too frustrating, allowing them to stay motivated and to believe in the fairness of the game.

In addition, in our experiment, we note that objective difficulty starts below 0.5, meaning that players face easier challenges at the beginning, when they are unfamiliar with the game, than at the end. Previous studies on the *hard/easy effect* rely on general knowledge questions, potentially enabling players to assess their knowledge and their chances of winning from the very first question. Therefore we may imagine that players' assessment of easy challenges is biased by their ignorance of the gameplay. However, the motor task has an almost flat progression curve, showing no evidence of an easy effect. Also, though both the sensory and logical tasks have easier challenges at the beginning of the session, for the logical task we seem to be nearing a small easy effect while for the sensory we see the opposite occurring, with players showing overconfidence for easy challenges. Here, therefore, oversampling easy challenges at the beginning of the session does not show a clear impact on the easy effect.

We may explain the differences in results between the sensory and both the logical and motor tasks by considering the nature of the subjective difficulty the players are asked to assess. As defined in our method in Sect. 4.3, the betting system focuses on the player's estimation of their performance, and this estimation is not always performed under the exact same conditions. For the sensory game, the player can select the squares before betting, thus experiencing some gameplay before interpreting their chances of failure. While they are not yet aware of their actual performance, they do go one step further toward the completion of the challenge than for the two other games. By assessing their chances of failure after having experienced the exercise they may have a more accurate feeling about the quality of their answer. For the two other games they perform no interaction and must guess the tasks' next steps. This design choice for the sensory task was made because we did not want to focus on memorization, but on the sensory aspect of detecting blinking squares.

Note that our results differ from those of psychophysical studies on subjective difficulty, where perceived difficulty seems to never reach a plateau and shows a more linear or exponential curve. We think that this is mainly because we ask player to predict the difficulty of a challenge rather than to evaluate it after many repetitions. Our approach, which more closely resembles those used in cognitive psychology, may be closer to what a player really feels while playing.

The motor task is the one where the quality of our model is the lowest ($R^2 = 0.28$). It is the fastest game to play - participants can complete quickly one turn after the other - and this may explain the higher objective difficulty variability. However, this feature is typical of action games. While slowing the game's pace may produce stable results, the experiment would be less representative.

6.2   Impact of the Player's Profile

We did not find any evidence of the influence of the players' profile on their estimations of difficulty. This appears to contradict studies on overconfidence. Certain aspects of our experiment may be responsible for this, however.

In a field study conducted within the profession of financial analysis, Barber and Odean [57] looked at whether overconfidence can explain the difference in trading performance based on gender. They concluded that men have a tendency to be more overconfident and less risk averse than women. We did not observe this in our experiment. This can be attributed to differences in experimentation protocol between our study and theirs. First, the median age of our participants was 15 while theirs was 50. Secondly, their participants held a certain degree of expertise in investment, whereas ours were ignorant of the content of the games before playing them. Finally, it may be that as our tasks are very abstract they are less prone to culturally induced gender differences.

Risk-aversion is also a determinant of excessive confidence [34,57]. However, we did not find any influence of risk on difficulty estimation error. In contrast to Barber's and Johnson's studies, the age of our participants was quite young. Also, as our questionnaire relies on mental calculus and probability assessments it may be less effective on adolescents.

Stone [58] shows that initial and positive self-efficacy assessment may reinforce participants' confidence and modify their performance. This was not evident in our study. In Stone's experiment, however, self-efficacy was assessed in relation to a given task, i.e. participants were asked to estimate their performance. In our study, we estimated self-efficacy using a general self-efficacy questionnaire [52,53]. However, if we use players' mean bet as a measure of self-efficacy, there is a clear relationship between self-efficacy (how high the mean bet is) and overconfidence (how high mean bet minus mean actual result is). This is not surprising, as objective difficulty is adapted to 0.5 for each player. In addition, we found no link between the mean bet and player performance.

6.3   Limitations of the Experiment

There are some limitations into our approach, particularly in the betting system.

The Bet System. Our approach is based on the use of a betting system to measure the difficulty estimation error of players. This approach is limited to specific tasks, where the rhythm of interaction can be combined with a recurrent question addressed to the player. Also important to note is the fact that betting is not strictly related to confidence as measured in cognitive psychology studies. For our games, the optimal strategy is to bet 7 when $D_{objective} > 0.5$, and 1 when $D_{objective} < 0.5$. Therefore our evaluation maybe less accurate than confidence scales. Moreover, as we said in Sect. 6.1, the betting system does not allow us to clearly distinguish between effort-based and skill-based subjective difficulties. Future experiments could improve the separation between them.

Dynamic Difficulty Adjustment. DDA is representative of how video games are designed, and should have a notable impact on the hard/easy effect. Such an adjusted curve should allow players to feel more confident in their chances of success, allowing us to observe a weaker easy effect and a stronger hard effect than in a purely random experiment. Our experiment shows than when using DDA, players do develop a strong feeling of confidence in two of the three tasks. Nevertheless, to be able to attribute this overconfidence to DDA we would need an A/B experiment comparing our results with results derived from the use of a random difficulty system.

Motivational Influences. The actual performance of a player depends on both task difficulty and players effort. If a player is not motivated enough, they may make a correct assessment of difficulty but play less well because they do not want to make the effort. Video game players experience various states of emotion [8,59], including boredom and anxiety. As such, these emotions should be taken account of for future experiments. We must also note that only the sensory and motor tasks induced a *near-miss effect*, while players were unaware of whether or not they were almost successful in the logical task. The *near-miss effect* may have convinced players that they were almost winning, leading them to overestimate their chances of success for the next turn [39,40].

7   Conclusion and Perspectives

In this article we described our study investigating player perception of difficulty. Our work builds upon previous psychophysical and cognitive psychology research by proposing a method to evaluate objective difficulty, focusing on video games.

First, results demonstrate the efficacy of our method for objective difficulty estimation. The mixed effect model allows us to easily take into account differences between players. Results show a predictive accuracy ranging from 61% for the motor task, to almost 70% for the other tasks. Estimated objective difficulty is consistent with DDA, showing a convergence of objective difficulty to 0.5 for all groups and levels. We were also able to see a learning effect, as a negative effect of time on objective difficulty for a given difficulty parameter value. This learning effect is relative to the nature of the tasks, with a higher learning effect for the logical task.

These results confirm the existence of an unrealistic evaluation of players' actual chances of failure. More specifically, players were always overconfident, except at low levels of difficulty in the motor and logical tasks. A strong *hard effect* was present for the motor and logical tasks, with no significant *easy effect* for all tasks.

We suggest that this strong overconfidence might be attributable the fact that our tasks are video games. First, players know that games are designed to be eventually mastered. Second, games allow players to improve, developing a sense of progression and mastery. Furthermore, the use of DDA would reinforce both these aspects. The absence of a hard effect on the sensory task may be understood by considering its design: the difficulty evaluation was performed after players had started the task, thereby potentially gaining additional insight into their performance.

Further experiments will be conducted in order to improve our understanding of difficulty perception in video games. In order to validate the impact of DDA on the hard/easy effect we plan to compare our results with a second experiment that uses a random difficulty curve. In addition, we plan to investigate the influence of previous turns on the player perception of difficulty. DDA creates a temporal relationship between the difficulty of subsequent turns thereby preventing us from performing this analysis on our experiment.

We also plan to investigate the impact of feedback on players' assessment of difficulty. Constant feedback about the decision process makes participants re-evaluate their judgments during the task, attaining a higher level of accuracy [60]. Giving users continuous feedback on their progress is a key feature of human computer interaction in general and video games in particular. It requires distinguishing between positive and negative feedback and testing the influence of its accuracy. Video games adopt various types of feedback, both positive and negative, designed to affect players in terms of increasing the uncertainty of outcomes enhancing enjoyment [49,59].

From a game design perspective, the presence of a hard effect has both benefits and disadvantages. The hard effect is a positive consequence of the game's motivational mechanics: if the player believes in their chances of success they may be motivated to play. However, having players believe that a challenge is easier than it is, particularly where difficulty is high, may also cause frustration because players will fail challenges they thought they could succeed in. The motivational aspects of the discrepancies between subjective and objective difficulty seem therefore worthy of further investigation.

Finally, we plan to expand our approach with other measures of mental effort like eye-tracking methods that have been used to assess cognitive load related to computer interface [61], specially about memory and logical related tasks [62].

Acknowledgment. Authors would like to thank Daniel Andler, Jean Baratgin, Lauren Quiniou, and Laurence Battais & Hélène Malcuit from *Carrefour Numérique*.

References

1. Juul, J.: The game, the player, the world: looking for a heart of gameness. In: Raessens, J. (ed.) Level Up: Digital Games Research Conference Proceedings, vol. 1, pp. 30–45 (2003)
2. Malone, T.W.: Heuristics for designing enjoyable user interfaces: lessons from computer games. In: Proceedings of the 1982 Conference on Human Factors in Computing Systems, pp. 63–68 (1982)
3. Lazzaro, N.: Why we play games: four keys to more emotion without story. In: Game Developers Conference, March 2004
4. Sweetser, P., Wyeth, P.: Gameflow: a model for evaluating player enjoyment in games. Computers in Entertainment (CIE) **3**(3), 3 (2005)
5. Nakamura, J., Csikszentmihalyi, M.: The Concept of Flow. In: Nakamura, J., Csikszentmihalyi, M. (eds.) Flow and the Foundations of Positive Psychology, pp. 239–263. Springer, Dordrecht (2014). doi:10.1007/978-94-017-9088-8_16
6. Allart, T., Levieux, G., Pierfitte, M., Guilloux, A., Natkin, S.: Difficulty influence on motivation over time in video games using survival analysis. In: Proceedings of Foundation of Digital Games, Cap Cod, MA, USA (2017)
7. Ryan, R.M., Rigby, C.S., Przybylski, A.: The motivational pull of video games: a self-determination theory approach. Motiv. Emot. **30**(4), 344–360 (2006)
8. Juul, J.: A Casual Revolution: Reinventing Video Games and Their Players. Mit Press, Cambridge (2009)
9. Juul, J.: The Art of Failure, 1st edn. The MIT Press, Cambridge (2013)
10. Hunicke, R.: The case for dynamic difficulty adjustment in games. In: Proceedings of the 2005 ACM SIGCHI International Conference on Advances in Computer Entertainment Technology, pp. 429–433. ACM (2005)
11. Andrade, G., Ramalho, G., Santana, H., Corruble, V.: Extending reinforcement learning to provide dynamic game balancing. In: Proceedings of the Workshop on Reasoning, Representation, and Learning in Computer Games, 19th International Joint Conference on Artificial Intelligence (IJCAI), pp. 7–12 (2005)
12. Vicencio-Moreira, R., Mandryk, R.L., Gutwin, C.: Now you can compete with anyone: Balancing players of different skill levels in a first-person shooter game. In: Proceedings of the 33rd Annual ACM Conference on Human Factors in Computing Systems, pp. 2255–2264. ACM (2015)
13. Rani, P., Sarkar, N., Liu, C.: Maintaining optimal challenge in computer games through real-time physiological feedback. In: Proceedings of the 11th International Conference on Human Computer Interaction, vol. 58 (2005)
14. Afergan, D., Peck, E.M., Solovey, E.T., Jenkins, A., Hincks, S.W., Brown, E.T., Chang, R., Jacob, R.J.K.: Dynamic difficulty using brain metrics of workload. In: Jones, M., Palanque, P. (eds.) CHI 2014 Proceedings of the SIGCHI Conference on Human Factors in Computing Systems, Toronto, Ontario, Canada, pp. 3797–3806. ACM, New York (2014)
15. Aponte, M.V., Levieux, G., Natkin, S.: Difficulty in videogames: an experimental validation of a formal definition. In: Romão, T. (ed.) Proceedings of the 8th International Conference on Advances in Computer Entertainment Technology, ACE 2011, Lisbon, Portugal, pp. 1–18. ACM, New York (2011)
16. Passyn, K., Sujan, M.: Skill-based versus effort-based task difficulty: a task-analysis approach to the role of specific emotions in motivating difficult actions. J. Consum. Psychol. **22**(3), 461–468 (2012)

17. Levieux, G.: Mesure de la difficulté dans les jeux vidéo. Thèse, Conservatoire National des Arts et Métiers CNAM Paris (2011)
18. Hunicke, R., LeBlanc, M., Zubeck, R.: MDA: a formal approach to game design and game research. In: Proceedings of the AAAI Workshop on Challenges in Game AI, San Jose, CA, USA. AAAI Press (2004)
19. Delignières, D., Famose, J.: Perception de la difficulté et nature de la tâche. Science et motricité **23**, 39–47 (1994)
20. Borg, G., Bratfisch, O., Dorni'c, S.: On the problems of perceived difficulty. Scand. J. Psychol. **12**(1), 249–260 (1971)
21. Slifkin, A.B., Grilli, S.M.: Aiming for the future: prospective action difficulty, prescribed difficulty, and fitts law. Exp. Brain Res. **174**(4), 746–753 (2006)
22. Delignières, D., Famose, J.P.: Perception de la difficulté, entropie et performance. Sci. Sports **7**(4), 245–252 (1992)
23. Delignières, D., Famose, J.P., Genty, J.: Validation d'une échelle de catégories pour la perception de la difficulté. Revue STAPS **34**, 77–88 (1994)
24. Delignières, D., Famose, J.P., Thépaut-Mathieu, C., Fleurance, P., et al.: A psychophysical study of difficulty rating in rock climbing. Int. J. Sport Psychol. **24**, 404 (1993)
25. Delignières, D., Brisswalter, J., Legros, P.: Influence of physical exercise on choice reaction time in sports experts: the mediating role of resource allocation. J. Hum. Mov. Stud. **27**(4), 173–188 (1994)
26. Fitts, P.M.: The information capacity of the human motor system in controlling the amplitude of movement. J. Exp. Psychol. **47**(6), 381 (1954)
27. Kahneman, D., Frederick, S.: A model of heuristic judgment. In: Holyoak, K.J., Morrison, R.G. (eds.) The Cambridge Handbook of Thinking and Reasoning, 1st edn, pp. 267–293. Cambridge University Press, Cambridge (2005)
28. Shah, A.K., Oppenheimer, D.M.: Heuristics made easy: an effort-reduction framework. Psychol. Bull. **134**(2), 207–222 (2008)
29. Kahneman, D., Tversky, A.: Judgment under uncertainty: heuristics and biases. Science (New York, N.Y.) **185**(4157), 1124–1131 (1974)
30. Russo, J.E., Schoemaker, P.J.H.: Managing overconfidence. Sloan Manag. Rev. **33**(2), 7–17 (1992)
31. Bessière, V.: Excès de confiance des dirigeants et décisions financières: une synthèse. Finance Contrôle Stratégie **10**, 39–66 (2007)
32. Moore, D.A., Healy, P.J.: The trouble with overconfidence. Psychol. Rev. **115**(2), 502–517 (2008)
33. Griffin, D., Tversky, A.: The weighing of evidence and the determinants of confidence. Cogn. Psychol. **411435**, 411–435 (1992)
34. Johnson, D.D.P., Fowler, J.H.: The evolution of overconfidence. Nature **477**(7364), 317–320 (2011)
35. Bandura, A.: Self-efficacy: toward a unifying theory of behavioral change. Psychol. Rev. **84**(2), 191–215 (1977)
36. Keren, G.: Facing uncertainty in the game of bridge: a calibration study. Organ. Behav. Hum. Decis. Process. **39**(1), 98–114 (1987)
37. Linnet, J., Gebauer, L., Shaffer, H., Mouridsen, K., Møller, A.: Experienced poker players differ from inexperienced poker players in estimation bias and decision bias. J. Gambl. Issues **24**, 86–100 (2010)
38. Park, Y.J., Santos-Pinto, L.: Overconfidence in tournaments: evidence from the field. Theor. Decis. **69**(1), 143–166 (2010)
39. Sundali, J., Croson, R.: Biases in casino betting: the hot hand and the gambler's fallacy. Judgm. Decis. Mak. **1**(1), 1–12 (2006)

40. Parke, J., Griffiths, M.: The psychology of the fruit machine: the role of structural characteristics (revisited). Int. J. Ment. Health Addict. **4**(2), 151–179 (2006)
41. Lichtenstein, S., Fischhoff, B.: Do those who know more also know more about how much they know? Organ. Behav. Hum. Perform. **20**, 159–183 (1977)
42. Klayman, J., Soll, J.B.: Overconfidence: it depends on how, what, and whom you ask. Organ. Behav. Hum. Decis. Process. **79**(3), 216–247 (1999)
43. Kahneman, D., Tversky, A.: Subjective probability: a judgment of representativeness. Cogn. Psychol. **3**(3), 430–454 (1972)
44. Croson, R., Sundali, J.: The gambler's fallacy and the hot hand: empirical data from casinos. J. Risk Uncertain. **30**(3), 195–209 (2005)
45. Gilovich, T., Vallone, R., Tversky, A.: The hot hand in basketball: on the misperception of random sequences. Cogn. Psychol. **17**(3), 295–314 (1985)
46. Langer, E.J.: The illusion of control. J. Pers. Soc. Psychol. **32**(2), 311–328 (1975)
47. Goodie, A.S.: The role of perceived control and overconfidence in pathological gambling. J. Gambl. Stud. **21**(4), 481–502 (2005)
48. Pulford, B.D., Colman, A.M.: Overconfidence: feedback and item difficulty effects. Pers. Individ. Differ. **23**(1), 125–133 (1997)
49. Costikyan, G.: Uncertainty in Games, 1st edn. MIT Press, Cambridge (2013)
50. Lankoski, P., Björk, S.: Game Research Methods: An Overview, 1st edn. ETC Press, Halifax (2015)
51. Bates, D., Mächler, M., Bolker, B.M., Walker, S.C.: Fitting linear mixed-effects models using lme4. J. Stat. Softw. **67**(1), 1–48 (2015)
52. Chen, G., Gully, S.M., Eden, D.: Validation of a new general self-efficacy scale. Organ. Res. Methods **4**(1), 62–83 (2001)
53. Bandura, A.: Guide for constructing self-efficacy scales. In: Urdan, T., Pajares, F. (eds.) Self-efficacy Beliefs of Adolescents, 1st edn, pp. 307–337. Information Age Publishing, Charlotte (2006)
54. Holt, C.A., Laury, S.K.: Risk aversion and incentive effects. Am. Econ. Rev. **92**(5), 1644–1655 (2002)
55. Nakagawa, S., Schielzeth, H.: A general and simple method for obtaining R2 from generalized linear mixed-effects models. Methods Ecol. Evol. **4**(2), 133–142 (2013)
56. Keren, G.: On the calibration of probability judgments: some critical comments and alternative perspectives. J. Behav. Decis. Mak. **10**(3), 269–278 (1997)
57. Barber, B.M., Odean, T.: Boys will be boys: gender, overconfidence, and common stock investment. Quart. J. Econ. **116**(1), 261–292 (2001)
58. Stone, D.N.: Overconfidence in initial self-efficacy judgments: effects on decision processes and performance. Organ. Behav. Hum. Decis. Process. **59**(3), 452–474 (1994)
59. Caillois, R.: Les jeux et les hommes : le masque et le vertige, 2nd edn. Gallimard, Paris (1958)
60. Arkes, H.R., Christensen, C., Lai, C., Blumer, C.: Two methods of reducing overconfidence. Organ. Behav. Hum. Decis. Process. **39**, 133–144 (1987)
61. Goldberg, J.H., Kotval, X.: Computer interface evaluation using eye movements: methods and constructs computer interface evaluation using eye movements: methods and constructs. Int. J. Ind. Ergon. **24**(November 2015), 631–645(1999)
62. Klingner, J., Tversky, B., Hanrahan, P.: Effects of visual and verbal presentation on cognitive load in vigilance, memory, and arithmetic tasks. Psychophysiology **48**, 323–332 (2011)

Improved Memory Elicitation in Virtual Reality: New Experimental Results and Insights

Joel Harman(✉), Ross Brown, and Daniel Johnson

Faculty of Electrical Engineering and Computer Science,
Queensland University of Technology (QUT), Brisbane, Australia
joel.harman@hdr.qut.edu.au

Abstract. Eliciting accurate and complete knowledge from individuals is a non-trivial challenge. In this paper, we present the evaluation of a virtual-world based approach, informed by situated cognition theory, which aims to assist with knowledge elicitation. In this approach, we place users into 3D virtual worlds which represent real-world locations and ask users to describe information related to tasks completed in those locations. Through an empirical A/B evaluation of 62 users, we explore the differences in recall ability and behaviour of those viewing the virtual world via a virtual reality headset and those viewing the virtual world on a monitor. Previous results suggest that the use of a virtual reality headset was able to meaningfully improve memory recall ability within the given scenario. In this study, we adjust experiment protocol to explore the potential confounds of time taken and tool usability. After controlling for these possible confounds, we once again found that those given a virtual reality headset were able to recall more information about the given task than those viewing the virtual world on a monitor.

1 Introduction

The ability to accurately gather knowledge is a non-trivial challenge with relevance to a variety of domains [1]. Furthermore, if this information is not gathered effectively, there is the potential for many complications to arise. For example, when attempting to formalize business practices, working with incorrect or incomplete information may lead to higher construction costs, longer development times or poor-quality products [2].

Many approaches have previously been explored which aim to elicit information from stakeholders [3]. These methods, however, usually produce a trade-off between the quality of information gathered and the time required to do so [1]. For example, questionnaires can usually be administered easily, but often yield inaccurate or incomplete information. Role-plays on the other hand, have been shown to be an effective means of gathering accurate information [4], but are used less often in a business setting [3]. It has been suggested that this may be due to issues related to the potentially high setup costs and co-location issues related to role-play [1]. Despite these issues, in this paper we will be considering

R. Bernhaupt et al. (Eds.): INTERACT 2017, Part II, LNCS 10514, pp. 128–146, 2017.
DOI: 10.1007/978-3-319-67684-5_9

a modified role-play approach due to the benefits it affords when looking to elicit accurate and complete information.

When performing a role-play, the individual steps in a task are usually executed in a specific sequence. The concept of memory chaining proposes that we are able to recall a piece of information more effectively if we are already thinking about the task it precedes [5]. This would suggest that even potentially mundane tasks, which may be ignored in other elicitation approaches (e.g. interviews), may initiate memory chains which could potentially yield relevant information. Furthermore, the rich context afforded during an in-situ role-play may also be sufficient in achieving a situated cognition response. Situated cognition is the theory that all knowledge is, to some extent, tied to the situations and contexts in which it was learned [6].

In our proposed approach, we look to leverage many of the benefits of a standard role-play. Rather than conduct the role-play within the real world, however, the session is instead conducted within a virtual environment closely resembling the real world location. By doing this, we aim to achieve many of the elicitation advantages associated with role-play, while mitigating many of the common detractors. Specifically, this approach may be preferable when a real world role-play would incur high setup costs, excessive risks, or have issues with co-location. For example, when looking to role-play a complex task, it may be difficult to arrange a time when all parties involved can be in the same location concurrently, without disrupting existing work commitments.

This is the third in a series of related studies exploring the potential recall benefits associated with proving situated context via a virtual world role-play. In our first study [7], we found that when comparing recall ability of participants provided with the virtual world stimuli and participants that weren't, participants given the stimuli were able to recall more information. In this first study, we conjectured that the stimuli provided by the virtual world was able to assist the users in recalling more information. Furthermore, we conjectured that if a more immersive interface was used (e.g. a virtual reality headset), a larger effect may potentially be observed. We later tested this theory in the second study and compared the recall ability of participants provided with a virtual reality headset with participants provided with a desktop display (monitor) [8]. The results of this experiment found that participants given the virtual reality headset were able to recall more information, but the experiment did identify some potential confounds which may have affected our results. In particular, we found that there were significant differences in both time taken and usability. Without further exploring these issues, we were unable to say with any degree of certainty whether the observed recall results were meaningfully due to the difference in viewing mechanism immersion, or some other secondary effect.

In the study presented in this paper, we aim to further explore this phenomenon and clarify the potential effect of confounds we found in our prior studies. In particular, we believe that the virtual world design and experiment setup we chose to use in our prior studies may have been too difficult for novice users, leading to issues with usability and subsequently affecting the time taken by participants experiencing these issues. As the participants given the virtual reality headset were using a new interface, we believe that this issue was more pronounced within this group, leading to the differences in usability and time taken between the two groups. In this study, we look to obtain insight into these issues by making the task easier to learn, understand and execute for participants.

2   Situated Cognition and Virtual Worlds

Applying the concept of situated cognition within virtual worlds has been extensively explored in literature. When situated cognition was first proposed in 1989, it considered the concept of situated learning [9] to be a related concept [6]. Situated learning postulates that students need to be taught information within the contexts in which it will be applied.

Situated learning research has primarily considered virtual worlds for their potential applications to distance learning [10]. The goal of these environments is to place students within virtual classrooms, in order to better situate them within an environment they associate with a student-teacher learning dynamic. Some research even suggests that this approach may be an improvement over typical distance-learning communication methods, such as conference calls [11].

Outside of the context of learning, there has been an absence of literature which has explored the theory of situated cognition and the appropriateness of virtual worlds for achieving the necessary degree of situated context. We found one theoretical paper, however, which discusses the appropriateness of existing measures, such as immersion, and their importance in achieving effective situated cognition responses within virtual worlds [12]. Immersion, within the context of this study, is the degree to which a person's senses are engaged [13]. For example, a movie with sound may be considered more immersive than one without, as it engages the person's sense of hearing. As this study discusses the potential for assisting memory recall within virtual worlds via situated cognition, we have decided to primarily explore whether differences in immersion may affect user recall performance.

3   Research Questions

In this study, we have looked to explore how differences in viewing immersion may affect participant behaviour and memory recall ability. This had led to the formation of two distinct research questions:

- **RQ1:** How do changes in viewing immersion affect memory recall performance of users when they are asked to describe information while role-playing within a related virtual world?

- **RQ2:** How do changes in viewing immersion affect the behaviour of participants when they are asked to describe information while role-playing within a related virtual world?

We have chosen to explore potential behavioural differences as our prior studies have suggested that there may be a relationship between participant behaviour and recall performance [8]. To examine the effect of this change in immersion, we will be comparing a virtual reality setup, using an HMD, with a standard desktop display. From the two above research questions, we have constructed two main hypotheses after exploring existing theory within related literature. The first hypothesis is:

- **H1:** Users asked to recall information while viewing a related virtual world within an HMD will recall more information than those viewing the virtual world on a desktop display.

In prior work, we found preliminary evidence to suggest that the context provided by a virtual world was able to assist participants with recalling information [7]. We conjecture, however, that while the virtual world provided some benefit, it did not, wholly, afford the necessary context to the user. Specifically, we believe that the embodiment and immersion afforded to the user by virtual reality will better situate the user and assist them in recalling more effectively. In addition to recall improvements, we believe that the added embodiment and immersion provided by the HMD will also result in certain behavioural changes between the two groups. This has led to the formation of our second hypothesis:

- **H2:** Users provided with the HMD will be more exploratory in their approach than those provided with the desktop display.

To better evaluate this hypothesis, we will be exploring two sub-hypotheses. These are:

- **H2(a):** Users provided with the HMD will traverse a larger portion of the virtual world than those provided with the desktop display.

- **H2(b):** Users provided with the HMD will adjust their view within the virtual world more often than those provided with the desktop display.

While we do not necessarily believe that virtual reality innately makes a participant more exploratory, we do believe that the interaction mechanisms it affords makes it easier for participants to operate in a way in which they are familiar and experienced. While this hypothesis was somewhat supported in our prior experiments [7], we look to confirm that these effects remain present if the user does not need to continually halt movement to enter descriptions of their actions. Furthermore, we believe the evidence for increases in emotions [14], telepresence and sexual presence [15] when using an HMD, rather than a desktop display, are all examples of how users appear to behave more naturally within virtual reality. We wish to understand if this more natural behaviour may lead to observable increases in recall ability for the subjects.

4   Artefact Design

Virtual worlds are synthetic environments which provide users with an avatar through which they can explore and interact with other users, or the environment itself, to perform various tasks [16]. For this study, we have constructed a virtual world which aims to be representative of a real world airport.

A common issue related to research within this area, however, is that the virtual worlds can be difficult for participants to use when they are unfamiliar with the features and have not been provided with extensive training within the environment [17]. To mitigate this issue, we have developed a virtual world specifically to explore this recall phenomenon.

The virtual world was developed using the Unity3D [18] game engine. The environment was constructed using a mix of both constructed and prebuilt assets available via the Unity 3D asset store. Furthermore, we have also looked at trying to improve the usability of the virtual world in previous experiments [19] and made modifications to improve usability where possible. We have endeavoured to reconstruct the airport as best as possible. For this reason, we have included both critical areas (check-in, security, boarding and the plane itself), and non-critical areas (parking, shops, luggage collection and restrooms). Figure 1 shows screen captures of the developed virtual world.

Fig. 1. Screen captures of the developed virtual world airport.

To navigate the virtual world, participants from both the HMD and desktop display conditions were both given an Xbox 360 game controller. This controller had two main functions:

- The left joystick controlled avatar movement.
- The right joystick controlled avatar view changes.

We chose to use a game controller for this study as it allowed both treatment groups to use similar mechanisms for both navigating and viewing the environment. It must be noted, however, that as a core component of the HMD is to assist with adjusting avatar view, the HMD was still responsible for view changes within this condition and the vertical view component of view change was disabled on the controller joystick. Furthermore, both treatment groups moved at the same constant speed and had the same turning speed when using the controller.

Unlike all prior experiments we have conducted to explore this phenomenon, the virtual world which was used in this experiment did not afford any interaction mechanisms to the user. Previously, participants were required to first look at an object or person within the virtual world, press a button to select the object and then write down the actions that they would normally complete with the object. While this approach greatly assisted in structuring the user responses, this did also present issues regarding usability. In this experiment, participants instead dictated all actions they would usually complete as they traversed through the virtual world.

5   Experiment Procedure and Measures

Participants who agreed to participate in the study were invited into a lab. They were then either presented with a 24 in. desktop monitor, or an HMD (Oculus Rift DK2), determined by random assignment. In addition to this, they were also provided with a game controller. A microphone was placed on the desk to record everything the participant said throughout the experiment. A between-subject design was chosen as we believed that participation in one treatment would meaningfully affect participant performance in the subsequent treatment. Upon entering the lab, participants read and signed the associated consent form and answered a series of control questions (e.g., knowledge of the boarding process, prior experience with virtual worlds). Following this, participants were placed into a virtual building, where they were trained to both view and traverse the environment. Participants were then instructed that for the experiment, they would be role-playing the task of boarding an airplane within a virtual airport. While doing this, participants were asked to verbally describe all the actions they would normally take within the environment, being as detailed and specific as possible. Participants were then placed into the airport to begin the experiment. No explicit time limit was placed on participants during their role-play. After participants were happy with their description of the task, they were asked to complete questionnaires related to presence and tool usability.

5.1   Recall Measure

The recall measure is the main item of interest in this study. To measure recall, we will be exploring the number of tasks described by participants within the two groups. This task count was generated by transcribing the logs from each session and manually assigning the phrases used by participants into individual tasks. For example, if a participant said "I hand my check in information to the boarding staff", it would be counted as a single task. If the participant had instead specified "I hand my check-in information and luggage to the boarding staff", however, this would instead be recorded as two different tasks (the giving of the check-in information and the giving of the luggage). We chose to use this approach as we emphasized to participants during the session that they should aim to be as specific as possible when describing the actions that they would need to take.

To provide further insight into this result, we will also be comparing the total number of words used by participants in the two treatment groups. While this is not necessarily a measure of recall performance, it does provide an objective measure of how much the participants in both groups spoke. This may provide some validation for our recall measure if the differences between the two groups are similar (e.g. Group A described more than Group B because they spoke more), or create interesting insights if the number of words spoken result is not reflected in recall performance (e.g. Why did Group A describe less than Group B, despite talking more? What were they saying?).

To ensure that both treatment groups had a similar understanding of the task, participants were asked to both state the number of times they had been on a plane in the last five years and to rate their subjective knowledge of the airplane boarding task. As we did not prime participants with a description of the task prior to the experiment, and each participant may have their own nuanced personal approach for completing the task in the real world, we have opted to not examine the results for correctness. We chose not to prime participants as it provides a much more ecologically sound basis for the study. If we had primed participants, it would not be measuring long-term memory ability, but instead short-term memory of the description they were given. We have, however, removed tasks from our first measure where the statement was immediately identified as erroneous (e.g. the participant described the same task several times in a row or backtracked to try and correct a mistake). Finally, it should be noted that this task, while exploring recall ability, is technically measuring task performance. We believe that this is valid, however, as memory tests often require the participants to constrain the information they recall to the requirements of a task (such as a quiz) (e.g. [20,21]).

5.2   Exploration

We have chosen to examine how the users traversed the environment as we believe that this may provide insight into the behavioural approach taken by the participants. This is important as we believe differences in behaviour may influence recall performance. In our prior study, we found that participants given the HMD treatment explored a larger portion of the environment than those given the desktop display [8]. To measure this, we once again split the virtual environment into 216 5 m × 5 m segments (virtual world units were designed to be approximately equivalent to real-world units). For this analysis, we compare the average number of segments traversed by the two groups.

In our prior study, we found that participants given the HMD traversed more of the environment than those given the desktop display. As the way the two groups traversed the environment did not fundamentally change in this study, we expect a similar result will be observed.

5.3   Change of View

We will be exploring change of view factors in order to better understand how the two treatment groups examined the virtual environment. This paper was primarily motivated by the concept that inserting a user into a situation with the appropriate context would assist them in recalling information related to that situation. For this to be an effective approach, however, the user must view and understand this context. For this reason, we conjecture that, to some degree, viewing more of the environment may result in participants recalling more information about the task.

For this study, participants given the desktop display adjusted their view entirely with the provided game controller, while participants given the HMD adjusted their view with both the controller and the HMD. We will be considering view change as the average change of vertical viewing angle per minute. We have chosen to use only the vertical component of view change as the participants, in addition to making horizontal view changes to examine the environment, also adjust their view horizontally when they need to turn. This means that horizontal view changes do not necessarily indicate that a user is looking to adjust their view of their avatar specifically to view a different part of the environment. As vertical view changes were exclusively performed in order to explore the environment, we believe that this is the more accurate measure in this scenario. To measure these view changes in both groups, we will be examining the rotation made by the avatar, rather than the raw HMD tracking data. We have chosen to do this as we wanted to keep this measure consistent between the two treatment groups. Furthermore, the functions controlling avatar jitter automatically removed HMD jitter, and should therefore more accurately reflect the intentional view changes made by the users.

In our prior study, we found that participants given the HMD adjusted their view more often than those given the desktop display. As the way the two groups view the environment did not change in this study, we expect to see a similar result in this study.

5.4   Time Taken

This time taken measure considers only the time taken from when the participant begins describing the task to when they finalise their description. The time taken for all other activities (e.g. questionnaire completion) is not included in this measure. We have chosen to examine the time taken by both groups in the virtual world as its relationship has remained uncertain in our prior experiments. One existing study found that participants who described tasks faster tended to perform better [22], but their approach did not provide the situated context central to the approach presented in this paper. In our prior work, we found that participants given the HMD both took longer to complete the task and performed better. As we found no existing literature which explored a potential link between the time spent viewing stimuli and recall performance, we were unable to adequately determine whether the differences in recall performance were due to differences in time taken between the two treatment groups, or due to the levels of immersion provided by the associated interfaces.

In our prior paper, we present several reasons why participants given the HMD may have taken longer to complete the task. For example, we identified that usability issues identified by participants given the HMD may have accounted for this difference in time taken. The design of this study aims to eliminate the differences in usability we found in our previous study by allowing participants to describe information verbally, rather than interacting with the world itself. For this reason, we will once again be examining time taken to determine whether there remains a difference in time taken by the two groups, despite the differences in experiment design.

5.5 Presence

Presence, as related to immersive virtual reality, is considered to be the concept of transportation. People are considered present when they report a sensation of being, to some degree, in the virtual world (e.g., you are there) [23]. We have chosen to measure presence in this study as existing literature suggests there may be a link between presence and recall performance [12]. In this study, we will be administering the Witmer and Singer presence questionnaire [24]. This questionnaire was chosen despite some criticism regarding its efficacy [25], as it remains the most widely administered survey for measuring presence in virtual worlds designed for non-game related activities.

In our prior study, we found inconclusive presence findings, with our quantitative results suggesting the HMD condition experienced lower presence while our qualitative findings suggested they experienced higher presence. We conjectured that this difference was due to the complexity of the task. Presence studies usually involve very simple tasks, where usability is not likely to be an issue. As this study aims to provide a much easier experience for the user to comprehend, we hope that the presence findings obtained in this experiment will not suffer from the inconsistencies encountered in our prior study.

5.6 Usability

We have chosen to measure usability as HMDs have been known to suffer from challenges with usability among novice users [26]. If a user has difficulty using the virtual environment, it may have ramifications on recall performance in addition to other aspects of the session. We have measured usability with the IBM usability satisfaction survey [27] as it remains a widely used measure for usability of software systems.

Furthermore, we are particularly interested in examining whether there are any usability differences between the two treatment groups as we found the HMD condition to have considerably lower usability in our previous study [7]. In this experiment, we have chosen to use a much simpler system for gathering information from participants, which we believe may mitigate this difference in usability between the two groups.

6 Results

Participants in this study were randomly assigned to either the HMD or desktop display conditions, with each condition having 31 participants. For comparing between the two conditions, we will be using two-tail Students-t tests when the data is both continuous and passes the Shapiro-Wilk W normality test (p < 0.05). If either of these conditions is not met, the two-tail Mann-Whitney U test will be used instead.

The average age of the participants was 24.84 (SD = 5.02). No significant difference was found between the age of those given the HMD and those given the desktop display (p = 0.39). Perceived understanding of the airport boarding scenario was quite high, with an average response of 5.40 (SD = 1.63) on a 7-point Likert scale. No statistically significant difference was found in perceived understanding between those given the HMD and those given the desktop display (p = 0.41).

Given the exploratory nature of the research presented and the relatively small sample size, we have not applied a Type I error correction (e.g., Bonferroni) to our analysis. Instead, we have elected to provide effect size calculations (Cohen's d) for all readings to provide the reader with a sense of the magnitude of all presented findings. Following Cohen (1992) [28], we treat all effect sizes between 0.2 and 0.5 as small, 0.5 and 0.8 as medium and greater than 0.8 as large. Due to the increased possibility of a Type I error, the findings presented in this study should be interpreted with a greater degree of caution. For consistency, we have used existing conversion formulas to convert the r effect sizes calculated for the Mann-Whitney U tests into comparable Cohen's d values [29].

6.1 Recall

In this study, we were primarily interested in comparing the recall ability of participants presented with the HMD and the desktop display. To evaluate H1, we compared the average number of tasks specified by both treatment groups. This test found that participants given the HMD were able to recall a larger number of tasks (M = 10.50, SD = 2.48) than those given the desktop display (M = 8.97, SD = 2.72, U = 327, z = 2.15, p < 0.05, d = 0.57).

To further explore this result, we also compared the average number of words spoken by both treatment groups. This test found that participants given the HMD spoke a larger number of words (M = 212, SD = 47.3) than those given the desktop display (M = 189, SD = 20.2, U = 272, z = 2.93, p < 0.005, d = 0.80).

6.2 Exploration

To evaluate Hypothesis 2(a), we have compared the mean amount of the environment traversed by the two groups. Results from this test found that participants given the HMD traversed a larger number of segments (M = 88.2, SD = 27.4) than participants given the desktop display (M = 66.0, SD = 20.9, $t(60)$ = 3.58, p < 0.001, d = 0.91).

6.3   Change of View

To evaluate Hypothesis 2(b), we have measured the average amount participants adjusted the vertical view of their avatar. Results from this test found that participants given the HMD adjusted the vertical view of their avatar more often per minute (M = 755, SD = 404) than those given the desktop display (M = 198, SD = 71, $t(60) = 7.56$, p < 0.0001, $d = 1.92$).

6.4   Presence

Participants reported higher presence in the HMD condition (M = 5.18, SD = 0.42) than the desktop display condition (M = 4.83, SD = 0.53, U = 282, z = 2.79, p < 0.05, $d = 0.76$).

6.5   Usability

No statistically significant difference in usability was found between participants given the HMD and participants given the desktop display (p = 0.16).

6.6   Time Taken

No statistically significant difference in time taken was found between participants given the HMD and participants given the desktop display (p = 0.09).

7   Discussion of Results

The primary aim of this study was to further confirm whether improvements to interface immersion (specifically viewing immersion) may directly translate into better long term episodic memory recall. This work has been motivated by the continuing need to develop elicitation techniques which can effectively gather knowledge from individuals. Accurately gathering knowledge is a core component of many domains [1].

The results of this experiment supported our first hypothesis that participants given the HMD would be able to recall more information about the given scenario than those given the desktop display. It must be noted, however, that when asking participants to recall information, it is possible that we may have been exposed to issues regarding cognitive load. Cognitive load refers to the total amount of mental effort being used with regards to working memory. For example, if a task was to greatly tax working memory capability, it would be considered high cognitive load. It is possible that while participants were experiencing higher cognitive load at more complex parts of the task, they may have become less focused on accurately articulating their thoughts verbally. This may have inadvertently lowered the recall scores of participants in both treatment groups, as they may not have been talking as much during the more complex parts of their description. This is somewhat supported, as participants in our previous study did tend to recall more information when asked to write down their knowledge of the task in a more structured manner. As both treatment groups were asked to describe the same task, however, the two treatments should have required similar levels of cognitive load. For this reason, we do not believe this finding invalidates the observed results. While the observed recall findings do suggest that the immersive system of virtual reality may be able to assist with allowing users to better recall information, we have also explored several other items of interest to better explain the observed result.

In addition to looking at memory performance, we have also explored behavioural differences between the two groups to determine whether any differences in behaviour may have also potentially affected recall performance. When examining how the two groups traversed the environment, we found that participants given the HMD explored more of the environment than those given the desktop display (supported by a large effect size). When examining how the two groups viewed the environment, we found that participants given the HMD adjusted their view more often than those given the desktop display. As participants given the HMD both traversed more of the environment and viewed more of the environment, we believe these findings support H2(b) and indicate that the participants given the HMD were more exploratory in their role-play approach. While it is likely this difference in view change was due to the ease at which the participants given the HMD were able to adjust their view to examine the environment, we do not believe that this diminishes the significance of the finding. The ability to easily change view is a fundamental affordance provided by the HMD. While we cannot say, with any degree of certainty, that these differences did result in better recall performance, these findings do seem to be consistent with existing literature which suggests that providing participants with adequate levels of context is important to best achieve a situated cognition effect [6].

No statistically significant difference in usability scores was found between those given the HMD and those given the desktop display. While this result is in no way conclusive, this suggests that the possible link between time taken and recall performance may not be as significant as our previous experiment suggested. This is an positive result, as one of the main reasons for running this study was to eliminate, or at least partially mitigate, the difference in usability between the two groups. Ensuring similar usability between the two treatments reduces the chance that usability differences may have affected any of the other results presented in this study.

In addition to usability, we also looked to explore any potential difference in time taken between the two groups, as differences in time taken presented a potential confound in our prior studies. In this experiment, we found no statistically significant difference in time taken between the HMD and desktop display conditions.

Finally, participants given the HMD reported higher subjective presence scores than those given the desktop display. These findings are consistent with prior research [23], which discussed a possible link between presence and memory performance within virtual worlds. Due to the increased levels of presence experienced by those given the HMD, we conjecture that the higher presence provided by the immersive properties of the HMD interface may be responsible for the improved recall ability. Further work will be required to better explore this phenomenon and adequately identify the exact mechanism, or mechanisms, facilitating better recall while immersed within virtual reality.

8 Synthesis from Overall Results

In this section, we will synthesise the findings discussed above with the data gathered in our prior studies. By doing this, we aim to identify patterns across different studies which may provide further insight into the overall approach. Specifically, we will be looking at the outcomes of this study and two prior studies to identify potential patterns and discuss possible reasons for differences in results across each of these studies. To assist with this, Table 1 provides a brief overview of the three experiments as well as a brief summary of the pertinent results. As we will be discussing multiple studies in this section, we will refer to the studies as they are numbered in Table 1, referring to the initial study we conducted as *Study One*, our prior study which also investigated recall differences between HMDs and desktop displays as *Study Two* and the study which was presented in this paper as *Study Three*.

Study One provided the initial motivation for the approach which was subsequently explored in Study Two and Study Three. Study One provided evidence that suggested the context provided by virtual worlds may assist in improving recall ability. Due to the differences in experiment design between the first study and the other two studies (e.g. differences in the virtual world visuals), we will not be making direct comparisons between the results of the first study and the results in the other two studies. We did feel that including this study in Table 1 was warranted, however, as it provided the initial results which assisted in designing the two subsequent studies. As both Study Two and Study Three had many similarities, however, we will be primarily comparing the results of these two studies and discussing potential causes for any differences in observed results.

In both Study Two and Study Three, we found that participants given the HMD were able to recall more information about the airport boarding task than those given the desktop display. This provides further evidence that the immersive qualities of the HMD were able to improve memory recall capabilities of participants.

Furthermore, in both Study Two and Study Three we found that participants given the HMD were also more exploratory in their approach, choosing to both traverse more of the environment and look at more of the environment. In Study Two, however, we found significant differences in the traversal patterns of the two groups. This was not the case in Study Three, whereby both groups traversed all areas of the airport, despite the HMD group traversing more on average. Furthermore, we found that both treatment groups traversed more of the environment than in Study Two. This may be due to the removal of the user interface, which forced users to stop moving and enter information into the system intermittently.

Table 1. Description and results summary for all related studies.

Study 1: No Context Compared with Virtual World Context [7]
This first study compared the recall ability of participants provided with a virtual world (viewed on a desktop display) with participants provided with a 2D process description environment. This study found: - Participants given the virtual world recalled more information - Participants given the virtual world completed the task faster
Study 2: HMD Compared with Desktop Display (Interactions) [19]
This second study compared the recall ability of participants provided with a virtual world viewed on either an HMD or a desktop display (monitor). Participants described information by interacting with objects and writing descriptions. This study found: - Participants given the HMD recalled more information - Participants given the HMD viewed and traversed more of the environment - Participants given the desktop display completed the task faster - Participants given the HMD reported lower subjective usability scores - Participants given the HMD reported lower subjective presence scores
Study 3: HMD Compared with Desktop Display (No Interactions)
The third study also compared the recall ability of participants provided with a virtual world viewed on either an HMD or a desktop display (monitor). Unlike in the second study, however, the participants could not interact with objects in the virtual world. Instead, users dictated the actions they would usually perform with each of the items or people as they traversed the environment. This study found: - Participants given the HMD recalled more information - Participants given the HMD viewed and traversed more of the environment - No significant difference was found in time taken between the two groups - No significant difference was found in usability between the two groups - Participants given the HMD reported higher subjective presence scores

In Study Three, we found no statistically significant differences in usability between the HMD and desktop display conditions. While not conclusive, this is a positive result, as the differences in usability identified previously in Study Two put many of our observed results into question. Issues with usability can manifest in a variety of ways and may have affected many, if not all of our results in some way. By simplifying the experimental setup and user requirements for this experiment, we have greatly mitigated any potential confounds posed by usability.

In Study Three, we also found no statistically significant difference in time taken between the HMD and desktop display conditions. Once again, this result is contrary to what we found previously in Study Two. This difference in time taken in our prior study was problematic, as we were unable to dismiss the possibility that the observed recall differences were not due to the differences in time viewing the given virtual world stimuli. This meant that it may not have been the immersive qualities of virtual reality producing differences, as we discussed in our research questions and hypothesis construction. In our prior experiment, we conjectured that a major reason for the difference in time taken between the two groups was due to the significantly lower usability scores reported by those given the HMD. If the participants given the HMD were finding the virtual world harder to use, it may mean that they would require longer to complete the task. This suggests that the observed difference in recall ability between the two treatment groups was likely a direct result of the way the two groups viewed the environment, rather than simply the time they spent viewing the virtual world stimuli.

Finally, Study Three found that participants given the HMD reported higher subjective presence scores than those given the desktop display. In Study Two, our presence findings were inconclusive. The subjective presence questionnaire suggested people given the HMD experienced lower levels of presence, while the semi-structured interviews suggested that they were experiencing higher levels of presence. After reflecting on the usage of the presence survey, however, we believe that the task we provided to participants in Study Two was not well suited to this particular questionnaire. After reviewing many of the papers which use this particular survey, the tasks given to participants tended to be very simple and contained a very unobtrusive user interface. In Study Two, however, the participants had to use a variety of menus and object interactions to describe their desired actions. We believe that these menus may have inadvertently affected the user presence scores on the chosen survey. Despite this, however, we have no way of knowing for certain which treatment group experienced greater levels of presence in Study Two. In Study Three, however, we have removed all menus from the task and the HMD subjective presence scores are now also significantly higher than the desktop display scores.

We believe that the study described in this paper has meaningfully clarified and explored the issues identified in our prior studies. Furthermore, this work has provided further rigor to our prior results and provided further evidence of a link between the added immersion provided by virtual reality and improved recall performance.

9   Design Insights

As we have now constructed multiple virtual worlds with varying interfaces, we believe it is prudent to discuss some of the insights we have gathered during the development, testing and refinement of these environments. While there are numerous design decisions made when looking to develop a virtual environment for eliciting information, our work in this area has generated particularly beneficial insights regarding how the virtual environments should be constructed and how the information should be elicited from the user.

Despite significant advancements to the tools and resources available for constructing these environments, the time required to accurately reconstruct environments manually is still greatly prohibitive to the overall approach. The environment used for this experiment was constructed in a matter of hours, but further time may be required for more complex environments, especially if objects within the environment needed to be created. Unless the virtual world reconstruction had already been developed for other purposes (e.g. training simulations), it would likely still be easier to conduct real-world role-plays, rather than manually attempt to reconstruct these environments. These environments do not manually need to be constructed, however, and may instead be generated via 3D scanning techniques (e.g. from a Matterport depth camera [30]). In our experiments, we chose not to use this approach as we did not want user experience within the real-world airport we chose to scan to confound our results. We have worked with these scanned environments, however, and we believe that they provide a sufficient level of detail for this particular approach, while greatly reducing the time required to generate these environments.

After working with both a structured approach (where participants manually entered their descriptions of individual tasks) and an unstructured approach (where participants dictated their descriptions of tasks), we also believe that providing some structure to the way in which participants provide their descriptions of each task is beneficial. In the experiment described in this paper, we believe that there may have been times where participants were role-playing the tasks they wished to complete within the environment, but forgot that they also needed to also describe their actions aloud. While this may have also occurred in our previous experiments, we do not believe it was so pronounced. This may be because participants given the structured approach believed they were constructing a list of required tasks for later review, while those dictating their actions believed they were describing their actions forthrightly. This is somewhat supported as many participants which described their actions using the structured approach refined their descriptions over time, while those dictating their descriptions were much less likely to make revisions. For these reasons, we believe that a structured approach is preferable when attempting to elicit information. This structure, however, may not necessarily have to be achieved by having participants manually enter descriptions. For example, this may instead be achieved by having the system only record while the user holds a button down. When the user then releases the button, the system then stores the description and allow the user to review and modify all of their prior recordings. Specifically, we believe that the key difference between these two approaches is the ease in which participants can review and revise their previous descriptions.

While we believe that these two areas are important when looking to develop a virtual world for elicitation, considerable future work is required to adequately explore the many design challenges associated with constructing a virtual world for this purpose.

10   Conclusion and Future Work

In this study, we have continued to explore the potential of using a virtual world role-play approach in order to assist in effectively eliciting knowledge. This approach was motivated by the theory of situated cognition, which postulates that by situating a user within a specific context, it becomes easier for them to recall related information. This study aimed to solidify the results of prior studies by exploring potential confounds related to usability, presence and time taken.

The results from this study indicated that participants using the HMD both described more tasks and spoke a larger number of words than those given the desktop display. When comparing the behaviour of the two groups, we also found that participants given the HMD also tended to traverse more of the environment and modify their view more often (supported by large effect sizes). Unlike in our prior study, no statistically significant difference in time taken or usability was found between the two treatment groups. In addition to this, the HMD condition reported higher presence than the desktop display condition. These results supported our prior conjecture that the interaction mechanisms presented by the virtual world in our previous experiment may have inadvertently affected the observed results.

In this experiment, however, we were measuring performance based on the dictation provided by participants. This does not necessarily adequately align with the actual recall ability of participants. There is a possibility that the areas of the task which would normally require high cognitive load may have resulted in participants actively describing less. Future work will be required to determine the effect that varying cognitive load may have on the ability of participants to adequately describe their knowledge. Furthermore, as both this study and prior studies used the same airport scenario, further research is required to adequately explore whether the observed results may generalise into other complex spatial scenarios, such as warehouse inventory management or hospital medical processes.

References

1. Davis, A., Dieste, O., Hickey, A., Juristo, N., Moreno, A.M.: Empirical results derived from a systematic review. In: Proceedings of Requirements Engineering, pp. 179–188. IEEE (2006)
2. Smith, E.A.: The role of tacit and explicit knowledge in the workplace. J. Knowl. Manag. 5(4), 311–321 (2001)
3. Zowghi, D., Coulin, C.: Requirements elicitation: a survey of techniques, approaches, and tools. In: Aurum, A., Wohlin, C. (eds.) Engineering and Managing Software Requirements, pp. 19–46. Springer, Berlin (2005). doi:10.1007/3-540-28244-0_2
4. Costain, G., McKenna, B.: Experiencing the elicitation of user requirements and recording them in use case diagrams through role-play. J. Inf. Syst. Educ. 22(4), 367 (2011)
5. Mace, J.H., Clevinger, A.M., Martin, C.: Involuntary memory chaining versus event cueing: which is a better indicator of autobiographical memory organisation? Memory 18(8), 845–854 (2010)
6. Brown, J., Collins, A., Duguid, P.: Situated cognition and the culture of learning. Educ. Res. 18(1), 32–42 (1989)

7. Harman, J., Brown, R., Johnson, D., Rinderle-Ma, S., Kannengiesser, U.: Augmenting process elicitation with visual priming: an empirical exploration of user behaviour and modelling outcomes. Inf. Syst. **62**, 242–255 (2016)
8. Harman, J., Brown, R., Johnson, D.: The role of immersion during situated memory recall within virtual worlds. In: Proceedings of the 28th Australian Conference on Computer-Human Interaction, pp. 1–10. ACM (2016)
9. Lave, J., Wenger, E.: Situated Learning: Legitimate Peripheral Participation. Cambridge University Press, Cambridge (1991)
10. Dede, C., Nelson, B., Ketelhut, D.J., Clarke, J., Bowman, C.: Design-based research strategies for studying situated learning in a multi-user virtual environment. In: Proceedings of Learning Sciences 2004, pp. 158–165 (2004)
11. Dickey, M.D.: Teaching in 3D: pedagogical affordances and constraints of 3D virtual worlds for synchronous distance learning. Distance Educ. **24**(1), 105–121 (2003)
12. Carassa, A., Morganti, F., Tirassa, M.: A situated cognition perspective on presence. In: Proceedings of Cognitive Science 2005, Sheridan Printing, pp. 384–389 (2005)
13. Mania, K., Chalmers, A.: The effects of levels of immersion on memory and presence in virtual environments: a reality centered approach. CyberPsychol. Behav. **4**(2), 247–264 (2001)
14. Riva, G., Mantovani, F., Capideville, C.S., Preziosa, A., Morganti, F., Villani, D., Alcaiz, M., Gaggioli, A., Botella, C.: Affective interactions using virtual reality: the link between presence and emotions. CyberPsychol. Behav. **10**(1), 45–56 (2007)
15. Renaud, P., Rouleau, J.L., Granger, L., Barsetti, I., Bouchard, S.: Measuring sexual preferences in virtual reality: a pilot study. CyberPsychol. Behav. **5**(1), 1–9 (2002)
16. Duncan, I., Miller, A., Jiang, S.: A taxonomy of virtual worlds usage in education. British J. Educ. Technol. **43**(6), 949–964 (2012)
17. Virvou, M., Katsionis, G.: On the usability and likeability of virtual reality games for education: the case of VR-ENGAGE. Comput. Educ. **50**(1), 154–178 (2008)
18. Unity Technologies: Unity - Game Engine (2016). Accessed 13 June 2016. http://unity3d.com
19. Harman, J., Brown, R., Kannengiesser, U., Meyer, N., Rothschädl, T.: Model as you do: engaging an S-BPM vendor on process modelling in 3D virtual worlds. In: Fleischmann, A., Schmidt, W., Stary, C. (eds.) S-BPM in the Wild, pp. 113–133. Springer, Cham (2015). doi:10.1007/978-3-319-17542-3_7
20. Roediger, H.L., Karpicke, J.D.: Test-enhanced learning taking memory tests improves long-term retention. Psychol. Sci. **17**(3), 249–255 (2006)
21. Ivanoiu, A., Adam, S., Van der Linden, M., Salmon, E., Juillerat, A.C., Mulligan, R., Seron, X.: Memory evaluation with a new cued recall test in patients with mild cognitive impairment and Alzheimers disease. J. Neurol. **252**(1), 47–55 (2005)
22. Claes, J., et al.: Tying process model quality to the modeling process: the impact of structuring, movement, and speed. In: Barros, A., Gal, A., Kindler, E. (eds.) BPM 2012. LNCS, vol. 7481, pp. 33–48. Springer, Heidelberg (2012). doi:10.1007/978-3-642-32885-5_3
23. Schumie, M.J., Van der Straaten, P., Krijn, M., Van der Mast, C.A.P.G.: Research on presence in VR: a survey. Cyberpsychol Behav. **4**(2), 183–202 (2001)
24. Witmer, B.G., Singer, M.J.: Measuring presence in virtual environments: a presence questionnaire. Presence: Teleoperators Virtual Environ. **7**(3), 225–240 (1998)
25. Schubert, T., Friedmann, F., Regenbrecht, H.: The experience of presence: factor analytic insights. Presence **10**(3), 266–281 (2001)
26. Sutcliffe, A.G., Kaur, K.D.: Evaluating the usability of virtual reality user interfaces. Behav. Inf. Technol. **19**(6), 415–426 (2000)

27. Lewis, J.R.: IBM computer usability satisfaction questionnaires: psychometric evaluation and instructions for use. Int. J. Hum.-Comput. Interac. **7**(1), 57–78 (1995)
28. Cohen, J.: A power primer. Psychol. Bull. **112**(1), 155 (1992)
29. Rosenthal, R.: Parametric measures of effect size. In: Cooper, H., Hedges, L.V. (eds.) The Handbook of Research Synthesis, pp. 231–244. Russell Sage Foundation, New York (1994)
30. Matterport: Immersive Spaces for Real-world Applications - Matterport (2016). Accessed 23 June 2016. http://matterport.com

Practice in Reality for Virtual Reality Games: Making Players Familiar and Confident with a Game

Jeffrey C.F. Ho[✉]

City University of Hong Kong, Kowloon Tong, Hong Kong SAR
jeffreycfho@gmail.com

Abstract. Game designers include training levels in video games to prepare players so that they can enjoy the game. The training levels of virtual reality (VR) games are typically assumed to be within the virtual world of the game. New players must learn about a new game in such an unfamiliar virtual world. A tutorial in the real world offers a potential way to enable players to learn about a new game and to practice the skills in a familiar world. To explore any effects of a real-world tutorial in VR games, an experiment was conducted, the results of which show that a real-world tutorial is effective in helping new players feel confident about and familiar with a VR game before playing it. However, it is not as effective as virtual-world tutorial in increasing game performance.

1 Introduction

Virtual reality (VR) headsets have become popular in recent years. VR technologies enable game designers to explore new forms of gameplay. Many players may be new to VR games and may require assistance in getting familiar with virtual environments and gaining basic skills. Therefore, game designers design tutorials in video games to prepare new players for a game.

Unique challenges arise when designing tutorials for VR games. Video game tutorials are typically presented within the video game environment. If the same approach is used in VR games, the tutorials would be presented in a VR environment that is new in every VR game. Players must wear a VR headset and fully immersed in an unfamiliar environment while simultaneously acquiring basic skills for the game. This is similar to someone new to basketball preparing for a basketball match that will be played on an unfamiliar court. Receiving training in the court may be helpful; however, he or she may feel more comfortable receiving basic training in a familiar place (e.g., his or her own backyard). In VR games, whether players can receive basic tutorials in a familiar place (e.g., their own living room) instead of the unfamiliar virtual environment of a VR game should be considered. This paper focuses on real-world tutorials for VR games.

Tutorials in the real world can help new players learn how to play a game. In the real world, designers can replicate certain objects (e.g., tools) from VR games. Such objects provide new players with an opportunity to experience the settings and interactions in a manner similar to that in the VR game. Thus, players can learn about a new

© IFIP International Federation for Information Processing 2017
Published by Springer International Publishing AG 2017. All Rights Reserved
R. Bernhaupt et al. (Eds.): INTERACT 2017, Part II, LNCS 10514, pp. 147–162, 2017.
DOI: 10.1007/978-3-319-67684-5_10

game in a familiar, real setting while acquiring some basic skills on how the game is played. Then, when they start playing a VR game, they can feel familiar with the game mechanics and achieve goals with the basic skills that they have acquired. This raises a concern of whether real-world tutorials can fulfill two purposes of game tutorials: (1) letting new players become familiar with the game, and (2) allowing them to acquire the necessary skills to play.

Tutorials in the real world provide opportunities for players to familiarize themselves with a new VR game because they are given in a familiar setting. Full immersion into the virtual world is not required until the players are prepared and start playing the VR game.

Another purpose of in-game tutorial is the acquisition of basic skills. An obvious concern about transferring game tutorials to the real world is whether the skills acquired in reality can be transferred to a VR world. VR simulation training for real-world tasks has become a common approach in training in many applications (e.g., military and aviation training). This suggests that skills can be transferred between virtual and real worlds. In other words, skills acquired in the real world are potentially transferable to a virtual world.

Real-world tutorials for VR games have practical benefits in certain applications. In most public VR public installations, such as those in shopping malls, few VR devices are available for people to use. Moreover, people must queue for a long time, yet they are typically allowed to enjoy the installation for only a few minutes. Tutorials in the real world would allow participants to practice while waiting and thus ensure that they are ready when it is their turn to play the VR applications.

This approach involves players' participation in two realities. The tutorial is given in a familiar setting (the real world) but the actual gameplay occurs in a virtual world. The research question in the present study thus concerns whether and how a tutorial in reality is effective in aiding new players with becoming familiar with and acquiring basic skills for playing a VR game.

2   Related Work

2.1   Tutorials and Practice in Video Games

A tutorial is a common feature in video games. A tutorial prepares players for gameplay by providing instructions and letting the players practice. The players' abilities must match the challenges in the game so that they can enjoy it [10]. If a tutorial is not available, new players can start with the first or second levels. However, players may spend their attention experimenting and developing skills during their gameplay in the initial levels instead of engaging themselves in the game content (e.g., narratives, visual aesthetics). Tutorials provide an opportunity for new players with limited ability to gain knowledge and ability before playing the main part of a game. Practice in the tutorial provides the same mechanism as the game, but with fewer constraints, such as the absence of a time limit. Examples include *Tom Clancy's Splinter Cell* (2002) and *Portal 2* (2011).

Tutorials have different formats. Some tutorials are aimed at providing information to new players. Tutorials that are mainly based on images and text can engage players in relatively complicated games [2]. Players may be able to learn how to play a game through experimentation [19].

When players play a VR game, they must become familiar with the virtual environment and how to use tools (e.g., shotguns) to interact with objects in the virtual world (e.g., shooting zombies). Practice-based tutorials may assist in overcoming this problem. Through practice, players can become accustomed to a tool, hold it, and use it as an extension of their body. Moreover, knowing the rules and tasks of a VR game is insufficient (e.g., an information-driven tutorial based on images and text); new players must be given an opportunity to actually practice using the tools (e.g., weapons in a game) to face challenges they encounter in the game (e.g., killing zombies).

A typical approach involves designing a training sequence in a VR game that enables players to experience the game before enjoying the main game content. This means that practice occurs in the virtual environment, which is new and unique in every VR game.

2.2 Influences Between Reality and Virtual Reality

Researchers in various disciplines have examined the relationship between experiences in real and virtual worlds. In human-computer interaction (HCI), researchers have explored training in a virtual environment with virtual human influence behavior in the real world [8, 9, 22]. For example, Chollet et al. [8, 9] used a virtual audience to train people in public speaking skills. In their user studies, they found that training with a virtual audience can improve trainees' public speaking skills. Trainees were also found to have improved eye contact and fewer unnecessary pause fillers in their talks.

In media studies, researchers have investigated the effects of media content on audiences' behavior in the real world. One research focus concerns whether and how violence in video games influences children's and adolescents' behavior [1]. The relevant findings have implications on policymaking and regulation. Such an influence can be perceptual to some gamers, rather than being behavioral. de Gortari et al. [26] interviewed gamers and found that some of them experienced difficulties in the perception of real-life events, elicitation of automatic thoughts, sensory perceptions, and dissociative experiences. This is called the game transfer phenomenon.

Most previous studies examining the relationship between experiences in the virtual world and the real world have mainly focused on the effect of the virtual world on experiences and behavior in reality, but not the converse. One exception is a study by Ho [18], who investigated the influence of real-world experiences on immersive experiences in the virtual world. The result suggests that the experience of a game in the real world causes experienced players to become more immersed in the VR game simulating it. The effect on inexperienced players is the opposite. However, the statistical result was not sufficiently strong to be conclusive.

One research area that evidently shows influences of VR on the real world is simulation training in motor learning literature, which is reviewed below.

2.3   Motor Skills and Practice

Playing VR games often involves some motor skills such as turning the head to inspect the environment and avoid obstacles. Thus, practice for VR games can be considered a type of motor skill training. According to research on motor learning [27], a skill is any ability that facilitates task completion with maximum certainty and minimum costs. Costs involves physical and mental energy as well as time. All skills comprise three elements: perception of the environment, decisions of what muscular actions to perform (and when to perform them), and the actual execution of such actions to achieve a goal.

Practice is the most crucial activity in learning a motor skill [27, p. 199]. A primary goal of practice is for learners to acquire a skill. They can improve their abilities to selectively perceive information that is crucial to achieving a goal and detect errors by themselves. Through the process of practicing, they can also reduce the amount of attention required to complete a task.

Another crucial goal of practice is skill transfer (also known as skill generalization), which refers to the concept that skills acquired from practice or experience with one task can be applied to another task. Learners are expected to transfer their skills from practice scenarios to novel scenarios that they have not encountered before. The transfer of a skill is referred to as positive if the skill is enhanced by practice but negative if the skill is reduced.

The degree of transfer depends on the similarity between the practice task and a target task [27]. The similarity between tasks can be decomposed into three aspects: (1) fundamental movement pattern, (2) perceptual elements, and (3) strategic and conceptual similarities. Fundamental movement patterns refer to the movement patterns involved in a task. If the fundamental movement pattern (e.g., arm movement in throwing a baseball) of practice and actual tasks are similar, skill transfer are likely to be successful. Moreover, if the perceptual cues involved in a practice task (e.g., perceiving a ball trajectory) are similar to those in the actual task, learners can react appropriately to different situations and thus the skill can be transferred. Skill transfer also depends on the similarity of strategic and conceptual elements. Different activities can have similar rules, strategies, guidelines, and concepts. For example, the similarity in road rules between commonwealth countries assists tourists from one commonwealth country when traveling in another commonwealth country, but this may cause a negative transfer effect if they travel to North America, where the road rules are different.

One application area that depends on the principles of skill transfer is simulation practice. A simulator is a device that replicates the features of a real-world target task in a virtual environment. Simulator training can be essential in situations where training with real-world tasks is expensive, when facilities are limited, or where practice in the real world is not feasible (e.g., surgery).

Researchers on training simulations have examined whether the skills acquired in VR training for serious tasks can be effectively transferred to the real world. Gallagher et al. [16] conducted two studies that involved surgical training—one in a VR simulation environment and one in the real world. They found that VR simulation improved skill levels in the real world, regardless of the level of previous experience of the trainees. Similar studies on the effects of training in a virtual simulation environment have also been conducted in military and aviation training [3, 14].

If the quality of a simulation is high, skill transfer to real-world application is expected to be effective. In the discussion of quality of simulation, two types of fidelity are concerned [23]. Physical fidelity refers to the extent to which the surface features (e.g., audiovisual elements) of a simulation and the target task are replicated. Psychological fidelity refers to the extent to which a simulation can produce behaviors and processes required for a target task. This type of fidelity is more concerned with the skills and behaviors required to perform a target task. The two types of fidelity should be complementary to each other.

2.4 Methodology of Studying Digital Games

An experiment is a standard research method in digital games (such as [5, 6, 12]). Researchers use this method for studying very specific aspects [4]. It is often done in a relatively controlled environment and carefully manipulate specific aspects of the stimulus (i.e. a game in game research). Researchers either select an existing game and modify the settings (e.g., [5, 11, 20]) or custom make their own game to suit specific purposes (e.g., [12, 13, 17]). In some cases, a custom-made game can be relatively simple such that one specific aspect can be focused in a study. For example, Depping and his colleagues [12] created a game called Labyrinth for their experiment aiming to study how players build trust in a game environment. Labyrinth was a 2-player game that requires cooperation to collect all the gems in a maze. The two players had different roles (so-called pusher and collector). They needed to communicate via voice chat to cooperate. The authors reported each pair of participants completed a round in 2 min. The game deliberately made simple such that they can be focused on how the challenges and cooperation in games can influence interpersonal trust. We took a similar approach in creating a simple game for our experiment.

3 Investigating Practice in Real World for VR Games

The real world is familiar to players and presents opportunities for practice sessions. On the basis of the perspectives covered in the previous section, the approach of real-world-based practice is analyzed in this section to examine its effectiveness in enhancing new players' confidence, familiarity, and skill learning. The research hypotheses are then proposed.

Practice in the real world provides a familiar environment for players to prepare themselves for a game. Players in a familiar environment may be more comfortable in learning about the mechanics of a game. As shown in previous research on and applications of simulation training, skills can be transferred from VR to the real world, which suggests that skills can be transferred between realities. Thus, real-world training for VR games should be effective as well.

Practicing in reality for VR games can involve tools and objects that replicate their counterparts in a VR game. Players can attempt challenges similar to those in the VR game. During practice, players can hold replicas of tools in the VR games, attach them to their bodies, and perform tasks similar to the challenges in the game. This attachment is considered a coupling process in the embodied interaction perspective [15].

Practice in virtual worlds and the real world differ in their strengths and weaknesses. Practice in a virtual world may be more effective for skill learning and transfer because of the high level of physical and psychological fidelity in simulations. The audiovisual effects in a VR practice environment can replicate those in a VR game (physical fidelity). Basic game rules and mechanics that require new players to strategically think and behave in a manner similar to how they would in a VR game can also be replicated in VR practice (psychological fidelity). The drawback with this approach is that it requires new players to be immediately immersed in an unfamiliar virtual world that they must learn about. By contrast, practice in the real world may be limited in creating a simulation with a high level of physical fidelity because recreating the audiovisual effects used in VR games may be impractical in the real world. However, a certain level of psychological fidelity can be realized if the real-world practice requires new players to think and behave in a manner that is similar to what is required in a VR game.

From this viewpoint, the key questions of the present study concern whether the experience gained in reality can help new players in a VR game, and if so, whether such practice is better offered in the real world or within a VR game itself.

3.1   Can Real-World Practice Prepare Players?

Practice-based tutorials enable new payers to experience a game's gameplay. If the challenges and tools in the practice-based tutorial are consistent with those in the VR game, players can attempt to use the tools. This paper focuses on three aspects of gameplay: confidence in playing the game, familiarity with the game, and game performance. To facilitate answering this question, hypotheses were formulated.

Confidence. Confidence refers to the extent to which players believe they can perform well in the game. Psychologists refer to this concept as self-efficacy [28]. The focus involves preparing new players for a VR game and therefore their confidence after any practice and before actual gameplay. Practice in the real world should develop new players' confidence in a VR game as long as the challenges and tools in the VR game are replicated in the real world. Thus, the proposed hypothesis is as follows:

H1.1: New players who practice in the real world will feel more confident playing a VR game than those who do not have any practice.

Familiarity. Familiarity refers to the extent to which players are familiar with a game before they actually play it. Although it is a different reality from the virtual world, the real world is a familiar reality to the players; therefore, they may benefit from such practice.

H1.2: New players who practice in the real world will be more familiar with a VR game than those who do not have any practice.

Players' familiarity with a game can also be observed form their behavior. If players are familiar with a VR game, they should be prepared to start the game as soon as they affix a VR headset. Players who are less familiar with a VR game will require more time to prepare.

H1.3: Once new players who practice in the real world enter a VR game, they will take less time to prepare and start the game than those who do not have any practice.

Game Performance. Game performance refers to players' actual measurable performance in playing a VR game. Practice in reality can enable players to gain certain basic skills. Skills acquired in the real world should be transferrable to a virtual world provided that the real-world practice simulates the game rules and mechanics of a VR game with a high level of psychological fidelity. Therefore, real-world practice should be an effective form of practice for VR games. Thus,

H1.4: New players who practice in the real world will perform better in a VR game than those who do not have any practice.

3.2   How Does Real-World Practice Compare with VR Practice?

The real world enables players to practice in a familiar reality. New players use tools with their body in the real world. By contrast, in VR practice, players must use tools in the virtual world with their characters' body in the virtual world using their own body and any game controllers in the real world.

Confidence. Practice in the real world enables players to face challenges in the VR game with concrete and realistic sensory-motor experience, similar to how they learn a new skill in their daily lives. However, the advantage of practice in the virtual world is that the players understand that they are practicing in the same world as that in which the actual gameplay takes place. The proposed hypothesis is as follows:

H2.1: New players who practice in the real world will feel more confident playing a VR game than those who practice in the virtual world.

Familiarity. In terms of familiarity that players can gain from practicing, the difference between real-world practice and VR practice is that the real world is a reality that new players are already familiar with. Arguably, players who receive practice in the real world should be aware that actual gameplay will occur in a different, virtual world. They might still be unfamiliar with the game after such practice. However, given that players understand that the challenges and tools are the same as those in the VR game, the concrete experience of touching these tools in the real world should provide them with a higher sense of familiarity.

H2.2: New players who practice in the real world will be more familiar with a VR game than those who practice in the virtual world.

The more familiar they are, the faster they can prepare once they enter the virtual environment. Following the same argument about familiarity, the following hypothesis is proposed:

H2.3: Once new players who practice in the real world enter a VR game, they will take less time to prepare and start the game than those who practice in the virtual world.

Game Performance. Regarding game performance, the key focus concerns whether practice in the real world trains players more effectively than that in the virtual world. Compared to practice in the real world, practice in the virtual world of a VR game provides a high level of physical and psychological fidelity. Therefore, virtual-world practice should be more effective than real-world practice.

H2.4: New players who practice in the virtual world will perform better in a VR game than those who practice in the real world.

The first three hypotheses concern about confidence and familiarity while the forth hypothesis is about game performance. We argue that practice in the real world benefits new players better in terms of confidence and familiarity because the real world is where people acquire skills since birth. It should allow people to feel confident about and familiar with a task (playing a game in this case) that they are going to engage in. In contrast, game performance here is concerned about how well new players actually perform in a game. Regarding performance, practice in virtual world should benefit new players better because the virtual world is more similar to the environment where the game takes place than the real world. This is based on the literature in motor learning regarding the influence of similarity between training environment and task environment.

4 Study Design

To test the hypotheses, an experiment was designed and conducted. Practice was the independent variable, which resulted in three conditions: no practice (Control Condition), practice in reality (Reality Condition), and practice in VR (VR Condition). The effects of treatments in preparing players for a VR game were investigated. Specifically, four areas corresponding to the hypotheses were examined: confidence with the game, perceived familiarity with the game, initial exploration time and game performance. Confidence and perceived familiarity were measured using a survey question with a 7-point Likert scale. The initial exploration time was measured according to the time after participants wore a VR headset and before they indicated that they were ready to start the game.

Regarding measuring players' performance, there are many different choices (e.g., [24, 25]). Studies use different measures for different types of games [21]. In our custom-made game, the task was to put five balls into the target container. If they have the skill to transfer balls to the target, they should be able to do so efficiently. In this experiment, the purpose of measuring performance is to investigate the effect of skill transfer across different realities. The game performance was measured according to the time each player required to complete the game (possible score: 5 points).

Sixty participants (52 women) with different levels of gaming experience were recruited. Their ages ranged from 19 to 28 years (mean (M) = 21.6, standard deviation (SD) = 1.9). Among these participants, 51 had experience playing video games, which ranged from 4 to 18 years. All of them indicate they have zero years of experience in playing VR games.

4.1 The Game

A VR game called "Hospital On Fire" was designed for this experiment. In the game narrative, the player is trapped in a hospital that is on fire. The player must extinguish the fire by triggering water sprinklers. However, the player can only move his or her head. A spoon-like tool is attached to the player's head. The player must move his or her head to catch a ball from a dispenser on his or her left and then transfer the ball to a target container on his or her right. For every ball the player puts into the target container, a water sprinkler is triggered to extinguish a portion of the fire. To complete the game, the player must put five balls into the target container. The game was developed using Unity and Oculus Rift DK2. Screenshots of the game are shown in Fig. 1. Two types of practice were created for the game: practice in reality and practice in VR.

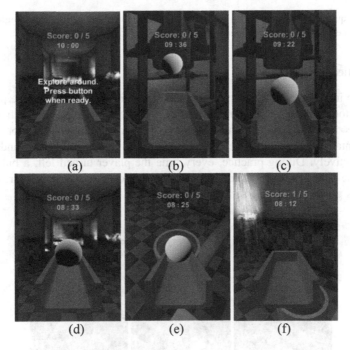

Fig. 1. (a)–(f) Screenshots of steps to gain one point in the game

4.2 Practice in Reality

For practice in reality, a replica of the spoon-like tool was created (see Fig. 2). The tool was attached to a pair of goggles. A small plastic bucket was placed on the right-hand side of the participant and was used as a physical replica of the target container. A researcher stood on the left-hand side of the participant. During practice, the participant affixed the goggles (with the tool attached). Every time the participant turned left, a researcher placed a ball in the spoon-like tool. The participant was asked to practice transferring balls to the small plastic bucket. Each participant was given 1 min to practice.

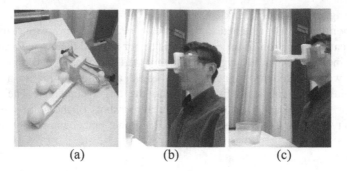

Fig. 2. (a) Equipment for practice in reality, (b) demonstration of wearing the goggles with the tool, and (c) demonstration of transferring a ball with the tool

4.3   Practice in VR

For practice in VR, a VR program was created (see Fig. 3). In the practice program, a spoon-like tool similar to that in the actual VR game was placed in front of the participant's face. The participant controlled the tool by moving his or her head. A target container and a ball dispenser were placed on the player's right- and left-hand sides, respectively. During practice, every time the player turned left, a ball was dispatched. The participant was asked to transfer balls to the target container. Each participant was given 1 min to practice.

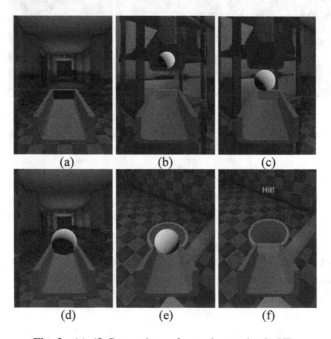

Fig. 3. (a)–(f) Screenshots of steps in practice in VR.

4.4   Procedure

Participants were randomly assigned to the three conditions. A total of 20 participants were included for each condition. When a participant arrived the laboratory, he or she was briefed and asked to read and sign a consent form. The participant then completed a questionnaire regarding background information, such as gender and age. A PDF document introducing the VR game was then shown to the participant. The introductory document presented the story, rules, and gameplay instructions with some screenshots. Participants in the Reality Condition then practiced within the reality program. Participants in the VR Condition practiced with the VR practice program. Participants in the Control Condition did not have any practice. Before playing the VR game, participants were asked about their confidence and familiarity with the game. They then affixed the VR headset. The game did not start immediately. The participants were reminded to explore the game environment. When the participant was prepared, he or she told the researcher to start the game. The researcher then helped the participant start the game, and the participant began playing the VR game. When they finished the game, they removed the VR headset. Finally, they were debriefed.

4.5   Results

An analysis of variance (ANOVA) on the confidence before gameplay showed significant differences among the conditions ($F(2, 57) = 7.40$, $p < .005$, $n^2 = .21$). Bonferroni test was performed to examine how the conditions compare with each other. The Bonferroni test revealed that confidence in the Reality Condition ($M = 4.75$, S.D. $= 1.45$) was significantly higher ($p < .005$) than confidence in the Control Condition ($M = 3.20$, S.D. $= 1.24$). Therefore, H1.1 is supported. No significant difference was identified between the Reality Condition and VR Condition ($M = 4.40$, S.D. $= 1.31$). Therefore, H2.1 is not supported.

Confidence in the VR Condition was found to be higher than that in the Control Condition, with statistical significance ($p < .05$). Tukey's-b test for homogeneous subset was performed to examine if there are additional groupings among the conditions. The result is shown in Table 1. It shows that the Reality Condition and VR Condition statistically belong to the same group with a higher level of confidence, whereas the Control Condition belongs to its own group with lower confidence.

Table 1. Result of Tukey's-b test for homogeneous subsets based on four dependent measures. Means and standard deviations (in brackets) of respective measurements of three groups are shown in the table cells

Conditions	Confidence		Perceived familiarity		Exploration time		Performance	
	Subset 1	Subset 2	Subset 1	Subset 2	Subset 1	Subset 2	Subset 1	Subset 2
No practice	3.20 (1.24)		2.85 (1.27)		20.6 s (5.55 s)		65.3 s (18.4 s)	
Practice in reality		4.75 (1.45)		4.40 (1.39)	20.0 s (7.57 s)		53.7 s (19.1 s)	
Practice in VR		4.40 (1.31)		4.25 (1.37)		15.4 s (6.03 s)		38.7 s (16.7 s)

An ANOVA on the self-reported familiarity before gameplay indicated significant differences among the conditions (F(2, 57) = 8.08, p < .005, n^2 = .22). In the post-hoc analysis, the Bonferroni test showed that familiarity in the Reality Condition (M = 4.40, S.D. = 1.39) was significantly higher than (p < .005) that in the Control Condition (M = 2.81, S.D. = 1.27). This supports H1.2. No statistical difference was identified between the Reality Condition and the VR Condition (M = 4.25, S.D. = 1.37). This does not support H2.2. Familiarity in the VR Condition was found to be significantly higher than that in the Control Condition (p < .01). Tukey's-b test for homogeneous subset-offered groupings is shown in Table 1. It shows that the Reality and VR Conditions statistically belong to the same group with higher familiarity, whereas the Control Condition belongs to its own group with lower familiarity.

An ANOVA on the exploration time showed significant differences among the conditions (F(2, 57) = 3.78, p < .05, n^2 = .12). In the post-hoc analysis, the Bonferroni test showed no statistical significance between the Control Condition (M = 20.55 s, S.D. = 5.55 s) and the Reality Condition (M = 20.00 s, S.D. = 7.67 s). Therefore, H1.3 is not supported. Exploration time in the VR Condition (M = 15.45 s, S. D. = 6.03 s) was found to be shorter than that in the Reality Condition, with marginal significance (p = .09). This does not support H2.3. Exploration time in the VR Condition was found to be significantly shorter than that in the Control Condition (p < .05). Tukey's-b test for homogeneous subset-offered groupings is shown in Table 1. It shows that the Control Condition and Reality Condition statistically belong to the same group, whereas the VR Condition belongs to its own group.

An ANOVA on the game performance showed significant differences among the conditions (F(2, 57) = 10.85, p < .001, n^2 = .28). In the post-hoc analysis, the Bonferroni test showed no statistical difference between the Control Condition (M = 65.30 s,   S.D. = 18.38 s)   and   the   Reality   Condition   (M = 53.75 s, S.D. = 19.09 s). Therefore, H1.4 is not supported. Game performance in the VR Condition (M = 38.75 s, S.D. = 16.65 s) was found to be significantly higher than that in the Reality Condition. Therefore, H2.4 was supported. Tukey's-b test for homogeneous subset-offered groupings is shown in Table 1. It shows that the No Practice and Practice variables in the Reality Condition statistically belong to the same group, whereas Practice in the VR Condition belongs to its own group. Table 2 shows a summary of the results.

Table 2. Summary of results

Dependent variables	Question 1: Is practice in reality effective?	Question 2: How does practice in reality compare with practice in VR?
Confidence	H1.1^	H2.1
Perceived familiarity	H1.2^	H2.2
Exploration time (actual familiarity)	H1.3	H2.3
Performance	H1.4	H2.4*

^Supported with statistical significance (p < .005). *Supported with statistical significance (p < .05).

5   Discussion

5.1   Real-World Practice Is Effective in Increasing Confidence and Perceived Familiarity

Practice in reality helps players feel more confident and familiar with a VR game. This is in line with our earlier discussion regarding the potential benefits of practice in a familiar reality. This suggests that our common understanding about practicing can be applied to reality and VR: practicing in a familiar place increases confidence and familiarity with the challenge to be faced in an unfamiliar place. Even if the players have not played the VR game, practicing in a familiar reality makes them feel as confident and familiar as someone who has practiced in the VR (as reflected by the groupings shown in Table 1).

However, the results show that even if practice in reality helps new players feel more familiar with a VR game, they still require time to prepare for the game when they first enter it. Their actual familiarity with the game is similar to conditions that they have no practice. This suggests that their perception of familiarity differs from their actual familiarity. Practice in reality makes them feel that they are familiar with a VR game before playing it, whereas they are actually not that familiar with it. This enhancement in perceived familiarity can potentially encourage new players to try out a VR game for the first time, which is crucial in game design [7].

This also implies that the effects of practice-based practice can be multidimensional. Future research in practice should investigate the effects of practice in different aspects.

5.2   Practice in Reality vs. Practice in VR

Our study provides evidence of the effects of experience in the real world on experience in VR. The results show that practice in VR is more effective than practice in reality in terms of actual familiarity and game performance. Practice in reality and VR are equally effective in increasing new players' confidence and familiarity.

These results do not show that the skills acquired through reality-based practice is applicable in confronting the challenges in a VR game. The acquired skills was not shown to reduce players' performance in VR games in this study; in other words, no negative skill transfer was observed. The results suggest that player performance can be improved through practicing in the virtual environment of a VR game. This is consistent with the skill transfer principles. Similarity is a determinant of skill transfer between reality and VR. This raises a concern of whether skill transfer between realities can be effective. If every VR game had its own version of reality, the skills acquired in one VR game might not apply to other VR games.

The effect of practice in reality on confidence is as beneficial as that of practice in VR. This means that practice in the real world helps players to be confident, as if they have practiced in VR, whereas their game performance is as if they had no prior training. This interesting finding suggests that practice in reality is beneficial to players in emotional and motivational aspects. Further research on psychological effects of real world practice is warranted.

5.3 Practical Implications

To game designers, this opens new opportunities for practice design. As mentioned, VR games are relatively new in major markets. The first experience is crucial in retaining players [7]. Encouraging new players to try out a VR game is crucial for success. One possibility involves helping them feel confident and familiar with a new game before they purchase it. Therefore, they would not be apprehensive. This result suggests that designing the practice to be experienced in reality helps new players feel more confident and familiar with it. Such practice may encourage players who are new to a VR game or VR games in general to try one. For example, in public VR installations, practice or some experience in the real world might encourage people who are new to, or even afraid, of an unfamiliar VR environment to gain confidence and become familiar with that environment.

This points to a potential new direction for tutorial design. The present paper suggests that practice in reality improves players' perceptions of their own confidence and familiarity. Game designers can consider including practice in tutorials in the real world. They can also explore the advantages of the real world, such as tools with materials other than plastic (which is often the case with VR headsets and controllers).

5.4 Limitations

Similar to other studies, the present study is not without limitations. The game designed for the experiment was relatively simple; it contained only one challenge (transferring balls) and one level. A typical VR game may contain different types of challenges and multiple levels. The key in the present study is to investigate the relationships between practice in reality and gameplay experience in VR. The simplicity of the game enables the isolation of the two factors being concerned through a high degree of control in the experimental conditions. The result offers evidence to support a causal relationship in certain aspects of gameplay experience.

In the experiment, the majority of the participants were female. This may reduce the generalizability of the results. We would like to point out that the game used in the study did not show nor imply the gender of the player character. The experimental procedure did not involve any gender-specific materials. We would argue that the influence of gender, if any, on the results would be very limited. Future studies may examine if gender moderates effects of practice in reality.

In the present study, the tasks in practice are assumed to be identical to those in actual gameplay. This means that practice in reality can only cover tasks in VR games that can be replicated in the real world. Therefore, this limits the applicability of this approach to VR games that contain challenges not replicable in reality, such as magic spells and killing zombies. However, practice in reality can be emphasized in the challenges that can be made available in the real world. Future research should focus on the influence of practice in reality on virtual experience in areas not covered by the practice.

6   Conclusion

The experiment reported offers evidence to show that practice can help new players of VR games in certain aspects, even if the practice is performed in the real world. Future research is required to further investigate the influences of such practice in other aspects of gameplay experience. Nonetheless, the result suggests a new approach to tutorial design for game designers to consider.

Acknowledgements. We thank all the participants for their participation and all the reviewers who have read and given feedback on the earlier versions of the manuscript.

References

1. Anderson, C.A., Gentile, D.A., Buckley, K.E.: Violent Video Game Effects on Children and Adolescents. Oxford University Press, Oxford (2007)
2. Andersen, E., O'Rourke, E., Liu, Y.-E., Snider, R., Lowdermilk, J., Truong, D., Cooper, S., Popovic, Z.: The impact of tutorials on games of varying complexity. In: Proceedings of the 2012 ACM Annual Conference on Human Factors in Computing Systems - CHI 2012, pp. 59–68. ACM Press, New York (2012)
3. Bell, H.H., Waag, W.L.: Evaluating the effectiveness of flight simulators for training combat skills: a review. Int. J. Aviat. Psychol. **8**, 223–242 (1998)
4. Cairns, P., Cox, A.L.: Research Methods for Human-Computer Interaction. Cambridge University Press, New York (2008)
5. Cairns, P., Cox, A.L., Day, M., Martin, H., Perryman, T.: Who but not where: the effect of social play on immersion in digital games. Int. J. Hum. Comput. Stud. **71**, 1069–1077 (2013)
6. Cairns, P., Cox, A., Nordin, A.I.: Immersion in digital games: review of gaming experience research. In: Handbook of Digital Games, pp. 337–361. Wiley, Hoboken (2014)
7. Cheung, G.K., Zimmermann, T., Nagappan, N.: The first hour experience: how the initial play can engage (or lose) new players. In: Proceedings of the First ACM SIGCHI Annual Symposium Computer Interaction Play - CHI Play 2014, pp. 57–66 (2014)
8. Chollet, M., Sratou, G., Shapiro, A.: An interactive virtual audience platform for public speaking training. In: Proceedings of the 2014 International Conference on Autonomous Agents and Multi-agent Systems, pp. 1657–1658 (2014)
9. Chollet, M., Wörtwein, T., Morency, L.-P., Shapiro, A., Scherer, S.: Exploring feedback strategies to improve public speaking: an interactive virtual audience framework. In: Proceedings of the 2015 ACM International Joint Conference on Pervasive and Ubiquitous Computing - UbiComp 2015, pp. 1143–1154. ACM Press, New York (2015)
10. Csikszentmihalyi, M.: Flow: The Psychology of Optimal Experience. Harper & Row, New York (1990)
11. Denisova, A., Cairns, P.: First person vs. third person perspective in digital games. In: Proceedings of the 33rd Annual ACM Conference on Human Factors in Computing Systems - CHI 2015, pp. 145–148 (2015)
12. Depping, A.E., Mandryk, R.L., Johanson, C., Bowey, J.T., Thomson, S.C.: Trust me: social games are better than social icebreakers at building trust. In: Proceedings of the 2016 Annual Symposium on Computer-Human Interaction in Play - CHI PLAY 2016, pp. 116–129. ACM Press, New York (2016)

13. Depping, A.E., Mandryk, R.L., Li, C., Gutwin, C., Vicencio-Moreira, R.: How disclosing skill assistance affects play experience in a multiplayer first-person shooter game. In: Proceedings of the 2016 CHI Conference on Human Factors in Computing Systems - CHI 2016, pp. 3462–3472. ACM Press, New York (2016)
14. de Winter, J.C.F., Dodou, D., Mulder, M.: Training effectiveness of whole body flight simulator motion: a comprehensive meta-analysis. Int. J. Aviat. Psychol. **22**, 164–183 (2012)
15. Dourish, P.: Where the Action is: the Foundations of Embodied Interaction. MIT Press, Cambridge (2004)
16. Gallagher, A.G., Seymour, N.E., Jordan-Black, J.-A., Bunting, B.P., McGlade, K., Satava, R.M.: Prospective, randomized assessment of transfer of training (ToT) and transfer effectiveness ratio (TER) of virtual reality simulation training for laparoscopic skill acquisition. Ann. Surg. **257**, 1025–1031 (2013)
17. Gutwin, C., Vicencio-Moreira, R., Mandryk, R.L.: Does helping hurt? Aiming assistance and skill development in a first-person shooter game. In: Proceedings of the 2016 Annual Symposium on Computer-Human Interaction in Play - CHI PLAY 2016, pp. 338–349. ACM Press, New York (2016)
18. Ho, J.C.F.: Effect of real-world experience on immersion in virtual reality games: a preliminary study. In: The Fourth International Symposium of Chinese CHI (2016)
19. Iacovides, I., Cox, A.L., Avakian, A., Knoll, T.: Player strategies: achieving breakthroughs and progressing in single-player and cooperative games. In: Proceedings of the First ACM SIGCHI Annual Symposium on Computer-Human Interaction in Play - CHI PLAY 2014, pp. 131–140. ACM Press, New York (2014)
20. Iacovides, I., Cox, A., Kennedy, R., Cairns, P., Jennett, C.: Removing the HUD: the impact of non-diegetic game elements and expertise on player involvement. In: Proceedings of the 2015 Annual Symposium on Computer-Human Interaction in Play - CHI PLAY 2015, pp. 13–22. ACM Press, New York (2015)
21. Jentzsch, T., Rahm, S., Seifert, B., Farei-Campagna, J., Werner, C.M.L., Bouaicha, S.: Correlation between arthroscopy simulator and video game performance: a cross-sectional study of 30 volunteers comparing 2- and 3-dimensional video games. Arthrosc. J. Arthrosc. Relat. Surg. **32**, 1328–1334 (2016)
22. Jones, H., Chollet, M., Ochs, M., Sabouret, N., Pelachaud, C.: Expressing social attitudes in virtual agents for social coaching. In: Proceedings of the 2014 International Conference on Autonomous Agents and Multi-agent Systems, pp. 1409–1410 (2014)
23. Kozlowski, S.W.J., DeShon, R.P.: A psychological fidelity approach to simulation-based training: theory, research, and principles. In: Salas, E., Elliott, L.R., Schflett, S.G., Coovert, M.D. (eds.) Scaled Worlds: Development, Validation, and Applications, pp. 75–99. Ashgate, Burlington (2004)
24. Loh, C.S., Sheng, Y., Li, I.-H.: Predicting expert–novice performance as serious games analytics with objective-oriented and navigational action sequences. Comput. Human Behav. **49**, 147–155 (2015)
25. Murias, K., Kwok, K., Castillejo, A.G., Liu, I., Iaria, G.: The effects of video game use on performance in a virtual navigation task. Comput. Hum. Behav. **58**, 398–406 (2016)
26. de Gortari, A.B.O., Aronsson, K., Griffiths, M.: Game transfer phenomena in video game playing. In: Evolving Psychological and Educational Perspectives on Cyber Behavior, pp. 170–189. IGI Global (2013)
27. Schmidt, R.A., Lee, T.D.: Motor Learning and Performance: From Principles to Application. Human Kinetics, Champaign (2014)
28. Terlecki, M., Brown, J., Harner-Steciw, L., Irvin-Hannum, J., Marchetto-Ryan, N., Ruhl, L., Wiggins, J.: Sex differences and similarities in video game experience, preferences, and self-efficacy: implications for the gaming industry. Curr. Psychol. **30**, 22–33 (2011)

Human Perception, Cognition
and Behaviour

I Smell Creativity: Exploring the Effects of Olfactory and Auditory Cues to Support Creative Writing Tasks

Frederica Gonçalves[1(⊠)], Diogo Cabral[1], Pedro Campos[1],
and Johannes Schöning[1,2]

[1] Madeira-ITI, University of Madeira, Funchal, Portugal
frederica.goncalves@m-iti.org,
diogo.cabral@staff.uma.pt, pcampos@uma.pt
[2] Human Computer Interaction, University of Bremen, Bremen, Germany
schoening@uni-bremen.de

Abstract. Humans perceive different objects, scenes or places using all their senses. Our sensory richness also plays an important role for creative activities. Humans also recall those sensory experiences in order to spark creativity, e.g. while writing a text. This paper presents a study with 100 students, divided in groups, that explores the effect of auditory and olfactory cues and their combination during a creative writing exercise. Our results provide useful insights suggesting that olfactory cues have an important role in the creative process of users and even when this type of cues are combined with auditory cues. We believe, that this type of modalities should gain more relevance on the development of creativity support tools and environments for supporting the creative writing process.

Keywords: Creativity support tools · Creativity · Olfaction · Odor · Sound · User studies · Creative writing

1 Introduction

Writing is among one of the top forms of human artistic expression [1]. Creative writing is also a central component to a range of different industries and disciplines (e.g. journalism, science fiction, advertisement, etc.) [2]. Even so the process of writing a text is often much unstructured, one can observe the following steps in a creation of a text: a writer starts with a prewriting, finishes the first draft, revises the draft, and then edits and finishes a final version of the work [1]. During this process, writers try to obtain their creativity from a very wide range of sources ranging from memories of dreams or television news reports, in a way in which they can imagine new characters or situations that can be included in their writings [3].

In our digital world 80% of our texts are created with the help of computer systems [4]. Therefore, different creativity support tools help people engage creatively with the world [5], and some researchers claim [6] that it is a challenge for human-computer interaction researchers and user interface designers to construct information technologies that support creativity. There are currently some possible solutions in creative

© IFIP International Federation for Information Processing 2017
Published by Springer International Publishing AG 2017. All Rights Reserved
R. Bernhaupt et al. (Eds.): INTERACT 2017, Part II, LNCS 10514, pp. 165–183, 2017.
DOI: 10.1007/978-3-319-67684-5_11

writing tools to foster the creativity of writers. One example, is writing prompts [7, 8] that are simple phrases meant to help writers trigger their creativity and start writing fluently without losing their time with a "writer's block", not being able to write a single line of text. Shneiderman [9] argues that there's an effort for developing creativity support tools, which enable us to explore, discover, imagine, innovate, compose and collaborate. Even with decades of creativity research, there is no single, agreed upon methodology for evaluating how well a creativity support tools to aid the creativity of its users [10]. Creative workers use artificial stimuli as inspirational guides, e.g., listening to music while writing or looking at images while drawing.

Certainly, well-designed creative writing tools can help users in generating multiple levels of creativity during the process of writing, particularly tools that can also generate different stimuli [11].

Olfactory cues are well known to have a strong emotional effect on arousal level and task on arousal level and task performance have also been suspected but not well explored in the literature [11]. Among other researchers, Seo [12] states that even though we often perceive odours in the presence of various background sounds, there is limited knowledge about the effects of background sound on odour perception. Spence [13], has studied the effect of background noise on the sensory-discriminative aspects of taste/flavour perception and on people's hedonic responses to food and beverage items. He highlights the impact of background music and/or soundscapes on food and beverage perception/consumption on people's sensory-discriminative and hedonic responses.

Therefore, this paper presents the first study on the effects of different modalities (sound and smell) on the creative writing process. The core contribution of this research is a novel between-subjects study to discover patterns in the influence of smell and sound on the participants' creativity while using a word processor in different environments. The research described below makes two supporting contributions. First, we triangulate qualitative and quantitative data from different sources to assess creativity of users in different writing conditions, giving us useful insights to develop a novel prototype for supporting the creative writing process. Second, although research on creativity has thus largely occurred within areas such as psychology and neuroscience and HCI, we believe other areas of computer science can also contribute to this domain.

2 Related Work

Researchers have investigated how to improve the creative writing *process* [14], e.g. by giving students the opportunity to interact with real readers of their work, showing that this could lead to an increased motivation to write. Advances in creative writing tools have been mostly made in very specific areas. Yannopoulos [15] proposed a symbolic language intended to express the content of films (motion pictures) much as notes provide a language for the writing of music, therefore bringing a new approach to the creative process of filmmaking. Goulet [16] focused on computer writing tools used during the production of documents in a professional setting. They report on a focus group conducted with professional writers, in which writers narrated their experiences using computer tools to write documents, describing their practices, pointing out the most important problems they encountered, and analyzing their own needs. Based on this work, they describe LinguisTech, a reference website for helping language professionals. Keeping in mind that one goal of digital tools for creative writing is to help users produce greater quantities of writing, Coughlan and Johnson [17] present three perspectives on creative interaction that have emerged from four years of empirical and design research. They argue that creative interaction can be usefully viewed in terms of *Productive Interaction* – focused engagement on the development of a creative outcome; *Structural Interaction* – the development of the structures in which production occurs; and *Longitudinal Interaction* – the long-term development of resources and relationships that increase creative potential.

Perception of Olfactory and Auditory Cues

Ho and Spence [18] investigate the differential effects of olfactory stimulation on dual-task performance under conditions of varying task difficulty. Their results provide the first empirical demonstration that olfactory stimulation can facilitate tactile performance, and highlight the potential modulatory role of task-difficulty in odour-induced task performance facilitation.

Some researchers, such as Xiang et al. [19] presented in their study a prototype system – Olfaction - that emits odour emoticons and it was applied in two contexts: online text chatting and voicemail receiving. Their results suggested that odour emoticons induced more chatting, and were easy to use, and helped participants to better perceive and convey emotions. Studies have been conducted with auditory cues in different areas such as consumer behaviours [20] and consumers' perception of food texture and quality [21].

Other studies were conducted to investigate the effect of visual cues on olfactory perception in humans [22]. Guest et al. [23], investigated whether similar auditory manipulations change people's perception of the roughness of abrasive surfaces and replicated the rubbing-hands manipulation of previous experimenters while participants rated either the perceived roughness or wetness of their hands. In these experiments, it was possible to demonstrate that auditory frequency manipulations can have an influence on the perceived tactile roughness and moistness of surfaces.

Creativity Support Tools

To properly investigate creativity, it is appropriate to adopt a variety of methods and perspectives to make it plausible and understanding. Creativity is a complex and multifaceted phenomenon [24] and includes discovery or invention of a significant idea, pattern, method, or device that gains recognition from accepted leaders in a field [25].

Over the last decades of creativity research there is no consensus on how to evaluate how well a Creativity Support Tool (CST) supports the creativity of its users [10]. As Joyce states [26] emerging computer-based tools can develop better and more creative solutions to the problems that we face in our days. Other researchers [27] considers that success during software development, despite of being a conceptually complex, knowledge intensive and cognitive activity, depends on the creativity of software engineers. Shneiderman [25] argues that it is a challenge to construct information technologies that support creativity and the goal of developing new CST can be obtained by building upon an adequate understanding of creative process. Also, the goal of CST is to develop improved software and user interfaces that make users become more productive, and more innovative [6]. Creativity and motivation enhancement can easily be aligned with the design of high-quality human-computer interaction and creativity can be viewed as any process which results in a novel and useful product, as stated by [28]. Researchers have also targeted other stimuli to support creativity, such as the visual stimuli, images and text, increase both originality and diversity of ideas during brainstorming [29–31]. Other such as Gonçalves et al. [32], studied UI Zen-based themes, composed of sound and images, foster inspiration, focus and immersion on creative writing tasks.

In the next two sections, we will describe the evaluations of the different environments, including the methods, participants, procedures and results of each. All data taken from the experiment was made completely anonymous.

3   User Study

We conducted a between-subjects experiment to investigate if olfactory or auditory cues affect peoples' creativity during a creative writing exercise. Since writing is part of everyday routine of our sample, the activity in this experiment involved writing a short story using Microsoft Word (MS Word) as the writing environment. We chose MS Word because the participants (high school students) were all familiar with.

3.1   Conditions

The writing activity was conducted under four different conditions: Neutral Environment (no cues); Smell Environment (cues alert/relax), Sound Environment (cues alert/relax) and Smell + Sound (both cues, sound/smell combined).

Neutral Environment. Our baseline (*session 1, N = 14*) without any cues.

Sound Environment. In this condition, we used two auditory cues: an alerting sound (*session 2, N = 17*) through which users might feel that they would be sitting in a cafe with the constant bustle of movement of people, machines and dishwashers, and a relaxing sound (*session 3, N = 14*), achieved using a natural soundtrack featuring water, birds and foliage.

Smell Environment. We used two types of olfactory cues: an alerting smell (*session 6, N = 12*) which was achieved by the actual fragrance of hot coffee that was spread around the room, and a relaxing smell (*session 4, N = 10*) for which we used a laurel fragrance.

Smell + Sound Environment. We used the combination of sound and smell in each condition – alert and relaxed. One group of students have smelled the real coffee and listen the sound of a café (*session 7, N = 21*), and the other group of students smelled the relaxing fragrance and listen the sound of nature (*session 5, N = 12*).

Smell Spread: To make sure that all students could smell the sense that was in the classroom, ten minutes before the session six and session seven started, we made coffee in the school's kitchen, and placed the coffee pot in the classroom, with doors and windows closed. To spread it we used a fan and small cups of coffee were placed next to each computer in case participants wanted to smell it more during the writing. In session four and session five we spread olfactory laurel fragrances using air fresheners' room spray by Air Wick[1], that remains for up to one hour and is propelled by 100% filtered air. Participants were exposed to smell during the session. Sessions of the different olfactory cues were done on different days.

Audio: To play back the audio we used two sound columns of 2×10 W output power.

Since this was a study conducted in a school environment, including students that were minors of age, a protocol was setup between parents, school and researchers regarding all the data gathered, even if anonymous, in order not to raise any privacy or security issues.

3.2   Task

Students had to write a short story about an "imaginary path on an island" [7, 33] Therefore, map[2] (Fig. 1) was handed out to all students before the activity. They were instructed to choose two points from the map, and through their own imagination and creativity they had to write a story about their path from a point A to point B. They had to initiate their writing from their own ideas. Participants were given 15 min as a time limit to complete the writing task in all conditions.

Fig. 1. Map used to trigger the writing task.

---

[1] http://www.airwick.us/products/room-sprays/.

[2] All rights reserved to Sofia Vasconcelos http://frommadeiratomars.com/pt/.

3.3 Participants

The study involved 100 students (45 female, 55 male), from the institution's population, aged between 15 and 19 years old ($M = 15.9$; $SD = 0.94$). They were recruited through the school's mailing list. All subjects were naïve to the experimental conditions. Everyone reported having a normal olfactory and auditory acuity.

3.4 Measures

We used the following measures for our experiment: Creative Behavior Inventory [34]; Flow Theory dimensions and Self-assessments; Creativity Support Index and Post-experiment interviews.

Creative Behaviour Inventory (CBI) is a psychometric tool to investigate ones past creative behaviour and activities [34]. The CBI was used to access the different creative levels of the participants. We used a subset of thirty items from the original CBI [34, 35], particularly the specific examples of creative activities such as: literature, miscellaneous, performing arts, science and music [36]. As Hocevar states [34], an item score was based on response category: zero points for never, one point for once, two points for twice, three points for 3–4 times and four points for more than five times. We classified subjects into two classes: subjects that had less than 30 points on the CBI as being *less creative*, and participants that had more than 30 points on the CBI as *highly creative* [10].

The Creativity Support Index (CSI) is a survey to assess a tool's creativity support which users provide ratings for six dimensions of creativity support: Enjoyment, Exploration, Expressiveness, Immersion, Results Worth Effort, and Collaboration [5].

We asked participants to self-rate their creativity [37], answering the question "*I consider myself a creative person*" ranking a seven-point Likert with the evidence scale for 1 (totally disagree) and 7 for (totally agree).

Another different approach to measuring creativity is the one of the Flow theory [38]. Csiksentmihalyi defines flow as "*a state in which people are so involved in an activity that nothing else seems to matter; the experience is so enjoyable that people will continue to do it even at great cost, for the sheer sake of doing it*" [38]. As the author argues, we all experience flow from time to time and we recognize its characteristics. When we are "*in the flow*" we typically feel strong, alert, in effortless control, unselfconscious, and at the peak of our abilities. Therefore, we focused on the following Flow Theory dimensions: concentration, sense of control, losing track of time, and loss of self-consciousness. These dimensions were evaluated by the participants while ranking the following 7-point Likert scale questions: "*I felt very concentrated during this task*"; "*I was able to solve this task without any problem*"; "*I lost track of time during this task*"; and "*I lost my attention during this task*".

To access participants' mental well-being, they were asked to choose up to three adjectives from the following list: Surprised, Delighted, Laid back, Depressed, Pacific, Happy, Tired, Bored, Sad, Satisfied, Frustrated, Angry, Serious, Animated, Distressed, Creative, and Frightened.

Finally, we collected qualitative data from all users with a set of questions such as: "*Did you enjoyed to write in this condition and why?*"; "*This condition gave you more immersive and emotionally engaging experience and why?"*; *"This condition felt more natural to you to write and why?"*; *"In this condition you felt more creative and why?"*; *"Did you fell more relaxed and why?"*; *"Did you fell more stressed and why?"*; *"Is there any comment that you would like to add?"*, in order to know the participant's opinion about the whole experience.

3.5 Procedure

The experiment was conducted in a classroom in the secondary high school (Fig. 2), during two weeks.

Fig. 2. Students from session 7, performing the study in the moment of the experience.

A preliminary evaluation was conducted with six participants to examine the feasibility and accuracy of the smell spread in the classroom. Three participants were in one classroom with the smell of coffee and the other three were in a classroom with the smell of laurel. For this purpose, we used a simple creative writing technique [36] that participants were presented with an image. They were asked to write a simple story during fifteen minutes. Following, participants were asked whether they could smell the odour during the writing task. The smell was already spread into the classroom as previously mentioned (*see 3.1 Conditions, Smell Spread*). Since participants reported that they smelled the odour, it was considered that the study may be conducted according the procedure.

In the main experiment, participants were brought to the classroom (Fig. 2), previously prepared for it. The experiment was conducted in a classroom equipped with computers on desks, and the time requirement for each session, including pre-questionnaire, instructions, experiment and debriefing took over an hour.

When participants entered the classroom, they delivered the document with the experiment protocol and the authorization to participate, which was previous delivered to them. Before starting each session, it was asked if the smell bothered any of the participants. First, participants were requested to fill the Creative Behaviour Inventory [31], and to self-rate their creativity [33]. After filling the inventory, the writing task was explained. Then, when they finished the writing task, they had to fill the Creativity Support Index [3], together with the very short survey based on Flow Theory [35] and to select up to three adjectives from the list that was mentioned before. Lastly, we interviewed them.

4   Results

To inquire the impact of olfactory and auditory cues on user's apparent and experienced creativity, we triangulated different data sources, such as behavioural data, users' verbal accounts during task execution, self-reports using psychometric scales of creativity and data from our exit interviews. We will refer to the creative writing conditions previously presented and shown in Table 1.

Table 1. Description of the creative writing conditions used.

Creative writing condition	Session	N
Baseline	Base	14
Sound alert	SA	14
Sound relax	SR	17
Smell relax	SmR	10
Smell + Sound relax	SmSR	12
Smell alert	SmA	12
Smell + Sound alert	SmSA	21

Are Our Samples Equally Creative?
Participants self-rated their creativity ($M = 4.85$; $SD = 1.17$) in a seven-point Likert Scale before starting the experience. Results are shown in Tables 2 and 3.

Table 2. Frequency and percentages *"I consider myself a creative person"*.

Seven-point Likert scale	Frequency	Percent
1	0	0%
2	0	0%
3	11	11%
4	31	31%
5	32	32%
6	14	14%
7	12	12%
Total	100	100%

Table 3. Descriptive of self-assessment about creativity in each creative writing conditions.

Sessions	Base	SA	SR	SmR	SmSR	SmA	SmSA
Mean	4.36	4.71	5.06	5.00	5.17	4.67	4.95
St. deviation	.84	1.38	1.19	1.49	1.03	.88	1.24
Std. error	.225	.370	.290	.471	.297	.256	.271
Minimum	3	3	3	3	3	3	3
Maximum	6	7	7	7	7	6	7

A chi-square test of independence was performed to examine the relation between students in each condition and their self-assessment of creativity. The relation between these variables was not significant, $X (24) = 17.992$, $p = .803$. Therefore, there is no statistically significant association between participants and their self-assessment of creativity, i.e., students consider themselves creative persons.

Through Cronbach's alpha, the CBI inventory was found to be highly reliable (30 items; $\alpha = .84$). Regardless of the self-report scale in the 30-item CBI that could capture a creative accomplishments and activities in past behaviours, our results suggest in terms of past creative actions that 42 students had more than 30 points on the CBI (*"highly creative"*) and 58 students had less than 30 points on the CBI (*"less creative"*). We compared the gender of the subjects with their creative level of the self-report scale in CBI to see if there were any difference between genders. On average, female participants reported greater creativity in past activities ($M = 30.78$; $SD = 16.40$) than male participants ($M = 25.86$; $SD = 14.99$). This difference was not statistically significant ($t (98) = 1.57, p > .05$). However, it did represent a small-sized effect $r = .13$.

We also compared the subjects in each condition (*session 1 to session 7*) and their creative level of the self-report scale in CBI. Some descriptive statistics are shown in Table 4.

Table 4. Average (SD) from CBI in each creative writing condition.

Sessions	Base	SA	SR	SmR	SmSR	SmA	SmSA
M (SD)	20.64 (12.73)	20.01 (14.93)	23.71 (9.50)	38.20 (15.55)	35.58 (14.40)	33.83 (23.26)	29.48 (13.38)

A chi-square test of independence was performed to examine the relation between the participants in each condition and their results in CBI (creativity in past activities). The relation between these variables was not significant, $X (288) = 296.04$, $p = .360$. Therefore, there is no statistically significant association between participants and their creativity and all groups were equally creative in past activities.

Did Olfactory or Auditory Cues Lead to Increased Flow?

To access the participants' mental well-being, we asked them to select up to three adjectives from the following list: Surprised, Delighted, Laid back, Depressed, Pacific,

Happy, Tired, Bored, Sad, Satisfied, Frustrated, Angry, Serious, Animated, Distressed, Creative and Frightened. Table 5 displays the percentages for each adjective, as selected by the participants on each creative writing environment.

We can see in Table 5 that Animated, Relaxed, Satisfied, Creative and Pacific were the most chosen adjectives.

A chi-square test of independence was performed to examine the relation between students and the adjectives selected in each creative writing condition. The relation between these variables was only significant for the adjective "Tired", X (6) = 20.490, p = .002. By looking at the data represented in Table 5, we can conclude that there is a statistically significant association between participants and their state of mental well-being in session one (baseline), session six (smell alert) and session seven (smell + sound relax); suggesting that students felt somehow tired in these sessions.

Table 5. Results in percentages for the adjectives chosen by participants in each creative writing condition.

Adjectives/Sessions	Base	SA	SR	SmR	SmSR	SmA	SmSA
Distressed	-	7.1	-	-	-	-	9.5
Animated	35.7	28.6	52.9	40.0	33.3	50.0	23.8
Satisfied	57.1	35.7	17.6	30.0	58.3	33.3	23.8
Bored	7.1	7.1	5.9	-	-	-	4.8
Pacific	21.4	21.4	52.9	20.0	50.0	33.3	14.3
Relaxed	78.6	64.3	52.9	60.0	75.0	66.7	52.4
Creative	57.1	57.1	70.6	40.0	75.0	83.3	57.1
Astonished	21.4	7.1	17.6	-	8.3	8.3	23.8
Serious	14.3	14.3	23.5	-	-	-	14.3
Fear	-	7.1	-	-	-	-	-
Frustrated	-	14.3	-	10.0	-	8.3	19
Happy	28.6	-	29.4	20.0	16.7	8.3	28.6
Delighted	14.3	-	-	-	-	8.3	4.8
Tired	7.1	-	–	-	-	8.3	33.3
Angry	-	-	10.0	-	-	-	-
Sad	-	-	10.0	-	-	-	-
Depressed	-	-	10.0	-	-	-	-
Total	N = 14	N = 14	N = 17	N = 10	N = 12	N = 12	N = 21

Thus, when we asked about how they felt in the writing task, participants reported similar thoughts to the creative writing conditions in this case, e.g., "*I did not have much creativity, so I felt tired of writing.*" [baseline, P12]; "*I got tired of writing and imagining the end of the story I was writing (...)*" [smell + sound relax, P10]; "*I did not feel like writing and I had no ideas to write.*" [smell alert, P2].

Some statistical results are shown in Table 6, to test differences between each creative writing environment from the answers in the survey based on Flow Theory [35] dimensions and ranked by participants in a seven-point Likert scale.

Table 6. Average (SD) for Flow Dimensions in each creative writing condition.

Sessions	Base	SA	SR	SmR	SmSR	SmA	SmSA
(i) Concentration	4.64 (1.82)	5.50 (1.74)	4.47 (1.80)	4.00 (1.25)	5.25 (1.29)	5.25 (1.95)	5.00 (1.81)
(ii) Sense of control	5.00 (1.75)	5.42 (1.60)	5.11 (1.69)	4.90 (1.85)	5.91 (.99)	5.17 (1.67)	4.90 (1.73)
(iii) Loss of self-consciousness	5.79 (1.37)	5.78 (1.93)	4.65 (2.19)	4.60 (1.89)	5.00 (1.70)	4.50 (2.28)	5.38 (1.69)
(iv) Lost track of time	3.79 (2.08)	2.71 (2.27)	3.35 (2.06)	3.50 (1.84)	2.41 (1.68)	2.67 (2.23)	3.47 (2.16)

A Skewness and Kurtosis and Kolmogorov-Smirnov test did not show a normal distribution of Flow Dimensions scores in each creative writing condition and, therefore, non-parametric tests were conducted. A Kruskal-Wallis test, showed that there was not a statistically significant difference in Concentration levels of participants' between the different creative writing conditions, H (6) = 8.36, p = .213 with a mean rank Concentration score of 46.21 for session 1 (baseline), 61.71 for session 2 (sound alert), 43.74 for session 3 (sound relax), 33.20 for session 4 (smell relax), 54.96 for session 5 (smell + sound relax), 57.88 for session 6 (smell alert) and 52.83 for session 7 (smell + sound alert). The Sense of Control level of participants was not significantly affected by the different sessions, H (6) = 3.192, p = .784 as well as the levels of Loss of Self-Consciousness, H (6) = 7.724, p = .259 and the levels of Lost of Track Time, H (6) = 6.391, p = .381.

Yet, by looking at the Table 6, one can see that the *Lost Track of Time* dimension was not a significant issue for any of the environments we evaluated. The *Sense of Control, Loss of self-consciousness*, and *Concentration* dimensions, results were most consistent in all environments.

Qualitative data revealed that students in the Smell + Sound Environment (33.3%) felt more stressed and others claim that the noise interfered with their concentration. 7.1% of the users in the Neutral Environment felt stressed because they knew they were contributing to a study. In the Sound Environment 12.9% of the users felt more stressed as 18.8% in the Smell Environment. Participants in these environments felt pressure to write under a limited time, but both the smell of the coffee and the laurel relaxed them, and the same for the sound cues. For instance, e.g., "*I felt stressed about knowing that I am contributing to an investigation.*" [baseline, P10]; "*Yes, I felt stressed, because I had a time limit to finish.*" [sound relax, P13]; "*Yes, the fact of having a time limit left me stressed, but it did not stop me from expanding my imagination.*" [sound alert, P14]; "*Yes a lot of pressure to write, however the smell of coffee allowed me to abstract a little.*" [smell alert, P2].

Did Olfactory or Auditory Cues Lead to Increased Output?

Regarding the stories written and the data dispersion, results showed (Table 7) that the participants in the session 4 (smell relax) wrote an average of 412.6 words ($SD = 97.3$), which contrasts with other creative writing conditions.

Table 7. Average (SD) for words written in each creative writing condition.

Sessions	Base	SA	SR	SmR	SmSR	SmA	SmSA
Words written	267.0 (132.1)	246.0 (90.23)	269.5 (105.7)	412.6 (97.3)	270.1 (90.0)	213.8 (79.7)	300.7 (79.6)

A Skewness and Kurtosis and Kolmogorov-Smirnov test did not show a normal distribution of words written in each creative writing condition and, therefore, non-parametric tests were conducted. A Kruskal-Wallis test, showed that there was a statistically significant difference between the words written by the participants' and the different creative writing conditions, H (6) = 20.449, p = .002. Mann-Whitney tests were used to follow up this finding with a correction at a .0083 level of significance, but we did not find statistically differences between sessions.

Did Olfactory or Auditory Cues Lead to Increased CSI?

We used the CSI [3] as a way of evaluating how well each environment (neutral, smell, sound or smell + sound) supported the creativity of the participants. 100 students generated an average overall CSI score as shown in Table 8 for creative writing task in each environment. Tables 9, 10 and 11 show the average factor counts, average factor score, and average weighted factor score for each of the six factors on the CSI in each environment session.

Table 8. Overall CSI score in each condition: average (SD).

Sessions	Base	SA	SR	SmR	SmSR	SmA	SmSA
Overall CSI score	54.43 (15.77)	71.03 (21.09)	58.49 (18.88)	51.37 (17.30)	77.60 (15.97)	74.03 (14.92)	51.73 (21.89)

The Shapiro-Wilk test did not show a normal distribution of CSI scores and, therefore, non-parametric tests were conducted. The Kruskal-Wallis test showed that there was a statistically significant difference in CSI scores between the different creative writing conditions, H (6) = 24.046, p = .01 with a mean rank CSI score 39.21 for Base (baseline), 60.71 for SA (sound alert), 45.29 for SR (sound relax), 37.50 for SmR (smell relax), 73.42 for SmSR (smell + sound relax), 70.46 for SmA (smell alert) and 37.12 for SmSA (smell + sound alert). Mann-Whitney tests were used to follow up this finding. A correction was applied and so all effects are reported at a .0024 level of significance.

CSI scores in SA (Mdn = 50.17) differ significantly from CSI scores in SmSR (Mdn = 81.33), U = 25.5, p = .002, r = −.59.

Table 9. CSI avg. factor counts (SD): sum of results of two questions by factor.

Sessions	Base	SA	SR	SmR	SmSR	SmA	SmSA
Results worth effort	11.29 (2.76)	14.50 (5.27)	11.88 (4.40)	9.70 (4.92)	17.00 (2.31)	15.50 (3.24)	12.14 (5.00)
Exploration	10.71 (2.43)	13.40 (5.27)	11.47 (3.79)	10.50 (3.60)	15.10 (3.78)	13.60 (3.41)	10.86 (4.29)
Enjoyment	10.36 (4.57)	14.70 (4.45)	12.06 (4.58)	9.80 (4.78)	15.30 (3.97)	15.30 (4.16)	6.38 (5.69)
Expressiveness	9.64 (4.67)	12.90 (5.32)	11.35 (4.34)	10.90 (4.25)	15.30 (3.13)	13.70 (3.23)	11.43 (4.61)
Immersion	11.86 (5.67)	17.30 (3.06)	11.35 (3.89)	8.80 (3.68)	15.40 (4.50)	16.70 (4.16)	11.19 (6.03)
Collaboration	11.57 (3.34)	14.50 (5.42)	12.18 (4.23)	10.50 (3.60)	13.90 (5.02)	14.20 (3.33)	7.43 (4.23)

Table 10. Avg. factor score (SD).

Sessions	Base	SA	SR	SmR	SmSR	SmA	SmSA
Results worth effort	2.14 (1.10)	2.40 (1.43)	1.94 (1.20)	2.70 (1.34)	2.40 (1.26)	2.60 (1.35)	2.24 (1.30)
Exploration	3.36 (1.15)	3.50 (1.08)	3.47 (1.46)	2.80 (0.92)	3.50 (1.08)	3.30 (1.16)	3.29 (1.15)
Enjoyment	2.00 (1.47)	1.10 (0.99)	2.18 (1.33)	2.30 (1.42)	2.20 (1.23)	1.10 (1.45)	1.71 (1.71)
Expressiveness	3.57 (1.60)	4.50 (0.53)	3.65 (1.22)	3.80 (1.14)	2.90 (1.66)	3.70 (1.25)	3.43 (1.57)
Immersion	1.71 (1.49)	2.40 (1.17)	2.18 (1.01)	2.00 (1.56)	2.20 (1.48)	2.40 (1.43)	2.90 (1.22)
Collaboration	2.21 (1.89)	1.10 (1.66)	1.59 (1.62)	1.40 (1.35)	1.80 (1.23)	1.90 (1.79)	1.43 (1.63)

Table 11. Avg. weighted (SD).

Sessions	Base	SA	SR	SmR	SmSR	SmA	SmSA
Results worth effort	24.71 (14.96)	31.00 (15.61)	25.00 (21.95)	28.80 (22.58)	42.00 (23.72)	40.10 (25.31)	28.81 (19.18)
Exploration	35.71 (14.35)	45.50 (22.42)	40.59 (20.77)	28.00 (10.91)	52.60 (22.10)	45.90 (21.88)	36.71 (19.23)
Enjoyment	21.21 (20.36)	16.50 (18.45)	25.94 (15.95)	25.10 (17.43)	36.20 (27.60)	18.60 (26.50)	10.33 (15.63)
Expressiveness	35.29 (25.16)	58.90 (26.27)	43.65 (27.73)	40.20 (20.33)	43.90 (25.99)	49.50 (18.85)	40.10 (24.17)
Immersion	19.43 (17.91)	43.20 (25.02)	25.24 (15.76)	18.60 (21.13)	33.00 (25.96)	39.70 (27.23)	32.29 (22.27)
Collaboration	26.93 (23.07)	18.00 (31.45)	15.06 (13.81)	13.40 (14.52)	25.10 (19.89)	28.30 (26.60)	8.95 (11.42)

There was a statistically significant difference in CSI scores from students in SmR (*Mdn* = 54.33) and SmSR (*Mdn* = 81.33) U = 12.0, p = .001, r = −.67. Also, CSI scores from SmR differ significantly from SmA (*Mdn* = 77.17), U = 12.0, p = .001, r = −.67.

CSI scores in SmSR (*Mdn* = 81.33) were statistically different from CSI scores in SmSA (*Mdn* = 50.33), U = 41.5, p = .001, r = −.55.

Finally, CSI scores in SmA (*Mdn* = 77.17), when compared with CSI scores in SmSA (*Mdn* = 50.33), U = 42.5, p = .001, r = −.55.

From the results, we can conclude that the combination of olfactory cues with auditory cues can significantly affect the level of support to the creative process of a digital creativity support tool, when compared to a condition that does not use any cue (olfactory or auditory). This holds true whether the cues are alerting or relaxing. Also, this is verified when there are only smell cues (alert or relax) in the creative writing task. However, when using only auditory cues, the results do not show any evidence of increased creative process support.

Triangulating the results with semi-structured interviews allowed us to support some of these results and observations. Students were curious to know what the writing task was, since none of the users had ever taken an experiment such as this one. In general, we observed that the participants were concentrated on the writing moment. It was clear that all participants felt somewhat creative during the experiment.

In the semi-structured interview, participants showed mixed feelings about how they felt creative in the creative writing conditions. 50% of students consider that they did feel more creative in the Neutral environment, 54.8% in the Sound Environment and 63.6% in the Smell + Sound Environment. 72.7% of the students in the Smell Environment considered themselves more creative in this creative writing condition.

90.9% of the participants enjoyed to write in the Smell Environment, expressing reasons such as: "*It made me relax, without any pressure.*" [smell_relax_P2]; "*(...) because we were very excited and happy*" [smell_relax_P5]; "*(...) because I think it helps to have more ideas*" [smell_relax_P5]; "*It was interesting - at first I was anguished and then more relaxed.*" [smell_relax_P10]; "*it made me want to work.*" [smell_relax_P7]; "*it allowed me to get immersed in the activity and be very creative. Although I did not have enough time to finish my story, I managed to create a creative and funny story, while not respecting some rules of grammar.*" [smell_alert_P9]; "*as the smell of coffee is comforting and makes it easier to express my ideas.*" [smell_a-lert_P7]; "*(...) because it allows a better flow of writing.*" [smell_alert_P3]; "*I think that it stimulated my creativity, imposing it on the work*" [smell_alert_P8].

In the Neutral Environment 57.1% of participants enjoyed writing in this environment as much as the 57.6% users in the Smell + Sound Environment. 77.4% of students enjoyed to write in the Sound Environment, expressing "*(...) because I felt completely oblivious of what was happening around me and I was just concentrated on what I had to do.*" [sound_relax_P11]; "*I was so focused writing that did not even notice the sounds around me.*" [sound_relax_P12]; "*music gives a good environment for writing and is relaxing.*" [sound_alert_P9]; "*(...) music has stimulated my creativity in writing*" [sound_alert_P3];

During the experience, we noted that participants were anxious and curious to know what they were supposed to do. In a qualitative way, we also observed them focused and in absolute concentration during the writing task in all conditions. According to the interviews, some participants were deeply involved in the creative writing task.

5   Discussion

This study aimed to explore which modalities, olfactory or auditory, were stronger triggers for creativity.

We identify that most of the students considered themselves creative persons, even though more than half of them were not usually engaged with creative activities, as reported by the CBI. These results indicate that the study was not biased by a highly critical self-assessment.

As stated by Csikszentmihalyi [35], every flow activity, whether they involved competition or any dimension of experience, had in common the sense of discovery, the creative feeling of transporting the person into a new reality. By giving a "writing challenge" we observed that students were immersed in the writing moment, and after they finished the activity, they felt creative, animated, relaxed and peaceful. This was especially evident during the smell and sound cues and during the combination of both (the smell + sound environment). From observation, in the Neutral Environment students were feeling more apathetic and they made more pauses in writing during the timeout. Although, through statistically analysis, we did not find significant results from the Flow Theory dimensions, from our qualitative data we noticed that sound cues could lead to lower levels of concentration. In addition, we noticed that they felt a little pressure towards writing with a time limitation, and this was probably the reason for the inexistence of substantial results in the Flow dimensions.

Triangulating the qualitative data from semi-structured interviews and results, indicates that 72.7% of students said they felt more creative in the Smell Environment, in contrast to other conditions that had higher values (50% in Neutral, 54.8% in Sound and 63.6% in Smell + Sound Environment) as well as that 90.9% of students enjoyed writing in the Smell environment and 77.4% in the Sound environment.

CSI did show significant difference through statistical analysis, confirming the benefit of olfactory and sound stimuli during a writing task. It is also important to observe a decay on the CSI value for the combination of Alert smell + sound when compared to the single conditions (only smell or sound), suggesting that such combination overwhelmed the participants. Such disturbance is confirmed by the qualitative data results.

The different results from our study show a strong influence of smell and sound cues during a creative writing task and with a highlight on olfactory cues. Therefore, answering our main research question *"Which modality, olfactory or auditory, sparks stronger triggers for creativity?"*. Such results become more relevant if we consider that previous research did not show any significant effect of odours on performance, as stated by Ho and Spence [17].

Our study suggests that olfactory cues should gain more relevance on the development of creativity support tools and environments. Novel smell dispensers [39] and their integration on current portable media devices as well as the olfactory augmentation of multisensory work environments could improve and foster creative tasks but their combination with other stimuli must be designed carefully to avoid disturbance.

6 Conclusion

Creative writing is a constant activity in many sectors and professions in the modern world. Because of today's diversity of possible technological ways to write, designing a creative writing user interface is hard work. Sometimes it is difficult to find a tool that keeps users focused whilst eliminating some of the hard work. In this paper, we presented a study that addresses the use of different modalities such as smell and sound on the creative writing process of users to enhance creativity.

In the between-subject study, we tested the influence of smell and sound on the participant's creativity in a writing task measured by the Creativity Support Index. We have created two types of auditory and olfactory cues each: an alerting smell was created using the actual fragrance of hot coffee that was spread around the room in small cups. Regarding the alerting sound, users might feel that they would be sitting in a cafe with the constant bustle of movement of people, machines and dishwashers. As for a relaxing scent, we used the fragrance of laurel, and the sound mode used was a natural soundtrack with water, birds and foliage.

We investigated which cue could promote higher levels of creativity and mental well-being – as measured by a survey based on the dimensions of Flow Theory.

We compared four different environments (neutral, smell, sound and smell + sound) using MS Word as a word processor. From a creative perspective, and triangulating qualitative and the statistical results, it is suggested that users considered to feel more expressive and more creative during the writing task, especially in the Smell Environment.

We found out that participants considered that the smell allowed them more creative times, thus being one of the decisive factors to abstract and to become concentrated. Our results provide interesting information regarding the smell and sound cues modalities. At the same time, for the combination of smell and sound in each category, in semi-structured interviews participants gave emphasis to these conditions in the creative moment of the writing task.

A significant problem faced by interaction designers that are involved in multi-sensory interaction is the timing of each multisensory interaction (*when* to apply the multisensory stimulus). Writing prompts – among other techniques such as using images like a map – are sometimes used to kick start the creative process, when writing. In this research, we highlight the value of smell and sound cues as an alternative, more powerful means to kick-start that same process more effectively.

There are many aspects of this study that remain open for future investigation such as our results about creativity combined with different modalities. Measuring creativity is an important approach that will lead us to different impacts of specific creative writing tools. These tools can have features to increase the creativity of writers and contribute to unblock writer's block. In future work, we think it is important to intensify the research on designing user interfaces that support creative writing and build novel tools that can be used by several people.

Acknowledgments. We would like to thank the students who participated in this research, as well as the teachers and the institutional support from Escola da APEL. This work was partially funded by ARDITI - Regional Agency for the Development of Research Technology and Innovation through the M14-20 Project - 09-5369-FSE-000001- PhD Scholarship, by FCT/MCTES LARSyS (UID/EEA/50009/2013 (2015–2017)), by IDE (ProCiência), SENSE-SEAT, through the M1420-01-0247-FEDER-000001 and by ERA Chair: Grant Agreement 621413.

References

1. Kroll, J., Harper, G.: Research Methods in Creative Writing. Palgrave Macmillan, Basingstoke (2013)
2. Morley, D.: The Cambridge Introduction to Creative Writing. Cambridge University Press, Cambridge (2007)
3. Myers, D.G.: The Elephants Teach: Creative Writing since 1880. University of Chicago Press, Chicago (2006)
4. Wang, D.: How people write together now: exploring and supporting today's computer-supported collaborative writing. In: CSCW 2016, Proceedings of the 19th ACM Conference on Computer Supported Cooperative Work and Social Computing Companion, San Francisco, California, USA (2016)
5. Cherry, E., Latulipe, C.: Quantifying the creative support of digital tools through the creativity support index. ACM Trans. Comput.-Hum. Interact. **21**(4), Article 21 (2014)
6. Shneiderman, B.: Creating creativity: user interfaces for supporting innovation, ACM Trans. Comput.-Hum. Interact. **7**(1), 114–138 (2000)
7. Digest, W.: The Writer's Guide to Creativity. F+W Media Inc., Blue Ash (2011)
8. Kroll, J.H.G.: Research Methods in Creative Writing. Palgrave Macmillan, Basingstoke (2013)
9. Shneiderman, B.: Leonardo's laptop: Human Needs and the New Computing Technologies. MIT Press, Cambridge (2002)
10. Carrol, E., Latulipe, C.: Triangulating the personal creative experience: self-report, external judments and physiology. In: Proceedings the Graphics Interface 2012 (GI 2012). Canadian Information Processing Society, Toronto, Ont. Canada, pp. 53–60, (2012)
11. Millot, J., Brand, G., Morand, N.: Effects of ambient odors on reaction time in humans. Neurosci **322**(2), 79–82 (2002)
12. Seo, H., Gudziol, V., Hähner, A., Hummel, T.: Background sound modulates the performance of odor discrimination task. Exp Brain Res. **212**(2) (2011)
13. Spence, C.: Auditory contributions to flavour perception and feeding behaviour. Elsevier Physiol. Behav. **107**(4), 505–515 (2012)
14. Magnifico, A.M.: Getting other's perspectives: a case study of creative writing environments and mentorship. In: Proceedings of the 9th Internacional Conference of the Learning Sciences (ICLS 2010), vol. 1, pp. 1151–1157 (2010)
15. Yannopoulos, A.: DirectorNotation: artistic and technological system for professional film directing. J. Comput. Cult. Herit. **6**(1), Article 2 (2013)

16. Goulet, M.D.A.: Focus group on computer tools used for professional writing and preliminary evaluation of LinguisTech. In: Proceedings of the Second Workshop on Computational Linguistics and Writing (CLW 2012): Linguistic and Cognitive Aspects of Document Creation and Document Engineering (EACL 2012), Stroudsburg, PA, USA, Linguistics, Association for Computational, pp. 39–47 (2012)

17. Coughlan, T., Johnson, P.: Understanding productive, structural and longitudinal interactions in the design of tools for creative activities. In: Proceedings of the Seventh ACM Conference on Creativity and Cognition (C&C 2009), pp. 155–164, ACM, New York, NY, USA (2009)

18. Ho, C., Spence, C.: Olfactory facilitation of dual-task performance, Neuroscience Letters, Elsevier (2005)

19. Xiang, W., Chen, S., Sun, L., Cheng, S., Bove, V.: Odor emoticon, Int. J. Hum.-Comput. Stud. 52–61 (2016)

20. Zampini, M., Spence, C.: The role of auditory cues in modulating the perceived crispness and staleness of potato chips, J. Sens. Stud. 347–363 (2005)

21. Seo, H., Hummel, T.: Influence of auditory cues on chemosensory perception. In: The Chemical Sensory Informatics of Food: Measurement, Analysis, Integration, American Chemical Society, pp. 41–56 (2015)

22. Demattè, L., Sanabria, D., Spence, C.: Olfactory discrimination: when vision matters? Chem. Senses **34**, 103–109 (2009)

23. Guest, S., Catmur, C., Lloyd, D., Spence, C.: Audiotactile interactions in roughness perception. Exp. Brain Res. **146**, 161–171 (2002)

24. Ward, T.: Creative cognition as a window on creativity. Elsevier Sci. Dir. Methods **42**(2007), 28–37 (2006)

25. Shneiderman, B.: Accelerating discovery and innovation. Commun. ACM **50**, 12 (2007)

26. Elam, J.J., Mead, M.: Can Software Influence Creativity? Inf. Syst. Res. 1–22 (1990)

27. Hegde, R., Walia, G.: How to Enhance the Creativity of Software. In: Proceedings of the 26th IEEE International Conference on Software Engineering and Knowledge Engineering, Vancouver, Canada (2014)

28. Selker, T.: Fostering motivation and creativity for computer users. Int. J. Hum.-Comput. Stud. **63**(4–5), 410–421 (2005)

29. Wang, H., Fussell, S., Cosley, D.: From diversity to creativity: Stimulating group brainstorming with cultural differences and conversationally-retrieved pictures. In: Proceedings of CSCW. ACM (2011)

30. Andolina, S., Klouche, K., Cabral, D., Ruotsalo, T., Jacucci, G.: InspirationWall: supporting idea generation through automatic information exploration. In: Proceedings of the 2015 ACM SIGCHI Conference on Creativity and Cognition (C&C 2015), New York, USA (2015)

31. Guzman, L., Kannan, N., Mendonza, K., Buenafe, S., Nunes, N., Nisi, V., Campos, P., Gonçalves, F., Campos, M., Freitas, P.: Yarn: a Product for Unraveling Stories. In: NordiCHI 2014 Industrial Program, Helsinki (2014)

32. Gonçalves, F., Campos, P., Hanna, J., Ashby, S.: You're the voice: evaluating user interfaces for encouraging underserved youths to express themselves through creative writing. In: C&C 2015 Proceedings of the 2015 ACM SIGCHI Conference on Creativity and Cognition, New York, USA (2015)

33. Writers Digest: http://www.writersdigest.com/qp7-migration-books/writing-better-lyrics-excerpt

34. Hocevar, D.: The Development of the Creative Behavior Inventory. In: Annual Meeting of the Rocky Mountain Psychological Association (1979)

35. Hocevar, D.: Measurement of creativity: review and critique. J. Pers. Assess. **45**(5), 450–463 (1981)
36. Silvia, P., Wigert, B., Reiter-Palmon, R., Kaufman, J.: Assessing Creativity With Self-Report Scales: A Review and Empirical Evaluation, Psychology Faculty Publications (2012)
37. Wiseman, R., Watt, C., Gilhooly, K.: Creativity and ease of ambiguous figural reversal. Br. J. Psychol. **102**, 615–622 (2011)
38. Csikszentmihalyi, M.: Flow: The Psychologic of Optimal Experience. Harper Perennial, New York (1991)
39. Amores, J., Maes, P.: Essence: olfactory interfaces for unconscious influence of mood and cognitive performance. In: Proceedings of the 2017 CHI Conference on Human Factors in Computing Systems, Denver, CO, USA (2017)

Night Mode, Dark Thoughts: Background Color Influences the Perceived Sentiment of Chat Messages

Diana Löffler[⊠], Lennart Giron, and Jörn Hurtienne

University of Würzburg, Würzburg, Germany
{diana.loeffler, joern.hurtienne}@uni-wuerzburg.de,
lenn.geh@gmail.com

Abstract. The discussion of color in HCI often remains restricted to issues of legibility, aesthetics or color preferences. Little attention has been given to the emotional and semantic effects of color on digital content. At the example of black and white, this paper reviews previous studies in psychology and reports an experiment that investigates the influence of black, white and gray user interface backgrounds on the perception of sentiment in chat messages on a social media platform (*Twitch.tv*). Of sixty-seven participants, those who rated the messages against a black background perceived them more negatively than those who worked against a white background. The results suggest that user sentiment perception can be influenced by interface color, especially for ambiguous textual content laced with irony and sarcasm. We claim that this knowledge can be applied in persuasive interaction and user experience design across the entirety of the digital landscape.

Keywords: Color · Affective bias · Sentiment analysis · User interface design · Online chat · Embodiment · Conceptual metaphor theory · Persuasive computing

1 Introduction

Dark themed user interfaces, night mode, low-power state - light and darkness are fundamental experiences in our very (digital) lives, both literally and metaphorically. As diurnal animals, humans are active at daytime, when their visual sense works best, and inactive during the night. Unsurprisingly, *black* and *white* are the first basic color terms that enter languages around the globe [5]. Interestingly, black and white also carry evaluative and affective metaphorical meaning. We talk about a *black cat* crossing one's path as a sign of bad luck. A *black sheep* represents a bad entity in an otherwise respectable group, while *blackmail* carries malicious intent. When we ask someone to *keep it dark*, we ask for his or her confidentiality. Across many cultures, the color *black* has unpleasant connotations, involving death, evil, the void, and secrecy. On the contrary, *white* is associated with innocence, benevolence, purity and the divine: A *white lie* is harmless or even beneficial in the long run. A *bright future* conveys hope, and a *bright*

© IFIP International Federation for Information Processing 2017
Published by Springer International Publishing AG 2017. All Rights Reserved
R. Bernhaupt et al. (Eds.): INTERACT 2017, Part II, LNCS 10514, pp. 184–201, 2017.
DOI: 10.1007/978-3-319-67684-5_12

girl is clever. Expressions of *white* and *black* relating to good and evil persist across an overwhelming majority of communities and cultures. Also, it has been shown that such metaphorical expressions are not mere figures of speech but instead reflect the underlying mental models of the speaker. As stated in Conceptual Metaphor Theory, many linguistic metaphors indicate how we think about the concepts linked by the process of metaphor [33, 34], and this approach can be applied to color psychology [36].

The dichotomous nature of *black* and *white* as opposites lends itself to facilitate the mental model of more abstract concepts like valence or morality, and has received support in cognitive linguistics as well as by empirical studies in the social sciences. For example, basic research in psychology demonstrated that the perception of *bright* vs. *dark* font color has an impact on the semantic categorization of affectively valenced word content. With 980 participants, diverse in terms of race, age, and geographical location, Meier and colleagues showed that response times in a two-alternative forced choice task are facilitated when word valence metaphorically matched font color (i.e., a positive word written in *white* font color) compared to when they did not match (i.e., a positive word written in black font color) [38].

Naturally, we also rely on color information when making inferences about digital information. As the personal computer is foremost a visual medium, the same effects may be replicable in the context of Human-Computer Interaction (HCI). Digital content is primarily conveyed via text, images, and video, all of which are realized by displaying contrast and color gradients to transmit information. Thus, HCI systems are inherently prone to subjecting users to cognitive biases caused by the perception and subconscious processing of black and white. So far, however, design recommendations involving color are almost exclusively restricted to issues of legibility, aesthetics or color preferences [37]. Comparably little attention has been given as to how it affects us emotionally and how it might influence the semantic interpretation of digital content and even interpersonal exchange [36].

To this extent, digitally mediated human communication is an intriguing area. Contrary to face-to-face communication, the clear majority of exchange in social media is conducted via textual messaging, stripped of many nonverbal signals, thereby increasing the ambiguity of the content. Messages with room for interpretation are particularly susceptible to incidental environmental cues [44]. The influence of black and white effects could have a significant impact on the judgment and interpretation of unclear, ironic or sarcastic messages. Digital chat rooms involving two or more users, a format still widely used and more prevalent than ever[1], bear potential for cognitive biases, as they require the users to engage from remote terminals with varying form factors and environmental conditions. This imposes the question if heterogeneous chat interfaces provide different messaging environments to such an extent that contents may be interpreted divergently on a semantic and affective level.

---

[1] (2017, January). Most popular mobile messaging apps worldwide as of April 2016, based on number of monthly active users (in millions), retrieved from https://www.statista.com/statistics/258749/most-popular-global-mobile-messengerapps/.

2 Related Work

2.1 Basic Research in Psychology on Affective Biases Related to Black and White

Much work has been done in perception psychology to investigate fundamental effects and biases when processing visual information of varying monochrome contrasts. For instance, Chiou and Cheng [11] employed an altered version of the classical Stroop-task [46] to study subconscious moral connotations of perceived font color (black vs. white). In the Stroop-task, participants are asked to name the font color of a task-irrelevant but color-relevant word. The closer the semantic relationship between word and font color, the higher the observed interference effect [27]. Chiou and Cheng found that the reaction time for color naming was faster when words related to immorality (rather than morality) were written in *black* (e.g. "malevolence"), and when words related to morality (rather than immorality) were written in *white*. This shows that although the semantic content of the to-be-classified words was irrelevant for the task, subjects nevertheless processed it and word meaning interacted with the primary task of font color categorization.

Similar effects could also be shown in other experimental setups. For example, when subjects are exposed to different levels of environmental illumination, the salience of moral considerations and the likelihood of engaging in ethical behavior is increased when the level of illumination is increased [11]. These results suggest that brightness might increase the mental accessibility of ethical behaviors. This affective bias induced by the perception of brightness could also be replicated in the context of purely visual information. Lakens, Fockenberg, Lemmens, Ham and Midden fairly recently discovered that brightness heavily influences the cognitive and emotional evaluation of affective pictures [31]. Over the course of multiple experimental setups, brighter pictures were evaluated more positively, whereas darker pictures received more negative judgment. Therefore, the perception of brightness seems to bias affective and moral interpretation, regardless of the conveying medium.

Another field of investigation is the directionality of the relationship between brightness and valence. In a study by Meier and colleagues, subjects' perception of gray-gradients was biased after being presented with morally connotated words [39]. Moral and ethical words, like *innocence, purity* and the like caused participants to judge different gray-gradients to be brighter. Similarly, when immoral terms were presented, participants subjected darker ratings, even though the colors were identical in both conditions. Findings like these suggest that the link between brightness and valence is bidirectional.

Some scholars focused on determining if the apparent link between brightness and valence is automatic. Meier et al.'s work indicates that these affective mappings are automatic in nature and thus elude conscious control without proper training [39]. On the contrary, Lakens, Semin and Foroni questioned the automaticity of the mapping and conducted a series of six experiments on the subject matter. Their experimental paradigm aimed at removing the factor of linguistic idiosyncrasy of one's native language by presenting the test subjects with foreign Chinese characters [32]. The Chinese alphabet is made up of ideograms, stylized depictions of superordinate ideas and concepts – like pictograms. For example, a vertical brush stroke with a horizontal line intersected with two diagonal lines branching from the top down and outwards constitute the word tree. Simplified, it is a symbolic depiction of a stem with branching twigs. Two of these "tree" characters side by side add up to the word forest. Lakens et al. instructed participants, devoid of any understanding of the Chinese language, to judge whether a correct translation for a character was presented on the screen while manipulating the font color (*black* vs. *white*). The authors found that when *white* font color was shown together with a positive translation and *black* font color with a negative translation, the correctness of the judgments was above chance. This indicates that the effect of perceiving *black* vs. *white* transcends peculiarities of individual languages and linguistic expressions, but instead represents the underlying conceptual metaphor GOOD IS BRIGHT – BAD IS DARK [3]. However, *white* only evoked positive associations when the negativity of *black* was co-activated but remained neutral when perceived alone. Thus, GOOD IS WHITE seems to be more context dependent that the association BAD IS BLACK.

Consequences of such cognitive biases are often reflected in behavior and decision making. Exposure to incidental light and dark visual contrasts tends to lead people to think in a "black and white" manner, as more extreme moral judgments follow than those which would occur otherwise [48]. Intuitive processes are affected in a way that leads to a polarization of moral judgment. Darkness appears to encourage moral transgressions. Zhong, Bohns and Gino found that it seems to induce a state of illusory anonymity which promotes egocentric behavior and dishonesty [49]. In their study, participants wearing sunglasses behaved more selfishly and cheated more often and systematically. This effect appears to scale from behavioral trivialities to severe crime. Regardless of factual anonymity, a psychological effect kicks in, suggesting impunity and a lack of repercussions, as darkness can conceal identity and thus legal pursuit. This is apparent in criminal statistics, as illumination directly correlates to the number and severity of criminal incidents [17]. In this vein, improved street lighting can have an immediate preventative effect on crime.

Similarly, the color *black* has been linked to behavioral aggression. In their classical study, Frank and Gilovich explored the effect of *black* uniforms and jerseys in professional sports in relation to the number of caused penalties. They found that throughout the course of their observations, teams wearing *black* jerseys constantly ranked among the top of the penalty statistics [19]. In the event a team switched from a *non-black* to a *black* uniform, an immediate increase in penalties was noticeable. Frank and Gilovich inferred that *black* uniforms lead to both biased judgments of referees and increased aggressiveness of the players themselves, which can be attributed to social perception and self-perception processes.

2.2 Affective Biases of Color Perception in HCI

In the field of HCI, the impact of colors on human behavior should be considered when designing User Interfaces (UIs). Predominantly, related work in this area is focused on the perception and effects of chromatic colors and their affective impact. For example, Hawlitschek, Jansen, Lux, Teubner and Weinhardt linked UI background color to reciprocation behavior via perceived warmth and color appeal [24]. In electronic commerce, manipulation of the affective state of mind is a potent tool in guiding reciprocity behavior and commercial purchasing power. The invocation of hedonistic notions like *desire, need* and *urge* regulates buying intentions [40]. This emotional reaction can be achieved by evoking and enhancing the customer's pleasure. According to Allagui and Lemoine, proficient color design increases pleasure, whereas inappropriate use of colors results in boredom, which in turn negatively effects mood and lessens the User Experience, leading to a significant decline of affective buying impulse [2].

Within the confines of digital chatting, color has widely been instrumentalized as an indicator of human sentiment and mood. *Sentiment* is defined as the attitude or state of mind toward or induced by something (contrasting to *mood*, which is defined as the affective state of mind lasting longer than mere emotions) [14, 15]. Together with emoticons, color provides the primary means of expressing and conveying affective states. For instance, Dos Santos, Gestraud, and Texier filed a patent for dynamically evaluating the mood of a chat user as a function of color and its intensity [43]. Back in 2006, Sánchez et al. suggested an instant messaging system tailored to convey mood and emotion [42]. Besides employing emoticons, colorful bubbles encompassing each message and font size maintain a record of current and past moods. An idea that has since been implemented in the globally popular Facebook Messenger[2], which allows for color personalization of any individual chat dialog or -group.

Since chromatic effects are so potent and powerful in guiding user behavior, comparatively little attention has been given to the domain of affective studies based on the sole perception of black and white in digital environments. Research in this domain is virtually limited to the topics of eye-strain, ergonomics (e.g. [29]) and workflow efficiency and -optimization (e.g. [10]). Although the presence of affective biases attributed to black and white in the digital context appears highly likely, validation studies are noticeably small in numbers [16]. This research gap is especially lamentable because perceptive *black/white* effects seem to be remarkably robust and replicable [38].

2.3 Automated Sentiment Analysis

Sentiment and mood have long been a growing area of interest in computer science. Today, the extraction of human sentiment and opinions from Big Data is one of the foremost researched topics [7, 8], involving data mining and using Artificial Intelligence and Machine Learning (especially Deep Learning), bearing immense potential for applications, both scientifically and commercially. As it sheds light on user desires, political and domestic satisfaction, as well as any other marketable area of life on a mass scale, the computational treatment of sentiment and subjectivity has received extensive attention. In the past years, major advancements in automated sentiment extraction have been made that enable a potent approximation of actual affective states conveyed in chats, blogs, social networks and other opinionated outlets.

For instance, a new approach to *Natural Language Processing* enabled Kouloumpis, Wilson, and Moore to analyze the sentiment on the popular micro-blogging service *Twitter* by identifying part-of-speech features combined with the presence of

---

[2] (2017, January). https://www.messenger.com/.

intensifiers, like emoticons and common abbreviations [28]. Through multiple itera-
tions of training data, they could achieve an accuracy of upwards to 75% for classifying
Tweets into the categories "positive", "neutral" and "negative", measured against a
human evaluation. Similarly, Godbole, Srinivasaiah, and Skiena developed a system
for large-scale sentiment analysis over large corpora of news and blogs [22]. By
assigning complexly computed scores, indicating positive or negative sentiment, this
system can describe the mood within any given text with each entity's sentiment
relative to other entities of the same class. This allows for spacial analyses and distribution of opinions and feelings to provide sentiment maps and thus give a comprehensive overview of a certain issue over large amounts of users. Given a certain
robustness and accuracy, sentiment extraction algorithms could function as an indicator
of ‚objective' chat sentiment, independent of particular UIs and their inherent tendency
to inflict cognitive and affective biases.

2.4   Research Question and Scope of the Empirical Study

In basic psychological research, the influence of *light* and *dark* on affective states has
been thoroughly examined. It has been validated that the perception of *black*, *white* and
chromatic colors ubiquitously and unconsciously takes part in governing cognition,
emotion and behavior. Furthermore, automated sentiment extraction receives growing
interest and scientific exploration in recent years. However, extensive sighting of the
related literature landscape revealed a blind spot of validation studies dedicated to the
reproduction of basic research on affective biases mediated by the perception of light
and dark in the context of HCI. Since the manipulation of color and contrast in digital
environments is one of the most trivial alterations to be made, research on the ensuing
effect on perceived sentiment and mood is highly warranted.

Legibility on computer screens is superior when using *dark* characters on a *light*
background. Alongside numerous studies coming to this conclusion, Bauer and
Cavonius found that participants were 26% more accurate and significantly faster
compared to reading from an inverse color scheme [4]. Conversely, with *light* text on
dark backgrounds, the iris opens wide to let in more light and causes a slight deformation of the lens, resulting in blurred letters which are marginally harder to perceive.
This effect is enhanced for people with astigmatism. However, especially near
night-time, prolonged exposure to *bright* computer screens negatively affects sleep,
circadian cycles and is known to cause headaches [9]. Consequently, *dark* themes
minimizing the presence of *bright* elements are widely used amongst professions that
heavily rely on working on computer screens. Additionally, digital services all over the
internet employ *dark themes* and interfaces for purely cosmetic reasons. The sheer
number of possibly affected people worldwide motivates and merits the investigation of
psychological effects of perceiving *light* or *dark*, *black* or *white* in the context of HCI.

Human communication lanced with irony and sarcasm provides ample grounds for
misinterpretation of affective intent and entails an enormous potential scope of severe
consequences, both on an interpersonal and professional level. Today, decades after its
inception, chatting persists as the primary means of digital communication globally.
Thus, this work aims at investigating the influence of a predominantly *white* interface
on perceived chat sentiment in contrast to a primarily *black* interface. It is expected that

when participants in an experimental study have to evaluate the sentiment of a chat excerpt with ambiguous messages, their judgments will be more negative when the background color is *black* compared to when the evaluation is performed in a predominantly *white* interface. If the interface color is gray or the sentiment analysis performed automatically, the judgments should be less extreme, as they are not influenced by a valence-related background color of the UI. Moreover, we argue that the expected effect is driven by the UI background color as opposed to the font color of presented messages, because the participants had to take the whole interface into account (video, chat log, chat message, answer keys) and the background is more prominent in the visual field of the subjects compared to most psychological studies that only present single words against a gray background, e.g. [38]. In such forced-choice reaction time tasks, the participants' full attention is directed to the target stimuli, thus inverting the prediction. Such inverted color effects are typically found in color psychology when single-color evaluations are extended to more applied contexts and interactions [25], thus questioning the transferability of results of basic research to more applied contexts.

3 Method

3.1 Participants

Test Subjects. Published effect sizes of related basic research in psychology were injected into *G*Power* [18], a statistical power analysis tool, to compute an approximation of required test subjects to find comparable effects in this study. These calculations indicated a sample size of 60 to 70 participants. The subjects were recruited through an online recruiting system in exchange for course credit. They were screened to meet *Twitch.tv's* target demographics of (predominantly male) 18 to 35 years old gaming savvy users. The total sample of 67 participants consisted of 24 women and 43 men aged 19 to 29 years ($M = 21.167$, $SD = 1.932$).

Expert Group. Six 'expert' evaluators could be won to participate in the study as a reference to the experimental groups. Subjects from this group were deeply involved with the subject matter of *Twitch.tv* streaming as a part of their professional occupation at a company situated in the social streaming market, as well as their everyday private lives. Due to their profound knowledge of vernacular and game mechanics, they are highly capable of disambiguating messages semantically with an outstanding sense of context and intention of the original author. This leaves less room for interpretational errors and approximates the true chat sentiment more closely, than the large group of test subjects. The expert sample consisted of 6 men aged 25 to 29 years ($M = 25.83$, $SD = 1.46$).

3.2 Procedure

In a single-blind between-subjects design, test subjects were assigned to either be part of condition white, processing the chat messages against a white background color, or condition black, where they encountered the black version of the UI (counterbalanced across both conditions). The study was set up as an online experiment that participants accessed through an email link. They received written instruction to rate the sentiment of presented chat messages based on their subjective perception and as fast as possible to emulate authentic reactions while reading a chat. To prevent participants from guessing the purpose of the experiment and thus falsifying resulting data, they were given a misdirecting study title, which was clarified upon completion. After completing the sentiment evaluation of 229 chat messages by labeling them as "positive" (+1), "neutral" (0) or "negative" (−1), an average sentiment score was calculated for each participant. In case a participant disregarded or missed a message, the denominator (i.e. total number of messages) was adjusted accordingly to produce a sound average. After having worked through all messages, a demographic questionnaire had to be completed with age, gender, average internet usage, gaming affinity, *Twitch.tv* familiarity, schadenfreude, mood, and tiredness. The whole procedure lasted 45–60 min.

As a reference measure for the experimental groups, two statistics have been employed. Firstly, another variant of the interface was generated in neutral gray [1, 21]. On this version, independently from the experimental conditions white and black, six *Twitch.tv* experts labeled the same chat excerpt as the experimental groups. Secondly, to access chat sentiment more objectively, a sentiment analysis algorithm was applied, eliminating human factors and thus susceptibility to cognitive biases and fatigue (see paragraph 3.1 Sentiment analysis algorithm).

3.3   Material

Chat Excerpt. Founded in June 2011, *Twitch.tv* has set out to become the world's leading social video platform and community for gamers. As of the time of this work, it is the largest contemporary facilitator of chat messages with an average volume of 200 billion messages per day[3]. *Twitch.tv* employs a chat with often hundreds or thousands of simultaneous participants. The publicly available nature of these open chat rooms allows for an easier approach to recording and logging prolonged exchanges of chat messages. This feature, combined with the fact that *Twitch.tv*'s sheer throughput dwarfs that of all of its competitors, has led to the decision to base this study on the example of *Twitch.tv*. By employing *Chatworkers* (bots that sit inside a specific channel and record the chat log), any arbitrary sequence of messages in any channel on *Twitch.tv* became obtainable. Moreover, *Twitch.tv*'s broadcasts and chats are accessible to the public and recorded and archived by default to be readily available as videos on demand for certain periods of time.

As eSports (professionally organized and managed competitive gaming) is driving the highest traffic per channel on *Twitch.tv*, we chose a chat excerpt with representative qualities for this format. The choice fell on a broadcast of a competitive contest of one of the most popular eSports games, DOTA 2, namely a match featuring competing teams *Natus Vincere* vs. *No Diggity* from *Dreamleague Season 5*, which aired 18:30 CEST on

---

[3] (2017, January). Twitch.tv message throughput. Retrieved from https://jobs.lever.co/twitch/ 61fb0c31-6f59-435b-a4f7-ea0e57a038b6.

April 05, 2016 on *Twitch.tv*. Recorded in its entirety, the encounter resulted in approximately two hours of video with its corresponding chat transcript.

When cropping down the recorded material to attain a prolific base of chat data for participants to evaluate, a segment of the recording was chosen that contained both a negative and a positive event, as well as the conclusion of the match, leading to mixed verdicts and opinions about performances throughout the course of the encounter. The chat excerpt accompanying the chosen content sequence, spanning the time of 10 min, originally consisted of 1172 messages. Early testing indicated a completion time of roughly 22 min per 200 labeled messages. To achieve an overall completion time of about an hour to avoid user fatigue, the chat log was trimmed down to a total of 229 unique messages and aliases were removed. Using a basic JSON script, the original log was processed to remove overly crude profanity, redundant messages, as well as messages with less than three characters. Although the excerpt was shortened drastically, much care was taken to preserve the chat's representative qualities as to prevent contortion of the content and flow due to overly manipulating the source material.

Evaluation Interface. To provide a functional environment for sentiment evaluation, video and condensed chat log were fed into a browser-based interface based on HTML/CSS framework Bootstrap. Messages could either be rated "negative" (Hotkey A), "neutral" (Hotkey S), "positive" (Hotkey D) or "undefined" (Hotkey X), with the latter being reserved for messages that by nature cannot be interpreted properly by sentiment. Examples for this case include Cyrillic characters, ad- and spam links, as well as a language other than English. Above the message field, the accompanying video scene was embedded. Initiated by triggering the "next" button, the clip would play back in real time until reaching the consecutive message of the processed chat log. From this labeling interface, three different versions were created. The *dark* version featured a *black* background (hex code #000000) with *white* font and button borders. Conversely, the *light* version consisted of a *white* background (hex code #FFFFFF) with *black* borders and font (see Fig. 1). For the expert group, a *gray* variant (hex code #7F7F7F) of the interface was generated. On the back-end, information for the labeling of any message was stored on a deployment of open source, multi-model database distribution *Couchbase*.

Auxiliary Data. The accompanying demographic questionnaire inquired information about gender, age and a range of possible moderator variables. Average daily internet usage, gaming affinity, and weekly *Twitch.tv* usage are likely to influence sentiment labelings of test subjects since they largely constitute a certain knowledge base of internet culture and language. Internet- and *Twitch.tv* usage data were gathered on a five-point Likert scale, ranging up to more than five hours per week.

Gaming affinity was queried on a five-point Likert scale ranging from "not familiar at all" to "very familiar". Furthermore, another factor which can potentially influence the evaluation of sentiment is the trait of *schadenfreude*, the pleasure at the suffering of others [45]. Depending on the character, a participant might find an insult, witnessed in the chat or on the video feed, either funny and gloat over someone's misfortune or offensive leading to rejection. To determine the experimental subjects' spitefulness and taste in humor, they were presented with three different insults that occurred in the captured broadcast before the segment chosen for the actual experiment. They were

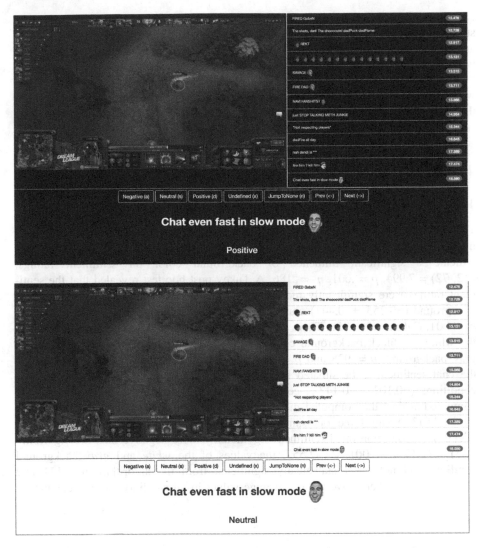

Fig. 1. Top: black interface variant. Bottom: white interface variant, with an exemplary message and Twitch.tv face emoji.

asked to assess whether they find these messages to be funny or rather offensive. Finally, the participants' condition and state of mind before conducting the labeling were inquired. Mood and tiredness, evaluated with four ordinal polytomous options, derived from the Epworth Sleepiness Scale [26], were inquired.

Sentiment Analysis Algorithm. Originally conceived to analyze sentiment in live Tweets, SentiStorm [47] was adapted to learn and interpret language specific to the platform *Twitch.tv*. The algorithm broke down every message word for word into tokens. Each token possesses a feature vector, containing 500 attributes. These attributes can be simple classifications (noun, verb, adjective) or more complex linguistic constructs, like *term frequency* or *inverse document frequency* – both related to language- and document occurrence of a word. Individual features were then equally weighted with a value between "0" and "1" and, in turn, produce an average numerical value from "−1" to "1". These values are then fed into a *Support Vector Machine*, that calculated in which category a message falls into, measured relatively against all other messages. For this to work, the algorithm had to be trained. For this purpose, 2000 messages from the stream broadcast before the experimental excerpt was used.

4   Results

4.1   Chat Sentiment

The impact of background color as the independent variable on sentiment ratings of the participants was tested using a one-way ANOVA. Alpha was set at .05. The results indicate a significant influence of background color on sentiment ratings, $F(2, 72) = 7.994$, $p = .001$, $\eta^2 = .186$. A Tukey post hoc test revealed that the sentiment ratings were significantly more negative when participants worked on a *black* background (-0.255 ± 0.441) compared to a *white* background (-0.069 ± 0.069), $p = .001$, *Cohen's d* = .958. There were no statistically significant differences between the white and black background color conditions and the experts working against a gray background, $p = .928$ and $p = .178$, respectively. The *Twitch.tv*-experts judged the chat sentiment to be situated between the numerical values of the experimental conditions (-0.101 ± 0.147), see Fig. 2. Next, the three participant groups were compared against the computed mean value of the employed sentiment algorithm of $M = -0.013$, using three one-sample *t*-tests. While the participants in the *black* background condition rated sentiment significantly more negative than the algorithm, $t(33) = 7.233$, $p < .001$, $d = 2.557$, the values of the *white* and *gray* background condition did not differ statistically significant from the algorithm, $p = .111$ and $p = .185$, respectively. Overall, the average values in all conditions were negative.

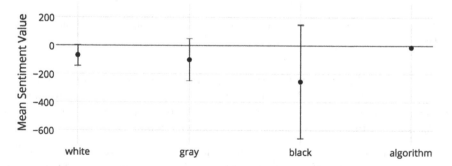

Fig. 2. Averaged sentiment judgments (−1 to 1) of the two experimental conditions (*black* vs. *white* background), expert group on *gray* background and algorithm; error bars, if applicable, indicate 95% confidence intervals.

4.2 Control Variables

As both experimental groups did not differ from each other regarding the collected control variables, values are reported for the whole group of test subjects. On average, participants stated that they spend three to four hours utilizing the internet daily. On a five-level Likert scale, ranging from "not familiar at all" to "very familiar", participants rated their familiarity with gaming contents as "familiar" ($M = 3.933$, $SD = 1.913$), and with eSports contents as "moderately familiar" ($M = 3.100$, $SD = 1.191$). Furthermore, participants rated their current mood before the experiment as "neutral" to "positive" ($M = 3.560$, $SD = 0.633$) on a second five-point scale. On average, participants rated their sleepiness on a four-point one-item scale, derived from the Epworth Sleepiness Scale and ranging from "would never doze" to "high chance of dozing", between categories "would never doze" and "slight chance of dozing" ($M = 1.950$, $SD = 0.746$). Qualitatively, weekly *Twitch.tv* usage averaged out to two to three hours on an ordinal categorical scale. Concerning schadenfreude, 26 participants declared the presented insults as being funny, whereas 34 found them to be offensive ($M = 1.567$, $SD = 0.500$, with the value "1" being coded for "funny" and "2" meaning "offensive").

To estimate the relative impact of the assessed control variables on the sentiment judgment of the participants, a multiple linear regression analysis was performed with interface color, sex, age, internet use, gaming-, eSports and *Twitch.tv* affinity, mood, tiredness and schadenfreude as independent variables and sentiment rating as dependent variable. The ten variables explain a significant amount of variance in sentiment ratings, $F(10, 59) = 3.295$, $p = .002$, $R^2 = .402$, *adj.* $R^2 = .280$. However, only interface color ($\beta = -.393$, $p = .002$) and schadenfreude ($\beta = -.436$, $p = .001$) were significant predictors of sentiment rating. If the interface background color was *white* and if a participant perceived written insults rather funny than offensive, the sentiment rating was more positive.

5 Discussion

This work set out to investigate the influence of *light* and *dark* chat interfaces on perceived sentiment. The resulting data suggests the presence of such affective biases, explored and validated in basic psychological research, in a digital environment. Sentiment ratings of participants in the *black* background condition were significantly more negative than those of participants in the *white* background condition, indicating affectively biased perception of mood in the chat excerpt. One alternative explanation for this result is that the participants' decisions were biased by differences in perceptual fluency. As *white* text on a *black* background is more difficult to read than *black* text on *white*, the perceptual fluency is lower, causing more negative judgments of the content [41]. Comparing the foreground/background contrast of both interfaces after the Web Content Accessibility Guidelines 2.0 using a tool provided by Hülsermann[4], no differences in contrast ratio and readability could be found. Moreover, the readability of the *gray* variant was notably lower than the *white* and *black* version, but experts did not

---

[4] (2017, January). http://joerghuelsermann.de/tool/kontrastrechner.

subject the lowest affective ratings. Therefore, this alternative explanation seems less likely. A second alternative explanation is the impact of familiarity, as more familiar things are judged more positive [20]. As the most consumed text is black font on white background, this could lead to a familiarity effect which could have impacted the interpretation of texts to a more positive sentiment of the white background. However, we could find similar ratings for white and gray (mid-gray is certainly less familiar than white background color). In addition, the black sentiment judgements were constantly negative over time (45–60 min exposure during the experiment), and a mere exposure effect (repeatedly perceiving things results in a positive bias) could not be observed. Therefore, we conclude that this does not offer a better explanation of the results than the brightness-induced affective bias hypothesis.

Although the sample size of the *Twitch.tv* expert group was small, their judgments, unbiased from the background color, do provide a frame of reference and valuable insight into more precise judgments of the inherent sentiment of the sample excerpt. Their cumulative ratings were situated numerically between those of participants using the *white* interface and those using the *black* interface. Statistical tests showed that while the *white* interface did not lead participants to rate the chat messages more positively, perceiving them against a *black* background dramatically decreased the perceived chat sentiment. This is in line with the literature that *black* automatically evokes negative associations, whereas *white* remains neutral when the negativity of *black* is not co-activated [32]. It is a subject to further research whether perceiving chat messages against a *white* background increases the perceived positive sentiment when a within-subjects design would have been employed. Moreover, future studies could employ a control condition that avoids an influence of color overall, for example by using an audio condition as baseline, and control for surrounding light sources.

Overall, the sentiment in the chat has been classified as slightly negative, as all average values are below "0". This fact has been anticipated since *Twitch.tv* is known to be somewhat notorious for a crude form of manners and verbal inconsideration amongst users.

To quantify inter-rater agreement across all messages, Fleiss' Kappa κ has been computed. In its unadjusted form, containing missing ratings where participants had omitted single messages and resulting in uneven counts of raters, the agreement was fair (κ = .509, SE = .0014), according to [35]. Standardized to 67 raters for each message, the measure of accordance fell to κ = .198, SE = .001. Over such many messages, and accounting for the highly subjective nature of mood perception, a low consensus is to be expected.

The distribution of age ($M = 21.167$, $SD = 1.932$) and sex (24 women to 43 men) of participants were within the intended demographic cohort, adding to the validity of gathered data about the factual user base of *Twitch.tv*[5] of 75% Millenial males. Of the collected control variables (age, sex, internet use, gaming-, eSports and *Twitch.tv* affinity, mood, tiredness and schadenfreude), only schadenfreude had a significant impact on sentiment ratings. The more the participants interpret insults against other people as humorous rather than offensive, the higher the perceived chat sentiment.

---

[5] (2017, January). http://twitchadvertising.tv/audience/.

Decreased empathy in online environments [6] together with exposure to very competitive surroundings, as is the case in eSports, likely explains spiteful and gloating tendencies like schadenfreude and in turn its effect on perceived chat sentiment [23].

Participants' mood before the experiment was rated "neutral" tending towards "positive", which is consequential when assessing affective sentiment, as one's state of mind will always factor into perception. Fortunately, the effects of potentially confounding factors mood and sleepiness on sentiment ratings were negligible in our data, as no significant contribution in the regression model could be found.

The experimental manipulation resulted in a decisively large effect size according to Cohen, signaling a strong statistical difference between the experimental conditions of different UI background color [13]. The employed ordinal scale for measuring sentiment with merely three different levels ("positive", "neutral", "negative") might have contributed to the strength of the effect. However, since only the control variable of schadenfreude had a slight impact on sentiment ratings and considering the random assignment of participants to the interface conditions, a potent and compelling effect on perceived sentiment attributed to the interface can be inferred.

Several limitations of this study need to be considered. First, the suitability of experimental subjects was not thoroughly validated. Although during recruitment the call for participation postulated gaming and eSports knowledge and prolific understanding of the English (internet-)language as prerequisites for attending this study, it is questionable if all participants truly possessed a thorough knowledge of gaming-related terms, idioms, and mechanics despite claiming to do so. A broader study in this endeavor should have employed a test to assess the gaming-savviness of participants.

Second, concerning the experimental design, a more finely grained scale for measuring sentiment may have yielded more revealing results. However, affective interpretation occurs automatic and instantaneously. If participants ponder too long to accurately assess the mood on an elaborate scale, the authentic replication of the actual human process of sentimental perception could be problematic. Additionally, in respect of a large number of to-be-evaluated messages, this might result in participant exhaustion and in turn produce unnecessary noise in the resulting data. A balance between authenticity and information entropy would have to be struck. Third, this study could have benefitted from supplementary qualitative data, interviews, and self-assessments of participants to further qualify empirical findings.

Fourth, the conceptualization of schadenfreude was merely evaluated on a nominal scale and assessed with only three items. Thus, the accuracy and explanatory power of this variable are limited. As the data suggests, schadenfreude, as a trait of character, plays a noteworthy role in the affective perception of online chats. This relationship could have been explored more extensively since the notion of equal distribution of experimental subjects with a higher schadenfreude score amongst the two conditions of the study was rejected for randomization over a bigger sample size. Fifth, the sample size of *Twitch.tv*-experts was very small. Given a larger cohort, test subjects using a neutral gray interface could have served as a better control group, further strengthening internal validity of the study.

Sixth, in respect to external validity, the extent of generalizability of found effects in the gaming content of *Twitch.tv* on digital chatting could be debated. Disregarding subject matter, large *Twitch.tv* channels feature an extreme chat fluctuation with an unparalleled rate of messages, which severely limits the potential of truly engaging in dialog. This is further deteriorated by spamming and trolling. Additionally, messages are often dubious in quality of content, information value and significance, which makes it difficult to guarantee similar valence of messages across larger portions of chats. Although the age of the participants was highly appropriate for *Twitch.tv*'s target demographic and user-base, the representativeness toward digital chat communication overall remains unexplored. Future work should therefore study the generalizability of the results, for example by trying to reproduce these findings for sentiment scoring of tweets with varying UI background colors.

6 Conclusions and Future Work

The presented findings bear value for application design across the entirety of the digital landscape, balancing issues of aesthetics, legibility and behavioral effects of color on user experience [30]. Depending on intent and use-case of a given service, employing a *black* or a *white* interface respectively might be either beneficial or hindering for the effect a software product is trying to achieve. For example, a grief counseling service comforting depressive or even suicidal patients would be ill-advised to implement a monochrome *black* interface. Ambiguous messages herein would be vulnerable to affective sentimental biases, possibly degrading the patients' condition unintentionally. Dating services, on the other hand, seek to bring people together and deepen mutual sympathy and thus would likely benefit from a *brighter* interface. In instances of critical importance of text and dialog, where objectivity and factual accuracy is paramount, one should refrain from providing purely *white* or *black* interfaces and make use of neutral gray styles instead. A minuscule influence could perchance be a crucial factor in decision making. As it is the case with high stakes business or governmental agreements, considerable repercussions and consequences could potentially ensue. Moreover, it is worthwhile investigating whether the results found in this study are only valid for black and white interfaces or extent to *lighter* and *darker* versions of different hues.

In mobile technology, organic light-emitting diode (OLED) displays are commonly used with Android and Windows Phone devices. In contrast to generic liquid crystal displays (LCDs) that filter light emitted from a built-in backlight, OLED screens display black by deactivating pixel elements altogether. This way, true deep blacks can be achieved without the consumption of any power. Battery life is one of the foremost concerns and bottlenecks in the smartphone industry today [12] since the portable form-factor inherently imposes capacitive limitations. Thus, on OLED mobile devices, black interfaces are heavily favored and deliberately utilized to improve battery efficiency (e.g. Android's power saving mode). These common IT-industry standards and practices might induce, or at least enhance, the vulnerability for affective biases on an immense scale, considering the global user base.

Future work following the direction of this study could explore the presence of these findings in more content-independent means of written and other visual communication. Excluding niche content will likely lead to the discovery of a universal affective brightness bias, in turn resulting in a broader applicability across a wide variety of digital domains. Adjacent research could investigate the influence on invoked emotion from reading fiction and novels. Especially considering e-readers and their color inverted night mode, the interface might affect intensity and direction of resulting emotion, which can be addressed in future research. In the long run, this might even affect the overall financial success of fiction literature within the confines of digital distribution, excluding print media. Similarly, any artistic endeavor appealing to con-jure emotion lends itself to scientific investigation.

By way of example, a digital environment for composing music, or the influence of a gaming interface on moral choice in video games provides promising research ventures. On a grander scheme, automated sentiment analysis could be deployed for an abundance of digital platforms over a large scale of big data to gather comparative sentimental reference, subject to the appearance of different interfaces, across a vast landscape of digital services. Moreover, not only the affective reception of online content biased by different interface colors should be a subject for future research, but also its production and potential interactions. Since digital communication and media assume increasingly dominant relevance in modern lifestyle, the true extent of affective influence and its magnitude gains more importance continuously. Perception and cognitive psychology have an entirely new field of application in the digital domain, as the zeitgeist shifts into intricately interwoven HCI systems across the entirety of the *virtuality continuum*.

References

1. Adams, F.M., Osgood, C.E.: A cross-cultural study of the affective meanings of color. J. Cross Cult. Psychol. **4**(2), 135–156 (1973)
2. Allagui, A., Lemoine, J.: Web interface and consumers' buying intention in e-tailing: results from an online experiment. Adv. Consum. Res. **8**, 24–30 (2006)
3. Baldauf, C.: Metapher und Kognition. Grundlagen einer neuen Theorie der Alltagsmetapher. Peter Lang Verlag, Bern (1997)
4. Bauer, D., Cavonius, C.: Improving the legibility of visual display units through contrast reversal. In: Ergonomic Aspects of Visual Display Terminals, pp. 137–142 (1980)
5. Berlin, B., Kay, P.: Basic Color Terms: Their Universality and Evolution. The David Human Series Philosophy and Cognitive Science Reissues, vol. 19, p. 178 (1969)
6. Bishop, J.: Representations of "trolls" in mass media communication: a review of media-texts and moral panics relating to "internet trolling." Int. J. Web Based Communities **10**(1), 7 (2014)
7. Cambria, E., et al.: Computational intelligence for big social data analysis [guest editorial]. IEEE Comput. Intell. Mag. **11**(3), 8–9 (2016)
8. Cambria, E., et al.: New avenues in knowledge bases for natural language processing. Knowl.-Based Syst. **108**(C), 1–4 (2016)
9. Chang, A.-M., et al.: Evening use of light-emitting eReaders negatively affects sleep, circadian timing, and next-morning alertness. Proc. Nat. Acad. Sci. **112**(4), 201418490 (2014)
10. Cheng, Z.: Effect of font and background color combination on the recognition efficiency for LCD displays. ProQuest Dissertations and Theses, p. 40, May 2015

11. Chiou, W.-B., Cheng, Y.-Y.: In broad daylight, we trust in God! Brightness, the salience of morality, and ethical behavior. J. Environ. Psychol. **36**, 37–42 (2013)
12. Chondro, P., Ruan, S.-J.: Perceptually hue-oriented power-saving scheme with overexposure corrector for AMOLED displays. J. Disp. Technol. **12**(8), 791–800 (2016)
13. Cohen, J.: Statistical Power Analysis for the Behavioural Sciences. Lawrence Earlbaum Associates, Hillside (1988)
14. Desmet, P.: Designing emotion (2002)
15. Desmet, P.M., Hekkert, P.: The basis of product emotions. In: Pleasure With Products: Beyond Usability (2002)
16. Elliot, A.J., Maier, M.A.: Color psychology: effects of perceiving color on psychological functioning in humans. Annu. Rev. Psychol. **65**, 95–120 (2014)
17. Farrington, D.P., Welsh, B.C.: Effects of improved street lighting on crime: a systematic review. Campbell Syst. Rev. **13**, 59 (2008)
18. Faul, F., et al.: G*Power 3: a flexible statistical power analysis program for the social, behavioral, and biomedical sciences. Behav. Res. Methods **39**(2), 175–191 (2007)
19. Frank, M.G., Gilovich, T.: The dark side of self-perception and social-perception - black uniforms and aggression in professional sports. J. Pers. Soc. Psychol. **54**(1), 74–85 (1988)
20. Garcia-Marques, T., Mackie, D.M.: The positive feeling of familiarity: mood as an information processing regulation mechanism. Psychology Press (2000)
21. Gil, S., Le Bigot, L.: Seeing life through positive-tinted glasses: color-meaning associations. PLoS ONE **9**(8), e104291 (2014)
22. Godbole, N., Srinivasaiah, M.: Large-scale sentiment analysis for news and blogs. In: Conference on Weblogs and Social Media (ICWSM 2007), pp. 219–222 (2007)
23. Greitemeyer, T., et al.: Playing prosocial video games increases empathy and decreases schadenfreude. Emotion **10**(6), 796–802 (2010). Washington, D.C.
24. Hawlitschek, F., et al.: Colors and trust: the influence of user interface design on trust and reciprocity. In: Proceedings of the Annual Hawaii International Conference on System Sciences, pp. 590–599 (2016)
25. Ho, H., et al.: Combining colour and temperature: a blue object is more likely to be judged as warm than a red object. Sci. Rep. **4**, 5527 (2014)
26. Johns, M.: A new method for measuring daytime sleepiness: the Epworth sleepiness scale. Sleep **14**(6), 540–545 (1991)
27. Klein, G.S.: Semantic power measured through the interference of words with color-naming. Am. J. Psychol. **77**(4), 576–588 (1964)
28. Kouloumpis, E., et al.: Twitter sentiment analysis: the good the bad and the OMG! Artif. Intell. **11**(164), 538–541 (2011)
29. Kwallek, N., et al.: Impact of three interior color schemes on worker mood and performance relative to individual environmental sensitivity. Color Res. Appl. **22**(2), 121–132 (1997)
30. Labrecque, L.I., et al.: The marketers' prismatic palette: a review of color research and future directions. Psychol. Mark. **30**(2), 187–202 (2010)
31. Lakens, D., et al.: Brightness differences influence the evaluation of affective pictures. Cogn. Emot. **27**(7), 1225–1246 (2013)
32. Lakens, D., et al.: But for the bad, there would not be good: grounding valence in brightness through shared relational structures. J. Exp. Psychol. Gen. **141**(3), 584–594 (2012)
33. Lakoff, G., Johnson, M.: Metaphors We Live By. University of Chicago Press, Chicago (1997)
34. Lakoff, G., Johnson, M.: Philosophy in the Flesh: The Embodied Mind and Its Challenge to Western Thought. Basic Books, New York (1999)
35. Landis, J.R., Koch, G.G.: The measurement of observer agreement for categorical data. Biometrics **33**(1), 159–174 (1977)

36. Löffler, D.: Color, Metaphor and Culture. Ph.D. dissertation, University of Würzburg, Würzburg (2017)
37. MacDonald, L.W.: Using color effectively in computer graphics. IEEE Comput. Graphics Appl. **19**(4), 20–35 (1999)
38. Meier, B.P., et al.: Black and white as valence cues: a large-scale replication effort of Meier, Robinson, and Clore (2004, 2015)
39. Meier, B.P., et al.: When "Light" and "Dark" thoughts become light and dark responses: affect biases brightness judgments. Emotion **7**(2), 366–376 (2007)
40. Pelet, J.-É., Papadopoulou, P.: The effect of colors of e-commerce websites on consumer mood, memorization and buying intention. Eur. J. Inf. Syst. **21**(4), 438–467 (2012)
41. Reber, R., et al.: Effects of perceptual fluency on affective judgments. Psychol. Sci. **9**(1), 45–48 (1998)
42. Sánchez, J.A., et al.: Conveying mood and emotion in instant messaging by using a two-dimensional model for affective states. In: Proceedings of VII Brazilian Symposium on Human Factors in Computing Systems, IHC 2006, p. 66. ACM Press, New York (2006)
43. Dos Santos, M., et al.: Method of dynamically evaluating the mood of an instant messaging user (2008)
44. Schwarz, N.: Feelings-as-information theory. In: Van Lange, P.A.M., Kruglanski, A., Higgins, E.T. (eds.) Handbook of Theories of Social Psychology: Collection, vol. 1 and 2, pp. 289–308. Sage, Thousand Oaks (2011)
45. Smith, R.H., et al.: Envy and schadenfreude. Pers. Soc. Psychol. Bull. **22**(2), 158–168 (1996)
46. Stroop, J.R.: Studies of interference in serial verbal reactions. J. Exp. Psychol. **18**(6), 643–662 (1935)
47. Zangerle, E., et al.: SentiStorm: Echtzeit-Stimmungserkennung von Tweets. HMD Praxis der Wirtschaftsinformatik **53**(4), 514–529 (2016)
48. Zarkadi, T., Schnall, S.: "Black and White" thinking: visual contrast polarizes moral judgment. J. Exp. Soc. Psychol. **49**(3), 355–359 (2013)
49. Zhong, C.-B., et al.: Good lamps are the best police: darkness increases dishonesty and self-interested behavior. Psychol. Sci. **21**(3), 311–314 (2010)

Subjective Usability, Mental Workload Assessments and Their Impact on Objective Human Performance

Luca Longo[(✉)]

School of Computing, Dublin Institute of Technology, Dublin, Ireland
luca.longo@dit.ie

Abstract. Self-reporting procedures and inspection methods have been largely employed in the fields of interaction and web-design for assessing the usability of interfaces. However, there seems to be a propensity to ignore features related to end-users or the context of application during the usability assessment procedure. This research proposes the adoption of the construct of mental workload as an additional aid to inform interaction and web-design. A user-study has been performed in the context of human-web interaction. The main objective was to explore the relationship between the perception of usability of the interfaces of three popular web-sites and the mental workload imposed on end-users by a set of typical tasks executed over them. Usability scores computed employing the System Usability Scale were compared and related to the mental workload scores obtained employing the NASA Task Load Index and the Workload Profile self-reporting assessment procedures. Findings advise that perception of usability and subjective assessment of mental workload are two independent, not fully overlapping constructs. They measure two different aspects of the human-system interaction. This distinction enabled the demonstration of how these two constructs cab be jointly employed to better explain objective performance of end-users, a dimension of user experience, and informing interaction and web-design.

1 Introduction

In recent decades the demands of evaluating usability of interactive web-based systems have produced several assessment procedures. Very often, during usability inspection, there is a tendency to overlook features of the users, aspects of the context and characteristics of the tasks. This tendency is also justified by the lack of a model that unifies all of these aspects. Considering features of users is fundamental for the User Modeling community [1,16]. Similarly, taking into consideration the context of use is of extreme importance for inferring reliable assessments of usability [3,36]. Additionally, during the usability assessment process, accounting for the demands of the task executed is core for describing user experience [20]. Building a cohesive model is not trivial, however we believe the construct of human *mental workload* (MWL) – often referred to as cognitive

© IFIP International Federation for Information Processing 2017
Published by Springer International Publishing AG 2017. All Rights Reserved
R. Bernhaupt et al. (Eds.): INTERACT 2017, Part II, LNCS 10514, pp. 202–223, 2017.
DOI: 10.1007/978-3-319-67684-5_13

load – can significantly contribute to such a goal and inform interaction and web-design. MWL, with roots in Psychology, has been mainly applied within the fields of Ergonomics and Human Factors. Its assessment is key to measuring performance, which in turn is fundamental for describing user experience and engagement. A few studies have tried to employ the construct of MWL to explain usability [2,24,41,46,50]. Despite this interest, not much has yet been done to investigate their relationship empirically. The aim of this research is to empirically test the relationship between subjective perception of usability and mental workload as well as their impact on objective user performance, which means tangible quantifiable facts (Fig. 1).

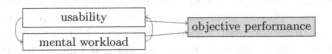

Fig. 1. Schematic overview of the empirical study

This paper is organised as follows. Firstly, notable definitions of usability and mental workload are provided, followed by an overview of the assessment techniques employed in Human-Computer Interaction (HCI). Related work is also presented, highlighting how the two constructs have been employed so far, distinctly and jointly. An experiment is subsequently designed in the context of human-web interaction, aimed at investigating the relationship between the perception of usability of three popular web-sites (Youtube, Wikipedia and Google) and the mental workload experienced by users after interacting with them. Results are presented and critically discussed, showing how these constructs interact and how they impact objective user performance. A summary concludes this paper pointing to future work and highlighting the contribution to knowledge.

2 Core Notions and Definitions

Widely employed in the broader field of HCI, usability and mental workload are two constructs from Ergonomics, with no crystal and generally applicable definitions. There is an acute debate on their assessment and measurement [4–6]. Although ill-defined, they remain extremely important for describing the user experience and improving interaction, interface and system design.

2.1 Definitions of Usability

The amount of literature covering definitions [21,48], frameworks and methodologies for assessing usability is vast. The ISO (International Organisation for Standardisation) defines usability as 'The extent to which a product can be used by specified users to achieve specified goals with effectiveness, efficiency, and satisfaction in a specified context of use'. Usability, according to Nielsen [38], is a method for improving ease-of-use in the design of interactive systems and technologies. It embraces other concepts such as efficiency, learnability and satisfaction. It is often associated with the functionalities of a product rather than being merely a feature of the user interface [39].

2.2   Measures of Usability

Often when selecting an appropriate procedure in the context of interaction and web-design, it is desirable to consider the effort and expense that will be incurred in collecting and analysing data. For this reason, designers have tended to adopt subjective usability assessment techniques for collecting feedback from users [21]. On one hand, self-reporting techniques can only be administered post-task, thus influencing their reliability with regard to long tasks. Meta-cognitive limitations can also diminish the accuracy of reporting and it is difficult to perform comparisons among raters on an absolute scale. On the other hand, these techniques appear to be the most sensitive and diagnostical [21]. Nielsen's principles, thanks to their simplicity in terms of effort and time, are frequently employed to evaluate the usability of interfaces [38]. The evaluation is done iteratively by systematically finding usability problems in an interface and judging them according to the principles [39]. The main problem associated to these principles is that they mainly focus on the user interface forgetting contextual factors, the cognitive state of the users and the underlying tasks.

The System Usability Scale [9] is a questionnaire that consists of ten questions (Table 9). It is a highly cited usability assessment method and it has been massively applied [7]. It is a very easy scale to administer, demonstrating reliability to distinguishing usable and unusable systems and even with small sample sizes [54]. Alternatives include the Computer System Usability Questionnaire (CSUQ), developed at IBM and the Questionnaire for User Interface Satisfaction (QUIS), developed at the HCI lab at the University of Maryland. The former is a survey that consists of 19 questions on a seven-point Likert scale of 'strongly disagree' to 'strongly agree' [25]. The latter was designed to assess users' satisfaction with aspects of a computer interface [49]. It includes: a demographic questionnaire, a measure of system satisfaction along six scales, and a hierarchy of measures of nine specific interface factors. Each of these factors relates to a user's satisfaction with that particular aspect of an interface as well as to the factors that make up that facet, on a 9-point scale. Although it is more complex than other instruments, QUIS has shown high reliability across several interfaces [19]. Many other usability inspection methods and techniques have been proposed in the literature [21,54].

2.3   Definitions of Mental Workload

Human Mental Workload (MWL) is an important design concept and it is fundamental for exploring the interaction of people with technological devices

[29,31,32]. It has a long history in Psychology with applications in Ergonomics, especially in the transportation industry [14,20]. The principal reason for MWL assessment is to quantify the cognitive cost associated to performing a task for predicting operator or system performance [10]. However, it has been largely reported that mental underload and overload can negatively influence performance [60]. On one hand, during information processing, when MWL is at a low level, individuals may frequently feel frustrated or annoyed. On the other hand, when MWL is at a high level, this can lead individual to confusion and decrease their performance in processing information and increases the chances of mistakes. Hence, designers who are interested in human or system performance require answers about operator workload at all stages of system design and operation so design alternatives can be explored and evaluated [20]. MWL is not a linear concept [30,43] but it can be intuitively defined as the volume of cognitive work necessary for an individual to accomplish a task over time. It is not 'an elementary property, rather it emerges from the interaction between the requirements of a task, the circumstances under which it is performed and the skills, behaviours and perceptions of the operator' [20]. However, this is only a practical definition, as many other factors influence mental workload [33].

2.4 Measures of Mental Workload

The measurement of MWL is an extensive area where several assessment techniques have been proposed [10,37,51,59,61,62]: (a) *self-assessment measures*; (b) *task measures*; (c) *physiological measures*; The category of *self-assessment measures* is often referred to as self-report measures. It relies on the subject perceived experience of the interaction with an underlying interactive system through the direct estimation of individual differences such as the emotional state, attitude and stress of the operator, the effort devoted to the task and its demands [14,20]. It is strongly believed that only the individual concerned with the task can provide an accurate judgement with respect to the MWL experienced, hence self-assessment measures have always attracted many practitioners. This has also been adopted in this study. The class of *performance measures* is based upon the assumption that the mental workload of an operator, interacting with a system, gain relevance only if it influences system performance. In turn, this class appears as the most valuable options for designers [45,53]. The category of *physiological measures* considers bodily responses derived from the operator's physiology. These responses are believed to be correlated to MWL and are aimed at interpreting psychological processes by analysing their effect on the state of the body. Their advantage is that they can be collected continuously over time, without requiring an overt response by the operator [40] but they require specific equipment and trained operators mitigating their employability in real-world tasks.

3   Related Work

In a recent review, it was acknowledge that usability and performance are two core elements for assessing user experience [46]. Lehmann et al. also emphasise the importance of adopting multiple metrics for tackling the problem of user engagement measurement, being usability and cognitive engagement part of these metrics [24]. OBrien and collaborators identified mental workload and usability as elements of user engagement, suggesting that a little correlation exists between the two constructs [41]. Nonetheless, this is under-investigated in their environment and, to the best of our knowledge, this study is the first real attempt aimed at exploring the relationship between subjective mental workload and perception of usability. Additionally, because the former area is less explored in interaction and web design, while the latter area has an extensive research endeavour [21,54], this section mainly covers related work on mental workload.

3.1   Applications of MWL for Design

At an early design phase, a system/interface can be optimised taking mental workload into consideration, guiding designers in making appropriate structural changes [60]. Specifically, in the context of web-applications, modern interfaces have become increasingly complex [35], often requiring more mentally demanding tasks with a consequent increments in the degree of mental workload imposed on operators [17,18]. As the difficulty of these task increases, due to interface complexity, mental workload also increases and performance usually decreases [10]. In turn, operator's response time increases, error are more recurrent and fewer tasks are completed per time unit [22]. In contrast, when task difficulty is minor, interfaces and systems can impose a low mental workload on operators. This situation should be avoided as it leads to difficulties in maintaining attention and increasing reaction time [10]. [63] noted how roles can be useful in interface design and proposed a role-based method to measure MWL applicable in HCI for dynamically adjusting mental workload and enhance performance in interaction.

3.2   Application of MWL Self-assessment Measures

Self-assessment measures of MWL include multidimensional approaches such as the NASA's Task Load Index ($NASATLX$) [20], the Subjective Workload Assessment Technique [42], the Workload Profile [52] as well as uni-dimensional measures such as the Copper-Harper scale [13], the Rating Scale Mental Effort [64], the Subjective Workload Dominance Technique [55] and the Bedford scale [44]. These procedures have low implementation requirements, low intrusiveness and high subject acceptability. The $NASATLX$ has been used for evaluating user interfaces in health-care [26] or in e-commerce, along with a dual-task objective methodology for investigating the effects on user satisfaction [47]. The Workload Profile [52], the $NASATLX$ and the Subjective Workload Assessment Technique [42] have been compared in a user study to evaluate different web-based interfaces [35]. Tracy and Albers adopted three different techniques for measuring MWL in web-site design: $NASATLX$, the Sternberg Memory

Test and a tapping test [2,50]. They proposed a technique to identify sub-areas of a web-site in which end-users manifested a higher mental worklaod during interaction, allowing designers to modify those critical regions. Similarly, [15] investigated how the design of query interfaces influence stress, workload and performance during information search. Here stress was measured by physiological signals and a subjective assessment technique – Short Stress State Questionnaire. Mental workload was assessed using the *NASATLX* and log data was used as objective indicator of performance to characterise search behaviour.

4   Design of Experiments

A study involving human participants executing typical tasks over 3 popular web-sites (Youtube, Google, Wikipedia) was set to investigate the relationship between perception of usability, mental workload and objective performance. One self-assessment procedure for measuring usability and two for mental workload:

- the System Usability Scale (*SUS*) [9]
- the Nasa Task Load Index (*NASATLX*), developed at NASA [20]
- the Workload Profile (*WP*) [52], based on Multiple Resource Theory [56,57].

Five classes of the objective performance of participants on tasks were set:

1. the task was not completed as the user gave up
2. the execution of the task was terminated because the available time was over
3. the task was completed and no answer was required by the user
4. the task was completed, the user provided an answer, but it was wrong
5. the task was completed and the user provided the correct answer.

These are sometimes conditionally dependent (Fig. 2). The experimental hypothesis are defined in Table 1 and illustrated in Fig. 3.

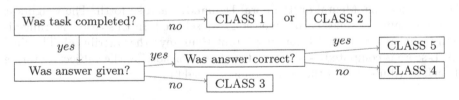

Fig. 2. Partial dependencies of classes of objective performance

Table 1. Research hypothesis

H_1	Usability and Mental workload are two uncorrelated constructs capturing difference variance (as measured with self-reporting techniques - SUS, NASATLX, WP)
H_2	A unified model incorporating a usability and a MWL measure can better predict objective performance than MWL alone

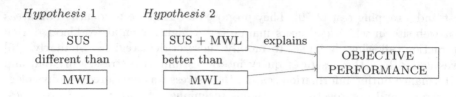

Fig. 3. Illustration of research hypothesis

4.1 Details of Experimental Subjective Self-reporting Techniques

The System Usability Scale is a subjective usability assessment instrument that uses a Likert scale, bounded in the range 1 to 5 [9]. Questions can be found in Table 9. Individual scores are not meaningful on their own. For odd questions (SUS_i with $i = \{1|3|5|7|9\}$), the score contribution is the scale position (SUS_i) minus 1. For even questions (SUS_i with $i = \{2|4|6|8|10\}$), the contribution is 5 minus the scale position. For comparison purposes, the SUS value is converted in the range $[1..100] \in \Re$ with $i_1 = \{1, 3, 5, 7, 9\}$, $i_2 = \{2, 4, 6, 8, 10\}$

$$SUS = 2.5 \cdot \left[\sum_{i_1}(SUS_i - 1) + \sum_{i_2}(5 - SUS_i) \right]$$

The NASA Task Load Index instrument [20] belongs to the category of self-assessment measures. It has been validated in the aviation industry and other contexts in Ergonomics [20,45] with several applications in many socio-technical domains. It is a combination of six factors believed to influence MWL (questions of Table 10). Each factors is quantified with a subjective judgement coupled with a weight computed via a paired comparison procedure. Subjects are required to decide, for each possible pair (binomial coefficient, $\binom{6}{2} = 15$) of the 6 factors, *'which of the two contributed the most to mental workload during the task'*, such as 'Mental or Temporal Demand?', and so forth. The weights w are the number of times each dimension was selected. In this case, the range is from 0 (not relevant) to 5 (more important than any other attribute). The final MWL score is computed as a weighed average, considering the subjective rating of each attribute d_i and the correspondent weights w_i:

$$NASATLX : [0..100] \in \Re \qquad NASATLX = \left(\sum_{i=1}^{6} d_i \times w_i \right) \frac{1}{15}$$

The Workload Profile (WP) assessment procedure [52] is built upon the Multiple Resource Theory proposed in [56,57]. In this theory, individuals are seen as having different capacities or 'resources' related to: • *stage of information processing* – perceptual/central processing and response selection/execution; • *code of information processing* – spatial/verbal; • *input* – visual and auditory processing; • *output* – manual and speech output. Each dimension is quantified through subjective rates (questions of Table 11) and subjects, after task completion, are required to rate the proportion of attentional resources used for performing a given task with a value in the range $0..1 \in \Re$. A rating of 0 means that the task placed no demand while 1 indicates that it required maximum attention. The aggregation strategy is a simple sum of the 8 rates d (averaged here, and scaled in $[1..100] \in \Re$ for comparison purposes):

$$WP : [0..100] \in \Re \qquad WP = \frac{1}{8} \sum_{i=1}^{8} d_i \times 100$$

4.2   Participants and Procedure

A sample of 46 people fluent in English volunteered to participate in the study after signing a consent form. Subjects were divided into 2 groups of 23 each: those in group A were different to those in group B. Participants could not interact with instructors during the tasks and they did not have to be trained. Ages ranges from 20 to 35 years; 24 females and 22 males evenly distributed across the 2 groups (Total - Avg.: 28.6, Std. 3.98; g.A - Avg. 28.35, Std.: 4.22; g.B - Avg: 28.85, Std.: 3.70) all with a daily Internet usage of at least 2 hours. Participants were required to execute a set of 9 information-seeking web-based tasks (Table 13) as naturally as they could, over 2 or 3 sessions of approximately 45/70 min each, on different non-consecutive days. Tasks differed in terms of difficulty, time-pressure, time-limits, interference, interruptions and demands on different psychological modalities. Two groups were created because the tasks were executed on web-based interfaces, sometimes altered at run-time (through a CSS/HTML manipulation) (as in Table 12). This manipulation was implemented, as part of a larger study [27,28,34], to enable A/B testing of web-interfaces (not included here). Interface alteration was not extreme, like making things very hard to read. Rather the goal was to alter the original interface to manipulate task difficulty and usability independently. The order of the tasks administered was the same for all the participants. Computerised versions of the SUS (Table 9), the $NASATLX$ (Table 10) and the WP (Table 11) instruments were administered immediately after task completion. Note that the question of the $NASA - TLX$ related to 'physical load' was set to 0 as well as its weight. Consequently, the pairwise comparison procedure was shorter. Some volunteer did not execute all the tasks and the final dataset contains 405 cases.

5   Results

Table 2 contains the means and standard deviations of the usability and the mental workload scores for each task, depicted also in Fig. 4.

5.1   Testing Hypothesis 1 - Difference Usability and Mental Workload

From an initial analysis of Fig. 5, it seems clear that there is no correlation between the usability scores (SUS) and the mental workload scores ($NASATLX$, WP). This is statistically confirmed in Table 3 by the Pearson and Spearman correlation

Table 2. Mental workload and usability - Groups A, B (G.A/G.B)

G. A Task	NASATLX avg	std	WP avg	std	SUS avg	std	G. B Task	NASATLX avg	std	WP avg	std	SUS avg	std
1	46.03	24.30	39.34	11.54	50.38	21.31	1	23.66	13.93	26.57	14.85	77.00	19.49
2	41.38	15.71	27.23	9.51	81.98	14.06	2	40.97	16.62	28.27	14.73	73.24	16.92
3	41.08	14.47	36.50	13.10	73.77	19.71	3	42.63	14.21	35.60	15.81	82.33	14.58
4	35.36	17.92	34.43	13.61	85.41	8.96	4	42.70	14.09	34.87	15.25	46.61	17.90
5	45.47	15.74	37.49	13.78	69.22	19.84	5	51.15	13.78	33.54	13.88	84.64	12.77
6	46.35	14.13	43.09	12.20	86.36	09.26	6	39.31	14.57	44.61	13.50	82.68	14.12
7	56.20	23.97	37.11	14.92	68.87	16.38	7	47.86	19.97	37.84	18.02	59.62	17.97
8	49.76	19.96	41.09	13.31	82.16	10.93	8	55.34	14.75	42.97	16.98	81.41	13.73
9	64.61	12.92	46.65	10.46	81.85	09.81	9	70.75	16.29	50.51	14.06	75.39	18.02

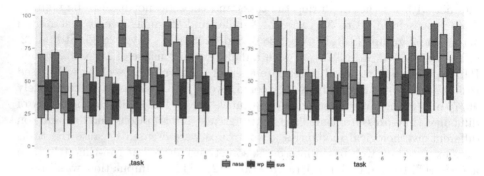

Fig. 4. Summary statistics by task

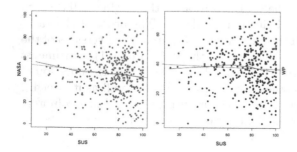

Fig. 5. Scatterplots of $NASATLX, WP$ vs SUS.

Table 3. Correlation coefficients

pearson	WP	SUS
NASA	0.55	-0.13
WP		-0.05

spearman	WP	SUS
NASA	0.53	-0.1
WP		-0.08

coefficients computed over the full dataset (Groups A, B). Person was chosen for exploring linear correlation while Spearman for monotonic relationship, not necessarily linear.

Despite perception of usability does not seem to correlate at all with mental workload, a further investigation of their relationship was performed on the scores obtained for each task. Table 4 lists the correlations between the MWL scores ($NASATLX, WP$) against the usability scores (SUS), and Fig. 6 their

Table 4. Correlations MWL vs usability. Groups A and B

G. B Task	Pearson Nasa/SUS	WP/SUS	Spearman Nasa/SUS	WP/SUS	G. A Task	Pearson Nasa/SUS	WP/SUS	Spearman Nasa/SUS	WP/SUS
1	-0.21	-0.39	-0.24	-0.42	1	-0.69	-0.06	-0.6	-0.11
2	-0.22	0.18	-0.1	0.01	2	-0.12	-0.15	-0.15	-0.23
3	-0.25	-0.13	-0.23	-0.08	3	-0.07	0.13	-0.05	0.11
4	-0.05	-0.11	-0.10	-0.09	4	-0.64	-0.34	-0.60	-0.34
5	0.14	-0.26	0.10	-0.27	5	-0.34	-0.08	-0.31	-0.08
6	-0.17	-0.01	0.04	0.06	6	-0.08	-0.14	-0.07	-0.12
7	-0.11	0.03	-0.10	0.03	7	-0.32	-0.2	-0.37	-0.30
8	-0.28	0.02	-0.13	-0.13	8	-0.08	-0.29	-0.04	-0.24
9	0.48	-0.15	0.57	-0.15	9	0.36	0.14	0.44	0.14

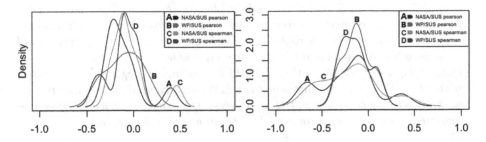

Fig. 6. Density plots of the correlations by task - Group A, B

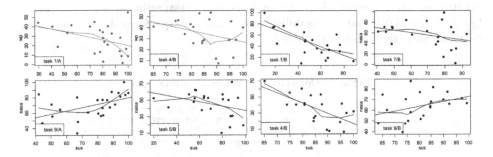

Fig. 7. Details of tasks with moderate/high correlation

densities. Generally, in behavioural/social sciences, there may be a greater contribution from complicating factors, as in the case of subjective ratings. Hence, correlations above 0.5 are regarded as very high, within [0.1–0.3] small and within [0.3–0.5] as medium/moderate (symmetrically to negative values) [12, p. 82]. For this analysis, only medium/high coefficients are considered. Yet, a clearer picture does not emerge and just a few tasks show some form of correlation between mental workload and usability. Figure 7 provides further details aiming at extracting further information and possible interpretations on why workload scores were moderately/highly correlated with usability.

- task 1/A and task 4/B: WP is moderately negatively correlated with SUS. This suggests that *when the proportion of attentional resources being taxed by a task is moderated and decreases, the perception of good usability increases.* In other words, when web-interfaces and the tasks executed over them require a moderate use of different stages, codes of information processing and input, output modalities (Sect. 4.1), the usability of those interfaces is increasingly perceived as positive.
- task 9/A and task 9/B: the $NASATLX$ is highly and positively correlated with SUS. This suggests that, even when time pressure is imposed upon tasks causing an increment in the workload experienced, and the perception of performance decreases because task answer is not found, than perception of usability is not affected if the task is pleasant and amusing (like task 9). In other words, *even if experienced workload increases but is not excessive, and even if the interface is slightly altered (task 9 group B), the perception of good usability is strengthened if tasks are enjoyable.*
- tasks 1/B, 4/B, 5/B, 7/B the $NASATLX$ is highly negatively correlated with SUS. This suggests that *when the MWL experienced by users increases, perhaps because tasks are not straightforward, perception of usability can be negatively affected even with a slight alteration of the interface.*

The above interpretations do not aim to be exhaustive; they are just our own interpretations, they cannot be generalised and are only confined to this study. To further strengthening the data analysis, an investigation of the correlation between the MWL and the usability scores has been performed by considering users on an individual-basis (Table 5 and Fig. 8).

Table 5. Correlation MWL-usability by user

User	Pearson Nasa/SUS	Pearson WP/SUS	Spearman Nasa/SUS	Spearman WP/SUS	User	Pearson Nasa/SUS	Pearson WP/SUS	Spearman Nasa/SUS	Spearman WP/SUS
1	-0.5	-0.43	-0.45	-0.32	24	0.19	0.32	-0.25	0.19
2	0.41	-0.11	0.57	-0.23	25	-0.62	-0.07	-0.38	-0.4
3	-0.4	0.18	-0.27	0.45	26	-0.69	0.29	-0.62	0.38
4	0.38	0.37	0.15	0.17	27	-0.38	-0.36	-0.55	-0.58
5	-0.66	-0.57	-0.7	-0.63	28	-0.13	-0.43	-0.2	-0.48
6	-0.15	-0.34	-0.06	-0.14	29	-0.11	0.28	-0.03	0.15
7	-0.17	-0.2	-0.17	-0.4	30	0.17	-0.22	0.22	-0.38
8	0.02	0.21	-0.36	0.01	31	-0.6	-0.42	-0.78	-0.48
9	-0.16	-0.4	-0.25	-0.08	32	-0.7	-0.4	-0.2	-0.22
10	0	0.26	-0.05	0.33	33	0.06	-0.67	0	-0.32
11	-0.47	-0.74	-0.52	-0.78	34	-0.41	-0.45	-0.32	-0.27
12	0.58	-0.33	0.46	-0.4	35	0.58	0.12	0.8	0.4
13	-0.17	0.18	-0.23	0.18	36	-0.39	-0.31	-0.54	-0.37
14	0.24	0.39	-0.22	0.16	37	-0.47	-0.08	-0.17	0.38
15	0.06	0.17	0.21	0.47	38	0.21	0.43	0.32	0.51
16	0.46	0.34	0.57	0.55	39	-0.17	-0.07	0.2	0.12
17	0.27	0.02	0.15	0.23	40	-0.34	0.93	0.1	0.87
18	-0.14	0.16	-0.15	-0.2	41	0.25	-0.23	0.37	-0.35
19	-0.57	0.13	-0.41	0.1	42	-0.67	-0.6	-0.65	-0.38
20	0.05	-0.21	0.27	0.18	43	0.36	0.34	0.28	0.25
21	0.36	-0.05	-0.07	0.07	44	-0.69	-0.69	-0.67	-0.51
22	-0.99	0.05	-1	0.4	45	-0.51	-0.22	-0.42	-0.27
23	0.29	-0.05	0.45	-0.17	46	0.39	0.59	0.2	0.36

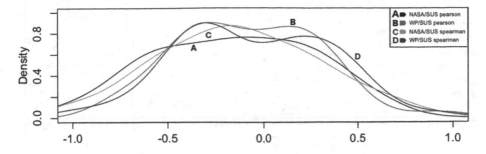

Fig. 8. Density plots of the correlations by user

As in the previous analysis (by task), just medium and high correlation coefficients (>0.3) are considered for deeper investigation. Additionally, because the results of Tables 3 and 4 were not able to systematically show common trends, the analysis on the individual-basis was reinforced by considering only those users for which a medium/high linear relationship (Pearson) and a monotonic relationship (Spearman) was detected between both the two MWL scores ($NASA$, WP) and the usability scores (SUS). Table 5 highlights these users (1, 5, 11, 12, 21, 22, 27, 39, 40, 46). The objective was to look for the presence of any particular pattern of user's behaviour or a complex deterministic structure. Figure 9 depicts the linear scatterplots associated to these users with a linear straight regression line and a local smoothing regression line (Lowess algorithm [11]). The former type of regression is parametric and stands on the normal distribution, while the latter is non-parametric and it is aimed at supporting exploration and identification of patterns, enhancing the ability to see a line of best fit over data not necessarily normally distributed. Outliers from scatterplot are not removed: the rationale behind this decision is justified by the limited amount of points – maximum 9 points that coincides with the number of tasks.

No clear and consistent patterns emerge from Fig. 9. However, by analysing the mental workload scores ($NASATLX$ and WP), it is possible to note that the 10 selected users have all achieved, except a few outliers, a score of optimal mental workload (on average between 20–72). In other words, these users did not perceive underload or overload while executing the nine tasks. From an analysis of the usability assessments, all the users achieved scores higher than 40, indicating that no interface was perceived not usable at all. This might indicate that *when the mental workload experienced by users is within an optimal range, and usability is not bad, then the combination of mental workload and usability in a joint model might not be fully powerful in explaining objective performance more than mental workload alone*. In the other cases, where correlation of mental workload and usability is almost inexistent, then a joint model might better explain objective performance. The following section is devoted to test this.

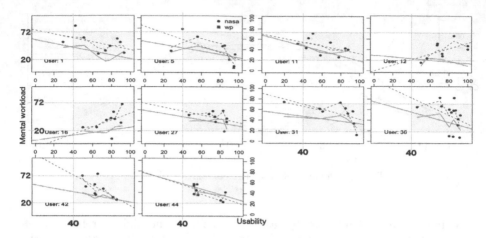

Fig. 9. Correlations MWL-usability for users with moderate/high Pearson and Spearman coefficients

5.2 Testing Hypothesis 2 - Usability and Mental Workload Impact Performance More than Just Workload

From the previous analysis it appears that the perception of usability and the mental workload experienced by users are not related, except few cases in which mental workload was optimal and usability was not bad. Nonetheless, as previously reviewed, literature suggests that these constructs are important for describing and exploring the user's experience with an interactive system. For this reason a further investigation of the impact of the perception of usability and mental workload on objective performance has been conducted to test hypothesis 2 (Sect. 4). In this context, objective performance refers to objective indicators of the performance of the volunteers who participated in the user study, categorised in 5 classes (Sect. 4). During the experiment, the measurement of the objective performance of users was in some case faulty. These were discarded and a new dataset with 390 valid cases was formed. The exploration of the impact of the perception of usability and mental workload on the 5 classes of objective performance was treated as a classification problem, employing supervised machine learning. In detail, 4 different classification methods were chosen to predict the objective performance classes, according to different types of learning:

- information-based learning: decision trees (with Gini coefficient);
- similarity-based learning: k-nearest neighbors;
- probability-based learning: Naive Bayes;
- error-based learning: support vector machine (with a radial kernel) [8, 23].

The distribution of the 5 classes is depicted in Fig. 10 and Table 6:

Clearly, the above frequencies are unbalanced. For this reason a new dataset has been formed through oversampling, a technique to adjust class distributions and to correct for a bias in the original dataset, aimed at reducing the negative

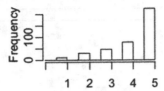

Fig. 10. Distribution of performance classes - original dataset

Table 6. Frequencies of classes

Class	Original	Oversampled
1	11	224
2	30	224
3	47	224
4	78	224
5	224	224
Total	390	1120

impact of class unbalance on model fitting. Random sampling (with replacement) the minority classes to be the same size as the majority class is used (Table 6). The two mental workload indexes ($NASA$ and WP) and the usability index (SUS) were treated as independent variables (features) and they were used both individually and in combination to form models aimed at predicting the 5 classes of objective performance (Fig. 11).

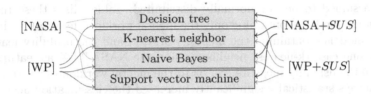

Fig. 11. Independent features and classification techniques

The independent features were normalised in the range $[0..1] \in \Re$ to facilitate the training of models and 10-fold stratified cross validation has been adopted in the training phase. In other words, the oversampled dataset was divided in 10 folds and in each fold, the original ratio of the distribution of the objective performance classes (Fig. 10, Table 6) was preserved. 9 folds were used for training and the remaining fold for testing against accuracy and this was repeated 10 times changing the testing fold. This generated 10 models and produced 10 classification accuracies for each learning technique and for each combination of independent features (Fig. 12, Table 7). It is important to note that training sets (a combination of 9 folds) and test sets (the remaining holdout set) were always the same across the classification techniques and the different combination of independent features (paired 10-fold CV). This is critical to perform a fair comparison of the different trained models using the same training/test sets.

To test hypothesis 2, the 10-fold cross-validated paired Wilcoxon statistical test has been chosen for comparing two matched accuracy distributions and to assess whether their population mean ranks differ (it is a paired difference test) [58]. This test is a non-parametric alternative to the paired Student's t-test

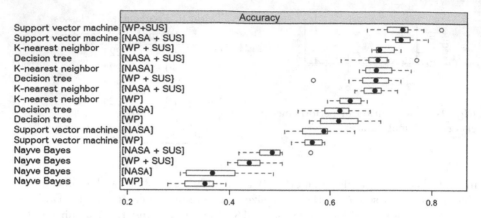

Fig. 12. Independent features, classification technique, distribution of accuracies with 10-fold stratified cross validation

selected because the population of accuracies (obtained testing each holdout set) was assumed to be not normally distributed. Table 8 lists these tests for the individual models (containing only the mental workload feature) against the combined models (containing the mental workload and the usability features). Except in one case (k-nearest neighbor, using the NASA-TLX as feature), the addition of the usability measure (*SUS*) to the mental workload feature (NASA or WP) always statistically significantly increased the classification accuracy of the induced models, trained with the 4 selected classifiers. This suggests how mental workload and usability can be jointly employed to explain objective performance measure, an extremely important dimension of user experience.

5.3   Summary of Findings

In summary, from empirical evidence, the two hypothesis can be accepted.

– H_1: *Usability and Mental workload are two uncorrelated constructs (as measured with the selected self-reporting techniques (SUS, NASA-TLX, WP).*

They capture different variance in experimental tasks. This has been tested by a correlation analysis (both parametric and nonparametric) which confirmed that the two constructs are not correlated. The obtained Pearson coefficients suggest that there is no linear correlation between usability (SUS scale) and mental workload (NASA-TLX and WP scales). The Spearman coefficients confirmed that there is no tendency for usability to either increase or decrease when mental workload increases. The large variation in correlations within different tasks and for different individuals is interesting and worth of future investigation.

– H_2: *A unified model incorporating a usability and a MWL measure can better explain objective performance than MWL alone.*

Table 7. Ordered distributions of accuracies of trained models

Classifier	Independent features	Min	1st Qu.	Median	Mean	3rd Qu.	Max
Support vector machine	WP, *SUS*	0.6726	0.7140	0.7422	0.7368	0.7506	0.8182
Support vector machine	NASATLX, *SUS*	0.7080	0.7285	0.7387	0.7430	0.7534	0.7928
K-nearest neighbors	WP, *SUS*	0.6754	0.6971	0.7027	0.7091	0.7185	0.7748
Decision tree	NASATLX, *SUS*	0.6216	0.6769	0.6933	0.6937	0.7111	0.7699
K-nearest neighbors	NASATLX	0.6339	0.6497	0.6815	0.6822	0.7101	0.7297
Decision tree	WP, *SUS*	0.5664	0.6645	0.6894	0.6816	0.7136	0.7387
K-nearest neighbors	NASATLX, *SUS*	0.6549	0.6704	0.6861	0.6848	0.6971	0.7143
K-nearest neighbors	WP	0.5676	0.6182	0.6355	0.6331	0.6510	0.6818
Decision tree	NASATLX	0.6216	0.6470	0.6578	0.6615	0.6696	0.7027
Decision tree	WP	0.5586	0.5813	0.6170	0.6179	0.6511	0.6991
Support vector machine	NASATLX	0.5664	0.6097	0.6233	0.6189	0.6323	0.6757
Support vector machine	WP	0.5225	0.5503	0.5644	0.5625	0.5812	0.5893
Naive Bayes	NASATLX, *SUS*	0.4182	0.4596	0.4844	0.4827	0.4989	0.5614
Naive Bayes	WP, *SUS*	0.3964	0.4194	0.4389	0.4411	0.4602	0.5045
Naive Bayes	NASATLX	0.2973	0.3400	0.3527	0.3597	0.3943	0.4091
Naive Bayes	WP	0.2793	0.3139	0.3524	0.3428	0.3671	0.3929

Table 8. Wilcoxon test of distributions of accuracies with different independent features and learning classifiers

Classifier	Model 1	Model 2	Accuracy (mean)		p-value	Difference
			Model 1	Model 2		
Decision tree	NASA	NASA, *SUS*	0.6615	0.6937	0.032	Yes
Decision tree	WP	WP, *SUS*	0.6179	0.6816	0.019	Yes
K-nearest neighbor	NASA	NASA, *SUS*	0.6822	0.6848	1	No
K-nearest neighbor	WP	WP, *SUS*	0.6331	0.7091	0.005	Yes
Nayve Bayes	NASA	NASA, *SUS*	0.3597	0.4827	0.001	Yes
Nayve Bayes	WP	WP, *SUS*	0.3428	0.4411	0.001	Yes
Support vector machine	NASA	NASA, *SUS*	0.6189	0.743	0.001	Yes
Support vector machine	WP	WP, *SUS*	0.5625	0.7368	0.001	Yes

This has been tested by inducing combined and individual models, using four supervised machine learning classification techniques, to predict objective performance of users (five classes of performance). The combined models were most of the times able to predict objective user performance significantly better than the individual models, according to the Wilcoxon non-parametric test.

Table 9. System Usability Scale (*SUS*)

Label	Question
SUS_1	I think that I would like to use this interface frequently
SUS_2	I found the interface unnecessarily complex
SUS_3	I thought the interface was easy to use
SUS_4	I think that I would need the support of a technical person to use this interface
SUS_5	I found the various functions in this interface were well integrated
SUS_6	I thought there was too much inconsistency in this interface
SUS_7	I would imagine that most people would learn to use this interface quickly
SUS_8	I found the interface very unmanageable (irritating or tiresome) to use
SUS_9	I felt very confident using the interface
SUS_{10}	I needed to learn a lot of things before I could get going with this interface

Table 10. The NASA Task Load Index (NASA-TLX)

Label	Question
NT_1	How much mental and perceptual activity was required (e.g. thinking, deciding, calculating, remembering, looking, searching, etc.)? Was the task easy or demanding, simple or complex, exacting or forgiving?
NT_2	How much physical activity was required (e.g. pushing, pulling, turning, controlling, activating, etc.)? Was the task easy or demanding, slow or brisk, slack or strenuous, restful or laborious?
NT_3	How much time pressure did you feel due to the rate or pace at which the tasks or task elements occurred? Was the pace slow and leisurely or rapid and frantic?
NT_4	How hard did you have to work (mentally and physically) to accomplish your level of performance?
NT_5	How successful do you think you were in accomplishing the goals, of the task set by the experimenter (or yourself)? How satisfied were you with your performance in accomplishing these goals?
NT_6	How insecure, discouraged, irritated, stressed and annoyed versus secure, gratified, content, relaxed and complacent did you feel during the task?

Table 11. Workload Profile (WP)

Label	Question
WP_1	How much attention was required for activities like remembering, problem-solving, decision-making, perceiving (detecting, recognising, identifying objects)?
WP_2	How much attention was required for selecting the proper response channel (manual - keyboard/mouse, or speech - voice) and its execution?
WP_3	How much attention was required for spatial processing (spatially pay attention around)?
WP_4	How much attention was required for verbal material (eg. reading, processing linguistic material, listening to verbal conversations)?
WP_5	How much attention was required for executing the task based on the information visually received (eyes)?
WP_6	How much attention was required for executing the task based on the information auditorily received?
WP_7	How much attention was required for manually respond to the task (eg. keyboard/mouse)?
WP_8	How much attention was required for producing the speech response (eg. engaging in a conversation, talking, answering questions)?

Table 12. Run-time manipulation of web-interfaces

Task	Manipulation
1	Left menu of wikipedia.com and the internal searching box have been removed. The background colour has been set to light yellow
2	Left menu of wikipedia.com and the internal searching box have been removed. The background colour has been set to light yellow
3	Each result returned by Google has been wrapped with a box with thin borders and the font has been altered
4	The left menu of google.com has been removed, the background colour set to black and the font colour to blue
5	The background colour of google.com has been set to black and the font colour to blue
6	The background colour of youtube.com has been set to dark grey
7	The background colour of wikipedia.com has been set to light blue and headings to white
8	The background colour of youtube.com has been set to black and each video was always displayed in 16:9, removing the right list of related videos
9	The background colour of youtube.com has been set to dark grey

Table 13. Experimental tasks (M = manipulated; g = Group)

Task	Description	Type	Task condition	Web-site	g.A	g.B
T_1	Find out how many people live in Sidney	Fact finding	Simple search	Wikipedia		M
T_2	Read the content of simple.wikipedia.org/wiki/Grammar	Browsing	Not goal-oriented and no time pressure	Wikipedia	M	
T_3	Find out the difference (in years) between the year of the foundation of the Apple Computer Inc. and the year of the 14th FIFA world cup	Fact finding	dual-task and mental arithmetical calculations	Google		M
T_4	Find out the difference (in years) between the foundation of the Microsoft Corp. & the year of the 23rd Olympic games	Fact finding	dual-task and mental arithmetical calculations	Google	M	
T_5	Find out the year of birth of the 1st wife of the founder of playboy	Fact finding	Single task by time pressure (2-min limit). Each 30 s user is warned of time left	Google		M
T_6	Find out the name of the man (interpreted by Johnny Deep) in the video www.youtube.com/watch?v=FfTPS-TFQ_c	Fact finding	Constant demand on visual and auditory modalities. Participant can replay the video if required	Youtube		M
T_7	a) Play the following song www.youtube.com/watch?v=Rb5G1eRIj6c and while listening to it, b) find out the result of the polynomial equation $p(x)$, with $x = 7$ contained in the wikipedia article http://it.wikipedia.org/wiki/Polinomi	Fact finding	Demand on visual modality and inference on auditory modality. The song is extremely irritating	Wikipedia	M	
T_8	Find out how many times Stewie jumps in the video www.youtube.com/watch?v=TSe9gbdkQ8s	Fact finding	Demand on visual resource and external inference: participant is distracted twice and can replay video	Youtube	M	
T_9	Find out the age of the blue fish in the video www.youtube.com/watch?v=H4BNbHBcnDI	Fact finding	Demand on visual and auditory modality, plus time-pressure: 150-s limit. User can replay the video. There is no answer	Youtube		M

6 Conclusion

This study attempted to investigate the correlation between the perception of usability and the mental workload imposed by typical tasks executed over three popular web-sites: Youtube, Wikipedia and Google. Prominent definitions of usability and mental workload were presented, with a particular focus on the latter. This because usability is a central notion in human-computer interaction, with a plethora of definitions and applications existing in the literature. Whereas, the construct of mental workload has a background in Ergonomics and Human Factors, but less mentioned in HCI. A well known subjective instrument for assessing usability—the System Usability Scale—and two subjective mental workload assessment procedures—the NASA Task Load Index, and the Workload Profile—have been employed in a user study involving 46 subjects. Empirical evidence suggests that there is no relationship between the perception of usability of a set of web-interfaces and the mental workload imposed on users by a set of tasks executed on them. In turn, this suggests that the two constructs seem to describe two not overlapping phenomena. The implication of this is that they could be jointly used to better describe objective indicator of user performance, a dimension of user experience. Future work will be devoted to replicate this study employing a set of different interfaces, tasks and with different usability and mental workload assessment instruments. The contributions of this research are to offer a new perspective on the application of mental workload to traditional usability inspection methods, and a richer approach to explain the human-system interaction and support its design.

References

1. Addie, J., Niels, T.: Processing resources and attention. In: Handbook of Human Factors in Web Design, pp. 3424–3439. Lawrence Erlbaum Associates (2005)
2. Albers, M.: Tapping as a measure of cognitive load and website usability. In: Proceedings of the 29th ACM International Conference on Design of Communication, pp. 25–32 (2011)
3. Alonso-Ríos, D., Vázquez-García, A., Mosqueira-Rey, E., Moret-Bonillo, V.: A context-of-use taxonomy for usability studies. Int. J. Hum.-Comput. Interact. **26**(10), 941–970 (2010)
4. Annett, J.: Subjective rating scales in ergonomics: a reply. Ergonomics **45**(14), 1042–1046 (2002)
5. Annett, J.: Subjective rating scales: science or art? Ergonomics **45**(14), 966–987 (2002)
6. Baber, C.: Subjective evaluation of usability. Ergonomics **45**(14), 1021–1025 (2002)
7. Bangor, A., Kortum, P.T., Miller, J.T.: An empirical evaluation of the system usability scale. Int. J. Hum.-Comput. Interact. **24**(6), 574–594 (2008)
8. Bennett, K.P., Campbell, C.: Support vector machines: hype or hallelujah? SIGKDD Explor. Newsl. **2**(2), 1–13 (2000)
9. Brooke, J.: SUS: a quick and dirty usability scale. In: Jordan, P.W., Weerdmeester, B., Thomas, A., Mclelland, I.L. (eds.) Usability Evaluation in Industry. Taylor and Francis, London (1996)

10. Cain, B.: A review of the mental workload literature. Technical report, Defence Research and Development Canada, Human System Integration (2007)
11. Cleveland, W.S.: Robust locally weighted regression and smoothing scatterplots. Am. Stat. Assoc. **74**, 829–836 (1979)
12. Cohen, J.: Statistical Power Analysis for the Behavioral Sciences. Lawrence Erlbaum Associates, Mahwah (1988)
13. Cooper, G.E., Harper, R.P.: The use of pilot ratings in the evaluation of aircraft handling qualities. Technical report AD689722, 567, Advisory Group for Aerospace Research and Development, April 1969
14. De Waard, D.: The measurement of drivers' mental workload. University of Groningen, The Traffic Research Centre VSC (1996)
15. Edwards, A., Kelly, D., Azzopardi, L.: The impact of query interface design on stress, workload and performance. In: Hanbury, A., Kazai, G., Rauber, A., Fuhr, N. (eds.) ECIR 2015. LNCS, vol. 9022, pp. 691–702. Springer, Cham (2015). doi:10.1007/978-3-319-16354-3_76
16. Fischer, G.: User modeling in human-computer interaction. User Model. User-Adapt. Interact. **11**(1–2), 65–86 (2001)
17. Gwizdka, J.: Assessing cognitive load on web search tasks. Ergon. Open J. **2**(1), 114–123 (2009)
18. Gwizdka, J.: Distribution of cognitive load in web search. J. Am. Soc. Inf. Sci. Technol. **61**(11), 2167–2187 (2010)
19. Harper, B.D., Norman, K.L.: Improving user satisfaction: the questionnaire for user interaction satisfaction version 5.5. In: 1st Annual Mid-Atlantic Human Factors Conference, pp. 224–228 (1993)
20. Hart, S.G.: Nasa-task load index (NASA-TLX); 20 years later. In: Human Factors and Ergonomics Society Annual Meeting, vol. 50. SAGE Journals (2006)
21. Hornbaek, K.: Current practice in measuring usability: challenges to usability studies and research. Int. J. Hum.-Comput. Stud. **64**(2), 79–102 (2006)
22. Huey, B.M., Wickens, C.D.: Workload Transition: Implication for Individual and Team Performance. National Academy Press, Washington, D.C. (1993)
23. Karatzoglou, A., Meyer, D.: Support vector machines in R. J. Stat. Softw. **15**(9), 1–32 (2006)
24. Lehmann, J., Lalmas, M., Yom-Tov, E., Dupret, G.: Models of user engagement. In: Masthoff, J., Mobasher, B., Desmarais, M.C., Nkambou, R. (eds.) UMAP 2012. LNCS, vol. 7379, pp. 164–175. Springer, Heidelberg (2012). doi:10.1007/978-3-642-31454-4_14
25. Lewis, J.R.: IBM computer usability satisfaction questionnaires: psychometric evaluation and instructions for use. Int. J. Hum.-Comput. Interact. **7**, 57–78 (1995)
26. Longo, L., Kane, B.: A novel methodology for evaluating user interfaces in health care. In: 2011 24th International Symposium on Computer-Based Medical Systems (CBMS), pp. 1–6, June 2011
27. Longo, L.: Human-computer interaction and human mental workload: assessing cognitive engagement in the world wide web. In: Campos, P., Graham, N., Jorge, J., Nunes, N., Palanque, P., Winckler, M. (eds.) INTERACT 2011. LNCS, vol. 6949, pp. 402–405. Springer, Heidelberg (2011). doi:10.1007/978-3-642-23768-3_43
28. Longo, L.: Formalising human mental workload as non-monotonic concept for adaptive and personalised web-design. In: Masthoff, J., Mobasher, B., Desmarais, M.C., Nkambou, R. (eds.) UMAP 2012. LNCS, vol. 7379, pp. 369–373. Springer, Heidelberg (2012). doi:10.1007/978-3-642-31454-4_38
29. Longo, L.: Formalising human mental workload as a defeasible computational concept. Ph.D. thesis, Trinity College Dublin (2014)

30. Longo, L.: A defeasible reasoning framework for human mental workload representation and assessment. Behav. Inf. Technol. **34**(8), 758–786 (2015)
31. Longo, L.: Designing medical interactive systems via assessment of human mental workload. In: International Symposium on Computer-Based Medical Systems, pp. 364–365 (2015)
32. Longo, L.: Mental workload in medicine: foundations, applications, open problems, challenges and future perspectives. In: 2016 IEEE 29th International Symposium on Computer-Based Medical Systems (CBMS), pp. 106–111, June 2016
33. Longo, L., Barrett, S.: A computational analysis of cognitive effort. In: Nguyen, N.T., Le, M.T., Świątek, J. (eds.) ACIIDS 2010, Part II. LNCS, vol. 5991, pp. 65–74. Springer, Heidelberg (2010). doi:10.1007/978-3-642-12101-2_8
34. Longo, L., Dondio, P.: On the relationship between perception of usability and subjective mental workload of web interfaces. In: IEEE/WIC/ACM International Conference on Web Intelligence and Intelligent Agent Technology, WI-IAT 2015, Singapore, 6–9 December, vol. I, pp. 345–352 (2015)
35. Longo, L., Rusconi, F., Noce, L., Barrett, S.: The importance of human mental workload in web-design. In: 8th International Conference on Web Information Systems and Technologies, pp. 403–409. SciTePress, April 2012
36. Macleod, M.: Usability in context: improving quality of use. In: Proceedings of the International Ergonomics Association 4th International Symposium on Human Factors in Organizational Design and Management. Elsevier (1994)
37. Moustafa, K., Luz, S., Longo, L.: Assessment of mental workload: a comparison of machine learning methods and subjective assessment techniques. In: Longo, L., Leva, M.C. (eds.) H-WORKLOAD 2017. CCIS, vol. 726, pp. 30–50. Springer, Cham (2017). doi:10.1007/978-3-319-61061-0_3
38. Nielsen, J.: Heuristic evaluation. In: Nielsen, J., Mack, R.L.E. (eds.) Usability Inspection Methods. Wiley, New York (1994)
39. Nielsen, J.: Usability inspection methods. In: Conference Companion on Human Factors in Computing Systems, CHI 1995, pp. 377–378. ACM, New York (1995)
40. O'Donnel, R.D., Eggemeier, T.F.: Workload assessment methodology. In: Boff, K., Kaufman, L., Thomas, J. (eds.) Handbook of Perception and Human Performance, pp. 42/1–42/49. Wiley-Interscience, New York (1986)
41. O'Brien, H.L., Toms, E.G.: What is user engagement? A conceptual framework for defining user engagement with technology. J. Am. Soc. Inf. Sci. Technol. **59**(6), 938–955 (2008). doi:10.1002/asi.20801
42. Reid, G.B., Nygren, T.E.: The subjective workload assessment technique: a scaling procedure for measuring mental workload. In: Hancock, P.A., Meshkati, N. (eds.) Human Mental Workload, Advances in Psychology, vol. 52, chap. 8, pp. 185–218. North-Holland, Amsterdam (1988)
43. Rizzo, L., Dondio, P., Delany, S.J., Longo, L.: Modeling mental workload via rule-based expert system: a comparison with NASA-TLX and workload profile. In: Iliadis, L., Maglogiannis, I. (eds.) AIAI 2016. IAICT, vol. 475, pp. 215–229. Springer, Cham (2016). doi:10.1007/978-3-319-44944-9_19
44. Roscoe, A.H., Ellis, G.A.: A subjective rating scale for assessing pilot workload in flight: a decade of practical use. Technical report 90019, Royal Aerospace Establishment, Farnborough (UK), March 1990
45. Rubio, S., Diaz, E., Martin, J., Puente, J.M.: Evaluation of subjective mental workload: a comparison of SWAT, NASA-TLX, and workload profile methods. Appl. Psychol. **53**(1), 61–86 (2004)

46. Saket, B., Endert, A., Stasko, J.: Beyond usability and performance: a review of user experience-focused evaluations in visualization. In: Proceedings of the Sixth Workshop on Beyond Time and Errors on Novel Evaluation Methods for Visualization, BELIV 2016, pp. 133–142. ACM, New York (2016). http://doi.acm.org/10.1145/2993901.2993903

47. Schmutz, P., Heinz, S., Métrailler, Y., Opwis, K.: Cognitive load in ecommerce applications: measurement and effects on user satisfaction. Adv. Hum.-Comput. Interact. **2009**, 3/1–3/9 (2009)

48. Shackel, B.: Usability - context, framework, definition, design and evaluation. Interact. Comput. **21**(5–6), 339–346 (2009)

49. Slaughter, L.A., Harper, B.D., Norman, K.L.: Assessing the equivalence of paper and on-line versions of the QUIS 5.5. In: 2nd Annual Mid-Atlantic Human Factors Conference, pp. 87–91 (1994)

50. Tracy, J.P., Albers, M.J.: Measuring cognitive load to test the usability of web sites. Usability and Information Design, pp. 256–260 (2006)

51. Tsang, P.S.: Mental workload. In: Karwowski, W. (ed.) International Encyclopedia of Ergonomics and Human Factors, 2nd edn., vol. 1, chap. 166. Taylor & Francis, Abingdon (2006)

52. Tsang, P.S., Velazquez, V.L.: Diagnosticity and multidimensional subjective workload ratings. Ergonomics **39**(3), 358–381 (1996)

53. Tsang, P.S., Vidulich, M.A.: Mental workload and situation awareness. In: Salvendy, G. (ed.) Handbook of Human Factors and Ergonomics, pp. 243–268. Wiley, Hoboken (2006)

54. Tullis, T.S., Stetson, J.N.: A comparison of questionnaires for assessing website usability. In: Annual Meeting of the Usability Professionals Association (2004)

55. Vidulich, M.A., Ward Frederic, G., Schueren, J.: Using the subjective workload dominance (SWORD) technique for projective workload assessment. Hum. Factors Soc. **33**(6), 677–691 (1991)

56. Wickens, C.D.: Multiple resources and mental workload. Hum. Factors **50**(2), 449–454 (2008)

57. Wickens, C.D., Hollands, J.G.: Engineering Psychology and Human Performance, 3rd edn. Prentice Hall, Upper Saddle River (1999)

58. Wilcoxon, F.: Individual comparisons by ranking methods. Biom. Bull. **1**(6), 80–83 (1945). doi:10.2307/3001968

59. Wilson, G.F., Eggemeier, T.F.: Mental workload measurement. In: Karwowski, W. (ed.) International Encyclopedia of Ergonomics and Human Factors, vol. 1, 2nd edn., chap. 167. Taylor & Francis, Abingdon (2006)

60. Xie, B., Salvendy, G.: Review and reappraisal of modelling and predicting mental workload in single and multi-task environments. Work Stress **14**(1), 74–99 (2000)

61. Young, M.S., Stanton, N.A.: Mental workload. In: Stanton, N.A., Hedge, A., Brookhuis, K., Salas, E., Hendrick, H.W. (eds.) Handbook of Human Factors and Ergonomics Methods, chap. 39, pp. 1–9. CRC Press, Boca Raton (2004)

62. Young, M.S., Stanton, N.A.: Mental workload: theory, measurement, and application. In: Karwowski, W. (ed.) International Encyclopedia of Ergonomics and Human Factors, vol. 1, 2nd edn., pp. 818–821. Taylor & Francis, Abingdon (2006)

63. Zhu, H., Hou, M.: Restrain mental workload with roles in HCI. In: Proceedings of Science and Technology for Humanity, pp. 387–392 (2009)

64. Zijlstra, F.R.H.: Efficiency in work behaviour. Doctoral thesis, Delft University, The Netherlands (1993)

What is User's Perception of Naturalness?
An Exploration of Natural User Experience

Sanjay Ghosh[✉], Chivukula Sai Shruthi, Himanshu Bansal,
and Arvind Sethia

Samsung R&D Institute Bangalore, Bengaluru, Karnataka, India
{sanjay.ghosh, ch.shruthi,
hibansal, arvind.s}@samsung.com

Abstract. Natural User Interfaces (NUI) is now a well-researched topic. The principles of NUI in literature primarily focus on designing the user interfaces to be intuitively easy to use. But is it enough for a software product to just have an intuitive user interface to give a natural experience? Designing for a product imbibing overall naturalness requires encompassing of all the aspects of user experience, which is beyond just an interface design. This study contributes by taking a holistic approach in identifying what users perceive to be natural and what experiences make them feel so. We involved 36 participants with diverse demographics and personalities, giving them a variety of stimuli to elicit their perceptions of naturalness. These were found to be a combination of what they perceived to be natural through visual, cognitive as well as real life past and present experiences. The insights from this research helped us in deriving inferences on designing for what we call as Natural User Experience (NUX). We found that the level of naturalness does not remain same over time for the users; rather it goes through a stage based cycle. We also evolved strategies for improving the naturalness by advancing user's experience across these stages.

Keywords: Natural User Experience · Natural User Interfaces · Intuitive interaction · Intuitive use · Naturalness of interaction

1 Introduction

The frequency of users' encounters with the variety of digital devices has now increased many folds. From the office to home, from inside the car to inside gym, while sitting to while walking, everywhere users encounter a variety of interfaces with a variety of interaction. All of these interfaces are designed to compete for user's engagement. With exposure to wearable devices, VR devices, social robots, new biometric authentication methods, new interaction modalities such as air gesture or gaze, users would expect their interaction experience to be more natural. Among these multitudes of digital experiences, the ones which will provide Natural User Experience would be preferred. User Experience is not just the experience of the interface alone and therefore we consider Natural User Experience is not just the natural mechanisms of user's interaction with the system. Our understanding of *Natural User Experience (NUX)* is derived from the Alben's classical definition of quality of experience [1];

© IFIP International Federation for Information Processing 2017
Published by Springer International Publishing AG 2017. All Rights Reserved
R. Bernhaupt et al. (Eds.): INTERACT 2017, Part II, LNCS 10514, pp. 224–242, 2017.
DOI: 10.1007/978-3-319-67684-5_14

focused on the naturalness aspect. It includes all the aspects of how people use an interactive product i.e. how naturally it feels in their hands, how naturally they understand its function from their existing skills, how natural do they feel while using it, and how naturally does it fits into their usage context.

Most of the prior literature dealing with naturalness were focused on Natural User Interfaces (NUI), which Wigdor and Wixon [2] defined as interfaces that make users act and feel natural. Being intuitive was considered the most fundamental for NUI design. There is high-level design guidelines for NUI in the literature as well [2, 3]. But the question we pitch is that, is it enough for a software product to just have an intuitive, easy to use interface to be close to being Natural for the users? Isn't it the experience that needs to be designed for naturalness and not just the interface? Norman [4] had also raised a valid question in these lines, "are natural user interfaces really natural?" Therefore, in this research, we took a holistic approach attempting to identify and understand what composes NUX.

In our research, we delved deeper to find out what are such cognitive processes and actions that drive naturalness and how those could be enabled through design. Although the results of this exploration on user's perceptions of naturalness may be generically applied across all digital experiences, but our objective was limited to NUX involved in the design of smartphones and similar products only. We investigated whether the perception of naturalness is similar across people or it differed; and does this perception of naturalness changed over time? Also, if it was ever changing then how should the design cater to it? It is important to understand these aspects to design a software product which imbibes NUX, which should not be intuitive for just the first encounter but should give natural experience in all subsequent usages.

2 Related Research

There have been some prior attempts to explore the experience aspects of NUI and tangible interfaces. Work by O'hara et al. [5] establishes naturalness aspects of touchless interfaces. Grandhi et al. [6] explored different aspects of touchless gesture interfaces like the motion, hand shape, form, imaginary object, and instruction; and derived what accounts for naturalness and intuitiveness. There are several prior works [7–9] that established various design methodology for intuitive interactions considering intuitiveness as an aspect of similar prior experiences. Hurtienne et al. [10] proposed designing intuitive tangible user interfaces with the help of 'image schemas' and their metaphorical extensions. Also, Asikhia et al. [11] had reported an approach for quantitatively evaluating the affective aspect or intuitive interaction. Also, similar to our exploration, Blackler et al. [12] had attempted to explore the notion of the intuitive use of the product and how to design for the same. Work by Baerentsen [13] and Turner [14] also explores intuitiveness of user interface. Most of these prior researches proved that intuition is a cognitive process that utilizes knowledge gained through prior experience, i.e. users' subconscious application of prior knowledge [15, 16]. Thus, there are several prior works which explore the intuitiveness aspect of user interfaces. But researches exploring the notion of naturalness and NUX are less. Celentano et al. [17] defined naturalness in using metaphors for designing tangible interfaces. To our understanding, there is a lack of relevant literature for NUX which could tie the insights from cognitive psychology into design directions for designing digital products; which we attempted to contribute through this research.

3 Research Methodology

We wanted to explore the perception of naturalness which was something so abstract that it was neither easy for us to communicate our questions to the participants nor it was easy for them to convey their thoughts. Thus, we had to make use of a variety of research techniques and had to include participants with personality and lifestyles as diverse as possible. The user research was conducted to collect perspectives of diverse people from real life instances, preferences on what they considered to be natural.

3.1 Participant Demographics

Our user research involved qualitative semi-structured, in-depth, personal interviews with 36 participants. For diversity among participants, we included people from different age groups, genders, primary personality types and professions; which segregates them in terms of socio-economic segments. We started by recruiting participants from various personal or professional or social network contacts according to age group and gender. A total of 61 respondents were telephonically contacted and asked about their profession and basic lifestyle, and were asked to attempt an online or a telephonic 'Basic Personality Evaluation'. We used 10 questions based brief version of the 'Big Five Inventory' [18]. Respondents were then grouped into 6 groups based on primary demographics of age and gender as mentioned in Table 1. Among the 8 to 13 people in each group, we recruited 6 participants for each, i.e. 36 participants in total, taking care to involve people with different personality types and professions, the secondary demographics, as much as possible. We had a rich variety of participants involving students, businessmen, surgeons, dentists, software developers, entrepreneurs, architects, lawyers, teachers, technicians, tele-callers, personal assistants, shopkeepers, musicians, retired, home makers, just to name a few.

Table 1. Participants demographics and distribution into 6 groups

Age	15–25 years		25–40 years		Above 40 years	
Gender	Male	Female	Male	Female	Male	Female
Group no.	I	II	III	IV	V	VI
Initially recruited	13	10	13	9	8	8
Finally recruited for interviews	6	6	6	6	6	6

3.2 User Session Protocol

Each participant sessions lasted for around two hours wherein each of them was engaged in four perception elicitation exercises described in the following section as per the sequence illustrated in Fig. 1.

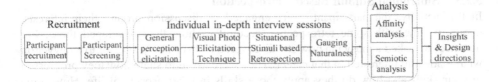

Fig. 1. Sequence of activities in the user research

3.2.1   General Perception of Elicitation of Naturalness

We began by asking participants to tell us what they consider as natural and unnatural by giving some examples from real life or from their personal awareness of digital gadget usage. Of course, this was a bit difficult for them to start responding to. The objective of this phase was to find the various attributes of "natural to use or do" to have a clear understanding of the term Natural and to also set the agenda of the session.

3.2.2   Visual Elicitation for Naturalness

Since the objective of our study was to extract the perception and preference of naturalness, which is abstract, subjective and not easy to convey, we conducted an activity based user-centered approach called Photo-elicitation technique [19]. A similar technique has been designed by Zaltman et al. [20] named as Metaphor Elicitation Technique which is applied to extract hidden knowledge, i.e. to find what people know subconsciously but can't articulate. Such research techniques have been popularly used in a variety of domains such as eliciting voice of the consumer in marketing [21], exploring the experience of powerlessness among women in sociology domain [22] etc. In this activity we printed 200 random photographs downloaded from the web and randomly spread them in front of the participants; see Fig. 2. They were asked to choose five images through which they wanted to convey what is the perception of naturalness to them or what is natural to use or to do. Post that, they were asked to explain the reason for their choices. They were asked to articulate what went in their minds while making those choices and were encouraged to give recent as well as past real life instances to support it. They were also asked to interpret the content in the chosen photographs and convey what aspect made it natural. This exercise acted as an ice breaker to motivate the users to share real life events and stories.

Fig. 2. Participant engaged in photo-elicitation technique with random photographs

3.2.3   Situational Stimuli Based Retrospection

In this activity, the participants were engaged in discussion around their interests, habits, routine with some retrospective account of how they developed those. For instance, we asked a musician how she discovered that she could sing, or to a lawyer on what made him interested in that career. They were asked to share how they progressed in their skills and how do they apply those skills in other aspects of life. How some things which they considered unnatural in the past have eventually become natural? Our objective was to understand the various stages of naturalness and reasons behind why something natural to someone may be unnatural to other.

3.2.4   Gauging Naturalness

During the three sessions mentioned above, participants mentioned various words that they related to the perception of naturalness. We kept hearing and noting those terms likes habit, instincts, addiction, reflex, routine, effortless, joy, to name a few along with relevant user stories and instances. As the fourth and last exercise participants were asked to relatively rank all those terms on a scale of low to high naturalness. On collating that we expected to get a progressive scale of various perceptions of naturalness. For each of the instances or stories shared by the participants, they were asked to categorize them into some action or cognition which made them feel natural. We expected to later infer some insights from these gathered experiences and stories focused on actions or cognition to derive naturalness. All the participant interactions were audio recorded and were transcribed later.

3.3   Analysis of Data

3.3.1   Affinity Analysis

We conducted affinity analysis of all the participant statements from all the activities with focus on two major aspects:

- What factors enabled naturalness ('naturalness enablers') and what role did they play in influencing NUX?
- How could those factors be utilized in design to enhance NUX?

In addition, we used two clusters in affinity analysis – naturalness driven from actions and naturalness driven from cognition, which were identified during the gauging naturalness activity. Most of the insights described later were derived from this analysis.

3.3.2   Semiotic Analysis of Visual Perception of Naturalness

Visual content can be examined from many points of view, such as intellectual, aesthetic, cognitive, social, etc.; ours was focused on personal preferences. We zeroed to the two most preferred photographs from the 36 participants. So, there were around 50 photographs for analysis (as some were common preferences). These were analyzed in a four step process using Saussure's semiotic approach [23], as illustrated in Fig. 3. As the first step, every visual element such as color, form, layout, material, object, etc., from the selected images were identified and enumerated. Next, they were analyzed as is for physical and direct representations and were listed as 'signifiers'. For instance, the sky is blue and clear, an object has an implicit shadow on the opposite direction of light. All these signifiers were then correlated with the context of the image and metaphorical or conceptual representations were interpreted as 'signified'. For instance, the sky is interpreted as vastness with a presence everywhere. As the fourth and final step, this signified list was synthesized into various representative themes for all visual elements based on participants' statements and interpretations. While all the insights were derived from the affinity analysis, one of the insights on visual perception of naturalness was based on this semiotic analysis.

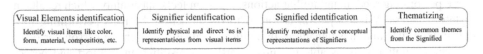

Fig. 3. Sequence of steps in semiotic analysis

4   What Composes NUX?

From our analysis of the qualitative data collected during the research, we arrived at various insights as to what is perceived as natural and how to enhance that aspect in NUX design. In summary, we found that there are three fundamental roots of naturalness, namely States of Naturalness, Action which drives Naturalness and Cognition which drives Naturalness. Now if people perceived what is natural based on the above-mentioned aspects, then why not the product UX use the similar philosophy to design a digital experience! Thus, for a product to elevate the NUX to a higher state either both or at least one of the two naturalness drivers (action and cognition) must elevate to a higher state. Further sections are focussed on these two naturalness drivers and various enablers for each of them, as summarized in Fig. 4. For each insight, we mentioned various observations that helped us derive it, and with some examples we explained related design directions for NUX.

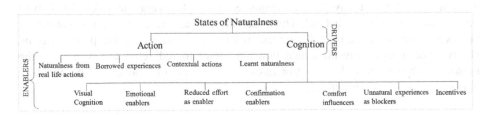

Fig. 4. Relationship among states of naturalness, naturalness drivers, and enablers

4.1   States of Naturalness

What we inferred regarding the changing states of naturalness was that, the transition from the 'State of Situational Control' to the 'State of Self Control' improved Naturalness. People felt relaxed and not being anxious when they were in their controlled environment or in a controlled situation where they can shape the course of action.

Perception of naturalness was logically inferred to have a progressive pattern from several user stories. Once in such state, they looked for anticipated progression. For instance, when a person performs a difficult task repeatedly, it becomes effortless for him, thereby shifting his experience towards higher naturalness. Anticipated exploration begins by following set patterns. Thus, we found that the state of naturalness is not stable but it is progressive. NUX would increase if the state of naturalness gets increased to a higher level. Figure 5 summarizes the overall states of naturalness in a scale from highly natural to unnatural based on how the participants ranked their different perceptions of naturalness in the activity of gauging naturalness. For example, while performing random unfamiliar actions, a person feels uncertainty which results in a state of stress. When a person is forced to do an action, he feels performing in a constrained state and thus unnatural. In a different situation, when the person performs an action intuitively, he is able to think effortlessly resulting in comfort and peacefulness, thereby shifting towards higher naturalness.

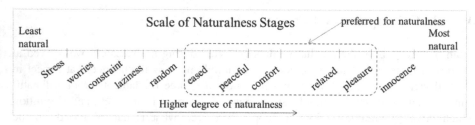

Fig. 5. Scale of naturalness stages inferred from participant inputs

4.2   Naturalness Derived from Action

Figure 6 shows the summary of how the participants ranked different actions be related to the drivers of naturalness. As evident from fig, to take the user to a higher naturalness state, the user's actions should be improved from being forced or with ignorance to that which is close to being playful, spontaneous or intuitive. We inferred that there are two different ways to use actions as drivers for naturalness i.e. 'freedom of action' and 'anticipated reaction'. The anticipation of any reaction to an action makes the experience more natural. 'Ignorance' refers to a state where the person has no clarity on occurrence or result of an action and 'Being forced' refers to a state where the person is subjected to follow a set of rules. Any reaction of product that propels user into such states is never natural.

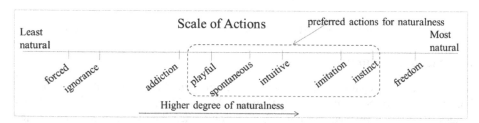

Fig. 6. Scale of action as naturalness driver inferred from participant inputs

From this, we understood that different level of actions drives different states of naturalness. Then how do we consciously enable those actions in a product? From the analysis of the participant statements, we were able to infer several ways to enable appropriate actions from which users would derive higher degrees of naturalness. Those were named as 'Action Enablers' and are as follows:

i. Digital naturalness enabled from real life actions
ii. Borrowed experiences from actions
iii. Contextual actions
iv. Learnt naturalness

Next, we describe each of these Action Enablers in detail with examples.

4.2.1 Digital Naturalness Enabled from Real Life Actions

Participants shared various instances of naturalness experiences from both physical and digital encounters. We found that there were pros and cons for both encounters that we identified as 'Incrementers' and 'Decrementers', respectively. Thus, four such 'Action Enablers' were identified as mentioned below with examples:

Physical Experience Incrementers (PEI) – e.g. muscle memory say while driving; rich sensorial immersions say for the sense of weight or temperature; or approximation of distance from a sound or facial expression.

Physical Experience Decrementers (PED) – e.g. randomness, time-taking non co-located communication through mails or letters.

Digital Experience Incrementers (DEI) – e.g. flexibility to redo any action, flexibility of customization, control over action time to act.

Digital Experience Decrementers (DED) – e.g. low trust factor due to hidden intentions and miscommunications in any software, awkwardness of using in public.

We found that people unconsciously related their natural experience of physical life into their digital encounters. Figure 7 summarizes the strategy of making use of real world naturalness drivers to reduce the effect of naturalness limiters in the virtual world. We concluded that *making use of real-world naturalness drivers to reduce the effect of naturalness limiters in the virtual world would enhance the NUX*. For example, in one of the e-books, the page turning interaction was designed very close to how one would do for turning the pages on a real book. This adds to the natural digital experience of the user. Therefore to design for natural digital experience, attempts should be made to translate the physical experience incrementers (PEI), maintain the digital experience incrementers (DEI), reduce the digital experience decrementers (DED) and avoid physical experience decrementers (PED). For e.g. software application which involves some online financial transaction that user doesn't trust, then such application may be designed with richer sensorial immersion, say haptic feedback, to make it more natural. Hence, for designing a digital product with NUX, first naturalness decrementers needs to be identified and be reduced or possibly neutralized through naturalness incrementers from physical life encounters.

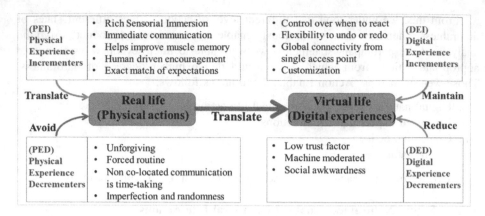

Fig. 7. Digital naturalness enabled from real life actions

4.2.2 Borrowed Experiences from Actions

There are many different skills that people develop based on their real-life experiences, such as being picture smart, detail oriented, goal oriented, efficient decision making, etc. We found that they borrowed attributes of such skills and utilized them into similar parts of other activities in digital encounters to feel natural, as illustrated in Fig. 8. For example, fiction reading hobbyists develop strong mental visualization of stories and are capable of borrowing that into the gaming experience. Similarly, detail oriented people find naturalness in fineness and depth of detailing in the digital world so they explore more and compare a lot in e-shopping. People with efficient decision-making skills tend to be efficient in following map routes, searching and online transactions. Likewise, a task oriented person will maintain proper check list and calendar to be task and time oriented. Thus we concluded that attribute or skill of one activity/habit makes a similar part of another activity natural. Therefore, *to design a new digital encounter we need to map the closely related attributes of Source Task actions to get the target task actions.* Given a target application to be designed, find out the appropriate kind of source instances according to the kind of user and map the appropriate attributes to the respective attributes of that source for NUX.

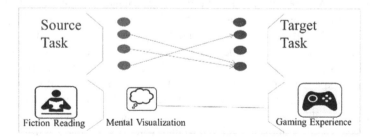

Fig. 8. Borrowed experiences from actions in earlier task enabling naturalness

4.2.3   Contextual Actions

We found that *to be natural, 'Actions' driven by 'Needs' should be in accordance with the 'Context'*. Most of the 'actions' of people are associated with one or the other 'needs'. For example, the need of social connection drives an action to associate with others through social media. Needs are fundamentally categorized according to expanded Maslow's hierarchy of needs [24]. We mapped various instances of real life actions as well as actions performed digitally, mentioned by the participants according to the fundamental needs from Maslow's hierarchy, as shown in the left portion of Fig. 9. For instance, real life action of decorating one's home, the digital action of photo editing or digital drawing, were mapped to the aesthetics need of the user. Also, we found that such digital actions were also hierarchical in nature as they mapped to the needs which were fundamentally hierarchical themselves. Moreover, from all the instances, we found that all familiar actions were considered natural only in an appropriate context; i.e. even a familiar action if not performed in suitable context, will turn out to be unnatural. For instance, two of the participants found video conferencing in a public place to be unnatural. Generically contexts could be majorly categorized into following five types:

– Time – involves periodicity, flexibility, and relativity of time
– Place – involves purpose of place, availability of resources and occasion
– Activity – involves importance and urgency of the activity
– People – involves number, relationship, culture and power-index of the people
– Self – involves age, gender, personality and state of emotion of self

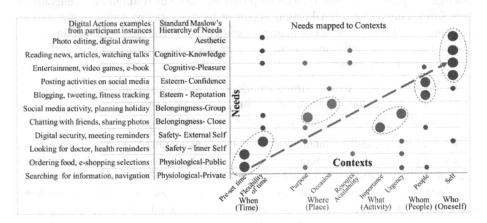

Fig. 9. Digital actions mapped to fundamental needs (left) and needs mapped to contexts (right) using the Need-Action-Context framework

We used these categories to evolve the mappings of Needs with Contexts from the various stories and instances that our participants shared during the interview session. For every instance that they shared, we asked them which Needs did it matched to and its most suitable context. Through these mapping what evolved was named as *"Need-Action-Context framework"*, which represents the relationship between different types of needs and relevant contexts. In Fig. 9 this is shown in form of a bubble chart, wherein the size of the bubbles represents the goodness of match between the need and corresponding context. For instance, a busy senior professional who is diabetic and needs to follow a regime of medicines, food, and exercise, the naturalness of his actions to have a healthy life (Need = Safety of inner self) will depend upon the availability of time from his professional routine (appropriate Context = Flexibility of time). Thus to assist him in this need with natural digital experience would include relevant reminders on his phone which understand his timings and lifestyle correctly. Instead, a basic timely reminder would be unnatural or may be annoying to him.

In Fig. 9, the diagonal progressive line reveals that for NUX relating to the higher level of needs, the equally higher level of context would be appropriate. In other words, context should be in accordance with the need. Thus we concluded that *actions performed by the users in digital encounters should be designed by taking utmost care of appropriate context*. For designing a digital experience for a particular action first 'root need' has to be identified and then appropriate context should be derived from this framework. Only then based on the relevant context appropriate action should be designed. As per the Need-Action-Context framework, contexts of Time and Place are less crucial and therefore the system can intervene or make recommendations on them. On the other hand contexts of People and Self being more crucial, the strategy would be to understand those well and design for user's needs.

4.2.4   Learnt Naturalness

By mastering an action one becomes confident on the nature of its reaction and thus removes any possible ambiguity, thereby progresses towards Naturalness. Generally, it starts from being an intentional action as part of behavior and progresses ultimately to an unintentional habit as a part of their personality. Our participants did mention about various instances of performing conscious or unconscious actions and related them to one of the following factors:

I.   Behavior – (e.g. writing strong emails, making approximations)
II. Habits – (e.g. longing to do something new, relating events)
III. Personality – (e.g. leadership, manipulation, solution orienteers, risk taking)

Each of these could be intentional as well as unintentional, the latter being more influential to naturalness. Generally there are three kinds of habit: Intellectual Habit (that deals with mental or psychological qualities of a person like applying past knowledge to new situations, building sensitivity towards few topics, etc.), Motor habit (what people perform physically like rolling a pen, shaking hands while talking, etc.) and Habit of Character (that people develop as a part of their personality over time and adopt them in any kind of situation). Therefore, as people keep repeating actions consciously or unconsciously they adopt those into their behavior which slowly gets progressed into the habit and finally becomes part of their personality. Behavior converts into habit through repetition and habit ultimately gets embedded into the personality. Now the question was which of these actions should be leveraged as naturalness enabler? In any case, there shouldn't be any external factor that should attempt to interfere or change user's habits or personality.

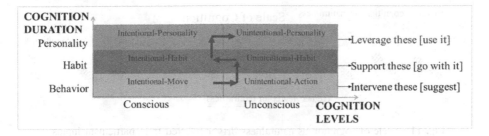

Fig. 10. Design direction to make use of user's behavior, habit, and personality

The highest level of naturalness experience in a product can be enabled through actions by leveraging or exploiting the personality of the user. For example, from the current pattern of email organization of a user who is organized personality, recommendations to apply the same pattern for files or apps could enhance his digital interaction naturalness. For the next level of impactful naturalness, user's habits should also be supported. For e.g. if a user is habituated in making particular typing mistakes, then it won't be appropriate for the system to point out each of them every time. Rather an ideal natural design would be to identify and correct them automatically and convey to the user. Figure 10 illustrates all these design strategies for making use of these kinds of actions. Also, we noted that naturalness does not get impacted if some of the users' behaviors are intervened. For instance, for people who wish to have their presence felt in community or social network, a social network application could be designed to make them feel unique. The application should enable them to make unique posts in a social network. Thus we concluded that *repetitive conscious or unconscious actions increases learnt natural behavior*. Digital system may intervene to enable user's conscious actions due to behavior but it should always support user's habit and must not attempt to change user's personality, rather leverage it.

4.3   Naturalness Derived from Cognition

As mentioned earlier, Cognition is one among the naturalness drivers. We further describe here how different levels of cognition, measured using a subjective scale, can influence different states of naturalness. From the analysis of the participant statements, we were able to infer several ways to trigger appropriate cognition effect from which users would derive higher degrees of naturalness as shown in Fig. 11. A higher level of naturalness is achieved if there is no involvement of rigorous thinking which is probably because being thoughtless is being without consideration of the consequences. From the instances shared by our participants, we could clearly observe that there was a clear preference of performing actions freely, without any constrains and without any prior thoughts. Thus we inferred that *decrease in response time and cognitive load increases naturalness*.

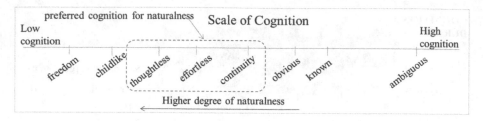

Fig. 11. Scale of cognition as naturalness driver inferred from participant inputs

Now, similar to 'naturalness derived from actions', the naturalness deriving cognition too had several enablers that a designer must design for NUX. These are named as 'Cognition Enablers' and are as follows

1. Visual cognition
2. Emotional enablers
3. Reduced effort as enabler
4. Confirmation enablers
5. Incentivizing, and
6. Avoiding Unnatural experiences

Next, we describe each of these Enablers in detail with examples.

4.3.1   Visual Cognition

From the design perspective, Naumann et al. [10] had studied the relation between aesthetic design characteristics and intuitiveness of interactive products. Visual cognition or visual perception is primarily derived from the semeiotic analysis as described earlier. It can be influenced by three factors: Color, Material, and Form.

'Color' is present everywhere and the people relate things with their colors as one of the visual aspects of naturalness. For example, change in color of a fruit from unripe to ripened state seems natural to them. Color helps to differentiate or relate something thereby enhancing NUX. One such way to assist this cognition process of the users would be the use of duotone color (two different shades of a color). Also, few colors symbolically represent some feeling; say vintage style colors rendered users with past or childhood memories. We observed that colors follow a progression from low to high or subtle to bright, similar to fruit ripening or changing the color of the sky according to the time of the day. So, the use of complementary colors showed progression and movement and naturalness as per the participants' reactions. Learned habits are represented with warm colors (yellow, orange) whereas conditioned habits are represented with cool colors (mostly blue). Generally, the natural colors perceived are *energetic, progressive* and *complementary* that enhances NUX.

'Material' is another such visual cognition aspect that affects natural UX experience. Materials are usually perceived in multiple layers which are one behind the other. The first layer acts as protective and accommodating while second acts as flexible and light. Each material combined together has its own identity as well as its cumulative identity. It is noted that all materials need to be organized in such a way that their existence complements each other. We observed that light and flexible materials provide comfort, which in turn takes closer to naturalness. Thus natural attributes of material are *protective, flexible, light* and *accommodating*.

'Form' is that visual element which is clearly distinct in people's real and digital experiences and hence plays a crucial role in imbibing naturalness. We observed that virtual reality and augmented reality interfaces added naturalness in experience due to the 3D forms. This is because these forms add a sense of depth (like a container) which users perceived to be supportive and sturdy. Forms are perceived as spherical and bulgy, to show continuity and repetitive cycle. This repetitiveness triggers learned habits which enhance the NUX. We inferred that the perceived attributes of natural forms are *supportive, continuity, connection,* and *binding*.

4.3.2 Emotional Enablers

Emotions play a very strong role in enabling naturalness provided it is rightly leveraged through intelligent design in any digital experience. Through semiotics analysis of the photos chosen by the participants, we attempted to infer the preferred emotions. Although, as obvious, we observed that mostly positive emotions were related to naturalness, but additionally we were able to infer few more insights relating to emotions for naturalness. Like, people preferred singularity of emotions to be natural, i.e. focusing only on one state of mind took user closer to naturalness. At the same time, the emotion of being independent or being comfortable in the company of own was found to be most strongly related to naturalness. Also emotionally people were reluctant to follow any kinds of rules or constraints from whatever digital gadget they used. To be natural, people indicated that they wanted to be emotionally free from all routines.

Further, people emotionally wished to see growth or progression in any activity to be natural. It is quite natural for human beings to do something faster and better next time and all consequent times. Without apparent progression boredom sets in which was found to be highly unnatural. For instance, changing TV channel – in a new TV, a user would be contented even if it shows some delay in switching as the user is learning to do. But once the user gets used to it the delays should also get reduced accordingly, else the user does not get an emotion of progression and boredom sets in. Thus, *for being close to natural the digital experiences should be designed to focus only on one positive emotion with some progression and not multitude of emotions.*

4.3.3 Reduced Effort as Enabler

We found that 'interests' are something that people consider close to natural, only once they clear a threshold with some efforts. For instance, playing a computer game could be of interest to someone but it is not natural unless the expertise is gained. Obviously, for expertise, the user has to put in a lot of efforts and of course for that he should be motivated enough. Now the key should be to somehow reduce this effort to enhance naturalness of an interest. From the instances shared by our participants we could identify two major ways of reducing the effort – first, by rapidly increasing the familiarity with the activity of interest; and second, by streamlining the exploration involved in the process of improving skills. Further, we have identified some primary and secondary mechanisms (as described in Fig. 12) which would enable these two ways to reduce the effort as described below:

- Frequent encounters: Repeated engagements with the activity are important to increase familiarity with it. The time interval between these encounters needs to be minimized with the support of constant motivation.
- Guidance: A coach or co-learner suggesting suitable techniques to perform certain part of the activity which they learnt from their experiences. Such techniques are beneficial to avoid mistakes during practice which will further reinforce increased familiarity and reduced exploration.
- Observed experience: These are the learnings received by observing someone else doing the similar activity. These are implicit ways of gaining experiences rather than explicitly getting guidance from others.
- Borrowed familiar experience: The user tries to utilize the past experience of different activity to current activity.
- Personalized routes: Everyone has their convenient way of doing an activity and enabling the person to look for those convenient ways reduces exploration.

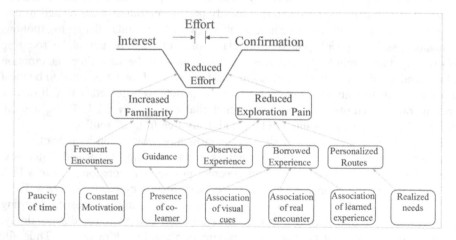

Fig. 12. Increased familiarity, reduced ambiguity, and reduced exploration enables naturalness

Thus we concluded that *increased familiarity reduced ambiguity and reduced exploration effort enables naturalness*. Below are two recommendations on design guidelines based on above inference:

- Provide 'guidance' to avoid diversions from intended path, but once sufficient expertise is achieved it should eventually disappear.
- Provide user with 'personalized route' through modified interaction flow and reorganized information based on user's identified need and goals.

4.3.4   Confirmation Enablers

In the minds of people, every activity goes through the progressive states of ignorance, difficulty, improvement, comfortable and then natural. To move from one state to other, one needs some confirmation about their self-capability regarding that activity. It is mostly an appropriate return/response that enables the confirmation and we have termed them as 'confirmation enablers'. Through participant statements, we have identified that these confirmation enablers progress towards naturalness. Prior literature [25] has also reported the fact that, for an expert user with heavy practice, decisions become intuitive. Figure 13 shows that, at what state of the user's activity, which confirmation enabler can confirm certain activity to be natural. In Fig. 13, the circles represent different confirmation enablers, which helps progress the perception of naturalness. The size of each circle represents how common that confirmation enabler is. Vertical alignment of the circles represents the corresponding confirmation states for which that confirmation enabler would be suitable. For example, in a difficult situation of the activity, absolute achievement gives confirmation to the person and repetitive achievements will make it feel very natural in performing that activity. In other words, for a new e-shopping user who is reluctant to make an online payment due to privacy concern, some extrinsic motivation may be effective. This motivation can be derived say from his peers who had 80% times successful transactions, or by observing others while transacting.

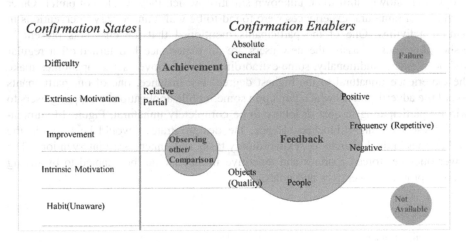

Fig. 13. Use of confirmation enabler for appropriate state initiates naturalness

Thus we concluded that *use of particular confirmation enabler for appropriate state initiates naturalness*. Natural UX for digital products should make use of appropriate confirmation enablers. The first step is to understand the particular state of action and how difficult would it be to make that action feel natural to the user. Accordingly confirmation enablers could be designed to boost the NUX.

4.3.5   Incentivizing

Incentive forces people to adapt new routines, and repetition of these routines becomes a natural habit. Actions repeated frequently and in a particular order become routine and natural habit to people. Most of these habits are from childhood, but as they grow up, they need an incentive to adapt to new habits. These incentives are motivational to people to adapt to new habits, progress and acquire naturalness. These motivations give fun, pleasure, satisfaction and spontaneity to the user. Thus we concluded, *an appropriate incentive at an appropriate stage would be capable of changing the course of naturalness progression.*

4.3.6 Unnatural Experiences as Blockers

Similar to our findings of naturalness enablers, we also found few unnatural experiences that degraded the NUX. Our participants also shared a lot of instances which resulted in not so natural experience. We tried to infer the pattern of those instances and various factors involved in making the experiences unnatural. We found that 'Forced routines' or tasks are the ones that user does unwillingly and found them slightly unnatural. Instead, as already discussed earlier, if any task is preferred by the user, then repeating the same would improve naturalness. In addition, the act of imitation is something natural to human but repeated imitation turns the experience to unnatural. For instance, one of our participants started to maintain schedules and reminders on her phone by imitating a habit of her boss. But after few days, she started to find it unnatural as she did not find it useful to her lifestyle. With repetition of imitations, people may slowly shift to an unknown situation which they would not prefer. Other instances of unnatural experiences were found to be with unnecessary interventions in natural activities. One of the participants mentioned that the chat bots present in e-shopping sites to assist the new users are an experience had turned-off a regular visitor like her. Additionally, some extraordinary tasks above user's capabilities make the experience unnatural to the highest degree. For instance, one of our participants found the advertisements which pop up in some mobile applications prompting users to win by participating in quiz or lottery to be completely unnatural. Figure 14 summarizes these naturalness blockers. Hence, the design strategy would be to avoid the higher ones in the hierarchy i.e. extraordinary tasks and unnecessary interventions. The lower ones i.e. forced routines and repetitive imitations can be adapted to by giving users appropriate incentives and goals.

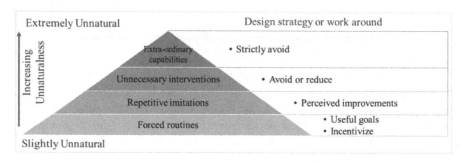

Fig. 14. Perception of unnaturalness which needs to be avoided

5 Conclusion

From this study, we were able to collate several insights on what in general users perceive as natural, what factors drive naturalness and how that can be enabled by making appropriate design choices. We applied user-centered design process with a diverse user group to explore the abstract notion of NUX. We realized that naturalness gets evoked when actions map to appropriate motor movements as well as cognition process. Through the three scales, i.e. scale of naturalness states, the scale of action and scale of cognition, we were able to subjectively define the causal dependency of the level of naturalness on the levels of actions and cognition. Also, we were able to identify various enablers for these actions and cognition which drives the experience towards being more natural. We also found that the perception of naturalness varied over time and context. We have explained the guidelines for NUX design through several examples related to design of digital software product for each. The guidelines developed in this study will enable designers to identify, evaluate and design NUX at different phases of the design process.

References

1. Alben, L.: Defining the criteria for effective interaction design. Interactions **3**(3), 11–15 (1996)
2. Wigdor, D., Dennis, W.: Brave NUI World: Designing Natural User Interfaces for Touch and Gesture. Elsevier, Amsterdam (2011)
3. Liu, W.: Natural user interface-next mainstream product user interface. In: IEEE 11th International Conference Computer-Aided Industrial Design & Conceptual Design (CAIDCD), vol. 1, pp. 203–205 (2010)
4. Norman, D.A.: Natural user interfaces are not natural. Interactions **17**(3), 6–10 (2010)
5. O'hara, K., Harper, R., Mentis, H., Sellen, A., Taylor, A.: On the naturalness of touchless: putting the "interaction" back into NUI. ACM Trans. Comput.-Hum. Interact. **20**(1), 5 (2013)
6. Grandhi, S.A., Joue, G., Mittelberg, I.: Understanding naturalness and intuitiveness in gesture production: insights for touchless gestural interfaces. In: ACM SIGCHI Conference on Human Factors in Computing Systems, pp. 821–824 (2011)
7. Blackler, A.L., Hurtienne, J.: Towards a unified view of intuitive interaction: definitions, models and tools across the world. MMI-interaktiv **13**, 36–54 (2007)
8. Blackler, A.L., Popovic, V., Mahar, D.P.: Intuitive interaction applied to interface design. In: International Design Congress - IASDR (2005)
9. Blackler, A.L., Popovic, V., Mahar, D.P.: Towards a design methodology for applying intuitive interaction. In: Design Research Society International Conference (2006)
10. Hurtienne, J., Israel, J.H.: Image schemas and their metaphorical extensions – intuitive patterns for tangible interaction. In: ACM Tangible and Embedded Interaction, pp. 127–134 (2007)
11. Asikhia, O.K., Setchi, R., Hicks, Y., Walters, A.: Conceptual framework for evaluating intuitive interaction based on image schemas. Interact. Comput. **27**(3), 287–310 (2015)
12. Blackler, A.L., Vesna, P., Douglas, P.M.: Intuitive use of products, pp. 120–134 (2002)
13. Bærentsen, K.B.: Intuitive user interfaces. Scand. J. Inf. Syst. **12**(1), 4 (2000)
14. Turner, P.: Towards an account of intuitiveness. Behav. Inf. Technol. **27**(6), 475–482 (2008)

15. Hurtienne, J., Blessing, L.: Design for intuitive use – testing image schema theory for user interface design. In: 16th International Conference on Engineering Design (2007)
16. Naumann, A., Hurtienne, J., Israel, J.H., Mohs, C., Kindsmüller, M.C., Meyer, H.A., Hußlein, S.: Intuitive use of user interfaces: defining a vague concept. In: Harris, D. (ed.) EPCE 2007. LNCS, vol. 4562, pp. 128–136. Springer, Heidelberg (2007). doi:10.1007/978-3-540-73331-7_14
17. Celentano, A., Emmanuel, D.: Metaphors, analogies, symbols: in search of naturalness in tangible user interfaces. Procedia Comput. Sci. **39**, 99–106 (2014)
18. Gosling, S.D., Rentfrow, P.J., Swann, W.B.: A very brief measure of the Big-Five personality domains. J. Res. Pers. **37**(6), 504–528 (2003)
19. Harper, D.: Talking about pictures: a case for photo elicitation. Vis. Stud. **17**(1), 13–26 (2002)
20. Zaltman, G.: Metaphor elicitation technique with physiological function monitoring, U.S. Patent No. 6,315,569, U.S. Patent and Trademark Office (2001)
21. Coulter, R.H., Zaltman, G.: Seeing the voice of the customer: metaphor-based advertising research. J. Adv. Res. **35**(4), 35 (1995)
22. Matheson, J.L., McCollum, E.E.: Using metaphors to explore the experiences of powerlessness among women in 12-step recovery. Subst. Use Misuse **43**(8–9), 1027–1044 (2008)
23. Chandler, D.: Semiotics: the Basics. Routledge, Abingdon (2007)
24. Maslow, A.H., Frager, R., Cox, R.: Motivation and Personality. In: Fadiman, J., McReynolds, C. (eds.) vol. 2, pp. 1887–1904. Harper & Row, New York (1970)
25. Dreyfus, S.E.: The five-stage model of adult skill acquisition. Bull. Sci. Technol. Soc. **24**(3), 177–181 (2004)

Information on Demand, on the Move, and Gesture Interaction

Presenting Information on the Driver's Demand on a Head-Up Display

Renate Haeuslschmid$^{(\boxtimes)}$, Christopher Klaus, and Andreas Butz

LMU Munich, Munich, Germany
`renate.haeuslschmid@ifi.lmu.de`

Abstract. Head-up displays present driving-related information close to the road scene. The content is readily accessible, but potentially clutters the driver's view and occludes important parts. This can lead to distraction and negatively influence driving performance. Superimposing display content only on demand – triggered by the driver whenever needed – might provide a good tradeoff between the accessibility of relevant information and the distraction caused by its display. In this paper we present a driving simulator study that investigated the influence of the self-triggered superimposition on workload, distraction and performance. In particular, we compared a gaze-based and a manually triggered superimposition with the permanent display of information and a baseline (speedometer only). We presented four pieces of information with different relevance and update frequency to the driver. We found an increased workload and distraction for the gaze- and manually triggered HUDs as well as an impact on user experience. Participants preferred to have the HUD displayed permanently and with only little content.

Keywords: Head-up display · Information on demand · Gaze interaction

1 Introduction

Head-up displays (HUDs) present driving-related information within the windshield area at an increased distance of approximately 2 m from the driver. This lets the driver read the HUD content faster because she can switch faster back and forth between the road scene and the display. In addition, it allows the driver to perceive the road scene ahead with peripheral vision when reading the HUD and thereby maintain a better lane position [7,11]. Compared to head-down displays (HDDs), drivers spend less time looking at the HUD than at HDDs [1,8,19] but still show faster reaction times [6,23]. To exploit those benefits it seems like an obvious choice to transfer more information onto the head-up display – especially information that is accessed frequently.

However, the HUD's location also increases the risk of distraction. Drivers cannot process the HUD content and the road scene simultaneously and hence show higher reaction times to road events when reading the HUD [12]. The HUD can capture the drivers' cognitive and visual attention ('cognitive capture'

© IFIP International Federation for Information Processing 2017
Published by Springer International Publishing AG 2017. All Rights Reserved
R. Bernhaupt et al. (Eds.): INTERACT 2017, Part II, LNCS 10514, pp. 245–262, 2017.
DOI: 10.1007/978-3-319-67684-5_15

Fig. 1. A participant on the baseline track with a permanently displayed speedometer.

and 'tunnel vision') and leave too little resources for the driving task without the driver being aware of it [21, 22]. This is related to change and inattentional blindness where the driver misses appearing or changing objects despite looking in their direction [24], e.g., driving directly into congested traffic without noticing [2].

The information usually presented on a HUD is relevant for driving and meant to increase safety by informing the driver, e.g., warning of hazards. But this additional information also increases the driver's load – potentially in a situation that is already highly demanding. The driver may actually react with an immediate glance away from the road simply when the content is updated [17]. Salient information or objects can capture the driver's attention, independently of their current urgency or relevance [15, 18, 20]. In addition, the HUD content can clutter the driver's view and occlude important parts of the driving scene, in turn causing distraction or an impeded perception of the surroundings.

To make use of the benefits of the well-accessible display location and at the same time decrease the risk of distraction of the continuously visible information, we propose to display the HUD content only on demand when the driver explicitly triggers it. We propose two methods to trigger the superimposition of the head-up display content: triggered by a glance into the HUD area and triggered by a shift paddle on the steering wheel. We compare these two methods with a permanent display and a baseline and measure the driving performance, user experience and the driver's workload and preferences.

2   Interaction Techniques in the Car

Contemporary cars provide a variety of input techniques. Each technique has characteristic advantages and disadvantages and hence a specific area of use. Kern et al. [10] analyzed modern cars (in 2007) regarding the integrated input modalities and developed a design space based on their findings. Haeuslschmid et al. [3] updated this design space (in 2016) specifically for head-up displays and proposed the following categories: touch & controls, gestures, speech, and gaze.

The group of *touch & controls* comprises haptic and hand-controlled input devices such as buttons, switches, multi-functional controllers, and touch screens. When placed on the steering wheel, the driver can leave both hands on the wheel while interacting with the car – which is considered safer than driving with one hand only. While drivers have learned to handle standard controllers blindly, touch interaction requires the driver to look at the display. Touch screens are still very limited in giving haptic feedback to the user and the corresponding interface and controller layout makes blind use almost impossible. As argued by Haeuslschmid et al. [3], touch interaction can only be applied to head-up displays in combination with an additional touch surface that controls the HUD remotely; touch is not applicable to the HUD itself.

The first cars with *gesture interaction* are currently entering the market; e.g. BMW series 7[1]. The midair gestures force the driver to remove one hand from the steering wheel but can be performed blindly without searching for a controller. This input technique is still developing and it remains unclear whether it is really practicable for in-car use. The gesture set is limited as the driver has to learn it by heart and seems to be applicable to only a small set of functions.

Similarly to gestures, *speech interaction* also shows potential for improvement. Speech interaction allows the driver to keep both hands and eyes focused on the driving task and is very suitable for text input but rather hard to use for object selection and manipulation [3] – the interaction procedure may become very long and cumbersome. Natural language understanding is a challenging task, especially in a noisy environment such as the car.

To our knowledge, there is no car on the market using *gaze interaction* as an explicit input method: The driver's gaze is monitored, e.g., for drowsiness warnings [25,26], but the driver can not actively select or manipulate in-car interfaces. Pomarjanschi et al. [18] showed that an assistance system that guides the drivers' gaze towards hazards leads to shorter reaction times to the event and a reduced gaze variation afterwards. The authors argue that gaze guidance can enhance driving behavior and increase safety. Haeuslschmid et al. [4] compared screen-fixed hazard warnings on a typical HUD to world-fixed – presumably gaze-guiding – ones and reported that the world-fixed warnings let the driver spend more time monitoring the driving scene, which suggests increased safety. Kern et al. [9] and Poitschke et al. [16] investigated gaze interaction as an active

---

[1] http://www.bmwblog.com/2016/01/05/new-control-concepts-from-bmw-showcased-in-new-7-series/; Accessed 30 Jan 2017.

interaction method for cars. Kern et al. [9] investigated an input technique that combines gaze- and button-interaction and compared it with speech interaction and conventional touch interaction. The driver's gaze point is used to preselect objects on a screen. By pressing a button on the steering wheel the driver can then confirm this selection. They found that the combined variant is slightly slower than the touch screen but significantly faster than speech interaction. It was further found to be more distracting than touch interaction. Poitschke et al. [16] compared gaze-based interaction with conventional touch interaction regarding task completion time, distraction and cognitive load. The authors found lower task completion times for gaze interaction, especially in situations with low demand. They also reported higher reaction times for gaze interaction than for the touch variant, However, the opposite was found for gaze experts. They argued that untrained users tended to stare at the objects and devoted their entire attention to it while trained users did not think about the process and acted fast. The participants rated gaze interaction more desirable and less demanding. We decided to test gaze interaction and shift paddle interaction in our study since both do not require the driver to remove a hand from the steering wheel. Gaze interaction seems to be a promising new interaction technique and is obvious since the driver needs to look at the display anyway in order to read it. Controller-based interaction is well-established and easy to use. Both, gaze and shift paddle, can be matched to the two status of HUD hidden/displayed easily and naturally. Speech interaction would require two commands and does not suggest a natural way of switching between the two states.

3   User Study

3.1   Pilot Study

We performed a pilot study in order to optimize the HUD application and implementation. We recruited six volunteers explicitly for the pilot study. The experienced a familiarization drive, driving with speedometer only, the permanent display as well as three information on demand concepts: shift paddle-triggered and two variants of gaze-triggered displays: A glance into the HUD area superimposes (1) the entire content (one large gaze-sensitive area) and (2) only the piece of information placed close to the gaze-point (four separate gaze-sensitive areas). While the first approach is comparable to the other display conditions regarding amount of and search for information (and the related distraction), the latter presents less information but rather requires knowledge about the location of the information and hence might lead to different search behavior.

By running this pilot study, we also evaluated the overall study design, the test setup and the reliability of the eye tracker. However, the major aim of the pilot study was to select one gaze interaction approach. The questionnaires as well as the individual feedback showed that there is a clear tendency towards the gaze interaction variant which controls the entire HUD content. Consequently, we decided to test this variant in the subsequent user study. Based on the results of the pilot study we also increased the distance between the gaze-sensitive area and the driving task by shifting it further to the lower edge of the display.

3.2 Participants

We recruited 20 participants by means of social networks. Our participants were on average 24 years old (SD = 2.4) and 18 of them owned a valid drivers license. Five participants had previously used a head-up display.

3.3 Study Design

We designed a within-subjects driving simulator study with four conditions: baseline (speedometer only), permanent display, gaze-triggered display, and shift paddle-triggered display of the HUD content. This corresponds to four driving tracks and one additional introductory familiarization drive. Therefore, we developed five different driving tracks. Each of them consisted of one individual driving video and a computer-generated ConTRe task (motion of arrow and brake light timing). The driving tracks were assigned in a counter-balanced way (Latin Square) to the display conditions. The order of the test tracks was also counter-balanced and participants were assigned randomly to one group. Each test track lasted 3 min; leading to an overall study duration of 60 min.

The aim of this study was to explore the user experience of information displayed on demand – triggered by gaze and a shift paddle. Therefore, we had to ensure that participants use the HUD and read the content frequently: We asked them to report changes in the HUD content verbally by naming the type of information that changed (except for the speedometer) and required driving at a constant speed (for which they had to use the speedometer). As for the secondary HUD monitoring task, we only measured the detected changes as the success rate. Since we did not aim to evaluate the information design or its memorability and since the comparability (of complexity and hence workload/distraction) of three content sets could not be ensured, we decided to use the same information set in all three HUD conditions. To avoid predictability, we altered the update timing of each piece of information for each driving track. To evaluate the driver's workload and user experience, we chose the NASA TLX[2] and UEQ[3] questionnaires. Furthermore, we designed an individual questionnaire that collects data about the driver's preferences and compares the four conditions directly.

Driving Task. We based our driving task on the continuous tracking and reaction task (ConTRe task) developed by Mahr et al. [13]. Instead of maneuvering a simulated car within the lane boundaries, the driver steers a cylinder ('self') to overlay another autonomously moving cylinder ('reference'). A red and a green light, similar to a traffic light, are placed above the autonomous cylinder and require an immediate braking or acceleration reaction of the driver when

---

[2] https://humansystems.arc.nasa.gov/groups/tlx/.
[3] http://www.ueq-online.org/.

switched on. We designed the task to be moderately hard according to the definitions of Mahr et al. [13]. The autonomous bar moves to 9 random positions within the lane boundaries per minute and remains at one position for 0 to 3 s. We adapted the standard task to our user study in order to reach a more realistic feeling of driving and a better interplay with the HUD information. Instead of an automated driving at a certain speed, we required a continuous control of the gas pedal for speed control and requested the participants to drive at a constant speed (120 km/h). Since additionally reacting to both green and red lights (according to the suggested timing) would be overwhelming and the mixed use of the gas pedal for speed control and traffic light response would be confusing, we decided to only collect the driver's response performance by the red light and limit the gas pedal to the speed control. The red light is turned on four times per minute: When the light switches on, the driver has to brake immediately; when it switches off (after 1 s), the driver has to accelerate to 120 km/h again. This allowed for the use of a speedometer – an information that changes continuously and has to be accessed frequently in order to reach a high driving performance – as head-up display content. We further used two arrows pointing at each other instead of two cylinders since we assume that this could lead to more precise steering.

The standard ConTRe task disconnects the steering behavior and the car's motion in the simulated world. This allows the use of footage of real driving instead of a simulated world. We recorded footage (30 fps, 1280 × 720 resolution) of driving on a straight highway with a speed of approximately 100 km/h. These videos were used in our driving simulator as a background scene; with an adjusted frame rate these videos were appropriate to simulate driving at a speed of 120 km/h. The participants received feedback about the current speed through the playback of the video; when they lowered the speed, the videos were played back slower. The speed decreased naturally by 1 km/h per second.

Head-Up Display Content. We selected four pieces of information with varying relevance for the driving task as well as varying update frequencies from 10 to 30 s, as depicted in Fig. 2. We selected information with low to high relevance for the driving task or the driver as a person based on the categorization for information according to its contexts [5]. Further, we chose continuous to singular updating, as we expect that the different display conditions might be suitable for different types of information.

1. **Speed:** The speedometer adjusts continuously to the gas pedal pressure and has to be monitored consistently. This information is available in all four conditions since it is of high relevance for the driving task, as in real driving.
2. **Personal message:** The personal message is of low relevance for driving but might be of high relevance for the driver. Its content is adjusted twice during each driving track.
3. **Gas:** The filling of the gas tank is of medium relevance for the driving task. Its value is designed to decrease naturally and changes 4 times during each driving track.

4. **Weather:** The weather information is of low relevance (as long as there is no risk of icy roads) and by nature very constant throughout the study duration. Consequently, this information was not updated.

Fig. 2. An example view of the driver. The driving simulator software runs an adjusted version of the ConTRe task and footage of real driving with superimposed HUD content.

The HUD information was placed in an area of −6° to 13° horizontally and −3° to 6° vertically. The vanishing point of the street constitutes 0°. These values also defined the gaze-sensitive area; a glance into this area superimposed the HUD content. In both information on demand conditions, the content was superimposed with a defined delay of 300 ms in order to avoid unintended display due to uncontrolled glance behavior. When the driver's gaze left the sensitive area or the shift paddle was released, the content remained visible for an additional 500 ms before it blanked out. The position of each piece of information is the same in each condition in order to avoid confusion or an implicit evaluation of the information placement: gas at −4°, speedometer at 0°, message at 6°, weather at 12° horizontally (corresponding to the center of the item).

3.4 Procedure

In a first step, participants had to complete a demographic questionnaire. Then, the experimenter introduced them to head-up displays in general and to the study goals and procedure. The experimenter asked the participants to take a seat in the setup and calibrated the eye tracker. The study started with a test drive during which participants familiarized themselves with the driving task and the setup. In the process, the experimenter explained the driving task in detail and instructed the participants to only use the right foot to control the pedals, as in a real automatic car. Then participants were introduced to the HUD information and asked to report content changes verbally. The participants then performed the four test tracks and filled in the UEQ and the NASA TLX questionnaires after each of them. After the study, they were asked to fill a final questionnaire.

3.5   Apparatus

Our test setup (see Fig. 1) used a 42″ display (1920 × 1080 px resolution) for the presentation of the driving simulator and a gaming steering wheel with pedals (Speedlink Drift O.Z.) for its control. The head-up display content was presented on the display and controllable through shift paddles and gaze. Two shift paddles were attached to the back side of the steering wheel, enabling interaction with both hands. The gaze interaction was realized by means of a Tobii REX eye tracker which was placed behind the steering wheel. The display was positioned at a distance of 1.65 m to the driver and shifted to the right (as was the windshield). The vanishing point of the road was set to be straight in front of the driver. Our driving simulator was based on footage of driving on a straight highway and the continuous tracking and reaction task (ConTRe task). We implemented the driving simulator, the head-up display and the interaction techniques in a single monolithic Java application.

4   Results

4.1   Driving Performance

To evaluate the driving performance, we measured the participants' accuracy in steering as well as the brake light reaction time and success rate. The mean values and standard deviations are depicted in Table 1. We analyzed each metric by means of repeated measures ANOVAs with Bonferroni-adjusted α-level.

Table 1. We measured the driving performance as steering accuracy and reaction time and success rate for the response to brake lights.

Display condition	Steering	Reaction time (ms)	Success rate
Speedometer	M = 9.4, SD = 4.8	M = 618, SD = 189	M = 0.4, SD = 0.5
Gaze-triggered	M = 15.3, SD = 11.1	M = 792, SD = 252	M = 2.0, SD = 2.2
Shift paddle-triggered	M = 11.4, SD = 4.9	M = 704, SD = 188	M = 1.1, SD = 1.5
Permanent display	M = 12.2, SD = 5.0	M = 715, SD = 204	M = 2.2, SD = 2.7

Steering. We measured the steering performance as the mean deviation between the reference arrow and the arrow representing the self. The ANOVA test showed a non-significant main effect (F(1.6, 26.4) = 3.9, p = .042). Post-hoc tests showed that driving with the speedometer only led to a significantly better steering performance compared to the permanent (p = .009), the gaze-triggered (p = .014), and the shift paddle-triggered HUD (p = .05). We did not find a difference between the two triggered HUDs. Neither we found a significant difference between the triggered HUD variants and the permanent HUD.

Brake Light Reaction. We measured the participants' reaction time to appearing brake lights as well as the missed brake lights. The ANOVA tests showed that the brake light reaction time (F(3.0, 51.0) = 4.2, p = .009) varied significantly. Post-hoc tests showed that the speedometer only variant leaded to significantly faster reaction times compared to the permanent HUD (p = .033), the shift paddle-triggered HUD (p = .39), and the gaze-triggered HUD (p = .007).

To analyze the missed brake lights, we performed a Friedman test with Wilcoxon post-hoc tests and found a significantly different success rate ($\chi^2(3) = 11.2$, p = .011). When driving with the speedometer only, the participants missed significantly fewer lights compared to the permanently displayed HUD (Z = −2.6, p = 0.1) and the gaze-triggered HUD (Z = −2.8, p = .004). Surprisingly, participants missed significantly fewer lights when driving with the shift paddle-triggered compared to the gaze-triggered HUD (Z = 2.0, p = .048).

4.2 HUD Monitoring Performance

We asked our participants to report updates of the HUD content verbally by naming the updated piece of information (e.g., 'message'). Overall, six updates occurred. A Friedman test with Bonferroni correction and Wilcoxon post-hoc tests showed a significant difference in update performance ($\chi^2(3) = 14.2$, p = .001). As expected, participants missed significantly more changes when information was displayed only on demand (gaze: M = 1.2, SD = 1.2, p = .003; shift paddle: M = 1.4, SD = 1.4, p = .002) compared to the permanent display (M = 0.2, SD = 0.4). There was no significant difference between the two self-triggered HUDs.

4.3 Workload

We measured the participants' workload by means of the standardized NASA-TLX questionnaire on a scale from 0 to 100; with 100 representing high workload. A repeated measures ANOVA showed that the workload depends on the display variants (F(2.3, 39.7) = 5.9, p = .004). We then analyzed this result by means of pairwise comparisons and found that the overall workload when using the gaze-triggered HUD (p = .008) and the shift paddle-triggered HUD (p = .007) is significantly higher compared to driving with the speedometer only. Although we did not find a statistically relevant result for the permanent display, the mean values indicates that it induces a workload level between the information-on-demand concepts and the baseline in our sample. Also, we did not find a statistically significant difference between the two self-triggered HUDs. The NASA-TLX is subdivided into the subscales mental demand, physical demand, temporal demand, overall performance, frustration level, and effort. We performed a repeated measures ANOVA with Bonferroni-adjusted α-level for each of the subscales and depicted the mean values and standard deviations in Fig. 3.

Mental Demand. The ANOVA test showed a significant difference in mental demand (F(2.7, 45.7) = 6.3, p = .002): The gaze-triggered (p = .002) and the shift paddle-triggered HUD (p = .001) as well as the permanently displayed HUD (p = .01) led to a significantly higher mental demand compared to the baseline.

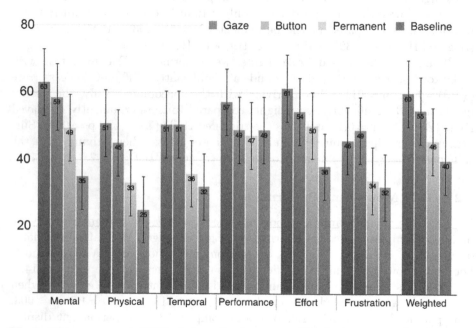

Fig. 3. The permanent HUDs induce the lowest workload; the more information is displayed the higher is the caused workload. The control of the HUD further increases the workload; the gaze-triggered HUD variant more than the shift paddle-triggered one.

Physical Demand. We found a significant influence of the display variant on the physical demand (F(2.8, 47.6) = 7.7, p < .001): The gaze-triggered (p = .001) and the shift paddle-triggered (p = .003) display as well as the permanently displayed HUD (p = .04) induced significantly higher physical demand compared to the baseline. Furthermore, the gaze-triggered information led to a higher physical workload than its permanent display (p = .007).

Temporal Demand. Also, the temporal demand depends on the display variant (F(2.7, 46) = 4.4, p = .01): The gaze-triggered (p = .027) and the shift paddle-triggered HUD (p = .02) led to a significantly higher temporal demand than driving with the speedometer only.

Overall Performance. The ANOVA test did not identify any statistically significant differences in the overall performance when using the HUD variants.

Frustration Level. We did not find a significant influence of the display variant on the frustration level. However, post-hoc tests showed that the shift paddle-triggered HUD leads to a higher frustration than the permanent HUD (p = .02) as well as the baseline (p = .025). We did not find a significantly higher frustration for the gaze-triggered HUD.

Effort. We found a significant effect of the display variants on the required effort (F(3.0, 51.0) = 4.8, p = .005): The participants had to invest significantly more effort when controlling the HUD with gaze (p = .004) and with shift paddle (p = .014) compared to the baseline. Also, the permanent display required more effort compared to the baseline (p = .05) by the participants. We rarely found statistically relevant results for the permanent display compared to the driver-triggered HUDs but the values indicate that the induced workload is between those and the speedometer only HUD in our sample.

4.4   User Experience

We applied the standardized UEQ questionnaire to measure the participants' experience when using the different display variants. The UEQ is subdivided into the aspects novelty, stimulation, dependability, efficiency, perspicuity, and attractiveness. The results for the single aspects are depicted in Fig. 4. We analyzed our data by means of Friedman and Wilcoxon tests and report the statistics below.

Novelty. We measured a significant difference for novelty of the four HUD variants ($\chi^2(3) = 17.9$, p < .001): The gaze interaction was rated the newest variant and received significantly higher values than the speedometer only HUD (Z = −3.4, p = .001) and also than the shift paddle-triggered variant (Z = −2.0, p = .044). Furthermore, we found a significant higher value for the shift paddle-triggered HUD compared to the baseline. (Z = −2.3, p = .023) The permanent variant with the full HUD content was also rated more innovative than the speedometer-only variant (Z = −3.5, p < .001).

Stimulation. We did not find any dependencies between the stimulation level and the display variants.

Dependability. We measured a significant difference in dependability ($\chi^2(3)=$ 18.5, p < .001): We found a significantly lower dependability rating for the gaze-triggered HUD compared to the permanently displayed HUD ($Z = -2.3$, p = .024). Furthermore, the speedometer only HUD received significantly higher values than the shift paddle-triggered HUD ($Z = -2.7$, p = .007), the gaze-triggered HUD ($Z = -3.5$, p < .001), and also than the permanent HUD ($Z = -2.6$, p = .01).

Efficiency. The perceived efficiency varies nearly significantly when using the different HUD variants ($\chi^2(3) = 9.8$, p = .021): The efficiency is rated lower for the gaze-triggered HUD ($Z = -2.4$, p = .017) and the shift paddle-triggered HUD ($Z = -2.6$, p = .009) compared to to the speedometer-only version. Surprisingly, the speedometer only HUD is perceived more efficient than the permanent HUD ($Z = -2.5$, p = .013).

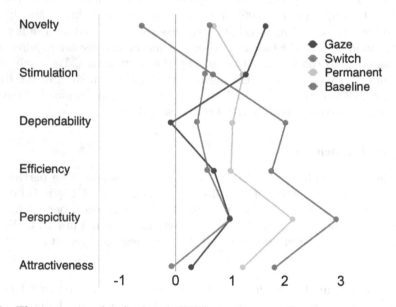

Fig. 4. The permanently displayed HUDs, and especially the variant with the speedometer only, provide a better user experience than the driver-triggered HUDs (UEQ results on a scale from −3 to 3).

Perspicuity. The perceived perspicuity varies significantly ($\chi^2(3) = 26.4$, p < .000): The permanently displayed HUD received significantly higher values than the gaze-interaction ($Z = -2.1$, p = .034) and the shift paddle interaction ($Z = -2.5$, p = .013) conditions. Also, the speedometer only HUD received significantly higher values than the gaze-interaction ($Z = -3.6$, p < .001) and the shift paddle interaction ($Z = -3.1$, p = .002) as well as the permanent HUD ($Z = -2.7$, p = .006).

Attractiveness. The HUD variants differ significantly in attractiveness ($\chi^2(3) =$ 25.24, p < .001): Participants found the two self-triggered HUDs less attractive than the speedometer only HUD (gaze: Z = −3.0, p = .003; switch: Z = −3.5, p < .001) as well as the permanent HUD (gaze: Z = −2.0, p = .047; switch: Z = −2.6, p < .008).

Summary. To sum this up, apart from *novelty* and *stimulation*, the minimal display of the speedometer led to the best user experience; followed by the permanent display of HUD. While gaze interaction was rated high for novelty and stimulation, it received comparably low values for the remaining aspects. The shift paddle-triggered variant received overall very neutral ratings.

4.5   Final Comparison and Qualitative Feedback

We used self-designed questionnaires with a 5-point Likert-scale (1–5) to gather insights into the participants' preferences and to collect qualitative feedback. Participants rated the driving task as medium realistic and demanding. The position of the HUD content felt intuitive and was easy to remember which suggests that there was no disadvantage in finding the information when it was presented only on demand.

The superimposition of information was more irritating for the participants when it was gaze-triggered (median = 4) and shift paddle-triggered (median = 3.5) compared to the permanent display (median = 2). The permanently displayed HUD was rated more distracting than the baseline (median = 1) but less distracting (median = 2) than the driver-triggered HUDs (median = 4).

Our participants felt less safe driving with the gaze-triggered HUD (median = 3) compared to all other conditions (median = 4). However, participants also stated that they played around more with the gaze interaction which suggests that the distraction and the perceived risk might be lower when participants are used to this interaction technique. The participants felt most in control of the HUD content when using the shift paddle-triggered variant (median = 5), closely followed by the permanent and the speedometer display (median = 4.5); our participants rated the feeling of control neutral when using the gaze-interaction (median = 3). The participants who stated that the gaze-triggered HUD was frequently displayed without their intend rated the gaze-triggered HUD lower in user experience and overall preferred the other HUD variants. A Spearman correlation showed that the likability of the gaze-triggered HUD correlates with the control over the display ($r_s = -0.579$, p = 0.012). The HUD information was displayed fast in all self-triggered HUD conditions (median = 5) but its access was faster in the permanent display (permanent:median = 5; gaze: median = 2.5; shift paddle: median = 4). Our participants mentioned that the gaze-controlled HUD superimposed information without their intent; showing need for improvement for our implementation but also potential for this interaction method in general. Further, they said that an acoustic feedback to content updates would be very helpful (permanent:median = 4; gaze: median = 4.5; shift paddle: median = 5).

Participants wanted to have the speedometer displayed on the HUD but are not as interested in other, non-driving related information and an explicitly triggered display. We expected that a combined version, e.g., a permanent speedometer which can be augmented with further information using gaze or a shift paddle, might be of interest to the participants but our results fail to support this thesis.

5   Summary and Interpretation of the Results

We conducted a driving simulator study on the potential of displaying an in-car head-up display only when explicitly triggered by the driver. We used the ConTRe task along with driving videos and adjusted it in order to reach a good compromise between study control and realism. As for the superimposition of the HUD we proposed two techniques: gaze- and shift paddle-based interaction.

This paper presents a first exploration of those two variants in a lab scenario but follow-up research should aim for a real world study. Below, we discuss our results as well as the limitations of the study design and setup and how we expect our results to hold in a real world scenario.

5.1   Discussion and General Limitations

The fact that participants reported most of the HUD content updates shows that they accessed the HUD and used the interaction methods. Hence, they are qualified to evaluate the tested HUD concepts. We found that driving performance was impeded by the head-up display and particularly by the gaze-triggered variant. This is not surprising since driving is a primarily visual task and hence driving and the HUD control competed for the visual attention. Participants stated that the information was superimposed fast when using the gaze interaction but also that it was displayed unintentionally, potentially leading to unwanted glances at the HUD. We expect that a more sophisticated eye tracking implementation may lead to better results, However, there will always be a delay between gaze shift and superimposition, which inevitably causes higher glance times.

Both the gaze- and the shift paddle-based interaction caused an increased workload. Although the difference to the permanent HUD display was not significant, values indicate consistently that a permanent display of the same amount of information requires less resources. Further, participants mentioned that they were able to concentrate most on driving when they were not in control of the HUD. We expected that the display of information only on demand could decrease the driver's workload but our results do not confirm this thesis. However, we think that the task of reporting the content updates forced the participants to access the information more often than they would do in real life. Also, a mixed approach – the permanent display of the speedometer and the superimposition of additional information – might further increase the demand.

The permanently displayed HUDs received higher user experience ratings than the information-on-demand concepts. For the gaze-triggered HUD we argue that a more reliable setup could improve the user experience. The implementation of the shift paddle-triggered HUD worked well and seven of our participants kept it triggered for longer than 20 s – utilizing it as a permanent display. In our opinion, it is questionable if a well-implemented information-on-demand approach can ever reach the user experience and workload level of a permanent display. We think that a long-term study is needed in order to find out whether and how the user behavior might change. Further, complementing the driver-triggered HUD with audio feedback might improve user experience and lower the workload.

5.2   Limitations of the Study Design and Setup

We performed a pilot study in order to validate our study design and setup and particularly to decide how to design the gaze-based interaction. Based on its results, we refined our study design and decided for a gaze interaction that controlled the entire HUD instead of single pieces of information. However, it seems that the eye-tracker had problems to track the eye gaze of some participants. Our results and the individual feedback from the participants indicated that it worked well for most of them but that the HUD content was occasionally displayed unintentionally for others. As we found that the likability of the gaze-triggered HUD depended on the control over the display, we think that a more sophisticated eye-tracker may lead to a higher rating in user experience.

Our study setup comprised one display for the driving simulator as well as the HUD content. The lack of distance between the road scene and the HUD content also disabled the foreground-background segregation which invites drivers to focus on the HUD [14]. Furthermore, it enabled the participants to switch faster between HUD and world and also to read the displayed information while visually focusing on the driving task (as mentioned by the participants). Also, our tasks forced participants to access the displayed information frequently – potentially more often than they would access it in real life. In a real car, participants might favor an explicitly triggered head-up display since the benefit of the simultaneous reading is lowered and the permanent display might be more distracting.

The switching times in a real car towards a real HUD will be higher than in our study. We assume they will be further increased for the gaze-triggered HUD compared to the shift paddle-triggered variant since the driver has to glance into the sensitive area but can only focus on the HUD once it is displayed. Presumably, the re-focusing in depth is separated from the glance into the HUD area – and potentially increases the switching time. This is not the case for the shift paddle-triggered HUD. Considering this and the better driving performance, we think that the shift paddle-triggered HUD is the safer alternative of the two.

The videos presented a real driving scene while driving simulators only present virtual and often unrealistic environments, e.g., without any other road users. The steering wheel did not affect the car's position in the world and gave feedback about the steering performance by adjusting the position of an arrow instead. Regarding the speed, the participants received feedback through the speed of the video playback. Our driving task differs from real driving – as every driving simulator does – however, our participants rated it as medium realistic.

6   Conclusions

The study presented in this paper explored the display of the HUD information only on demand – triggered by gaze or a shift paddle – and compared it to its permanent display. Our results show that the overall workload increased, although the information was displayed for a shorter time. Further, the user experience of the two information-on-demand variants was generally rated lower which might be caused by the eye-tracker. Participants rated the gaze- and shift paddle-triggered HUD as more distracting from the primary task. The fact that participants liked the speedometer-only HUD more than the full HUD content shows that they are generally not as interested in having driving-irrelevant information cluttering their view on the road. However, their statements indicate that a display on demand showing driving-related but not permanently needed information complemented with audio notifications might be more desirable. As follow-up research, we propose a real world study that utilizes a gaze- or shift paddle-triggered HUD. We further think, that a long-term study would be very interesting since prior research showed that gaze interaction becomes less demanding [12,16] and user behavior may change over time.

References

1. Briziarelli, G., Allan, R.W.: The effect of a head-up speedometer on speeding behaviour. Percept. Mot. Skills (1989)
2. Dellis, E.: Automotive head-up displays: just around the corner. Automot. Eng. **96**(2) (1988)
3. Haeuslschmid, R., Pfleging, B., Alt, F.: A design space to support the development of windshield applications for the car. In: Proceedings of the 2016 CHI Conference on Human Factors in Computing Systems, CHI 2016, pp. 5076–5091. ACM, New York (2016). http://doi.acm.org/10.1145/2858036.2858336
4. Haeuslschmid, R., Schnurr, L., Wagner, J., Butz, A.: Contact-analog warnings on windshield displays promote monitoring the road scene. In: Proceedings of the 7th International Conference on Automotive User Interfaces and Interactive Vehicular Applications, AutomotiveUI 2015, pp. 64–71. ACM, New York (2015). http://doi.acm.org/10.1145/2799250.2799274
5. Haeuslschmid, R., Shou, Y., O'Donovan, J., Burnett, G., Butz, A.: First steps towards a view management concept for large-sized head-up displays with continuous depth. In: Proceedings of the 8th International Conference on Automotive User Interfaces and Interactive Vehicular Applications, Automotive'UI 2016, pp. 1–8. ACM, New York (2016). http://doi.acm.org/10.1145/3003715.3005418
6. Iarish, I., Wickens, C.D.: Attention and huds: flying in the dark? In: Society for Information Display International Symposium Digest of Technical Papers, XXII, pp. 461–464 (1991)

7. Kaptein, N.A.: Benefits of in-car head-up displays, TNO report no.: TNO-TM 1994 B-20. Technical report, TNO Human Factors Research Institute (1994)
8. Kato, H., Ito, H., Shima, J., Imaizumi, M., Shibata, H.: Development of hologram head-up display. Technical report, SAE Technical Report Paper No. 92060 (1192)
9. Kern, D., Mahr, A., Castronovo, S., Schmidt, A., Müller, C.: Making use of drivers' glances onto the screen for explicit gaze-based interaction. In: Proceedings of the 2nd International Conference on Automotive User Interfaces and Interactive Vehicular Applications, AutomotiveUI 2010, pp. 110–116. ACM, New York (2010). http://doi.acm.org/10.1145/1969773.1969792
10. Kern, D., Schmidt, A.: Design space for driver-based automotive user interfaces. In: Proceedings of the 1st International Conference on Automotive User Interfaces and Interactive Vehicular Applications, AutomotiveUI 2009, pp. 3–10. ACM, New York (2009). http://doi.acm.org/10.1145/1620509.1620511
11. Kiefer, R.J.: Effect of a head-up versus head-down digital speedometer on visual sampling behaviour and speed control performance during daytime automobile driving. SAE technical report paper no. 910111. Technical report, SAE (1991)
12. Liu, Y.C.: Effects of using head-up display in automobile context on attention demand and driving performance. Displays 24(4–5), 157–165 (2003). www.sciencedirect.com/science/article/pii/S0141938204000022
13. Mahr, A., Feld, M., Moniri, M.M., Math, R.: The ConTRe (continuous tracking and reaction) task: a flexible approach for assessing driver cognitive workload with high sensitivity. In: Adjunct Proceedings of the 4th International Conference on Automotive User Interfaces and Interactive Vehicular Applications (AutomotiveUI 2012), Portsmouth, NH, USA, pp. 88–91 (2012)
14. Mazza, V., Turatto, M., Umiltà, C.: Foreground-background segmentation and attention: a change blindness study. Psychol. Res. 69(3), 201–210 (2005). http://dx.doi.org/10.1007/s00426-004-0174-9
15. Mulckhuyse, M., van Zoest, W., Theeuwes, J.: Capture of the eyes by relevant and irrelevant onsets. Exp. Brain Res. 186, 225–235 (2008). Experimentelle Hirnforschung Experimentation Cerebrale
16. Poitschke, T., Laquai, F., Stamboliev, S., Rigoll, G.: Gaze-based interaction on multiple displays in an automotive environment. In: 2011 IEEE International Conference on Systems, Man, and Cybernetics, pp. 543–548, October 2011
17. Poitschke, T.M.: Blickbasierte Mensch-Maschine Interaktion im Automobil. Ph.D. thesis, Universität München (2011)
18. Pomarjanschi, L., Dorr, M., Barth, E.: Gaze guidance reduces the number of collisions with pedestrians in a driving simulator. ACM Trans. Interact. Intell. Syst. 1(2), 8:1–8:14 (2012). http://doi.acm.org/10.1145/2070719.2070721
19. Sojourner, R., Antin, J.F.: The effects of a simulated head-up display speedometer on perceptual task performance. Hum. Factors 32(3), 329–339 (1990)
20. Theeuwes, J., Kramer, A.F., Hahn, S., Irwin, D.E.: Our eyes do not always go where we want them to go: capture of the eyes by new objects. Psychol. Sci. 9, 379–385 (1998)
21. Trent, V.: Keeping eye and mind on the road. Ph.D. thesis, Uppsala University (2005)
22. Weintraub, D.J.: HUDs, HMDs and common sense: polishing virtual images. Hum. Factors Soc. Bull. 30, 1–3 (1987)
23. Wickens, C.D., Long, J.: Conformal symbology, attention shifts and the head-up display. In: Proceedings of the 38th Human Factor and Ergonomics Society Annual Meeting, pp. 6–10. Human Factors Society (1994)

24. Wickens, C.D., Horrey, W.: Models of attention, distraction, and highway hazard avoidance. In: Regan, M.A., Lee, J.D., Young, K.L. (eds.) Driver Distraction Theory, Effects, and Mitigation, pp. 57–69. CRC Press, Boca Raton (2008)
25. Yeo, J.H.: Driver's eye detection method of drowsy driving warning system. US Patent 6,130,617, October 2000. http://www.google.com/patents/US6130617. Accessed 9 June 1999
26. Yeo, J.H.: Driver's drowsiness detection method of drowsy driving warning system. US Patent 6,243,015, June 2001. http://www.google.com/patents/US6243015. Accessed 17 June 1999

Seeing Through the Eyes of Heavy Vehicle Operators

Markus Wallmyr[1,2(✉)]

[1] Mälardalen University, Västerås, Sweden
markus.wallmyr@mdh.se
[2] CrossControl, Uppsala, Sweden

Abstract. Interaction Designers of heavy vehicles are challenged by two opposing forces, the increasingly information-driven systems resulting in higher visual load, and a must to support a focus on the area of operation. To succeed in the interaction design and application of new technology, a good understanding of the user and the activity is needed. However, field studies are related with substantial efforts for both researcher and operator. This paper investigates and shows how quick non-intrusive studies can be held, by bridging practice from one HCI area into another, i.e. applying guerilla testing approaches used in mobile and web development into the heavy vehicles domain, an area not used to this practice. An exploratory study is performed, on a diverse set of vehicles in the field. This study describes and presents examples how both qualitative and quantitative conclusions can be extracted on the user attentiveness to digital systems and surrounding.

Keywords: Off-highway vehicles · Eye tracking · User studies · Guerilla HCI

1   Introduction

Demands on production performance, cost efficiency, personal safety and environmental considerations, among others, push the creation of even more intelligent industrial systems. From the beginning of the industrial era, technological advances have changed the users' behavior and tasks performed. For each new generation, machines are becoming more and more automated. Availability of information technology in terms of sensors, computing performance, and software capabilities increases over time, and so does the use of information systems enabled by the big amount of data produced.

This direct the machine users (i.e. operators) activities, towards information processing and spatial awareness, rather than controlling the machine. They spend more time monitoring and gaining information from built in, or retrofitted information systems. For example, Global Positioning System (GPS) based navigation systems, aided visual systems using cameras, Industrial Control System (ICS), etc.

Current industrial approach to present the increasing information in vehicles is to add more instrumentation and graphical displays. A tractor can, for example, contain more than five different displays. One for the main instrumentation cluster, one for tractor configuration and information, one for the precision farming system, one for the

R. Bernhaupt et al. (Eds.): INTERACT 2017, Part II, LNCS 10514, pp. 263–282, 2017.
DOI: 10.1007/978-3-319-67684-5_16

implement attached to the machine and one for monitoring cameras. This does not include additional screens, such as the operators' cell phone or additional implement displays. While future scenarios involve augmented reality and see-through interfaces [1, 2], there is currently a limitation in cabin space.

Even at the current state, there are issues with user acceptance. For example: When the author were making a pilot field study at a larger Swedish farm and asked the operator about the usability of the touch screen, the operator answered: "I don't use the touch screen, only the joystick". In this case, the machine was a potato harvester attached to a tractor, where the touch screen was used to configure and show information from the harvester's implement. The user was regarded a skilled machine operator in terms of driving and operating the equipage, but he was limited in his computer related interaction. Instead, the manager of the farm made the configuration and tuning of the system.

The observation above is supported by other studies addressing obstacles for operators to embrace new technology. In agriculture, for example, Kutter et al. express that precision farming is less frequent than expected [3]. Precision farming systems are information intelligence systems that include positioning information, maps, and sensory data in order to provide farm managers and operators a better overview and control of their production. Ultimately this leads to decision support systems that optimize production and reduce the use of treatments that has an environmental impact [4, 5]. Although precision farming has existed for decades, its main adopters are younger full-time farmers with higher education, operating at larger farms [6], making the potential benefits not fully exploited. Assuming that other industrial vehicle domains have a similar situation there is still much to be done in terms of operator interaction design with these types of system.

1.1 The Challenge of Gaining Understanding

Creating interaction with these systems require a diligent understanding of operator's behavior [7]. However, doing field studies can take a significant amount of time [8]. Also, participatory techniques can be difficult to perform, because in many of these vehicles the cabin is too small to ride along with the operator. Thus, one is limited to observe from a distance, making it difficult to detect operator attention and actions that are not visible. Performing interviews or surveys with users is an approach that can give lots of valuable information. However, when they are made separate from the actual operation the answers may not fully include the actually performed operation, or be biased by opinions [9]. As argued by Nielsen, designers should "pay attention to what users do, not what they say" [10, 11].

One method to acquire knowledge about a user's behavior and attention is by using eye tracking. Eye tracking is carried out using a camera that measures the eyes focus point, i.e. the gaze fixations [12]. These fixations can then be referenced against information in front of the user, for example, a monitor presenting a web page. This makes it possible to observe where the user puts his or hers focus of attention and analyze the information seeking pattern.

In literature, many eye tracking examples relates to marketing and different types information retrieval studies, such as forms evaluation and web pages [12]. In road vehicle situations eye tracking has been frequently used to study drivers behavior and attention [13]. Eye tracking has also been used in different off-highway vehicle setups, some examples from different areas being: Forestry, where eye tracking has been used to identify dwell patterns and focus areas for harvester operators [14]. In mining, where it has been used to track user attention and, combined with additional sensors, identifying factors for operators ergonomics [15]. Eye tracking has been used in agriculture to measure differences between drivers experience levels and to measure how a higher level of automation increases utilization of vehicle display systems [16]. It has moreover been used in trains, for example, to measure how in-train traffic management systems affect the visual attention to the outside of the cab [17]. In the property construction area, "considerably less attention has been paid to its potential to improve the design and construction processes" according to Yosefi et al. [18].

Traditional eye tracking has been related with bungle some in equipment as well as time-consuming methods. Historically, equipment such as cameras had to be mounted in cabins, taking up valuable production time when doing field studies. With the availability of head-worn tracker solutions, the tracker follows the user movements while looking around. This is beneficial in applications where the user is not focusing at one single area, such as a form or a screen. Instead, it can record how the user looks around in the scenery, such as in mobile machines, were the driver can have a wide area of attention and a frequent change of focus. Still, head worn trackers have until recently been associated with a high cost and have thus been a tool for researchers or enterprises with deep pockets that spend significant efforts in user understanding. Also, recommendations on the number of participants to include in studies are above 30 people for quantitative conclusions and six users for qualitative studies [19]. Not only do this consume time in the field, it also makes analysis of data an effort consuming activity. Combining a gaze map with 30 users on a static screen is considerably easier than combining 30 people performing a freely moving activity.

1.2 Re-Setting the Scenery

With shortened time to market and a design practice that is becoming increasingly incorporated into the product development [20], it is of interest to understand how we can complement more rigorous user studies with lightweight approaches. In the user experience community (UX), cost effective methods are proposed where practitioners quickly go out to gain user understanding, for example when approaching persons in a coffee shop to ask for feedback on a design, also known as guerilla HCI [21, 22].

What if the same type of cost effective methods could be used to gain understanding in other domains, more specifically for heavy vehicles? Though, in a café, it can be assumed a visitor's participation will not interfere with the work of a complete team.

Here we come back to eye tracking, where availability of simpler and cheaper equipment [23, 24], opens up for a more widespread use [25], as a probing tool to identify where additional usability testing resources can be focused. With eye tracking plus a recording of the user's operation, it is possible to get a view of the attention and how the user is performing the task at hand. If the operator could quickly be hooked up with the equipment and then continue with the work, such approach could offer a time and effort efficient method to conduct field studies. Giving minimal interference to operators and their team's ongoing work and a tool to collect, and share, user perception of a product or a solution, with a physically distributed engineering and design team.

Additionally, Rozalinski et al. present that even simplified methods of eye tracking and a limited test sample "allowed us to discover several usability problems [...] not discoverable through traditional usability testing methods. Moreover, eye tracking provided a more detailed understanding of usability issues already uncovered by traditional usability testing" [26].

The rest of this paper will present an experience report where eye tracking was performed in a guerilla usability testing manner. This combination of approaches within the industrial setting is uncommon in literature and show how practitioners can quickly get real field data. The used technical setup will be presented as well as the practice where industrial sites were approached to find users to study. Following thereafter is a presentation of the recording analysis and findings, a discussion of results including practical lessons learned and finally a conclusion.

2 Study Setup

The purpose of this study was to evaluate how eye tracking can be used to make quick probing studies of operator attention when using off-highway machines, as well as to gain knowledge about their use of the digital information systems in vehicles. For this study, a diverse set of machines and environments were approached, rather than a higher amount of a specific type. The machines were:

- A forestry harvester, performing thinning operations.
- A wheel loader working in a stone crusher zone, moving and loading crushed material to trucks.
- An excavator performing supportive functions during leveling of a shaft.
- An articulated dump truck transporting soil from a digging zone to an unloading zone.
- A wheeled excavator working with leveling of a property ground.
- A mobile crane, lifting prefabricated concrete walls at a property building.

The study was done at different working sites located in central region of Sweden. Swedish was the natural language for all participants. The conductor, also Swedish, stemmed from the industrial vehicle domain, thus having basic knowledge about machines, operation process, domain terminology etc. All machines visited were operated by male operators, ranging from young adults to middle-aged men. Unfortunately, we didn't meet any females.

The field work was constrained in time, motivated, as described above, by an interest to get real-life information quickly and without costly setups and long planning. In practice that meant that 4 of the vehicles was visited in one day. The other at separate days.

A mix of operators worked alone and with other people/machines. The harvester worked alone. The excavators and the crane worked with other persons. The wheel loader and dump truck were mostly alone, though occasionally approached by other machines. This mix was looked-for, it gave a diverse sample. A lower variety would be of interest, in a detailed study.

For some of the above machines, there was enough space for an additional passenger that could ride along and observe the operator behavior and interaction, in this case, the dump truck and the harvester. In the other machines, there wasn't enough space to fit more than the operator.

On-road moving vehicles, such as trucks, were deliberately not included as these type of vehicles work in different conditions and with a different working pattern.

Our assumption was that, using eye trackers that record what is in front of the operator, analysis can be made of real word operation in a detailed manner where it is difficult observe from aside or through testimonials, in areas such as users attention while doing operation, how they interact with other workers and to what level the systems built-in Human Machine Interface (HMI) is used. Observing the user's gaze can also give input on factors in the HMI, for example, if excessive time is spent comprehending the HMI, or if information is not detected, such as notification or alarm messages. The diversity and size of the sample set would not give quantitative results, but prove the study approach and give input of interest for further, more detailed, studies.

3 Technical Setup

The eye tracking equipment was based on a pair of eye tracking glasses from Pupil labs [27]. The glasses capture the pupil position using emission of infrared light that illuminates the user's eye and detects the pupil position based on the reflected light [24]. This is done via two eye cameras, making it possible to track both eyes for higher accuracy. These cameras are placed on an adjustable arm at the lower outer side of the spectacle frame. In the center of the spectacles frame there is a camera pointing forward, the world camera. This camera records what's in front of the operator, in other words, what the operator sees.

The gaze tracking and eyesight recording are done via software on a connected computer. A lightweight laptop computer was used, running Ubuntu 14.04 and the pupil labs open source software (Pupil Capture v.0.7.3).

The glasses features a 120 Hz infrared camera for eye capture rate and a full HD (1080p) scene in front. However, in the recordings, the resolution was limited to 60 Hz framerate and HD (720p) resolution. This was selected to reduce the file size of the recordings and to preserve computer battery lifetime, due to the high CPU load when using highest settings. Sound was also recorded, using the laptops built-in microphones.

The analysis was performed in the accompanying player application, Pupil Player. The windows version v.0.6.9 was used. This application can play back the video from the front camera together with the eye tracking data overlaid on the recorded image.

4 On-Site and User Approach

The first visit was the forest thinning site. It involved a few hours of travel, hence the operator was contacted in advance and the study was briefly described. This was the only visit where the operator knew about the evaluation in advance. The subsequent site was contacted via phone to clear the visit with site management before approaching the site, the rest of the sites were approached directly.

At the site, the responsible manager was approached for clearance before approaching any operator. The purpose of the visit was described, how the eye tracking study should be performed as well as the ambition to introduce as minimal as possible disruption to ongoing production. Everyone approached was very positive to the purpose and every visited place accepted the request to study one or more operators. For the machines approached there was occasionally a shorter time period where the machine wasn't operating, for example, while waiting for material or for others work. Unless when escorted by local managers, this was the time when machine operators were approached.

In order to produce valid data, the glasses have to be calibrated. This calibration was done with the operator staying in the cabin. Not only did this make the setup sequence quick. It also avoided the glasses to become repositioned on the head while entering the vehicle and it helped to get world camera set up in a good angle, to record the correct part of the visible area.

The calibration process was performed using the recording applications screen calibration process, where the computer display was held in height of the operator's head and as close as possible to the front windscreen. This type of calibration process does not result in the highest accuracy when looking at longer distances, it was, however, a tradeoff for getting accuracy when looking inside the cabin. The glasses have an accuracy of 0.6% in good conditions [24] and the eye gaze position accuracy provided what can be considered as a satisfying result for the need, to capture attention to different areas and not specific details in the scenery or cabin.

Once calibrated the recording was started and the computer stowed away in the cabin. The whole setup procedure was completed a few minutes, depending on a number of questions asked by the operator. After activation of the recording, the operator was left to continue the work. The length of each recording session followed the natural breaks occurring during in operation.

4.1 User Acceptance

After shortly presenting the study, including the eye tracking equipment, the operators were asked if they were interested in participating. Neither of them had ever tried anything like this before, but pleasingly all were positive to be part of the test.

The use of glasses turned out to be a very suitable technology. It was natural for the user to put them on and easy to calibrate. They also seemed to give some amusement, with operators giving comment to other colleagues like "terminator is here" when wearing the glasses. The glasses was not reported to disturb their operation. However, some users reported them as a bit unaccustomed to wear and in the beginning they glanced at the eye tracking recording cameras, visible in their outer lower field of vision.

When natural breaks occurred, or when it was possible to ride along in the vehicle, questions were asked to gain more understanding. This also gave an impression about the operators, where the harvester, wheeled excavator and crane operator showed a genuine interest in their machine and technology. The excavator and Dump Truck operator seemed knowledgeable but didn't show the same interest. The wheel loader operator seemed least interested. However, this can be biased by the operator's social appearance. Firm information about user knowledge, background etc. would require formal questions, thus counteracting the aim of minimal interruption.

5 Gaze Recording Analysis

Apart from evaluating the acceptance and use of eye tracking as a method and tool to conduct quick on-site studies with different types of heavy machines, there was a purpose for the study as such. The purpose was to perform a mix of phenomenological research [28] and objective indications. The phenomenological research objective was to acquire information on operators work in natural conditions and to get an understanding about their steps of operation and focus of attention. The following section will provide examples of analysis results from each of the visited machine.

5.1 Forestry Harvester

The forestry harvester was performing thinning in the forest. The purpose of the thinning procedure is to select which trees to keep for further growth and which trees to remove in order to give the kept trees improved conditions and room for further growth. The selection of trees to keep and remove is in some cases done before actual felling, but in this case, it was done by the operator while driving.

During felling and movement of the crane, the focus was mostly on the harvester head, as exemplified in Fig. 1, with glances in other directions to check felling directions as well to ensure enough open space for the tree being fed through the harvester head.

Fig. 1. Forestry harvester and operators gaze points when processing a birch tree.

The display, placed centrally in the lower part of the windscreen, was glanced upon shortly to verify that the selection of assortment was correct and that the fed length was reasonable. In other words, making sure everything was operating as expected. This was only done for trees considered to have a value, pulpwood was just cut in the pre-set length without checking the screen. However, when feeding of the tree was not proceeding as expected, the display was used to find out information about what could have gone wrong. For example, if the display showed that the diameter or length wasn't as expected, this provided an indication that additional stems had been taken in the harvester head and thus obstructing the length measurement system.

In addition to the selection of trees to fell, the operator must also plan the travel path for the machine. Whether or not he will reach a tree from the current passage or have to go another way. During movement of the vehicle, the gaze moves around more freely. Sweeping from identification of the tree to fell, if the crane reaches there, scanning of the ground for good passage, estimating if trees are possible to pass or if the wheel will hit them in tight passages or during reversing. The operator must also choose how to fell the trees in a good way, both to avoid damages on trees that should be kept, as well as being able to collect cut trees into piles which the forwarder can later come and collect. Still, the focus is mostly ahead, because the whole cabin can be rotated instead of only the crane.

Figure 2 shows the level of attention through the cabin windows and at different areas in the cabin. Areas are divided into left window, front window, right window, upper window, lower part of the front window and the computer display.

Fig. 2. Level of attention in different areas for the harvester.

Being a machine so computerized and with the display placed centrally in front of the operator, its attention was remarkably lower than expected. There is, however, a possible reason, related to the task performed. During thinning trees with less value are removed, while the maximum output of each tree is the focus during final felling. Because of this, according to the operator, the thinning work involve less screen usage than final harvesting. In other words, there wasn't much focus on selecting optimal lengths and cuts, which is one of the primary information on the display.

5.2   Wheeled Excavator

Next was the wheeled excavator, it was adding gravel to a property ground in order to level it. Gravel was collected from one pile and transported it to the leveling area. Reaching the unloading area the operator scanned the surface, looking for the next place to fill, see example in Fig. 3. Then the gravel was poured out and thereafter evened with the shovel. The final adjustment was done manually by another person.

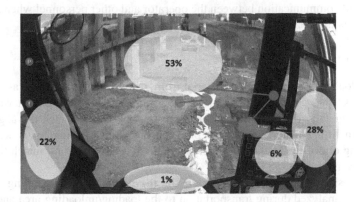

Fig. 3. Level of attention in different areas for the wheeled excavator.

In a site like this, with several machines and persons working simultaneously, the operator reported that he routinely checked the rearview mirrors before starting to roll the excavator. This was also confirmed by the eye tracking. However, during leveling, the focus was on the task at hand, with only a few indications that the operator was looking at something else than the shovel operation and the partner on the ground.

The machine was equipped with a height sensing system, giving the operator guidance on the height of the shovel. The final measuring was however done by the external person using laser measuring, not making it necessary for the operator to do precision operation based on the machine measurement indication. Additionally, the measurement system also had a useful feature where the whole screen shifted color between blue, green and red, depending if the shovel was too low, at correct height or too high. This signal was probably indication enough for the operator's peripheral view while having focus on the task at hand.

In relation to the harvester, the excavator had much higher values on display usage, in other words, use of precision positioning system, see Fig. 3. This despite having ground support. In terms of attention, the excavator also shows relatively high numbers at the sides, even though the operator had the possibility to rotate the cabin with the boom, in the same way as the harvester. One reason for this was the wheeling. The path was partly over a narrow road built using sleepers, with the purpose to even the ground pressure. There the operator looked out of the side windows to ensure the correct wheel placement. Another reason was the communication with the ground person where the operator often rotated the machine and looked through the side window, not to have the boom close to persons.

5.3   Mobile Crane

The mobile crane was lifting concrete pre-fabricated wall segments from a truck to a building ground. This was performed in close range to the mobile crane and with good visibility. Unfortunately, for eye tracking recording, the weather changed from cloudy to sunny before recording was started, i.e. the sunlight became strong enough to affect the pupil detection. Although no valid gaze plots could be made, the recording from the front camera could still give valuable information. For example about the sequence of operation and communication between the operator and other personnel when attaching wall segments and placing them.

5.4   Wheel Loader

The wheel loader was transporting material from a stone crusher to a pile as well as to passing trucks that came to collect gravel. During loading, the attention was on the bucket. Presumably to watch the bucket filling up, but also to watch the angle of the bucket when lifting material from the pile. During unloading the focus was on the gravel falling out of the bucket, in order to obtain a steady flow and match the falling gravels placement.

Figure 4 shows the areas of attention for the operator. The mapping of visual attention was analyzed during transportation to the loading/unloading area and loading of a dump truck flatbed. As shown by the numbers, the major focus was ahead of the machine. Very little attention was focused through the side windows, even while the loading involved reversing operations. Though, some attention was put at the rearview mirrors which were visible through the front windows. It is also noticeable that the instrumentation, placed low in the cabin and containing an integrated reversing camera, was never visible during the session analyzed. This may indicate that placement of information providers, in this case reversing camera and mirrors, can affect usage. We will come back to this for the articulated dump truck.

Fig. 4. Level of attention in different areas for the wheel loader.

5.5 Excavator

The excavator was supporting ground personnel to level a shaft, wheeling to get material and distributing it on places indicated by the ground personnel. During wheeling, the operator's attention was freely moving as the transportation was straight ahead without obstacles. During unloading the attention was however swiftly moving between the ground leader, indicating by gestures how much material to pour out, to observation of the gravel falling out from the shovel and where it landed.

Figure 5 shows the attention of the operator during the supporting face. As the work was carried out in a shaft on the left side of the machine the attention is focused on the left side. And since the workers in the shaft controlled depth and alignment of the ground, the vehicle's information system was hardly used at all. Using the video recording, it was also noted, in terms of input to the system and ergonomics, that the operator did quite excessive shakes of the joysticks. This in order to get an even pour of gravel.

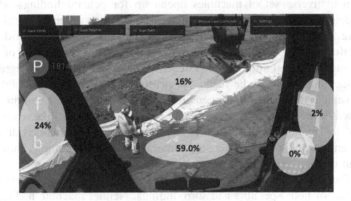

Fig. 5. Level of attention in different areas for the excavator.

5.6 Articulated Dump Truck

Lastly, the articulated dump truck whose task was more related to vehicle driving than control of machine operation, such as crane arm operation. Still, while the control of the dump truck isn't related to advanced processing control systems, the display systems usage was surprisingly high in, comparison with the other vehicles, see Fig. 6.

One reason for this was due to the reversing and unloading operations, where the operator constantly switched focus between the rear view mirrors and the reversing camera display. Looking into the mirrors make up for 11% and 8% of the side windows gaze time respectively. In relation to the wheel loader, it can be noted that the placement of the reversing camera display, more aligned with the mirrors could be one factor for the higher utilization. It can also be noted that the placement of the rear view mirrors makes the operator look more on the sides.

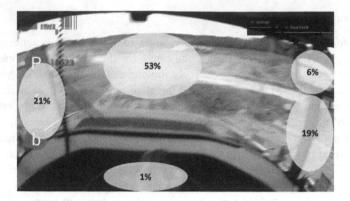

Fig. 6. Level of attention in different areas for articulated dump truck.

5.7   General Findings

Sampling on a diverse set of machines opens up for general findings where it is possible to detect similarities in use, or differences, between different machines. Such examples are when problems occur. Then the operators looked at the display for additional information. Another example is during normal movement of crane or machine, where the digital information systems were used to a very low degree, if used at all. This fact shall probably be seen as reassuring since focus should preferably be outside the vehicle rather than on screens inside the vehicle. As told by the operators the display was however used more frequently in certain scenarios, like when the crane lifts material to locations with limited visibility. The earlier mentioned difference in display placement and use of reversing camera is also an example showing how learnings can be discovered by matching different designs.

An additional area affecting all of these machine types is safety, where operation should be safe for both operators and surroundings. Neither machine had any system for detection of surrounding persons or objects, so the operator had to keep track of people in range of the machine. However, when doing work that required some form of precision, the gaze mapping clearly showed a focused attention to the task at hand and the persons directly involved in the task, resulting in a limited attention to the surroundings. The surrounding environment does, of course, affect the possibility of someone being in the vicinity of the machine, for example being alone in the forest versus a building site with several machines and persons close by.

For all machines, the machine structure caused limited visibility, but it was most noticeable for the wheel loader, with its bucket in front of the operator. Additionally, the visibility was very limited when doing operation with the bucket raised high, for example when unloading material in the truck bed.

6   Measuring Display Usage

One objective of the study was to measure attention to the graphical display interface in the different vehicles. This measurement was done by observing a clip from each machines recording, each containing a few sequences of repeating operation. For example, tree cuts, lifts, transportation loops, etc. For each of these clips, the time when the user was having a focus on any graphical display in the cabin was measured, starting with a fixation on the display and ending with a fixation outside the display. For calculation, the frame counter presented by the pupil player software was used.

The result is listed in Table 1, indicating the time spent looking at the vehicle graphical display(s) in percent of the total time for each recording clip. In some cases, the numbers in the table differ in relation to the numbers in the figures above (Figs. 2, 3, 4, 5 and 6). The reason for this is that the measurement of display usage was performed over another timespan than the measurement of where the operator looked in the whole cabin/surrounding environment.

The numbers were generally lower than what was expected prior to the study. It was expected that vehicles with richer information systems that presented process and site information should have at least 5% display attention. Such vehicles were the harvester with its centrally placed display presenting key metrics presented, as well as the wheeled excavator using a precision positioning system.

Table 1. Percentage gaze time on vehicle display when performing operation for the measured time

Machine	Display usage	Time (minutes)	Sequences
Harvester	1%	5	9 trees
Wheeled excavator	<1%	9	4 gravel unloading and evening sequences
Dump truck	7%	8	1 drive including 4 reversing periods
Wheel loader	0%	9	8 lift and unload sequences
Excavator	1%	6	2 gravel acquire and unloading sets

The other systems had a more basic information system (instrumentation type and reversing cameras. It was expected that the usage for these vehicles should be low. In this respect, the dump truck stands out with the highest registered usage at 7%, and the wheel loader, who did not use the built-in display at all.

One vehicle is missing from the above table, the mobile crane. As mentioned above this vehicle was left out because of weather conditions, making the recorded data untrustworthy for measurement. However, the indication was that screen usage was limited. Something that was also supported by the operator when describing that he did not use the support from the vehicle information system when lifting in close range and good visibility. The aiding systems, that display height, load, wind, and pressure on supporting legs was, however, more frequently used when lifting longer distances and when direct visibility is hindered.

As a diverse set of vehicles was selected for the study, findings cannot be considered quantitative representative, they rather provide an indication for future more detailed research. Both for individual machine types and also for identification of possible similarities between machines. Following is an example that illustrates this.

As mentioned, the dump truck has the highest display usage. This while being the vehicle with the lowest level of information system support. The other graphical information system in the vehicle was a dot matrix display in the center console. However, the secondary display was frequently used for a specific activity, reversing. During reversing, attention was divided between the mirrors and the reversing camera. Subsequently, the attention to the reversing camera display increases to 23.8% when looking only at reversing time, which occurred 4 times during the clip.

Simultaneously, the wheel loader had no display usage. The wheel loader was also equipped with reversing camera capabilities. The operation pattern between the dump truck and the wheel loader did also have similarities: Something is loaded in the bucket of the wheel loader, or the tipping body of the dump truck, the machine thereafter reverses, travels to the unloading zone and unloads. What could then be the reason for this difference in attention? One possible explanation could be the cabin design. In the dump truck, the rear view camera display is placed at the same level as the rear view mirrors. Making the eye movement flow naturally between the mirrors and the display. In the wheel loader, on the other hand, the display showing the reversing camera is placed in the lower right instrumentation cluster, far away from the operator's normal attention. Perhaps this makes the time and effort needed to look at the display too high.

More data can be extracted from the recorded material. Still, the paper exemplifies that also a limited study and analysis can give insights and pinpoint future detailed studies. It shall be noted that great care shall be taken when comparing the figures and before making firm conclusions. The use of different information sources must be put into context. For example, the excavator did not have to use any assistive functionality for the work he was doing. The display usage indicated by the numbers was instead used during crawling, to change from slow speed into fast speed.

7 Discussion

Looking into the imminent future, development investments in heavy vehicles will to a high degree be in the digital domain. Studies indicate that up to 40% of a cars production cost is due to electronics and software [29]. Heavy vehicles are also be connected and integrated into the information value chain. For examples through wireless real-time productivity improvements in construction sites [30] and information driven farming [31].

With more functionality realized through electronics and software it can be expected that more information will have to be presented to the operator, already today the HMI in a car can provide access to more than 700 functions [32]. Still, the attention of the operator cannot be too diverted from the task at hand. Sørensen et al. mention that, in farming, the "increasing use of computers and the dramatic increase in the use of the internet have to some degree improved and eased the task of handling and processing of internal information as well as acquiring external information. However, the acquisition and analysis of information still proves a demanding task" [31]. Neither does the availability of data warrant the understanding or usefulness of the data to the user [33].

As more information has to be presented, space in vehicle cabins can be a limiting factor and as window area to look outside of the cabin is of the essence, thus putting demands on efficient communication through limited display sizes. One method is to combine different information providers together. However, as described by Holstein et al. there are challenges in building homogenous interfaces consisting of a diversified set of haptic and visual interfaces and software providers [34]. Sanches et al. state that "the need for research that informs the design of effective, intuitive, and efficient displays is a pressing one." [16].

It can also be assumed that the connected vehicles will be updated more frequently and that agile development methods will be increasingly used. This is already happening in the automotive industry where continuous software deployment is starting to become practiced. Such examples are the Tesla vehicles, or the recent Volvo XC90 platform, where software is deployed every two days [35].

To aid the design of these information driven and more continuously improved systems there is a need for efficient validation of usefulness and stakeholder acceptance. Buur et al. observed, doing user studies of forklift operators, that the skilled operators perform many operations in parallel, as well as, tasks far beyond the everyday notion of 'lifting', 'carrying' and 'dropping' a load [36]. The knowledge must therefore be based system use and adoption "in the wild", thus giving a true understanding of use to complement laboratory tests and prior assumptions [37, 38]. Benyon notes that designers need to understand the people who will use their systems and products. They need to understand the activities that people want to undertake and the contexts in which those activities take place [39]. With a diligent understanding of operator behavior, the systems could be made better at combining and presenting relevant and valid information for the current task, as well as automating tasks, thus easing operator's task fulfillment [7].

The purpose of this paper is not to provide design guidance, but rather a way to quickly gain insights. The combination of eye tracking and guerilla approach is, to our knowledge, uncommon in industry settings. Eye tracking can give a lot of qualitative and quantitative information on comparable interfaces. But instead of studying a single machine type, to draw more objective conclusions, we targeted diversity, to get input on the general approach in industrial vehicle settings. This is a big area in itself, as only in the area of advanced agriculture and construction there are over 800 K vehicles created yearly [40]. We also believe that the combination of guerilla and eye tracking can be considered universal and useful in many settings needing a lightweight approach.

Additionally, we perceived eye tracking as a door opener to approach users, making it interesting and easy for the operators to accept our request. This, in turn, gave good informal discussions. It shall be noted that social context, gender, organizational structure, culture etc. could affect the accessibility of working sites as well as the openness of operators and would be interesting to study further.

Availability of affordable eye tracking equipment and light weight processes opens up for new ways to acquire information. Not only could more research organizations do first person studies, it could also be used to expand the potential sample ground for product development teams. For example, a global sales and support organization with access to eye tracking equipment could provide first person views from a diverse global user group and more detailed information about occurring issues.

However, the use of non-trained usability professional doing operator recordings may open up to ethical considerations, as recording data from real operation could impose personal or professional issues. Common guidelines, such as the principles of research ethics, states that participants in studies should be informed of the purpose, be asked for consent, be handled with highest possible confidentiality, and, that the result should only be transferred or used by others that commit to the same principles as the person(s) performing the study [41]. One implication in this regard could be that persons with limited training in user studies might not follow the ethical guidelines. Establishing a formal structure, including consent forms etc. can be one solution. Though, even in professional settings this is not commonly used. Only 45% of usability professional have participants to sign audio/video consent forms [42]. Also, having a process that is heavy on the formality, may harm the objective of evaluations that are minimal-intrusive and easily performed. As it will interfere with operators work and they could potentially be deterrent from participation by "legal disclaimers". It can also be difficult to guarantee that recorded data gets handled in a de-personified way when sharing information.

In this study, the use of vehicle information systems was rather limited according to the gaze patterns recorded, less than expected in advance. This may partly relate to the activities being performed by the operators, an assumption supported by the conversations with the studied operators. The harvester operator, both types of excavator operators and the mobile crane operator all said that the use of vehicle information systems differs depending on the task performed. Furthermore, they described that the display usage was relatively low for the tasks performed during recording.

Nevertheless, as indicated by the study, efficient vehicle information systems are highly valuable in certain situations. For example, to get specific information, such as an indication of the correct height of ground when using the excavator. Or, to find out what is going on when the automation systems aren't behaving as expected. Additionally, the information systems are used for increased visibility, for example when reversing or when the crane operator had limited visibility.

The design of the user interfaces, as well as cabins, is in this sense a vital factor for efficient interaction, as possibly indicated by the utilization of the reversing camera between the dump truck and wheel loader. This difference in usage may also affect the ergonomic situation for the user. Edger et al. points out that need for the operator to look in extreme angles causes operator injuries [15]. Using cameras or additional sensors to extend visualization around the vehicle could assist the operator, not only in increased situational awareness but also in terms of less operator strain. Given that the cabin is appropriately designed to support usage.

Looking into the future, new technologies, such as see-through interfaces and augmented reality, could also increase productivity, visibility, and placement of information. For example, placing information in line of sight using Head-up-displays has indicated benefits in information exchange and productivity for heavy vehicles [2]. But for these new means of interaction, there is still a strong need to understand the user attention and the task performed in daily operation.

7.1   Lessons Learned from the Setup and Usage

As we learn from the mistakes made and the way we overcome problems, a section of practical lessons learned is included below.

It is recommended to have a lightweight recording computer with a touch display as it eases operation in tight cabin spaces. The initial approach was to use an Intel Compute Stick as recording computer, together with a Wi-Fi connected tablet for calibration and configuration. This would give a small and lightweight solution. This approach was however disbanded, because of low processing power and connectivity issues with the tablet. After several tryouts, a working setup was established using a touch screen enabled laptop computer running Linux.

The recordings were saved to a USB stick. This enabled easy transfer of information to the analysis computer as well as the possibility to add more storage when needed. During the initial runs, the software crashed after a longer period of usage, resulting in corrupt recordings. This was related to the fat32 file system, used per default on USB sticks. Reformatting the USB sticks with a file system supporting a larger file size limit solved this issue (NTFS). A separate hard drive would have been another option. But this makes the solution more bungle some. The limited power supplied from the USB outlet was also an issue, causing the glasses to turn off. The use of a USB cable with two ports for power consumption solved this issue.

Sometimes the recordings showed a slightly staggered position in regards to what could be considered the operator's visual focus. This was probably due to the working environment, where the operator is exposed to shocks and vibrations, resulting in the glasses slight movement on the operator's head. In these cases, the eye fix position was retrospectively recalibrated against what could be considered credible focal points, by manually adjusting the offset in the X and Y axis plane. For more detailed tracking, for example, to track exactly what was read on an operator screen, this process of recalibration could raise uncertainties on data validity and a more secure way to fit the glasses on the operators head would be needed.

The CPU performance required for video recording and gaze tracking is rather high, thus quickly draining the computer battery. For longer recording sessions it is advised to have some sort of charging equipment that can be attached to the machine. It was however not used for these evaluations, as it would have added more time and complexity during the setup phase.

The optics on the world camera provide a good field of view, still, the visual area to cover is even bigger. Additional cameras added at strategical places could provide additional useful information. For example, detailed visibility of display content, even when the user looks in another direction. Or, how the controls are used by the operator. The drawback, again, is increased vehicle setup effort as equipment needs to be mounted in the cabin. This would also extend the time needed for analysis because several sources of information would have had to be stitched together.

8   Conclusions

The paper presents a way for designers to gather information using relatively affordable equipment and a method of acquiring data that doesn't interfere with the subject of study. This was done by combining the guerilla HCI approach on heavy vehicle user studies and relatively cheap eye tracking equipment. This combination of approaches within the industrial setting is uncommon in literature and shows how practitioners can quickly acquire real field data, with limited interference in ongoing work. The experience report demonstrates that it is possible to observe an operators work and attention, even when it is not possible to be physically located together with the operator in the cabin. The limited sample spectrum for this specific study makes it difficult to ground design directions. But it indicates the usefulness of quick sample studies to gain knowledge and identify areas for further observation, or limitations in existing designs. For example, the difference in use based on display placement, how interaction minimizing focus on the screen can provide useful assistance, or how limited visibility might affect the use.

Moreover, the study as such contributes to the understanding of operator use of vehicle information systems and how the tracking result can be used to learn about operator behavior and attention in addition to the statistical data than can be extracted. While sheer numbers of HMI display usage show low levels, the systems were used in certain situations, for example when the machine was not performing as expected or for reversing camera usage. Also, cabin design is something that might prohibit vehicle HMIs where, for example, placement of displays out of sight of operator attention area may result in information being left unattended.

9 Future Work

As a continuation of this work, it is of interest to perform a larger analysis with more vehicles and operators and more objectives for measurement. It is also of interest to refine the method and technical approach. For example using visual tags to automatically detect areas of interest, making it easier to analyze longer sessions. Or integrating additional sensor or cameras to further enhance quality, while still facilitating a quick and easy setup. It is also of interest to target the studies to specific activities that are more information system related, for example, when making machine configuration and administration, or when performing precision control.

References

1. Wang, X.: Improving human-machine interfaces for construction equipment operations with mixed and augmented reality. In: Balaguer, C., Abderrahim, M. (eds.) Robotics and Automation in Construction. InTech, Rijeka (2008)
2. Lagnel, O., Engstr, J.: Bättre arbetsmiljö med Head Up Display (2015)
3. Kutter, T., Tiemann, S., Siebert, R., Fountas, S.: The role of communication and co-operation in the adoption of precision farming. Precis. Agric. **12**, 2–17 (2011)
4. Precision agriculture. https://en.wikipedia.org/wiki/Precision_agriculture. Accessed 19 June 2015
5. Herring, D.: Precision farming. http://earthobservatory.nasa.gov/Features/PrecisionFarming/. Accessed 24 June 2015
6. Daberkow, S.G., McBride, W.D.: Farm and operator characteristics affecting the awareness and adoption of precision agriculture technologies in the US. Precis. Agric. **4**, 163–177 (2003)

7. Wallmyr, M.: Understanding the user in self-managing systems. In: Proceedings of the 2015 European Conference on Software Architecture Workshops - ECSAW 2015, pp. 1–4. ACM Press, New York (2015)

8. Kjeldskov, J., Graham, C.: A review of mobile HCI research methods. In: Chittaro, L. (ed.) Mobile HCI 2003. LNCS, vol. 2795, pp. 317–335. Springer, Heidelberg (2003). doi:10. 1007/978-3-540-45233-1_23

9. Hughes, M.: Talking out loud is not the same as thinking aloud. http://www.uxmatters.com/mt/archives/2012/03/talking-out-loud-is-not-the-same-as-thinking-aloud.php

10. Nielsen, J.: First Rule of Usability? Don't Listen to Users. https://www.nngroup.com/articles/first-rule-of-usability-dont-listen-to-users/. Accessed 14 Apr 2016

11. Nielsen, J., Levy, J.: Measuring usability: preference vs. performance. Commun. ACM 37, 66–75 (1994)

12. Poole, A., Ball, L.J.: Encyclopedia of Human Computer Interaction. IGI Global, Hershey (2006)

13. Dukic, T., Hanson, L., Holmqvist, K., Wartenberg, C.: Effect of button location on driver's visual behaviour and safety perception. Ergonomics 48, 399–410 (2005)

14. Häggström, C.: Human Factors in Mechanized Cut-to-Length Forest Operations (2005). http://pub.epsilon.slu.se/12208/2/haggstrom_c_150511.pdf

15. Eger, T., Godwin, A., Henry, D.J., Grenier, S.G., Callaghan, J., Demerchant, A.: Why vehicle design matters: exploring the link between line-of-sight, driving posture and risk factors for injury. Work 35, 27–37 (2010)

16. Sanchez, J., Duncan, J.R.: Operator-automation interaction in agricultural vehicles. Ergon. Des. Q. Hum. Factors Appl. 17, 14–19 (2009)

17. Naghiyev, A., Sharples, S., Carey, M., Coplestone, A., Ryan, B.: ERTMS train driving in-cab and outside: an explorative and eye-tracking field study. In: Sharples, S., Shorrock, S. (eds.) Contemporary Ergonomics and Human Factors 2014, pp. 343–350. CRC Press, Southampton (2014)

18. Yousefi, M.V., Karan, E., Mohammadpour, A., Asadi, S.: Implementing eye tracking technology in the construction process. In: 51st ASC Annual International Conference Proceedings, pp. 752–759, College Station, TX (2015)

19. Pernice, K., Nielsen, J.: How to Conduct Eyetracking Studies (2009)

20. Lindell, R.: Crafting interaction: the epistemology of modern programming. Pers. Ubiquit. Comput. 18, 613–624 (2014)

21. Nielsen, J.: Guerrilla HCI: using discount usability engineering to penetrate the intimidation barrier. Cost-Justif. Usab. 245–272 (1994)

22. Nudelman, G.: One Dollar Prototype. DesignCaffeine Publications, San Francisco (2014)

23. Ferhat, O., Vilariño, F., Sánchez, F.J.: A cheap portable eye–tracker solution for common setups. J. Eye Mov. Res. 7, 1–10 (2014)

24. Kassner, M., Patera, W., Bulling, A.: Pupil: an open source platform for pervasive eye tracking and mobile gaze-based interaction. In: Proceedings of the 2014 ACM International Joint Conference on Pervasive Ubiquitous Computing, pp. 1151–1160. Adjunct Publication (2014)

25. Jacob, R.: Eye tracking in human–computer interaction and usability research: ready to deliver the promises. In: Hyönä, J., Radach, R., Deubel, H. (eds.) The Mind's Eye, pp. 573–737. Elsevier, Amsterdam (2003)

26. Rozanski, E.P., Karn, K.S., Haake, A.R., Vigliotti, A.M., Pelz, J.B.: Simplified eye tracking enhances problem understanding and solution discovery in usability testing. 49th Annual Meeting of Human Factors and Ergonomics Society HFES 2005, pp. 2090–2094 (2005)

27. Pupil labs. https://pupil-labs.com/

28. Gray, D.E.: Doing Research in the REAL WORLD (2014)

29. Broy, M.: Challenges in automotive software engineering. In: Proceeding of the 28th International Conference on Software Engineering - ICSE 2006, p. 33. ACM Press, New York (2006)
30. Rylander, D.: Productivity Improvements in Construction Site Operations Through Lean Thinking and Wireless Real-Time Control Productivity Improvements in Construction Site Operations Through Lean Thinking (2014)
31. Sørensen, C.G., Fountas, S., Nash, E., Pesonen, L., Bochtis, D., Pedersen, S.M., Basso, B., Blackmore, S.B.: Conceptual model of a future farm management information system. Comput. Electron. Agric. **72**, 37–47 (2010)
32. BMW technology guide: iDrive. www.bmw.com/en/insights/technology/technology_guide/articles/idrive.html
33. Chinthammit, W., Duh, H.B.-L., Rekimoto, J.: HCI in food product innovation. In: Proceedings of the extended abstracts of the 32nd annual ACM conference on Human factors in computing systems - CHI EA 2014, pp. 1111–1114. ACM Press, New York (2014)
34. Holstein, T., Wallmyr, M., Wietzke, J., Land, R.: Current challenges in compositing heterogeneous user interfaces for automotive purposes. In: Kurosu, M. (ed.) HCI 2015. LNCS, vol. 9170, pp. 531–542. Springer, Cham (2015). doi:10.1007/978-3-319-20916-6_49
35. Bosch, J.: Jan Bosch keynote presentation at the 25th Anniversary INCOSE International Conference (2014)
36. Buur, J., Caglio, A., Jensen, L.C.: Human actions made tangible. In: Proceedings of the 2014 Conference on Designing Interactive Systems - DIS 2014, pp. 1065–1073. ACM Press, New York (2014)
37. Chilana, P.K., Ko, A.J., Wobbrock, J.: From user-centered to adoption-centered design. In: Proceedings of the 33rd Annual ACM Conference on Human Factors in Computing Systems - CHI 2015, pp. 1749–1758. ACM Press, New York (2015)
38. Buxton, B.: Sketching User Experiences. Morgan Kaufman, Burlington (2007)
39. Benyon, D.: Designing Interactive Systems. Pearson, London (2014)
40. Stieler Technologie- & Marketing Beratung: Assessment of the Market for Advanced Electronics used in Industrial Vehicles (2012)
41. Vetenskapsrådet: Forskningsetiska principer, pp. 1–17 (2002)
42. Hinderer, D., Nielsen, J.: 234 Tips and Tricks for Recruiting Users as Participants in Usability Studies (2003)

TrackLine: Refining touch-to-track Interaction for Camera Motion Control on Mobile Devices

Axel Hoesl[(✉)], Sarah Aragon Bartsch, and Andreas Butz

LMU Munich, Munich, Germany
{axel.hoesl,sarah.aragon.bartsch,andreas.butz}@ifi.lmu.de

Abstract. Controlling a film camera to follow an actor or object in an aesthetically pleasing way is a highly complex task, which takes professionals years to master. It entails several sub-tasks, namely (1) selecting or identifying and (2) tracking the object of interest, (3) specifying the intended location in the frame (e.g., at 1/3 or 2/3 horizontally) and (4) timing all necessary camera motions such that they appear smooth in the resulting footage. Traditionally, camera operators just controlled the camera directly or remotely and practiced their motions in several repeated takes until the result met their own quality criteria. Automated motion control systems today assist with the timing and tracking sub-tasks, but leave the other two to the camera operator using input methods such as touch-to-track, which still present challenges in timing and coordination. We designed a refined input method called TrackLine which decouples target and location selection and adds further automation with even improved control. In a first user study controlling a virtual camera, we compared TrackLine to touch-to-track and traditional joystick control and found that the results were objectively both more accurate and more easily achieved, which was also confirmed by the subjective ratings of our participants.

Keywords: Camera motion · Motion control · Image-based control · User interface · User-centered design

1 Introduction

New technologies such as drones, gimbals or industrial robots have substantially advanced physical cinematographic camera motion and motion control within the last decade. These systems provide smooth camera motion and image stabilization. They offer more accuracy and reproducibility to experts and simultaneously lower the entrance barrier for novices. As these systems are motor-driven, they can be operated remotely, often by manipulating input hardware or virtual interface elements on the touch screen of a mobile device.

In fact, mobile devices are particularly appealing as they offer additional functionality, such as reviewing the video stream of live or recorded material and

© IFIP International Federation for Information Processing 2017
Published by Springer International Publishing AG 2017. All Rights Reserved
R. Bernhaupt et al. (Eds.): INTERACT 2017, Part II, LNCS 10514, pp. 283–292, 2017.
DOI: 10.1007/978-3-319-67684-5_17

quick editing of sequences. They also allow to flexibly control different systems with one controller or to share material with others. On the other hand, touch devices also introduce their own challenges, most prominently, a loss in control precision. Particularly the lack of haptic and kinesthetic feedback makes the already complex task of camera control even more challenging.

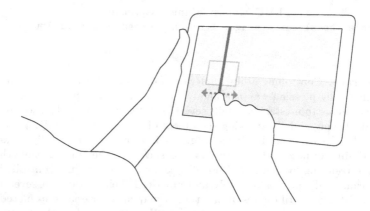

Fig. 1. Users can predefine the axis at which a moving object should be framed by dragging the TrackLine (blue) at the desired position (Color figure online)

Manufacturers have introduced automatic functions, such as object tracking using computer vision (CV) to overcome some of these new challenges, sometimes allowing image-based motion control directly on the video stream. Instead of continuously controlling the movement with a hard- or software joystick, operators can now specify the expected results (e.g. the framing of a moving object in the image). A motor-driven gimbal system can then not only keep the camera steady, but also maintain framing when following the moving object[1].

For such image-based control, systems often use the touch-to-track (TTT) approach for the selection of an object to be tracked and followed. With TTT, users tap on the object or person in the video stream and the system then continuously adjusts the camera position to keep the selected object at the same position within the frame. This design entangles object selection, framing and timing in one interaction, making it fast, but also prone to errors as the touch interaction needs to be timed precisely. The object might be moving out of the frame without being selected or the user might not be able to tap on the object at the right moment. In this case, the user needs to perform a select-and-correct move to adjust the framing position: with a drag-and-drop gesture on the touch screen, the object is moved to its correct framing position. As the correction is performed while recording, the resulting film material can only be used after the select-and-correct move has been carried out. Performance with this manual selection of a moving object can also be expected to decrease for faster moving targets [6] as in car commercials, sports-broadcasting or high-speed recordings.

---

[1] Example system: http://www.vertical.ai/studio.

1.1 Contributions

To overcome the issues of existing image-based motion control methods, we developed TrackLine as an alternative method, untangling the interactions of a touch-to-track design. TrackLine (Fig. 1) lets operators define the desired tracking position in advance and delegates the correct timing to an assisting system. A vertical line, displayed on top of the video stream, serves as a motion trigger. It can easily be positioned by drag and drop gestures before the recording is started. As soon as a moving object intersects with the line in the image space, the camera starts moving automatically, framing the object at the predefined position. By defining the desired tracking position in advance, select-and-correct moves can be avoided and the selection of fast objects is no longer tied to human reaction time. We compared our approach to existing approaches, namely software joystick and touch-to-track. Our results show that, TrackLine is more *efficient* (fewer retakes) and more *precise* (smaller distance from intended position). In addition, it was perceived as easy and effective to use as well as quick to learn by our participants.

2   Related Work

Focusing on physical camera motion, Chen and Carr [3] presented an in-depth survey on autonomous camera systems. They identified core tasks and summarized twenty years of research-driven tool development and evaluation. Besides traditional cinematography, further work was conducted in automated lecture recording [12,18–20], tele-conferencing [10,21] or event broadcasting [1,2,4,9]. Regarding high-level control in particular, as in our case, the most prominent approaches are Through-the-Lens [7], image-based [14] or constraint-based [8,13] control. Our design uses image-based control on a *virtual* camera, but today's motorized motion control systems already show that results for virtual camera control can be applied to remotely controlled real cameras. To evaluate designs the use of standardized tasks is common. For comparing different techniques in cinematographic tasks however, we found no well-established methodology in the literature. Of course, systems have been evaluated before in their unique ways. In [16] a computer-vision supported crane was evaluated by following a target that was moved by an industrial robot. In [12] a motorized slider was used to move an action figure, which served as a tracking target for a computer vision based panning system. Without standardized tasks at hand, a system's capabilities are also often documented by picture series as in [15] or by referencing a video as in [11]. These approaches, however, are often limited to subjective interpretation. To enable *objective* comparisons with a task that is also native to cinematography, we chose a framing task and measure similar to [12] and [17].

3   Study Comparing TrackLine to the State of the Art

In a user study, we compared our TrackLine approach to the current state of the art, which is the software joystick for continuous and touch-to-track for assisted control, representing the baselines for two different control paradigms (Fig. 2).

Using the software joystick, the camera could be translated manually along the x-axis, while with TTT, the motion was triggered by tapping on the target at the desired tracking position. With our TrackLine approach, the users had to drag the motion axis at the desired position before starting the recording. For the assisted methods, visual feedback was given by indicating the automated tracking with a green box around the target.

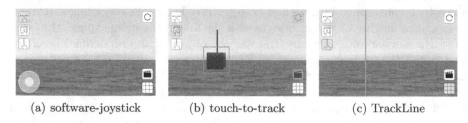

| (a) software-joystick | (b) touch-to-track | (c) TrackLine |

Fig. 2. The status quo designs software-joystick and touch-to-track (Figs. 2(a) and (b)) and our TrackLine alternative (Fig. 2(c)) as implemented and evaluated (Color figure online)

To test our approach early in the design process, we used a virtual camera and environment for a prototypical implementation. The concept was implemented in Unity 5.3. running on an off-the-shelf Android tablet.

(a) Deviations (blue) from lane center   (b) Deviations (blue) from desired framing

Fig. 3. The SDLP [17] for estimating the quality of control in a driving task (Fig. 3(a)), our adaptation (Fig. 3(b)) to determine *precision* in a cinematographic task (Color figure online)

For the study we wanted to collect quantitative data with a task that is native to cinematography. We therefore adapted an appraoch from the automotive domain, namely the standard deviation of lateral position (SDLP) [17]. The SDLP measure follows the idea that when driving – usually in a simulator – during the course of a study participants will deviate from the center of the lane they are driving on (Fig. 3(a)). These differences from the ideal pathway are recorded and analyzed. The closer the participants' trajectory matches the ideal pathway, the better is their driving performance.

Our adaption is based on the Rule of Thirds[2]. Beyond its aim to provide a visually pleasing framing for the audience, it can also be understood as a

---

[2] Guideline for image composition where the image space is divided into thirds (horizontally and vertically). Objects of interest are best placed at one of the intersections.

goal-oriented task for the operator. The goal-orientation allows to measure how accurately the goal is achieved. Similar to the SDLP, we use the distance between the moving object's actual and ideal position. The ideal position in our case is the first third in movement direction within the image space (Fig. 3(b)). The smaller the distance from the ideal position, the better we rate the control performance.

3.1 Study Design

We used a within-subjects study design with the independent variables user interface (3 levels) and task (3 levels). To avoid learning effects both variables were counter-balanced with a Latin-Square Design.

3.2 Participants

We recruited 12 participants (3 female). The average age was 24, with ages ranging from 21 to 27. Vision was normal or corrected to normal for all. Also, all were familiar with touch screens and 3 acquainted with camera operation.

3.3 Study Tasks

In our study, a horizontally moving object (red cube) should be followed and framed according to the Rule of Thirds. In detail, when the recording was started by tapping on a button, a text countdown of three seconds was displayed on screen, before the cube moved into the scene from the left. The users were asked to frame the cube at 1/3 of the screen, e.g., the first third in movement direction. To find the target position more easily, a thirds grid could be displayed by the participants. Additionally, the center of the cube was marked with an antenna. The camera motion should be stopped when a red signal was presented on the display. To vary the workload, we developed three variations of this task: *direction change* (movement direction changes), *fast object* (object moves at high velocity) and *track&pan* (transition from tracking to panning). Within the latter, the users had to smoothly transition the camera motion from a translation along the x-axis to a rotation around the y-axis when the red signal was shown. For manual control, we therefore implemented a second software joystick. When using the assisted techniques, the users only hat to tap on the background of the screen to trigger the transition.

3.4 Procedure

After welcoming the participants and explaining the structure and the context of the study, a consent form was handed out. Given their consent, the participants were asked to fill out a demographic questionnaire. They were then given an introduction to the application and could familiarize with the controls during a five minute training task in which the cube moved from left to right at moderate speed. Following the training task, the specifics of each task variation were explained in detail ahead of each condition. After finishing each task, the participants were asked to fill out a questionnaire and the next task was prepared. To be consistent to the mobile usage context, we asked the participants to carry out the tasks while standing. The study ended with a final questionnaire and semi-structured interview, asking the users to give a rating of the techniques in direct comparison.

3.5   Measurements

Participants were asked to repeat the task until they did not expect a further increase in performance anymore. They were assessing their results based on their own subjective impression. As a measure for *efficiency*, we thus counted the number of trials. We consider this a relevant measure, as in real world productions a reduced number of trials effectively saves time and money. For estimating *precision*, we used our adaptation of the SDLP described above. We continuously logged the distance of the moving cube to the ideal position.

4   Data Analysis and Results of the User Study

For the data collected on *efficiency* and *precision* the conducted Shapiro-Wilk Tests showed significance. Thus normality of the data cannot be assumed. In the following data analysis we therefore used non-parametric tests (Friedman's ANOVA, Wilcoxon Signed-Rank) to test for statistical significance. Bonferroni correction was applied in post-hoc tests to make up for pairwise comparisons ($\alpha^* = .016$). These were conducted only after a significant main effect was found.

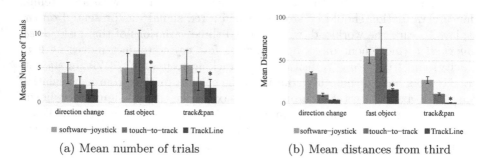

(a) Mean number of trials   (b) Mean distances from third

Fig. 4. Results on *efficiency* and *precision* of the studied interfaces

4.1   Efficiency

In number of trials, the *fast object* and *track&pan* tasks showed noteworthy effects. For *fast object*, TTT needed the most trials and for *track&pan* the software-joystick did. For each task one approach would perform better and therefore seems better suited. However, TrackLine outperformed both interfaces in both tasks. For *fast objects* ($\chi^2(2) = 19.96$, p $\leq$ .001), participants did 5.08 trials on average (SE $\leq$ .06) with software-joystick, while they did 7.08 (SE $\leq$ 1.0) with TTT and only 3.17 with TrackLine (SE $\leq$ .56). Post-hoc pairwise comparisons showed that using TrackLine resulted in significantly fewer trials than software-joystick (Z $\leq$ 3.11, p $\leq$ .002, η^2 $\leq$ .81) and TTT (Z $\leq$ 2.96, p $\leq$ .003, η^2 $\leq$ .73). For *track&pan* ($\chi^2(2) = 21.04$, p $\leq$ .001), the participants did 5.50 trials on average with software-joystick (SE $\leq$ .62), with TTT 3.17 (SE $\leq$ .39) and only 2.17 (SE $\leq$ .37) with TrackLine. Post-hoc tests indicate that TrackLine needs less trials than software-joystick (Z $\leq$ 3.08, p $\leq$ .002, η^2 $\leq$ .79) and TTT (Z$\leq$2.81, p $\leq$ .005, η^2 $\leq$ .66).

4.2   Precision

For *fast object* ($\chi^2(2)$ $\leq$ 13.17, p $\leq$ .001), the software-joystick resulted in a 55.22 px distance on average (SE $\leq$ 8.07), TTT in 63.60 px (SE $\leq$ 25.80), and TrackLine only in 16.26 px (SE $\leq$ 1.30). In pairwise comparison, we found participants to be closer the ideal position with TrackLine than with software-joystick (Z $\leq$ 2,98, p $\leq$ 0.06, η^2 $\leq$ .74) and TTT (Z $\leq$ 2,75, p $\leq$ 0.03, η^2 $\leq$ .63). For the *track&pan* task ($\chi^2(2)$ $\leq$ 22.17, p $\leq$ .001), the average distances were 27.62 px with software-joystick (SE $\leq$ 3.85), 11.45 px with TTT (SE $\leq$ 25.80) and only 1.34 px with TrackLine (SE$\leq$0.17). Pairwise comparisons reveal that TrackLine led to a smaller distance to the ideal position than software-joystick and TTT (for both: Z $\leq$ 3,06, p $\leq$ 0.02, η^2 $\leq$ .78). Additionally, it helped avoiding misses that occurred especially with TTT resulting in a larger variance (see error bars in Fig. 4(b)).

4.3   User Feedback

We collected self-reported data on the efficiency, ease of use and comfort via 5-item rating scales. The software-joystick was rated low in efficiency (Mdn = 2) and ease of use (Mdn = 2), but as comfortable to hold (Mdn = 4.5). TTT was rated to be efficient (Mdn = 4) and easy to use (Mdn = 4), but lowest in comfort (Mdn = 3.5). TrackLine was perceived as very efficient (Mdn = 5), easy to use (Mdn = 5) and comfortable to hold (Mdn = 5). In the debriefing interviews, participants pointed out that extension in future work should include fostering exploration and expressiveness of the technique. '*I liked the joystick best, because I had the most control, even if the technique is potentially more imprecise than the TrackLine.*' (P09). But the same participant also acknowledged the resulting jerkiness of the motion '*If this would have been a real recording, it would have become pretty jerky.*' (P09). Participants also felt that the software-joystick occupied more cognitive resources. Three participants stated that it was harder to react to the presented stop signal when using the software-joystick, because they were occupied with focusing on the cube.

5   TrackLine: Effective and Precise – Yet Limited

In our study we observed an expected decrease in *efficiency* and *precision*, especially for fast moving objects. Regarding state of the art designs, depending on the task, one or the other seems preferable. Despite these particularities provoked by the different tasks, our approach could address the performance issues in all cases. It resulted in more precise camera motion when controlled with a touch screen device and helped to avoid select-and-correct moves. Still, the observed performance issues could not be totally avoided, but their frequency and consequences could at least be minimized. Additionally, we found that in the participants' perception the gain in precision comes at a trade-off in expressiveness. The expressiveness of tools for the support of creative tasks such as cinematography is an important aspect. It is thus often tested in the evaluation of such tools, for example with the Creativity Support Index by Cherry and Latulipe [5]. Therefore, the missing expressiveness needs to be addressed in future work. This means in particular, (a) to extend the functionality of the TrackLine approach and (b) to combine manual continuous control elements fostering exploration and expressiveness with a content-based approach providing efficiency and precision.

To assess data and insights early in the design process, we implemented our system in a virtual environment. This environment, of course, provides perfect information, which would be more noisy in real world systems. This is likely to uniformly affect all performance aspects we measured, especially regarding *precision*. The collected data should thus be considered with caution on an absolute level. Our results are mainly suited for a comparison of the design alternatives on a conceptual level. It thus can help to inform the design of real-world implementations. While future work is surely necessary to asses the feasibility of our approach in the wild, we think that given today's existing technology, an enhanced version of our approach could already be implemented on top of established systems. However, such an implementation still needs to address the issues discussed above.

6   Conclusion

To overcome the issues of existing image-based motion control methods, we developed a refinement for high level camera motion control on mobile devices (TrackLine). TrackLine lets operators define the desired tracking position in advance and delegates the correct timing to an assisting system. Our approach counteracts select-and-correct moves and separates performance, especially in selecting fast objects, from human reaction time. To evaluate our design, we compared it to two established techniques (software-joystick and touch-to-track). Our results indicate that with TrackLine, operators are more *efficient* while simultaneously being more *precise* compared to established techniques. In addition to the increased performance, users perceived the technique as efficient, easy to use, quick to learn and comfortable to operate.

References

1. Carr, P., Mistry, M., Matthews, I.: Hybrid robotic/virtual pan-tilt-zom cameras for autonomous event recording. In: Proceedings of the 21st ACM International Conference on Multimedia, MM 2013, pp. 193–202. ACM (2013)
2. Chen, C., Wang, O., Heinzle, S., Carr, P., Smolic, A., Gross, M.: Computational sports broadcasting: automated director assistance for live sports. In: 2013 IEEE International Conference on Multimedia and Expo (ICME), ICME 2013, pp. 1–6. IEEE (2013)
3. Chen, J., Carr, P.: Autonomous camera systems: a survey. In: Workshops at the Twenty-Eighth AAAI Conference on Artificial Intelligence, pp. 18–22. Québec City, Québec, Canada (2014)
4. Chen, J., Carr, P.: Mimicking human camera operators. In: IEEE Winter Conference on Applications of Computer Vision, pp. 215–222. WACV 2015. IEEE (2015)
5. Cherry, E., Latulipe, C.: Quantifying the creativity support of digital tools through the creativity support index. ACM Trans. Comput.-Hum. Interact. (TOCHI) **21**(4), 21 (2014)
6. Chiu, T.T., Young, K.Y., Hsu, S.H., Lin, C.L., Lin, C.T., Yang, B.S., Huang, Z.R.: A study of Fitts' Law on goal-directed aiming task with moving targets. Percept. Mot. Skills **113**(1), 339–352 (2011)
7. Christie, M., Hosobe, H.: Through-the-lens cinematography. In: Butz, A., Fisher, B., Krüger, A., Olivier, P. (eds.) SG 2006. LNCS, vol. 4073, pp. 147–159. Springer, Heidelberg (2006). doi:10.1007/11795018_14
8. Christie, M., Normand, J.M.: A semantic space partitioning approach to virtual camera composition. Comput. Graph. Forum **24**(3), 247–256 (2005)
9. Foote, E., Carr, P., Lucey, P., Sheikh, Y., Matthews, I.: One-man-band: a touch screen interface for producing live multi-camera sports broadcasts. In: Proceedings of the 21st ACM International Conference on Multimedia, MM 2013, pp. 163–172. ACM, Barcelona, Spain (2013)
10. Gaddam, V.R., Langseth, R., Stensland, H., Griwodz, C., Halvorsen, P., Landsverk, Ø.: Automatic real-time zooming and panning on salient objects from a panoramic video. In: Proceedings of the 22nd ACM International Conference on Multimedia, pp. 725–726. ACM (2014)
11. Galvane, Q., Fleureau, J., Tariolle, F.L., Guillotel, P.: Automated cinematography with unmanned aerial Vehicles. In: Christie, M., Galvane, Q., Jhala, A., Ronfard, R. (eds.) Eurographics Workshop on Intelligent Cinematography and Editing. WICED 2016. The Eurographics Association (2016)
12. Hulens, D., Goedem, T., Rumes, T.: Autonomous lecture recording with a PTZ camera while complying with cinematographic rules. In: Proceedings of the 2014 Canadian Conference on Computer and Robot Vision, pp. 371–377. CRV 2014. IEEE Computer Society, Washington, DC, USA (2014)
13. Lino, C., Christie, M., Ranon, R., Bares, W.: The director's lens: an intelligent assistant for virtual cinematography. In: Proceedings of the 19th ACM International Conference on Multimedia, MM 2011, pp. 323–332. ACM, Scottsdale, Arizona, USA (2011)
14. Marchand, E., Courty, N.: Image-based virtual camera motion strategies. In: Fels, S., Poulin, P. (eds.) Proceedings of the Graphics Interface 2000 Conference, GI 2000, pp. 69–76. Morgan Kaufmann Publishers, Montral, Qubec, Canada (2000)
15. Stanciu, R., Oh, P.Y.: Designing visually servoed tracking to augment camera teleoperators. In: IEEE/RSJ International Conference on Intelligent Robots and Systems, IRDS 2002, vol. 1, pp. 342–347. IEEE (2002)

16. Stanciu, R., Oh, P.Y.: Feedforward-output tracking regulation control for human-in-the-loop camera systems. In: Proceedings of the 2005, American Control Conference, ACC 2005, vol. 5, pp. 3676–3681. IEEE (2005)
17. Verster, J.C., Roth, T.: Standard operation procedures for conducting the on-the-road driving test, and measurement of the standard deviation of lateral position (SDLP). Int. J. Gen. Med. 4(4), 359–371 (2011)
18. Wulff, B., Fecke, A.: LectureSight - an open source system for automatic camera control in lecture recordings. In: 2012 IEEE International Symposium on Multimedia (ISM), ISM 2012, pp. 461–466. IEEE (2012)
19. Wulff, B., Rolf, R.: Opentrack-automated camera control for lecture recordings. In: 2011 IEEE International Symposium on Multimedia (ISM), ISM 2011, pp. 549–552. IEEE (2011)
20. Zhang, C., Rui, Y., Crawford, J., He, L.W.: An automated end-to-end lecture capture and broadcasting system. ACM Trans. Multimedia Comput. Commun. Appl. (TOMM) 4(1), 6 (2008)
21. Zhang, Z., Liu, Z., Zhao, Q.: Semantic saliency driven camera control for personal remote collaboration. In: IEEE 10th Workshop on Multimedia Signal Processing, MMSP 2008, pp. 28–33. IEEE (2008)

Understanding Gesture Articulations Variability

Orlando Erazo[1(✉)], Yosra Rekik[2], Laurent Grisoni[2],
and José A. Pino[3]

[1] Universidad Técnica Estatal de Quevedo, Quevedo, Ecuador
oerazo@uteq.edu.ec
[2] University of Lille Science and Technology, CNRS, INRIA, Lille, France
yosra.rekik@inria.fr, laurent.grisoni@univ-lillel.fr
[3] Department of Computer Science, University of Chile, Santiago, Chile
jpino@dcc.uchile.cl

Abstract. Interfaces based on mid-air gestures often use a one-to-one mapping between gestures and commands, but most remain very basic. Actually, people exhibit inherent intrinsic variations for their gesture articulations because gestures carry dependency with both the person producing them and the specific context, social or cultural, in which they are being produced. We advocate that allowing applications to map many gestures to one command is a key step to give more flexibility, avoid penalizations, and lead to better user interaction experiences. Accordingly, this paper presents our results on mid-air gesture variability. We are mainly concerned with understanding variability in mid-air gesture articulations from a pure user-centric perspective. We describe a comprehensive investigation on how users vary the production of gestures under unconstrained articulation conditions. The conducted user study consisted in two tasks. The first one provides a model of user conception and production of gestures; from this study we also derive an embodied taxonomy of gestures. This taxonomy is used as a basis for the second experiment, in which we perform a fine grain quantitative analysis of gesture articulation variability. Based on these results, we discuss implications for gesture interface designs.

Keywords: Mid-air gestures · Whole body gestures · Gesture articulation · Gesture variability · Gesture taxonomy

1 Introduction

Mid-air gestural interactions are increasingly popular, with applications for entertainment [20], operating rooms [11], museums [23] or public spaces [44]. Although the evolution of new hardware devices, such as MS Kinect or Intel RealSense, has contributed significantly to this proliferation, there are still some challenges that need to be addressed. One of these challenges is the association between gestures and meanings/commands. There are various proposals that could be used for this goal, which mainly focus on a one-to-one mapping (e.g., [27, 45]). However, users may perform a specific gesture in different manners expecting it has equal meaning. For example, a user may display a menu by "drawing" in the air a letter "M" in the horizontal/vertical/sagittal

R. Bernhaupt et al. (Eds.): INTERACT 2017, Part II, LNCS 10514, pp. 293–314, 2017.
DOI: 10.1007/978-3-319-67684-5_18

plane, using one or two hands, performing one or more strokes, holding a hand pose, or also using other body part(s). The absence of this variability of user's gestures in the mapping between gestures and commands is a design limitation that may conduct to poor user experiences. This problem may be tackled by understanding gesture articulations; i.e., the ways in which users produce gestures in the air.

Regardless of the usefulness of gestures, little is known about how users articulate gestures. One of the focuses of previous work is how to choose gestures to define a gesture vocabulary. Several criteria may be used for this purpose. One of them may be the appropriateness of the candidate gestures to the intended meaning by considering features like user preferences [14, 24, 27, 45], social acceptability [35], teaching/learning [15], or memorability [25]. The time efficiency to perform the various gestures is another criterion to select gestures [10]. Other researchers have focused on notations or formal gesture specifications [6, 38], gesture recognition [43], and also studied specific gestures [13, 26]. Though some efforts have been made for analyzing user behavior on performing gestures [2, 12], variability of gesture articulations has only been studied in the case of multi-touch input [32, 33]. However, those findings should not be directly applied to mid-air gestures given the different behavior and body parts that can be involved. Moreover, most studies have focused on gestures produced with hands; the few ones related to gestures made with other body parts have not analyzed variability in depth (e.g., [17, 28]). Consequently, the answers to the following questions are still missing: How do users perform gestures moving their hands in the air? Do they use only hands or also use other body parts? Do they use one or two hands? Do they perform gestures using one or several movements?

Given these open questions, we advocate in this work for the need of more in-depth user studies to better understand how users articulate gestures without haptic contact under unconstrained conditions toward finding a relation between many gestures to one command. We are mainly interested in analyzing the variability of gesture articulations produced by a same user for a same gesture type, but we also summarize results for all participants and also identify differences among participants. To reach this goal, we conducted a two-phase user study in which participants produced various articulations for the same gesture type. The study was done from a broad perspective, not focusing just on hand gestures; i.e., participants were neither instructed nor restricted to use only the hands. The collected data allowed analyzing the variability of user's gestures, and the results show users' preferences to produce the same gesture type in various articulations.

Thus, this paper contributes as follows: (1) a qualitative model to understand user's gestures execution; (2) a taxonomy of whole body gestures, utilized to classify the performed gestures and make comparisons with related works; (3) a detailed qualitative and quantitative analysis of gesture variability; (4) implications for designing applications based on gestures. We hope our results will prove useful to designers and practitioners interested in maximizing the flexibility of gestures set designs. In the long run, the presented exploration and contributions are first steps toward designing many gestures to one command.

2 Related Work

The main design problems of gesture interfaces are shifting toward finding the optimum mapping from gesture to function. To tackle this issue, a set of toolkits have been designed to advise practitioners on how to obtain a high recognition rate or help them on how to organize gesture sets [4]. Spano et al. [38] proposed GestIT, a compositional, declarative meta-model for defining gestures based on Petri Nets. Choi et al. [6] developed a method to organize and notate user-defined gestures in a systematic approach. These works can help develop gesture interfaces and notate gestures respectively, but they are restricted to gesture specification and do not cover execution of those gestures according to users' mental models. Other similar work could be borrowed from touch interfaces but with the same limitation. Model-based evaluation can also be used to analyze gestures. Current existing models allow estimating performance scores to produce mid-air gestures [9, 10, 39] that can be used to compare gestures and/or to create gesture sets, but they do not consider the possibility of performing a same gesture in different manners.

Consequently, two options have been defined in order to find the best mappings: (1) designers can rely on their own expertise or (2) organize user studies. However, the first option often leads to arbitrary gesture sets [36] that do not take into account users' mental model or opinions, resulting in misdesigns and frustrating user experiences [8]. Involving users into the design process represents a viable alternative for collecting important data to inform design. Wobbrock et al. [45] introduced a methodology for eliciting gesture commands from users. Follow-up work verified this methodology for mid-air gestures [17, 28, 29, 31, 37, 40]. The methodology consists of presenting non-technical users the effects of gestures and eliciting the causes meant to invoke them. Later, Morris et al. [24] proposed that user elicitation studies could be improved by generating various gestures, priming users, and involving partners. Furthermore, Hoff et al. experimentally tested the first and second suggestions in a follow-up work [14]. Though this and other methodologies that can be found in the literature (e.g., [27]) are user-centered, they only considered the relation between one gesture and one command.

Other previous studies have reported on users' gestures articulation variations and preferences. Nancel et al. [26] demonstrated that bimanual gestures were faster than the one-handed ones for panning and zooming given that these actions are complementary. Next, trying to understand mid-air hand gestures, Aigner et al. [2] found that users would prefer both different types of gestures and number of hands depending on the meaning of the gesture. Actually, as Silpasuwanchai and Ren [37] explain and suggest, a same gesture may not be valid in all cases, and hence, more than one gesture should be used for one command when needed. Meanwhile, two works focusing on user defined gestures for augmented reality and controlling robots, showed that more than half of gestures proposed by participants for the requested tasks fell in the dynamic category (i.e., gestures are expressed using strokes) or unimanual category [28, 31]. Later, Henschke et al. [12] verified that user's gestures changed over repetitions. Despite this progress, articulation variability of gestures has not been analyzed in a comprehensive way.

Recently, Rekik et al. [32] presented a comprehensive investigation on how users vary multi-touch gestures under unconstrained articulation conditions. Based on a proposed taxonomy, they evaluated user gesture variability and concluded that users equally use one or two hands and gestures are achieved using parallel or sequential combination of movements. They also noted that it is important to know whether their findings "can be applied to other type of gesture detection devices which do not require a contact surface" [32]. However, no study yet exists for investigating the various manners in which users could articulate mid-air gestures. This work tries to fill this gap by collecting and analyzing gesture articulations variability. Hence, we followed the methodology of [32], making the needed modifications, to understand mid-air gestures.

3 User Study

Our study was composed of two tasks. Like Rekik et al. [32], the goal of the first task was to familiarize participants with the experimental setup and to analyze their interaction styles using an uncontrolled experimental procedure. The analysis of this data served as a basis to derive both a qualitative model on user conception and production of gestures, and a taxonomy of whole body gestures. This taxonomy and this model were used to analyze the second task. The goal of the second task, like [32], was to perform a quantitative analysis of how users articulate mid-air symbolic gestures by following some specific instructions and exploring several ways to do it. The remaining details of our study are described below.

3.1 Participants

Twenty people (mean age = 27.5 years, SD = 4.3, 6 female) took part in the study. They were invited by mailing lists and social networks. Eighteen participants were right-handed. Graduate students and researchers from Europe, South America, Africa and Asia agreed to volunteer for the study (UI designers were not allowed participating). Ten participants self-declared having some previous experience on mid-air interaction for gaming (e.g., using Kinect).

3.2 Apparatus

The hardware setup, mounted in our laboratory, consisted of a notebook, a Kinect sensor and a display. The Kinect and the display were connected to a notebook equipped with an Intel Core i7 processor, 8 GB of RAM. Participants stood about 2.5 m away from the display (with a size of 1.8 × 1.4 m and a resolution of 1024 × 768 pixels). The Kinect was placed below the display at a height of 1 m. Kinect RGB data was used to videotape the interaction and give participants some feedback while performing gestures. The developed application interface consisted of an augmented video blending UI controls and the real environment. Augmented video was used trying to avoid participant distractions while performing the tasks [9, 10]. It means participants were able to see themselves in the projected display like looking in a mirror. Also, the application showed the instructions to participants (i.e., the name of each required gesture type), the progress, and whether the gesture was considered right or wrong (i.e., a green check or a red "X" respectively). Inputs were considered right if participants followed the instructions correctly. No additional visual feedback was provided to prevent some effect [10, 32].

In addition, we decided to make use of a Wizard of Oz design [7, 12, 27] taking into account that participants were instructed to perform gestures in the articulation they preferred rather than being limited to the capabilities of a recognition system. The main idea was participants believe they are interacting "normally" with the system that provides the results/information when responses are in fact given by an experimenter (the "wizard"). Hence, the experimenter pressed some keys with the aim the system responded according to the participant's input (i.e., start, end, and right/wrong).

3.3   Procedure and Tasks

Participants were given the exact procedure for each task in paper sheets to avoid instructing them in various manners. They executed the gestures guided by the software when they were ready to start. Participants were also requested and encouraged to think-aloud while performing each gesture in both tasks (i.e., perform each gesture describing it aloud) [32]. Moreover, they had a short rest at the end of each task. Finally, we asked participants to provide some information by filling out a question-naire. The specific instructions and differences of each task are described below.

Task 1: Open-Ended Gestures. We asked participants to produce as many gestures as possible that came to their minds such as gestures that had a meaningful sense to them or gestures that they would use to interact with applications (i.e., gestures had to be realistic for practical scenarios, easy to produce, easy to remember, and different enough from one another that they could be used for different actions). In addition, participants were asked to describe the gestures they performed using the think-aloud protocol. Participants decided when to start and stop. Thus, this task finished when participants could not produce additional gestures.

Task 2: Goal-Oriented Gestures. Participants received more explicit instructions to carry out the second task. They had to create gestures for a set of 20 gesture types (see Fig. 1). The gestures set includes geometric shapes, letters, numbers, and symbols similar to the ones used in previous works on touch and touchless interactions [3, 10, 32–34, 42]. The selection of these gestures aimed to be general enough trying participants could articulate them without visual representations and under unconstrained conditions [33]. Moreover, this task focused on symbolic mid-air gestures instead of gestures for traditional actions utilized in mid-air interactions (e.g., pan, zoom, rotate, etc.), given the versatility of symbols to be generalized for other applications [34].

The software randomly asked participants to perform a gesture by showing only its name. Paper sheets were presented on demand just for the case in which a participant was not familiar with the corresponding gesture type. Participants had to think of the gesture articulations in which they would produce the gesture type after reading its name. They were instructed to create as many different gesture articulations as possible, trying to increase variety and creativity [24]. Though participants were free to select the different gesture articulations, we gave them the requirement that executions should be

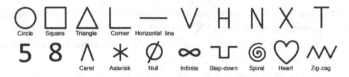

Fig. 1. The set of 20 gesture types used in the experiment.

realistic for practical scenarios, i.e., easy to produce and reproduce later. Furthermore, we provided no instructions on the body part(s) to be used to produce gestures. This decision enabled us to analyze whether users could use and/or prefer using body parts other than hands to articulate gestures.

4 Open-Ended Task Results

The first task of the study consisted in producing gestures by following an uncontrolled experimental procedure. Participants had to appeal to their imagination to carry out the task. Thus, the gathered data allowed analyzing the various gesture articulations conceived and produced by participants.

4.1 General Observations

Regarding the collected quantitative data, participants performed a total of 117 gestures in this task. Each participant performed from 3 to 14 gestures (mean = 6, SD = 3, median = 5, mode = 3). We obtained the following features by analyzing all these gestures:

- All participants performed drawing or writing symbolic gestures (such as shapes, letters, or numbers). Furthermore, participants executed gestures for traditional interactions/actions. For instance, 12 participants produced gestures for scale, swipe, drag & drop, etc. 14 participants produced gestures for actions like typing in the air, wave, tap, clap, etc. One participant added gestures for selecting a group of objects while another participant added gestures for making a copy or paste actions.
- Participants produced both stroke and hold (keep a pose a short period of time) gestures. For instance, 17 participants performed at least one gesture stroke. Nine participants utilized poses at least once.
- Gestures were produced using one or more body parts. 15 participants executed gestures using both one and two upper limbs (i.e., arms, hands or fingers). From the remaining five, four utilized only one upper limb for all gestures, whereas one used both upper limbs (but he also utilized the whole body in a few cases). Moreover, four out of the 20 also employed other body parts (different than upper limbs).
- 18 participants performed gestures using both single and multiple movements. The two remaining participants executed only single movement gestures, whereas nobody used only multiple movement gestures. Multiple movements were either parallel or sequential.

– 19 participants executed most of the gestures starting from a resting position, whereas the remaining one performed 75% of his gestures continuously, i.e., participants produced the gestures without adopting positions of resting or relaxation between strokes/movements only in a few cases. Resting positions consisted in having both hands/arms down and close to the hips or to the torso in most cases.

4.2   GCP: A Model for Gestures Conception and Production

Before analyzing in detail variability of gesture articulations it is necessary to understand how users conceive and produce gestures. Related works from psychology and neuroscience provide the basis to reach this goal. On the one hand, the framework proposed by Wong et al. [46] to define motor planning can be adapted and used to explain the user gesture conception. On the other hand, Kendon's and McNeill's proposals allow for analyzing gestures produced in midair [16, 22]. Based on both these related works and the aforementioned results, we derived GCP, a qualitative model for gestures conception and production (see Fig. 2).

According to GCP, a user initially needs to mentally prepare (think) before executing a gesture. During the mental act phase, which was adapted from [46], the user establishes/defines a motor goal (i.e., "what" processes), and then, s/he specifies the manner in which s/he will achieve that goal (i.e., "how" processes). In other words, the mental act consists of perception and gesture planning.

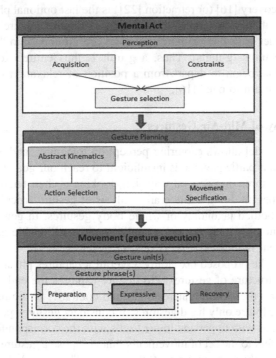

Fig. 2. GCP, a model on user conception and production of gestures (based on [16, 22, 46]).

The user selects/defines/forms motor goals during perception. Perception consists of three processes: (1) acquisition or identification of proposed symbols/referents; (2) application of rules/constraints to perform gestures (e.g., the instructions given in our study); and (3) selection of the gesture to be performed.

Gesture planning in turn refers to how the required gesture will be produced; i.e., it defines the specific movement(s) to execute the gesture. It also involves several processes that may occur in sequence or in parallel. These processes are: (1) abstract kinematics of the gesture (i.e., how the gesture will look), which is optional for single gestures such as pointing; (2) selection of body end-effector(s) action (i.e., how the effectors/body parts will achieve the goal); (3) complete specification of motor commands needed to produce the gesture. The occurrence of these processes allows translating the motor goal into the movement that will correspond to the intended gesture.

Several phases can be observed when the user executes the gesture. Actually, the results obtained in the first task of our study are consistent with the temporal nature of gestures, which is described in terms of phases, phrases, and units [16, 18, 22]. The gesture execution starts with an optional physical preparation of the effectors selected during the mental act. During this preparation phase, the user moves the body part(s) from a resting or relaxation position to the position in which the meaning of the gesture is manifested. The peak of effort and shape are clearly expressed in the expressive phase, which is an obligatory phase. It must take the form of either stroke or hold [18]. These two phases, preparation and expression, are encapsulated in a gesture phrase (g-phrase). At the end of a g-phrase, the user may produce another one or continues to the next phase. Recovery [16] (or retraction [22]) is the last optional phase in which the effectors return to their initial or resting positions. Recoveries are not part of any g-phrase but together with one or more g-phrases are grouped into "kinematic units" labeled as gesture units (g-units). Thus, a g-unit is the "entire excursion from the moment the effectors begin to depart from a position of relaxation until the moment when they finally return to one" [16].

4.3   A Taxonomy of Mid-Air Gestures

Despite the GCP model allows capturing perception, planning, and execution of gestures proposed by our participants, it is insufficient to reach our goal. GCP only models the execution of gestures in a general way (i.e., looking at their temporal nature), and hence, it does not permit doing a fine grain analysis of gesture articulation. Therefore, we propose an embodied taxonomy of whole body gestures. In general, the different levels of this taxonomy cannot be seen serially or as partitionable attributes because these levels represent indivisible aspects of user gestures.

Table 1 depicts the proposed taxonomy. Overall it captures physicality, movement composition, and structure of gestures. Physicality captures the end-effectors or body parts used to perform the gesture. Interestingly and contrarily to multitouch input [32], this level does not capture only hand gestures; it considers gestures performed with the whole body as well as with upper and lower limbs with the corresponding subdivisions. Movement level refers to the set of movements that compose a gesture. When a gesture is composed of more than one movement, these movements can be entered in parallel (i.e., multiple movements are articulated at the same time, e.g., using two hands to draw two sides of a "heart" shape at the same time) or in sequence (i.e., one movement after the other, such as in drawing the "plus" sign with one hand). However, not all gestures can be produced with parallel movements. In fact, only gestures containing a symmetry can be performed with parallel movements. Interestingly, wherever a gesture presented a symmetry, participants produced synchronous parallel movements to create that part of the gesture (i.e., some movements of the gesture were articulated with one movement at the same time and others were articulated in parallel, e.g., using two hands at the same time to draw the two diagonal symmetric lines of a "triangle" shape and then one hand to draw the horizontal line). The gesture may also involve a sequence of parallel movements (e.g., use both hands at the same time to articulate the two vertical lines of the "square" shape and then again use both hands to articulate the two horizontal lines). The last level refers to the structure of the gesture, which captures the state of the articulated movements. Considering this, a gesture may be a combination of single (static) or a series (dynamic) of poses that follow or not a path (like in [45]).

Table 1. A taxonomy of mid-air gestures.

Physicality	Whole body		
	Upper limbs	Arms	One-arm
			Two-arms
		Hands	One-handed
			Two-handed
		Fingers	One-finger
			Multi-fingers
	Lower limbs	Legs	One-leg
			Two-legs
		Feet	One-foot
			Two-feet
	Other, (e.g., head)		
Movement	Single		
	Multiple	Parallel	
		Sequential	Sequence of single movement
			Sequence of parallel movement
			Sequence of single and parallel movement
Structure	Static pose		
	Dynamic pose		
	Static pose with path		
	Dynamic pose with path		

5   Goal-Oriented Task Results

This section presents the results obtained from the second task in which participants produced various gesture articulations for specific symbolic gesture types.

5.1 Gesture Variations

Participants were instructed to propose as many articulation variations as possible for each gesture type. We collected 1,237 total samples for our set of 20 gesture types. On the average, our participants proposed 3.1 variations per gesture type (SD = 0.4, see Fig. 3), a result that is in agreement with the findings of [30] for action gestures (mean 3.1, SD = 0.8). A Friedman test revealed a significant effect of gesture type on the number of variations ($\chi^2(19) = 96.053$, $p < .001$). The "*" and "step-down" gestures presented the lowest number of variations (2.2 and 2.6 variations on the average respectively). The gesture with the maximum number of variations was "X" (3.9 on the average) for which our participants managed to easily decompose it into individual strokes that were afterward combined in many ways in time and space using different gesture physicality and structure (see Fig. 4). For example, only 3 participants produced less than 4 gesture articulations for "X". These first results suggest that the specific geometry of the gesture enables users with different affordances of how to articulate that shape. Likely, the mental representation of a gesture variation implies a particular type of articulation which is tightly related to the gesture shape. We can also remark that for all gesture types the maximum number of variations was 4 or 5, except "triangle" and "V" that had 6 variations. The minimum number of variations was 1, except "square", "corner", "X", and "T" with 2 variations. Meanwhile, the means (averaged over all subjects) of the percentages of the gesture types for which each participant produced at least 4, 3, and 2 gestures were 49%, 70%, and 91% respectively. This result also suggests that, for some users and for some gesture types, the number of gesture articulation variations can be limited which can be explained by the previous practice but also by the geometrical shape of the gesture.

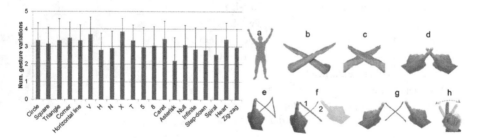

Fig. 3. Number of variations for each gesture type.

Fig. 4. Various articulation patterns for the "X" symbol produced with several poses (a–d); number of strokes (e–h), sequential (f), and parallel movements (g, b–d), using the whole body (a), arms (b), hands (c) and fingers (d–h). Numbers on strokes indicate stroke ordering.

5.2 Physicality Breakdown

Figure 5 shows the ratios (averaged over all users) of gestures for each gesture type and overall. We used only single levels for arms, fingers and lower limbs to simplify the

Table 2. Friedman tests for gesture type on level types.

Physicality		Movement		Structure	
Type	$\chi^2(19)$	Type	$\chi^2(19)$	Type	$\chi^2(19)$
Whole body	91.40	Single	128.02	Static body pose	75.78
Arms	125.84	Parallel	144.58	Static arm pose	138.53
One-handed	122.12	Sequential	67.82	Static hand pose	91.21
Two-handed	46.92			Static hand pose and path	102.08
Fingers	85.70			One finger pose	121.77
Lower limbs	39.01			Other	62.92

análysis. A Friedman test revealed a significant difference in the ratios (averaged over all symbols) between the six physicality types ($\chi^2(5) = 17.84$, $p < .001$). Post-hoc Wilcoxon signed-rank tests confirmed not significant differences only between arms and two-handed levels.

Friedman tests also revealed significant effect of gesture type on the ratio of the physicality types (Table 2). Referring to each physicality level, participants preferred one-handed gestures in all cases (53.4% on the average), especially for gesture types that may be considered as more difficult or strange to articulate. This is precisely the case of "spiral" that got the highest value and differed significantly from the other gesture types (except "infinite") according to the corresponding post hoc test. Similarly, the gesture types "asterisk", "infinite", and "zig-zag", that also obtained high values, were not significantly different from one another; and they showed differences between the other gesture types (except for "H", "N", and "5"). The next types are gestures made with fingers (one or multiple) and with two hands but with a short difference according to overall values (17.7% and 13.9% respectively). Notably, the highest values of finger type were for gesture types that represent numbers (i.e., "5" and "8", with no significant differences between them), which could be attributed to the fact that numbers can be easily represented using fingers. Actually, no significant differences were found between "5" and "8", as well as between them and other gesture types that can also be easily mapped into fingers (such as "circle", "square", "triangle", "V", "H"). Furthermore, finger gestures did not obtain high values for all gesture types (excluding one-handed type). For instance, some gestures were easier to map into two hands (e.g., "square", "T" and "step-down") and arms (e.g., "horizontal line", "V" and "X"). In addition, though whole-body type is represented in a relatively negligible ratio (5.8%), ratios between 14% and 20% were obtained for a few gestures (e.g., "heart" and "zig-zag"). Finally, gestures executed with lower limbs were observed only for six gestures with rates lower than 6%. Summing up, our participants produced their gestures mainly using one hand, and then, with fingers and two hands.

Although types of gestures produced with more than one upper limb did not get the best ratios, we performed an additional analysis of them given that about one third of gestures fell in these physicality types. 428 gestures performed with two-arms, two-hands, and fingers of both hands were analyzed according to the spatial relation of them. This relation can be as follows: folded (limbs act as a unit), act on each other (limbs act upon each other in a dynamic contact), symmetrical, complementary (e.g., one hand acts as a reference while the other one is moved), and independent.

Effectors are in touch in the first two cases, whereas they are separated in the other cases. Figure 6 shows the global ratios of the five levels for each kind of effectors and overall. A Chi-square test revealed that the percentage of the spatial relation significantly differed by used effectors ($\chi^2(8) = 175.43$, $p < .001$). Actually, Fig. 6 shows participants used most often two arms (67.4%) or several fingers (87.9%) as a unit, whereas they preferred employing both hands symmetrically (55.6%). The other levels are negligible (less than 14% in all cases).

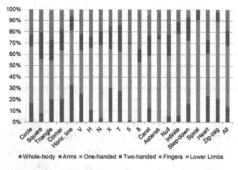

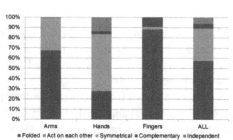

Fig. 5. Gesture physicality ratio.

Fig. 6. Upper limb ratios according to spatial relation.

5.3 Movement Breakdown

Figure 7 shows gesture ratios for each gesture type according to movement synchronization type. The three types of sequential gestures were subsumed under a general sequential type due to the small number of occurrences especially in the case of sequence of parallel movements and sequence of parallel and single movements. A Friedman test revealed significant difference in the ratios (averaged over all gesture types) between the three movement synchronization types ($\chi^2(2) = 30.70$, $p < .001$). Post-hoc tests confirmed significant differences between all the movement synchronization types.

Similarly, gesture types showed a significant effect on the ratio of these three synchronization types as reported on Table 2. Overall participants performed more often single gestures; its average (60.5%) almost doubles the one of parallel gestures. However, parallel gestures were preferred to produce gesture types having a symmetry axis (e.g., "X", "triangle", and "T", etc.), a finding in agreement with previous work [32, 34], only symmetric gestures can be conveniently parallelized during articulation. Post-hoc tests showed significant differences between these three gesture types ("X", "triangle", and "T") and the remaining ones, except for the following pairs: ("triangle", "rectangle"), ("T", "rectangle"), ("T", "V"), and ("T", "8"). All these gesture types can be produced using two end-effectors with ease, e.g., crossing the arms/hands/fingers to form an "X" (Fig. 4 b, c and d). Other gesture types, such as "8" and "square", got in parallel type ratios lower than in single type, but they demonstrated a behavior similar to the previously described for "X", "triangle", and "T". Concerning sequential type, its overall ratio was very small (6.6%), but non-negligible ratios were observed for three

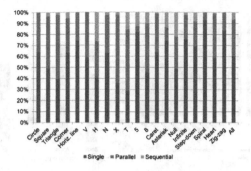

Fig. 7. Gesture movement composition ratio.

gesture types: "H", "null", and "T". These gesture types showed no differences between them, as well as significant differences between them and the other gesture types (except between "*" and "null", and "*" and "T"). This finding suggests that participants may have produced gestures composed of a sequence of movements only when it was worth doing it; they still preferred the other two types.

5.4 Structure Breakdown

This section provides details of gesture articulations based on both the dynamics (i.e., poses and paths) of gestures and the used end-effectors. The five structure types with highest scores were selected, while the remaining levels were grouped into another one labeled as "other". Figure 8 shows the corresponding ratios for each gesture type. Significant difference in the ratios between these six structure types was found ($\chi^2(5) = 74.11$, $p < .001$). Post-hoc tests confirmed not significant differences between static body pose and the levels one finger pose and "other". Likewise, Friedman tests revealed a significant effect of gesture type on the ratio of structure levels (see Table 2). In particular, participants preferred gestures made with one hand pose plus path (62.3%) to produce all gesture types, especially for those ones that may be considered more difficult or strange (e.g., "spiral", "infinite" and "zig-zag", which showed no difference from one another). Although static hand pose had a relatively non-negligible average ratio of 19.5%, it got the second place in most cases. It was outperformed by static arm pose to produce two gesture types, "horizontal line" and "X" (there was no difference between them), that could be mapped better into arms as explained above. Also, static poses held with the whole body or with one (index) finger of both hands were rarely used. Participants employed them especially for articulating the gesture types "X" and "T" (with significant differences between them and the other gesture types, but no difference between both), which were in fact the gesture types more fairly distributed among the five structure types (excluding "other"). "Other" level was observable basically for "step-down" and "asterisk".

Figure 9 shows global ratios for each effector type according to structure levels. It reveals that participants performed few dynamic pose gestures (about 2%), and they mostly produced gestures that followed a path (63%) in comparison to only hold poses (37%); i.e., participants most often executed their gestures by holding a single (hand) pose while drawing the corresponding gesture type.

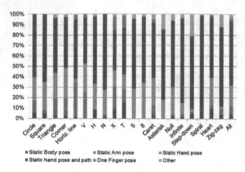

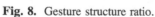

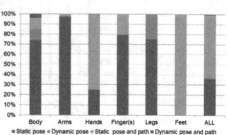

Fig. 8. Gesture structure ratio.

Fig. 9. Gesture structure ratio by used effectors.

5.5 Mental Model Observations

At a high level, GCP facilitates the analysis and understanding of the second task. A user doing the task identifies the current symbol and defines a gesture for it (see Fig. 2). Next, s/he executes that gesture departing from a resting position, and returning to it or going to another one. Overall we observed that participants executed their gestures in this manner, both gestures composed of single movement as well as those ones composed of multiple movements. Actually, only one subject tried to perform the gestures consecutively in most cases, i.e., without having a retraction. Contrary to a general/common participants' behavior, there are several particular observations that are worth mentioning:

- **Gesture shape complexity influences mid-air gesture input.** Overall participants were able to produce various articulations for the predefined gesture set, but they felt less creative for gesture types with complex/strange geometry (e.g., "spiral"). Two participants proposed exclusively drawing gestures in all cases. Nonetheless, they still used both hands and/or sequential movements to "draw" their symbolic gestures.
- **Preference for vertical plane.** While we did not constrain participants on the direction of the plane when articulating a gesture, all participants performed their gestures in the vertical plane. As an exception, one participant executed some gestures in the horizontal plane.
- **Gesture position, size and direction can be a source of variation.** Several participants in some cases changed the used hand, starting point, size and/or direction of paths to produce various articulations.
- **Gestures in ways few technologies could detect.** Though we instructed participants to articulate a gesture for each gesture type, some of them gestured in ways current technologies could not detect. One participant counted the number of fingers to define a number. Another participant touched his heart to define the "heart". One user walked by making three steps to define the "zig-zag". Furthermore, a participant proposed a few gestures by drawing a part of the shape, and next, performing another movement to deform it and get the desired figure. For example, he drew a horizontal line with a hand, and then, he put his hands apart on the line and moved them down to form the step-down symbol.

6 Discussion: Comparison with Elicitation Studies

The results described above provide evidence on how users articulate gestures, which should be compared with previous results. Table 3 shows a comparison between several previously proposed taxonomies and the one proposed in this work. Those taxonomies were proposed as part of studies on user-defined gestures for scenarios such as augmented reality [31], humanoid robot [28], storytelling [17], controlling a drone [29], and video games [37]. The values included in the table are given as the percentage of gestures that participants proposed for each gesture type in each work. Some levels were removed because there were not equivalent levels in one or other taxonomy (e.g., see physicality level).

Table 3. Comparison with other taxonomies.

		This work	[28]	[17]	[31]	[29]	[37]
Physicality	Whole body	5.8	34.8	41.0		13.0	3.0
	One-handed	53.4	40.9	42.0		45.0	40.0
	Two-handed	13.9	24.2	17.0		42.0	35.0
	One-leg	0.8					16.0
	Two-legs						4.0
	Other						2.0
Movement	Single	60.5					
	Parallel	33.0			12.9		
	Sequential	6.6			4.4		
Structure	Static pose	35.7	15.7	45.0	10.1	11.0	
	Dynamic pose	1.3			10.8		
	Static pose with path	62.3	84.3	55.0	71.0	89.0	
	Dynamic pose with path	0.6			8.1		

Referring to physicality level, (one) hand was the most used end-effector in both our study and the other four studies that considered various body parts (i.e., [17, 28, 29, 37]). Though Piumsomboon et al. [31] only reported hand gestures, they also found a preference for one-handed gestures. Similarly, users may also prefer using one hand for gesturing in scenarios like product exhibition or public displays [1, 5, 21]. Actually, passers-by who stop to interact with a public display could hold a mobile phone or carry things on one hand [1, 21]. On the contrary, there is evidence in favor of two-handed gestures [26]. However, users may prefer bimanual gestures depending on the nature of the tasks or the performed gestures, e.g., when one hand is employed as a reference or for zooming [2, 5]. Likewise, we found that participants employed more parallel movements than sequential movements. This finding is comparable with the results reported by Piumsomboon et al. [31] for the symmetric and asymmetric levels respectively. Concerning structure level, four of the works (i.e., [17, 28, 29, 31]) shown in Table 3 reported that participants articulated gestures using more strokes than holds, which is consistent with our results. Likewise, we found a high preference toward static hand pose with path gestures similar to [31].

In addition, although our study had other focus, we might also do another comparison with gesture elicitation studies, namely referring to production of gestures to enhance this type of studies. Morris et al. [24] suggested using five gestures, whereas Ho et al. [14] advised that requesting participants to produce more than three gestures would impact on practical utility of gesture elicitation. Though our participants were shown symbol names instead of desired effects of actions, they proposed at least three "natural" gestures for 70% (SD = 30%) of the utilized symbols on the average. Our study also included a first task in which the participants performed several gestures in a free manner, which could be comparable to priming. However, our participants were not able to reach the threshold of three gestures in all cases despite of this "priming". In conclusion, this finding suggests that proposing more than three gesture articulations can be not natural, which is consistent with [14] but different than [24].

Finally, our participants' characteristics are similar to those who took part in the studies used in Table 3 (i.e., [17, 28, 29, 31, 37]), but a difference between our work and the others must be noticed. While those works were mainly focused on finding gestures for specific scenarios (especially based on Wobbrock et al.'s methodology [45]), we are interested in analyzing the various manners in which users could produce gestures for a same command. In fact, participants were asked to propose a set of gestures for the needed actions in those works, whereas we asked participants to propose various gestures for a set of symbols (Task 2).

7 Design Implications

Informed by our findings, we are able to outline a set of guidelines for designing mid-air gestures interfaces that address gesture ergonomics, design and recognizers with the aim of enabling several gestures to one command.

7.1 Mid-Air Gesture Ergonomics

Our findings indicate that strokes are preferred instead of poses to articulate gestures. These strokes were especially expressed by following a path, mostly with hands. Our findings also demonstrate that producing paths with hands matters to users more than the posture maintained while they do it. The participants generally kept the same pose while executing a gesture; i.e., they rarely used more than one posture between different strokes. Specific hand postures would be needed if users should discriminate between drawing paths and displacing the hand to the point where the path (or a part of it) starts (i.e., the system is not capable of doing this distinction automatically), for example, to perform multi-stroke gestures. Likewise, and contrary to the findings for multi-touch gestures [32], paths performed with a variable number of fingers should not be a problem because users would adopt a single pose (e.g., putting together middle and index fingers, or touching the tips of thumb and index fingers).

Despite the high preference for drawing gestures reported here, we do not advocate that gestures based on poses should not be employed. They have proven to be useful in various scenarios (e.g., finger spelling [39]), but an additional issue is that postures should be learned to interact with applications [15]. Beyond this possible limitation, our results show that static poses maintained not only with hands/fingers may be suitable just for gesture types that could be easily produced through this structure (e.g., letter "X" or "T" and numbers). This finding indicates that the use of postures would depend on the facility to map gestures into the corresponding end-effectors. On the other hand, our results suggest that users would prefer static poses instead of dynamic poses, given that the second ones were very scarce in the second task.

Gestures expressed using either single strokes or single holds should be preferred according to the results of the second task. Although parallel movements may be used as a complement, sequential movements may not result "natural" to users. Unexpectedly, when participants produced the candidate multi-stroke gestures (i.e., gestures for symbols "H", "X", "T", "asterisk", and "null") using static hand poses with paths, they did it frequently using single strokes. Furthermore, participants did not worry or notice a need to discriminate between drawing paths and just moving hands.

Concerning used end-effectors, participants clearly preferred employing hands and fingers to produce symbolic gestures. Despite the high tendency to use one hand, the presence of two-handed, two-arms, and multi-finger gestures was also noticeable. Our findings suggest that users would use both hands symmetrically (principally to produce static hand pose with path gestures) more than folded hands. Conversely, two arms and several fingers would be mainly used in touch acting as a unit. Moreover, unlike previous work [2, 32], we observed no two-handed gestures in which a hand was used as a reference and the other one was used to express the gesture. Additionally, overall the use of arms or whole-body to execute gestures would be preferred depending on the ease to map gestures into them as mentioned above. Finally, more gestures executed with feet may have been expected, but they were hardly ever used by the participants. This may have happened due to any of these causes: the instructions were insufficient, the participants did not imagine these gestures, or simply, foot gestures were not good enough or "natural" to participants.

7.2 Mid-Air Gesture Design

Our findings show that inferring flexible input when articulating gestures would be more suitable when users are provided with little to no instructions or when symbols are unfamiliar or difficult to them. Otherwise, UI designers and researchers should observe how users articulate a gesture set before designing it. Familiar shapes should also be preferred to unfamiliar ones, and gesture articulations should be connected to users' previous gesture practice whenever possible. Additionally, gesture shapes with complex geometries should be used with care, and learning and memorization should be integrated into the design of such gesture shapes. Moreover, the available methods to analyze the difficulty of symbolic gestures (e.g., [10, 34, 42]) should be taken into account during the design.

7.3 Mid-Air Gesture Recognizers

Many of the gestures we witnessed had strong implications for gesture recognition technology. Our results demonstrate that UI designers and researchers should design flexible recognizers that are invariant to users' preferred articulation patterns. Gesture recognizers should be trained with different articulation patterns in terms of physicality, synchronization, and structure. For example, for the same gesture type, our participants articulated it using different number of strokes that are combined sequentially or in parallel using arms/hands/fingers etc., and mixing path and pose structures, such as [3, 19, 33, 41].

8   Conclusion and Next Steps

We presented an investigation of users' gestures articulations variability. We outlined a model for gestures conception and production (GCP), and a taxonomy for mid-air gestures to carry out a qualitative and quantitative analysis. Our findings indicate that, additionally to hands, users would use other body parts to articulate gestures if the proposed gesture type can be mapped better into other body parts to hold postures. Similar to multi-touch input [32], gestures in mid-air could be articulated with single as well as multiple movements entered in sequence or in parallel. Our findings also suggest that users would prefer producing gestures in mid-air mainly using one hand to iconically describe single motion paths. This preference does not mean that users would not produce gestures in other articulations. These findings are important in the context of proposing new interaction techniques that make use of the variability of user gestures, and hence, this study is a first step toward enabling designers to use more than one gesture for a same command. These many-to-one mappings should lead to better user interaction experiences by giving more flexibility and avoiding penalization.

As a future work, we plan to study gesture variability in more interactive scenarios. The same or a similar methodology used here may be followed, but users would have to propose gestures for concrete applications. It may be similar to elicitation studies but adding variability analysis. Other aspects may be also considered in this future work, such as cultural differences (with a larger population) and different contexts.

Acknowledgments. This work was partially supported by INRIA Lille (France), Institut Français du Chili, SENESCYT (Convocatoria Abierta 2011, Ecuador), NIC Chile (DCC, Universidad de Chile), European Funds for Economic Development (ERDF), ANR (Equipex IRDIVE), and CPER Mauve.

References

1. Ackad, C., Clayphan, A., Tomitsch, M., Kay, J.: An in-the-wild study of learning mid-air gestures to browse hierarchical information at a large interactive public display. In: Proceedings of the 2015 ACM International Joint Conference on Pervasive and Ubiquitous Computing, UbiComp 2015, pp. 1227–1238. ACM, New York, NY, USA (2015). http://doi.acm.org/10.1145/2750858.2807532

2. Aigner, R., Wigdor, D., Benko, H., Haller, M., Lindbauer, D., Ion, A., Zhao, S., Koh, J.T.K.V.: Understanding mid-air hand gestures: a study of human preferences in usage of gesture types for HCI. Technical report, November 2012. https://www.microsoft.com/enus/research/publication/understanding-mid-air-hand-gestures-a-study-ofhuman-preferences-in-usage-of-gesture-types-for-hci/

3. Anthony, L., Wobbrock, J.O.: A lightweight multistroke recognizer for user interface prototypes. In: Proceedings of Graphics Interface 2010, GI 2010, pp. 245–252. Canadian Information Processing Society, Toronto, Ontario, Canada (2010). http://dl.acm.org/citation.cfm?id=1839214.1839258

4. Barkhuus, L.: Television on the internet: new practices, new viewers. In: CHI 2009 Extended Abstracts on Human Factors in Computing Systems, CHI EA 2009, pp. 2479–2488. ACM, New York, NY, USA (2009). http://doi.acm.org/10.1145/1520340.1520351

5. Chen, L.-C., Chu, P.-Y., Cheng, Y.-M.: Exploring the ergonomic issues of user-defined mid-air gestures for interactive product exhibition. In: Streitz, N., Markopoulos, P. (eds.) DAPI 2016. LNCS, vol. 9749, pp. 180–190. Springer, Cham (2016). doi:10.1007/978-3-319-39862-4_17

6. Choi, E., Kim, H., Chung, M.K.: A taxonomy and notation method for three-dimensional hand gestures. Int. J. Ind. Ergon. 44(1), 171–188 (2014)

7. Dahlbäck, N., Jönsson, A., Ahrenberg, L.: Wizard of Oz studies: why and how. In: Proceedings of the 1st International Conference on Intelligent User Interfaces, IUI 1993, pp. 193–200. ACM, New York, NY, USA (1993). http://doi.acm.org/10.1145/169891.169968

8. Dezfuli, N., Khalilbeigi, M., Mühlhäuser, M., Geerts, D.: A study on interpersonal relationships for social interactive television. In: Proceedings of the 9th International Interactive Conference on Interactive Television, EuroITV 2011, pp. 21–24. ACM, New York, NY, USA (2011). http://doi.acm.org/10.1145/2000119.2000123

9. Erazo, O., Pino, J.A.: Predicting task execution time on natural user interfaces based on touchless hand gestures. In: Proceedings of the 20th International Conference on Intelligent User Interfaces, IUI 2015, pp. 97–109. ACM, New York, NY, USA (2015). http://doi.acm.org/10.1145/2678025.2701394

10. Erazo, O., Pino, J.A., Antunes, P.: Estimating production time of touchless hand drawing gestures. In: Abascal, J., Barbosa, S., Fetter, M., Gross, T., Palanque, P., Winckler, M. (eds.) INTERACT 2015. LNCS, vol. 9298, pp. 552–569. Springer, Cham (2015). doi:10.1007/978-3-319-22698-9_38

11. Gallo, L., Placitelli, A.P., Ciampi, M.: Controller-free exploration of medical image data: experiencing the kinect. In: 2011 24th International Symposium on Computer-Based Medical Systems (CBMS), pp. 1–6, June 2011

12. Henschke, M., Gedeon, T., Jones, R.: Touchless gestural interaction with wizard-of-Oz: analysing user behaviour. In: Proceedings of the Annual Meeting of the Australian Special Interest Group for Computer Human Interaction, OzCHI 2015, pp. 207–211. ACM, New York, NY, USA (2015). http://doi.acm.org/10.1145/2838739.2838792

13. Hespanhol, L., Tomitsch, M., Grace, K., Collins, A., Kay, J.: Investigating intuitiveness and effectiveness of gestures for free spatial interaction with large displays. In: Proceedings of the 2012 International Symposium on Pervasive Displays, PerDis 2012, pp. 6:1–6:6. ACM, New York, NY, USA (2012). http://doi.acm.org/10.1145/2307798.2307804

14. Ho, L., Hornecker, E., Bertel, S.: Modifying gesture elicitation: do kinaesthetic priming and increased production reduce legacy bias? In: Proceedings of the TEI 2016: Tenth International Conference on Tangible, Embedded, and Embodied Interaction, TEI 2016, pp. 86–91. ACM, New York, NY, USA (2016). http://doi.acm.org/10.1145/2839462.2839472

15. Ismair, S., Wagner, J., Selker, T., Butz, A.: Mime: teaching mid-air pose-command mappings. In: Proceedings of the 17th International Conference on Human-Computer Interaction with Mobile Devices and Services, MobileHCI 2015, pp. 199–206. ACM, New York, NY, USA (2015). http://doi.acm.org/10.1145/2785830.2785854

16. Kendon, A.: Gesture: Visible Action as Utterance. Cambridge University Press, Cambridge (2004)

17. Kistler, F., André, E.: User-defined body gestures for an interactive storytelling scenario. In: Kotzé, P., Marsden, G., Lindgaard, G., Wesson, J., Winckler, M. (eds.) Human Computer – Interaction INTERACT 2013 14th IFIP TC 13 International Conference, pp. 264–281. Springer, Heidelberg (2013). doi:10.1007/978-3-642-40480-1_17

18. Kita, S., van Gijn, I., van der Hulst, H.: Movement phases in signs and co-speech gestures, and their transcription by human coders. In: Wachsmuth, I., Fröhlich, M. (eds.) GW 1997. LNCS, vol. 1371, pp. 23–35. Springer, Heidelberg (1998). doi:10.1007/BFb0052986

19. Kratz, S., Rohs, M.: Protractor3D: a closed-form solution to rotation-invariant 3D gestures. In: Proceedings of the 16th International Conference on Intelligent User Interfaces, IUI 2011, pp. 371–374. ACM, New York, NY, USA (2011). http://doi.acm.org/10.1145/1943403. 1943468

20. Leyvand, T., Meekhof, C., Wei, Y.C., Sun, J., Guo, B.: Kinect identity: technology and experience. Computer **44**(4), 94–96 (2011)

21. Mäkelä, V., Korhonen, H., Ojala, J., Järvi, A., Väänänen, K., Raisamo, R., Turunen, M.: Investigating mid-air gestures and handhelds in motion tracked environments. In: Proceedings of the 5th ACM International Symposium on Pervasive Displays, PerDis 2016, pp. 45–51. ACM, New York, NY, USA (2016). http://doi.acm.org/10.1145/2914920. 2915015

22. McNeill, D.: Hand and Mind: What Gestures Reveal about Thought. University of Chicago (1992)

23. Mehler, A., Lücking, A., Abrami, G.: Wikinect: image schemata as a basis of gestural writing for kinetic museum wikis. Universal Access in the Information Society, pp. 333–349 (2015)

24. Morris, M.R., Danielescu, A., Drucker, S., Fisher, D., Lee, B., Schraefel, M.C., Wobbrock, J.O.: Reducing legacy bias in gesture elicitation studies. Interactions **21**(3), 40–45 (2014). http://doi.acm.org/10.1145/2591689

25. Nacenta, M.A., Kamber, Y., Qiang, Y., Kristensson, P.O.: Memorability of predesigned and user-defined gesture sets. In: Proceedings of the SIGCHI Conference on Human Factors in Computing Systems, CHI 2013, pp. 1099–1108. ACM, New York, NY, USA (2013). http:// doi.acm.org/10.1145/2470654.2466142

26. Nancel, M., Wagner, J., Pietriga, E., Chapuis, O., Mackay, W.: Mid-air pan-and-zoom on wall-sized displays. In: Proceedings of the SIGCHI Conference on Human Factors in Computing Systems, CHI 2011, pp. 177–186. ACM, New York, NY, USA (2011). http:// doi.acm.org/10.1145/1978942.1978969

27. Nielsen, M., Störring, M., Moeslund, T.B., Granum, E.: A Procedure for Developing Intuitive and Ergonomic Gesture Interfaces for HCI. In: Camurri, A., Volpe, G. (eds.) GW 2003. LNCS, vol. 2915, pp. 409–420. Springer, Heidelberg (2004). doi:10.1007/978-3-540-24598-8_38

28. Obaid, M., Häring, M., Kistler, F., Bühling, R., André, E.: User-defined body gestures for navigational control of a humanoid robot. In: Ge, S.S., Khatib, O., Cabibihan, J.-J., Simmons, R., Williams, M.-A. (eds.) ICSR 2012. LNCS, vol. 7621, pp. 367–377. Springer, Heidelberg (2012). doi:10.1007/978-3-642-34103-8_37

29. Obaid, M., Kistler, F., Kasparavičiūtė, G., Yantaç, A.E., Fjeld, M.: How would you gesture navigate a drone?: a user-centered approach to control a drone. In: Proceedings of the 20th International Academic Mindtrek Conference, AcademicMindtrek 2016, pp. 113–121. ACM, New York, NY, USA (2016). http://doi.acm.org/10.1145/2994310.2994348

30. Oh, U., Findlater, L.: The challenges and potential of end-user gesture customization. In: Proceedings of the SIGCHI Conference on Human Factors in Computing Systems, CHI 2013, pp. 1129–1138. ACM, New York, NY, USA (2013). http://doi.acm.org/10.1145/2470654.2466145

31. Piumsomboon, T., Clark, A., Billinghurst, M., Cockburn, A.: User-Defined Gestures for Augmented Reality. In: Kotzé, P., Marsden, G., Lindgaard, G., Wesson, J., Winckler, M. (eds.) INTERACT 2013. LNCS, vol. 8118, pp. 282–299. Springer, Heidelberg (2013). doi:10.1007/978-3-642-40480-1_18

32. Rekik, Y., Grisoni, L., Roussel, N.: Towards many gestures to one command: a user study for tabletops. In: Kotzé, P., Marsden, G., Lindgaard, G., Wesson, J., Winckler, M. (eds.) INTERACT 2013. LNCS, vol. 8118, pp. 246–263. Springer, Heidelberg (2013). doi:10.1007/978-3-642-40480-1_16

33. Rekik, Y., Vatavu, R.D., Grisoni, L.: Match-up & conquer: a two-step technique for recognizing unconstrained bimanual and multi-finger touch input. In: Proceedings of the 2014 International Working Conference on Advanced Visual Interfaces, AVI 2014, pp. 201–208. ACM, New York, NY, USA (2014). http://doi.acm.org/10.1145/2598153.2598167

34. Rekik, Y., Vatavu, R.D., Grisoni, L.: Understanding users' perceived difficulty of multi-touch gesture articulation. In: Proceedings of the 16th International Conference on Multimodal Interaction, ICMI 2014, pp. 232–239. ACM, New York, NY, USA (2014). http://doi.acm.org/10.1145/2663204.2663273

35. Rico, J., Brewster, S.: Usable gestures for mobile interfaces: evaluating social acceptability. In: Proceedings of the SIGCHI Conference on Human Factors in Computing Systems, CHI 2010, pp. 887–896. ACM, New York, NY, USA (2010). http://doi.acm.org/10.1145/1753326.1753458

36. Sheu, J.S., Huang, Y.L.: Implementation of an interactive TV interface via gesture and handwritten numeral recognition. Multimedia Tools Appl. **75**, 1–22 (2015). http://dx.doi.org/10.1007/s11042-015-2739-6

37. Silpasuwanchai, C., Ren, X.: Designing concurrent full-body gestures for intense gameplay. Int. J. Hum. Comput. Stud. **80**, 1–13 (2015)

38. Spano, L.D., Cisternino, A., Paternò, F.: A compositional model for gesture definition. In: Winckler, M., Forbrig, P., Bernhaupt, R. (eds.) HCSE 2012. LNCS, vol. 7623, pp. 34–52. Springer, Heidelberg (2012). doi:10.1007/978-3-642-34347-6_3

39. Sridhar, S., Feit, A.M., Theobalt, C., Oulasvirta, A.: Investigating the dexterity of multi-finger input for mid-air text entry. In: Proceedings of the 33rd Annual ACM Conference on Human Factors in Computing Systems, CHI 2015, pp. 3643–3652. ACM, New York, NY, USA (2015). http://doi.acm.org/10.1145/2702123.2702136

40. Vatavu, R.D.: User-defined gestures for free-hand TV control. In: Proceedings of the 10th European Conference on Interactive TV and Video, EuroiTV 2012, pp. 45–48. ACM, New York, NY, USA (2012) http://doi.acm.org/10.1145/2325616.2325626

41. Vatavu, R.D., Casiez, G., Grisoni, L.: Small, medium, or large?: estimating the user-perceived scale of stroke gestures. In: Proceedings of the SIGCHI Conference on Human Factors in Computing Systems, CHI 2013, pp. 277–280. ACM, New York, NY, USA (2013). http://doi.acm.org/10.1145/2470654.2470692

42. Vatavu, R.D., Vogel, D., Casiez, G., Grisoni, L.: Estimating the perceived difficulty of pen gestures. In: Campos, P., Graham, N., Jorge, J., Nunes, N., Palanque, P., Winckler, M. (eds.) INTERACT 2011. LNCS, vol. 6947, pp. 89–106. Springer, Heidelberg (2011). doi:10.1007/978-3-642-23771-3_9

43. Vikram, S., Li, L., Russell, S.: Writing and sketching in the air, recognizing and controlling on the fly. In: CHI 2013 Extended Abstracts on Human Factors in Computing Systems, CHI EA 2013, pp. 1179–1184. ACM, New York, NY, USA (2013). http://doi.acm.org/10.1145/2468356.2468567
44. Walter, R., Bailly, G., Valkanova, N., Muller, J.: Cuenesics: using mid-air gestures to select items on interactive public displays. In: Proceedings of the 16th International Conference on Human-computer Interaction with Mobile Devices & Services, MobileHCI 2014, pp. 299–308. ACM, New York, NY, USA (2014). http://doi.acm.org/10.1145/2628363.2628368
45. Wobbrock, J.O., Morris, M.R., Wilson, A.D.: User-defined gestures for surface computing. In: Proceedings of the SIGCHI Conference on Human Factors in Computing Systems, CHI 2009, pp. 1083–1092. ACM, New York, NY, USA (2009). http://doi.acm.org/10.1145/1518701.1518866
46. Wong, A., Haith, A., Krakauer, J.: Motor planning. Neuroscientist **21**(4), 385–398 (2015)

Watching Your Back While Riding Your Bike

Designing for Preventive Self-care During Motorbike Commuting

Tomas Sokoler[1(✉)] and Naveen L. Bagalkot[2]

[1] Digital Design Department, IT University of Copenhagen,
Copenhagen, Denmark
sokoler@itu.dk
[2] Srishti Institute of Art, Design and Technology, Bangalore, India
naveen@srishti.ac.in

Abstract. This paper presents our early exploratory work investigating if, and how motorbike riders would engage with visual cues on lower-back posture to adjust their body posture while riding, and in turn prevent lower back injuries due to physical stress. The design exploration reported is part of a larger series of investigations looking into the broader question of integrating measures for preventive self-care with existing everyday activities (e.g. daily motorcycle commute) by means of digital technology. We are guided by the concept of embodied self-monitoring grounded in theories on the embodied and circumstantial nature of human actions, a construct previously used to guide design oriented research in the domain of out-of-clinic physical rehabilitation. We follow a research-through-design approach with the sketching of user experience as our primary mode of inquiry, as we look to expand opportunities for interaction design in the domain of preventive self-care. We report on the outcome of in-situ enactments performed by four motorbike riders as co-explorers engaging with our interactive soft&hardware sketches while actually riding in traffic. In-situ enactments and follow-up interviews with the riders encourage us to (a) further elaborate our interactive sketches for motorbike commuting, and (b) investigate more broadly the design of digital technology in support of preventive self-care as an integrated part of mundane activities such as, in the case at hand, the daily motorcycle commute.

Keywords: Motorbike riding · Embodied self-monitoring · Constructive design research · Interactive sketching

1 Introduction

"If you know bikes at all, you can tell a lot about a man by how he rides. Abdullah rode from reflex rather than concentration. His control of the bike in motion was as natural as his control of his legs in walking. He read the traffic with a mix of skill and intuition. Several times, he slowed before there was an obvious need, and avoided the hard braking that other, less instinctive riders were forced to make. Sometimes he accelerated into an invisible gap that opened magically for us, just when a collision seemed imminent" [14].

© IFIP International Federation for Information Processing 2017
Published by Springer International Publishing AG 2017. All Rights Reserved
R. Bernhaupt et al. (Eds.): INTERACT 2017, Part II, LNCS 10514, pp. 315–323, 2017.
DOI: 10.1007/978-3-319-67684-5_19

In this paper, we explore the design of digital technology aimed at mitigating the risk of lower back pain injuries caused by the physical stress experienced as part of the daily motorcycle commute through dense urban traffic. In particular, we look into the design of a system that, by making cues on the rider's back posture available seeks to enable and encourage bike riders to carry out preventive measures as an integrated part of riding.

A large number of people use motorcycles to commute in India. As per Bangalore Traffic Police, Bangalore had about 3.8 million two-wheelers (which includes both motorbikes and scooters) in March 2015. Commuting in Indian traffic involves not only negotiating dense traffic, but also traffic that is erratic with no lane-discipline, and bad road conditions (see Fig. 1).

Fig. 1. Riding in traffic

Motorbike commuting in such conditions is physically stressful, as the rider rides for longer durations while in uncomfortable positions required to balance the motorbike in slow moving and erratic heavy traffic [16]. It requires the rider to continuously adjust the steering utilizing the upper body [9]. The constant adjustments of the upper body lead to high repetitive loading on the musculoskeletal system, particularly in lower back region [16]. Furthermore, research has shown that maintaining the same lean-forward posture for longer duration, while navigating the city traffic causes fatigue in lower back muscles [15]. Orthopedics and physiotherapists suggest the riders to strengthen their core back muscles to reduce the musculoskeletal strain through core strengthening exercises [1]. However, adhering to this kind of traditional exercising require that the riders take time out of their busy schedule to exercise as a distinct activity beyond, and detached from, the daily commute. Realising this challenge, therapists suggest that the riders perform back stretching exercises while sitting on the bike either during a break or immediately before or after riding (see Fig. 2).

Fig. 2. Recommended preventive self-care exercises for the motorbike riders (From: http://www.bmf.co.uk/news/show/7-tips-to-reduce-motorcycle-pain)

We see this as an example of a general move in the field of physiotherapy towards a more individualized approach (for e.g. [11–13]) aiming to better integrate exercising as part of existing everyday activities. Saving time, one could imagine that riders, for example, would do the stretching exercises while holding still at traffic lights. However, as we observe in Indian city traffic most bike riders do not make a complete stop at traffic lights, but instead push the bikes using their feet to get in position (see Fig. 1).

Taking the suggestions by the physiotherapists even further we want to explore if and how part of the most basic lower-back strengthening exercises could be integrated with the activity of actually riding the bike. Grounded in related research on the design for physical rehabilitation [2–6] we speculate that presenting the riders with an opportunity to perform preventive self-care as part of riding will lead to a higher degree of adherence. In particular, guided by the theoretical construct of 'embodied-self-monitoring' [2, 4], we explore if and how, digital technology could help bring forward opportunities for the riders to perform basic adjustments to their ride posture while riding. As a first principle, our design to support in-situ body posture adjustment obviously has to take second place to the primary task of navigating the motorbike safely through dense traffic. Hence, basic adjustment of posture involves simple stretching and activation of the muscles of the lower back while leaving the hands free for the most crucial task of steering.

Without having any clear preconceived constraints to our design, other than the before mentioned first principle, and general therapist input on relevant basic adjustments, we set out to explore and narrow in on the kind of experience and interaction a system like this should enable. We did so by engaging in a process of co-exploration with riders experiencing our interactive sketch while riding. In terms of a broader research framing, the work reported is part of a series of research-through-design studies guided by the overall vision of mobile and pervasive digital technologies designed to encourage and enable people in turning mundane activities of everyday life into opportunities for preventive self-care.

2 Design Exploration

We take a construction oriented research-through-design approach [10]. In particular, we engage in a process of sketching where interactive soft&hardware sketches act as our main vehicle for inquiry as the key facilitator of in-situ co-exploration with actual riders while riding. Hence, we seek to engage stakeholders in a dialogue, and process of co-exploration, anchored in actual, however brief and sketchy, first hand experience.

In line with Buxton [7] we emphasize the evocative nature of sketching throughout this process and how what we look for in the collaboration with the riders are suggestions and openings for further design towards the overall experience rather than conclusive statements on the usability of the concrete sketches. Informed by initial observations of motorcycle rides and guided by the theoretical construct of embodied self-monitoring, we started to envision, through scenarios, how data on back postures could be made available to encourage acts of preventive self-care while riding. At the same time, and as a fully entangled part of the envisioning process, we started work on the interactive ReRide soft&hardware sketch that would allow us to engage four riders as in-situ co-explorers.

2.1 Adding Cues on Back Posture to the Experience of Motorbike Riding

To get an initial report on the world of motorbike commuting in dense traffic one of the authors wore a GoPro camera on his helmet to video-record a ride from work to home. Inspection of the video soon turned our attention to the ways the rider, like Abdullah, constantly engage with a range of cues as he weaves in and out of traffic. The most easy to identify cues at play had to do with the presence and movement of nearby vehicles, the condition of the road, and of course the movements of the motorcycle experienced through the rider's direct bodily interaction with the bike.

What if data on Abdullah's body posture were made available alongside the many other cues that he experiences from the environment and the bike as he skillfully moves through traffic? How would Abdullah experience this? Could taking in visual cues on his back posture and adjusting his back accordingly be fully worked-in as part of Abdullah's driving?

Looking further to the rider's interaction with the bike we notice how cues from the environment, in many cases experienced as direct bodily interaction with the bike, is combined with visual cues taken in by the occasional glance at the dashboard with its selection of standard gauges (speedometer, tachometer oil pressure, fuel level, etc.) availing data on the state of the motor cycle. This seems to suggest a presentation of cues designed for continuous presence in the rider's field of view but at the same time, most important, designed with a low demand for attention along the lines of the design for glanceability [8], as we aim for a minimum of interference with the primary task of navigating the bike safely through traffic. In a first attempt, this made us look for ways to piggyback on the dashboard design and placement as well as the rider's familiarity with the reading-at-a-glance of the standard gauges. In effect, this opened a much broader space of opportunity for design as it, in general, encouraged us to expand the kind of information made available on a motorbike to encompass not only data on the state of the bike but also data on the condition of the rider.

2.2 The ReRide Scenario

As one of the very first steps in the process of sketching we formulated the idea of ReRide, as captured by the following scenario: *Diva commutes to her work on her motorbike daily. She has been doing so for the past 5 years, and now is in the danger of developing repetitive strain injury of her lower back. To prevent the injury she has to perform stretching exercises, but she does not have the time or the energy at the end of day to do so. She then starts using ReRide. ReRide consists of two parts: (a) A belt that is worn on the lower back sensing the position of the back (see Fig. 3) and (b) a display unit that displays this information real-time, next to the motorbike's speedometer. As Diva rides her bike through the traffic she gets continuous feedback of her lower-back posture and adjusts her riding position in accordance with advice from her physiotherapist on preventive exercising.*

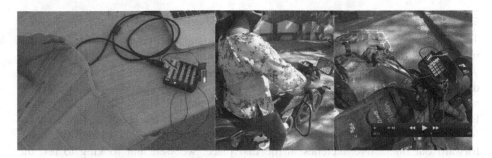

Fig. 3. ReRide interactive sketch. rider with the belt. The display next to speedometer

2.3 The ReRide Interactive Sketch

In line with the open-ended nature of our early explorations we constructed a very basic interactive soft&hardware sketch using the Arduino platform. We fixed a passive resistor based flex sensor on a back support belt as the sensing unit (see Fig. 3). Data from the belt was input to the Arduino and in turn used to drive a LED bar display. When the rider bends their lower-back, resistance of the flex sensor increases. The Arduino board detects this increase as a change in analog input signal level and lights up a LED on the LED bar; the more the rider bends their lower-back the more number of LEDs light up on the LED bar. Our mapping of the increase in resistance in the flex sensor to the LED bars is an approximation aimed purely at exploring the basic experience of a real-time coupling between lower-back posture and display while riding. The data measured this way clearly lacks the precision needed if they were to be considered as 'true' measurements of the rider's lower-back posture.

The LED bar display was placed on the dashboard of the motorbike (see Fig. 4).

Fig. 4. Riding with the ReRide display positioned as part of the existing dashboard

2.4   Experiencing ReRide

The interactive sketches helped us establish a dialogue with riders grounded in actual in-situ, however brief, first hand experience of what it would be like to have data on your lower-back posture available as visual cues while riding your bike. We asked four daily motorbike commuters, two men and two women, to go for rides with our ReRide sketch. One of the authors was riding pillion during this trial, with a video camera focusing on the rider and the ReRide display. Each ride lasted about 20 min and was followed by a brief discussion about the experience. Reiterating the intent of bringing forward our interactive sketches in the first place, we were not looking to test the particular design but rather trying to tap into riders reflections on the overall experience while aiming to get further input on where to take the general notion of making information on lower-back posture available as part of the riding experience.

2.5   What the Riders Did and Said

All the four riders mentioned that having access to their lower back data helped them to get a sense of their posture during the ride. One participant said, "Being able to see (data about) my posture helps, as I am usually aware of my bad posture only when it (lower back) starts to hurt." While the riders' opinions varied on how they would engage with the data if riding with a 'real system', they agreed that it added another layer of information for them to consider during the short ride with the sketch. In summing up the riders' experience of riding with ReRide we focus on two points brought forward across riders when discussing the role of lower-back cues as part of the act of riding.

"How About the Time Spent in the Same Posture?"

During the post-ride interview riders suggested that some kind of indication of the accumulated time spent in the same 'bad' back posture would help them make the decision on whether to adjust their back posture or not. Further, riders suggested that combining these accumulated back posture data with some sort of measure on time left to reach their destination would help them prioritize their decision to change posture in relation to their primary goal of reaching their destination safe and on time. We observed several instances where preventive self-care clearly took second place to getting to the destination on time.

In one such instance, the rider had to brake as he approached a parked car and hence had to bend his back to balance the bike. This was reflected by the ReRide display increasing the lit LEDs from one to two. Slowing down could have been an opportunity for him to change his back posture, straightening it. However, as he at the same time identified a gap in oncoming traffic he immediately started to speed up, again stressing his back, with the LEDs increasing further from two to three. Later, he was very explicit when explaining how it is more important for him to overtake, than worry about posture when in busy traffic. He went on to mention how he would sit in the right posture, if there were no traffic. This statement however, was contradicted by our video observations showing how after seeing a clear stretch of road with no traffic, he did not slow down and sit with back straightened. Instead he accelerated till he got close to the car ahead, and 4 LEDs lit up. When he was showed this video, he commented that if he had known for how long he was sitting in a bad posture, and how he was doing on making it to his destination on time, he would have adjusted his posture. Future sketching and in-situ enactments with a modified ReRide system making available the data the rider asked for will have to show whether this is the case or not.

All together, these observations, further emphasizes to us, that any design seeking to enable preventive measures for self-care as part of riding needs to present itself as subtle and suggestive, but by no means demanding or directive, if they are to be considered relevant by the riders in the first place.

"Vibration May Help, But I Will Have to Learn to Drive With It"

Also during the post-ride interview with riders the idea of having of non-visual cues of back posture made manifest by means of haptic and audio was brought forward.

One rider in particular suggested that non-visual presentation would be helpful for her. She was quite experienced in navigating the traffic, as she was a rider for 20 years. She never looked at her speedometer, which by the way, had stopped working. However, she was a very cautious rider, anticipating bumps and potholes well in time to slow down and correct her posture immediately after she hit a speed-breaker. She kept glancing at the display before correcting her posture. During the discussion she mentioned that even though she hardly looks at the dashboard when riding, she did look this time, as she wanted to know her lower-back posture. As part of the study we did not insist that the riders look at the display, but we had explained that it displays the data about lower-back posture, which may have influenced her actions.

She mentioned how over time she would stop looking at the display, as she will develop a habit of adjusting her posture whenever she slows down. Further she mentioned that an on-body haptic feedback maybe better to develop such a habit. However, when asked if such a display would disturb her riding experience, she mentioned that it might initially, but over time she will have to learn to ride with it. We take these suggestions as an important indication that we should work on broadening the notion of 'glanceability' to make cues available by means other than visual display.

3   Concluding Remarks

We engaged in an open-ended exploration of the idea of making back posture data available as visual cues to motorbike riders in order to encourage them to do in-situ adjustments of their lower back while riding to prevent lower-back injuries.

Using our ReRide interactive soft&hardware sketch we asked four riders to go for a ride and experience first hand what it is like to engage with data on their lower-back posture while riding. In subsequent interviews we asked the riders to reflect on their experience and through this bring forward suggestions for where to take the design of a ReRide system. Overall, we got promising feedback from the riders encouraging us to further explore the design of digital technology in support of performing preventive basic lower-back adjustments while riding. In particular, all the four riders mentioned the importance of having access to lower back information while riding, while offering suggestions for future directions for our work. As such, our interactive sketches successfully made it possible for the riders to directly engage as co-explorers based on actual experience rather than de-contextualized speculations on what it might be like to ride with systems the like of ReRide.

The riders' experience and feedback brought forward two concrete suggestions both pointing out the need to prioritize concerns for a healthy riding position with concerns for safe and effective driving. Based on these suggestions we will start exploring how to present real-time lower-back posture data in combination with data on the duration spent in an unfavorable posture and the estimated time left to reach the destination. Further, we will explore the use of alternative modalities in the interaction with posture data while emphasizing that such an exploration clearly need to also focus on how the riders could learn to ride with such systems, without compromising the safety and ability to navigate traffic. Beyond an immediate response to the four riders' input, we are currently expanding our initial design exploration to (1) include more sensor data acquired through a Bluetooth based personal area network of pressure and movement sensors, some wearable and some integrated with the bike, (2) integrate data on the condition of both bike and rider in one and the same display space, and finally (3) build on a cloud-based Internet-of-Things architecture (e.g. Amazon Web Services IoT) where data generated across rides and riders can be accumulated, analyzed, and made available as a shared pool of data accessible for inspection through the riders' preferred personal devices before and after rides.

Finally, our work on ReRide demonstrated to us that the theoretical construct of embodied self-monitoring can be successfully transferred as a generative design ideal in support of people turning mundane activities of everyday life into opportunities for preventive self-care.

Acknowledgements. We thank the four riders who spent time exploring the idea with us.

References

1. Akuthota, V., Ferreiro, A., Moore, T., Fredericson, M.: Core stability exercise principles. Curr. Sports Med. Rep. **7**(1), 39–44 (2008). doi:10.1097/01.CSMR.0000308663.13278.69
2. Bagalkot, N.L., Sokoler, T.: Designing for lived informatics in out-of-clinic physical rehabilitation. Hum. Comput. Interact. (2017, in print). doi:10.1080/07370024.2017. 1312405
3. Bagalkot, N.L., Sokoler, T., Baadkar, S.: Reride: performing lower back rehabilitation while riding your motorbike in traffic. In: Proceedings of the 10th EAI International Conference on Pervasive Computing Technologies for Healthcare, PervasiveHealth 2016, pp. 77–80. ICST, Brussels, Belgium: ICST (Institute for Computer Sciences, Social-Informatics and Telecommunications Engineering) (2016)
4. Bagalkot, N.L., Sokoler, T.: Embodied-self-monitoring: embracing the context for adherence to physical rehabilitation in the design for self-monitoring. In: 2013 7th International Conference on Pervasive Computing Technologies for Healthcare (PervasiveHealth), pp. 192–199 (2013)
5. Bagalkot, N.L., Sokoler, T., Shaikh, R.: Integrating physiotherapy with everyday life: exploring the space of possibilities through ReHandles. In: Proceedings of the 6th International Conference on Tangible, Embedded and Embodied Interaction, pp. 91–98. ACM (2012)

6. Bagalkot, N., Sokoler, T.: Unboxing the tools for physical rehabilitation: embracing the difference between the clinic and home. In: Proceedings of the 7th Nordic Conference on Human-Computer Interaction: Making Sense Through Design, pp. 597–606. ACM (2012)
7. Buxton, B.: Sketching User Experiences: Getting the Design Right and the Right Design. Morgan Kaufmann Publishers Inc., Burlington (2007)
8. Consolvo, S., McDonald, D.W., Toscos, T., Chen, M.Y., Froehlich, J., Harrison, B., Klasnja, P., et al.: Activity sensing in the wild: a field trial of ubifit garden. In: Proceedings of the SIGCHI Conference on Human Factors in Computing Systems CHI 2008, pp. 1797–1806. ACM, New York (2008)
9. Either, P.: Motorcycle-Rider Servomechanism Steering Theory (2000). http://papers.sae.org/2000-01-3565/. Accessed 09 Jan 2016
10. Koskinen, I.K., et al.: Design Research Through Practice From the Lab, Field, and Showroom. Morgan Kaufmann, Burlington (2012)
11. Mastos, M., Miller, K., Eliasson, A.C., Imms, C.: Goal-directed training: linking theories of treatment to clinical practice for improved functional activities in daily life. Clin. Rehabil. **21**(1), 47–55 (2007)
12. National whitepaper on rehabilitation (2004). http://www.marselisborgcentret.dk/fileadmin/filer/hvidbog/hvidbog.pdf
13. Nicholls, D.A., Gibson, B.E.: The body and physiotherapy. Physiother. Theory Pract. **26**(8), 497–509 (2010)
14. Roberts, G.D.: Shantaram. Abacus (2012)
15. Velagapudi, S., Balasubramanian, V., Babu, R., et al.: Muscle fatigue due to motorcycle riding, SAE Technical Paper 2010-32-0100 (2010)
16. Sai Praveen, V., Ray, G.G.: A study on motorcycle usage and comfort in urban India. In: Proceedings 19th Triennial Congress of the IEA, Melbourne (2009). http://e-journal.um.edu.my/public/article-view.php?id=1488. Accessed 9–14 Aug 2015

Interaction at the Workplace

FeetForward: On Blending New Classroom Technologies into Secondary School Teachers' Routines

Pengcheng An[(⊠)], Saskia Bakker, and Berry Eggen

Department of Industrial Design, Eindhoven University of Technology,
Eindhoven, The Netherlands
{p.an, s.bakker, j.h.eggen}@tue.nl

Abstract. Secondary school teachers have complex, intensive and dynamic routines in their classrooms, which makes their attentional resources limited for human-computer interaction. Leveraging principles of peripheral interaction can reduce attention demanded by technologies and interactions could blend more seamlessly into the everyday routine. We present the design and deployment of FeetForward - an open-ended, and foot-based peripheral interface to facilitate teachers' use of interactive whiteboards. FeetForward was used as a technology probe to explore the design of new classroom technologies which are to become peripheral and routine. The deployment took place with three teachers in their classrooms for five weeks. Based on in-depth and longitudinal interviews with the teachers, we discuss about how FeetForward integrated into teachers' routines, what its effects were on teaching and whether its foot-based interaction style was suitable for peripheral interaction. Subsequently, implications on design of peripheral classroom technologies were generalized.

Keywords: Peripheral interaction · Classroom technology · Foot-based interaction · Secondary school teacher · Calm technology · Interactive whiteboard

1 Introduction

With normally 30 or more students to serve and various tasks to fulfil, secondary school teachers have busy everyday routines, characterized by multitasking [1], unpredictability [2] and complexity [3]. While teaching, teachers need to constantly remain aware of students' progress, frequently confront interruptions, and reflect on their goals or plans for the lesson [1]. As such, they need to divide or shift their attention among different tasks, which consequently makes the teachers' attention a valuable yet limited resource in this context.

Nowadays, secondary schools in developed countries usually offer good access to technologies through well-built ICT infrastructures [4] and devices such as (laptop/tablet) computers, interactive whiteboards, smartphones. Various applications are available to support teachers to organize and track the class (e.g. Google Classroom [5]), to demonstrate and explain the content (e.g. SMART Notebook [6]), and to access relevant

R. Bernhaupt et al. (Eds.): INTERACT 2017, Part II, LNCS 10514, pp. 327–347, 2017.
DOI: 10.1007/978-3-319-67684-5_20

internet resources (e.g. Pocket [7]). However, such classroom technologies are designed for focused interaction [8]: users have to continuously pay attention to the graphical user interface to perform interactions successfully. As a result, such technologies unintentionally bring new complexity into teachers' work and the frequency of using technologies for educational purposes is relatively low [9, 10].

Classroom technologies could be more seamlessly blended into teachers' routines when they require less focused attention while still supporting teaching tasks [1]. We believe this can be achieved by leveraging the principles of peripheral interaction [11], a human-computer interaction paradigm which enables not only interaction with focused attention, but also interaction which takes place in the periphery of attention, and allows seamless shifts between the two.

With the purpose of exploring how new classroom technologies can be designed to become peripheral and routine for secondary school teachers, this paper presents the research-through-design [12] study of FeetForward, a foot-based peripheral interface to facilitate secondary school teachers' use of interactive whiteboards (See Fig. 1). We have deployed this simple yet new technology with three secondary school teachers in their classrooms for a period of five weeks. In this study, we used FeetForward as a technology probe [13] to gather implications for the design of peripheral classroom technologies. In particular, we aimed to study how FeetForward as a peripheral interaction design, could impact pedagogical activities, what may influence a new classroom technology to integrate into teacher's routines, and whether foot-based interaction styles were suitable for peripheral interaction.

Fig. 1. FeetForward: a foot-based peripheral interface to support teachers' use of interactive whiteboards. See [14] for a demo video. (Color figure online)

The remainder of this paper will discuss related work, theoretical background, the design process and rationale of FeetForward and the process of deployment and data gathering. Subsequently, we address the findings of the study and conclude generalized implications for design.

2   Related Work

In their renowned paper on calm technology, Weiser and Brown [15] envisioned that as computing devices become increasingly ubiquitous in our lives, users should be enabled to interact with these devices not only in the center but also in the periphery of their attention, and shift back and forth between the two. This vision inspired various related research areas. Peripheral displays [16] or ambient displays [17], for example, study how to present relevant information without requiring focused visual attention. More recently, the field of peripheral interaction [11] was introduced, studying how physical interactions with computing systems can shift to the periphery of attention.

In the context of education, a few examples of ambient displays are known. Lernanto [18] presents glanceable information about the real-time performance of students, to support differentiated instructions. Lantern [19] uses interactive lamps to display ambient information about work status of student teams to facilitate teacher-students communication. ClassSearch [20] aims to create ambient awareness of web search activities in the class, to facilitate social learning and teacher-led discourse. Similarly, Lamberty et al. [21] present an ambient display which shows each student's real-time design work, to improve peer awareness in learning. Sturm et al. [22] described an ambient display which gives feedback to a teacher about the attention and interest level of students being lectured.

While above mentioned ambient displays are helpful in providing relevant information during lessons, we believe teachers can be further supported in their daily routines if physical interactions would also become available in the periphery of attention. However, examples of peripheral interaction are mainly found in the office context. The unadorned desk [23], for example, uses gestures at the periphery of the workspace to trigger frequently used shortcuts in a desktop context. Probst et al. [24] explored subtle movements or gestures on a chair, such as tilting left and right, to trigger common web-browsing commands, such as next and previous webpage. Few related research explorations are known in educational settings. Notelet [25], is a bracelet interface, enabling a teacher to take a picture of the class through a camera mounted in a corner of the classroom to later remind the teacher about a certain behavior of a student. FireFlies [26] is an interactive system which allows teachers to quietly and unobtrusively communicate short messages to children using a tangible tool. Both these examples were explored in a primary school setting. This paper contributes an exploration of peripheral interaction for secondary school teachers, a target group that differs considerably in terms of teaching styles [27] and everyday routines.

Different from earlier explorations of peripheral classroom technologies, this paper particularly explores foot-based interaction as a style for peripheral interfaces. Foot-based interaction has been studied since the very beginning of the HCI realm [28], and has before that been used as a supportive or secondary modality to manual tasks of people such as potters, organists, or drivers. Because humans have highly developed abilities to manipulate artifacts by hand, feet are not often the first choice for performing human-computer interaction. However, foot-based interaction could be suitable in specific scenarios in which the hands are occupied [29].

Related to educational technology, Daiber et al. [30] explored foot navigation while interacting with geospatial data on a large display, and suggested the interaction style may be beneficial in "teacher-apprentice setting". In the area of peripheral interaction, Probst [31] explored foot kicking and rolling as interaction styles in the context of desktop computing (in sitting posture). Velloso et al. [28] presented a comprehensive review of foot based HCI, in which they also pointed out that since a lot of work of this area has been done in laboratory settings, more field deployments for extended periods of time are still needed. The work presented in this paper contributes a field deployment of a foot-based interface specifically aimed at shifting some of teachers' interactions with the interactive whiteboard to the periphery of attention.

3 Habituation and Peripherality

During their everyday routines, people frequently perform interactions with everyday objects in the periphery of their attention [32]. For example, when reading a newspaper, one could pick up a coffee cup and take a sip without consciously paying attention to it. Or when talking to a friend, you could still put something into your pocket, or straighten your jacket. The reason why these secondary activities can be performed peripherally is two-folded. On one hand, the cognitive or motor resources required by these tasks do not conflict with those required by the main tasks, which makes them possible to be performed in parallel with the main tasks (according to multiple resource theory [33]). On the other hand, these tasks have been repeated for many times in our familiar daily contexts, thus have become automatic to certain degree. The process of activities becoming automatic after repeatedly performing it, is also referred to as habituation [34].

As suggested by dual-process theories [35], our behaviors can be carried out along two competing pathways: a deliberative route, and an automatic route [36]. When we are performing novel activities, or when we are in unfamiliar contexts, our performance normally requires continuous attention in order to perceive new information and respond appropriately. Contrarily, when we are performing habitual activities in a familiar context, we do not have to pay continuous, or focused attention to our performance [34]. Along the automatic route, a behavior is performed peripherally, and therefore can save us cognitive resources for more focused or unfamiliar activities.

Habituation is a key determinant of automaticity [37–39]. New interactions also require a certain extent of habituation (learning and unlearning) before it can be performed in the periphery of attention [40]. In the domain of peripheral interaction, it is therefore valuable to investigate the habituation of interactions when evaluating designs, as it may indicate a design's integration into the personal contexts and existing routines of a user. In the study presented in this paper, we therefore use habituation (habit strength) as an indicator in the evaluation of peripheral interaction design.

4 Designing FeetForward

4.1 Understanding the Context

Secondary schools in developed countries are widely equipped with interactive whiteboards. they are generally seen as a useful tool for teaching and learning [41, 42].

However, various disadvantages restrict the use of interactive whiteboard. For example, effective use requires advanced skill training [42, 43], teachers often find using the interactive whiteboard time-consuming [43], and they argue that there is not enough customizable space [42].

The aim of the study presented in this paper is to explore how to shift some of the teachers' interactions with the interactive whiteboard to the periphery of attention. To better understand teachers' use of the interactive whiteboard, we observed two teachers while using the interactive whiteboard during a regular lesson, and we invited each of them to participate in an ideation session with several designers. While interacting with the board, both teachers were occasionally observed walking to their computer to fulfil operations such as opening an application, opening a webpage, resizing or moving a window, and pausing or replaying a video. Although such operations could also be done using touch or stylus interaction on the board, the teachers preferred using the mouse or keyboard of their computers, interactions to which they were more accustomed. From the observations and discussions with the teachers, it became clear that their operations on the interactive whiteboard or through computer required focused attention, even though these operations were considered secondary tasks. The ideation sessions therefore brought forward the idea to make such actions available through a peripheral interface, so that the tasks become easier to perform, and teachers do not have to walk to their computers that often.

Additionally, we observed that, while standing in front of the whiteboard, teachers' hands were often in use, holding tools such as (interactive) mark pen, textbook and paper documents. On the other hand, teachers' lower limbs were free to move. Unlike when sitting at a desk, while standing, foot movement can be observed through peripheral vision. This lead to the choice of exploring a foot based peripheral interface, and the design of FeetForward.

4.2 FeetForward Design

Peripheral behavior has a highly personal nature [40], new interactions usually become peripheral only when they are meaningful in the specific context to the specific user. Depending on factors such as teaching experience or subjects, teachers often have diverse teaching routines [1]; therefore, we designed FeetForward as an open-ended system. FeetForward consists of four pedals placed under the interactive whiteboard, which can be pressed using the foot, see Fig. 1. Each pedal can be connected to a personalized shortcut operation on the interactive whiteboard. Teachers can personalize the functions of the pedals to make them meaningful to their own contexts.

Each pedal of FeetForward can detect two states of foot operation: hovering and pressing (see [14] for a demonstrating video). When a foot is hovering above the pedal, an icon will pop up on the whiteboard indicating the function that is activated when the pedal is pressed. This augmented feedforward [44] was designed to help users remember or confirm the function before pressing the pedal. Additionally, the four pedals were tagged with different colors (yellow, red, green, and blue) to be differentiated from each other at a glance. These colors match the colors of the icons of the connected functionality. The FeetForward prototype deliberately involved straightforward functionality and relatively easy foot gestures (toe tapping [28, 29]), to ease the process of habituation and to enable interactions to shift to the periphery of attention.

The FeetForward design was developed into a functional prototype. Each pedal of the prototype contained a proximity sensor to detect hovering of a foot, and a tactile switch to detect pressing. Four pedals were connected to an Arduino microcontroller, which was connected to a teacher's laptop computer that ran a dedicated java-based program to achieve the personalized operations.

5   Methodology

The research presented in this paper was conducted using an approach inspired by research-through-design [12] and technology probes [13]. We designed and deployed our dedicated peripheral interface, FeetForward, with the purpose of expanding knowledge on the design of peripheral classroom technology. The aim of deploying this probe was to answer the following research questions: (1) What impacts may peripheral classroom technology have on teaching? (2) What may influence a new classroom technology to become peripheral and routine? (3) Can foot-based interaction be a possible style for peripheral interaction design?

A process of habituation is needed for any interaction to become peripheral [40]. We therefore deployed the FeetForward prototype in secondary school classrooms for a period of five weeks, which would also help obviate the novelty effect.

5.1   Study Setup

Two identical prototypes of FeetForward were implemented into two classrooms of different secondary schools. Three teachers (see Table 1) participated in the deployment. In the following parts of this paper we refer to these participants by their aliases: Peter, Sandy, and Mary. Peter and Mary taught mathematics at the same school. During the deployment, Peter taught 5 lessons per week in the classroom equipped with FeetForward, while Mary taught 2 lessons a week in that classroom. Sandy taught chemistry at a different school, and she taught 4 lessons a week in the equipped classroom. All three teachers had been using interactive whiteboards for teaching before this study.

A FeetForward prototype was installed in each classroom for around two months. Due to school holidays and examinations, the actual usage period for each teacher was five weeks. At the start of the deployment, we demonstrated the prototype with its four pedals assigned to functions we chose based on observations (opening a folder, opening a website, opening an application, and switching among opened application). Subsequently, we asked each participant to indicate what personalized functions they may want to use, and a researcher implemented these functions into the prototype. During the deployment, the researcher visited each participant once a week to see if they wished to change the personalized functions. These informal meet-ups also triggered conversations between teachers and the researcher, which could reveal additional insights into the use and experience of FeetForward.

Since FeetForward has four pedals, at most four functions could be assigned to it in each week. Table 1 lists the functions of FeetForward chosen by each participant during the whole deployment. As the table shows, we refer to the interactions with FeetForward to achieve teachers' personalized functions as **Fi,j**. Correspondingly, the interactions teachers had been doing before the study through interactive whiteboard or computer to achieve the same functions were referred to as **Fi,j'**.

During the deployment, each teacher joined four rounds of data gathering: (1) At the beginning of the deployment (we refer to it as **Week 0**), (2) after one week of using FeetForward (**Week 1**), (3) after three weeks of deployment (**Week 3**), and (4) at the end of the five weeks (**Week 5**). In each round, the teacher was asked to fill in a questionnaire, take an interview, and have one of his or her lessons video-recorded. The researcher was not present during these video-recording sessions. Questionnaires and interviews were conducted either in the teacher's classrooms or at the university.

Table 1. A list of personalized functions applied by each participant with their descriptions in the brackets. The weeks in which each function was implemented were also indicated.

Peter Function (description), week	Sandy Functions (description), week	Mary Functions (description), week
F1,1 (open folder), 1–5	F2,1 (switch webpages), 1–5	F3,1 (open webpage), 1–5
F1,2 (switch applications), 2–3	F2,2 (open webpages), 1–5	F3,2 (open "File" menu), 2–5
F1,3 (open webpage), 2–5	F2,3 (exit virtual desktop), 1–5	F3,3 (switch applications), 1–5
F1,4 (screen shot), 2–5	F2,4 (resize window), 2–5	F3,4 (open folder), 1–4
F1,5 (resize window), 4–5	F2,5 (open folder), 1	F3,5 (resize window), 5

5.2 Questionnaire Design

The questionnaire used in each round was designed to gather subjective quantitative data on the habituation of, and effort required for, interactions with FeetForward. In each data gathering round, the participants were asked to rate nine interactions on the Rating Scale Mental Effort (RSME) [45] and on the scale of the Self-Report Behavioral Automaticity Index (SRBAI) [46].

Measures of mental effort (using RSME [45]) have been adopted in related studies on peripheral interaction (e.g. [26]). Interactions which are experienced to demand less mental effort are assumed to require less attentional resources, which could indicate they may be performed in the periphery of attention. The SRBAI [46] was chosen to assess habituation of an interaction. When a behavior becomes more habitual, it uses cognitive resources more efficiently, and requires less attentional resources. Additionally, habituation may reveal how well a behavior is adopted into the everyday routine.

SRBAI is a streamlined version of Self-Report Habit Index (SRHI). SRHI was developed as a standardized and reliable scale of habit which contains 12 items. Four items of it were selected and validated to construct SRBAI to afford parsimonious measure of habit strength which especially focusing on the characteristic of automaticity [46]. Automaticity is the key effect led by habit which contributes to peripherality of an interaction, and parsimony is valuable for this study since multiple interactions were assessed over a period of time. As a result, SRBAI was used to evaluate interaction behaviors in this study.

In each session, up to nine interactions were given to a teacher to rate using RSME and SRBAI. These included the four functions connected to the four pedals of FeetForward, and the four interactions which would normally be used to trigger these functions. Both these interactions were included to enable comparison and evaluation of changes in habituation and effort over time. For example, Peter assigned the red pedal of FeetForward to the function of opening a frequently used folder. He was therefore asked to rate the interaction "opening my frequently used folder with the red pedal of FeetForward" and the interaction "opening my frequently used folder with my computer". Additional to these eight interactions, the teachers were asked to rate the activity of "turning on the lamps in my classroom" (which we refer to as **L**). We assumed that this behavior was relatively stable and habitual in teachers' everyday routines, and unlikely to change during the deployment. This interaction was used as a warm-up and as a reference when analyzing the data.

5.3   Qualitative Data Gathering and Analysis

We chose a phenomenological approach [47] to gather and analyze qualitative data. This approach is used to describe and explain lived experiences of several (1–10) individuals [47], which is particularly suitable for answering our qualitative research questions regarding the integration of peripheral interfaces in teachers' routines.

Qualitative data was collected using semi-structured interviews, as is conventional in the phenomenological approach [48]. As mentioned above, each participant was interviewed four times. Each interview was conducted with an individual participant and consisted of three parts, aimed to gain insights into (1) the users' general experience of using FeetForward including perceived advantages and disadvantages, (2) peripherality of the interactions including perceived effort and routineness, and (3) the users' experience of foot-based interaction, their experience in learning and practicing how to use the interface, and their allocation of attention to the pedals and visual feedforward. As each participant was interviewed four times, participants usually also reflected on changes in their experiences.

Using [49] as a reference, the transcribed qualitative interview data were analyzed using the following steps: (1) the first author read through the transcripts to gain an overall understanding of the data, (2) phrases or sentences which were considered relevant to a research question were highlighted, (3) these selected phrases were clustered into emerging topics under each research questions, and finally (4) these clusters were re-contextualized by adding concrete descriptions provided by the participants.

6   Quantitative Findings

Self-report Effort. Figure 2 shows the results of the Rating Scale Mental Effort (RSME), in which teachers rated the mental effort required for interactions with FeetForward, and for counterpart interactions with their laptop or interactive whiteboard to achieve the same functionalities. It is shown in Fig. 1 that all the interactions

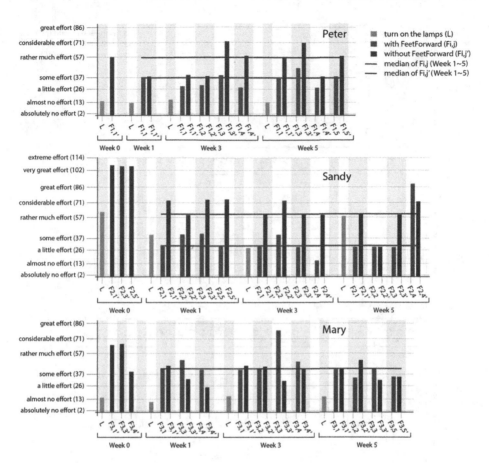

Fig. 2. Results of RSME. The rated value of RSME could range from 0 to 150: the higher an interaction is rated, the more effort a subject experiences. The medians of tasks with/without FeetForward during the five-week deployment were also shown.

with FeetForward were considered as more effortless than those without FeetForward for Peter. For sandy, FeetForward also took much less effort except F2,4 rated in the last week. Mary found interaction F3,1 and F3,2 are a bit more effortless; But F3,3 and F3,4 were felt more difficult than F3,3' and F3,4'. As the comparisons of the medians in Fig. 1 shows, using FeetForward was generally considered no more effortful than performing previously practiced interactions. And it was especially considered as more effortless than previous interactions for Peter and Sandy.

Self-report Automaticity. Figure 3 shows the results of the Self-Report Behavioral Automaticity Index (SRBAI), the four-item rating scales participants used to indicate the perceived automaticity of interactions to achieve the personalized functions, with and without use of FeetForward. The higher the rating, the more habitual/automatic the behavior is experienced. The results in Fig. 3 indicate that after the deployment, the perceived automaticity of most tasks with FeetForward (F1,2, F1,5, F2,3, F2,4, F2,5,

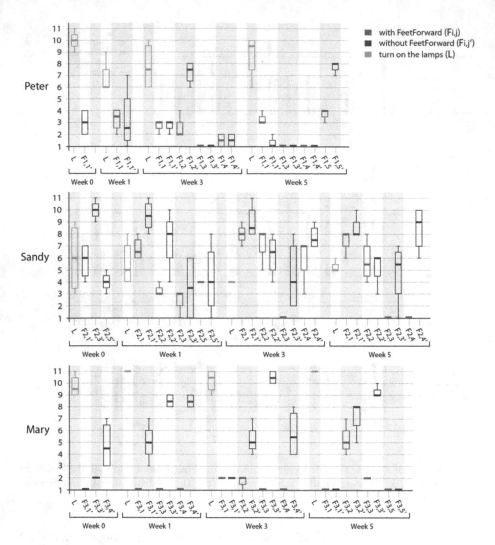

Fig. 3. Results of SRBAI gathered using eleven-point Likert scales, where 1 stands for 'strongly disagree', 6 stands for neutral attitude, and 11 stands for 'strongly agree' to statements of SRBAI (e.g., "Behavior X is something I do without thinking."). The results are represented by box-and-whisker plots (indicating median, quartiles, and max/min values).

F3,3, and F3,4) had not increased, even though some of them (F1,5, F2,3, F2,5) were experienced as considerably more effortless than their counterparts (see Fig. 2), and some of them (F2,3, F3,3, F3,4) had been implemented for four or five weeks (see Table 1). There were also some tasks to be found not automatic at all both with or without using FeetForward (F1,3, F1,4, F3,1, F3,5, and their counterparts). However, as shown in Fig. 3, there were also a few of interactions (F1,1, F1,5, F2,1, F2,2, F3,2) with FeetForward that had clearly gained self-report automaticity. For example, data from Week 1 and Week 3 show that the automaticity levels of F1,1 and F1,1' were about the same, but in Week 5, F1,1 had become more automatic than F1,1'. F2,2 was evidently less automatic than F2,2' in Week 1, but they had become comparably automatic in Week 3 and Week 5. The same change happened to F3,2 from Week 3 to Week 5. Additionally, while F2,1' is quite automatic to Sandy, F2,1 had quickly become automatic (since Week 1), and remained the level which is quite close to F2,1'. In general, for most of the interactions with FeetForward, the five-week deployment might be too short to see an evident increase of behavior automaticity, or a replacement to a previously practiced interaction; However, a few of operations with FeetForward did show a clear rise of self-report automaticity.

Interaction Duration. In order to gain insights into the routineness of the interactions with FeetForward, we video-recorded one lesson of each teacher during each data gathering session. Additionally, the prototype logged interactions during the deployment. These data were used to interpret the duration of each interaction with FeetForward. We defined this interaction duration as the duration between the moment the user started to glance down at the pedals, and the moment that the user pressed the pedal. This total interaction duration consists of two sub-durations: *glancing down* (from starting to look down at the pedals to moving the foot above the pedal and an icon appearing) and *foot hovering* (from the moment the foot hovers above a pedal until the pedal is pressed). These two sub-durations were measured separately. Foot hovering was measured by the prototype, using the proximity sensor and tactile button. The numbers of interactions logged by the system were 26 from Peter, 26 from Sandy, and 23 from Mary. Glancing down was measured through video analysis, in which the number of frames within the sub-duration was measured as the original value, and converted into seconds (The framerate of the analyzed videos was 30f/s). The numbers of interactions which were captured by video and analyzed were 7 for Peter, 11 for Sandy, and 12 for Mary. The mean values and standard deviations of interaction durations of each participant are presented in Table 2. As the table shows, the total durations of Peter and Mary were below 4 s, while Sandy's duration was 2.68 with the standard deviation of 1.64 (1.04 – 4.32), which is generally below 4 s. Therefore we can conclude that interactions with FeetForward were mostly performed in less than 4 s. This is within the duration range of microinteractions [50], which considered a minimal interruption of primary tasks according to the Resource Competition Framework [51].

7   Qualitative Findings and Discussion

In this section, corresponding to each of our three research questions, we address and discuss in-depth qualitative findings from longitudinal interviews with the participating teachers, while also including some discussion about the quantitative findings presented in previous section.

Table 2. The results of interaction duration (in seconds), which are formatted as: mean ± SD.

Subject	Glancing down	Foot hovering	Total duration
Peter	1.56 ± 0.51	0.54 ± 0.33	2.1 ± 0.84
Sandy	1.85 ± 0.93	0.83 ± 0.71	2.68 ± 1.64
Mary	1.3 ± 0.5	0.97 ± 1.01	2.27 ± 1.51

7.1   What Impacts May Peripheral Classroom Technology Have on Teaching?

Saving Effort. As RSME and interaction duration data shows (see Fig. 2 and Table 2), interactions with FeetForward were generally perceived to demand no more effort than the existing interactions, and were mostly performed within 4 s. The interviews also revealed that all participants agreed that FeetForward saved them time and effort to achieve certain functions. For example, Peter thought the pedal connected to the function of resizing a window (F1, 5) made the task much easier, "*because it's hardest to do* [with the stylus on the interactive whiteboard]". Sandy indicated that when she was interacting with her computer, "*I have to walk* [to the desk from the whiteboard] *and I have to look at the small screen, I have to bend over... and it takes a while.*" She thought with the task simplified by FeetForward, that "[I] *don't have to walk always from computer to board back and forth. It's much quicker.*" and that she could "*keep on talking to my class while I'm doing it*". Mary agreed: "*It saves me walking to the computer. It helps me not concentrating at the computer screen. I look at the pedals and I can also pay attention to the pupils.*" In summary, by reducing effort, and enacting minimal interruption to the main task, FeetForward can possibly enable some side tasks to be performed quasi-parallel with other tasks. These experiences therefore echo the core intention of peripheral classroom technology.

Fulfilling Personal Needs. Freedom of function personalization of FeetForward triggered conversations between the participants and researchers, revealing the teachers' diverse routines and needs. For example, the pedal that had become most habitual to Mary with FeetForward was connected to the function of calling the "File" menu to open recently used files (F3, 2, see Fig. 3). She used this function frequently, but the problem she faced without using FeetForward, was that the 'open' button is located at the top area of the interactive whiteboard, and she could not easily reach it. "*I am not going to jump in front of students*". Therefore, she had to go to her computer to fulfil the task. Sandy shared this difficulty with her, "*I cannot reach the top button*". Besides, she used different web pages in her lessons, therefore she chose for a pedal to switch between opened tabs whose buttons are on the top area of the internet browser (F2,1). This pedal also had gained the most automaticity among the four (See Fig. 3). Peter's "*most useful*" pedal connected to opening a folder which stores resources relevant to the current lesson topics (F1, 1), and it had become more automatic than the previously practiced interaction (using computer). Although Peter considered that pedal most useful, the other participants did not find this function very relevant. These findings show that different functions of FeetForward blended into different routines, which was supported by the open-ended nature of the peripheral interface. Furthermore, we found that this open-endedness motivated teachers to think about more possibilities of the classroom technology which fit to their own contexts. Sandy reported that after she got more used to FeetForward, *"I started to more and more think about possibilities of pedals... you want make use of it. I haven't tried the possibilities. ...I can think about a hundred things to do"*.

Improved Integration of Technology. By making side tasks more effortless, and satisfying diverse personal needs, peripheral classroom technology may also lead to improved integration of technology into classrooms. FeetForward made our participants use certain functions more often. Before Peter had the pedal connected to a frequently used folder, he already put relevant pictures into that folder with the intention to use them during his lesson. However, *"I didn't use it often [...]. Maybe with FeetForward it's easier for me to access, and I will use it more often"*. Sandy talked about the pedal to switch webpages: *"because I think it's convenient to switch [using] the pedal, it makes me use the web browser more"*. That also made her use online exercises more often. *"I can switch more easily, so that made me search for web-based applications I could use with the students... Instead of assigning them as homework, I can use these exercises in the class"*. Additionally, effortless access may lead to more flexible use of technology. Peter, for example, found the function of resizing and repositioning a window helpful when two applications needed to be shown or used at the same time. Due to the effort required to do this with the stylus, he usually did this before the lesson with the computer. *"It's something I do mostly when preparing my lesson... But sometimes I have to do when I am in front of the classroom"*. Using the pedal, the task became easier, especially in unexpected situations. This also held for the frequently used folder; he normally tried to *"foresee"* which pictures might be used in the lesson, and collected them in one document beforehand. But with FeetForward, *"when the students ask about their homework, and I didn't anticipate, [...] at that moment we could retrieve the picture from the folder with FeetForward"*. The flexibility offered by FeetForward may thus enable teachers to interact with technologies more extemporaneously during teaching activities, possibly enhancing their use of digital resources.

7.2 What May Influence a New Classroom Technology to Become Peripheral and Routine?

Although FeetForward facilitated or simplified teachers' individually relevant side tasks in relatively short interaction durations without requiring much mental effort, we had not seen that all the new interactions completely became more automatic than previously practiced interactions during the five weeks. The study results indicated that it requires a relatively long period of time for designed peripheral interaction to really become peripheral, and many factors could have an influence on this process. In this sub-section, user's experiences about factors that may influence a new technology to become peripheral and routine will be addressed and discussed.

Consistent Accessibility. Throughout each week, each of our participants taught in different classrooms of which only one was equipped with FeetForward. Mary for example, used two classrooms. She thought it would be *"really helpful"* if prototypes were equipped in all classrooms. She spent more time in the classroom in which no FeetForward was available. She indicated that, since the two classrooms "*look alike,* [..] *I perceive they* [the two classrooms] *are the same,* [..] *so I have to remember they* [pedals of the prototype] *are here to actually use them*". Likewise, Sandy emphasized the importance for the classrooms to have consistent settings for a new technology; "*not* [teaching] *in the same classroom takes long time for me to get used to it* [FeetFordward]". To explain this further, she indicated that "*working in different classrooms is like cooking in different kitchens ...it takes me a while to adjust ...*". The inconsistency of the settings demanded extra mental effort to adapt to, as Sandy said, it "*requires thinking*", which made it difficult to adopt the new technology. In Mary's thought, if FeetForward would only be available one classroom, "*most of the teachers will just use the whiteboard* [not the pedals]". As experienced by our participants, consistent accessibility is important for a new technology to blend into a teacher's routines.

Existing Habits. Due to the function of FeetForward, we were able to compare effort and automaticity of interactions with the pedals to those of interactions teachers had been previously doing, to achieve the same operations. As seen in respectively Figs. 2 and 3, we found that although some interactions with FeetForward were rated as more effortless than the existing interactions, perceived automaticity of these interactions had not exceeded the existing ones during the deployment. All participants reported several times in interviews that they sometimes forgot to use the pedals, but automatically used their computers or whiteboards. For example, "*Afterwards...* [I noticed] *Oh I could have used FeetForward*" (Peter), or "*When I want to open my frequently used folder, first thought is to go to the computer. [..] Sometimes on my way to the desk and I think oh wait I can use the pedal*" (Mary). Sandy indicated that she forgot to use FeetForward especially when experiencing high mental load or stress, for example when "*the lesson isn't going as I planned*". She furthermore mentioned "*When something happened, you have to switch to your automatic pilot*". Although walking to the computer to operate the interactive whiteboard may objectively be less economical compared to using FeetForward, it seems to be strongly habitual. Given the attention demanding nature of teacher's main tasks, it seems that side tasks are prone to be performed in a habitual way. Such strong existing habits seem difficult to be replaced by a new habit; the period of five weeks may not have been enough to completely achieve this.

Frequency of Practice. Repetitive performance in certain context gradually raises the automaticity of a certain behavior [34]. Although using the pedals did not replace existing habits during the deployment, all participants agreed that their frequency of usage effected how they got used to FeetForward. "*The less I used it, the less automatic it is*" (Mary). Mary believed that using the prototype "*continuously*" and "*repetitively*" would help it to become part of her routines more quickly. The deployment of FeetForward was conducted in the last two months of a semester. Therefore the three teachers had fewer lessons to teach than earlier in that semester. As Peter experienced, "*teaching frequency is at low point*", and "*if I had more lessons, the more quickly I will adjust to FeetForward*". Besides lesson schedule and perceived usefulness, it was also pointed out by the teachers that physical presence of a new technology may have influence on frequency of its usage. As mentioned in the previous sub-subsection,

participants sometimes forgot to use FeetForward. However, the visibility of the prototype reminded our participants to use the new technology, when they came into the
classroom. *"It's visible because it's on the floor"* (Sandy). *"When I come in I see them
[the pedals], when I switch on the board the pedals are under it"* (Mary). Additionally,
Peter thought the physicality of FeetForward had benefits *"because it's a physical
button, it's not part of the smart board"*. When he was using the interactive whiteboard,
*"actual computer functions, they are more in the back of my head... maybe the physical
buttons make me use some computer functions more often"*. This could indicate that,
because the pedals offer users physical affordance, or inherent feedforward [44] to
some functions which were previously hidden behind the interface of interactive
whiteboard, these functions might be more frequently used.

Learnability. As an open-ended system, FeetForward required participants to map the
four pedals to four customized functions. It took longer than expected for teachers to
remember these functionalities. *"Four pedals are quite a lot"*, Peter experienced, *"it
will take time for us to remember which pedal does what"*. Sandy indicated *"I still have
to think about the color. I made mistakes... I have to remember [the colors]"*. During
the deployment, we found that the position and order of the pedals were remembered
by the teachers earlier compared to the colors. Peter indicated that when he was
glancing down at the pedals, what he focused was *"positions of the four pedals mostly,
not onto colors"*. In Sandy's classroom, she located the green and the yellow pedal at
the left and right ends under the board. And for her, *"the green and yellow ones are first
to remember... The left the right, they are at the ends, easy to locate"*. Similarly, Mary
indicated that it was easier for her to remember *"Positions, not the colors... If you
change the color to all yellow, I don't think it will make a difference to me"*. Clearly,
the functions of pedals were first remembered by the teachers using spatial memory.

7.3 Can Foot-Based Interaction Be a Possible Style for Peripheral Interaction Design?

Challenges. Foot-based interaction was new to our participants, and may be new to
many users. This seems to have made it more difficult to habituate to it. *"If the pedals
would have been here when the smart board have been, then I would probably use
them equally, I guess"* (Peter). At a standing posture, users' lower limbs have to support
their body weight. This makes foot-based interaction limited when teaching. Peter told
us that it was not convenient for him to switch from pedals close by to the pedal far
away; *"[I] have to move my supporting foot"*. Mary experienced that it is more difficult
to interact with pedals when wearing high heels; *"I am afraid to lose my balance. High
heels are not practical in classrooms"*. Mary also pointed out that if a foot task is
performed with a manual task at the same time, switching eyesight between the board
and the ground will be *"effortful"*, *"because you have to move you eyesight and mind"*.

Benefits. Despite these issues might be solved with a more sophisticated prototype, for
which the foot does not have to be tilted very high and the pedals are more perceivable
to peripheral vision. We believe that foot-based interaction seems promising for
peripheral interfaces. Mary thought that foot-based interaction was supportive to the

main tasks she performed on the interactive whiteboard. "*I think it adds something, adds some more options*". It was especially helpful when her hands were occupied, or when she had to operate the top area of the display. "*I use my pen to interact with whiteboard, and I am right handed, when I want to click on it I have to give the pen to the left hand... Top part, I have to jump toward it*". Similarly, Sandy described specific moments in which she experienced foot-based interaction as supportive; "*I had four test tubes, I was holding them, and they* [students] *had questions, and I had to go to different slides* [to explain the question]." Moreover, since the feet are within the user's eye-sight, the teachers could easily get used to the interface, as also evidenced by the observation that interactions were often preceded by briefly looking down at the pedals (See Table 2).

8 Discussion and Implications

Used as a technology probe, FeetForward gathered rich contextual information to answer our research questions. Based on discussed findings, we generalize implications to inform the design of peripheral classroom technology.

Towards Seamless Integration of Technology. In current classrooms, in which no peripheral interaction designs are installed, teachers tend to perform many computer-related tasks during lesson preparation. For example, Peter prepared pictures for students, or opened and resized the windows of applications, and Sandy opened webpages she wanted to use before the lesson. This often made them feel pressured at the start of lessons (as also found in [1]). However, such preparations are convenient because conducting these operations ad-hoc during lessons demands effort and attention away from the main task of teaching. In our field study with FeetForward, we have replaced some of these attention-demanding focused interactions by more readily available foot-operations. Our findings show that although teachers need to get used to these new interactions, they seem to demand less time and effort and therefore potentially shift to the periphery of attention where they can be performed in parallel to main tasks. Additionally, we found that the open-endedness of the peripheral interface made it easy for the teachers to blend it into their own routines. As we discussed, the personalized functions with FeetForward which were found to have perceivably gained automaticity seemed also to be especially relevant to teachers. Furthermore, when the interactions got more effortless, teachers were triggered to use the technology more frequently and more extemporaneously. Given these promising findings, it seems that peripheral classroom technology is meaningful to enact a more seamless integration of technology into this context.

Design for Habituation. Interactions that are capable to perform peripherally are meaningful for users whose attentional resources are occupied by multiple tasks. However habituation, or automatization, is needed before their peripherality could be leveraged. It is not easy for users to add new interactions into their flow of routines, and it is especially difficult if the new interactions compete with a previously practiced interactions, as revealed by our study. It has also been found that perceived relevance, consistency and learnability of the interface and frequency of use could have effects on the habituation of new interactions. These factors need to be considered while designing for habituation. Through the deployment we found that flexibility of personalization of the new technology helped itself to identify individually relevant function and make its way to blend in differentiated routines of the teachers. Consistency may be important for any interface, but they are especially crucial for peripheral interfaces, since peripheral, or automatic behaviors only involve limited attentional resources and therefore are less sensitive to changes in the context. For example, in our study, teachers experienced that if all of their classrooms were equipped with FeetForward, they would get habituated to it more quickly. It is also very important for a designed peripheral interaction to be easy to learn and practice [40]. By inquiry into how the teachers remembered the functions of FeetForward, it has been found that spatial memory may play an important role in getting habituated to a new interface, which can be further exploited in the design of peripheral interaction (as also explored by related work such as [23]). It was also found that the physical presence of FeetForward served as an intuitive cue for the users to practice using it, and it also provided affordances for some computer functions that are otherwise "hidden" in the interactive whiteboard. Inspired by this we believe that more functions could be derived from the current centralized interfaces (such as computer, interactive whiteboard), and distributed into physical objects (such as a pedal, a pen, or a wearable) around teachers to make these functions more visible and accessible and therefore easier to be practiced and used ad-hoc. Additionally, our study also implied that although some interactions were considered effortless, it didn't necessarily mean that they were at the moment with enough peripherality to be performed automatically by the users. Therefore, behavior habituation, or automatization could be used as additional assessments in longitudinal evaluations of peripheral interactions.

Leveraging Foot-based Interaction. The study presented in this paper explored foot-based interaction as a means to peripherally interact with large displays while in standing posture. Based on the experiences of our participants, we have seen that foot-based operations can help users to interact with components which are far to reach (e.g. the top area of the display). Furthermore, with feet leveraged for supportive or secondary tasks, users could utilize their hands for more relevant or elaborate tasks, which may enhance quasi-parallel task performance (e.g. using stylus, or holding demonstration materials). However, our study also revealed challenges, which should be considered when designing foot-based peripheral interaction. While the fact that our participants could visually see the interface made it easier to get used to the interactions (possibly using peripheral vision), such foot operations should not demand focused visual attention, since the eyesight switch from the display to the foot area can result in unwanted interruptions. Therefore it could be helpful to consider how to make the foot interface easy to locate and to operate through user's peripheral vision. Additionally, we found that, with the interface designed for a standing posture, it can be challenging for users to keep balance, for example when the user has to frequently move the supporting foot to reach a certain part of the interface. These challenges could be addressed by decreasing the height of the foot-pedals, or by attaching sensors to the user's shoes, such that smaller foot movements are required to trigger the needed operations.

9 Conclusion

In this paper, we presented FeetForward, a foot-based peripheral interface aimed to support teachers' secondary tasks when using the interactive whiteboard. Designed as a peripheral foot-based interface, FeetForward was considered to facilitate side tasks for teachers, and was operated in short periods of time with minimal interruptions to the main tasks. It was experienced to support multiple-task situations as well as ad hoc and extemporaneous use of technology while teaching. However, it was also shown that a field deployment lasting five weeks was not long enough for interactions with FeetForward to exceed the previously practiced interactions in terms of behavior automaticity. Although using FeetForward was objectively economical, occasionally, previous interactions were subconsciously performed especially while the users are with relatively high mental-load. This indicates that a prolonged deployment will be needed in order to see FeetForward being fully integrated into the users' habitual task flow. Nonetheless, a few tasks with FeetForward which are especially individually meaningful to the users had gained perceivable automaticity during the deployment, showing the potential of FeetForward to blend into different routines of the teachers. Based on our findings, we discussed the possible impact peripheral technology may have on teaching, and the factors that may influence a new technology to become peripheral and routine, as well as the opportunities and challenges of employing foot-based interaction into peripheral interaction design. Subsequently, based on the discussions, we generalized the implications for design. By presenting FeetForward as a novel peripheral classroom technology, and evaluating it in the real context of use, this paper contributes insights into the design of interfaces that can help integrate classroom technologies more seamlessly into teacher's everyday routines.

References

1. An, P., Bakker, S., Eggen, B.: Understanding teachers' routines to inform classroom technology design. Educ. Inf. Technol. **22**, 1347–1376 (2017)
2. Doyle, W.: Learning the classroom environment: an ecological analysis of induction into teaching (1977)
3. Brante, G.: Multitasking and synchronous work: complexities in teacher work. Teach. Teach. Educ. **25**, 430–436 (2009). doi:10.1016/j.tate.2008.09.015
4. Ten Brummelhuis, H., Kramer, M., Post, P., Zintel, C.: Vier in balans-monitor 2015. In: Kennisnet (2015). https://www.kennisnet.nl/fileadmin/kennisnet/publicatie/vierinbalans/Vier_in_balans_monitor_2015.pdf
5. Google Classroom. https://classroom.google.com/
6. SMART Notebook. https://education.smarttech.com/
7. Pocket. https://getpocket.com/
8. Bakker, S., Niemantsverdriet, K.: The interaction-attention continuum: considering various levels of human attention in interaction design. Int. J. Des. **10**(2), 1–14 (2016)
9. Cuban, L., Kirkpatrick, H., Peck, C.: High access and low use of technologies in high school classrooms: explaining an apparent paradox. Am. Educ. Res. J. **38**, 813–834 (2001). doi:10.3102/00028312038004813

10. Urhahne, D., Schanze, S., Bell, T., et al.: Role of the teacher in computer-supported collaborative inquiry learning. Int. J. Sci. Educ. **32**, 221–243 (2010). doi:10.1080/09500690802516967

11. Bakker, S., Hausen, D., Selker, T.: Introduction: framing peripheral interaction. In: Bakker, S., Hausen, D., Selker, T. (eds.) Peripheral Interaction. HIS, pp. 1–10. Springer, Cham (2016). doi:10.1007/978-3-319-29523-7_1

12. Zimmerman, J., Forlizzi, J., Evenson, S.: Research through design as a method for interaction design research in HCI. In: Proceedings of SIGCHI Conference on Human factors Computing Systems - CHI 2007, pp. 493–502 (2007) doi:10.1145/1240624.1240704

13. Hutchinson, H., Hansen, H., Roussel, N., et al.: Technology probes. In: Proceedings of Conference on Human factors Computing System - CHI 2003, p. 17. ACM Press, New York, USA (2013)

14. FeetForward. https://vimeo.com/196859949

15. Weiser, M., Brown, J.S.: The coming age of calm technology. In: Denning, P.J., Metcalfe, R.M. (eds.) Beyond Calculation, pp. 75–85. Springer, New York (1997). doi:10.1007/978-1-4612-0685-9_6

16. Matthews, T., Rattenbury, T., Carter, S.: Defining, designing, and evaluating peripheral displays - an analysis using activity theory. Hum.-Comput. Interact. **22**, 221–261 (2007). doi:10.1080/07370020701307997

17. Mankoff, J., Dey, A.K., Hsieh, G., et al.: Heuristic evaluation of ambient displays. In: Proceedings of Conference on Human factors Computing System - CHI 2003, p. 169. ACM Press, New York, USA (2003)

18. van Alphen, E., Bakker, S.: Lernanto. In: Proceedings of 2016 CHI Conference on Extended Abstract Human Factors Computing Systems - CHI EA 2016, pp. 2334–2340. ACM Press, New York, USA (2016)

19. Alavi, H.S., Dillenbourg, P.: An ambient awareness tool for supporting supervised collaborative problem solving. IEEE Trans. Learn. Technol. **5**, 264–274 (2012). doi:10.1109/TLT.2012.7

20. Moraveji, N., Morris, M., Morris, D., et al.: ClassSearch: facilitating the development of web search skills through social learning. In: Proceedings of SIGCHI Conference on Human Factors Computing System, pp. 1797–1806 (2011)

21. Lamberty, K.K., Froiland, K., Biatek, J., Adams, S.: Encouraging awareness of peers' learning activities using large displays in the periphery. In: Proceedings of 28th International Conference on Extended Abstracts on Human factors in Computing Systems - CHI EA 2010, pp. 3655–3660 (2010)

22. Sturm, J., Iqbal, R., Terken, J.: Development of peripheral feedback to support lectures. In: Renals, S., Bengio, S. (eds.) MLMI 2005. LNCS, vol. 3869, pp. 138–149. Springer, Heidelberg (2006). doi:10.1007/11677482_12

23. Hausen, D., Boring, S., Greenberg, S.: The unadorned desk: exploiting the physical space around a display as an input canvas. In: Kotzé, P., Marsden, G., Lindgaard, G., Wesson, J., Winckler, M. (eds.) INTERACT 2013. LNCS, vol. 8117, pp. 140–158. Springer, Heidelberg (2013). doi:10.1007/978-3-642-40483-2_10

24. Probst, K., Lindlbauer, D., Haller, M.: A chair as ubiquitous input device: exploring semaphoric chair gestures for focused and peripheral interaction. In: CHI 2014 Proceedings of 32nd International Conference on Human Factors Computing Systems, pp. 4097–4106 (2014)

25. Bakker, S., van den Hoven, E., Eggen, B., Overbeeke, K.: Exploring peripheral interaction design for primary school teachers. In: Proceedings of Sixth International Conference on Tangible, Embed Embodied Interact - TEI 2012 1:245–252 (2012). doi:10.1145/2148131.2148184

26. Bakker, S.: Design for peripheral interaction (2013). doi:10.6100/IR754544
27. Sulaiman, T., Hassan, A., Yi, H.Y.: An analysis of teaching styles in primary and secondary school teachers based on the theory of multiple intelligences. J. Soc. Sci. **7**, 428–435 (2011)
28. Velloso, E., Schmidt, D., Alexander, J., et al.: The feet in human-computer interaction. ACM Comput. Surv. **48**, 1–35 (2015). doi:10.1145/2816455
29. Alexander, J., Han, T., Judd, W., et al.: Putting your best foot forward: investigating real-world mappings for foot-based gestures. In: Proceedings of 30th International Conference on Human factors Computing System (CHI 2012), pp. 1229–1238 (2012)
30. Daiber, F., Schöning, J., Krüger, A.: Whole body interaction with geospatial data. In: Butz, A., Fisher, B., Christie, M., Krüger, A., Olivier, P., Therón, R. (eds.) SG 2009. LNCS, vol. 5531, pp. 81–92. Springer, Heidelberg (2009). doi:10.1007/978-3-642-02115-2_7
31. Probst, K.: Peripheral interaction in desktop computing: why it's worth stepping beyond traditional mouse and keyboard. In: Bakker, S., Hausen, D., Selker, T. (eds.) Peripheral Interaction. HIS, pp. 183–205. Springer, Cham (2016). doi:10.1007/978-3-319-29523-7_9
32. Bakker, S., van den Hoven, E., Eggen, B.: Acting by hand: Informing interaction design for the periphery of people's attention. Interact. Comput. **24**, 119–130 (2012). doi:10.1016/j.intcom.2012.04.001
33. Wickens, C.D.: Multiple resources and performance prediction. Theor. Issues Ergon. Sci. **3**, 159–177 (2002). doi:10.1080/14639220210123806
34. Wood, W., Quinn, J.M., Kashy, D.A.: Habits in everyday life: thought, emotion, and action. J. Pers. Soc. Psychol. **83**, 1281–1297 (2002). doi:10.1037/0022-3514.83.6.1281
35. Chaiken, S., Trope, Y.: Dual-process theories in social psychology. Guilford Press, New York City (1999)
36. Gardner, B., de Bruijn, G.-J., Lally, P.: A systematic review and meta-analysis of applications of the self-report habit index to nutrition and physical activity behaviours. Ann. Behav. Med. **42**, 174–187 (2011). doi:10.1007/s12160-011-9282-0
37. De Bruijn, G.-J., Kremers, S.P.J., De Vet, E., et al.: Does habit strength moderate the intention–behaviour relationship in the theory of planned behaviour? The case of fruit consumption. Psychol. Health **22**, 899–916 (2007). doi:10.1080/14768320601176113
38. Kremers, S.P., de Bruijn, G.-J., Visscher, T.L., et al.: Environmental influences on energy balance-related behaviors: A dual-process view. Int. J. Behav. Nutr. Phys. Act. **3**, 9 (2006). doi:10.1186/1479-5868-3-9
39. Lally, P., van Jaarsveld, C.H.M., Potts, H.W.W., Wardle, J.: How are habits formed: modelling habit formation in the real world. Eur. J. Soc. Psychol. **40**, 998–1009 (2010). doi:10.1002/ejsp.674
40. Bakker, S., van den Hoven, E., Eggen, B.: Peripheral interaction: characteristics and considerations. Pers. Ubiquitous Comput. **19**, 239–254 (2014). doi:10.1007/s00779-014-0775-2
41. Manny-Ikan, E., Dagan, O., Tikochinski, T.B., Zorman, R.: Using the interactive white board in teaching and learning – an evaluation of the SMART CLASSROOM pilot project. Interdiscip. J. E-Learn. Learn. Objects **7**, 249–272 (2011)
42. Bannister, D.: Guidelines for Effective School/Classroom Use of Interactive Whiteboards. Brussels (2010)
43. Jang, S.J., Tsai, M.F.: Reasons for using or not using interactive whiteboards: perspectives of Taiwanese elementary mathematics and science teachers. Australas J. Educ. Technol. **28**, 1451–1465 (2012)
44. Wensveen, S.A.G., Djajadiningrat, J.P., Overbeeke, C.J.: Interaction frogger: a design framework to couple action and function through feedback and feedforward. In: DIS 2004 Proceedings of 5th Conference on Designing Interactive System Processing Practice methods, Techniques, pp. 177–184 (2004)

45. Zijlstra, F.R.: Efficiency in work behaviour: a design approach for modern tools. Delft Univ Press, pp. 1–186 (1993). ISBN 90-6275-918-1
46. Gardner, B., Abraham, C., Lally, P., de Bruijn, G.-J.: Towards parsimony in habit measurement: testing the convergent and predictive validity of an automaticity subscale of the self-report habit index. Int. J. Behav. Nutr. Phys. Act. **9**, 102 (2012). doi:10.1186/1479-5868-9-102
47. Creswell, J.W.: Qualitative Inquiry and Research Design: Choosing Among Five Approaches. Sage Publications, Thousand Oaks (2007)
48. Starks, H., Trinidad, S.B.: Choose your method: a comparison of phenomenology, discourse analysis, and grounded theory. Qual. Health Res. **17**, 1372–1380 (2007). doi:10.1177/1049732307307031
49. Anderson, E.H., Spencer, M.H.: Cognitive representations of AIDS: a phenomenological study. Qual. Health Res. **12**, 1338–1352 (2002). doi:10.1177/1049732302238747
50. Ashbrook, D.L.: Enabling mobile microinteractions. Georgia Institute of Technology (2010)
51. Oulasvirta, A., Tamminen, S., Roto, V., Kuorelahti, J.: Interaction in 4-second bursts. In: Proceedings of SIGCHI Conference on Human factors Computing Systems - CHI 2005, p. 919, ACM Press, New York, USA (2005)

Human-Building Interaction: When the Machine Becomes a Building

Julien Nembrini[✉] and Denis Lalanne

Human-IST Research Center, University of Fribourg, Fribourg, Switzerland
{julien.nembrini,denis.lalanne}@unifr.ch
http://human-ist.unifr.ch

Abstract. Acknowledging the current digitalizing of buildings and their existence as interactive objects, this article sets out to consolidate Human-Building Interaction (HBI) as a new research domain within HCI. It exposes fundamental characteristics of HBI such as user immersion in the "machine" and extensive space and time scales, and proposes an operational definition of the domain. Building upon a comprehensive survey of relevant cross-disciplinary research, HBI is characterized in terms of dimensions representing the interaction space and modalities that can be invoked to enhance interactions. Specific methodological challenges are discussed, and illustrative research projects are presented demonstrating the relevance of the domain. New directions for future research are proposed, pointing out the domain's potentially significant impact on society.

Keywords: Human-Building Interaction · Home automation · Smart home · Interactive architecture · Comfort · Energy efficiency

1   Introduction

In the environment we inhabit, we spend most of the time inside buildings. The way we experience these environments as users can be very different, depending on the nature and purpose of the buildings, on the social context, on the specific environmental conditions they provide, on our emotional state, etc. These multiple influences make buildings a complex and dynamic construct which architecture has to deal with. Since many interaction contexts happen within built space, many HCI research examples are linked to the built environment [24]. This includes research on home (e.g. [22,29]) and work environments (e.g. [34,39]). In these examples, the focus is on describing and analysing interactive artifacts in their context of use, while the built environment which hosts such context appears more as a backdrop than as interactive element in itself. Usually considered as an invariant, the affordances of the built substance may prove to actually have a non-negligible role in these contexts.

Meanwhile, the field of building automation, as understood by building engineers, has begun to install more and more building sensing and automation systems, motivated by the quest for energy efficiency. These systems are designed

R. Bernhaupt et al. (Eds.): INTERACT 2017, Part II, LNCS 10514, pp. 348–369, 2017.
DOI: 10.1007/978-3-319-67684-5_21

through a development centered on automatic control and optimisation of technical installations. Energy consumption standards play a central role, requiring quantitative proof of performance and bypassing the uncertainty and diversity of user behaviour to support automatic solutions [36]. As a result, a series of negative user experiences have become stereotypes of the work environment: automated blinds with a behaviour that seems erratic to the user, extremely controlled environments leading to a feeling of being controlled by the building oneself, sick building syndrome [26], etc. With this automation paradigm now reaching the housing context through energy efficiency requirements, such negative experiences are being broadened to a wider set of users and situations. Recent progress in different sensing and actuation techniques for the built environment (think IoT [29]) and their shrinking prices can be seen as signs of even more profound changes to come.

Indeed, the digitalizing of buildings and their existence as interactive objects does not appear to be a question of the near future, but a fact of the present whose implications need to be studied with methodologies able to fully take into account users and usage. This context represents an opportunity for HCI research to play a role in studying the use of existing or newly proposed digital artifacts in relation to the built structure, and also in fostering interactions with non-digital elements of the building through digital means. As a goal to seek with as little energy consumption as possible, the notion of *comfort* is central to the built environment [26]. It relates to a very specific characteristic of built environment interactive contexts: users are physically *immersed* within the interactive object, bearing the consequences of their interactions in a multi-sensory way, possibly going as far as creating their own lack of comfort.

The present article builds on research contributions from engineering [48] and HCI [4,5] to present and consolidate the concept of *Human-Building Interaction* (HBI). It proposes a common and operational definition through the systematic mapping of the dimensions that are relevant to HBI and the modalities with which these dimensions can be acted upon. Pursuing the aim to establish HBI as a relevant component of HCI research, the article first provides a cartography of the fields that comprise HBI (Sect. 2). Drawing from a large span of cross-disciplinary contributions, the focus is then put on characterizing HBI in terms of dimensions (Sect. 3) and interaction modalities (Sect. 4). The methodological challenges raised are then discussed (Sect. 5) and some examples of research are presented (Sect. 6). Finally, new directions for future research are proposed (Sect. 7).

2   A Definition of HBI

To define HBI in general is a difficult task, and its interdisciplinary nature has resulted in the lack of a single clear definition. As a contribution to the consolidation of the field, we propose to construct a definition in several steps. First, we will develop the immersive specificity of HBI mentioned in the introduction. Second, we will draw an outline of HBI through a cartography of the fields that compose it. In a third step we will enumerate the different dimensions that can be involved when considering a user in interaction with a building. In the final step, the modalities that can be used to affect these dimensions will be described. Together, these steps represent an operational definition of HBI: by evaluating whether a particular dimension is impacted by the use of a specific modality allows the assessment of whether a particular interaction context is part of our definition of HBI.

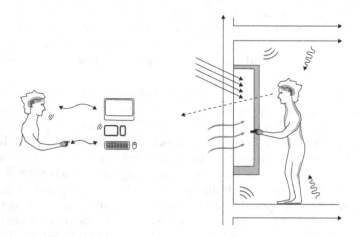

Fig. 1. Standard HCI (left) compared to Human-Building Interaction specificity (right). Interaction feedback uses potentially multiple sensory channels: tactile, acoustic, visual, radiative, convective or olfactory

2.1   Specificity of HBI

With regard to a more standard conception of HCI in which a user interacts with a machine through well-defined and circumscribed modalities, HBI considers users as completely immersed in an interactive object. The building contains its users and influences their experience through multiple channels (e.g. heat radiation, light or sound reflections, air movement, etc. see Fig. 1). An important consequence is that the user cannot terminate the interactive session without leaving the space. Conversely, users' actions may have a more important impact given this immersion, possibly leading to physiological changes in the user, sometimes to the point of making the interactive space inhospitable.

In addition to this immersive aspect, due to the building's physical behaviour, users' actions may have repercussions on very different time scales. Opening a window in the middle of a summer afternoon may have the immediate effect of inducing fresh air convection, but also lets heat enter, which can have consequences on comfort in the days to come. Space is also present at different scales: the comfort sensation can be influenced by minute air movement around the body, as well as by the radiative heat produced by a far away sun.

In the semantic field of HCI, such an interactive context could be seen as an ambient interface pushed to the extreme [59], or more precisely to the conjunction of the extremes of an ambient and a tangible interface. The field of *ambient intelligence* (AmI) presents an overlap with the HBI approach by linking sensing, reasoning, action, HCI and privacy to achieve intelligent environments and thus shares this immersive component [8,18]. Aarts and de Ruyter [1] present a particularly interesting discussion sharing many aspects developed in the present article, which however reveals that AmI emphasis lies on digital means to solve tasks and mainly considers interaction with digital artifacts, considering the building structure as a backdrop. For example, Thomas and Cook [64] consider energy efficiency of smart buildings as a task of intelligent turning off of unused appliances, without tackling the comfort question. In contrast, HBI's primary concern is to consider the built structure as an interactive element whose inclusion is essential to grasp the full complexity of interactions. As a result, the discussion here reflects this change of perspective.

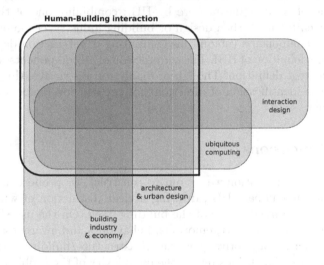

Fig. 2. Cartography of the HBI-relevant research fields

2.2   HBI Field Cartography

The first step of our definition is to propose a mapping of the fields composing HBI, that is able to provide a means to attribute to or exclude existing research work from HBI (see Fig. 2). In this process, four fields are identified as components. The component that appears most relevant is the one of architecture and urban design. This component can be understood as an existing or future physical object, but also as a design process. It encompasses complex multidisciplinary issues related to the definition of the built environment and entails by nature strong cultural differences. In the present paper, we will not consider the urban scale and concentrate only on the scale of buildings.

The building industry and the economy within which it develops constitute the second component. It includes building material availability, and the different processes inherent to the production of buildings, such as norms and laws. This component is strongly influenced by regional differences. By being the context that ultimately adopts a candidate innovative solution, in our opinion this component plays a central role in defining relevant research axes.

The third component represents the technological availability—at an affordable price—of sensors, screens, actuators, algorithms, etc., as well as the recent proliferation of connected personal artifacts. This dimension is encompassed in the concept of ubiquitous computing, and the current developments of IoT and AmI are part of it. This component is less impacted by regional differences, except for differences to privacy laws and technology/Internet access or adoption.

The final component represents the HCI contribution. It encompasses interface design, development and evaluation, but also the study of users' behaviour with existing interactive architectural elements.

Once these components are defined, it becomes possible to propose a more precise outline of what is meant here by HBI: combining one of the first two dimensions (architecture/urban design or building industry/economy) with one of the last two components (ubiquitous computing or interaction design) would result in a large definition of HBI. The conjunction of all components would result in a more stringent definition. Though probably too restrictive, this last definition enables the identification of directions for project development to broaden research impact.

3   HBI Dimensions

Contributing to the definition we set out to construct, we propose a mapping of the dimensions that impact HBI, drawing a clear distinction of whether these affect users or the infrastructure of the building itself. On the users' side, these dimensions encompass comfort, emotions, behaviours and awareness; and quality, usability, efficiency and privacy on the infrastructure/building side. Interrelations between these dimensions reflect the complexity of the problem considered (see Fig. 3, right).

In a research article close to the present argument, Rodden and Benford [59] use as basis the "Site, Structure, Skin, Services, Space plan, Stuff" decomposition by Brand [12] to develop an HCI approach to buildings. Supporting our argument on the immersive aspect of HBI, they acknowledge that "Site", "Structure" and "Skin" receive less attention in HCI research than the remaining dimensions. However, we believe that in following Brand [12], their approach has too strong an architectural edge. Instead, we propose to keep the same emphasis on the built structure while considering a user-oriented approach to grasp the whole depth of human-building interactions.

Comfort. Taking its origin in the 19th century hygienist movement for building salubrity, the notion of comfort is ubiquitous in the building context and is

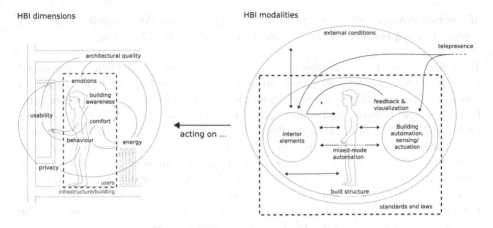

Fig. 3. Proposed HBI dimensions and some of their interrelations (left), and HBI modalities acting on these dimensions (right)

related to its immersive specificity: as main purpose of a dwelling, comfort is a space quality to be guaranteed. We draw here a distinction between comfort measured at the building environment scale and at the individual scale. Typically, the time scales differ and are larger when measuring at the building scale. Many studies have looked at factors influencing user comfort in buildings; see [30,56] for reviews on the subject. Perceived comfort, which is the translation in the users' mind of a body's response into a perceived comfort sensation, can be culturally and psychologically influenced [26,42]. For this reason, we categorize this part as a users' emotions.

At the building scale, the Fanger model [28], widely used in the building industry, allows to compute the Predicted Percentage of Discontent (PPD) as a function of objective variables such as temperature, humidity, etc. but also user clothing and activity. Aimed more at fully controlled environments, this model has been completed by the adaptive model that takes into account the fact that buildings may be naturally ventilated [17]. For comfort at an individual scale, measurements consist of skin temperature, conductivity, or eye movement to capture the actual response of the users' body to the environmental conditions [38]. Such responses present large individual differences and have been shown to be gender-dependant [42]. Ranjan and Scott [58] propose to use thermal imaging to infer thermal comfort while Knecht et al. [44] investigate the use of wearables for thermal comfort.

While it must be evident to the HCI community that perceived comfort is the one that matters, it is comfort measured at the environment scale that is used during the architectural design process. This measure is efficient for bringing the project forward without having to care about the users' variability, unknown at the design time, and which is typically prone to change during the building lifetime. Consequently, this model is applied during all design phases, in very diverse cultural and climatic contexts, which contributes to a global standardization of interior environments and technology requirements. As a result, many HCI research examples rely on the Fanger model, including [17, 39, 66].

User Emotions. By users' emotions we mean emotions and feelings generated by or in interaction with the built environment. Beyond comfort perception as already stated, there are numerous examples, starting from the happiness or calm felt by a view towards a specific landscape (thus representing interaction with "Site" [12]), to the annoyance created by the arbitrary and alienating behaviour of automatically controlled blinds. Other examples are more subtle, or even subject to discussion, such as boredom or disenchantment generated by low quality architecture. This emotional aspect plays an important role in the users' perception of their environment [7]. A building presenting a special architecture can become an iconic reference that contributes to identification and pride to be one of its users (see the work of the studio Lacaton-Vassal as an example [62]).

User Behaviour. By behaviour, we mean here the practices consisting in interacting with the different building elements. These behaviours are often part of a culture and function symbiotically with the architecture; for example, closing the windows during the hot part of the day in conjunction with high ceilings and the practice of a siesta in Mediterranean countries. This dimension is fundamental to the building's function and durability, as improper practices may rapidly degrade it, waste energy, raise security issues or lower comfort. From an engineering perspective, Haldi and Robinson [32] and Langevin et al. [48] present studies of occupants' interaction with windows or building elements, while Crabtree and Tolmie [23], following an ethnographic approach, thoroughly document interactions with "things" within a day in a domestic environment.

The recent evolution of comfort conventions in the occidental world (uniformly heated space, mechanical air renewal, electric lighting, etc.) in parallel with energy and economic efficiency needs have led to increased automation in the building context, ranging from thermostatic valves to sensor-activated lighting. However, it has been shown that the impossibility to act upon one's environment in order to adapt one's comfort induces an increased intolerance to non-standard comfort conditions [33, 41, 56]. The very fact of giving the possibility to interact thus has important implications in terms of perceived comfort. Social dynamics may significantly influence individual perception [66], while the building itself may have an important influence on the relations between users (e.g. through a bad acoustic in a meeting). Following Rodden and Benford [59], HBI should also consider as users the different stakeholders of the building context: users, designers, landlords, engineers, building facility managers, etc.

Building Behaviour Awareness. Through the conjunction of multiple time scales, the influence of external conditions, user presence or not, as well as the physical behaviour of its elements, building behaviour is dynamic and complex. Most interactions actually happen to counter-act or influence building fluctuations, for instance due to changing weather conditions (e.g. lowering blinds, opening windows, turning on lights). To have adequate practices requires a given awareness of such behaviour [25].

This awareness can be acquired by cultural transmission, by experience, or through direct experimentation with the building. In this sense, building automation can induce different biases: the automation concept may not be adapted to the cultural context (for instance the habit of leaving a window open during winter nights in a high performance building equipped with heat recovery HVAC), may induce the user to acquire experience with the automation itself which tends to rapidly become obsolete, or presents irregular (irrational) behaviour in the eyes of the experimenting user.

Architectural Quality. If architectural quality is especially difficult to define, and strongly depends on its function and cultural aspect, an argument is nevertheless commonly accepted: a building presents a certain quality if stakeholders in society invest funds to preserve it, be it for socio-economical or cultural reasons. Even if the reasons to renovate or demolish a building tend to change, this corresponds to a sustainability objective [62]. Indeed, buildings that last are those that are able to adapt to evolutions in functions and use [12]. Optimization of building functions, such as energy optimization, is actually going against such adaptability by tightening the range of possible building behaviour. HBI should thus support the production of quality architecture, for instance by providing measures of space use in different conditions or by augmenting existing buildings with digital artifacts to make them more adaptable.

Building Usability. The design of the building and of the elements modifying its dynamics may by their affordances induce specific behaviours, both positive or problematic. Through their non-definitive and manual aspect, they can induce an interactive behaviour, possibly even fostering experimentation. For example, in the housing buildings by the studio Lacaton-Vassal, thermal comfort in some part of the apartments requires the manipulation of insulating curtains [62]. Inhabitants must therefore actively interact in order to benefit from the space, and typically need an adaptation period after moving in to understand its functioning. This exemplifies an approach where users are asked to take responsibility in a mixed-mode approach (see Sect. 4).

Energy Efficiency. To preserve comfort in the building context, energy is used to heat, cool, lighten or ventilate, in order to preserve interior space from climatic fluctuations or evacuate pollutants emitted by interior activities. The building stock has been identified as presenting the most important energy saving potential through retrofitted of highly efficient new buildings [50]. In order to activate this potential, more and more stringent efficiency constraints are being enforced, while maintaining high comfort levels [68]. In order to achieve quantifiable results, this process often encourages building automation: if the SmartHome concept has yet to demonstrate wide adoption [15], energy efficient buildings have integrated a level of automation that makes the dimension of energy particularly relevant in terms of interaction [52].

In parallel, the same energy resource context has generated a large body of work on "behaviour change": inducing users to change their behaviour with the aim of lowering their energy consumption. Abrahamse et al. [2] presents a review of interventions aimed at energy conservation, while Pierce and Paulos [57] review and discuss how such intervention acquire meaning for HCI by involving digital artifacts. More recent examples include [3,10,58,70], among others. Intertwined with comfort and related to the immersive context, the dimension of energy efficiency is of primary importance for HBI.

Private Sphere. One of the functions of a building and its interior design is to articulate a physical boundary between public and private. New technologies with their multiple sensing devices and wireless approaches tend to blur this physicality, both from the point of view of information leakage and of limit perception from the user: a wall is more tangible as a limit than a firewall software [31]. It is important to address these questions of perception and the corresponding mental models in order to understand the articulation between physical and digital limits as they are felt by the user [16,40]; even more since data mining techniques are becoming able to infer users' behaviours [6,19].

4   HBI Modalities

Once the dimension set spanning the HBI space is defined, the different levers or techniques able to influence these dimensions can be discussed. We set out this task by presenting a schematic representation (see Fig. 3, right) and developing each element. Here, instead of using the architecturally-centered framework of Brand [12], as used in [59], which for instance differentiates "Skin" and "Structure", we propose a decomposition centered on change from the user perspective.

External Conditions. Outdoor conditions are important to users inside through the relationship between the outdoor (diurnal/seasonal) and indoor timescales. Comfort perception is influenced by outside conditions [26], while transitions between the outdoor and indoor environment can lead to temporary perceptions of discomfort [38]. Daylight access, but also view access, has an influence on perceived comfort and user health [56]. With lowered heating energy consumption, lowering lighting energy through daylighting strategies has become more important. Gaver et al. [31] present a research study of the implications of digital mediation of outside conditions towards inside users.

Built Structure. Volume, access, openings, circulations, etc. are essential elements channelling user experience, inducing a reaction or its absence [24]. This modality represents all permanent elements typically not open to short term changes from the user and thus represents the immersive constraint. If, for this reason, the elements may appear as static, the building's dynamic physical behaviour (mechanical, visual, thermal and acoustic) has an important impact on user perception and comfort. Users' actions may influence and exploit this behaviour, depending on their awareness of it.

This cooperation between user and structure has a long tradition in the built environment, going back to vernacular architecture, and is strongly related to social and technological settings. For instance, occidental comfort requirements, but also organisation of work, are translated into the structure in the form of insulation, ventilation systems and window sizes, for instance. To start considering the user in relation to this permanent structure and how the digital component relates to this structure is a new area of research for HCI. In studying energy aware behaviour, Chetty et al. [16] elicited the important role of the built infrastructure or site location in user behaviour.

Interior Elements. By interior elements is meant here all elements that are in reach of interior user manipulation to influence the user's immersive context. On top of contributing to space perception, each of these elements presents its own affordances, which translate into use patterns [23], which in turn influence user experience on several scales and dimensions. For instance, a window with several aperture modes will influence air renewal modes and strategies, the relation with the outside, or the building's thermal behaviour. HCI may be involved in studying the existing digital component of these interior elements or adding one to it, but also in influencing interactions with non-digital elements through digital means.

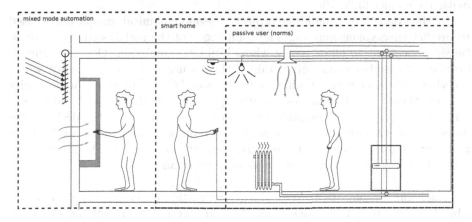

Fig. 4. Illustration of the underlying user model, in the actual normative framework (right), in the mart home concept (middle) and in the proposed mixed mode automation (left).

Building Automation, Sensing/Actuation. To avoid potential discomfort within the immersive context, elements of building control are often essential to contemporary buildings to maintain comfort conditions, for instance in terms of heating/cooling, lighting or air renewal. Control is achieved through the help of sensors and actuators able to take into account user behaviour, possibly only indirectly. However, due to the difficulty to take users' behaviour variability into account in building system automation [55], building system concepts and user models steering their reactivity are mainly based on a passive user [36], often confining them to the role of preference definition, as some examples related to the SmartHome concept [52]. If HCI involvement in the context of interfaces for automation systems seems evident and necessary [10,39,66], progresses in terms of sensors, automation and data analysis, in conjunction with a user-centered approach, could contribute to define a larger interaction space [11].

User Participation, Mixed-Mode Automation. The notion of active adaptive users, responsible both for their comfort and for their energy-related impact is more and more taken into account by building industry professionals [41,56], held back though by current conservative norms. Research from the building industry has studied building users' behaviour extensively [36,48,67]. However, the main driver in this research has been to reduce uncertainties in models and system control. The impact on perceived comfort, as well as the necessity to improve system robustness, are arguments for a mixed mode approach [37] combining an automatized part while leaving large autonomy to the user—ideally playful and engaging—thereby calling for HCI involvement (see Fig. 4), which corresponds to findings in [46]. In the mixed-mode context, the use of machine learning techniques to infer user preferences has shown limited success [69], while user suggestions may achieve better performance as well as acceptance than automatic techniques [3,20,70].

In the context of a building project, thermodynamical simulation is used to predict energy consumption. The complexity of the real system forces drastic simplifications to allow yearly whole building simulation. One such simplifications is user behaviour, often taking the form of occupancy density, which together with space programming, define heat and CO_2 production or electricity consumption. It is in this case essentially a passive user who defines building performance forecasts. This simplification towards passiveness at the design stage induces a bias towards automatic solutions. The behaviour difference between real users and their simplified simulated counterparts ironically translates then into differences between real and predited performance [27].

Feedback and Visualization. With the generalization of sensing it becomes possible for users to get feedback from their interaction with building elements. Here different time scales are relevant, from direct feedback needed to confirm an action to presenting data recorded over time [66]: by analysing building data it becomes possible to offer users a mirror of their behaviour, through ambient or collective visualizations, to trigger awareness or even behaviour change. There is already work from HCI along this line related to buildings, examples include [21,60]. Schwartz et al. [63] present a critical investigation into user perception of energy feedback. Such visualizations, together with data analysis methods, may also prove useful for other stakeholders such as expert engineers or building facility managers [13,49,53].

Telepresence. New communication and working modes induce a reconsideration of space perception, whose interaction questions have been addressed by the field of HCI [54]. However, implications in terms of space redefinition, for instance for teleworking, raise questions related to the modalities mentioned earlier, e.g. the mediation of external conditions or interior elements/use [31], but possibly reaching as far as modifying the built structure. Through its ability to transcend the limits of distance and material boundaries drawn by structure, telepresence naturally extends to implications in terms of private sphere.

Standards and Laws. Standards and laws, harmonized at the European level, are extremely present in the built environment context. Some represent what users expect in terms of comfort and energy performance, while others formulate user presence and behaviour models that serve as a base to forecast energy consumption, as well as dimensioning and control of building systems. In a study about user perception of energy consumption, Chetty et al. [16] emphasize: "infrastructure not just as a set of technical arrangements that provision the smart green home, but also as a set of commercial, legal, and governmental arrangements". Since demonstrating standard compliance is easier through automated systems, the involvement of the HCI community could allow the evolution of such standard user models towards more realistic—and more active—personas [56].

5 HBI Methodologies

Through its immersive and multimodal aspects involving processes over large spatial and time scales, the HBI context is a typical one in which isolating variables is highly difficult. Fundamental methodological questions thus arise to address this context from the HCI point of view, such as drawing the limits of the system under study or repeating conditions with multiple users to achieve significance. However, we are convinced that HCI methods are particularly adapted to help design and evaluate user-centered buildings. In light of the proposed HBI modalities, some remarks are in our opinion relevant in the evaluation of interactive built environments.

New Comfort, Energy and Usability Metrics. The building automation modality with its general aim to optimize comfort with energy consumption relies on very specific metrics. For comfort, standards define several metrics such as the maximal number of overheating hours to the Percentage of Predicted Discontent (PPD) [28]. These metrics originate from very specific conditions, the climatic chambers, implying mostly user passiveness, and thus inducing a bias towards controlled environments [26]. Moreover, the PPD metrics (and their corresponding Predicted Mean Vote PMV) presuppose the precise determination of several variables such as clothing levels or metabolic rate which are often difficult to evaluate [38]. Additionally, it is now accepted that this set of metrics does not always faithfully reflect the comfort as perceived by the users themselves, as examples have shown that this perception may be modified by user action possibilities [26]. Such metrics would not be suitable for instance to prove the usefullness of a mixed-mode approach. The PMV/PPD metrics consequently need to be decomposed into measurable quantities and user appreciation to discriminate the contribution of each component and their interrelation.

Although energy metrics are less subjective, there are many different strategies to allow comparison of different energy sources, for instance using CO_2 production equivalence or primary energy use, depending on the focus of the quantification. The different energetic consumption metrics are important to test interfaces aimed at fostering behaviour change. However, being aggregates, these metrics are difficult to convey to lay users [14,43]. Moreover, Chetty et al. [16] pointed out that users have difficulties understanding energy units, such as the difference between energy (in kWh) and power (in kW), and would prefer units of cost; whereas this preferred unit may become less meaningful in the future in light of the electricity market liberalisation [3].

The above methodological difficulties are related to the prevalence of standards and laws in the built environment context. In order to make sense of building users' behaviour, HBI methods need to take this modality into consideration, with the aim to untangle the influence of what had to be constructed/installed for compliance. This in particular calls for interdisciplinary approaches.

Human-Building Interaction Metrics. Research effort should strive towards developing a measure of the usability of a given space, whether as a consequence of its built structure, or at the level of interior elements. The ability to capture and quantify the different ways of interacting with the elements of space, whether digital or not, has the potential to inform building design. In this respect, the difference in methodologies between HCI [23] and building physics [32] is substantial.

In the scope of evaluating building digital interfaces, standard HCI acquisition methods such as logging interactions or occulometry are directly applicable. On the other hand, if building physical dynamics influence the interactive process, measurement tools need to acquire the relevant physical dimensions, such as temperature, humidity, etc. The HBI immersive specificity implies more important setups and possibly larger time scales. As an example, if occulometric measurements normally happen in the constrained environment of a display screen, physiological visual comfort acquisition in space should be able to measure eye movement in the larger context of a room, and measure a longer time sequence to capture modifications linked to sunlight exposure changes [7].

The acquisition of user interaction with the building may benefit from sensors available through the building infrastructure [32]. However, given that sensors are primarily installed for system control reasons, it is often difficult to infer user behaviour from this data [65]. A method to acquire interactions spanning from users' movement in space to the manipulation of building elements needs to be formalized and tested; the same being true for a method to acquire the different components of comfort [38]. A longitudinal survey bridging both topics can be found in [48].

Evaluation Methods. Similarly to HCI, interactive HBI elements can be evaluated in controlled environments or directly in "in the wild" situations. In the case of controlled environments, techniques consisting in comparing within or between groups while treating independent variables are applicable. However, to address the HBI immersive specificity, the physical dimension should be taken into account, requiring an important infrastructure that allows to repeat conditions (e.g. thermal conditions), even possibly conduct experiments in parallel in the case where external conditions play a role (e.g. sunlight). For "in the wild" experiments, ethnographic or sociological qualitative techniques are used, consisting in observing and annotating videos, or conducting, transcribing and coding interviews, such as in [3,16,63], among others. These methods suffer from the limited time scale that can be covered. The analysis of sensor data through data mining techniques represents a new evaluation source with longer time scales and potentially high relevance [19,65], but whose true potential remains to be discovered.

6   HBI Examples

We present here a subset of our research projects to illustrate how the modalities proposed for HBI could translate in actual research effort. These projects are developed within the smartlivinglab structure, which represents the collaboration between three Swiss academic institutions [47]. The smartlivinglab is a research program dedicated to the future of the built environment from the technical and societal perspectives. Its aim is to imagine living spaces of the future, focusing on inhabitants' well-being and environmental concerns. In this context, the research center Human-IST (Human Centered Interaction Science and Technology) is responsible for developing and evaluating technologies able to enhance human-building interactions.

Measured and Perceived Comfort. The gap between perceived comfort and environmental comfort is a fundamental incentive for mixed-mode automation. One research project uses sensors together with interactive techniques to tackle this subject. By proposing a personal emphatic object reflecting comfort conditions in the near environment—a sort of comfort companion—this project aims first at acquiring and understanding user comfort data, and second at directly reflecting comfort conditions to the user, thus also addressing the feedback/visualization modality. Usability studies in this case allow to characterize the dynamics induced by feeding back such information on user behaviour and his felt comfort. Implications in terms of architectural design remain speculative, but it is foreseeable that results from the project may inform the design process of sustainable buildings. Reaching this state would situate the project in the strong definition of HBI as proposed in Sect. 2.2.

In a parallel project using the experience sampling method [35], a mobile application is used to acquire comfort as felt by the user (thermal, acoustic and visual comfort) through simple questionnaires (see Fig. 5), in order to compare this information with measured data from sensors available on the mobile platform [45]. Compared to the previous project, this approach has the advantage of easily scaling up, for instance to gather user perception in a public building, and may use building automation data for feedback. Similar research examples also use the experience sampling approach [38], some with the aim to close the loop by adjusting HVAC services to comfort results [39,66].

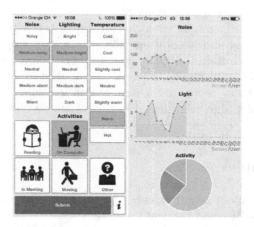

Fig. 5. Through simple user questionnaires following the experience sampling approach, users' comfort perception is compared with smartphone sensor data.

User Behaviour Analytics. As initial steps addressing the methodological challenge of understanding user interactions with and within space, two different contexts are considered. First, a networking event is digitally augmented through participants' location tracking in order to induce more targeted interactions. Through fixed RFID readers detecting users' RFID tags, passive indoor location within zones is possible [61], recording only participants' presence within detection range. Real time visualizations inform participants of others' interests, while allowing to locate them (see Fig. 6). The system has been able to track up to a hundred participants in real events.

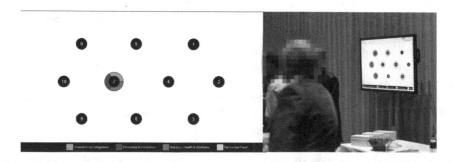

Fig. 6. Live visualizations of tracking to support networking during social events.

Second, the smartlivinglab premises are studied as a day-to-day research office context. Bluetooth beacons on users' wrists track occupants in the building to know how they behave in space [65]. The granularity of the tracking is macroscopic since the technology only allows to detect in which room a specific user is at a given time. The aim is deliberately to extract patterns from data traces to understand who are the occupants and their needs, and to assess the space in terms of occupancy, in order to inform the design process and build better work places, which corresponds to the strong definition of HBI. Further research is needed to refine the granularity of the tracking towards capturing more minute interactions and enlarging the context towards true "in the wild" studies.

Building Data Visualizations. For automation purposes, buildings produce great amounts of data which represent their dynamic non-linear behaviour. In addition to the obvious building automation modality, the exploitation of such data has the potential to nurture research on modalities as different as the external conditions, the built structure, or user implication. Visualizations representing such data can be targeted towards user feedback, but may also represent value for experts trying to guarantee comfort levels and/or optimize energy consumption, who are in need of efficient tools to explore such datasets [49].

As an example, a user study involved experts using interactive visualizations to explore real building data that they did not previously know. Within a limited time span (up to 20 min), they were able to spot various behaviours specific to the building which were not possible to infer from raw data, such as spotting malfunction and identifying non-trivial relations between measured variables [9] (see Fig. 7). A similar example addresses energy portfolio analysis [13]. In these cases, the conjunction of interactive technologies in a building design or industry context qualifies for the strong definition of HBI.

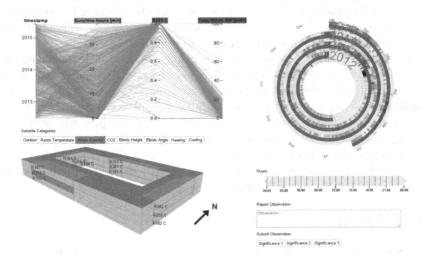

Fig. 7. Interactive visualization of building data

7   Discussion

From the exposition of the dimensions and modalities of the field of HBI, together with the presentation of numerous research works and example projects, some considerations emerge that in our view should contribute to establishing stronger foundations for this approach:

Unification. The survey presented here encompasses several research fields from HCI, ubiquitous computing, applied psychology, HVAC engineering, building physics, etc. What has appeared is that such different fields do not share the same methodologies, and despite the great quality of the work referenced here, some research projects that are sound in one field may present obvious flaws in another, and vice-versa. So it is clear that some exchange, confrontation and unification in the methodologies is needed to bootstrap a process of cross-fertilization among disciplines. To a certain extent, the formulation of the field itself and the possibility for research projects to claim to be part of HBI is an initial step [5].

Consolidation. As a corollary of the previous topic, research in the field of HBI needs to be consolidated. New metrics and methodologies need to be defined and tested, that specifically apply to the challenges found in building settings. Interdisciplinary projects need to be formulated and conducted with success. Funding agencies need to be convinced to appreciate the different quality of this field, also with regard to high infrastructure costs.

Recognition. In the field of building engineering, the mindset "You can come with your interface when the technical job is done" is still very entrenched and the sector is, for liability reasons, very conservative. The need for HCI often appears either superfluous or straightforward to many stakeholders. Establishing the field of HBI requires an effort to convince these stakeholders that it is able to contribute significantly to current problems involving users, as faced in the building industry. The two previous considerations will contribute to increase recognition, but because of conservatism, researchers should take an active role in disseminating their results to practice.

Further Work. From the mapping of dimensions and modalities, some research topics have appeared very popular, such as energy-related behaviour change, while others suffer from an apparent lack of interest. For instance, the relationship between private sphere and buildings is not very articulated, even in the advent of IoT. While user comfort and trust in the presence of dynamic intelligent automation, as well as setting the right limit for user involvement in contrast to automation are topics that see burgeoning interest. Related to this question, the notion of designing for user involvement in the dynamic behaviour of buildings is still largely uncovered.

8   Conclusion

The present articles presents a series of arguments to consider Human-Building Interaction as a promising research topic in need of appropriation and consolidation by the HCI community. This domain aims at studying human interactions with and within buildings, as well as the development and evaluation of interactive technologies to encourage user-building interactions. The fundamental characteristics of this context, namely user immersion in the "machine" and extensive space and time scales, are believed to be more than anecdotal and represent a challenge for HCI which justifies an appropriate and specific methodology.

Through the proposition of a taxonomy of HBI dimensions, an enumeration of the different modalities to influence users in this context, blended with a comprehensive survey of cross-disciplinary research addressing the topic, the paper raises research themes relevant for the HCI community. These include energy efficiency, comfort and user awareness of building dynamics improvements.

Although striving for an exhaustive and systematic approach, it is probable that our contribution overlooked some dimensions or research efforts. We thus rely on the HCI community to contribute to this initial proposal. We believe that exposing the concept of HBI not only allows to raise the interest of HCI community members in the specifics of such a context, but also allows to influence building engineering fields with a new approach and its corresponding methods.

As a conclusion, a fundamental transition in the way we interact with buildings is probable; and probably towards styles of interactions that are central research themes of the HCI community. To let users and society as a whole profit from it, it is important from this research community to assert its expertise for proposing human-centered—instead of technology-centered—solutions.

Acknowledgements. The authors would like to thank Agnes Lisowska for her suggestions and English language corrections, as well as the anonymous reviewers for their constructive comments.

References

1. Aarts, E., de Ruyter, B.: New research perspectives on ambient intelligence. J. Ambient Intell. Smart Environ. **1**(1), 5–14 (2009)
2. Abrahamse, W., Steg, L., Vlek, C., Rothengatter, T.: A review of intervention studies aimed at household energy conservation. J. Environ. Psychol. **25**(3), 273–291 (2005)
3. Alan, A.T., Shann, M., Costanza, E., Ramchurn, S.D., Seuken, S.: It is too hot: an in-situ study of three designs for heating. In: Proceedings of the 2016 CHI Conference on Human Factors in Computing Systems, CHI 2016, pp. 5262–5273. ACM, New York (2016)
4. Alavi, H.S., Churchill, E., Kirk, D., Nembrini, J., Lalanne, D.: Deconstructing human-building interaction. Interactions **23**(6), 60–62 (2016)
5. Alavi, H.S., Lalanne, D., Nembrini, J., Churchill, E., Kirk, D., Moncur, W.: Future of human-building interaction. In: Proceedings of the 2016 CHI Conference Extended Abstracts on Human Factors in Computing Systems, CHI EA 2016, pp. 3408–3414. ACM, New York (2016)
6. Alcalá, J., Parson, O., Rogers, A.: Detecting anomalies in activities of daily living of elderly residents via energy disaggregation and cox processes. In: Proceedings of the 2nd ACM International Conference on Embedded Systems for Energy-Efficient Built Environments, BuildSys 2015, pp. 225–234. ACM, New York (2015)

7. Andersen, M.: Unweaving the human response in daylighting design. Build. Environ. **91**, 101–117 (2015)
8. Augusto, J.C., Callaghan, V., Cook, D., Kameas, A., Satoh, I.: Intelligent environments: a manifesto. Hum.-Centric Comput. Inf. Sci. **3**(1), 12 (2013)
9. Baeriswyl, R.: Visualization of multivariate building data by spatiotemporal building models. Technical report, Human-IST research Centre, University of Fribourg, Fribourg, Switzerland (2015)
10. Balaji, B., Koh, J., Weibel, N., Agarwal, Y.: Genie: a longitudinal study comparing physical and software thermostats in office buildings. In: Proceedings of the 2016 ACM International Joint Conference on Pervasive and Ubiquitous Computing, UbiComp 2016, pp. 1200–1211, ACM, New York (2016)
11. Bier, H.: Robotic building(s). Next Gener. Build. **1**(1), 83–92 (2014)
12. Brand, S.: How Buildings Learn: What Happens After They're Built. Viking, New York (1994)
13. Brehmer, M., Ng, J., Tate, K., Munzner, T.: Matches, mismatches, and methods: multiple-view workflows for energy portfolio analysis. IEEE Trans. Vis. Comput. Graph. **22**(1), 449–458 (2016)
14. Brewer, R.S., Verdezoto, N., Rasmussen, M.K., Entwistle, J.M., Grønbæk, K., Blunck, H., Holst, T.: Challenge: getting residential users to shift their electricity usage patterns. In: Proceedings of the 2015 ACM Sixth International Conference on Future Energy Systems, e-Energy 2015, pp. 83–88. ACM, New York (2015)
15. Brush, A.B., Lee, B., Mahajan, R., Agarwal, S., Saroiu, S., Dixon, C.: Home automation in the wild: challenges and opportunities. In: Proceedings of the SIGCHI Conference on Human Factors in Computing Systems, CHI 2011, pp. 2115–2124. ACM, New York (2011)
16. Chetty, M., Tran, D., Grinter, R.E.: Getting to green: understanding resource consumption in the home. In: Proceedings of the 10th International Conference on Ubiquitous Computing, UbiComp 2008. pp. 242–251. ACM, New York (2008)
17. Clear, A.K., Morley, J., Hazas, M., Friday, A., Bates, O.: Understanding adaptive thermal comfort: new directions for UbiComp. In: Proceedings of the 2013 ACM International Joint Conference on Pervasive and Ubiquitous Computing, UbiComp 2013, pp. 113–122. ACM, New York (2013)
18. Cook, D.J., Augusto, J.C., Jakkula, V.R.: Ambient intelligence: technologies, applications, and opportunities. Pervasive Mob. Comput. **5**(4), 277–298 (2009)
19. Cook, D.J., Krishnan, N.: Mining the home environment. J. Intell. Inf. Syst. **43**(3), 503–519 (2014)
20. Costanza, E., Fischer, J.E., Colley, J.A., Rodden, T., Ramchurn, S.D., Jennings, N.R.: Doing the laundry with agents: a field trial of a future smart energy system in the home. In: Proceedings of the SIGCHI Conference on Human Factors in Computing Systems, CHI 2014, pp. 813–822. ACM, New York (2014)
21. Costanza, E., Ramchurn, S.D., Jennings, N.R.: Understanding domestic energy consumption through interactive visualisation: a field study. In: Proceedings of the 2012 ACM Conference on Ubiquitous Computing, UbiComp 2012, pp. 216–225. ACM, New York (2012)
22. Coughlan, T., Brown, M., Martindale, S., Comber, R., Ploetz, T., Leder Mackley, K., Mitchell, V., Baurley, S.: Methods for studying technology in the home. In: CHI 2013 Extended Abstracts on Human Factors in Computing Systems, CHI EA 2013, pp. 3207–3210. ACM, New York (2013)
23. Crabtree, A., Tolmie, P.: A day in the life of things in the home, pp. 1736–1748. ACM Press (2016)

24. Dalton, N., Green, K.E., Dalton, R., Wiberg, M., Hoelscher, C., Mathew, A., Schnädelbach, H., Varoudis, T.: Interaction and architectural space. In: CHI 2014 Extended Abstracts on Human Factors in Computing Systems, CHI EA 2014, pp. 29–32. ACM, New York (2014)
25. Day, J.K., Gunderson, D.E.: Understanding high performance buildings: the link between occupant knowledge of passive design systems, corresponding behaviors, occupant comfort and environmental satisfaction. Build. Environ. **84**, 114–124 (2015)
26. de Dear, R.J., Akimoto, T., Arens, E.A., Brager, G., Candido, C., Cheong, K.W.D., Li, B., Nishihara, N., Sekhar, S.C., Tanabe, S., Toftum, J., Zhang, H., Zhu, Y.: Progress in thermal comfort research over the last twenty years. Indoor Air **23**(6), 442–461 (2013)
27. de Wilde, P.: The gap between predicted and measured energy performance of buildings: a framework for investigation. Autom. Constr. **41**, 40–49 (2014)
28. Fanger, P.O., et al.: Thermal Comfort. Analysis and Applications in Environmental Engineering (1970)
29. Fischer, J.E., Crabtree, A., Rodden, T., Colley, J.A., Costanza, E., Jewell, M.O., Ramchurn, S.D.: "Just whack it on until it gets hot": working with IoT data in the home. In: Proceedings of the 2016 CHI Conference on Human Factors in Computing Systems, CHI 2016, pp. 5933–5944. ACM, New York (2016)
30. Frontczak, M., Wargocki, P.: Literature survey on how different factors influence human comfort in indoor environments. Build. Environ. **46**(4), 922–937 (2011)
31. Gaver, W., Boucher, A., Law, A., Pennington, S., Bowers, J., Beaver, J., Humble, J., Kerridge, T., Villar, N., Wilkie, A.: Threshold devices: looking out from the home. In: Proceedings of the SIGCHI Conference on Human Factors in Computing Systems, CHI 2008, pp. 1429–1438. ACM, New York (2008)
32. Haldi, F., Robinson, D.: Interactions with window openings by office occupants. Build. Environ. **44**(12), 2378–2395 (2009)
33. Haldi, F., Robinson, D.: On the unification of thermal perception and adaptive actions. Build. Environ. **45**(11), 2440–2457 (2010)
34. Hanssens, N., Kulkarni, A., Tuchida, R., Horton, T.: Building agent-based intelligent workspaces. In: International Conference on Internet Computing, pp. 675–681. Citeseer (2002)
35. Hektner, J.M., Schmidt, J.A., Csikszentmihalyi, M.: Experience Sampling Method: Measuring the Quality of Everyday Life. SAGE (2007). Google-Books-ID: 05e5dKBYY0C
36. Hong, T., Yan, D., D'Oca, S., Chen, C.F.: Ten questions concerning occupant behavior in buildings: the big picture. Build. Environ. **114**, 518–530 (2017)
37. Horvitz, E.: Principles of mixed-initiative user interfaces. In: Proceedings of the SIGCHI Conference on Human Factors in Computing Systems, CHI 1999, pp. 159–166. ACM, New York (1999)
38. Huang, C.C.J., Yang, R., Newman, M.W.: The potential and challenges of inferring thermal comfort at home using commodity sensors. In: Proceedings of the 2015 ACM International Joint Conference on Pervasive and Ubiquitous Computing, UbiComp 2015, pp. 1089–1100. ACM, New York (2015)
39. Jazizadeh, F., Ghahramani, A., Becerik-Gerber, B., Kichkaylo, T., Orosz, M.: Human-building interaction framework for personalized thermal comfort-driven systems in office buildings. J. Comput. Civil Eng. **28**(1), 2–16 (2014)
40. Kang, R., Dabbish, L., Fruchter, N., Kiesler, S.: My data just goes everywhere: user mental models of the internet and implications for privacy and security. In: Symposium on Usable Privacy and Security (SOUPS) (2015)

41. Karjalainen, S.: Should it be automatic or manual–the occupant's perspective on the design of domestic control systems. Energy Build. **65**, 119–126 (2013)
42. Kingma, B., van Marken Lichtenbelt, W.: Energy consumption in buildings and female thermal demand. Nat. Clim. Change **5**(12), 1054–1056 (2015)
43. Kluckner, P.M., Weiss, A., Schrammel, J., Tscheligi, M.: Exploring persuasion in the home: results of a long-term study on energy consumption behavior. In: Augusto, J.C., Wichert, R., Collier, R., Keyson, D., Salah, A.A., Tan, A.-H. (eds.) AmI 2013. LNCS, vol. 8309, pp. 150–165. Springer, Cham (2013). doi:10.1007/978-3-319-03647-2_11
44. Knecht, K., Bryan-Kinns, N., Shoop, K.: Usability and design of personal wearable and portable devices for thermal comfort in shared work environments. In: Proceedings of the 30th International BCS Human Computer Interaction Conference: Fusion!, HCI 2016, pp. 41:1–41:12. BCS Learning & Development Ltd., Swindon (2016)
45. Kueper, R.: Relationship between subjective comfort perception and smartphone sensor data. Technical report, Human-IST research Centre, University of Fribourg, Fribourg, Switzerland (2015)
46. Lahoual, D., Fréjus, M.: Sustainability at home: an exploratory study on monitoring needs and energy management actions of solar power producers. In: Kotzé, P., Marsden, G., Lindgaard, G., Wesson, J., Winckler, M. (eds.) INTERACT 2013. LNCS, vol. 8120, pp. 125–132. Springer, Heidelberg (2013). doi:10.1007/978-3-642-40498-6_9
47. Lalanne, D., Alavi, H.S., Nembrini, J., Verman, H.: Human-building interaction in the smart living lab. In: Future of Human-Building Interaction Workshop at the 34rd Annual ACM Conference on Human Factors in Computing Systems (CHI 2016). ACM (2016)
48. Langevin, J., Gurian, P.L., Wen, J.: Tracking the human-building interaction: a longitudinal field study of occupant behavior in air-conditioned offices. J. Environ. Psychol. **42**, 94–115 (2015)
49. Lehrer, D., Vasudev, J.: Visualizing energy information in commercial buildings: a study of tools, expert users, and building occupants. Technical report, Center for the Built Environment, UC Berkeley (2011)
50. Lucon, O., Ürge-Vorsatz, D., Ahmed, A.Z., Akbari, H., Bertoldi, P., Cabeza, L.F., Eyre, N., Gadgil, A., Harvey, L.D., Jiang, Y., et al.: Buildings. In: Mitigation of Climate Change. Contribution of Working Group III to the Fifth IPCC Report, pp. 671–738. Cambridge University Press, Cambridge, and New York (2014)
51. Mennicken, S., Kim, D., Huang, E.M.: Integrating the smart home into the digital calendar. In: Proceedings of the 2016 CHI Conference on Human Factors in Computing Systems, CHI 2016, pp. 5958–5969. ACM, New York (2016)
52. Mennicken, S., Vermeulen, J., Huang, E.M.: From today's augmented houses to tomorrow's smart homes: new directions for home automation research. In: Proceedings of the 2014 ACM International Joint Conference on Pervasive and Ubiquitous Computing, UbiComp 2014, pp. 105–115. ACM, New York (2014)
53. Miller, C., Nagy, Z., Schlueter, A.: Automated daily pattern filtering of measured building performance data. Autom. Constr. **49**(Part A), 1–17 (2015)
54. Mynatt, E.D., Rowan, J., Craighill, S., Jacobs, A.: Digital family portraits: supporting peace of mind for extended family members. In: Proceedings of the SIGCHI Conference on Human Factors in Computing Systems, CHI 2001, pp. 333–340. ACM, New York (2001)
55. Nguyen, T.A., Aiello, M.: Energy intelligent buildings based on user activity: a survey. Energy Build. **56**, 244–257 (2013)

56. O'Brien, W., Gunay, H.B.: The contextual factors contributing to occupants' adaptive comfort behaviors in offices - a review and proposed modeling framework. Build. Environ. **77**, 77–87 (2014)
57. Pierce, J., Paulos, E.: Beyond energy monitors: interaction, energy, and emerging energy systems. In: Proceedings of the SIGCHI Conference on Human Factors in Computing Systems, pp. 665–674. ACM (2012)
58. Ranjan, J., Scott, J.: ThermalSense: determining dynamic thermal comfort preferences using thermographic imaging. In: Proceedings of the 2016 ACM International Joint Conference on Pervasive and Ubiquitous Computing, UbiComp 2016, pp. 1212–1222. ACM, New York (2016)
59. Rodden, T., Benford, S.: The evolution of buildings and implications for the design of ubiquitous domestic environments. In: Proceedings of the SIGCHI Conference on Human Factors in Computing Systems, CHI 2003, pp. 9–16. ACM, New York (2003)
60. Rogers, Y., Hazlewood, W.R., Marshall, P., Dalton, N., Hertrich, S.: Ambient influence: can twinkly lights lure and abstract representations trigger behavioral change? In: Proceedings of the 12th ACM International Conference on Ubiquitous Computing, UbiComp 2010, pp. 261–270. ACM, New York (2010)
61. Rouvinez, T.: Real time tracking and visualization of indoor social interactions. Technical report, Human-IST research Centre, University of Fribourg, Fribourg, Switzerland (2015)
62. Ruby, A.: Lacaton & Vassal. Editions HYX, Orléans (2009)
63. Schwartz, T., Stevens, G., Jakobi, T., Denef, S., Ramirez, L., Wulf, V., Randall, D.: What people do with consumption feedback: a long-term living lab study of a home energy management system. Interact. Comput. **27**(6), 551–576 (2015)
64. Thomas, B.L., Cook, D.J.: Activity-aware energy-efficient automation of smart buildings. Energies **9**(8), 624 (2016)
65. Verma, H., Alavi, H.S., Lalanne, D.: Studying space use: bringing HCI tools to architectural projects. In: CHI 2017, Denver, CA, USA, 06–11 May 2017
66. Winkler, D.A., Beltran, A., Esfahani, N.P., Maglio, P.P., Cerpa, A.E.: FORCES: feedback and control for occupants to refine comfort and energy savings. In: Proceedings of the 2016 ACM International Joint Conference on Pervasive and Ubiquitous Computing, UbiComp 2016, pp. 1188–1199. ACM, New York (2016)
67. Yan, D., O'Brien, W., Hong, T., Feng, X., Burak Gunay, H., Tahmasebi, F., Mahdavi, A.: Occupant behavior modeling for building performance simulation: current state and future challenges. Energy Build. **107**, 264–278 (2015)
68. Yang, L., Yan, H., Lam, J.C.: Thermal comfort and building energy consumption implications - a review. Appl. Energy **115**, 164–173 (2014)
69. Yang, R., Newman, M.W.: Learning from a learning thermostat: lessons for intelligent systems for the home. In: Proceedings of the 2013 ACM International Joint Conference on Pervasive and Ubiquitous Computing, UbiComp 2013, pp. 93–102. ACM, New York (2013)
70. Yang, R., Pisharoty, D., Montazeri, S., Whitehouse, K., Newman, M.W.: How does eco-coaching help to save energy? Assessing a recommendation system for energy-efficient thermostat scheduling. In: Proceedings of the 2016 ACM International Joint Conference on Pervasive and Ubiquitous Computing, UbiComp 2016, pp. 1176–1187. ACM, New York (2016)

Investigating Wearable Technology for Fatigue Identification in the Workplace

Christopher Griffiths, Judy Bowen$^{(\boxtimes)}$, and Annika Hinze

The University of Waikato, Hamilton, New Zealand
cjgg1@students.waikato.ac.nz, {jbowen,hinze}@waikato.ac.nz

Abstract. Fatigue has been identified as a significant contributor to workplace accident rates. However, risk minimisation is a process largely based on self-reporting methodologies, which are not suitable for fatigue identification in high risk industries. Wearable technology which is capable of collecting physiological data such as step and heart rates as an individual performs workplace tasks has been proposed as a possible solution. Such devices are minimally intrusive to the individual and so can be used throughout the working day. Much is promised by the providers of such technology, but it is unclear how suitable it is for in-situ measurements in real-world work scenarios. To investigate this, we performed a series of studies designed to capture physiological and psychological data under differing (physical and mental) loading types with the intention of finding out how suitable such equipment is. Using reaction time (simple and choice) as a measure of performance we found similar correlations exist between loading duration and our measured indicators as those found in large-scale laboratory studies using state of the art equipment. Our results suggest that commercially available activity monitors are capable of collecting meaningful data in workplaces and are, therefore, worth investigating further for this purpose.

1 Introduction

Fatigue is, by nature, cumulative, and is influenced by many variables such as activity, time of day, sleep levels and social pressures. The impact of high fatigue levels, especially in high-risk workplaces, can lead to increased risk for employees, and is seen as a large contributor to workplace accident rates [12,19,29]. Risk assessment processes include attempts to assess the impact of workplace activities on fatigue levels. Typically these use qualitative self-reporting methodologies rather than quantitative data measurements. This type of data collection in workplace contexts is susceptible to response bias [24] and can result in a generalised view of risk. However the actual impact of activity upon fatigue is individualised. For example, tasks performed by a young person impacts fatigue levels to a lesser extent than tasks performed by an older person [2].

Many studies investigating the impact of activity upon performance have been undertaken. Most identify that an individual's performance is negatively

© IFIP International Federation for Information Processing 2017
Published by Springer International Publishing AG 2017. All Rights Reserved
R. Bernhaupt et al. (Eds.): INTERACT 2017, Part II, LNCS 10514, pp. 370–380, 2017.
DOI: 10.1007/978-3-319-67684-5_22

impacted by activity, both physical and mental [9,16,23,27]. Each of these studies collected data using different methods, but the majority are conducted in a laboratory setting with large numbers of participants. In real-world work environments, individuals encounter naturally occurring stressors that may not be observed in laboratory experiments. Similarly the longer-term nature of fatiguing activities in the workplace and the limited number of participants who can be measured in in-situ studies may make it hard to reproduce known results.

The rise in popularity of wearable devices has provided additional tools for quantification of individualised activity levels. These devices are designed to operate autonomously and enable the real-time collection of quantifiable data in the field throughout the day. Physiological markers such as step and heart rates can be used to determine workload intensities, especially in physically-biased roles. Conversely, changes in the balance of the autonomic nervous system can be used to quantify cognitive loading. However, it is unclear how accurate these measures are when using commercial products designed primarily for the personal user. As a first investigation into this, we performed a series of single-person studies designed to see if we could reproduce known correlations between activity (both mental and physical) and response times. If we find similar correlations can be identified by these devices then it is worth further investigating their use in real-world work environments.

In this paper, we present the results of these initial studies investigating the use of low cost commercially available devices as a means of collecting data that has sufficient accuracy and granularity to identify physiological changes associated with mental and physical activity types which may indicate fatigue. We examine the suitability of such devices for use in the field, specifically for gathering data and monitoring of forestry workers throughout their working day.

1.1   Motivation

The forestry industry in New Zealand has a poor Health and Safety record with some 12,921 active Accident Compensation Corporation (ACC) claims between 2008 and 2013. More importantly the number of reported fatalities for the same period is 32. Such high levels of fatalities are concerning to the industry with reforms being planned to address safety of employees. Suggestions based on experimental data are limited, and difficult to source. Currently, the only practicable solution is seen as increasing the level of mechanisation resulting in removal of the employee from the worksite.

Recently (2014), the large numbers of incidents reported prompted the Independent Forestry Safety Review [1], designed to investigate factors that impact on health and safety within the forestry industry and to provide guidelines designed to minimize the number of incidents. It was identified that the forestry industry is one of the most dangerous occupations in New Zealand. Employees are 15 times more likely to suffer a workplace injury compared to other NZ based industries.

The physical nature of the work, long working days and tasks requiring high levels of concentration can all exacerbate the impact of fatigue [13,28] with high demand tasks requiring more energy to complete. In workplaces with high task demands employees may experience the effects of fatigue earlier. There is also a recognition that the lack of welfare facilities in the forestry environment may be an additional contributor to fatigue.

1.2   Measurements

There are numerous physiological indicators that can be used to quantify activity. Step and heart rates have been successfully used to quantify physical activity [8], whereas changes in the balance of the autonomic nervous system have been used as an indicator of cognitive activity [25].

Currently seen as the gold standard for measurement of these variables are step counting for ambulatory activity and, electrocardiography for heart rate data collection. However, we must remember that in our proposed domain the devices we choose need to be minimally intrusive and capture data autonomously. Before we can assess suitable devices for the data collection we must first consider what the appropriate data to collect is. We discuss proposed identifiers of activity next, these will then inform subsequent choices of appropriate apparatus for data capture.

Step Rate: The use of pedometers to measure an individual's daily activity has been used many times in differing domains. Designed to capture accelerations of the hip during gait cycles they count the number of steps taken by an individual over a given time period. Using the number of steps taken we can gain an insight into how role-based activity may contribute to excessive fatigue levels. This method has been used successfully to differentiate activity levels by role types in forestry harvesting operations [17] with large differences between manual and mechanised activity types being identified.

Heart Rate: Heart rate data captured throughout the course of a work period can be an used as an indicator of task demand. Higher heart rates typically accompany higher periods of physical activity as higher levels of oxygenated blood are required due to increased physiological demand. Increases in heart rate are individualized with demand being dependent on such criteria as age and fitness levels. However, maximal heart rate can be calculated from the general formula equation Maximal Heart Rate = 220 minus Age [20]. The resultant figure can then be used in conjunction with resting heart rate to determine periods of high and low activity where activity is defined as deviation from the resting heart rate.

Heart Rate Variability (HRV): Heart rate variability is the time interval between successive heart beats. Shorter periods are indicative of active loading while longer time periods are indicative of rest. There are a large number of variables that can be extracted from collected data each providing an insight into autonomic nervous system activity. For our studies we use the low frequency/high frequency ratio of the power spectrum density of the heart. This variable has been found to correlate well with mental activity across differing levels of cognitive load [7, 10, 26].

Workload Intensity: Workload intensity, or how hard an individual perceives their workload can be an indicator of increasing fatigue levels. Monotonous or repetitive tasks have been identified as a contributor to motivational levels [22] with individual performance slowing as motivational levels decrease [34]. The Task Load Intensity Tool (TLX) developed at the Ames Research Center is designed as a self-reporting estimator of how difficult an individual perceives their workload. Using a six point scale it provides a workload score for workplace activities [18]. Increasing workload scores for tasks where the only change is duration can indicate increasing workplace fatigue [3].

Performance: Reaction time (both simple and choice) has been used many times to measure individual performance. It is a measure of the elapsed time between the presentation of a given stimulus and the participant's response. In simple reaction time the user responds to one stimulus whereas in choice reaction time the user must identify the correct response from a set of choices. Reaction time has been found to deteriorate with increasing fatigue [5,13,21] furthermore the time difference between choice and simple reaction time can give insights into the speed of mental processing.

2 State of the Art Methods and Tools

When considering our methodologies for collecting data we must also consider the accuracy of our proposed devices. The most accurate measure for step counting is manual counting. However, this is impractical for many purposes and in particular for our chosen domain - one cannot manually count steps in the workplace. The Yamax range of pedometers are widely regarded as the most accurate equipment for automatic step counting [32] and have been used in many studies investigating step rates [6,8,30]. When comparing the accuracy of our chosen device (Fitbit Charge HR) many studies have found good agreement between actual and recorded steps taken [14,15].

Real-time data collection of cardiovascular activity in the workplace presents additional challenges. This type of data collection is typically done using an electrocardiograph and is undertaken at hospitals or dedicated research laboratories. The equipment can be bulky and cumbersome with an individual having wired sensors placed on the body. As previously discussed, our proposed domain is forestry operations in which traditional ECG measurement is not practical.

Wearable devices exist that are designed to capture data in free living activities. These devices range from chest strap based monitoring through to smart clothing containing electrodes to capture the electrical signals produced during a heart beat cycle. Devices are designed to be minimally intrusive to the individual and collect data autonomously facilitating use in the field.

The Polar range of products have been used extensively in studies investigating the cardiovascular system. For example, Paritala's work investigating the effects of physical and mental activity used the Polar RS800 monitor to capture the heart rate of 24 participants during laboratory testing [25]. In a similar study the relationship between markers of work related fatigue and HRV of 28 participants used Polar devices for the data capture [33].

In the above section we have discussed the gold standards for data collection and identified limitations for use in workplace domains. Tools for performance and perceived workload intensity are numerous however, given our proposed domain our choice is limited. Any devices used to measure our required metrics will be worn throughout the working day by forestry workers and so should not cause discomfort during their physical activities. In order to collect data we therefore selected to use Fitbit Charge HR activity trackers to collect ambulatory data and the Polar RS8020CX fitness watch paired with a Polar chest strap to collect heart-rate data. In addition, field-based testing must be quick to conduct to minimise the impact on both productivity and the individual and as such we implemented an electronic version of the unweighted NASA TLX to collect data on perceived workload intensity as this will be quicker than a paper-based survey. For performance data we selected the Deary-Liewald Reaction Time application developed by the Centre for Cognitive Ageing and Cognitive Epidemiology [11]. It is an application specifically designed for conducting reaction time testing using portable computing devices.

3   Studies

The aim of these initial studies was to investigate whether the tracking devices and tools listed above could be used to replicate the results of large-scale, laboratory-based tests which investigate the effects of activity on fatigue. Performing monitoring studies of forestry workers is time-consuming and requires considerable buy-in from a number of different entities (forestry owners, contracting companies, health and safety organisations and the workers themselves). Before undertaking the field studies with workers, we therefore wanted to be certain that our equipment choices would be suitable and we could gather meaningful data. As such we focussed on evaluating combinations of different measurements across different activity types. Each of the studies described below were conducted with a single participant over short periods of time (the course of a day or a focussed activity) as a means to conduct such an evaluation.

3.1   Activity and Recovery

To assess the impact of activity on the physiological and psychological systems our first study was designed to assess the impact of differing loading types (physical and mental) on performance and psychological indicators. During physical loading the measurements were undertaken in an ad-hoc manner as and when opportunities presented themselves. Workload intensity was measured using an electronic implementation of the NASA TLX running on a dedicated server and measured at the same time as reaction time testing. Apparatus was worn for the duration of the monitoring exercise.

3.2   Physical Loading

Monitoring sessions were undertaken over the course of a working day. The participant worked as a floor team member at a large retail outlet, a position requiring large amounts of ambulatory activity. Both ambulatory activity and heart rate data collection commenced at the start of the work day and concluded at the end of the work period. Workload intensity and performance measurement was undertaken at the start and end of the work period and at the participant's designated break times (2×15min and 1×30min).

When extracting data for heart rate variability, the raw data is put through an analysis program that computes the various indicators of cardiographic activity. For this task we used the gHRV software developed by Milegroup based at the University of Vigo in Spain. The application is specifically designed for the analysis of heart rate variability.[1]

As mentioned in 1.2, we use the ratio of low frequency to high frequency of the power spectrum density of the heart as an indicator of autonomic nervous system activity, inferring increasing fatigue from the increase of this ratio. The large datasets we create during monitoring can be used to provide point data, however, for our estimation of increasing fatigue we use the cumulative mean of the data over the duration of the monitoring period.

When assessing performance as the speed of mental processing (choice reaction time minus simple reaction time) we see an initial period of improvement followed by a period of slowing as the workday lengthens. The psychological impact was found to increase across duration with increasing perceived task intensity being reported (Fig. 1).

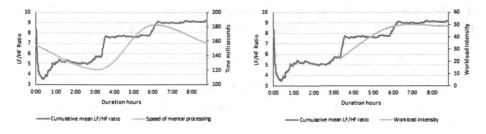

Fig. 1. Speed of mental processing (left) and workload intensity (right) vs cumulative mean LF/HF ratio

Activity during this period was measured as 22,322 steps (18.8 km) with the majority occurring within the first 6 h of the work session. The graphs indicate that speed of mental processing and perceived workload intensity are impacted by this high physical loading.

3.3   Cognitive Loading

To investigate the impact of cognitive load we conducted experiments where driving was used as the mental activity and stressor. Driving is a task requiring constant vigilance and high levels of spatial awareness. The experimenter

---

[1] Available from https://milegroup.github.io/ghrv/doc.html.

performed a 3 h driving exercise on real roads encountering typical driving conditions. Reaction time testing in conjunction with workload intensity monitoring was undertaken at 30 min intervals for the duration of the experiment. On completion of the driving exercise monitoring was continued to assess performance through a recovery period.

We found a similar increasing trend as that in physical loading however, the increase in LF/HF ratio was found to be higher. Workload intensity and performance were also negatively impacted over the duration of the experiment (Fig. 2).

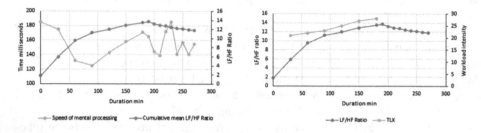

Fig. 2. Speed of mental processing (left) and workload intensity (right) v cumulative mean LF/HF ratio for driving experiment

The higher number of data points collected during the driving experiments facilitates further analysis of existing relationships between our variables. We identified a good correlation for the majority of our measured variables. Table 1 presents the results of the correlation between our measured variables.

Table 1. Correlation of physiological and psychological variables

Condition	Correlation R	Comments
Driving v speed of mental processing	0.73	Speed of mental processing increases with loading duration
Driving v workload intensity	0.98	Perceived workload increases with loading duration
Driving v LF/HF ratio	0.89	LF/HF ratio increases with loading duration
Recovery v speed of mental processing	−0.69	Speed of mental processing decreases on loading cessation
Recovery v LF/HF ratio	−0.75	LF/HF ratio decreases on cessation of loading
LF/HF ratio v workload intensity	0.92	LF/HF ratio increases with increasing workload perception
LF/HF ratio v speed of mental processing driving	0.72	Speed of mental processing increases with increasing LF/HF ratio
Speed of mental processing v workload intensity	0.56	Speed of mental processing increases with increasing perceived workload

4   Discussion

When examining the results of our studies, we can see that each of our measured variables indicate an impact resulting from activity. In both physical and cognitive loading types, we see a reduction in performance across loading duration indicated by slowing of reaction times. We also observe that this reduction in performance occurs as the cumulative mean of low frequency/high frequency ratio increases (Fig. 1). Furthermore, we note that cognitive load impacts the cumulative mean of low frequency/high frequency ratio to a greater extent than physical loading with higher values being recorded (Fig. 2) for our driving study. These results are similar to the findings of other studies investigating the impact mental and physical loading on the autonomic nervous system [10, 23, 27].

In our driving study, we found a good correlation between our measured variables (Table 1) indicating relationships between performance and increasing levels of the high frequency/low frequency ratio. We also identified that performance continues to degrade on cessation of activity prior to improvement facilitated through a recovery period. These findings agree with those of previous studies investigating the impact of loading on the autonomic nervous system [9, 10].

Similar to other studies [9], we found perceived workload intensity increases as loading duration lengthens, individuals report higher workload scores later in the day for the same tasks. The perception of workload intensity was also found to relate to our measured physiological indicators. We identified higher workload scores were reported with increasing cumulative mean low frequency/high frequency ratios.

What we are seeking to identify here is the suitability of wearable devices for capturing meaningful data. As such the results described are not intended to prove relationships between activity, fatigue and response times per se. But rather act as a proof of concept that such methods and tools can replicate known correlations in such data. Given that they indicate this is possible, we can then move on to study their use in the field within our larger-scale studies with forestry workers.

5   Conclusions and Future Work

Our research question asked if low cost lightweight methods can be used for meaningful data collection of data pertaining to physiological indicators related to the impact of activity on performance. As found in other studies [4, 31] the Fitbit Charge HR successfully collected data on ambulatory activity. Having a similar footprint to a wrist watch we found the device minimally intrusive, and caused no discomfort to the individual.

The Polar chest strap used for the collection of heart rate variability proved to be capable of collecting meaningful data. However, the practicality of this device can be called into question. We found the fastening clasp on the chest strap can cause discomfort to the individual, resulting in reluctance to wear the device over longer periods. We also note a period of spiking may be present due to insufficient moisture between skin and electrode to accurately record heart rate data. This can be overcome by the application of electrode gel prior to the commencement of data capture.

As in other studies [3,16,29], our results indicate workplace activity impacts both physiological and psychological states. We identify increasing values of the cumulative mean low frequency/high frequency ratio as loading duration extends. Furthermore, we identify that cognitive loading has a greater impact on the individual than physical loading. We have also identified that on cessation of activity performance continues to degrade prior to improvement. We acknowledge that monitoring undertaken during our study was brief and extended data collection over longer time frames is required to further identify any trends that maybe present. Furthermore, we acknowledge that the data collected represents a single individual as such future studies should incorporate a larger participant base to gain a better understanding of the physiological and psychological impact of workplace activity.

In conclusion, we assessed commercially available fitness monitoring devices as tools for physiological data capture under differing loading types. We found that the selected activity trackers are capable of collecting meaningful data providing researchers with additional tools for monitoring activity in free living. The use of the cumulative mean of the power spectrum density of the heart may be a useful indicator of the impact of activity on the autonomic nervous system and as such may be useful for the determination of workplace role/task intensity.

References

1. Adams, G., Armstrong, H., Cosman, M.: Independent forestry safety review. Final report (2014)
2. Avin, K.G., Law, L.A.F.: Age-related differences in muscle fatigue vary by contraction type: a meta-analysis. Phys. Ther. **91**(8), 1153 (2011)
3. Baulk, S.D., Kandelaars, K.J., Lamond, N., Roach, G.D., Dawson, D., Fletcher, A.: Does variation in workload affect fatigue in a regular 12-hour shift system? Sleep Biol. Rhythms **5**(1), 74–77 (2007)
4. Bowen, J., Hinze, A., Cunningham, S.J., Parker, R.: Investigating the use of activity trackers to observe high-risk work environments (2015)
5. Brisswalter, J., Arcelin, R., Audiffren, M., Delignieres, D.: Influence of physical exercise on simple reaction time: effect of physical fitness. Percept. Mot. Skills **85**(3), 1019–1027 (1997)
6. Castillo-Retamal, M., Hinckson, E.A.: Measuring physical activity and sedentary behaviour at work: a review. Work **40**(4), 345–357 (2011)
7. Chandola, T., Britton, A., Brunner, E., Hemingway, H., Malik, M., Kumari, M., Badrick, E., Kivimaki, M., Marmot, M.: Work stress and coronary heart disease: what are the mechanisms? Eur. Heart J. **29**(5), 640–648 (2008)
8. Choi, S.W., Lee, J.H., Jang, Y.K., Kim, J.R.: Assessment of ambulatory activity in the Republic of Korea Navy submarine crew. Undersea Hyperb. Med. **37**(6), 413 (2010)

9. Cinaz, B., La Marca, R., Arnrich, B., Tröster, G.: Monitoring of mental workload levels. In: Proceedings of IADIS eHealth conference, pp. 189–193 (2010)
10. Collet, C., Averty, P., Dittmar, A.: Autonomic nervous system and subjective ratings of strain in air-traffic control. Appl. Ergon. **40**(1), 23–32 (2009)
11. Deary, I.J., Liewald, D., Nissan, J.: A free, easy-to-use, computer-based simple and four-choice reaction time programme: the Deary-Liewald reaction time task. Behav. Res. Methods **43**(1), 258–268 (2011)
12. Dobbie, K.: Fatigue-Related Crashes: An Analysis of Fatigue-Related Crashes on Australian Roads Using an Operational Definition of Fatigue. No. OR 23. Australian Government, Department of Infrastructure and Regional Development, Road Safety Publications, Australia (2002)
13. Ellis, H.D.: The effects of cold on the performance of serial choice reaction time and various discrete tasks. Hum. Factors **24**(5), 589–598 (1982)
14. Evenson, K.R., Goto, M.M., Furberg, R.D.: Systematic review of the validity and reliability of consumer-wearable activity trackers. Int. J. Behav. Nutr. Phys. Act. **12**(1), 159 (2015)
15. Ferguson, T., Rowlands, A.V., Olds, T., Maher, C.: The validity of consumer-level, activity monitors in healthy adults worn in free-living conditions: a cross-sectional study. Int. J. Behav. Nutr. Phys. Act. **12**(1), 42 (2015)
16. Galy, E., Cariou, M., Mélan, C.: What is the relationship between mental workload factors and cognitive load types? Int. J. Psychophysiol. **83**(3), 269–275 (2012)
17. Griffiths, C.J.G.: Investigating tools and methods for data capture of forestry workers. Ph.D. thesis, University of Waikato (2016)
18. Hart, S.G., Staveland, L.E.: Development of NASA-TLX (Task Load Index): results of empirical and theoretical research. Adv. Psychol. **52**, 139–183 (1988)
19. Haslam, R.A., Hide, S.A., Gibb, A.G., Gyi, D.E., Pavitt, T., Atkinson, S., Duff, A.: Contributing factors in construction accidents. Appl. Ergon. **36**(4), 401–415 (2005)
20. Karvonen, M.J., Kentala, E., Mustala, O.: The effects of training on heart rate; a longitudinal study. In: Annales Medicinae Experimentalis et Biologiae Fenniae, vol. 35, p. 307 (1957)
21. Lim, J., Dinges, D.F.: Sleep deprivation and vigilant attention. Ann. N. Y. Acad. Sci. **1129**(1), 305–322 (2008)
22. MacDonald, W.: The impact of job demands and workload on stress and fatigue. Aust. Psychol. **38**(2), 102–117 (2003)
23. McDuff, D., Gontarek, S., Picard, R.: Remote measurement of cognitive stress via heart rate variability. In: 2014 36th Annual International Conference of the IEEE Engineering in Medicine and Biology Society (EMBC), pp. 2957–2960. IEEE (2014)
24. Morrel-Samuels, P.: Getting the truth into workplace surveys. Harv. Bus. Rev. **80**(2), 111–118 (2002)
25. Paritala, S.A.: Effects of physical and mental tasks on heart rate variability. Ph.D. thesis, Kakatiya University, India (2009)
26. Patel, M., Lal, S., Kavanagh, D., Rossiter, P.: Applying neural network analysis on heart rate variability data to assess driver fatigue. Expert Syst. Appl. **38**(6), 7235–7242 (2011)
27. Pichot, V., Bourin, E., Roche, F., Garet, M., Gaspoz, J.M., Duverney, D., Antoniadis, A., Lacour, J.R., Barthélémy, J.C.: Quantification of cumulated physical fatigue at the workplace. Pflügers Arch. **445**(2), 267–272 (2002)
28. Pilcher, J.J., Nadler, E., Busch, C.: Effects of hot and cold temperature exposure on performance: a meta-analytic review. Ergonomics **45**(10), 682–698 (2002)

29. Rosa, R.R.: Extended workshifts and excessive fatigue. J. Sleep Res. **4**(s2), 51–56 (1995)

30. Soroush, A.: A 6 month physical activity intervention in university staff: effectiveness and health outcomes-the ASUKI step study. Inst för biovetenskaper och näringslära/Dept of Biosciences and Nutrition (2013)

31. Takacs, J., Pollock, C.L., Guenther, J.R., Bahar, M., Napier, C., Hunt, M.A.: Validation of the fitbit one activity monitor device during treadmill walking. J. Sci. Med. Sport **17**(5), 496–500 (2014)

32. Tully, M.A., McBride, C., Heron, L., Hunter, R.F.: The validation of Fitbit Zip physical activity monitor as a measure of free-living physical activity. BMC Res. Notes **7**(1), 952 (2014)

33. Völker, I., Kirchner, C., Bock, O.L.: Relation between multiple markers of work-related fatigue. Saf. Health Work **7**(2), 124–129 (2016)

34. Wright, R.A., Pantaleo, G.: Effort processes in achieving performance outcomes: interrelations among and roles of core constructs. Behav. Brain Sci. **36**(06), 705–706 (2013)

Leveraging Conversational Systems to Assists New Hires During Onboarding

Praveen Chandar[1(✉)], Yasaman Khazaeni[1], Matthew Davis[1], Michael Muller[1], Marco Crasso[2], Q. Vera Liao[3], N. Sadat Shami[4], and Werner Geyer[1]

[1] IBM Research, Cambridge, MA, USA
{pcravich,yasaman.khazaeni,davismat,michael_muller,
werner.geyer}@us.ibm.com
[2] IBM Research - SilverGate, Buenos Aires, Argentina
crasso@ar.ibm.com
[3] IBM Research, Yorktown, NY, USA
vera.liao@ibm.com
[4] IBM, Armonk, NY, USA
sadat@us.ibm.com

Abstract. The task of onboarding a new hire consumes great amounts of resources from organizations. The faster a "newbie" becomes an "insider", the higher the chances of job satisfaction, retention, and advancement in their position. Conversational agents (AI agents) have the potential to effectively transform productivity in many enterprise workplace scenarios so applying them to the onboarding process can prove to be a very solid use case for such agents. In this work, we present a conversational system to aid new hires through their onboarding process. Users interact with the system via an instant messaging platform, to fulfill their work related information needs as if it were a human assistant. We describe the end-to-end process involved in building a domain specific conversational system and share our experiences in deploying it to 344 new hires in a month-long study. The feasibility of our approach is evaluated by analyzing message logs and questionnaires. Through three different measures, we observed an accuracy of about 60% at the message level and a higher than average retention rate for the agent. Our results suggest that this agent-based approach can very well compete with the existing tools for new hires.

Keywords: Artificial intelligence · Conversational agents · Personal assistants · Evaluation · NLP

1 Introduction

Lave and Wenger [11] showed that people join a community or an organization slowly, through a process of "legitimate peripheral participation," in which they must first learn their new environment, then tentatively test their knowledge, and

© IFIP International Federation for Information Processing 2017
Published by Springer International Publishing AG 2017. All Rights Reserved
R. Bernhaupt et al. (Eds.): INTERACT 2017, Part II, LNCS 10514, pp. 381–391, 2017.
DOI: 10.1007/978-3-319-67684-5_23

finally begin to act as fully competent members. Organizations and their new-hires would benefit from speeding up this process from "newbie" to "insider."

With all the challenges that come with being a new hire, the path for every employee to go from the "newbie" stage to an "insider" depends on how fast they acquire enough knowledge to feel comfortable at their new workplace. Obviously this depends on the size of the company and the direct group who will be working with the employee, the job rank, his/her number of years of previous experience, whether there is a change in the type of job and his/her personality and ability to deal with uncertainty. In [14] seven different information seeking tactics (overt questions, indirect questions, third parties, testing limits, disguising conversations, observing, surveillance) are studied which are used by new hires in an organization to seek information.

This paper describes how a conversational agent can be used to augment the onboarding process and details our experience with building and deploying an end-to-end system. We explain the various steps involved from curating a domain-specific knowledge base to evaluating the system using message logs and questionnaires. The main advantage of our proposed system is that unlike humans, conversational agents can be available 24/7 to answer new hire questions and unlike existing web-based tools the agent provides a human-like interaction. Additionally, the agent can help with compliance by sending proactive messages to the user which could be helpful in reminding new employees of their tasks to be completed.

The primary goal of our proposed system is to cater to the work-related informational needs of the newcomers in an organization. The system is designed to provide an answer for questions on company policies and procedures, or search the company's Intranet. In addition, the system can help new hires connect with co-workers by allowing them to find experts on certain topics as well as looking up co-workers through an intelligent directory look-up service. While information retrieval is an essential objective for our agent, social behavior and interaction capabilities are equally important. A number of works have dealt with how conversational agents should interact and behave with humans [7,24,28]. As noted by previous works, we anticipated the anthropomorphic chit-chat behavior and implemented a chit chat module providing a more natural human/agent interaction.

The use of conversation in information systems goes back to the 1950s [25]. More recently, success in the field of natural language processing and machine learning has led to rapid adaptation of state of the art chat bot technologies for information access in various fields including education [22], health care [5], or accounting [15]. Conversational systems have been an active area of research with focus areas including user experience [18,23], personalization [10], and dialog modeling [16,26,29]. Most conversational systems proposed in the literature are evaluated on datasets created for artificial tasks or in a laboratory. Our work focuses on the process involved in building an end-to-end conversational agent evaluated in the field.

The rest of this paper is organized as follows. Section 2 describes the system design and the steps involved in building a conversation system for a domain specific application. Section 3 provides details of the study design followed by the results of our user study in Sect. 4. We conclude the paper with a discussion and directions for future work.

2 System Description

We designed a conversational agent named *Chip* to aid new hires with their information needs and ease their way into the organization. The agent was available on a company wide instant messaging service that the new hires could add to their buddy list and start interacting. We conducted a user study to gain insights into the user's experience with system and estimate system performance. In this section, we describe the capabilities of the system along with design in detail.

2.1 System Capabilities

Knowledge Base: The primary goal of the agent was to address the information needs of newcomers in an organization. We compiled a set of frequently asked questions on a variety of topics to address their needs (refer to Sect. 2.2 for more details on the methodology used to identify these questions). The knowledge base also contained question variations that enabled our system to provide the same answer to different versions of the same underlying question. The knowledge base consisted of answers for each question. An example question-answer pair is show below:

User Request: How can I host a teleconference?
Chip's Response: Before you can host a teleconference,
you have to sign up for a host code. You can visit this link
to register. For complete instructions, check out
this link on audio conferencing.

Chit Chat: Our goal was not only to build a question answering system but also to provide a human touch to the interactions. It has been shown that "anthropomorphism" can solicit social responses from users such as trust, empathy, etc., and also helps with conversation [2]. Casual conversations such as chit chat is one possible way to humanize an agent [12]. We developed a chit chat module to handle casual conversation pertaining to agent trait (e.g. *who are you?, what do you like?, etc.*), agent status (e.g. *how are you?, what are you doing?, etc.*), compliments (e.g. *you are great!, you are smart, etc.*). The agent could even tell jokes.

Search Capabilities: The agent had the ability to search over a set of documents in the organization's intranet. We restricted the search index to contain documents related to company policies and HR related pages. An inverted index was used to rank documents (webpages) in decreasing order of relevance for a given information need.

Lookup Capabilities: In addition to the search, the users could use lookup services such as:

- *Employee Demographics Lookup*: Users could search the employee directory by asking natural language questions. For example, the users can ask the agent to "Look up John Smith's phone number and address" and the agent would understand the intent and extract names entity (e.g. "John Smith") to search the employee directory.
- *Experts Lookup*: Employees joining an organization often have a hard time finding domain experts within the company. To ease this problem the agent was equipped with the ability to search an internal social media portal to return a list of domain experts along with their contact information.
- *Wikipedia Search*: The agent allowed the users to search Wikipedia for a given natural language query.

Proactive Reminders: New hires joining an organization have to complete a set of tasks within a specified time frame. These tasks include signing up for health insurance, join relevant mailing lists, etc. Our agent was designed to send proactive messages to users reminding them of their tasks and answer question related to the tasks. Proactive reminders also served as a way to remind the users about the availability of the agent.

2.2   System Design

The process that we followed to develop the conversational system for new hires can roughly be divided into three different phases: (1) Curating the knowledge base; (2) Building a conversational agent; (3) Tuning the performance.

Knowledge Base Curation: In order to build a comprehensive knowledge base consisting of question-answer pairs relevant to our new hire use case, we used call records obtained from the company's employee service center (ESC). The call records were composed of email conversations between employees and customer service representatives organized in the form of threads. The ESC call records contained a broad range of topics, including topics that were irrelevant to our new hire use case. In order to refine the topics in the call records, we performed topic modeling to identify prominent topics in the call records using the Latent Dirichlet Allocation [6] technique. The topics guided us to manually define a diverse set of candidate questions to be included in the knowledge base. Once the questions were finalized, a subject matter expert went through them to provide a short and concise answer to each of these questions.

Conversational Agent: The goal of our conversational agent was to return a text-based response for a given user request in natural language. Prior work on short text conversational systems can be categorized into retrieval-based [8] and generation-based methods [17]. Retrieval-based methods select the best possible answer from a set of predefined responses whereas generation-based methods create a natural language response for a given question. We used a retrieval based method in this work and the steps involved in obtaining a response are explained below:

1. *Intent identification:* Identifying the intent for a given question is key to understanding the user's information need. We annotate every incoming user message with a predefined intent using a natural language classifier. The classifier used in this work was a multi-layer convolution neural network similar to the one used in [9]. The goal of the intent classifier was to categorize the user's information need into chit chat, knowledge base question, Wikipedia search, employee or expert lookup. In practice, we found that splitting the chit chat and knowledge base question category into more granular intents was more effective. For instance, we decompose the knowledge base question into a list of topics such as health insurance, benefits, IT Help, etc. The use of CNN models enabled us to generalize our approach beyond exact matches. For example, a user can ask for: "information on health-care benefits", or "where can I find my health benefits information?"; both will be matched to the answer containing the appropriate web page for health benefits.

2. *Entity Extraction:* Additionally, each user request was also annotated with named entities and keywords (noun phrases) present in the text. We use the AlchemyAPI to extract entities and keywords [1] to be used in the answer selection step.

3. *Answer Selection*
   - *Knowledge Base and Chit Chat*
     Once the intent classifier has identified the user request as a chit chat or knowledge base question, the next step was to retrieve the most likely response from a pool of predefined responses. Similar to the previous step, we use a multi-layer convolution neural network based classifier to select the best response. The intent and answer selection classifier returned a confidence score along with the most likely class label. The agent returned the selected answer as a response only when both were above threshold t_1 for intent classifier and t_2 for answer selection classifier.
   - *Inverted Index*
     When the intent classifier's confidence was above a threshold t_1 and answer selection classifier's confidence was below a threshold t_2, we used the search index as a fall-back. A query was created by removing the stop-words from the user request to search an inverted index created using the Lemur toolkit [21]. A sequential dependency model [13] was used to find relevant documents, and the top three documents along with the snippets were returned as a response.
   - *Employees and Expert Lookup*
     An internal employee lookup service was used by passing in the extracted person entity as arguments. The keywords extracted are passed as an argument to the expert lookup service and the output was returned as a response.

– *Wikipedia Search*

The extracted keywords are passed to the Wikipedia Search API as a query. The top ranked document along with the snippet is returned as a response.

Finally, the agent had to handle questions that were out of scope. The thresholds t_1 and t_2 described above were used to determine out-of-scope questions and a generic "Sorry, I don't understand you question" response was returned.

Performance Tuning: The thresholds t_1 and t_2 have a direct influence on system performance because they determine when a question is out of scope or when the agent must search the inverted index.

Determining optimal values for t_1 and t_2 is a non-trivial task so as an ad-hoc solution, in this work, we divided our user study into three different cohorts and used the user data from first cohort to tune the values for thresholds t_1 and t_2.

3   User Study

The conversational agent was made available to 344 new hires of a large organization for 4–5 weeks. The participants were recruited in three cohorts and were mostly college graduates with different backgrounds, including software engineering, consulting, product design, administration, and sales. The participants were located at different work locations across a single country and they attended a mandatory new hire orientation program organized by the company. A member of our research team was present at the orientation to demonstrate the capabilities of the agent. Upon adding the agent to their instant messenger's "friend list", the participants were able to interact with agent. For example, a new hire could ask the agent about benefits – "how do I set up my health insurance", lookup directory information – "what is John's phone number" or even find experts in their field of interest – "find an expert in machine learning", etc. The system was introduced as an experimental tool and the participants were requested to provide feedback by sending a *#FAIL* message for incorrect agent responses.

3.1   Post Study Questionnaire

We followed up with a post study questionnaire sent to participants after about a month of usage. Similar to other studies [3, 4, 30], we developed a version of the questionnaire to capture user opinion. To understand the user's self assessed accuracy of the system, we included the following question: *What percent of questions was Chip able to answer for you?*

The users were also asked to rate a series of statements on a Likert scale. The following statements were included in the questionnaire to estimate the user-perceived efficacy of the agent. We replaced the agent name below with Chip for blind review.

– The answers Chip gave me were of high-quality answers.
– I would continue to use Chip if he were available to me.

We also included the following question on comparing the agent to other sources.

– I tended to ask Chip before turning to a coworker for help.
– Chip was able to help me when I would otherwise have called the Employee Service Center.
– I thought to ask Chip for help before emailing my onboarding Specialist.

Additionally, we asked the survey takers to rank the following sources by their ability to answer questions about the company's knowledge and process that is required for a new hire: (1) Co-worker (2) Intranet Search (3) *Chip* (4) onboarding Specialist assigned to the employee by the human resources (5) Employee Service Center.

4   Results

4.1   System Usage

In this section, we present the descriptive statistics of all user messages to *Chip*. Overall, *Chip* received a total of 5984 messages throughout the study from 322 users (average of 18.58 messages per user).[1] The messages received could be a request with an information need, chit chat, a lookup for employee demographics, search for domain experts, Wikipedia search, or "#FAIL" reporting system failure. Among them, 75.8% users have 5 or more unique interactions with *Chip*. Table 1 shows the usages statistics across the three cohorts.

Table 1. Usage statistics across all three cohorts

	Tot. users	Tot. messages	Messages/user
Group 1	89 (82)	1383	16.9
Group 2	124 (115)	2513	21.9
Group 3	131 (125)	2088	16.7

As an agent that aims to provide continuous interactions, a critical design goal of *Chip* is to encourage users' long-term engagement. We observed that 25% messages came in the second two weeks of the user's access time to *Chip* compared to 75% coming in the first two weeks. Considering the effect of introduction to a new tool in the first week or so, this shows users didn't only use to system as a toy tool but for actual retrieval of information. Additionally, we observed a considerable number of active users[2] during the second half of the study, 26.1% of were using the system in the latter half compared to 69.3% in the first half. This shows a much higher retention rate compared to what is reported for most chatbots at lower than 10% in the first month [31].

---

[1] About 6.3% of the users never used *Chip*.
[2] Users with five or more unique interactions were considered active users.

4.2 System Effectiveness

To assess the accuracy of the system at the message level, we randomly sampled 149 of request-response pairs from the message logs. The pairs were annotated by a researcher with a four point scale: correct, needs improvement, wrong and out of scope. Table 2 shows the result we get from this annotation. Among 149 question, we found around 58% answered correctly while around 13% answers were wrong.

Table 2. Annotation results

Total	Correct	Improvement needed	Wrong	Out of scope
149	87	16	19	27
	58.4%	10.7%	12.8%	18.1%

As described in Sect. 3.1, we also measured user satisfaction through questionnaires in which the user evaluated the quality of response, compared the agent with other sources, etc. We distributed the survey to all participants, however, only 37% completed the questionnaire. Table 3 shows the results for two types of questions in the survey to measure satisfaction. The users rated the statements related to *efficacy* and *comparison to other sources* on a Likert scale. We convert the nominals to continuous scale by assigning 7 for strongly agree and 1 for strongly disagree (neutral is 4).

Table 3 shows that users in general agreed that the answers were of high quality and showed a strong intent to continue using the agent. The results also show that, as the first source of answers, users preferred to start with *Chip* before contacting their co-workers, onboarding specialist or the ESC.

We also asked the users to rank the different sources by their general ability to answer questions on company policies. While it is evident from Fig. 1 that

Table 3. Questionnaire data analysis

Efficacy	Mean (SD)
The answers Chip gave me were high-quality answers	4.75 (1.6)
I would continue to use Chip if he were available to me	5.44 (1.63)
Comparison to other sources	
I tended to ask Chip before turning to a coworker for help	4.59 (1.98)
Chip was able to help me when I would otherwise have called the employee service center	4.8 (1.69)
I thought to ask Chip for help before emailing my onboarding specialist	5.67 (1.59)
What percent of questions was Chip able to answer for you?	62.2% (27.5%)

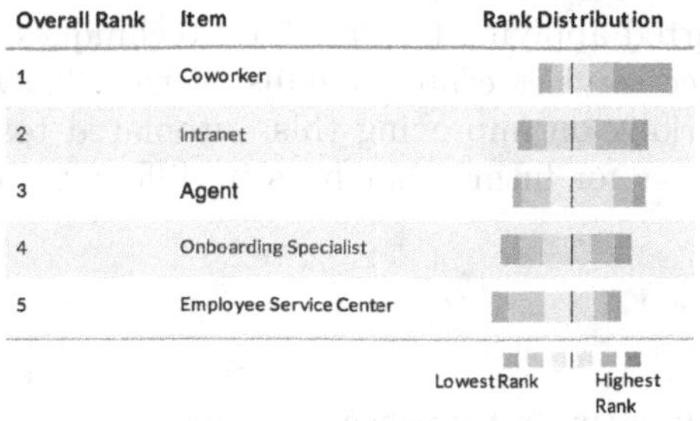

Overall Rank	Item	Rank Distribution
1	Coworker	
2	Intranet	
3	Agent	
4	Onboarding Specialist	
5	Employee Service Center	

Lowest Rank   Highest Rank

Fig. 1. Source of information ranked by their ability to answer questions for new hires from the questionnaire data.

co-workers are the preferred choice to obtain reliable and correct answer, *Chip* is in the same level as intranet, ESC, and onboarding specialists.

The users' ratings of system accuracy at the message level was 63%, which is very close to 58% we get from the annotation results. A second estimate of accuracy comes from the users' #FAIL messages. However, users do not always report system failures, nevertheless, it serves as a reasonable metric to measure system effectiveness, we observed that "#FAIL" was used for about 8.5% of the messages.

5   Discussion and Conclusion

In this paper, We presented a conversational agent (chat bot) that supports new hires with their informational needs during their onboarding phase. We described system capabilities and outlined design consideration in building such an agent. Evaluating domain specific retrieval-based conversational systems is a challenging open research problem, mixed results have been reported through objective vs subjective evaluations [19,20,27]. We approached evaluation through a live deployment and a field study with 344 new hires in a large organization and measured system effectiveness based on the data collected "in the wild," and post-deployment surveys. Our results are highly encouraging: The system we built can well compete with existing informational means such as call center or onboarding experts. We observed accuracies of around 60% (or 70% counting both correct answers and those that needed some improvement but still provided value) using both objective (message level annotations) and subjective (questionnaire) evaluations. Even with this average accuracy, subjective evaluation indicated a users' intent for continued use. In our experience, objective evaluations are effective in fine tuning the performance while subjective evaluations measure user satisfaction more effectively.

One of the most challenging and labor-intense aspects of building an informational agent is the curation of the knowledge base. It involves the manual generation of questions and their natural language variations with the guidance from subject matter experts from the employee service center. To automate this process, We have started applying text analytic techniques to the content provided by the employee services center (emails, tickets, knowledge documents). We are currently working on improving this automated text analytics process so that knowledge bases for future chat bots in different domains can be built more effectively.

References

1. AlchemyAPI (2010). http://www.alchemyapi.com
2. Bickmore, T., Cassell, J.: Relational agents: a model and implementation of building user trust. In: Proceedings of the SIGCHI Conference on Human Factors in Computing Systems, pp. 396–403. ACM (2001)
3. Bickmore, T., Pfeifer, L., Schulman, D.: Relational agents improve engagement and learning in science museum visitors. In: Vilhjálmsson, H.H., Kopp, S., Marsella, S., Thórisson, K.R. (eds.) IVA 2011. LNCS, vol. 6895, pp. 55–67. Springer, Heidelberg (2011). doi:10.1007/978-3-642-23974-8_7
4. Bickmore, T.W., Pfeifer, L.M., Jack, B.W.: Taking the time to care: empowering low health literacy hospital patients with virtual nurse agents. In: Proceedings of the SIGCHI Conference on Human Factors in Computing Systems, pp. 1265–1274. ACM (2009)
5. Bickmore, W.T., Utami, D., Matsuyama, R., Paasche-Orlow, K.M.: Improving access to online health information with conversational agents: a randomized controlled experiment. J. Med. Internet Res. **18**(1), e1 (2016)
6. Blei, D.M., Ng, A.Y., Jordan, M.I.: Latent Dirichlet allocation. J. Mach. Learn. Res. **3**(Jan), 993–1022 (2003)
7. Cassell, J.: Embodied conversational interface agents. Commun. ACM **43**(4), 70–78 (2000)
8. Ji, Z., Lu, Z., Li, H.: An information retrieval approach to short text conversation. arXiv preprint arXiv:1408.6988 (2014)
9. Kim, Y.: Convolutional neural networks for sentence classification. In: Proceedings of the 2014 Conference on Empirical Methods in Natural Language Processing, EMNLP 2014, pp. 1746–1751 (2014)
10. Kiseleva, J., Williams, K., Jiang, J., Hassan Awadallah, A., Crook, A.C., Zitouni, I., Anastasakos, T.: Understanding user satisfaction with intelligent assistants. In: Proceedings of the 2016 ACM on Conference on Human Information Interaction and Retrieval, pp. 121–130. ACM (2016)
11. Lave, J., Wenger, E.: Situated Learning. The Language of Science Education. Cambridge University Press, New York (1991)
12. Liao, Q.V., Davis, M., Geyer, W., Muller, M., Shami, N.S.: What can you do?: Studying social-agent orientation and agent proactive interactions with an agent for employees. In: Proceedings of the 2016 ACM Conference on Designing Interactive Systems, pp. 264–275. ACM (2016)
13. Metzler, D., Croft, W.B.: A Markov random field model for term dependencies. In: Proceedings of the 28th Annual International ACM SIGIR Conference on Research and Development In Information Retrieval, pp. 472–479. ACM (2005)
14. Miller, V.D., Jablin, F.M.: Information seeking during organizational entry: influences, tactics, and a model of the process. Acad. Manag. Rev. **16**(1), 92–120 (1991)
15. Pickard, M.D., Burns, M.B., Moffitt, K.C.: A theoretical justification for using embodied conversational agents (ECAs) to augment accounting-related interviews. J. Inf. Syst. **27**(2), 159–176 (2013)

16. Ritter, A., Cherry, C., Dolan, W.B.: Data-driven response generation in social media. In: Proceedings of the Conference on Empirical Methods in Natural Language Processing, EMNLP 2011, pp. 583–593. Association for Computational Linguistics, Stroudsburg, PA, USA (2011). http://dl.acm.org/citation.cfm?id=2145432.2145500

17. Shang, L., Lu, Z., Li, H.: Neural responding machine for short-text conversation. In: Proceedings of the 53rd Annual Meeting of the Association for Computational Linguistics, ACL 2015, pp. 1577–1586 (2015)

18. Shechtman, N., Horowitz, L.M.: Media inequality in conversation: how people behave differently when interacting with computers and people. In: Proceedings of the SIGCHI Conference on Human Factors in Computing Systems, pp. 281–288. ACM (2003)

19. Silvervarg, A., Jönsson, A.: Subjective and objective evaluation of conversational agents in learning environments for young teenagers. In: Proceedings of the 7th IJCAI Workshop on Knowledge and Reasoning in Practical Dialogue Systems (2011)

20. Silvervarg, A., JÃűnsson, A.: Subjective and objective evaluation of conversational agents in learning environments for young teenagers. In: 7th IJCAI Workshop on Knowledge and Reasoning in Practical Dialogue Systems (2011)

21. Strohman, T., Metzler, D., Turtle, H., Croft, W.B.: Indri: a language model-based search engine for complex queries. In: Proceedings of the International Conference on Intelligent Analysis, vol. 2, pp. 2–6. Citeseer (2005)

22. Tegos, S., Demetriadis, S.: Conversational agents improve peer learning through building on prior knowledge. J. Educ. Technol. Soc. **20**(1), 99–111 (2017)

23. Trappl, R. (ed.): Your Virtual Butler. LNCS (LNAI), vol. 7407. Springer, Heidelberg (2013). doi:10.1007/978-3-642-37346-6

24. Traum, D., DeVault, D., Lee, J., Wang, Z., Marsella, S.: Incremental dialogue understanding and feedback for multiparty, multimodal conversation. In: Nakano, Y., Neff, M., Paiva, A., Walker, M. (eds.) IVA 2012. LNCS, vol. 7502, pp. 275–288. Springer, Heidelberg (2012). doi:10.1007/978-3-642-33197-8_29

25. Turing, A.M.: Computing machinery and intelligence. Mind **59**(236), 433–460 (1950)

26. Vinyals, O., Le, Q.: A neural conversational model. arXiv preprint arXiv:1506.05869 (2015)

27. Walker, M.A., Litman, D.J., Kamm, C.A., Abella, A.: Paradise: a framework for evaluating spoken dialogue agents. In: Proceedings of the Eighth Conference on European Chapter of the Association for Computational Linguistics, pp. 271–280. Association for Computational Linguistics (1997)

28. Wang, Z., Lee, J., Marsella, S.: Towards more comprehensive listening behavior: beyond the bobble head. In: Vilhjálmsson, H.H., Kopp, S., Marsella, S., Thórisson, K.R. (eds.) IVA 2011. LNCS, vol. 6895, pp. 216–227. Springer, Heidelberg (2011). doi:10.1007/978-3-642-23974-8_24

29. Williams, J., Raux, A., Ramachandran, D., Black, A.: The dialog state tracking challenge. In: Proceedings of the SIGDIAL 2013 Conference, pp. 404–413 (2013)

30. Xiao, J., Stasko, J., Catrambone, R.: An empirical study of the effect of agent competence on user performance and perception. In: Proceedings of the Third International Joint Conference on Autonomous Agents and Multiagent Systems-Volume 1, pp. 178–185. IEEE Computer Society (2004)

31. Yao, M.: 4 critical steps to maximize chatbot retention & engagement (December 2016). http://www.topbots.com/4-critical-steps-to-maximize-chatbot-retention-engagement/

RemindMe: Plugging a Reminder Manager into Email for Enhancing Workplace Responsiveness

Casey Dugan[1(✉)], Aabhas Sharma[1], Michael Muller[1], Di Lu[2],
Michael Brenndoerfer[3], and Werner Geyer[1]

[1] IBM Research, Cambridge, MA, USA
{cadugan, michael_muller, Werner.Geyer}@us.ibm.com,
Aabhas.Sharma@ibm.com
[2] University of Pittsburgh, Pittsburgh, PA, USA
dil6@pitt.edu
[3] IBM, Rueschlikon, Switzerland
BRE@zurich.ibm.com

Abstract. Reminding others to do something or bringing something to some-one's attention by sending reminders is common in the workplace. Our goal was to create a system to reduce the cognitive overhead for employees to manage their email, specifically the incoming and outgoing requests with their col-leagues and others. We build on prior research on social request management, interruptions, and cognitive psychology in the design of such a system that includes an email reminder creation algorithm, with a built-in learning mecha-nism for improving such reminders over time, and a reminder delivery user interface. The system is delivered to users through a browser plugin, allowing it to be built on top of an existing web-based email system within an enterprise.

Keywords: Reminders · Email · Request management · Browser plugin

1 Introduction

Email is used for many purposes [13, 30] and the burden of managing it is a core part of the work environment [8, 13, 20, 44]. This is particularly true as many use email for task management [4, 5, 14, 20, 34, 40]. In this paper, we consider tasks represented in incoming and outgoing requests in email in the work place. While such requests can occur in many kinds of channels (real-time messaging, social collaboration platforms etc.), recent research has shown that email is still the predominant channel for requests in the workplace [34]. We have observed that a common strategy in managing requests in the workplace involves reminding others to do something or bringing something to someone's attention by sending reminders. However, this involves significant cognitive overhead for employees: *I asked Bob for that file a couple of days ago, is it too soon to remind him to send it?* As such, we sought to create a system that proactively reminds users of such request-based emails that require their attention – before their colleagues need to.

© IFIP International Federation for Information Processing 2017
Published by Springer International Publishing AG 2017. All Rights Reserved
R. Bernhaupt et al. (Eds.): INTERACT 2017, Part II, LNCS 10514, pp. 392–401, 2017.
DOI: 10.1007/978-3-319-67684-5_24

A significant challenge in attempting to build such a system is that the very act of reminding users could distract them from their tasks at hand. Most studies of reminding have involved the unsolicited presentation of a message – i.e., an "interruptive notification" [36]. In workplaces, notifications interrupt on-going work, and are therefore stressful [33] and can result in negative emotional experiences of work [22, 36]. While researchers have studied the impact of interruptions [7] and recovery from interruptions [37] as a matter of cognitive load and task boundaries [22], there is also evidence that people prioritize interruptions in terms of content and social relationships [16]. Despite the emotional and cognitive costs, users in organizations continue to prefer to receive interruptions, because those notifications provide awareness of others' work and needs [23].

In our work, we adopt an unobtrusive way of notifying users. Instead of interrupting the user's on-going work, we provide a slowly-changing, ambient series of non-interruptive notifications. These are presented in a dedicated region, directly within the context of a user's mail client. This allows the user to be aware of such pending tasks, while being in control of the decision of whether the interruption is important enough to act upon right now.

Another significant challenge in creating such a system is determining which emails a user should be reminded about. While it is relatively easy to classify emails into binary categories such as spam-vs.-ham [15], or single dimensions such as sentiment [6], the automated analysis of emails to determine which contain requests, or actions a receiver must take, has proven more challenging. Some researchers have explored classifying emails and email-like messages into categories [17]. Early work analyzed rule-based classification of messages similar to emails [31]. Increasingly, researchers are using machine-learning methods to classify emails in general (e.g., [1, 15], for activities [12], for meeting requests [26], and for specific purposes such as prioritization [45]. The most relevant work in this area is predicting the likelihood of a user responding to a given email [11], or the end of a conversation [29]. While such work discusses how a reply prediction algorithm could be used to make users aware of emails they need to reply to (such as through annotating received emails), they stop short of proposing a reminder system. We believe this comes back to balancing the required reply behavior (as opposed to expected) against the cost of the interruption. For example, just because I typically reply with "Thanks" when a colleague fulfills my requests, the system likely shouldn't remind me to do so a week later if I forgot.

To address these challenges, we report on a system architecture for RemindMe, which supports identifying, presenting and acting on reminders from within complex email interfaces, as part of a longer-term goal of providing automated support to help users manage their requests and reminders. Our envisioned systems would be similar in spirit to the opportunistic agents of Dey and Abowd [10] and Myers and Yorke-Smith [35], but would focus on *social reminders* among collaborating colleagues. This paper constitutes a first step, which solves the problem of managing social reminders. It takes a novel approach in delivering such reminders to users, balancing interruption and awareness. It builds on prior machine learning work in determining which emails likely require responses. And it incorporates mechanisms to gather user feedback, necessary for the algorithm to be able to learn the user's preferences towards the nature of requests that they would like to be reminded about and better identify when to remind users about such requests.

2 Context, Challenges, and Technical Approach

Enterprise users face challenges with email overload [29, 44] and social request management [34], and are most likely to need proactive reminding capabilities. To help them, we designed and built RemindMe within the context of IBM.

In evaluating how to build the reminder system, context, pluggability and generalizability were taken into account. Reminding users within the context of a mail application was important to ensure they were currently focused on their regular email activity and minimize the interruptions of reminders [26]. Pluggability focused on the ability to extend an existing IBM email tool, rather than building a new one. Generalizability related to building the tool in a way to allow for testing with users from other organizations with minimal development costs.

To support reminding within an existing mail application context, we designed our solution to extend IBM's popular web-based email client, through the use of a browser plugin. As Firefox was the most popular browser used to access the mail platform within IBM, we first focused on a Firefox plugin.

The plugin format also helped with the generalizability of the solution. We could give selected users the plugin to install for testing purposes, who could uninstall it if they chose to. We also gained significant control over modifying the existing mail interface, and the ability to modify the plugin to support different web-based email systems supporting generalizability. The downsides of this approach are that our system couldn't automatically be rolled out to all IBM users simultaneously (since it requires installation), we support only Firefox browser users, and we are only able to collect data and remind users while they use the mail site within their browser.

While the Browser Plugin focuses on the interface and limited, light-weight analysis, a server component is required to conduct more computationally intense analysis including storage and processing of a user's email, request identification, and reminder creation, storage, and feedback.

As shown in Fig. 1, the ReminderMe system consists of three overall modules. The first module is responsible for generation of Reminders. The email synchronization is responsible for collecting the user's emails and is the only part of this module that

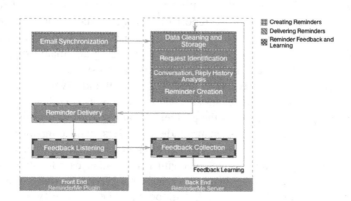

Fig. 1. Flowchart depicting interactions of the different system components

operates within the plugin. The mail data collected is then analyzed on the RemindMe server, which also generates the reminders.

The second module is responsible for delivering the system-generated reminders to the user; it operates entirely within the plugin. Finally, the third module is responsible for obtaining feedback from the user, analyzing the information and providing this to the Reminder creation module in the form of feedback learning. This module is divided across both the RemindMe plugin and back-end server.

3   Creating Reminders

3.1   Email Synchronization

As part of the reminder creation process, email data must first be collected from the underlying enterprise mail system and sent to the RemindMe server for storage and processing (Fig. 1). When the user authenticates via the email service's web interface, the browser activates the RemindMe plugin. The plugin then continuously queries the same mail retrieval REST APIs used to populate the mail interface and sends the results to the RemindMe server for synchronization. Polled emails include both incoming and sent emails. We periodically re-poll to check for changes such as deletes and changes to state (such as unread/read).

3.2   Data Cleaning and Storage

Emails arriving at the server are stripped of HTML and rich text, reply histories (in the case of replies to threads), and email signatures. New line whitespace is preserved, resulting in an optimized line-based representation of the textual content (both subject and body) of the emails. The procedure is similar to [9].

3.3   Request Identification

Within the RemindMe system, we chose to focus on reminding users about emails containing requests, rather than focusing on other features related to reply prediction [11]. To identify such requests within email messages, we use a third-party "action identification" API from Watson Workservices, found at https://api.watsonwork.ibm. com. This is a machine-learning classifier that analyzes provided text and returns a set of identified requests, questions etc. (such as "please send the file"), the position in the text where these were found, confidence scores etc. We run this identification on each textual content line from the body of an email, as well as the subject.

3.4   Conversation Analytics, User-Reply-History Analysis

In addition to the storage of individual emails, we also store a representation of overall conversation threads, which tracks which emails are replies to other emails (e.g., [24, 41]). For each RemindMe user we also calculate statistics on their reply patterns with other users, similar to [29]. These statistics include how often they receive emails from another user and reply to those emails, as well as how long it takes them to reply to those emails on average.

3.5   Reminder Creation

Users are frequently overwhelmed with the volume of work items to manage [3, 43], email in general [29, 44], and email-requests in particular [28, 34]. However, users are reluctant to do extra work to mark emails as needing reminders [4]. Therefore, in RemindMe, we try to automatically determine whether a user is likely to need a reminder about a given email in the future. To do so, the results of the Request Identification analysis described above are used to determine the likelihood that a given message contains a request (based on the subject or body of the email including questions, requests, etc., with a probability score above a certain threshold, see [11] for a related approach). However, in practice, request identification alone is not sufficient, because certain emails users are unlikely to reply to were found to have correctly identified requests, such as spam emails asking "Have you checked your credit score?" Therefore, we also analyze the reply-statistics for a given user to determine how likely they are to reply to this particular user. If they have received many emails, but replied to none, a reminder is not created. In addition to automatically generating reminders, reminders are also created for emails a user has manually flagged as requiring follow-up. However, as only 5% of IBM users actively use this feature of the under-lying mail system (see also [4]), most reminders are automatically determined.

For each reminder created, we need to determine when it should be shown. As an initial approximation of this, we again make use of the reply history between user *dyads* – i.e., a sending and receiving user (see also [29]), to determine the average reply time for the message receiver. If a reply to this message is not processed by the system by the time this period has elapsed, a reminder about the message is activated for the user (Fig. 1). This works in both directions, for requests a user has sent to others where replies have not been received as well as requests sent to the user.

Finally, for each reminder, we need to determine what information from the original email should be included as part of the reminder message. To do so, we draw upon the significant body of research in the field of cognitive psychology that studied the effect of providing reminders on the performance of prospective memory (or a person's capability to remember to do an activity in the future) since the 1990s. Guynn et al. [18] found that the most effective reminders referred both to the information about the trigger event of the task and to the intended activity. More recently, Baldwin [2] showed that text-only reminders had a limited period of impact, which could be extended by including a picture implying the task. As such, for each reminder, in addition to storing a reference to the original request email and when the reminder should be activated, we store a "trigger event" description (i.e. "Bob made a request to you in an email with subject 'Customer Briefing' on May 1st"), "intended activity" text determined from an identified request within the email with the highest confidence score (i.e. "Send the file"), as well as a photo of the related person (i.e. the sender if the user is the recipient of the request).

4 Delivering Reminders

While most prior reminder systems have operated through intrusive alerts [26], a key design consideration for RemindMe was to deliver reminders in a fashion that grabs the user's attention, but not enough to distract them from their other email activity, allowing users to make their own decisions about potential interruptions. The interface attempts to strike this balance by creating a dedicated visual 'reminder area,' which is injected by the browser plugin directly above the email viewing space, as shown in Fig. 2. This area presents the user with exactly one reminder at a time, to prevent reminder overload. Reminders determined by the server to be currently active then appear in this area and the plugin continuously polls the server for newly activated reminders.

Fig. 2. RemindMe browser plugin injects interface components into existing mail application, including: A. Minimal active reminder view. B. Maximized view. C. Contextual reminder information for a selected email. D. Reminder annotations on list views

The interface automatically transitions from the current reminder to the next active reminder after a set time, to provide ambient awareness, avoiding additional notification overload. However, this automated transition between active reminders can be personalized through user settings (a popup accessed through the Settings icon shown on the right of Fig. 2A). The user can toggle between automatic scrolling vs. manual scrolling. Additionally, the user can manually transition from the currently shown reminder to other active reminders by using two on-screen arrow keys.

The dedicated visual reminder area begins in a "minimized" state, or the area shown in Fig. 2A, which includes only the "trigger event" description and photo of the user associated with the reminder, as described in Sect. 3.5. This is done to minimize the area used by the reminder, which takes away space devoted to reading messages within the mail interface. However, if the user chooses to see more information about the current reminder or interact with it in some way, s/he can click on it to expand the reminder space, to include the area shown in Fig. 2B. The maximized view of the reminder display region includes the "intended activity" text described above as well as options for facilitating replies and providing other feedback on the reminder. The user has the option of viewing the entire conversation thread related through a "See Conversation" button. A "Reply" button also enables the user to write their response to original reminder-triggering email directly from the RemindMe plugin interface. Choosing either of these options causes the relevant content to open up in a new tab rather than disturbing the current state of the email interface.

5 Reminder Feedback and Learning Mechanisms

As reminder creation in RemindMe involves various aspects of machine learning (learning user reply behaviors, request identification etc.), we have designed the system to collect, store, and learn from both implicit and explicit user feedback on these reminders (Fig. 1). Three of the four user interface regions highlighted in Fig. 2 include feedback mechanisms for the identification of emails requiring reminders as well as the selection of the appropriate time to present a reminder.

The maximized area shown in Fig. 2B addresses currently active reminders. Here, the user can give feedback on both the validity as well as the timing of the reminder. For example, clicking the "Reply" button in this area informs the RemindMe server a request was completed, which deactivates the reminder and removes it from this area. While both the "Done" and "Remove" buttons trigger the removal of the current reminder, they provide different feedback. With the "Done" option, the user provides feedback that the identified request was valid, they have simply already completed it. This feedback tells the system that more work may be necessary to automatically identify completion of requests like these in the future. The "Remove" button, in contrast, provides feedback to the RemindMe server that the current reminder was misidentified. This feedback can be used to tune a personalized machine learning classifier of messages that should be treated as reminders for this user.

The final functionality of Fig. 2B is a set of "snooze" options that allow the user to simultaneously give feedback to the system that this was a valid reminder given at the wrong time, while also enabling the user to reschedule it for a better time. The interface provides four options to snooze a currently active reminder: fixed durations of thirty minutes, two hours and one day, and a user-adjustable interval.

The areas shown in Fig. 2D and C present alternate methods of making users aware of emails which are likely to trigger reminders in the future. The area in Fig. 2D presents annotations in the inbox while the area in Fig. 2C presents additional reminder details about the currently viewed email. As shown in Fig. 2D, in the email list, the plugin adds a small annotation next to messages that are classified as future reminders. The annotation contains the estimated time within which the reminder will activate. This indication allows the user to identify and view an email of interest in a more direct fashion as well as gain early awareness of future reminding activity. As shown in Fig. 2C, when a given email is displayed, an added reminder bar affords the user the ability to view, modify and give feedback on whether the respective reminder is active, scheduled for the future, or does not exist. If the current email is not marked as a reminder, the user can manually schedule a future reminder for it, which acts as feedback to the system of a potentially missed request. Should the current email be marked as an upcoming reminder, the user can view the estimated time within which this email would enter the user interface as an active reminder and manually modify that activation time if necessary. Again, by doing so, the user informs the RemindMe server of a more suitable time to present the relevant reminder. This feedback can serve as ground truth to tune a different machine-learning algorithm that is focused on personalized time intervals.

6 Conclusion

We designed and built a novel proactive reminder system that helps enterprise users cope with work requests buried in email. Our work is informed through previous research [3–5, 11, 14, 19, 20, 26, 28, 30, 31, 42–44] and, to the best of our knowledge, describes the first system design that combines various components and algorithms together into an integrated system that tackles "email overload" [44] from a reminder perspective, while balancing between intrusive notifications [26] and ambient information. We presented an architecture that allowed the system to be integrated into an existing web-based mail application through the use of a browser plugin. The interface design was informed by prior research on social request management and interruptions, as well as work in the area of cognitive psychology on the effect of types of reminder information on prospective memory [18, 21].

While our system incorporates prior research and functions as an end-to-end request management tool, there is room for improvement in future work. The system currently uses a simplistic model of request "fulfillment" - it assumes a reply to a given email negates the need for a reminder. However, we understand that in practice the process may be much more complex (i.e. a user replies that they will send a file at a later date, rather than sending the file). As such, we plan to incorporate a more detailed method of determining if a given reply satisfies the request from a previous email, using a method as described in [25]. Another possible improvement to the system could come in the form of sensing the user's current task or task boundaries, such as in [22, 23], in choosing when to remind them about certain emails.

Early feedback collected on the system has already established a need to expand on how users can respond to email requests through the reminder interface. For example, a feature can be added through which the system helps the user compose a reminder message. A user also asked for a feature to delay request response delivery until the user's average reply time to the request sender has been reached. A detailed user study is planned to test the personalized learning mechanisms related to reminder identification and timing described in the Reminder Feedback section. The user study would also uncover additional user needs and preferences in using such a system, such as any burden of giving manual feedback on accuracy of timing and content of reminders, and users' privacy requirements in the automated analysis of their email. Finally, through the current system design and through above mentioned improvements, we believe such a reminder system can change how we interact with email in the future.

References

1. Alberts, I., Vellino, A.: The importance of context in the automatic classification of email as records of business value: a pilot study. Proc. AIST **50**, 1–2 (2013). Article no. 113

2. Baldwin, M.: The effects of reminder distinctiveness and anticipatory interval on prospective memory. MS thesis, Clemson University (2014)

3. Barreau, D., Nardi, B.A.: Finding and reminding: file organization on the desktop. SIGCHI Bull. **27**(3), 39–43 (1995)

4. Bellotti, V., Dalal, B., Good, N., Flynn, P., Bobrow, D.G., Ducheneaut, N.: What a to-do: studies of task management towards the design of a personal task list manager. In: Proceedings of the CHI 2004, pp. 735–742 (2004)

5. Bellotti, V., Ducheneaut, N., Howard, M., Smith, I.: Taking email to task: the design and evaluation of a task management centered email tool. In: Proceedings of the CHI 2003, pp. 345–352 (2003)

6. Bogawar, P.S., Bhoyar, K.K.: Soft computing approaches to classification of emails for sentiment analysis. In: Proceedings of the ICIA 2016, Article no. 22 (2016)

7. Bogunovich, P., Salvucci, D.: The effects of time constraints on user behavior for deferrable interruptions. In: Proceedings of the CHI 2011, pp. 3123–3126 (2011)

8. Bota, H., Bennett, P.N., Awadallah, A.H., Dumais, S.T.: Self-Es: the role of emails-to-self in personal information management. In: Proceedings of the CHIIR 2017, pp. 205–214 (2017)

9. Carvalho, V.R., Cohen, W.W.: Learning to extract signature and reply lines from email. In: Proceedings of the Conference on Email Anti-Spam (2004)

10. Dey, A.K., Abowd, G.D.: CybreMinder: a context-aware system for supporting reminders. In: Thomas, P., Gellersen, H.-W. (eds.) HUC 2000. LNCS, vol. 1927, pp. 172–186. Springer, Heidelberg (2000). doi:10.1007/3-540-39959-3_13

11. Drezde, M., Brooks, T., Carroll, J., Magarick, J., Blitzer, J., Pereira, F.: Intelligent email: reply and attachment prediction. In: Proceedings of the IUI 2008, pp. 321–324 (2008)

12. Drezde, M., Lau, T., Kushmerick, N.: Automatically classifying emails into activities. In: Proceedings of the IUI 2006, pp. 70–77 (2006)

13. Ducheneaut, N., Bellotti, V.: Email as habitat. Interactions **8**(5), 30–38 (2001)

14. Flores, F., Graves, M., Hartfield, B., Winograd, T.: Computer systems and the design of organizational interaction. ACM TOIS **6**(2), 153–172 (1988)

15. George, P., Vinod, P.: Machine learning approaches for filtering spam emails. In: Proceedings of the SIN 2015, pp. 271–274 (2015)

16. Grandhi, S.: Human interruptability: a relational perspective. In: Proceedings of the GROUP 2007, Article no. 2 (2007)

17. Grbovic, M., Halawi, G., Karnin, Z., Maarek, Y.: How many folders do you really need? Classifying email into a handful of categories. In: Proceedings of the CIKM 2014, pp. 869–878 (2014)

18. Guynn, M.J., McDonald, M.A., Einstein, G.O.: Prospective memory: when reminders fail. Mem. Cogn. **26**(2), 287–298

19. Gwizdka, J.: Email task management styles: the cleaners and the keepers. In: Proceedings of the CHI 2004, pp. 1235–1238 (2004)

20. Gwizdka, J.: Reinventing the inbox –supporting the management of pending tasks in email. In: Proceedings of the CHI 2002, pp. 550–551 (2002)

21. Gwizdka, J.: Supporting prospective information in email. In: CHI EA 2001, pp. 135–136 (2001)

22. Iqbal, S.T., Bailey, B.P.: Effects of intelligent notification management on users and their tasks. In: Proceedings of the CHI 2008, pp. 93–102 (2008)

23. Iqbal, S.T., Horvitz, E.: Notifications and awareness: a field study of alert usage and preferences. In: Proceedings of the CSCW 2010, pp. 27–30 (2010)

24. Joty, S., Carenini, G., Murray, G., Ng, R.T.: Exploiting conversation structure in unsupervised topic segmentation for emails. In: Proceedings of the EMNLP 2010, pp. 388–398 (2010)

25. Kalia, A., Nezhad, H.R.M., Bartolini, C., Singh, M.: Identifying business tasks and commitments from email and chat conversations (2013). http://citeseerx.ist.psu.edu/viewdoc/download?doi=10.1.1.643.5660&rep=rep1&type=pdf
26. Kamar, E., Horvitz, E.: Jogger: models for context-sensitive reminding. In: Proceedings of the AAMAS 2011, pp. 1089–1090 (2011)
27. Kaptein, M., Halteren, A.: Adaptive persuasive messaging to increase service retention: using persuasion profiles to increase the effectiveness of email reminders. Pers. Ubiquit. Comput. **17**(6), 1173–1185 (2013)
28. Karger, D.: Creating user interfaces that entice people to manage better information. In: Proceedings of the CIKM 2011, p. 1 (2011)
29. Kooti, F., Aiello, L.M., Grbovic, M., Lerman, K., Mantrach, A.: Evolution of conversations in the age of email overload. In: Proceedings of the WWW 2015, pp. 603–613 (2015)
30. Mackay, W.E.: More than just a communication system: diversity in the use of electronic mail. In: Proceedings of the CSCW 1998, pp. 344–353 (1998)
31. Mackay, W.E., Malone, T.W., Crowston, K., Rao, R., Rosenblitt, D., Card, S.K.: How do experienced information lens users use roles? In: Proceedings of the CHI 1989, pp. 211–216 (1989)
32. Mandic, M., Kerne, A.: Using intimacy, chronology, and zooming to visualize rhythms in email experience. In: CHI EA 2005, pp. 1617–1620 (2005)
33. Mark, G., Gudith, D., Klocke, U.: The cost of interrupted work: more speed and stress. In: Proceedings of the CHI 2008, pp. 107–110 (2008)
34. Muller, M., Dugan, C., Brenndoerfer, M., Monroe, M., Geyer, W.: What did I ask you to do, by when, and for whom? Passion and compassion in request management. In: Proceedings of the CSCW 2017, pp. 1009–1023 (2017)
35. Myers, K., Yorke-Smith, N.: Proactive behavior of a personal assistive agent. In: Proceedings of the AAMAS 2008 (2008)
36. Paul, C., Komlodi, A.: Emotion as an indicator for future interruptive notification experiences. In: CHI EA 2012, pp. 2003–2008 (2012)
37. Salvucci, D.D.: On reconstruction of task context after interruption. In: Proceedings of the CHI 2010, pp. 89–92 (2010)
38. Scupelli, P., Kiesler, S., Fussell, S.R., Chen, C.: Project view IM: a tool for juggling multiple projects and teams. In: Proceedings of the CHI 2005, pp. 1773–1776 (2005)
39. Singh, N., Tomitsch, M., Maher, M.L.: A time and place for preparatory methods in email. In: Proceedings of the CHINZ 2013, Article no. 4 (2013)
40. Siu, N., Iverson, L., Tang, A.: Going with the flow: email awareness and task management. In: Proceedings of the CSCW 2006, pp. 441–450 (2006)
41. Thomas, G., Zahm, M., Furcy, D.: Using a sentence compression pipeline for the summarization of email threads in an archive. J. Comp. Sci. Coll. **31**(2), 72–78 (2015)
42. Venoglia, G., Dabbish, L., Cadiz, J.J., Gupta, A.: Supporting email workflow (2001). http://research.microsoft.com/en-us/groups/coet/01-88.pdf
43. Whittaker, S., Jones, Q., Nardi, B., Creech, M., Terveen, L., Isaacs, E., Hainsworth, J.: ContactMap: organizing communication in a social desktop. ACM TOCHI **11**(4), 445–471 (2004)
44. Whitaker, S., Sidner, C.: Email overload: exploring personal information management of email. In: Proceedings of the CHI 1996, pp. 276–283 (1996)
45. Yoo, S., Yang, Y., Carbonell, J.: Modeling personalized email prioritization: classification-based and regression-based approaches. In: Proceedings of the CIKM 2011, pp. 729–738 (2011)

The Cost of Improved Overview: An Analysis of the Use of Electronic Whiteboards in Emergency Departments

Morten Hertzum[(⊠)]

University of Copenhagen, Copenhagen, Denmark
hertzum@hum.ku.dk

Abstract. Forming and maintaining an overview of an information space is key to competent action in many situations and often supported by overview displays. We investigate the cost of the improved overview associated with the introduction of electronic whiteboards in four emergency departments (EDs). In such a dynamic environment the work that goes into keeping the whiteboard current is, we contend, an indicator of the cost of maintaining an overview. On the basis of log data for the period 2012–2014 we find that the ED clinicians make an average of 1.91 whiteboard changes per minute to keep the whiteboard current. Performing these changes takes an estimated 6647 h a year in each ED. While the whiteboard is well-like and has improved the clinicians' overview, our cost-of-overview estimation shows that it consumes substantial staff resources. This reflects the value the clinicians assign to having an overview but also reveals the amount of resources removed from other activities to maintain this overview.

Keywords: Cost of use · Overview formation · Electronic whiteboard · Healthcare

1 Introduction

Professionals in engineering, healthcare, management, and other dynamic domains are confronted with large amounts of information in their daily work and must be able to navigate it competently. Relatedly, common non-work activities involve monitoring continuously evolving social media for updates of interest and searching vast information spaces for items about specified topics. The sheer amount of information has made it challenging for users to maintain the overview necessary to navigate the information and has made overview displays an important part of many systems [1, 2]. One indication of the importance of overview displays is Shneiderman's [3] visual information-seeking mantra: "Overview first, zoom and filter, then details-on-demand". Before users know where to zoom in and what to filter away, they first need an overview of the information space. However, an overview does not come for free. It is especially demanding to maintain an overview when the information space changes dynamically because the overview decays quickly and therefore has to be continuously updated to stay current. That is, while an initial overview may be necessary, it is not

R. Bernhaupt et al. (Eds.): INTERACT 2017, Part II, LNCS 10514, pp. 402–410, 2017.
DOI: 10.1007/978-3-319-67684-5_25

sufficient. This study investigates the amount of work involved in maintaining an overview of the dynamically evolving state of an emergency department (ED).

EDs are the common entry point to hospitals for most patients with acute problems. In the ED the patients are assessed (triaged) to determine the severity of their problem [4]. Patients with high-severity problems are attended straight away to arrive at an initial diagnose and then transferred to the appropriate inpatient department for further treatment. Patients with low-severity problems may wait for hours before they are seen by a clinician. This patient flow means that most patients stay in the ED for a brief period only. But the patient volume is large, and every now and then it exceeds the available ED resources [5, 6]. Initial information about the patients' condition will tend to be rudimentary and additional information must be acquired quickly, reliably, and often under time pressure. Any oversight about a patient's condition may be detrimental to her health but this pressure toward detailed patient examinations must be balanced against the need to see a number of patients quickly. These work conditions create an environment in which it is important to have, and continuously maintain, an overview of the current state of the ED: Which patients are in more urgent need of attention? Which clinicians are responsible for which patients? What are the health problems of my current patients? What treatment should be administered to these patients? What is the status of this treatment? Are new patients about to arrive? And so forth.

We have for several years been involved in a project aiming to support ED clinicians in maintaining an overview of their work [e.g., 7–9]. This project has consisted of technically developing, organizationally implementing, and systematically evaluating an electronic whiteboard in the EDs in Region Zealand, one of the five healthcare regions in Denmark. The whiteboard (Fig. 1) supplements the electronic patient record by providing selected information about all patients currently in the ED. For each patient the whiteboard provides one row of information, including time of arrival, triage level, responsible physician, responsible nurse, working diagnose, current treatment activity, lab-test results, and – if relevant – the time at which the patient will be transferred to an inpatient department. The coordinating nurse plays a key role in keeping the whiteboard current but whiteboard updates are made by all physicians and nurses as well as by some other staff groups. In the present study we analyze almost three years of log data from the whiteboards in the four EDs of the region to assess the amount of work that goes into keeping the whiteboard current. We take this work as an indicator of the work-related cost of maintaining an overview.

It is important to note that the whiteboard has been successful in supporting the ED clinicians in forming and maintaining an overview of their work. In interviews conducted as part of our activities relating to the whiteboard a physician at ED3, for example, expressed that "*It gives a great overview. I cannot imagine that we could do without it.*" More formally, a survey at ED1 and ED2 showed that the clinicians experienced an improvement in their overview of their work when the electronic whiteboard replaced the former dry-erase whiteboards [10]. In addition, before/after measurements at ED4 showed that the nurses' mental workload decreased at the beginning of their shifts when they form an overview of the ED [11]. That is, the work that goes into changing the whiteboard to keep it current has improved the clinicians' overview of their work and is, we contend, an indicator of the cost of the improved overview.

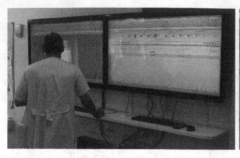

Fig. 1. The electronic whiteboard (a pair of 52-inch touch screens) in two of the EDs.

2 The Notion of Overview

Hornbæk and Hertzum [1] emphasize the distinction between overviews (displays in a user interface) and overviewing (a user's awareness of an aspect of an information space). While the whiteboard is an example of an overview display, it appears risky to assume that overviewing will ensue simply from attending to the whiteboard. Yet, Spence [12] and others take the term overview to imply that the user becomes aware of information in a rapid or even pre-attentive manner, that is without cognitive effort. This suggests that overviewing requires little more than periodically glancing at the whiteboard. Other researchers describe the process of acquiring an overview as more active, thereby suggesting that the user makes sense of the information space through active involvement with the overview display. For example, Bossen and Jensen [13, p. 257] tentatively define the process of achieving an overview as "how health care professionals arrive at a sufficiently informed, accountable and coherent understanding of a situation, so that they are capable of acting consciously and with confidence." This definition states that to provide competent patient treatment the ED clinicians must form and maintain an overview based on which treatment decisions can be made. That is, overviewing is a central clinical activity. In addition, the definition suggests that users need to engage with the displayed information to make sense of it. Glancing at the whiteboard may be key to this engagement but it is not sufficient.

In order for a display to support its users in forming and maintaining an overview it must contain accurate information. While previous research on overviewing [1] – and related notions such as sensemaking [14] and situation awareness [15] – accentuates that in dynamic environments the users' understanding of the situation must evolve to stay current, it speaks less about the work that goes into keeping overview displays and other external representations current. In their investigation of the cost structure of sensemaking, Russell et al. [16] found that the main cost was associated with finding and encoding the relevant information. This activity amounted to over 75% of the total time even though it appears that the information space (a set of documents) was known and static. We contend that in a dynamic environment the continuous work of finding the relevant information and encoding it on an overview display is, by far, the biggest cost that comes with using the display to maintain an overview.

3 Method

The four EDs in Region Zealand introduced the same electronic whiteboard in December 2009 (ED1), January 2010 (ED2), January 2011 (ED3), and May 2011 (ED4). The EDs were part of medium-sized hospitals that collectively served a population of approximately 820000 citizens. Some of the whiteboard data, such as lab-test results, were automatically updated when new data became available, but most of the whiteboard data were entered and updated manually. This study is exclusively about the data that were entered and updated manually. Prior to conducting the study we obtained approval from the healthcare region.

3.1 The Log Data

All changes of the whiteboard content were automatically logged. For the purpose of this study the whiteboard vendor, Imatis, produced a version of the logs from which all patient names, clinician names, and other information that might identify persons had been removed. These anonymized log data covered the three-year period 2012–2014. However, we had to discard the periods January 2013–January 2014 (ED1) and November 2013–January 2014 (ED2–ED4) from the analysis because they contained long intervals of no data. After also removing 741 outliers (defined as ED visits longer than seven days, i.e. more than 50 times the median length of stay), the dataset comprised 380611 ED visits. The data for these visits consisted of more than 10 million log entries, each documenting a manually performed change of the whiteboard content. A log entry contained a timestamp, an event type, any values associated with the event, and a system-generated identifier of the visit to which the event pertained. For example, the event type 'TRIAGEChanged' along with the event value '5' showed that a clinician had changed the patient's triage level to 5 (indicating a life-threatening condition).

3.2 Data Analysis

We used the timestamp and the visit identifier of the log entries to determine the number of change events per minute and per patient. We also calculated the month-by-month evolution in the number of change events and their distribution onto day (08–16), evening (16–00), and night (00–08) shifts. These calculations served to assess whether the cost of the improved overview was evenly distributed across time.

   To convert the number of change events into time spent we needed an estimate of the average duration of a change event. On the basis of an experiment with 18 clinicians from ED2, Rasmussen and Hertzum [17] found that it took the clinicians an average of 26.2 s to make a change on the whiteboard, including the time to log on to the whiteboard (by briefly holding a personal token onto a reader). Most whiteboard interactions consist of logons to make one or two changes. The clinicians in the experiment were experienced users of the whiteboard and they made fairly simple changes. To avoid overestimating the duration of a change event we set it to 20 s.

   Before the introduction of the electronic whiteboard the EDs used dry-erase whiteboards. To provide an, admittedly rough, estimate of the added time involved in using the electronic rather than the dry-erase whiteboard we estimated that it took equally long to make a change on the electronic and dry-erase whiteboards and that the electronic whiteboard was changed 82% more often than the dry-erase whiteboard. Our basis for estimating that it took equally long to make changes on the two whiteboards was that, depending on the kind of change, Rasmussen and Hertzum [17] found either no difference in the time required to change the whiteboards or slightly longer times for the electronic whiteboard. Our basis for estimating that the electronic whiteboard was updated 82% more often than the dry-erase whiteboard was that Hertzum and Simonsen [7] arrived at this relationship between the number of changes on the two whiteboards in ED3. It should however be noted that the relationship was determined on the basis of few data, all of which from day shifts. That is, our estimate of the added time involved in using the electronic rather than the dry-erase whiteboard should be treated as merely suggestive.

4 Results

As a preamble to the analysis we note that all four EDs saw 30–40 thousand patients a year. That is, they were about equally busy.

4.1 Number of Whiteboard Changes

Table 1 shows the number of changes the ED clinicians made to the content of the whiteboard in the period covered by the dataset. The lower number of patients for ED1 was due to the shorter period for which we had data for this ED. While there was some variation across EDs, the general picture in all EDs was one of frequent changes. Across the four EDs the clinicians made an average of 26.63 whiteboard changes per patient, corresponding to an average of 1.91 changes per minute. Thus, the clinicians' improved overview of their work after the introduction of the electronic whiteboard was achieved by devoting a substantial amount of work to keeping the whiteboard current.

At the beginning of 2012 (the start of the dataset) the EDs had been using the whiteboard for between half a year and two years. Thus, it could be expected that the use of the whiteboard had had time to stabilize and that the clinicians had arrived at a work practice with a fairly standardized number of whiteboard changes per patient.

Table 1. Number of changes to the content of the whiteboard

ED	Number of change events	ED visits (i.e., patients)	Changes per patient	Changes per minute
ED1	1905328	63759	29.88	1.92
ED2	2669736	110479	24.17	1.85
ED3	2200990	95308	23.09	1.53
ED4	3360537	111065	30.26	2.34
Total	10136591	380611	26.63	1.91

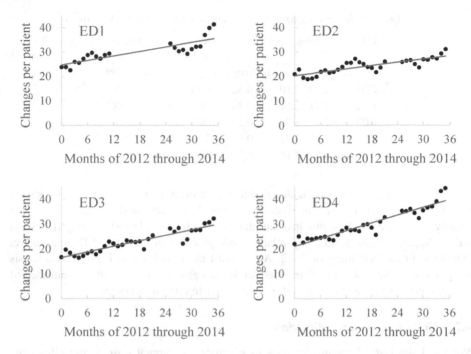

Fig. 2. Month-by-month evolution in the number of whiteboard changes per patient

Figure 2 disproves this expectation. All four EDs experienced an increasing trend in the work that went into obtaining the improved overview provided by the whiteboard. The trendlines (see Fig. 2) from a linear regression of the month-by-month evolution in changes per patient had a positive slope for all four EDs and explained 70% (ED1), 69% (ED2), 84% (ED3), and 89% (ED4) of the variance in the data. Because the increasing trend was in changes per patient it was not caused by a change in the number of patients. In addition, the trend occurred during a period with no increase in the number of clinicians. Rather, it appears that the clinicians gradually found more ways of using the whiteboard to improve their overview and that these new ways of working involved that the same number of clinicians made more frequent whiteboard changes.

Unsurprisingly, the changes of the whiteboard content were not evenly distributed across work shifts (Table 2). The clinicians changed the whiteboard content more frequently during day (08–16) and evening (16–00) shifts than during night (00–08) shifts because the number of patients was larger during day and evening shifts. Thus, most of the work that went into changing the whiteboard content was performed during the shifts in which the ED clinicians were most busy attending to patients. It is more noteworthy that the largest increase in the number of whiteboard changes (calculated by comparing the number of changes in December 2014 to that in January 2012) was also during the day and evening shifts, see Table 2. Presumably, the clinicians discovered more new ways of utilizing the whiteboard during the more busy day and evening shifts than during night shifts, thereby suggesting that the whiteboard offered the largest potential to improve the clinicians' overview of their work when the

Table 2. Increase in whiteboard changes divided onto work shifts

ED	Changes per minute			Increase (Jan. 2012 to Dec. 2014)		
	Day	Evening	Night	Day	Evening	Night
ED1	2.84	2.10	0.82	65%	89%	51%
ED2	2.71	2.11	0.74	56%	34%	43%
ED3	2.24	1.78	0.57	124%	116%	59%
ED4	3.31	2.71	0.98	122%	134%	50%
Average	2.77	2.18	0.77	92%	93%	51%

workload was high and it was challenging to maintain an overview. Table 2 also shows that the larger increase in whiteboard changes during day and evening shifts was mainly due to the two EDs that had introduced the whiteboard most recently (ED3 and ED4). Apparently, the whiteboard-related work practices in these two EDs had not yet stabilized in the beginning of 2012. Along with the trendlines in Fig. 2 this analysis suggests that the last part of the dataset is more representative of the number of whiteboard changes associated with obtaining an improved overview.

4.2   Cost-of-Overview Estimation

We used the last 12 months of data to estimate the annual cost of the clinicians' improved overview of their work, see Table 3. According to our estimates the EDs spent an average of 6647 h updating the whiteboard during these 12 months, corresponding to an increase of 2991 h compared to the time they previously spent updating the dry-erase whiteboards. The cost of the improved overview was similar at EDs 1, 2, and 3 and somewhat higher at ED4.

Table 3. Cost-of-overview estimation for 12 months of whiteboard use

ED	Number of change events	Hours spent (estimated)	Added hours (estimated)
ED1	1019331	5663	2548
ED2	1084920	6027	2712
ED3	1098681	6104	2747
ED4	1582644	8792	3957
Average		6647	2991

5   Concluding Discussion

The clinicians change the content of the whiteboard more than twice a minute during day and evening shifts and more than once every two minutes during night shifts. In the dynamic ED environment these changes are necessary to keep the whiteboard current. Importantly, the use of the whiteboard is merely recommended, not mandated, by hospital management; the ED clinicians spend time updating the whiteboard because they find that the improved overview justifies the time spent. We estimate that the time spent amounts to 6647 h a year in each of the EDs or the equivalent of about 1.7 extra full-time clinicians compared to the previous use of dry-erase whiteboards.

The cost-of-overview estimate shows the large value the clinicians assign to having an overview of the state of the ED. It is also evident that this overview is a collaborative accomplishment: Multiple clinicians must contribute updates to keep the whiteboard current and, in return, the whiteboard supports multiple clinicians in forming and maintaining an overview. This collaborative aspect of overview has previously been investigated by, for example, Bossen and Jensen [13], who note that novice and experienced clinicians form an overview in quite different ways but still contribute to the collaborative accomplishment of an overview. Relatedly, several studies show that the value of whiteboards is, in part, that they create a place where people meet face to face and information is exchanged [7, 18, 19]. Meeting at the whiteboard is a valued occasion for consulting experienced colleagues, for obtaining details not on the whiteboard as well as for glancing at the whiteboard. In addition, the cost-of-overview estimate shows the potential of automating the whiteboard updates by deriving them from data in the electronic patient record. Such automation requires high-quality data because bypassing manual data entry also means bypassing a clinical judgement of whether the data make sense. However, automatic updates appear to be the only way to reduce the cost of overview while at the same time increasing the number of whiteboard changes in order to improve the overview further.

Two limitations should be remembered in interpreting the results of this study. First, the dataset is from one work domain and one country. While the four EDs provide evidence that the results are not peculiar to one hospital, we acknowledge that the results may be specific to healthcare and to Denmark. Second, the conversion of the number of change events to hours spent is no better than the estimate of the duration of the events and that of the ratio of electronic to dry-erase whiteboard changes. The latter estimate, in particular, is based on few empirical data. Much more research is needed to quantify the cost of overview. This study proposes that in dynamic environments the number of changes needed to keep an overview display current is indicative of this cost and shows that it may be substantial.

Acknowledgements. This study is part of the Clinical Communication project, which is a research and development collaboration between Roskilde University, University of Copenhagen, Imatis, and Region Zealand. The interview quote at the end of Sect. 1 is from an interview conducted in collaboration with Jesper Simonsen from Roskilde University. Special thanks are due to Rasmus Rasmussen at Imatis for making the anonymized version of the log data.

References

1. Hornbæk, K., Hertzum, M.: The notion of overview in information visualization. Int. J. Hum.-Comput. Stud. **69**(7&8), 509–525 (2011)
2. Card, S.K., Mackinlay, J.D., Shneiderman, B. (eds.): Readings in Information Visualization: Using Vision to Think. Morgan Kaufmann, San Francisco (1999)

3. Shneiderman, B.: The eyes have it: a task by data type taxonomy for information visualizations. In: Proceedings of the 1996 IEEE Conference on Visual Languages, pp. 336–343. IEEE Press, Los Alamitos, CA (1996)

4. Fitzgerald, G., Jelinek, G.A., Scott, D., Gerdtz, M.F.: Emergency department triage revisited. Emerg. Med. J. **27**(2), 86–92 (2010)

5. Moskop, J.C., Sklar, D.P., Geiderman, J.M., Schears, R.M., Bookman, K.J.: Emergency department crowding, part 1 - concept, causes, and moral consequences. Ann. Emerg. Med. **53**(5), 605–611 (2009)

6. Hoot, N.R., Aronsky, D.: Systematic review of emergency department crowding: causes, effects, and solutions. Ann. Emerg. Med. **52**(2), 126–136 (2008)

7. Hertzum, M., Simonsen, J.: Visual overview, oral detail: the use of an emergency-department whiteboard. Int. J. Hum.-Comput. Stud. **82**, 21–30 (2015)

8. Rasmussen, R., Fleron, B., Hertzum, M., Simonsen, J.: Balancing tradition and transcendence in the implementation of emergency-department electronic whiteboards. In: Molka-Danielsen, J., Nicolaisen, H.W., Persson, J.S. (eds.) Selected Papers of the Information Systems Research Seminar in Scandinavia 2010, pp. 73–87. Tapir Academic Press, Trondheim (2010)

9. Rasmussen, R., Hertzum, M.: Visualizing the application of filters: a comparison of blocking, blurring, and colour-coding whiteboard information. Int. J. Hum.-Comput. Stud. **71**(10), 946–957 (2013)

10. Hertzum, M.: Electronic emergency-department whiteboards: a study of clinicians' expectations and experiences. Int. J. Med. Inform. **80**(9), 618–630 (2011)

11. Hertzum, M., Simonsen, J.: Effects of electronic emergency-department whiteboards on clinicians' time distribution and mental workload. Health Inform. J. **22**(1), 3–20 (2016)

12. Spence, R.: Information Visualization: Design for Interaction, 2nd edn. Prentice Hall, Harlow (2007)

13. Bossen, C., Jensen, L.G.: How physicians 'achieve overview': a case-based study in a hospital ward. In: Proceedings of the CSCW2014 Conference on Computer Supported Cooperative Work & Social Computing, pp. 257–268. ACM Press, New York (2014)

14. Weick, K.E., Sutcliffe, K.M., Obstfeld, D.: Organizing and the process of sensemaking. Organ. Sci. **16**(4), 409–421 (2005)

15. Endsley, M.R.: Toward a theory of situation awareness in dynamic systems. Hum. Factors **37**(1), 32–64 (1995)

16. Russell, D.M., Stefik, M.J., Pirolli, P., Card, S.K.: The cost structure of sensemaking. In: Proceedings of the INTERCHI1993 Conference on Human Factors in Computing Systems, pp. 269–276. ACM Press, New York (1993)

17. Rasmussen, R., Hertzum, M.: Consider the details: a study of the reading distance and revision time of electronic over dry-erase whiteboards. In: Proceedings of the Danish HCI Research Symposium, DHRS2012, pp. 24–27. University of Southern Denmark, Sønderborg, DK (2012)

18. Scupelli, P., Xiao, Y., Fussell, S.R., Kiesler, S., Gross, M.D.: Supporting coordination in surgical suites: physical aspects of common information spaces. In: Proceedings of the CHI 2010 Conference on Human Factors in Computing Systems, pp. 1777–1786. ACM Press, New York (2010)

19. Whittaker, S., Schwarz, H.: Meetings of the board: the impact of scheduling medium on long term group coordination in software development. Comput. Support. Coop. Work **8**(3), 175–205 (1999)

Interaction with Children

An Interactive Elementary Tutoring System for Oral Health Education Using an Augmented Approach

Mitali Sinha and Suman Deb[(✉)]

Department of Computer Science and Engineering,
National Institute of Technology, Agartala, India
mitalisinha93@gmail.com, sumandebcs@gmail.com

Abstract. The conventional elementary education system in India is mostly guided by formal content development, focusing on areas like math, language, science and social-science. Children tend to retain very little knowledge about other important areas of learning like heath care, which needs to be developed in their foundation years. The education on oral health is one such example which is not given the focus they ought to be. Considering its importance in early education, we propose a learning environment where children would gain knowledge through constant interaction with an intelligent tutoring system. The system addresses the challenges in developing a learning environment for children by introducing audio-visual effects, 3D animations and customizing the tutoring process to provide user-controlled pace of learning. It also employs the Wii Remote for imparting a tangible hardware interaction with the interface. This paper describes the proposed system and the studies conducted on treatment and control groups to evaluate its efficacy and compare the learning outcome at various domains. Experimental results depict positive effects on learning in the proposed technology-enhanced environment and paves a way for the deployment of more interactive, technology-driven learning process in the elementary education system.

Keywords: Intelligent tutoring system · Wii remote · Tangible interaction

1 Introduction

Intelligent systems are rapidly becoming a part of the modern education environment which leads to what is known as technology enhanced learning (TEL). Although TEL is often related to e-learning, we can also refer to it as a hardware or ICT (Information and Communication Technology) based teaching environment. The teaching and learning process is highly benefited with the advent of technologies like computers. Turning computers into an intelligent tutoring system (ITS) and designing careful instructional strategies helps in building a learner-centric process. Our work presents the design and evaluation of an oral health based ITS for young children. The children must be educated at a very early stage and realize the importance of learning about oral

© IFIP International Federation for Information Processing 2017
Published by Springer International Publishing AG 2017. All Rights Reserved
R. Bernhaupt et al. (Eds.): INTERACT 2017, Part II, LNCS 10514, pp. 413–430, 2017.
DOI: 10.1007/978-3-319-67684-5_26

health and hygiene. With a goal of designing a learner-centric process, an intelligent tutoring system is proposed which keeps track of a learner's progress and guide him or her by generating feedbacks throughout the process. Our idea is to introduce a gaming element in the tutoring system along with learning contents, as research indicates that children show a high degree of interest and engagement in a playful learning environment [1]. There is some evidence that favors the understanding of abstract concepts more easily with physical artifacts and tangible user interfaces [2, 3]. The Nintendo Wii remote is introduced as a tangible tool to enhance the interaction with the system. The interface allows 3-dimensional interactions with the user delivering knowledge at both visual and auditory channel. By effective use of animations and audio-visual effects throughout the play, the system aims to successfully deliver educational contents to the learners.

Our research work also compares the learning outcomes between the traditional learning environment and the technology-enhanced learning environment in the cognitive domain. We have also assessed the outcomes in the affective domain and investigated the development of psychomotor skills among the children.

2 Background and Related Work

An intelligent tutoring system possesses important features like personalization, interaction, and engagement in learning. In a traditional learning environment, the teaching and learning system often becomes a one-way process where the teacher acts as a controller of the pace of learning. In a large classroom environment, it becomes difficult for an instructor to keep track of the progress of each student individually. Research works suggested that learning outcome increases with the introduction of private tutors in the process [4]. Private tutors are able to monitor the learning curve of individuals and suggest remedies whenever required. Thus, in the absence of private tutors, ITS can be used for tutoring different concepts. Unlike the traditional process, an ITS is designed carefully to deliver knowledge in a learner-controlled pace. It strives to understand the level of tutoring to be provided to the individual learners and delivers educational contents accordingly. There are also many examples where intelligent tutoring systems are employed and found to be effective [5–9].There is some evidence that shows an increasing interest and motivation in learning with the appropriate use of technology at early childhood stages [10, 11]. The research works of Montessori also provided hints of young children grasping complex knowledge very easily in a playful environment with the help of physical artifacts [1]. Thus, in quest of providing an augmented tangible interaction to the users, the Nintendo Wii remote is employed in the system as a tangible tool.

The system also introduces a notion of game-based learning where children learn different skills and knowledge through a game. The significance and effects of digital games in educational domains are studied extensively. A multiuser learning game called Quest Atlantis resulted in learning gains for various topics and adopted in multiple school environment [12]. Also, a game-based approach to teaching nutritional course depicted good results on learning [13]. As an experimental example, the oral health based tutoring system is proposed in our work which aims at imparting knowledge about dental hygiene. A limited number of research work has been carried out in the field of dental health education being addressed by an intelligent tutoring system. The study of Ho et al. [14] employs a Wii remote to investigate its effect as a TUI (Tangible User Interface). Their study showed improvement in memorability and fun factor in learning but does not provide better results in cognitive development among the users. Gerling et al. proposed a serious interface design for dental health based on the Wii remote interaction by introducing additional gaming elements [15]. Another serious game was designed by Chang et al. which focused mostly on developing the psychomotor skills and did not keep an account of the interest and motivational factors which may result in dissatisfaction in the future [16]. Although, the above studies were successful in including gaming instincts, by carefully adapting user-centric designs and including better methodologies can definitely result in better learning outcomes.

The proposed system attempts to provide a balanced learning system which includes both educational contents and fun factor. To make the learning interesting our system is developed in a 3-dimensional environment with the use of proper animations and visual effects. Finally, a detailed study of outcomes in cognitive, affective and psychomotor domain helps in strengthening the idea of employing an intelligent tutoring system in learning educational contents.

3   System Architecture

The system provides an enhanced learning environment to the users with the help of animations, hardware interactions and a tutoring process running in the backend. It aims for a proper blending of factual knowledge and its application. Animations and picture clips along with audio effects render the factual knowledge about dental health and hygiene. Users are asked to perform different tasks or solve a problem depending upon the factual knowledge gained at different levels (As an instance, the user is asked to match the name of a tooth to the 3D model of the tooth displayed on screen). As the user works through the task, the system keeps track of his or her actions and help in progressing towards the solution through feedbacks.

The system is divided into different modules on the basis of their functionality as shown in Fig. 1. It comprises of a user interface through which the users interact with the system, a profile base that keeps the profile information and history of interactions for individual users, a hardware interaction module which facilitates the hardware interactions with the system, a knowledge evaluator that evaluates the knowledge of the user with the help of the task formation module and knowledge repository, a tutoring module which tutors the user throughout the task with necessary feedbacks with the aid of a feedback module.

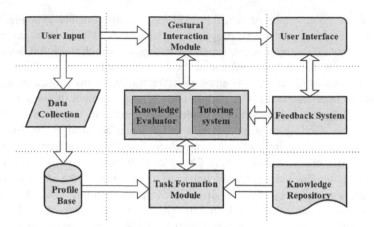

Fig. 1. System interconnection modules

3.1 User Interface and Gestural Interaction Module

The user interface facilitates interaction with the system. It is developed in a 3D designing environment using tools like Unity3D and Blender for experiencing an enhanced interaction and better understanding of the concepts. The system employs the Nintendo Wii remote for a tangible interaction. The Wii remote is a remote controller for a Japanese gaming console called Wii. Its motion sensing capability differentiate it from other traditional remotes. It has the ability to digitally manipulate items allowing gesture recognition and pointing of objects on a screen. The gesture recognition is guided by the three-axes accelerometer and its infrared sensing capability determines the location on the screen where the remote is pointing. The Wii remote connects with a computer via Bluetooth connection and thus provides a simple and wireless communication medium. It is employed as a tangible device in the system where it imitates the movement of a 3- dimensional brush model on the screen thus providing an augmented interaction with the system. The application includes a section where the user performs a gameplay with the Wii remote and learn few psychomotor skills.

3.2 Profile Base Module

The Profile base module is responsible for keeping the details of every user along with their performance history. The system is designed to impart knowledge to different groups of users with varying capacity and methods of learning and accepting information. This division is based on the Piaget's theory of cognitive development [17] where he proposed four stages of cognitive development as shown in Fig. 2. According to Piaget, at the sensorimotor stage the children understands through senses and actions, at the preoperational stage they understand through language and mental images, at the concrete operational stage, they tend to gain knowledge through logical thinking and finally through hypothetical thinking and scientific reasoning at the formal operational stage. The proposed system focused on parts of the preoperational and concrete operational stages forming two levels namely POP (5–7 years) and COP

(8–10 years). The user starts experiencing the system by first interacting with the user profile based module and entering their details (where the primary factor is the age group). The User_Name field helps the system to interact with the user with his/her name throughout the gameplay giving a sense of empowerment and making them in-charge of their actions. The Age field is used by the system to direct the user to either POP or COP level where depending upon the level, information is provided to the users. Thus, data collected by the profile base module guide the tutoring system to continue the process of further evaluation.

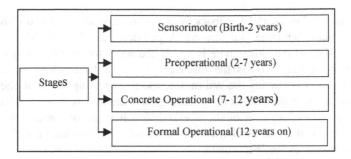

Fig. 2. Piaget's stages of cognitive development

3.3 Knowledge Repository and Task Formation Module

The knowledge repository is a metadata store that holds information regarding each concept, the problems generated and their solutions. Whenever a solution to a problem is submitted by the user, it is processed by the knowledge evaluator with the help of the knowledge repository. The task formation module is responsible for creating tasks for the user at different levels.

3.4 Feedback Module

The feedback module is responsible for guiding the users through stimulant learning and task solving. Three types of feedback mechanisms are designed as follows: audiovisual feedback serving as problem hints, movement-based feedback, and report-based feedback.

Audio-visual Feedback. As the user initiates a task, the feedback module generates audio-visual feedbacks whenever the user finds difficulty in solving a problem. The feedbacks are generated in the form of text, video clips or animations on the screen. To build up the interest of the user during the gameplay, they are also greeted for successful completion of the task. Figure 3 shows a snapshot of scenarios before and after the play. After successful completion of a level, the system appreciates the user's effort by displaying smileys and congratulating them. This kind of interactions helps in accelerating user engagement by addressing them emotionally and boosting their confidence.

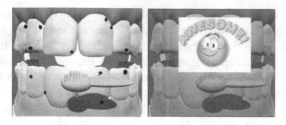

Fig. 3. Scenario before and after the successful completion of task (left to right)

Movement Based Feedback. Feedback is also generated to help the user for making correct movements with the Wii remote. A pre-determined threshold value for the accelerometer data of the Wii remote is set. If the accelerometer data acquired at any instant during the play crosses the threshold value, a feedback is generated. For example, if the user is moving the Wii remote too fast crossing the limit, then the user is prompt on screen to slow down the pace. Again if the user is showing no movement for a preset amount of time, he or she is asked to either quit or continue the play as a result, the movement based feedback helps in developing psychomotor skills by limiting the movement of the Wii remote.

Report Based Feedback. At the completion of each level, a performance report is presented to the user giving a brief description of the outcome of the play. This report generation at the end of each level provides a basis for determining the level of difficulty to be adapted in next stage of the play and also helps in monitoring the psychomotor development in children.

3.5   Tutoring System

The users are tutored throughout the process by the tutoring system with the help of the information gathered from the profile base module, knowledge evaluator, and feedback modules. The tutoring system is guided by some predefined rules depending on which it determines the level of knowledge provided to the particular user. It then interacts with the user through the feedback module. On the basis of the information from the knowledge evaluator, the tutoring system decides the level of factual knowledge delivered. It processes knowledge at two levels (POP or COP) depending on the pretest results. Figure 4 gives the illustration of a generic scenario of problem-solving by the tutor system. As a problem is given to the user, the tutoring system helps him or her through the process by providing hints or explanations regarding the problem. The users are tutored with textual, video or animations by the feedback module. A problem is then presented to the user based on the concept discussed to decide whether to further tutor the user or move on and take next actions.

Figure 5 represent a more specific scenario in case a user fails to give a valid answer. A problem is displayed on the screen and the user is asked to choose the correct answer. Since the user failed to give the correct answer, the tutoring system displays a hint on screen. A molar tooth model is displayed along with an audio instruction playing in the background.

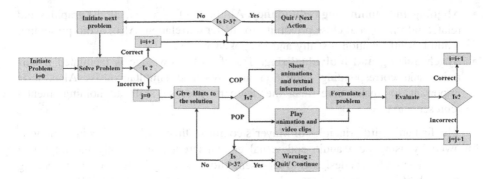

Fig. 4. Automatic feedback generation process by tutor module

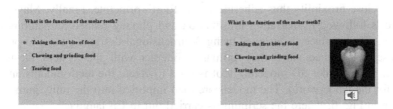

Fig. 5. Problem displayed on screen; hint generated by tutoring system

4   The Application Development

The application is developed with a goal of blending learning content and gameplay effectively. In quest of finding ways to provide a tangible learning experience, the Nintendo Wii remote was selected. Therefore, the user gets a multi-model interactive environment where the sense of sight and hearing is exploited by the user interface and the sense of touch is provided by the Wii remote.

4.1   The Interface Design

The interface design constraints are guided by the principles of Mayer's cognitive theory of multimedia learning [18]. Mayer proposed five principles for effective multimedia design for the better understanding of educational contents as follows:

- **Off-loading.** Moving some essential information from visual channel to the auditory channel would help in the better transfer of knowledge.
- **Segmenting and pre-training.** Better outcomes are observed when lessons are presented in learner-controlled segments allowing time between successive segments. Also providing pre-training like knowing the names and behaviors of the system would facilitate the learning process.
- **Weeding and Signaling.** Excluding extraneous materials and including signals results in better understanding of a specific concept.

- **Aligning and eliminating redundancy.** Aligning refers to placing the graphics and related information at close proximity for better correlation. Also, avoid presenting redundant information visually and in spoken words.
- **Synchronizing and individualizing.** Transfer of knowledge is facilitated if narration and corresponding animation are presented simultaneously. Also, it is important to make sure that the learners possess skill at holding mental representations.

The first and third principles of Mayer's cognitive theory of multimedia learning is followed by using both audio and visual contents representing only the important materials. The system is designed to represent knowledge at different levels depending upon the ability of the user to grasp the concepts. Thus the second principle is justified by allowing a user-controlled pace of learning. The design is thoroughly revised for any redundant information being delivered and also placing graphics and related information in close proximity thus adhering to the fourth principle. Finally, Mayer's fifth principle is followed by narrating information and playing related animations simultaneously. The interface is designed using 3-dimensional designing tools to provide a better user experience since they primarily interact with the system through the interface. The Blender 3D modeling tool is used to create the teeth models and other objects for the game world. The models are then imported into the unity game engine as shown in Fig. 6, where the scripting is carried out in C# language.

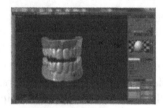 

Fig. 6. Teeth model in blender; teeth and brush model imported in Unity 3D game engine.

4.2   The Game Concept

The game supports two stages of learning as mentioned earlier i.e. the POP and COP stage. The POP stage is designed for the children belonging to the age group of 5-7 years while the COP stage is for the age group of 8-10 years. Although the underlying idea of the game is same for both the stages, the knowledge representation is slightly different. In the POP stage, the factual knowledge is represented to the user mostly through storytelling, animations, and auditory means. While in the COP stage, concepts are represented more broadly using textual, audio and video contents. The pre-knowledge test helps the system decide to either provide the user with the POP or COP stage. This is important because if the user starts with the COP stage and he or she is unaware of the basic concepts and terminologies explained in the POP stage, it may result in a gap in the learning process. Again if the user is given with the POP stage and finds the facts repetitive, he or she may lose interest in learning.

The idea of the game is to first provide factual knowledge to the users and then evaluate them by proposing simple tasks. As an instance, in the POP stage at first, the user is tutored and introduced to the shapes and names of the teeth by animating each tooth model on the screen along with audio effects. After each such sessions, the users are asked to answer some questions or solve a problem related to the concepts explained which are then evaluated by the knowledge evaluator. If the submitted answer is incorrect, the system provides some hints dynamically or suggests the user revise the concepts by going back to the animations as depicted in the Fig. 3.

The interface also includes three buttons which help to switch between three sections namely "Facts", "Stories", and "Play". The "Stories" section includes small concepts related to dental health in the form of stories since storytelling tends to have a positive impact on learning among small children [19]. The "Play" section helps in developing psychomotor skills of children by helping them to learn proper brushing techniques.

The Nintendo Wii remote is employed in the environment as a tangible tool to imitate the brush model on screen. The user needs to hold the Wii remote and gently clean away the black dots making small circular movements as shown in the Fig. 3. The gameplay is designed using an adaptive algorithm with different levels. If the user is not able to solve the assigned task at the first level, then the subsequent level is made easy by altering some game elements (like a number of black dots or time limits) to maintain his or her level of satisfaction. Similarly, if the user completes the task very quickly then the next level is made more difficult to hold his or her interest in play. The system also provides tips and hints to the user throughout the play and feedbacks are dynamically generated by the system whenever required. A report based feedback helps to increase the level of interest as they can assess their own improvement at the end of each session. To adhere to the gaming standards, our gameplay introduces certain gaming aspects as follows:

- **Challenges.** Various challenges are included in the play to uphold the interest of the users. A timer is set at the start of each level and the user needs to complete the task within the time constraint. Also, the accelerometer data acquired from the Wii remote is used to restrict the user movement and generating warning when it accesses the predefined threshold value.
- **Animations.** The game effectively makes use of animations which scales down the cognitive load and thus facilitates learning.
- **Personalizing information.** A login system is employed in the system which helps in personalizing user information to boost their interest and consciousness towards the play.
- **Fantasy context.** Involvement of technologies like the computer and the Wii remote in the education process add a fantasy context to increase engagement and motivation of the users.

Our system thus successfully maps to the Bloom's Taxonomy of Learning Domain [20]:

- **Affective Domain.** The system manages to uphold the motivation and satisfaction level of the users by personalizing the game, introducing different in-game challenges and various feedbacks.
- **Cognitive Domain.** The "Facts" and "Stories" section impart the factual knowledge in form of textual, animations and audio-visual effects.
- **Psychomotor Domain.** The "Play" section helps in developing the motor skills to facilitate the proper brushing techniques of the users.

5   Research Methodology

Our research work primarily focuses on investigating the outcomes of learning in the cognitive and affective domain. It also includes an assessment process tracking the psychomotor development of the children throughout the play. Our study tries to address one overarching question and three sub-questions as follows:

Overarching Research Question. Does the proposed technology enhanced learning environment helps in improving children's outcome of learning?

Sub-research Question 1. Does the system accelerate cognitive learning in children?

Sub-research Question 2. Does the system arouse learning interest and improves learning outcome at affective domain?

Sub-research Question 3. Does the system help in developing psychomotor skills at the end of the learning process?

5.1   Study Design

An experimental study design was adopted using a pre-test and post-test interventions. Our focused group for user study was grade-3 and grade-4 students of a primary school in Tripura, India. The experimental design comprised of 80 students (grade-2 and grade-3 students) divided into two groups i.e. the treatment group and the control group (40 students each). The treatment group went through the experimental setup and completed their tasks as instructed (each participant were asked to play or interact with the system using the Wii remote). On the contrary, the control group was provided with a traditional classroom environment, where an instructor was teaching a group of students. In the case of the control group, the instructor did not use any technology-aided tools for teaching and they learned new concepts by listening to the instructor. Thus, both the groups are delivered same knowledge base about dental hygiene but experienced different environments of learning.

To ensure that the members of the two groups (treatment and control groups) are equivalent prior to the treatment, a matched random assignment technique was considered. This technique is adopted to normalize the assignments of participants to different groups based on characteristics like age and their familiarity with playing video games (which was recorded by interviewing the participants and their parents). A sample of the matched random sampling is shown in Table 1.

Table 1. Matched random assignment

Participant ID	Age	Played video games	Group
01	8	Yes	Treatment
02	9	Yes	Control
03	8	No	Treatment
04	8	No	Control
05	9	Yes	Control
⋮	⋮	⋮	⋮
80	9	No	Treatment

5.2 Instruments

Our user study comprised of different instruments used to assess the learning outcomes at various domains.

Cognitive domain. The pre-tests and post-tests interventions served as an instrument to investigate the outcomes at the cognitive domain for both the treatment and control groups. Before conducting the experiment, a pre-test was carried out on the topic of dental hygiene and the scores of each participant (treatment and control groups) were recorded. At the end of the experiment, a post-test was conducted depending upon the knowledge being delivered through the process. Some of the questions are listed as follows:

- Name the different types of teeth?
- What is the function of a molar and canine teeth?
- What is the cause of cavities?
- What is the name of the tooth model? (An animation of a tooth model is displayed on screen)

The pre-test and post-test results were analyzed to find whether there was a significant difference between the learning curve of the treatment and the control groups. An analysis of the variance was carried out by One-Way ANOVA using the SPSS statistical tool.

Affective Domain. The affective domain plays a transparent role in education. Emotional needs act as an unseen bridge between the physiological needs and self-realization or success. Therefore, it is equally important to take care of the affective domain in learning along with other factors like cognitive and psychomotor skills in children. To assess the affective domain in our study, we used an anecdotal report for each individual, a checklist and finally survey questionnaires.

Anecdotal report. The first instrument for assessing the affective domain was an anecdotal report which provided a brief narrative account of the participant's actions in intervals throughout the session. One of the observers present in the experimental area recorded a detailed description of each participant's activity carefully. The process was carried out for both treatment and control groups at three intervals each with a duration of 120 s. To provide a strong support to the anecdotal report created by the observers, we also recorded the experiments and captured users' reactions which were used later to interpret their behavior. During the observation, information was collected regarding how children communicated verbally or nonverbally. Physical gestures and movements, reactions towards the teacher or the game-based learning environment, and interactions with peers were also summarized. Figure 7 shows an example anecdotal record (record presented here shows a part of the collected data). Only observable actions were recorded in the anecdotal report and no generalization of the attitude and causes were written.

ANECDOTAL REPORT

Participant's Name: *Meenakshi Das* Played Video games**:** *Yes* Date: *1/11/XX* Age: *8 years* Group: *Treatment* Observer: *Mitali Sinha*

Interval I: Meenakshi came into the classroom and took a seat. She wished the instructor "Good Morning". As the instructor gave instruction she looked at him. She raised a hand to ask a query as the instructor was explaining. She asked if she will be rewarded for her victory in the game.

Interval II: She sat in front of the computer and took the device in her hand. She started reading the instruction on screen and proceed as suggested by the instructor.

Interval III: At the middle of the activity, at times she exclaimed Wow!. She also informed the instructor "Sir, I want to know more about our teeth and how they catch cavities.

Fig. 7. A sample anecdotal report

Checklists. Checklists were used as our second instrument for information gathering. In this method, a number of specific traits or behavior was pre-defined by the researchers that are relevant to their work or motive of research. We designed our codes by studying various existing literature based on classroom observations [21, 22]. One of our observers sat with the checklist and recorded the actions of both the treatment and control groups. Each participant of both groups was observed at three intervals (120 s for each interval) and their behaviors were recorded positive or negative depending on their gestures and reactions. Table 2 shows the sample checklist of both treatment and control group at an instant.

Table 2. Sample checklist for recording behaviors of treatment and control group (Interval I).

Behaviors	Treatment Group						Control Group				
	1	2	3	4	5	40	1	2	3	4	40
Looking at Instructor/ Screen	✖						✖		✖		✖
Asking queries to Instructors								✖			
Looking outside classroom			✖	✖							
Feeling Sleepy	✖	✖	✖	✖					✖		
Talking with others (on irrelevant topic)	✖		✖								
Doing other works					✖		✖		✖		✖
Sharing thoughts with peers after activity			✖						✖		✖

Survey Questionnaire. The third instrument used in our study was the survey-questionnaire. Keeping in mind the young age of the participants the survey was conducted orally. The observers asked relevant questions to the participants in order to draw effective conclusions regarding their engagement and interest throughout the activity. The young participants were asked to describe the activity in their own words. Some of the survey questionnaires are as follows:

- How do you feel in learning by playing games?
- Did you enjoy studying?
- Would you like to learn and play again?

The accumulated reactions and comments were grouped as positive, negative and neutral. Comments including adjectives like "Awesome", "Wow", "Good", "Superb", "Fun", and "Cool" were grouped as positive comments. While statements including words like "not fun", "boring" etc. were grouped into negative comments. The neutral group comprised of statements that were irrelevant to the topic, providing neither positive nor negative views. Such group contained statements including words like "Okay", "interesting but too easy", "not my type" etc. The treatment and control group were compared against these three partitions of reaction (positive, negative and neutral) to investigate which group (treatment or control) had more positive comments. The group that showed higher positive comments were concluded as providing more engagement to the participants and thus better performance.

Psychomotor Domain. To investigate the effect of the proposed system in the psychomotor development of the children, the mean error (in performing correct gesture i.e. correct brushing technique) of each participant of the treatment groups were observed. The system keeps track of the psychomotor development of each individual and produces a report. This report is analyzed to assess whether the children developed the skills after going through the experiment.

6 Results and Discussions

6.1 Cognitive Domain

A pretest was carried out at the beginning to evaluate the internal validity of the experiment conducted, where both the groups were evaluated on their pre-knowledge about dental health and care. The test was based on the educational content to be delivered throughout the experimental process. The pretest questions consist of some basic to advanced questions regarding oral health. At the end of the experiment, a posttest was conducted to assess the learning outcomes of the participants. A One-Way Analysis of Variance (ANOVA) was formulated using the SPSS tool to evaluate the null hypothesis that there is no difference in the learning outcomes among children in the traditional learning environment and the proposed learning system ($N = 80$). Table 3 shows the mean of the difference between pretest and posttest results of participants in the treatment group ($M = 3.33$, $SD = 3.724$) and control group ($M = 1.68$, $SD = 3.362$). The mean value of 3.33 of treatment group depicts that the difference between the pretest and posttest results in the treatment group is more significant than the difference in the control group with the mean value of 1.68.

Table 3. Mean score table

Group	Mean	Std. deviation	N
Control	1.68	3.362	40
Treatment	3.33	3.724	40
Total	2.50	3.621	80

The assumption of homogeneity of variances was tested and found tenable using Levene's Test, $F (1, 78) = 0.05$, $p = 0.943$. The results of ANOVA was significant as shown in Table 4 with $F (1, 78) = 4.327$, $p = 0.039$. Thus, there is a sufficient evidence to reject the null hypothesis and conclude that there exists a significant difference in the learning outcomes of the children in the treatment and control group.

Table 4. One-way ANOVA test results.

	Sum of squares	df	Mean square	F	Sig
Between groups	54.45	1	54.450	4.327	0.039
Within groups	981.55	78	12.584		
Total	1536.00	80			
Corrected total	1036.00	79			

6.2   Affective Domain

Analysis of Anecdotal Records. To determine affective learning among the participants of the treatment and control group, we first performed a detailed analysis of the anecdotal records prepared by the observer. A report was produced for each participant in both treatment and control groups noting down their behaviors at three intervals. The sample individual report is shown in Table 5. Since the anecdotal report provides a detailed study of each individual, we broke down the observed behaviors into few set of behaviors (which was not pre-defined) for the sake of comparison. Mean score was calculated out of the three intervals for each individual participant. Again the mean scores of each participant in treatment and control group against enlisted behaviors were tallied and a final score for the two groups was presented. The final table of comparison between treatment and control group for the anecdotal report is described in Table 6.

Analysis of Checklist report. Our second instrument that is Checklists provides a means of quickly recording the presence or absence of a behavior amongst the participants. Unlike the anecdotal report, the checklist comprises of pre-defined rubrics on which we performed the comparisons. The checklist for the first interval for both treatment and control group is shown in Table 2. After three intervals the observations were compared and the final results were obtained by calculating the mean scores of treatment and control group towards the enlisted behaviors. This is shown in Table 7.

Table 5. Sample individual report at three intervals and their mean scores.

Behavior	Intervals			Mean (%)
	I	II	III	
Not paying attention to activity	✖		✖	33.33
Trying to understand the instructions	✖			66.67
Actively participating during the procedure		✖		66.67
Feeling bored	✖		✖	33.33
Interested in other topics not related to current	✖			66.67
Concentrating on others' works	✖	✖		33.33

Table 6. Comparison between treatment and control group for anecdotal report

Behavior	Treatment		Control	
	Mean	SD	Mean	SD
Not paying attention in activity	26.66	0.01	66.66	0.01
Trying to understand the instructions	73.33	0.02	30.00	0.03
Actively participating during the procedure	66.66	3.02	36.66	0.02
Feeling bored	29.99	0.03	36.66	0.02
Interested in other topics not related to current	50.00	3.33	46.66	0.02
Concentrating to others' works	29.99	0.03	30.00	0.03

Table 7. Comparison between treatment and control group for checklist report

Behavior	Treatment		Control	
	Mean	SD	Mean	SD
Looking at instructor/Screen	71.26	0.02	35.01	0.03
Asking queries to instructors	69.67	2.03	35.21	0.02
Looking outside classroom	21.23	0.02	50.53	0.03
Feeling sleepy	32.26	0.02	36.20	0.01
Talking with others (on irrelevant topic)	25.00	2.27	39.89	0.01
Doing other works	28.78	0.03	27.63	0.03
Sharing thoughts with peers after activity	68.82	0.03	25.43	0.02

Analysis of Survey Questionnaire. Further ambiguity check of the intended results was carried out by conducting a post-activity survey. In the post-activity survey, each participant of treatment and control groups were asked about their experience during the experiment. The answers of each participant were recorded and grouped into three categories i.e. positive, negative and neutral. Figure 8 shows the distribution of the comments for both the treatment and control groups. The graph depicts that the treatment group showed more positive response than the control group. Also, the control group produced a more negative reaction in comparison to the treatment group. A few participants' reaction in both the groups were neutral and showed the least interest in both cases. However, we found a major number of participants interested in learning in the treatment group and thus get some evidence of better performance in the treatment scenario.

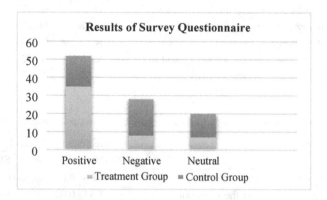

Fig. 8. Survey questionnaires results

6.3 Psychomotor Domain

The report generated by the system at each level corresponding to each individual is analyzed to check the improvement in psychomotor skills among the children. The system recognizes the number of attempts of each participant during the experiment and the mean error is calculated from the results. The Fig. 9 shows the comparisons between the mean error values at the first and last levels. As depicted by the graph, the mean error of many participants decreased eventually from the first level to the last level. This fact gives an evidence that the participants were making less error in the movement of the Wii remote and were successful in completing the levels in the game. Thus, we conclude that the participants showed improvement in developing the skills generating less mean error at the last level in comparison to the first level of the game play.

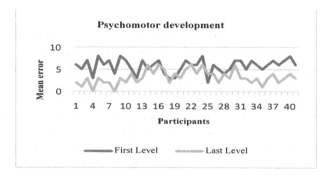

Fig. 9. Comparison between mean error values of the participants at end of the treatment

7 Conclusion

In this paper, we presented an enhanced learning environment which is guided by an intelligent tutoring system and investigated its effect on the learning outcomes of the children. Our work tries to address the areas of learning which is important but not very widely included in the education system's curriculum at present. We try to introduce an environment of the education system where we can enhance the outcomes of learning by increasing the interest and motivation of children towards learning new concepts. The proposed system was able to successfully deliver educational contents to the children and help in their cognitive development. By introducing the notion of the game and 3-dimensional contents in the application, the system was able to gain the attention of the participants thus improving the affective domain. Also at the end of the experiment, the participants were able to improve psychomotor skills by the technology-enhanced environment. Thus, the use of technology and enhanced interactions depicted better learning outcomes arousing the interests of young children in learning.

We now discuss a few limitations and future directions to our research work. The proposed system was developed to address primarily the dental health based contents. To generalize the educational contents proper care must be taken considering the target users else it would not be able to produce the desired results. Although our study depicted positive effects on learning, large-scale testing of the system with varying target groups is to be done in the future.

References

1. Montessori, M.: The Montessori Method: Scientific Pedagogy as Applied to Child Education in "the Children's Houses". Translated by Anne E. George. Heinemann (1937)
2. Papert, S.: Mindstorms: Children, computers, and powerful ideas. Basic Books Inc, New York (1980)
3. Resnick, M., Ocko, S., Papert, S.: LEGO, logo, and design. Children's Environments Quarterly, pp. 14–18 (1988)
4. Reiser, B.J., Anderson, J.R., Farrell, R.G.: Dynamic student modelling in an intelligent tutor for LISP programming. IJCAI **85**, 8–14 (1985)
5. Ritter, S., Anderson, J.R., Koedinger, K.R., Corbett, A.: Cognitive tutor: applied research in mathematics education. Psychon. Bull. Rev. **14**(2), 249–255 (2007)
6. Papadimitriou, A., Grigoriadou, M., Gyftodimos, G.: Interactive problem solving support in the adaptive educational hypermedia system MATHEMA. IEEE Trans. Learn. Technol. **2**(2), 93–106 (2009)
7. VanLehn, K., Lnch, C., Schulze, K., Shapiro, J.A., Shelby, R., Taylor, L., Treacy, D., Weintein, A., Wintersgill, M.: The andes physics tutoring system: five years of evaluations. NAAL ACADEMY ANNAPOLIS MD (2005)
8. Fossati, D., Di Eugenio, B., Brown, C.W., Ohlsson, S., Cosejo, D.G., Chen, L.: Supporting computer science curriculum: Exploring and learning linked lists with iList. IEEE Trans. Learn. Technol. **2**(2), 107–120 (2009)

9. Gertner, A.S., Van Lehn, K.: Andes: a coached problem solving environment for physics. In: Gauthier, G., Frasson, C., VanLehn, K. (eds.) ITS 2000. LNCS, vol. 1839, pp. 133–142. Springer, Heidelberg (2000). doi:10.1007/3-540-45108-0_17

10. Van Scoter, J., Ellis, D., Railsback, J.: Technology in early childhood education: Finding the balance. Northwest Regional Education Laboratory, Portland (2001)

11. Anderson, D.R., Pempek, T.A.: Television and very young children. Am. Behav. Sci. 48(5), 505–522 (2005)

12. Barab, S., Thomas, M., Dodge, T., Carteaux, R., Tuzun, H.: Making learning fun: quest Atlantis, a game without guns. Educ. Tech. Res. Dev. 53(1), 86–107 (2005)

13. Yien, J.-M., Hung, C.-M., Hwang, G.J., Lin, Y.-C.: A gamebased learning approach to improving students' learning achievements in a nutrition course. TOJET: Turkish Online J. Educ. Technol. 10(2) (2011)

14. Ho, J.H., Zhou, S.Z., Wei, D., Low, A.: Investigating the effects of educational game with wii remote on outcomes of learning. In: Pan, Z., Cheok, A.D., Müller, W., Chang, M. (eds.) Transactions on Edutainment III. LNCS, vol. 5940, pp. 240–252. Springer, Heidelberg (2009). doi:10.1007/978-3-642-11245-4_21

15. Gerling, K., Klauser, M., Masuch, M.: Serious interface design for dental health: wiimote-based tangible interaction for school children. In: CEUR Workshop Proceedings, Vol 634 (2010)

16. Chang, Y.C., Lo, J.L., Huang, C.J., Hsu, N.Y., Chu, H.H., Wang, H.Y., Chi, P.Y., Hsieh, Y. L.: Playful toothbrush: ubicomp technology for teaching tooth brushing to kindergarten children. In: proceedings of the SIGCHI conference on human factors in computing systems, pp. 363–372. ACM(2008)

17. Piaget, J.: Piaget's theory of cognitive development. childhood cognitive development: the essential readings, pp. 33–47 (2000)

18. Mayer, R.E.: Multimedia learning. Psychol. Learn. Motiv. 41, pp. 85–139 (2002)

19. Ryokai, K., Cassell, J.: StoryMat: a play space for collaborative storytelling. In: CHI 1999 Extended Abstracts on Human factors in computing systems. ACM. pp. 272–273 (1999)

20. Bloom, B.S., Krathwohl, D.R., Masia, B.B.: Bloom taxonomy of educational objectives. Allyn and Bacon, Boston, MA. Copyright© by Pearson Education (1984). <http://www. coun.uvic.ca/learn/program/hndouts/bloom.html

21. Roehrig, A.D., Christesen, E.: Development and use of a tool for evaluating teacher effectiveness in grades K-12. In: Shute, V., Becker, B. (eds.) Innovative Assessment for the 21st Century. Springer, Boston (2010)

22. Sawada, D., Piburn, M.D., Judson, E., Turley, J., Falconer, K., Benford, R., Bloom, I.: Measuring reform practices in science and mathematics classrooms: The reformed teaching observation protocol. School Sci. Math. 102(6), 245–253 (2002)

Empowered and Informed: Participation of Children in HCI

Janet C. Read[✉], Matthew Horton, Daniel Fitton, and Gavin Sim

University of Central Lancashire, Preston PR4 6RU, UK
{jcread,mplhorton,dbfitton,grsim}@uclan.ac.uk

Abstract. The participation of end users in design, research and evaluation has long been a feature of HCI. Traditionally these end users consent to participate in the general belief that they are contributing some knowledge that will eventually improve things for themselves or others. The involvement of children in research in HCI creates new challenges for ethical participation. This paper brings together current research on ethical participation and models of participation, and presents three tools, CHECk, ActiveInfo and PICO- Art, as well as a set of practical ideas, for researchers to adapt and use in their work with children. The paper explores how effective different aspects of the different tools are, and offers a set of practical suggestions based on observational assessments. The main contribution is a culturally adaptable ethical toolkit and a protocol for ethical working with children in HCI.

Keywords: Children · Ethics · Participation · Impact · Empowerment

1 Introduction

The HCI community is a reflective community that has actively sought to explore several key themes around its practices and its methods. One area of interest is the ethical participation of individuals in research studies. When research is being done with children, there is a pressing need to examine what participation in research means. Several papers have individually explored the involvement of children in research, design and evaluation studies but these tend to be relatively pragmatic considering the happiness of children, the means by which they can participate, and the design of tools and techniques to make their participation possible. The ethics around the participation of children, in terms of being able to justify their inclusion, explain their roles and determine their influence has not been so well studied nor has there been to date any attempt to improve the practices of gaining informed consent and working openly in research with children in HCI. This paper therefore brings to the surface the key issues around children participating in HCI research and proposes some solutions that can help researchers work in more ethically appropriate ways with children.

R. Bernhaupt et al. (Eds.): INTERACT 2017, Part II, LNCS 10514, pp. 431–446, 2017.
DOI: 10.1007/978-3-319-67684-5_27

2 Related Work

In this section previous work is presented on ethics and their role in HCI, the participation of children in HCI research, and then the ethics of children's participation.

2.1 Ethics and Values

Ethical values are concerned with what is right and what is wrong [1] and it is common for research to be governed by ethical codes. Typically, these are determined by ethical boards within institutions that examine research and determine if it is ethical. Codes of ethics tend to focus on several key themes:

- Beneficence (that work does good)
- Avoidance of harm
- Truthfulness
- Not discriminating
- Appropriately acknowledging rights of property
- Respecting privacy and confidentiality

Central to ethics in terms of research is consent. Consent is where a human participant agrees to be included in a research study. The principle of informed consent is where an individual agrees to participate based on being fully informed about the research that is being done. Consent is related to risk. The higher the risk associated with research the more severe are the requirements for informed consent. Thus medicine and psychology typically have more tightly defined consent processes than design and ethnography where the risk associated with participation is much reduced.

Informed consent has been much discussed in the literature. Of interest in this debate is:

- Who should give it
- When is it needed
- How is it gathered
- How is it tested
- How is it receded

In terms of who should give consent, the generally accepted view is that to give consent one has to be 'legally competent' as well as physically and mentally capable of giving consent [2]. Aspects of this definition have been challenged with regard to competence to consent especially highlighted in the famous 'Gillick competence'[1] which resulted in the understanding that 'A competent child is one who has sufficient understanding and intelligence to enable him or her to fully understand what is proposed and also sufficient discretion to enable him or her to make a wise choice in his or her own interests.'

---

[1] Gillick v West Norfolk and Wisbech Area Health Authority and another
    [1985] 2 BMLR 11.

In HCI work, consent is always considered to be needed when images and data are being gathered from participants. Less clear is the extent to which consent should be sought when a researcher is gathering ideas or, as is the case in some HCI work and ethnographic work, working undercover in some way such as by passively observing individuals. Sometimes referred to as deep cover research in HCI, such work certainly requires consent at the 'reveal' moment [3], this being the traditional way of gaining consent in many Wizard of Oz studies [4].

Typically, a signature attached to a consent form assumes consent. The general principle is that an information sheet is produced that outlines the research and then signatures are gathered. The readability of such forms has been studied in some detail and is often considered to be a problem [5].

The understandability of such information, and the test of whether or not the participants really are informed is associated with both the readability of consent documents but also with the general understanding of the participants as to the extent of, and possible impact of, what the research aims to do. This is the very essence of informed consent. That the consenting individual has to know what the research is about. It is argued that this understanding should be tested [6] in some way otherwise it is wrong to assume it.

In most cases individuals consent to participate in research before they start a study and a core principle is that there should be a 'right to withdraw'. How consent is withdrawn rather depends on what is being consented to. Actioning the removal of consent after the surgical removal of a limb for instance is impossible, but data from a HCI study should be withdrawable.

2.2 Children and Participation

The participation of children in research is highlighted as especially problematic in terms of consent. Much of the debate in this has come from medicine where the right of a child to consent (or not) to a medical procedure has been widely debated. This was indeed the case in which *Gillick competence* was derived. Traditionally, research ethics boards refer to all adults under the age of 18 as minors and demand special considerations in terms of informed consent. This focus on age as opposed to activity is historic and is rooted in legal argument. Age based lineation has been wieldy challenged as research consent has moved beyond the operating theatre to consent to participate in research across a multitude of disciplines.

Concern about the child as a participant in research has been brought to the fore as thinking has changed from seeing a child as an object or subject to seeing the child as a social actor. Ethically, this move in position leads to new considerations including what Hill et al. [7] refer to as 'negotiation not imposition' in terms of what is being done with the child in research. In 2002, Christensen [8] introduced the idea of ethical symmetry in research work where the concern is to be ethically appropriate to 'the other' and where children are treated no differently from adults in terms of being informed and included in research work. This requires a move towards more personalized ethics where responsibilities are shared, embracing the philosophy of Jean Paul Sartre that the 'primacy of system over individual' does not remove responsibility of the individual to take ethics onboard. In [8] Christensen further refers to cultures of communication where practices in research should be in line with children's experiences, values and everyday routines.

This move towards individual responsibility is a theme for our own work. Believing in the three principles from Thomas in regard to participatory research with children [9] that (a) their inclusion depends on their active agreement, (b) that they should be able to withdraw and (c) they should have some choice in terms of the research methodology, our approach is based on going beyond the ethics review board and seeking ways to make HCI research work with children in mutually beneficial ways.

Our long term objective is to develop means to make research meaningful and fun for children, acknowledging the pressures of tie and attention, [10] whilst promoting a move from 'research on' through 'research with' to 'research by' children as provoked by Kellet in 2005 [11].

2.3   Children's Participation in HCI Research

Models of participation in research exist in the literature both within HCI and beyond. The earliest studies of participation were less about children and more about adults and many of the papers in this area come from the fields of sociology where the participation of different actors in society is studied and categorized. Participation can be described in many ways but one useful definition is that it is "*the social process of taking part (voluntarily) in formal or informal activities, programs and/or discussions to bring about a planned change or improvement in community life, services and/or resources*" [12]. This definition is especially useful for HCI as it stresses the voluntary aspect of participation which can be a point of tension. In many situations, when working with children in schools and clubs, children are not always empowered to decline participation if they do not wish to take part. Bracht [12] refers to participation as being something that results in a 'change' outcome. This is also pertinent to the HCI debate and it raises the question, if children are participating without there being an expectation that something changes, can they be assumed to have participated at all?

Participation is generally regarded as being something that occurs at different levels; one can participate in a sperficial way, or in a deep way and for those seeking to promote participation as an ideal, the aim is generally to maximize participation in order to maximize both individual and collective potential [13].

Modeling the effect and depth of participation has been a theme of considerable research. One of the most useful models for the HCI community comes from Hart [14] who conceptualized youth participation aligning to rungs on a ladder, (see Fig. 1), showing increasing autonomy, increasing knowledge and increasing influence as the participant moves up the rungs.

In Hart's model, the lower three rungs are considered to be 'not participation'. These refer to children as decoration, as having a token involvement and as being manipulated. These are strong words and they need to be considered by the HCI community when justifying inclusion of children in studies. Others model participation in terms of the depth, as opposed to the autonomy of the involvement; an example can be seen in the literature review by Nielsen et al. [15] where studies of participation were categorized against what was being done in terms of the 'mass' or density of

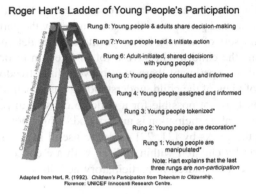

Fig. 1. Hart's model of participation

participation. In HCI a depth style model is proposed by Druin [16], who modeled the participation of children in HCI design activities in terms of the roles the children take on (Fig. 2).

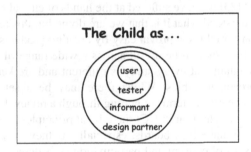

Fig. 2. Participation according to roles

In this model the emphasis is on the perceived increasing influence of the child as the circles expand. The design partner is also, in this view, an informant and the informant a tester and so on. This model has been heavily used in HCI to allow researchers to distinguish between the roles of children. It was the main model used in a review of Interaction Design and Children design research found in [17].

The involvement of children within participatory research in HCI is known to be beneficial as it allows children to gain knowledge in social action and helps them to prepare for active participation in democratic society. Participation is believed to strengthen social development and is, to varying extents, a right of the modern child [18].

In HCI, children typically participate as evaluators of a product, as contributors to a research study, or as designers of ideas and products [19]. In considering these three roles, it is pertinent to consider to what end the child is contributing, to what extent that child understands his or her contribution, and what, if anything, is the value of the contribution made.

It is recognized in other fields that conflict can occur in 'adult' participation when the 'agenda' is set by a third party rather than it being set by the participants [20]. In the HCI community, the sort of activity being promoted will determine the agenda. In some design sessions the child might have a lot of freedom to do as he or she likes whereas in a controlled experiment there may be very little freedom.

From the point of view of the child, understanding participation is central to the act of informed consent. It is not possible for a child to consent to participate unless the extent of, and the effect of, participation is understood. Whilst not directly associated to participation per se the works by [21, 22] could be useful in the ongoing study of the effect of participation by children within HCI as both are concerned with identifying the contributions made by children in participatory activities.

3   Ethical Participation in Action

HCI research can take many guises, it can be design and it can be experimentation, it can be about the effect of technology on people, or it can be all about the performance of the technology. Given that it can have many guises, the process of completing a University ethics application to carry out research in HCI can be fraught with difficulties. With others in the HCI field [23] we have suffered at the hands of ethical review boards in the process of making understood what it is that we are doing but this tension has enthused us to make application for ethics approval easy by creating products and processes that can be validated and be shown to be useful across a wide range of research scenarios. That said, we also maintain that every study is different and are keen to not suggest a one-size fits all approach to ethics. Whilst there may be a set of forms that can approximate to most scenarios in terms of getting through a review board, our own view is that when working with children in HCI the ethical principles used should transcend any variance in institutional ethics boards, especially as they may not appreciate the more sophisticated issues of consent and participation considered here.

In the following sub heading, our own work towards ethical participation is presented in three sections. The first section is concerned with how we communicate to children what we are doing and how we set up research studies. The next section describes how we challenge ourselves in terms of why we are doing what we are doing by exposing the values of the research team. In the third section we describe how we start to understand how children feel at the end of the research activity in terms of how they have participated.

3.1   Basic Information - ActiveInfo

Early in our work we chose to go beyond just gathering parental consent to actively seek consent from children. Active consent requires the children to be informed and to be engaging with the process of being informed. An early attempt was the production of information packs for children, built as three page booklets. These packs started with the creation of usernames (Fig. 3) as well as activities that could be either done at the start of the research study while things were being handed out, or could be used as filler activities for children completing a research task early etc.

Fig. 3. Choosing a secret username

Activities in the booklets, which were designed differently for three different age groups, included coloring, word games and collecting researcher autographs (Fig. 4). These side-activities are also helpful to have in the cases where a child may want to withdraw from the research activity. They provide something for the child to do without creating a problem for the research study and without drawing attention to the themselves. The children can also take these booklets home and talk to their parents about what they did at school. Each booklet has a contact number and the group website so parents can find out more if they want to.

In addition, these information booklets sought to explain something about data and research, as well as providing information about what we would be doing with the research outputs (Fig. 5).

These information booklets were designed for the children we were working with so were aligned to their abilities and their cultures. We have not stuck only with these designs, we have incorporated secret names and filler activities into many information booklets but we have always sought to make the booklet suit the activity and the children.

3.2   Examining Our Values – the CHECk Tools

Value centered design explains itself as 'frontloaded ethics' [24, 25] and promotes an early look at the values that are incorporated in design. As written by Friedman [26], *'Human values and ethical considerations no longer stand apart from the HCI community but are fundamentally part of our practice. This shift reflects, at least in part, the increasing impact and visibility that computer technologies have had on human*

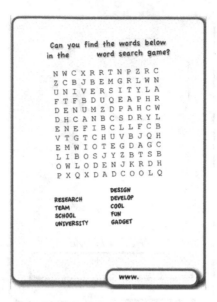

Fig. 4. Fun activities like word searches

Fig. 5. Explaining what research is

lives'. Whilst accepting that technology conveys and supports values, researchers and designers are also called to be 'value conscious' [27] and to deliberately clarify their ethical objectives in design by considering who's values are being considered. Central to value conscious and value centered design is the need to examine our own values; as adults enabling research practices with children. To that end we have developed two *values checklists* to assist in this process [28].

CHECk1

CHECk1 is a value checklist for use prior to a research study. Six questions ask:

1. What are we aiming to research or design?
2. Why are we *concerned* with this?
3. What platform/technologies or methods are we planning to use with the children?
4. Why are we using *these*?
5. Which children will we work with?
6. Why are we working with *these* children?

In completing this value checklist each 'why' question is required to be answered twice. The first time we answer with our first excuse for the work, the second time wereflect on this and seek to really get down to the real reasons for each response. An example makes this clear. In recent work with children in a very well-funded private school in the US, the research team was working with children to design a game for children in rural Africa. In asking 'why' in question 2, the excuse would be that we wanted *to improve the lives of children in Africa*, the more honest answer might refer to *the need to write an Interact paper* or the *desire to study design practices*. In question 4, our excuse might be to *gain great design ideas* but in an honest view it might be that *a study of the PD process* was being couched in the research activity. Question 6 is especially important. Often researchers will 'justify' a group of children on the basis of their *unique position to inform research* but more realistically the inclusion of a specific group of children is probably more likely to be that that group had a headteacher who *said yes on the day of a phone call*.

As can be seen in the example, the purpose of this checklist is to expose some of the tensions that are relevant to the research space. Having completed the checklist it is then down to the researcher, or the research team, to critically consider where the honest answers conflict with the excuses and where the excuses are not defensible.

CHECk2

CHECk2 is a consent checklist that seeks to assist in the formulation and communication of research to children. Like CHECk1, CHECk2 has a series of questions; some of which directly feed from CHECk1. As with CHECk1, the questions arrive in pairs with the second question of each pair informing the researcher on how to talk to the children about the research. The questions are as follows:

1. Why are we (the research team) doing this research project?
2. What do we tell (the children)?
3. Who is funding, and/or who are the stakeholders in, this research project?
4. What do we tell (the children)?
5. What might happen to the information /data /ideas that we take away in the long term?
6. What do we tell (the children)?
7. What might we publish /share /exploit from this project and who will read it?
8. What do we tell (the children)?

In completing CHECk2 the intention is to look before and beyond the research activity in order to better frame, for the children, the landscape of the work so they can better consent to participate. In completing this second checklist, researchers find that they better understand the ethics of their own work as well as finding that the research is done in more honest ways.

The CHECk tools are designed to assist thinking. We believe these to be cross-cultural in terms of their usefulness as they are simply prompts for thinking. Having answered the two checklists, the researcher is then in a strong position to talk to the children about the work they will be doing.

3.3 Explaining HCI Research to Children

Once the research team understands what they have to tell children, the next challenge is to convey this to children in ways that they can understand.

Our experience is that the way to talk with children is to engage with them and use images and examples to explore concepts. Our narrative, on coming to a group of children is firstly to introduce ourselves, then to talk about Universities, Research, Science, Funding, Publishing and finally Consent. Each of these needs explaining in an appropriate way so children can understand. Thus, when we talk about Universities we describe how they are similar to, but a bit different from, schools. We explain that research is more than finding out about things that are already known and is about discovering new things; we use examples of scientific enquiry, like talking with children about how we could find out if playing out was better for them than sitting at a computer all day. We talk about how research is paid for and ask children to suggest who they wouldn't want to be paying for research. We then talk to children about the possibilities for the outcomes from their research and this is possibly the hardest part of this process as it is far removed from their usual experiences.

PICO-Art

Discussion about outcomes is complicated by the different ways that children participate in research. Given that HCI research is so often multi-faceted, for example a research scientific style study with then some design ideas, we have found it complex to be able to explain to children how these different things will be used. To that end we have chosen to visualize what we consider to be the four different aspects of participation using meaningful images for children, referred to here as PICO-Art where P is for participation, I for influence, C for control and O is for outcomes. We can explore these four aspects with imagery. We do not see that there is single set of images for PICO-Art, rather that this is a way of thinking about expressing complex ideas to children and as such we would encourage all researchers to make their own culturally sensitive PICO-Art. Figure 6 shows our UK PICO-Art that is appropriate for our location and for the children in the schools we work with. Four images describe different positions on the participation continuum as it pertains to HCI. They allow us to talk to the children about how participation affords control, influence and outcomes.

The first of these images represents the 'no control' and 'no influence' end of participation. Here, in our PICO-Art, the image shows a child being taken to the supermarket mostly against his /her will; we associate this with the child as *object* or

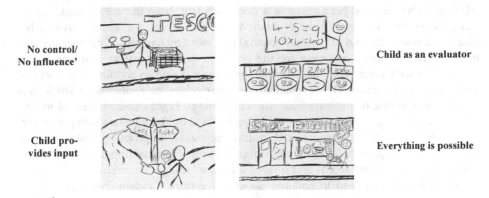

Fig. 6. Being taken to the shops by the parents, voting on the teacher, choosing the next direction and having a chance to do anything

maybe as *research subject*. A position where the child could be any child, he/she bringing little to the research and having little control. In the second image the child as an evaluator is portrayed. Here the child gets to vote on the performance of his/her teacher. If the teacher performs well maybe he or she will get to carry on in the job, if badly, then who knows. The child here has some control over what happens next to the teacher to a small extent. The child has a voice and is making a judgment that is considered to have some value.

The third image tends towards the classic research study where the child provides input towards a question that could have lasting impact. The child here is with the adult but the child is making the decision so this conveys the idea of more control than the 'you must come along because that is how it is' supermarket visit. In the fourth image the child has almost too much freedom and can do whatever he/she wants. Everything is possible and all the choices are his/hers in the shop of everything.

A PICO-Art set can be used at the start of a study to explain what is being planned but the abstractness of research makes it more useful after a study has taken place. Recently we have used these as a means to evaluate how children have felt about their participation. In Fig. 7, children voted for the participation descriptor that they most

Fig. 7. Using PICO-Art to gauge how children feel about research participation

felt fitted what they had been doing in a research study. Note the use of masks so we can photograph children. All these children had been doing the same activities but given a choice, at the end of their participation, to stand by any one of the four images; twice as many thought they were solving problems (the signposts as in image 3, that coming up with great ideas and having the chance to do everything (the shop of everything as in image 4); no children see themselves as evaluators (which was encouraging as that is not something we were doing). Eight children seemed to find themselves rather un-empowered by choosing to stand by the reluctant shopper image.

The PICO-Art images can be used in different ways – as props for children to tak about as well as signposts for children to align towards. The most important thing about PICO-Art is that all the words and images used are locally meaningful.

Having actively talked to children about universities, funding, participation and science in several research studies we have had interesting discussions with children about the possibility of their research being used to make money, about where that money should go (should it materialize) and about what data is and where it is to be used. Discussions on the possible profit from design work have been inclusive and informative; groups of children have been seen to draw towards a consensus decision.

4 Discussion

Applying these processes to our work has had several consequences. The first is that we have established a protocol by which research has to be explained to children before, and after each study using, as appropriate, tools from our toolkit described here. Sometimes researchers have used only narrative to explain things to children, in other cases they have used ActiveInfo in the form of booklets and worksheets. We have also embarked on a series of studies to 'evaluate' the effectiveness of our tools and our protocols. In these evaluations we have discovered that some concepts are harder than others for children to understand. In particular, children find the concept of research as discovery of new knowledge to be quite difficult to understand; having a tendency to see it as a way to answer a question for which the answer is known but just needs to be unearthed. This is a subtle idea and one that we will need to work harder on as it impacts on how children consider they contribute. If children are simply helping us find an existing answer or evidence this is slightly different than helping us invent. The idea of publication, which we have framed as 'exposing or advertising your answers' we have found children struggled to understand, but funding from 'good' and 'bad' sources and the idea of a university being like a school are easy concepts for children to grasp.

As has been shown in Fig. 7. Children may all do one activity and see it in a different way. This is perhaps a little surprising but given that an activity that we propose is designed in a certain way, that does not immediately map to the child perceiving it in that same way. This exposes that each child comes to an activity as an individual with expectations, their own understandings and then their own interpretations. We recently explored the individualization of participation with a class of twenty-seven 7 and 8-year-old children who were doing design and evaluation in two different research activities. In this work, the children were mainly engaged in a participatory design activity (Fig. 8), creating sketches of ideas, of a game to teach children about hygiene in which they were working in groups of three and four and then they were being taken out, in groups of four, to carry out an evaluation of an iPad game in which they were being asked for opinions on how to improve it.

Fig. 8. The participatory study

Children had brought bears to school that day and so, within the ActiveInfo concept we asked them to use their bears' names as their secret usernames for their research activities.

We asked children, before and after each activity about how much influence they felt they would have and had on the outcomes from the two activates. In other words, they were asked to what extent they imagined their designs might be used in the eventual game and to what extent what they said about the iPad game would be included in future instances.

As can be seen in Fig. 9, the children expected to be pretty influential in both the design and the evaluation activities with over half the children expecting to contribute loads or quite a lot of ideas /comments /content. But, and this is important, quite a few of the children though did not expect to have much influence. There is a real possibility that these children see their inclusion in the research in quite a negative way and in much the same way as the children who voted in Fig. 7, to align to the 'dragged to the

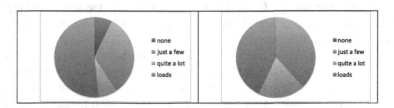

Fig. 9. Children's self-report on perceived influence

supermarket image', so these children were not able to imagine their individual value to the research study.

In this instance, the children were introduced to the PICO-Art at the end of the two activities and it was used as a tool to talk to the children about what they had been doing rather than as a tool to evaluate how they had felt. Having heard what we said about the research activities, the teacher lead a fifteen minute conversation with the class about participation while one of the research team took notes.

From this discussion it was clear that the children understood about freedom and control as portrayed in the PICO-Art images and they had also identified with the idea of being able to choose or make choices.

One aspect that the teacher explored with the children, prompted by the PICO-Art, was the 'shop of everything'. The teacher took a straw poll to get a sense of the children's enthusiasm for completely open activities and it was interesting to note that almost a third of the class voted for each possibility 'yes please', 'not sure', 'no thanks'. This confirms what we have observed over many studies with children, that some are very happy with open ended work whilst others much prefer structure. In proposing more freedom for children to influence participation levels in research, and in moving their involvement higher up the Hart's ladder, we mustn't lose sight that this might be a very uncomfortable place for some children to be.

5   Empowering and Informing Children in HCI Research

This paper has reviewed literature on the ethical participation of children in HCI. A set of three culturally adaptable reflective ethical 'tools' have been described, each providing additional value to HCI research with children. Practically these tools can be used in many different ways according to the situation and context of the work. We would always encourage, in all cases, the use of the CHECk toolkits as this is done away from the children and will always provide a means for the research team to reflect on what they are doing and on what they are going to say to the children. Having understood this, researchers can then consider how that information is best given to the children in terms of ActiveInfo. Whether this is a booklet or a single sheet of paper, whether a small passport is used for the bear's secret name, that is part of the research environment design. Consideration should be given to whether there is an intention, or willingness, to evaluate the extent if understanding after the research activity. If this is the case, then some post-activity questions can be asked or some notes made of discussion with a teacher or with one of the research team. Understanding how children have felt about their participation can be done in different ways, one way is to do a short before and after survey, às we did with the study with the seven and eight year olds, another is to explore their deeper sense of what they have been doing suing PICO-Art in an appropriate way.

Going forward there is a need for the HCI community to seek ways to better understand the impact of child participation on the children, on the community and on the society and systems beyond academia. That children gain from participating in research and design activities is a commonly stated justification for participation but it may be that this has to be challenged. Whilst an activity may not be harmful to a child, it may still not be the best use of their time. Given the extent of child participation in HCI studies; the community needs to grapple with this as a matter of some urgency.

Understanding the value of children's contributions will be complex. As a community the obvious place to begin is in understanding what these children bring to our field and then we can start to look beyond what they bring to us towards what they bring to each other and to society. Tools we create to help talk about participation with children may end up being useful prompts for our own discussion.

We need to be able to explain what participation means to the children who freely give their time and talents to our endeavors. This is possibly the biggest challenge for our research community to date.

References

1. Spriggs, M.: Understanding consent in research involving children: the ethical issues. In: A Handbook for Human Research Ethics Committees and Researchers. Melbourne: Children's Bioethics Centre, The Royal Children's Hospital, Melbourne (2010)
2. World Medical Association: World medical association declaration of helsinki. Ethical principles for medical research involving human subjects. Bull. World Health Organ. **79**(4), 373 (2001)
3. Williamson, J.R., Sundén, D.: Deep cover HCI: the ethics of covert research. Interactions **23** (3), 45–49 (2016)
4. Dahlback, N., Jonsson, A., Ahrenberg, L.: Wizard of oz studies - why and how. Knowl. based syst. **6**(4), 258–266 (1993)
5. Young, D.R., Hooker, D.T., Freeberg, F.E.: Informed consent documents: increasing comprehension by reducing reading level. IRB: Ethics Hum. Res. **12**(3), 1–5 (1990)
6. Flory, J., Emanuel, E.: Interventions to improve research participants' understanding in informed consent for research: a systematic review. JAMA **292**(13), 1593–1601 (2004)
7. Hill, M., Laybourn, A., Borland, M.: Engaging with primary aged children about their emotions and well-being: methodological considerations. Child. Soc. **10**, 129–134 (1996)
8. Christensen, P., Prout, A.: Working with ethical symmetry in social research with children. Childhood **9**(4), 477–497 (2002)
9. Thomas, N., O'Kane, C.: The ethics of participatory research with children. Child. Soc. **12**, 336–348 (1998)
10. Barker, J., Weller, S.: "Is it fun?" Developing children centred research methods. Int. J. Sociol. Soc. Policy **23**(1/2), 33–58 (2003)
11. Kellett, M.: Children as active researchers: a new research paradigm for the 21st century? (2005)
12. Bracht, N.: Health Promotion at the Community Level. Sage, Newbury Park (1990). 320
13. Israel, B.A., et al.: Review of communitybased research: assessing partnership approaches to improve public health. Annu. Rev. Public Health **19**(1), 173–202 (1998)
14. Hart, R.A.: Children's Participation: from Tokenism to Citizenship. UNICEF International Child Development Centre, Florence (1992)
15. Hrastinski, S.: What is online learner participation? A literature review. Comput. Educ. **51**, 1755–1765 (2008)
16. Druin, A.: The role of children in the design of new technology. Behav. Inf. Techno. **21**(1), 1–25 (2002)

17. Isola, S., Fails, J.A.: Family and design in the IDC and CHI communities. In: Proceedings of the 11th International Conference on Interaction Design and Children, pp. 40–49. ACM, Bremen (2012)
18. Checkoway, B., Richards-Schuster, K.: Youth participation in community evaluation research. Am. J. Eval. 24(1), 21–33 (2003)
19. Yarosh, S., et al.: Examining values: an analysis of nine years of IDC research. In: IDC 2011, ACM Press, Ann Arbor (2011)
20. Minkler, M., Wallerstein, N. (eds.): Community- Based Participatory Research for Health. Jossey-Bass, San Francisco (2003). 490
21. Guha, M.L., et al.: Mixing ideas: a new technique for working with young children as design partners. In: IDC 2004. ACM Press, College Park, Maryland (2004)
22. Read, J.C., Fitton, D., Horton, M.: Giving ideas an equal chance: inclusion and representation in participatory design with children. In: IDC 2014, pp. 105–114. ACM Press, Aarhus (2014)
23. Munteanu, C., et al.: Situational ethics: Re-thinking approaches to formal ethics requirements for human-computer interaction. In: Proceedings of the 33rd Annual ACM Conference on Human Factors in Computing Systems. ACM (2015)
24. van den Hoven, M.J.: Design for values and values for design. Inf. Age 7(2), 4–7 (2005)
25. van den Hoven, J.: Moral methodology and information technology. In: Himma, K.E., Tavani, H.T. (eds.) The Handbook of Information and Computer Ethics, pp. 49–69. Wiley, New York (2008)
26. Friedman, B.: Value sensitive design. In: Bainbridge, W.S. (ed.) Berkshire Encyclopedia of Human Computer Interaction, Berkshire Publishing Group, Great Barringham (2004)
27. Manders-Huits, N.: What values in design? The clhallenge of incorporating moral values in design. Sci. Eng. Ethics 17, 271–287 (2011)
28. Read, J.C., et al.: CHECk: a tool to inform and encourage ethical practice in participatory design with children. In: CHI 2013 Extended Abstracts on Human Factors in Computing Systems, pp. 187–192. ACM, Paris (2013)

Gaze Awareness in Agent-Based Early-Childhood Learning Application

Deepak Akkil[1(✉)], Prasenjit Dey[2], Deepshika Salian[3],
and Nitendra Rajput[4]

[1] University of Tampere, Tampere, Finland
deepak.akkil@uta.fi
[2] IBM Research, Bangalore, India
prasenjit.dey@in.ibm.com
[3] Kidzee Kindergarten Domlur, Bangalore, India
kidzeedomlur6@gmail.com
[4] Infoedge India Limited, New Delhi, India
nitendra@acm.org

Abstract. Use of technological devices for early childhood learning is increasing. Now, kindergarten and primary school children use interactive applications on mobile phones and tablet computers to support and complement classroom learning. With increase in cognitive technologies, there is further potential to make such applications more engaging by understanding the user context. In this paper, we present the Little Bear, a gaze aware pedagogical agent, that tailors its verbal and non-verbal behavior based on the visual attention of the child and employs means to reorient the attention of the child, when distracted from the learning activity. We used the Little Bear agent in a learning application to enable teaching the vocabulary of everyday fruits and vegetables. Our user-study (n = 12) with preschoolers shows that children interacted longer and showed improved short-term retention of the vocabulary using the gaze aware agent compared to a baseline touch-based application. Our results demonstrate the potential of gaze aware application design for early childhood learning.

Keywords: Gaze · Touch · Pedagogical agent · Early-childhood learning · Vocabulary building · Games · Mobile devices · Engagement · Comparative study

1 Introduction

The use of developmentally and pedagogically appropriate technology to promote early childhood learning is on the rise. Recently, a variety of technological tools, such as digital whiteboards [29], touch sensitive tabletops [10], Kinect sensors for whole body gestural interaction [17], and tangible objects [6] are beginning to be applied in the early childhood pedagogical environment. In addition, mobile phones and tablet computers are among the most popular technological devices applied in early

This work was done when Nitendra Rajput was working for IBM Research.

R. Bernhaupt et al. (Eds.): INTERACT 2017, Part II, LNCS 10514, pp. 447–466, 2017.
DOI: 10.1007/978-3-319-67684-5_28

childhood learning environment. Growing popularity and access to technology enable learners to become familiar in interacting with these devices at a very young age and provide scope for designing innovative, ubiquitous, and constructive learning experiences [34].

Currently, touch-based interaction is the most common technique in learning applications on mobile devices. Direct-touch interactive applications enhance learning compared to non-interactive video viewing [1] and is also known to be both easier and preferred by children than indirect interfaces such as a mouse [26]. However, there are also several challenges in designing touch-based interactive applications for children. Plowman and Mcpake [31] note that if children do not understand what they need to do, the interactivity offered by such devices may be counter-productive to learning. Touch interactions require the children to reach to the screen and tap the screen or do specific touch gestures, to perform an action. This requires careful design of the stimuli and prompts to make it intuitive [16]. Further, reaching to touch the screen maybe difficult depending on how the screen is positioned in front of the child [35]. Also, for early learners, the problem of accidental touches, and need for fine motor skills to perform complex actions has been recognised as challenges for using touch interactivity.

Another challenge in designing optimal learning experiences for young children is that the children have very limited attention span and get easily distracted (e.g. a noise from the hallway or colorful object in the tablet screen of a peer) [12]. Luna [27] notes that younger the child is, the more easily distractible they are. It is hence important in educational applications designed for early learners to be aware of children's attention and employ ways to reorient the attention when the child is distracted to facilitate continuous learning.

Recent advancements in computer vision software and hardware technology, have made gaze tracking cheaper, more accurate and ergonomic to use. The technology is increasingly seen as a viable and potentially beneficial interaction technique in mobile devices [22]. Gaze tracking has been previously used with children. For example, as a methodology in early developmental research [11], as a tool to diagnose and understand different psychiatric disorders in young children [39], and as an assistive technology for children with physical [5, 18] or learning [37] disabilities. However, the potential of gaze-based interaction remains unexplored for early childhood learning, among the general children population.

Gaze provides implicit information about the attention, intention, and rich cues of the interest of a child. Unlike touch-based interaction which needs an explicit action, a gaze-based application could adapt itself based on visual attention of the child, integrating learning with their curious visual exploration [20] of young minds, providing a rich and embodied experience. Gaze aware applications could also keep track of the visual attention of the child and employ means to reorient the attention, when the child is distracted from the learning activity.

In this paper, we present the Little Bear, a gaze-aware pedagogical agent designed for early childhood learners. The Little Bear tailors its verbal and non-verbal behavior in response to the visual attention of the child. The agent also exhibits emotional responses of sadness and boredom when the user is distracted from the learning activity, to help reorient the attention of the child to the learning activity. We developed an educational application using the Little Bear as the central character, to teach the vocabulary of everyday fruits and vegetables. Further, to evaluate the feasibility and usefulness of the gaze-aware pedagogical agent, we conducted two user studies with children from the 4–5 years age group. The purpose of the first study was to understand how children interacted with the application using the Little Bear and compare it with a baseline application that makes use of conventional touch-based interaction. The purpose of the second study was to understand the feasibility of integrating the gaze-aware agent in a touch-based application.

1: Comparing gaze-aware application with the baseline touch-based application: Different fruits and vegetables appeared onscreen and the learner was free to explore them. When the user activated an object, by either looking at it (*LittleBear*) or touching the item (*baseline*), the agent spoke interesting details about the item. Additionally, in the *LittleBear* application, the agent exhibited verbal and non-verbal behavior to help reorient the attention of the child, when the child looked away from the tablet screen. In this study, we wanted to understand how learners interacted with the application based on the conditions and observe differences in engagement, if any.

2: Feasibility of combining gaze and touch input: The agent asked a question regarding an onscreen fruit or vegetable (e.g. *could you show me the fruit banana*) and the learner had to touch the corresponding fruit. The agent proactively encouraged the learner if they gazed at the correct item before touching it or provided clues to guide the learner to the correct fruit if they gazed at the wrong item without touching it. With this observational study, we wanted to know if the two modalities can be combined in the current state of the technologies for children.

We begin by reviewing the relevant related work. We then describe the agent-based learning application we developed and the two user studies we conducted with it. Next, we report the results, followed by discussion of our key findings and observations.

2 Background Literature

2.1 Touch-Based Interaction for Early Learners

Aladé et al. [1] studied the pedagogical value of touchscreen technology for preschoolers and found that such interactive technology can facilitate and enhance learning compared to conventional mediums. Previous research has also investigated the challenges of using a touchscreen by young children. Hourcade [19] notes that children under the age of seven have underdeveloped fine motor skills and not yet well established hand preferences, and these affect how they use touch to interact. Vatavu et al. [38] studied touchscreen interaction for children between 3 to 6 years and found that children are significantly slower than adults and made more mistakes in performing simple touch interaction tasks. They partly attributed this to the under-developed finger dexterity and visuospatial processing abilities. Nacher [28] investigated the feasibility of multi-touch gesture for pre-kindergarten (2–3 years) children and found that some gestures such as double tap, long tap and two finger rotations are especially difficult to perform. McKnight and Fitton [13] studied young children's abilities to use touchscreen and found that children are more prone to accidental or unintended touches.

Complementary input modalities such as gaze tracking are expected to be available in mobile devices in the future. Our work investigates the feasibility and usefulness of applying gaze as an input modality in an agent-based learning application.

2.2 Animated Pedagogical Agent-Based Learning Application

Animated pedagogical agents are virtual characters designed to teach or guide users in an educational environment. While the pedagogical value of such agents are still debated [14], a well-established benefit of having a life-like tutoring agent is the engagement and motivational benefit it provides. Studies have shown that even the mere presence of a lifelike agent, even if not interactive, is capable of fostering interest and attention. Black et al. [4] studied how children converse with virtual agents and humans. They found that children tend to smile more, sit up and stay oriented towards the dyad when speaking to an agent rather than with humans.

Atkinson et al. [2] showed that the visual presence of the agent when combined with spoken instruction is more effective at promoting learning than an agent incapable of speaking. Krämer and Bente [23] note that improvement in non-verbal communication is required for agents to be more successful. While pedagogical agents were widely expected to transfer the benefits of human-human tutoring, the current generation of agents do not exhibit sophisticated non-verbal communication nor do they exert a social influence. Pedagogical agents that tailor their behaviour based on the emotional and cognitive state of the learner and show capacities for non-verbal communication, may have more pedagogical value [23].

Our study extends the previous knowledge on animated pedagogical agent. We designed an animated pedagogical agent capable of oral communication that is also aware of the visual attention of the learner. The agent exhibits emotional states, depending on whether the user is paying attention to the learning activity and, also uses the gaze information of the user to establish joint attention (agent looks where the child is looking), then guides the user based on the visual interest.

2.3 Gaze-Aware Virtual Agents

Gaze awareness has been studied in virtual agents previously. Lahiri et al. [25] studied how gaze data of adolescents with autism, recorded while interacting with a virtual agent could be used to provide personalised feedback regarding appropriateness of gaze behaviour. Similarly, Ramloll et al. [32] developed a gaze contingent environment for fostering social attention in autistic children, using an avatar that rewards socially appropriate gaze behaviour of the user. Eichner et al. [9] investigated gaze awareness in virtual agents capable of giving oral presentations and found that agents that tailor the presentation based on interest and disinterest of the user provide a more natural interaction experience. Bee et al. [3] notes that agents that use the gaze information of the user to exhibit socially acceptable mutual gaze and gaze aversion behaviour are rated more positively. D'Mello et al. [7] studied gaze aware tutoring agents for young adults and found that using audio prompts such as *"please pay attention"* was an effective way in dynamically orienting the user's attention.

Previous research on gaze-aware virtual agents has shown they provide therapeutic benefits for children with autism, and can make the interaction more natural and effective for normal users. Our work complements the previous work in this by investigating the value of gaze-ware agents, exhibiting emotional response, for early learners.

3   Comparing Gaze-Aware Application with Baseline Touch-Based Application

3.1   Design of the Gaze-Aware Learning Application

We designed a learning application with the "Little Bear", a bear character, as the pedagogical agent. The application was designed to teach children the names of different everyday fruits and vegetables. The application was set in a garden-like 3D environment, where the agent would take the child for a walk. Different fruits and vegetables would appear on screen at pre-defined locations during the walk. The environment was chosen to provide a realistic context to the learning, similar to a human companion taking the child to a garden and teaching about the different items (see Fig. 1). Once a fruit or vegetable appeared on screen, it could be activated by glancing at the fruit, making the agent speak an interesting detail about the fruit.

Fig. 1. Learning application using the Little Bear. The red semi-transparent boxes indicate the gaze interactive area. The application used in the baseline condition also had the same visual appearance and layout (Color figure online)

For gaze tracking, we used an off-the-shelf gaze tracker. Since accuracy of tracking maybe affected by the frequent movement of children, the gaze reactive areas were made slightly larger than the size of the fruit (see Fig. 1). When the fruits were visible, background image was dimmed, so that the fruits are the most salient objects in the vicinity to reduce the probability of the child looking something in the background activating the fruit. Once the fruit was activated, a short animation was played where the fruits were scaled to 25% larger than their size then back to the original size and the agent also spoke an interesting detail about the fruit. The agent communicated orally using pre-recorded voice generated using the IBM Watson Text-to-Speech service. The parameters for speed of speech, pitch and, pauses between words were carefully chosen to make the speech feel natural, fitting to the character and easy to understand. The agent knew four different facts about each fruit (colour, size, where it grows etc.) and told one fact at a time in order, once the item was activated. Every fact included the name of the fruit (e.g. *"apple is red in colour"*). Once a fruit was activated, the agent speech lasted 3–5 s and during this window the application did not respond to any other gaze activations of fruits until the agent finished speaking.

In addition to speaking about the fruit or vegetable based on the current visual attention of the child, the agent also used the gaze information to reorient the attention of the child back to the learning activity when distracted. When the child is distracted and does not look at the tablet screen, the character becomes sad (see Fig. 2a) and uses speech to attract attention by saying *"I become sad when you do not look at me"*.

Fig. 2. Agent non-verbal behaviour in response to visual attention of the child. (a) A frame from the 'sad' animation when the child does not look at the screen. (b)–(e) Head orientation of the bear changes based on the visual attention of the child (agent looks where the child is looking).

Further, when the agent was not speaking, the head of the agent was oriented towards the direction the user is looking at (obtained from gaze tracker), giving an implicit feedback of gaze tracking and helping establish joint attention (see Fig. 2(b)–(e)). However, when the agent was speaking, the head of the character was oriented directly ahead, abiding by the established social conventions of eye contact during face to face conversation. To further improve the realism of the agent, the agent also exhibited realistic lip movement and blink behavior to complement the speech.

3.2 Design of the Baseline Touch-Based Application

The baseline touch-based application used the identical learning context and visual appearance of the agent as in the gaze-aware application (See Fig. 1) and the difference was only in the interaction mechanism. In the baseline condition, touching the on-screen fruit or vegetable activated it and the agent was not aware of attention of the child and always appeared happy with the head oriented directly ahead. We did not employ methods to predict to the attention using the frequency of touch activity (e.g. assuming that the child is not attending to the screen, if no touch activity is detected for a specific duration). Our application design was based on the affordances offered by modality, i.e., gaze has a strong association with attention, and looking away strongly indicates distraction, while a gap in touch interaction need not always mean lack of attention. Table 1 lists the verbal and non-verbal behaviour of the agent depending on the visual attention of the child.

Table 1. Description of various behavior of the agent-guided interaction for various modalities in the application.

Agent response	Trigger in *LittleBear* condition	Trigger in *baseline* condition
Agent shows signs of sadness and utters *"I become sad when you do not look at me"*	User is distracted and looks away from the screen for 1.25 s	Not possible
The agent acts happy and energetic	User attends to the screen	Always
The agent orients its head in real-time to the direction the user is looking at	User looks around different parts of the screen without activating any onscreen object	Not possible
The agent utters *"I love the attention you are giving me, but did you notice the fruits we just found?"*	User looks at the agent for a predefined duration (3.5 s) without looking at other fruits and vegetables on the screen	User taps the agent
The agent speaks a detail about the item each time it is activated. E.g. name of the fruit, its colour, size etc.	User looks at the fruit or vegetable for 500 ms	User taps a fruit

3.3 User Study

The purpose of the study was to understand and compare the engagement and learning benefits provided by gaze awareness in agent-based learning application compared to the baseline touch-based application. We initially conducted a pilot study with 2 participants (1 male and 1 female) of the age group 4–5 years. The values for the dwell-duration for the character (3.5 s), duration to activate the fruits (500 ms), the duration of time for which the user looked away from the screen before the character responded visually (1.25 s) and verbally (6 s) with sad emotion were chosen based on the pilot evaluation. The chosen value for dwell duration for activating a fruit was short (500 ms). The median fixation duration for children (4–6 yrs) in free viewing task is 280 ms [15] and it is also known that children have less ability to perform longer fixations at a target than adults [40]. We noticed that a longer dwell was considerably difficult for our pilot participants. Choosing a relatively short dwell time allowed our application to be implicitly reactive to the interest/visual attention of the child than requiring an explicit gaze action.

Participants

We worked with Kidzee Kindergarten in Bangalore, India for the user study. We invited 12 children (5 females, 7 males) enrolled at the kindergarten to take part in the study. The participants were between the age group 4–5 years old and all participants had normal vision. English was not the first language of any of the participants and the participants were nominated by the teachers based on the English language proficiency. All the participants were familiar with mobile devices. The kindergarten itself has the policy of using learning applications on mobile devices, allowing every child to play with the devices once a week. Informed consent for the study was received from the teachers. No personally identifiable data of the child was collected or maintained.

Design

We chose a within-subject design. The two experimental conditions were labelled as follows: *LittleBear*: participants used the gaze-aware learning application with the Little Bear agent and used gaze input only and *Baseline*: participants interacted using touch input only (see Table 1).

We constructed two lists of 20 fruits and vegetables each for the test. Each list was constructed such that both had approximately the same number of everyday and uncommon fruits, making it safe to assume that participants were equally likely to know the names of the same number of fruits in both the lists before the test. The two lists were used in the application for the two different conditions. The order of the condition and the list for the condition were counter-balanced.

There were three dependent measures: *(i)* the duration of time participants interacted with the application, *(ii)* the number of times on average the participants activated each fruit, and *(iii)* the short-term retention of the vocabulary soon after the interaction as measured using a paper-based evaluation at the end of the session. For the paper-based evaluation, we showed the participant a paper with pictures of four fruits each and asked them to point at a specific fruit (e.g. *can you show me the fruit banana?*). The evaluation consisted of 10 such questions for each condition and was conducted soon after the interaction for the condition.

To test for differences between the *LittleBear* and *Baseline* conditions we used a non-parametric pair-wise (Monte Carlo) randomisation test [8]. In the randomisation test, the null hypothesis is that pair-wise differences are equally likely to be positive or negative. Repeated resampling (n = 10,000) with a random assignment of signs for the difference between the conditions gives us a sampling distribution of the mean difference. The observed mean difference is compared to the sampling distribution to estimate how likely the observed difference is by chance.

Apparatus

The learning application was developed using Unity 5.3 on a Microsoft surface pro 4 touchscreen tablet. We used a Tobii EyeX gaze tracker to record the gaze information. The tracker was mounted at the bottom of the tablet. See Fig. 3(a) for the experimental set up.

Fig. 3. (a) Experimental setup. (b) A frame from the interactive introduction of the Little Bear gaze-aware agent. The green dot indicates the current gaze point of the user. (Color figure online)

Procedure

The test was conducted in the Kidzee kindergarten premises. The participants were seated facing the tablet, which was positioned on a table in normal viewing position, approximately 40 cm away (similar to situations when using tables with special holders for mobile devices). In the baseline condition, the participants were free to lean forward or re-position themselves as they felt comfortable. The gaze tracker was first calibrated. We used the built-in Tobii EyeX "pop the dots" calibration process. It used seven calibration points. The visual stimuli used for the calibration were coloured dots, which burst when the user looked at one for a specific duration. We used the built-in calibration procedure because we felt the playful element in the calibration procedure was well-suited for children.

Before the *LittleBear* condition, a short interactive introduction was shown to the participant. In the introduction material, the character spoke "*I will tell you a secret. I have eyes and I know where you are looking*". We used the metaphor that the agent has eyes to convey the gaze awareness feature of the application. In the interactive introduction, the child could see the smoothened gaze point of where they were looking and the character would also look at the same area (shown in Fig. 3(b)). The bear also showed the emotions of sadness and boredom when the participant did not look at the screen. The moderator encouraged the participants to look away from the screen and observe the response of the character (as shown in Table 1). After the interactive character introduction, the learning application was started.

In both the conditions, the character introduced the environment as a garden with a lot of fruits and vegetables and encouraged the participant to walk with him to find interesting items. The character then turned around and started walking in the garden, where we used background animation and music to give a perception of a virtual tour around the garden. At different points during the walk, four different fruits/vegetables appeared at the sides of the screen (see Fig. 1). The character encouraged the participant to explore the fruits by saying, for example, "*we just found more fruits, do you know what these are?*".

In total, there were five phases for each condition and each phase had four items appear onscreen (altogether 20 fruits/vegetables). In the first phase, the moderator encouraged the participant to activate the different onscreen fruits (by touching them or dwelling at them by using gaze) and this phase was treated as practice and excluded from all the analysis. For each condition, the participant was encouraged to interact with the different onscreen fruits and vegetables, listen to what the agent said and repeat after the character. The application did not require the participants to activate any fruits to go to the next phase. When the participant wanted to go to the next location they had to press the "NEXT" button (see Fig. 1) on the screen, which made the character walk to a new location and four new items then appeared on screen, starting the next phase.

After each session, we used a five level smiley-meter [41] to record participant response along with qualitative feedback. We used the smiley-meter with two questions: *"Did you like the game you played?"* and *"Did you like the bear character?"* and the participants had to respond by selecting an appropriate smiley face from the smiley-meter shown on paper. In addition, we also logged the interaction events for further analysis.

Results

Average Time Spent per Phase

Figure 4(a) shows the time spent per phase interacting with the application for the two conditions. This study was about free exploration and the application did not have any restriction on how many times user had to activate each fruit. The extent of time spent on each phase was hence completely controlled by the child in both conditions. Therefore, we can assume that the time spent in each of the phases in different conditions reflects the overall engagement. The median value indicates that our participants spent almost twice as much time interacting with the application in the *LittleBear* condition than baseline. The difference was found to be statistically significant using the pair-wise randomisation test (p = 0.02).

Average Activations per Fruit

Figure 4(b) shows the average number of activations per fruit for the two conditions. The median value indicates that participants activated each fruit almost twice as often in the *LittleBear* condition as in the baseline condition and hence indulged in more learning activity. The difference was found to be statistically significant using the pair-wise randomisation test (p = 0.001).

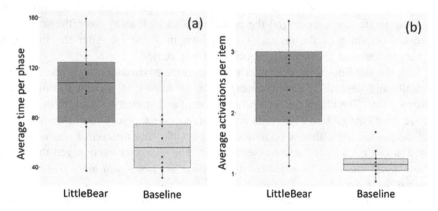

Fig. 4. (a) Average time (in seconds) spent per phase for the two conditions. (b) Average number of activations per fruits for the two conditions

Number of Items Retained After the Interaction

Figure 5 shows the boxplot for the number of correct answers in the paper-based evaluation following each condition. This evaluation was used as a measure of the *short-term retention* of the vocabulary, following the interaction. The median values indicate that our participants retained about 23% more names of fruits and vegetables after using the gaze-based learning application when compared to touch-based interaction. The difference was found to be statistically significant using the pair-wise randomisation test (p = 0.03).

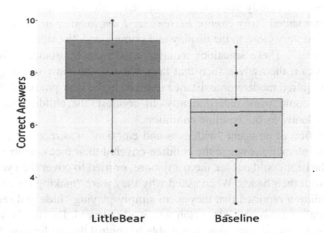

Fig. 5. Boxplot showing the number of fruits the participants recalled correctly in the paper-based evaluation following the interaction. There were in total 10 questions and each question had four different alternatives.

Smiley-Meter Data

We did not notice any difference between the Smiley-Meter data for the questions *"Did you like the game?"* and *"Did you like the little bear character?"* for the two conditions. Both the conditions were rated very highly (4 or 5 out of the 5 levels) for both the questions. Randomisation test showed that the differences were not statistically significant (p > 0.05).

Other Observations: Children Interacting with Gaze-Aware Agent

Using the agent's emotion to regain the child's visual attention was a useful technique. All the participants reported that they did not want to make the character sad or tried their best to keep the character happy. This proved helpful in two ways: first, to attract the participant's attention when they were distracted or looking away from the screen and second, the participants could successfully tell when the agent could not see them (i.e. gaze tracker could not track their eyes) as the bear appeared sad (e.g. when the child moved out of the view of the tracker), and hence re-positioned themselves, making the agent happy again.

Often, our participants would be distracted by external factors, e.g. by the objects or noise in the environment. However, this made the agent appear sad and was a motivator for them to return their attention to the application. This was also clear in two separate scenarios when two of the participants were casually interacting with the application after the test, in the presence of other children observing them. The users specifically wanted the observers to leave the room as their presence and conversations were distracting the user, which in turn was making the character appear sad.

Further, our participants sometimes made significant movements of their head and upper body while interacting with the application. This, at times, meant that they moved out of the view of the tracker, which again made the character appear sad. In the beginning phase of the study this sometimes caused confusion. For example, one of the participants commented "*why cannot he see me, I am looking at him?*" and another participant leaned very close to the display and commented "*he still cannot see me, my bear has bad eyes*". These situations required moderator assistance to help the participants re-position themselves such that they were in the view of the gaze tracker. However, the required moderator assistance reduced in the later phases of the study and the participants could work independently. In contrast, the children worked almost always independently in the baseline condition.

Also, the notion of an agent "with eyes and emotion" was received positively and sparked playful interactions where the children covered their faces, deliberately moved away so that the bear could not see them anymore, or tried to cover the eyes of the bear on the screen with their hands. When asked why they were "making the character sad", in all cases, children reported that they were simply playing "hide and seek" with the character. Overall, gaze-based interaction was well received. During the test, children did not show any signs of confusion or not able to control the application with the eyes due to Midas Touch. They could correctly associate the fruit that they looked and the spoken description of the agent. Figure 6 shows a representative gaze distribution pattern for the participant P11, interacting with the Little Bear.

Fig. 6. An example gaze distribution pattern for the LittleBear condition (Color figure online)

4   Feasibility of Combining Gaze and Touch for Children

Next, we wanted to understand the feasibility of combining implicit gaze-input and explicit touch input for children in their early learning years. There are numerous previous works that have investigated the combination of interaction techniques for adults [30]. While touch is a familiar, and the primary, input modality in mobile devices, gaze provides a wealth of information from a pedagogy point of view. Gaze could be used as a cue to evaluate common ground in conversational interfaces, be useful to predict intentions to provide proactive guidance (like in our Study-2), as a reliable way to evaluate comprehension etc. Hence, gaze and touch is a valuable combination of input modalities for early learners. We extended the gaze-aware agent application that we used in the previous comparative evaluation. The main difference was that instead of allowing the users to freely explore the fruits and vegetables, the agent asked the user a question (e.g. *can you show me the fruit banana?*) and the user had to touch the correct fruit, out of the four on-screen alternatives. The agent implicitly used the gaze information to understand if the user was confused or unsure about the answer. For example, if the user glanced at the wrong fruit for 500 ms, the agent would proactively tell the user how the fruit they were looking at is different in terms of size and colour from the fruit they need to find (e.g. *"you are looking at apple, apple is red in colour, while banana is yellow in colour"*) or if the user looked at the correct fruit while being hesitant to touch it, the agent would encourage the user to touch it (e.g. *"Yes, that is the one, go ahead and touch it!"*). When the user touched the wrong fruit, the agent gave the same response, comparing the fruit that was touched with the fruit they needed to find. If the user touched the correct fruit, the agent thanked the user for helping him find the fruit and danced for a few seconds, before moving to the next location where the user had to help find a different fruit.

We felt that with such gaze-based proactive intervention could potentially reduce the cognitive load associated with selecting a choice, and even possibly enhance learning [36]. The focus of the study was to observe how children would interact with an application that combines implicit gaze-input with explicit touch input and understand the real-world feasibility of combining gaze and touch input, in the current state of the technology, in an early childhood learning application.

4.1   User Study

We used the same participants and same experimental set up as in the previous study. The participants completed 4 onscreen questions and each question had four onscreen alternatives (same as Fig. 1). We used the fruits/vegetables which the participants had incorrectly answered in the paper-based evaluation of Study-1. In a few cases, the participants had less than 4 incorrect answers in paper-based evaluation after Study-1. In those cases, we used a predefined set of fruits which were not part of the evaluation to be used in the Study-2. The task for the participants was to find the specific fruit asked for by the agent among other onscreen fruits and touch it.

Results and Observations

As we had anticipated, almost all participants had one or more questions about which they were noticeably unsure or had selected the wrong answer at first. However, gaze-based guidance was rarely invoked due to issues with gaze tracking. Figure 7 shows the gaze data loss for each participant. The gaze data loss was calculated based on the number of valid samples expected, based on the approximate sampling rate of the tracker and the number of actual valid samples returned by the tracker.

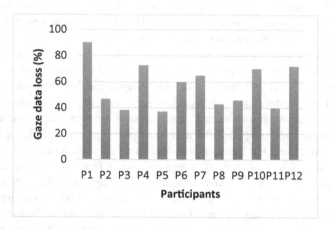

Fig. 7. Percentage of time gaze data could not be tracked for the participants.

There were two separate issues that caused problems in gaze tracking:

1. Short arms of the participants meant that, as soon as a question was asked by the agent, they leaned forward to touch the screen and the distance from the screen was insufficient for the gaze tracker to work. Optimal working distance of Tobii EyeX tracker is 40–90 cm.
2. In our study, the tracker was positioned at the bottom part of the tablet. This meant that normally when the children used their hands to touch the screen, the hands would obstruct the gaze tracking sensor causing tracking issues.

There were also differences between how participants interacted with the application. E.g. P1 was always close to the tablet making gaze tracking difficult almost all the time, while P3 and P4 moved closer when the interaction required touch activation. For all participants, there were problems in gaze tracking just before and while they were touching the screen for interaction. In the discussion section, we reflect on the technological improvements required to make the combination of gaze and touch work smoothly for early learners.

5 Discussion

We investigated the value of gaze awareness in an agent-based learning application for children. Before the study, we did not know if the gaze input is feasible; how children would react to the notion of an "agent with eyes"; nor how it compares against baseline touch-based interaction. Our results from study-1, suggest that an application that uses the attention information of the children to tailor the agent's verbal and non-verbal behavior may lead to better engagement, help develop a closer connection with the agent and provide learning benefits than a baseline touch-based application, that is unaware of the attention of the user.

All the participants in our experiment (study-1) completed both the conditions successfully. While we did encounter challenges with continuously gaze tracking the user when the children moved a lot, we did not face any issues with gaze tracker calibration and accuracy of tracking. Our study shows the feasibility of gaze-based interaction in early childhood learning applications. Our participants also reacted very positively to the concept of a gaze-aware pedagogical agent or "bear with eyes and emotions". Our results from Study-1 suggest that such gaze-aware applications are not only engaging but could also help motivate the children to attend to the learning material, and prove beneficial in learning as indicated by our results on improved short-term retention. In the *LittleBear* condition, our participants developed a closer emotional connection with the agent and all the participants reported that they did not want to make the agent sad. The agent, who became sad when not looked at, may have motivated the participants to attend more to the on-screen items.

There are two different factors that could have jointly contributed to the improved overall engagement and performance in the paper-based evaluation in the *LittleBear* application. First is the input modality that was used to activate the fruits. The Little Bear used the visual attention of the user to tailor its response and spoke about the fruits and vegetables that were of current interest to the user. Eichner et al. [9] showed that an agent that tailor its verbal response based on the attention of the user improves the overall engagement in adult users. In some situations, interacting with the application may have been easier with gaze than using explicit touch actions; for example, when the user wanted to activate the same fruits multiple times. While interacting with the Little Bear, children often exhibited a gaze behavior where they kept looking at the same fruit even after the agent had finished speaking a detail for that fruit. A cue that can be considered as if the child "wants to know more" about that fruit. This meant that the agent continued explaining the next detail about the same fruit, as opposed to the baseline condition which required another explicit touch action for the next activation. The fact that our participants spent more time using the application in the LittleBear condition could have influenced how well they performed in the paper-based evaluation.

Second, Little bear also exhibited feelings of sadness when the child looked away, as a mean to reorient the attention of the user back to the learning activity. D'Mello et al. [7] have shown that using simple audio prompts to regain the attention of a distracted user to a learning application could produce significant learning gains, even at deeper levels of comprehension. This emotional response may have motivated our participants to focus on the learning activity and this additional engagement possibility may also be one of the reasons the users interacted longer with the Little bear compared to the baseline condition. Overall, our results show the strong potential of gaze-based educational applications for early learners.

Our participants rated both the conditions very highly in the smiley-meter based questions. There could be two plausible explanations for this. First, it could be because our participants did not have any strong preference between the two conditions and enjoyed using both equally well. Touch-based interaction used in the baseline condition was a familiar interaction technique for our participants. While our participants were noticeably more engaged interacting with the Little Bear using gaze, they were also noticeably more confident and independent in the baseline condition. Second, it could have been a problem with our methodology of getting feedback from the participants. Previous research had also reported similar results using a smiley-meter with rural Indian children of age group 6–7 years. Kam et al. [21] note that their participants chose smiling faces, simply because they were more aesthetically appealing than frowns. We keep this as an important area to address in future studies.

Further, we also investigated the feasibility of combining gaze and touch-based interaction for early learners. Both gaze and touch modalities worked well when used as the sole interaction techniques, however, we faced unexpected technical challenges relating to gaze tracking robustness when using the combination of gaze and touch to interact. The two main reasons for the tracking issue was the sub-optimal working distance of gaze trackers, and hands obstructing the tracker view while interacting by using touch. In the current state of the gaze tracking technology, it seems difficult to combine gaze-input with touch interaction in mobile devices for early learners. Technological improvements are needed before the combination would work seamlessly. In the next section, we discuss the technological improvements required for gaze tracking to be useful for field applications for children.

5.1 Technological Improvement Required in Gaze Trackers

When using touch-based interaction, children position the mobile device very close to them, to perform easy touch actions. This distance is often less than the optimal working distance of commercial gaze trackers. Unlike adult users, children are even more restless and move a lot while interacting with technological devices. It would hence be beneficial for gaze trackers to have a larger range of operating distance and a larger field of view to efficiently track children.

Further, almost all gaze trackers are mounted below the screen, possibly to avoid the occlusion of the eyes by the eyelid and get a clearer image of the pupil. However, when mounted below the screen, frequent touch-based operations would cause the hands to obstruct the view of the tracker. While this is also an issue with older users [30], it is aggravated in the case of young users, as they do not show any specific preference of hands when touching the screen [19], and as we noticed in our study, sometimes even use both hands together to point at and touch an item. A potential solution to this would be to mount the camera above the screen or use multiple gaze tracking cameras to improve the accuracy and robustness of tracking.

Further, collaborative learning is common and encouraged in early childhood pedagogical environment (e.g. two children sharing a tablet). In our study, two of our participants wanted the few curious onlookers to leave the room because they were distracting the participant, which in turn was making the agent sad. While this shows that our approach of using agent emotion to reorient the child's attention may not be conducive to collaborative learning, this is also an inherent problem with gaze trackers. Currently, commercial gaze trackers do not support tracking multiple users simultaneously. It would hence be beneficial for gaze tracking devices, that are meant to be applied in early childhood learning environments, to support the inherent pedagogical practices of collaborative learning and playing.

5.2   Limitations and Future Work

We have identified five limitations in our study. First, the study was conducted by a trained external moderator and the reported results are based on short-term evaluation. There is growing understanding in the Child-Computer Interaction research community for the need of long-term evaluation of technologies in naturalistic settings. The presence of the moderator, who is unfamiliar to the children may have influenced how long they interacted with the systems. Novelty of the gaze-based interaction may have influenced the engagement. Future work will investigate the long term engagement and pedagogical value of gaze-aware learning applications, for example, by training the teachers to help in the data collection [33].

Second, the task used in our study-1 involved only simple selection/activation of fruits (with either gaze in the *LittleBear* condition or touch in the *baseline* condition). Using gaze as the sole input modality may only be suitable for such simple interaction tasks. Other input modalities such as touch/tilting the device affords more complex interaction possibilities. The purpose of the study was to demonstrate the engagement possibility and learning benefit offered by gaze awareness in an agent-based application for children and further research is required to understand how this gaze awareness can be best combined with other expressive interaction.

Third, we placed the device in a viewing position. In study-1, baseline condition, the children were free to lean forward or re-position themselves as they felt comfortable. However, in a naturalistic setting children may position the device differently (e.g. on the lap or flat on the table). The positioning of the device may have an influence on how children interact with the device using touch [35]. Further research is required to understand the effect of device positioning on our results.

Fourth, the small sample size (N = 12) is a limitation of the study. While many of the reported results were statistically significant, a larger number of participants could have been beneficial to understand any difference based on gender of the participant, or familiarity of mobile devices.

Finally, all our participants were between the age group of 4–5 years old and from an urban community. Age and culture may have an influence on how people respond to novel technologies, pedagogical agents, or the acceptable social gaze behaviour [24] with the agent. Future work should also investigate if our results could be applicable to children of different age groups and cultural representation.

6 Conclusion

We investigated how children of the age group 4–5 years interact and engage with a gaze-aware pedagogical agent that tailors both its verbal and non-verbal behaviour to the visual attention of the user. Our results suggest that gaze is a promising input modality for early learners. Gaze awareness in the agent-based application not only improved the children's engagement with the application, but also improved their short-term retention of the vocabulary learnt, and helped develop a closer connection with the agent. We further investigated the feasibility of combining implicit gaze and explicit touch input in a learning application. While the combination of modality has strong potential in applications for children, our results suggests that several technical improvements are required for this combination to work seamlessly for children.

Acknowledgement. We thank Nathalie Henry Riche for her valuable inputs while shepherding this paper. We also thank the staff members at Kidzee Kindergarten, Domlur, Bangalore for their support to conduct the study.

References

1. Aladé, F., Lauricella, A.R., Beaudoin-Ryan, L., Wartella, E.: Measuring with Murray: touchscreen technology and preschoolers' STEM learning. Comput. Hum. Behav. **62**, 433–441 (2016)
2. Atkinson, R.K.: Optimizing learning from examples using animated pedagogical agents. J. Educ. Psychol. **94**(2), 416 (2002)
3. Bee, N., Wagner, J., André, E., Charles, F., Pizzi, D., Cavazza, M.: Interacting with a gaze-aware virtual character. In: Proceedings of the 2010 workshop on Eye Gaze in Intelligent Human Machine Interaction, pp. 71–77. ACM (2010)
4. Black, M., Chang, J., Chang, J., Narayanan, S.: Comparison of child-human and child-computer interactions based on manual annotations. In: Proceedings of the 2nd Workshop on Child, Computer and Interaction, p. 2. ACM (2009)
5. Borgestig, M., Sandqvist, J., Parsons, R., Falkmer, T., Hemmingsson, H.: Eye gaze performance for children with severe physical impairments using gaze-based assistive technology: a longitudinal study. Assist. Technol. **28**(2), 93–102 (2016)
6. Chipman, G., Druin, A., Beer, D., Fails, J.A., Guha, M.L., Simms, S.: A case study of tangible flags: a collaborative technology to enhance field trips. In: Proceedings of Conference on Interaction Design and Children, pp. 1–8. ACM (2006)
7. D'Mello, S., Olney, A., Williams, C., Hays, P.: Gaze tutor: a gaze-reactive intelligent tutoring system. Int. J. Hum.-Comput. Stud. **70**(5), 377–398 (2012)
8. Dugard, P.: Randomization tests: a new gold standard? J. Context. Behav. Sci. **3**(1), 65–68 (2014)
9. Eichner, T., Prendinger, H., André, E., Ishizuka, M.: Attentive presentation agents. In: Pelachaud, C., Martin, J.-C., André, E., Chollet, G., Karpouzis, K., Pelé, D. (eds.) IVA 2007. LNCS, vol. 4722, pp. 283–295. Springer, Heidelberg (2007). doi:10.1007/978-3-540-74997-4_26
10. Evans, M.A., Drechsel, E., Woods, E., Cui, G.: Multi-touch tabletop computing for early childhood mathematics: 3D interaction with tangible user interfaces. In: Proceedings of the 9th International Conference of the Learning Sciences, pp. 274–275 (2010)

11. Feng, G.: Eye tracking: a brief guide for developmental researchers. J. Cogn. Dev. **12**(1), 1–11 (2011)
12. Fisher, A.V., Godwin, K.E., Seltman, H.: Visual environment, attention allocation, and learning in young children when too much of a good thing may be bad. Psychol. Sci. **25**(7), 1362–1370 (2014)
13. McKnight, L., Fitton, D.: Touch-screen technology for children: giving the right instructions and getting the right responses. In: Proceedings of the 9th International Conference on Interaction Design and Children, pp. 238–241. ACM (2010)
14. Heidig, S., Clarebout, G.: Do pedagogical agents make a difference to student motivation and learning? Educ. Res. Rev. **6**(1), 27–54 (2011)
15. Helo, A., Pannasch, S., Sirri, L., Rämä, P.: The maturation of eye movement behavior: scene viewing characteristics in children and adults. Vis. Res. **103**, 83–91 (2014)
16. Hiniker, A., Sobel, K., Hong, S.R., Suh, H., Kim, D., Kientz, J.A.: Touchscreen prompts for preschoolers: designing developmentally appropriate techniques for teaching young children to perform gestures. In: Proceedings of International Conference on Interaction Design and Children, pp. 109–118. ACM (2015)
17. Homer, B.D., Kinzer, C.K., Plass, J.L., Letourneau, S.M., Hoffman, D., Bromley, M., Hayward, E.O., Turkay, S., Kornak, Y.: Moved to learn: the effects of interactivity in a Kinect-based literacy game for beginning readers. Comput. Educ. **74**, 37–49 (2014)
18. Hornof, A.J., Cavender, A.: EyeDraw: enabling children with severe motor impairments to draw with their eyes. In: Proceedings of the SIGCHI Conference on Human Factors in Computing Systems, pp. 161–170. ACM (2005)
19. Hourcade, J.P.: Interaction design and children. Found. Trends Hum.-Comput. Interact. **1**(4), 277–392 (2008)
20. Gottlieb, J., Oudeyer, P.Y., Lopes, M., Baranes, A.: Information-seeking, curiosity, and attention: computational and neural mechanisms. Trends Cogn. Sci. **17**(11), 585–593 (2013)
21. Kam, M., Rudraraju, V., Tewari, A., Canny, J.: Mobile gaming with children in rural India: contextual factors in the use of game design patterns. In: Proceedings of 3rd Digital Games Research Association International Conference (2007)
22. Kangas, J., Akkil, D., Rantala, J., Isokoski, P., Majaranta, P., Raisamo, R.: Gaze gestures and haptic feedback in mobile devices. In: Proceedings of the SIGCHI Conference on Human Factors in Computing Systems, pp. 435–438. ACM (2014)
23. Krämer, N.C., Bente, G.: Personalizing e-learning. the social effects of pedagogical agents. Educ. Psychol. Rev. **22**(1), 71–87 (2010)
24. LaFrance, M., Mayo, C.: Cultural aspects of nonverbal communication. Int. J. Interc. Relat. **2**(1), 71–89 (1978)
25. Lahiri, U., Warren, Z., Sarkar, N.: Design of a gaze-sensitive virtual social interactive system for children with autism. IEEE Trans. Neural Syst. Rehabil. Eng. **4**, 443–452 (2014)
26. Lu, C., Frye, D.: Mastering the machine: a comparison of the mouse and touch screen for children's use of computers. In: Tomek, I. (ed.) ICCAL 1992. LNCS, vol. 602, pp. 417–427. Springer, Heidelberg (1992). doi:10.1007/3-540-55578-1_88
27. Luna, B.: Developmental changes in cognitive control through adolescence. Adv. Child Dev. Behav. **37**, 233–278 (2009)
28. Nacher, V., Jaen, J., Navarro, E., Catala, A., González, P.: Multi-touch gestures for pre-kindergarten children. Int. J. Hum.-Comput. Stud. **73**, 37–51 (2015)
29. Ovaska, S., Hietala, P., Kangassalo, M.: Electronic whiteboard in kindergarten: opportunities and requirements. In: Proceedings of the 2003 Conference on Interaction Design and Children, pp. 15–22. ACM (2003)

30. Pfeuffer, K., Alexander, J., Chong, M.K., Gellersen, H.: Gaze-touch: combining gaze with multi-touch for interaction on the same surface. In: Proceedings of the 27th Annual ACM Symposium on User Interface Software and Technology, pp. 509–518. ACM (2014)
31. Plowman, L., McPake, J.: Seven myths about young children and technology. Child. Educ. **89**(1), 27–33 (2013)
32. Ramloll, R., Trepagnier, C., Sebrechts, M., Finkelmeyer, A.: A gaze contingent environment for fostering social attention in autistic children. In: Proceedings of the 2004 Symposium on Eye Tracking Research & Applications, pp. 19–26. ACM (2004)
33. Robertson, J., Macvean, A., Howland, K.: Robust evaluation for a maturing field: the train the teacher method. Int. J. Child-Comput. Interact. **1**(2), 50–60 (2013)
34. Rogers, Y., Price, S., Randell, C., Fraser, D.S., Weal, M., Fitzpatrick, G.: Ubi-learning integrates indoor and outdoor experiences. Commun. ACM **48**(1), 55–59 (2005)
35. Romeo, G., Edwards, S., McNamara, S., Walker, I., Ziguras, C.: Touching the screen: issues related to the use of touchscreen technology in early childhood education. Br. J. Educ. Technol. **34**(3), 329–339 (2003)
36. Schroeder, E.L., Kirkorian, H.L.: When seeing is better than doing: preschoolers' transfer of STEM skills using touchscreen games. Front. Psychol. **7**, 1–10 (2016)
37. Sibert, J.L., Gokturk, M., Lavine, R.A.: The reading assistant: eye gaze triggered auditory prompting for reading remediation. In: Proceedings of the 13th Annual ACM Symposium on User Interface Software and Technology, pp. 101–107. ACM (2000)
38. Vatavu, R.D., Cramariuc, G., Schipor, D.M.: Touch interaction for children aged 3 to 6 years: experimental findings and relationship to motor skills. Int. J. Hum.-Comput. Stud. **74**, 54–76 (2015)
39. Vidal, M., Turner, J., Bulling, A., Gellersen, H.: Wearable eye tracking for mental health monitoring. Comput. Commun. **35**(11), 1306–1311 (2011)
40. Ygge, J., Aring, E., Han, Y., Bolzani, R., Hellström, A.: Fixation stability in normal children. Ann. N. Y. Acad. Sci. **1039**(1), 480–483 (2005)
41. Zaman, B., Abeele, V.V., De Grooff, D.: Measuring product liking in preschool children: an evaluation of the Smileyometer and this or that methods. Int. J. Child-Comput. Interact. **1**(2), 61–70 (2013)

Puffy: A Mobile Inflatable Interactive Companion for Children with Neurodevelopmental Disorder

Franca Garzotto[1](✉), Mirko Gelsomini[1], and Yosuke Kinoe[2]

[1] Department of Information, Electronics and Bioengineering,
Politecnico di Milano, Milan, Italy
{franca.garzotto,mirko.gelsomini}@polimi.it
[2] Department of Intercultural Communication, Hosei University, Tokyo, Japan
kinoe@hosei.ac.jp

Abstract. Puffy is a robotic companion that has been designed in cooperation with a team of therapists and special educators as a learning & play companion for children with Neurodevelopmental Disorder (NDD). Puffy has a combination of features that support multisensory stimuli and multimodal interaction and make this robot unique with respect to existing robotic devices used for children with NDD. The egg-shaped body of Puffy is inflatable, soft, and mobile. Puffy can interpret child's gestures and movements, facial expressions and emotions; it communicates with the child using voice, lights and projections embedded in its body, as well as movements in space. The paper discusses the principles and requirements underlying the design of Puffy. They take into account the characteristics of NDD and the special needs of children with disorders in the NDD spectrum, and provide guidelines for designers and developers who work in socially assistive robotics for this target group. We also compare Puffy against 21 existing commercial or research robots that have been used with NDD children, and briefly report a preliminary evaluation of our robot.

Keywords: Neurodevelopmental Disorder · Children · Inflatable robot · Soft robotics · Socially assistive robotics · Autism · Down syndrome · Intellectual disability

1 Introduction

Neurodevelopmental Disorder (NDD) is an umbrella term for a group of disabilities with onset in the developmental period that vary from specific limitations of learning and control of executive functions to deficits in social skills and intelligence, affecting personal, social, academic or occupational functioning [1].

Several researchers highlight the importance of early interventions to mitigate the NDD effects on the person's life and pinpoint how interactive technology can help in this respect. Particularly, the use of interactive robots has been proven promising in this arena and a number of studies have investigated the potential of these technologies (particularly for subjects with autism) to help children with NDD to develop cognitive, motor, and social skills. Still, given the wide range of NDD conditions and the specific

© IFIP International Federation for Information Processing 2017
Published by Springer International Publishing AG 2017. All Rights Reserved
R. Bernhaupt et al. (Eds.): INTERACT 2017, Part II, LNCS 10514, pp. 467–492, 2017.
DOI: 10.1007/978-3-319-67684-5_29

characteristics of each single subject, there is space for new exploratory experiences involving robotic interaction to identify new forms of therapeutic and educational interventions for this target group.

The paper presents an innovative robotic companion called Puffy that has been designed as a learning & play tool for children with different forms of NDD. Puffy is the latest outcome of a set of robotic companions that we have developed for this target group in cooperation with a team of NDD specialists, and evaluated at different therapeutic and education contexts [9, 10, 19]. Puffy engages users in free play and in game-based goal-oriented tasks, e.g., to promote imagination, communication, memory, or space and body awareness. Puffy has a combination of features that makes it unique with respect to existing robotic devices for children with NDD. It is mobile and has an egg-shaped inflatable soft body. It supports multimodal interaction, interpreting its body manipulation as well as user gestures, movements, facial expressions and emotions. It provides multisensory stimuli through voice, lights and projections embedded in its body, and movements in space. After a review of the state of the relevant literature (Sect. 2), we describe some general requirements for the design of robots devoted to children with NDD (Sect. 3) that offer guidelines for designers and developers who work in socially assistive robotics for this target group. The requirements take into account the characteristics of NDD and are grounded on the state of the art, the lessons learned from our previous projects, and the feedbacks from the NDD specialists who have collaborated in the development of Puffy. We then discuss the design of our robot (Sect. 4) and how it can be used in educational and therapeutic contexts (Sect. 5). After presenting the enabling technology of (Sect. 6), we evaluate Puffy from two perspectives. In Sect. 7 we compare Puffy against 21 existing robots used for subjects with NDD and highlight the originality and completeness of our robot. This analysis exploits an evaluation schema that is based on the requirements discussed in Sect. 2 and can be used as benchmarking framework for comparing future robots in this field. In Sect. 8 we report a preliminary evaluation of Puffy involving NDD specialists and two children with NDD. Section 9 draws the conclusions and depicts the future directions of our research.

2   Related Work

The review in this section focuses on Socially Assistive Robotics (SAR) and inflatable robots in relationship to NDD. While there is a wide number of study that explore the benefits of SAR in general, and some specific SAR features in particular, for subjects with NDD, the application of inflatable robots for this target group is unexplored.

2.1   SAR and NDD

Socially assistive robots are characterized by the capability of communicating and interacting with users in a social and engaging manner [25, 68]. In the last years, many researchers have investigated their application for NDD subjects, mainly considering children with ASD - Autism Spectrum Disorder (e.g., [15, 16, 21–23, 39, 47, 54, 60, 64, 68]). In contrast to other devices such as computers, tablets, and smartphones, socially assistive robots can play, learn and engage with children in the real world physically, socially and emotionally, and offer unique opportunities of guided, personalized, and controlled social interaction for specific learning purposes [67]. Many of the socially assistive robots used in NDD therapy are remotely controlled by caregivers [39, 40, 64]. Autonomous behavior is implemented only in few cases, to support a single type of tasks and to achieve a specific therapeutic goal [59] [TEO] such as imitation, communication or question answering. Autonomous socially assistive robots have been used successfully to attract attention, stimulate imitation, and improve communication, socialization, and behavioral skills [9, 38] needed for independent living.

2.2 Socially Assistive Robots: Body Shape and Mobility

Several researches explore the shape and movement capability of robots in relationship to NDD. Different shapes have been explored, from abstract ones to cartoon-like, simplified humanoids, or realistic human-like faces [15]. For example, the shape of Teo [9], a robot designed specifically for children with autism, resembles the popular cartoon characters of Minions or Barbapapà. Results from several researches pinpoint that individuals with NDD show a preference for something that is clearly "artificial" with respect to agents that have human-inspired characteristics [20, 58]. The research reported in [6, 51] shows that subjects with NDD may respond faster when cued by robotic movement than human movement, and some socially assistive robots used in NDD therapy can move body parts [39, 60, 65, 66]. Mobility in the physical environment offers opportunities to engage children in space-related tasks. IROMEC [59] and Labo-1 [21] for example are mobile differential drive robots but their movements are slow and clumsy movements so that children may lose attention in the interaction. QUEBall [63] has a simple spherical morphology of a relatively small dimension and rolls while moving. It provides multiple visual and sound effects to encourage the child to play but, to enabling rolling, it offers limited tactile affordances and stimuli. Teo [10] includes a holonomic (omnidirectional) base that enables it to move at a speed of up to 1.2 m/sec in any direction, which resembles the mobility capability of human beings. Teo supports space-related game tasks involving "joint" (robot + child) movements in the space which exploit the infrared and sonar distance sensors embedded in the robot body and an external depth sensor (Kinect).

2.3 Socially Assistive Robots: Emotional Features

Several SAR systems exploit emotional features that seem to benefit children with NDD. Keepon [39, 40] is a creature-like robot that is only capable of expressing its attention (directing its gaze) and emotions (pleasure and excitement). The empirical studies with autistic children showed that the robot triggered a sense of curiosity and security, and the subjects spontaneously approached Keepon and engaged in dyadic interaction with it, which then extended to triadic interactions where they exchanged with adult caregiver's pleasure and surprise they found in Keepon. KISMET [12] is an emotional robot which possesses eyebrows, ears, and mouth and expresses emotions depending on the way a human interacts with the robot. The robot's emotional behavior is designed to generate an analogous social interaction for a robot-human dyad as for an infant-caretaker dyad. Teo [10] supports users' emotional manifestation through the personalization of the robot. It is equipped with a set of a detachable pieces like eyes, eyelids, or mouths that can be attached to its body and enables children to create face expressions. In addition, as Teo's sensorized body can distinguish among caresses, hugs, and two levels of violent punches or slaps, the robot can react emotionally to different manipulations, using light, sound, vibrations, and movement to express different emotional states – happiness, angriness, or fear.

2.4   Inflatable Robots

Inflatable robots [43, 52, 69] have recently received the interest of the research community as they have several advantages over rigid robots. A soft lightweight inflatable body contributes the increased safety and robustness. It is less likely to cause harm to humans during interaction and works as a shock absorber in a case of an accidental collision or an unexpected fall [4], protecting embedded sensors and devices from a potential damage. The use of inflatable robots has been investigated in some critical environments such as disaster relief and field exploration [43]. To our knowledge, their application to children's learning and play is unexplored. Still, inflatable robots have a potential for children with NDD as they meet the requirements for robustness and safety that are needed, and their deformable structures offer manipulation experiences that can be particularly engaging.

3   Design Requirements

The requirements (Rs) that informed the design of Puffy are grounded on several design guidelines that are available in the literature about robots for autistic children [15, 31, 47]. Starting from the analysis of the state of the art, existing design principles have been filtered, revised, and enriched to address the broader target of children with NDD. We also capitalize on our own prior experience in assistive technology for children with NDD [9, 10, 19, 71, 72] and on the collaboration with therapists and special educators specialized in NDD who have been collaborating in our past research and in the design of Puffy. A general consideration that pervades many of the requirements described below concerns the characteristics of the sensory and perceptual system of most children with NDD, and how these affect functioning and behavior. Subjects with NDD often have an abnormal capability of sensory discrimination (the ability of focusing on, and discriminating between, certain stimuli) and sensory integration (the ability of processing and properly interpreting multiple sensory signals at the same time). These deficits are thought to be one of the main reasons for irritability, difficulty in selective and sustained attention, or hyperactivity that characterize many subjects with NDD; They generate discomfort, frustration, and disengagement, and make enormously difficult to accept, express and interpret emotions, and to sustain social relationships. These deficits are also thought to originate functional deficits related to own body awareness and space awareness, elementary mechanisms of abstraction and generalization, problem solving, planning, and language [18, 62].

3.1   Visual Appearance (R1)

As most of children with NDD are visual learners and have frequent loss of attention, the visual appearance of the robot body is fundamental in the experience with the robot. The robot body is a mean to attract the child's attention and engage her in an experience, as well as to communicate and convey meaning. Considering the sensory problems described above and the consequent risk of distress, the robot should *avoid* visual *overstimulation*, as the one created by different brightly colored body parts and aggregation of (moving) components of different shapes [31, 61]. Few *neutral colors* should be used for the body and harmonized to promote relaxation and trust [35]. Their visual attributes should be functional to their affordance and to the goal they are meant to support during interaction. The use and amount of different colors should be carefully calibrated considering the sensorial characteristics of each child and different visual configurations should be available for the same task. The *shape* of the robot should evoke a *familiar* element, possibly something that the subject likes such as cartoon characters. Considering Mori's conjecture about the uncanny valley [48], and the difficulty of NDD subjects to interpret the multiple signals expressed by the complexity of human faces and body, *abstract minimalistic "harmonic"* shapes are thought to be preferable to realistic representations (e.g., human like) [58, 61]. Still, it is important that some facial components are included, particularly eyes, so that the child could easily understand where the robot is facing and "looking at", and establish eye contact with the robot. Children with NDD (especially those with autism) are uncomfortable in making eye contact with humans, and simulating eye contact with the robot might help them to generalize this concept in human-human relationships [57]. To facilitate eye contact with the robot, the most appropriate *size* for the robot should correspond to the average size of the target group [10, 57, 60].

3.2   Multimodality (R2)

Multimodality, i.e., the provision of different interaction modes that involve different (sets of) skills and sensory stimuli, have a number of advantages for children with NDD. Supporting multiple modes of interacting with the robot opens up opportunities to engage the children in different ways, each one focused on specific and evolving learning needs, and to promote cause-effect understanding skills which derive from experiencing the action-feedback loop in different situations. Still, multimodality involves some potential risks for this target group. The perceptual experience of subjects with NDD is often abnormal and these persons may have impairments in filtering or processing simultaneous channels of visual, auditory and tactile inputs. They may perform poorly across different interaction modes and during conditions that require processing different requests and stimuli. The robot should offer a gamut of "single mode" interactions that can be used one by one, and also enable progressive combinations or concatenations of different interaction modes. These must be carefully calibrated so to enable children to practice tasks at the proper level of sensory complexity and to master the difficulty of perceiving inputs across multiple modes. According to the current literature, the interaction modes that have been proved effective for children with NDD are *spatial*, *tangible*, *vocal*, and *emotional*.

3.3 Spatial Interaction (R3)

Spatial interaction exploits how humans use the space to regulate the reactive behavior of an interactive technological artifact, and has recently been emphasized as one of the important design aspect of a social assistive robot [45, 49, 55]. Spatial interaction requires that the robot is able to move as naturally as possible in the space, to sense and interpret the user position, orientation, movement, direction, and to react consistently. Spatial interaction help children with NDD to learn spatial awareness, i.e., the ability to be aware of oneself in space, which is often weak in these subjects. Spatial awareness requires the creation of a contextualized body schema representation - a sense of where your body is in the space, and involves the understanding of the relationship between physical objects and oneself in the space, both when objects are static and when they change position, learning concepts like distance, speed, "near", "behind", and similar.

3.4 Tangible Interaction (R4)

Manipulation and tactile experiences plays a fundamental role in the development of sensory-motor capabilities as well as cognitive functions [70]. Several therapeutic tasks for children with NDD involve touch and manipulation of physical materials as a means to improve the capability to interpret stimuli processed by the tactile system and to improve own-body awareness. Similar skills can be promoted in a playful, safe, and controlled way through tangible interaction with the robot, enabling touch and physical manipulation of its body associated to consistent feedbacks. Physical touch is also one of the most basic, but at the same time most important forms of human communication. Through physical interaction with the robot children with NDD can learn to express and interpret this form of communication. Particularly, while an inappropriate tactile interaction with a human (e.g., pushing) would lead to a negative reaction which can be enormously frustrating for subjects with NDD, the similar action on a robot can trigger stimuli that help them reflect on their behavior and build a sense of stability and confidence [56]. Tactile interaction involving the feature of being "huggable" is recently emphasized as one of important aspects in the design of Robot Assisted Therapy [9, 10, 20, 68].

3.5 Vocal Interaction (R5)

Children with NDD may have deficits in speech production and understanding - a complicated process involving the coordination of motor, auditory, somatosensory systems and several cognitive functions. Many therapy programs for these subjects include activities to help them communicate verbally in a useful and practical way. A robot equipped with vocal interaction can support vocalization capability and in principle be integrated in existing speech-therapy treatments. The controlled study reported in [24] show more positive effects on vocalization and speech capability when the considered robot interacted through remotely arm, ears, mouth, and eye movements *and* speech (remotely generated and controlled by the investigator) compared to the effects achieved when voice features were missing. Qualitative observations emerging from empirical studies on Teo [9] highlights that vocal interaction through reward phrases and songs (generated after a task completion) promotes engagement and fun.

3.6   Emotional Interaction (R6)

Emotional information exchange plays an important role in human-human interaction. Current SAR research considers emotional interaction one of the principal ways to achieve trust and believability [8], making the user feel that the robots "understand" and "care" about what happens in the world. In addition, a robot that can both manifest its emotional states and interpret users' emotions helps subjects with NDD to develop the capability of emotional information exchange, i.e., to learn how to interpret and manifest emotions, which is fundamental for human interpersonal communication. Emotions can be expressed through different signals depending on the actuation characteristics of the robot: different face expressions, music, voice tones, movements in space or body movement rhythms convey different emotional signal.

3.7   Multisensory Feedback (R7)

The action-feedback mechanism which is intrinsic in interaction promotes two basic and fundamental skills: cause-effect understanding and sense of agency, i.e., the feeling of being able to exercise control and of obtaining a coherent response. Once these skills are established, a person learns that (s)he can also affect different situations and people, and is motivated, for example, to use communication in its many forms (e.g., by requesting, questioning, or refusing) to manipulate situations. Reward stimuli, to acknowledge the correct completion of a multi-action task should also be explicitly acknowledged so that the child feels gratified for the achievement [61]. For example, lighting up part of the robot body or playing music or songs, showing animations is thought to be particularly engaging and encouraging [27, 47]. Still, for the reasons discussed at the beginning of this section, all stimuli must be carefully designed, and calibrated properly to avoid overstimulation and discomfort.

3.8   Safety (R8)

The robot should be "be harmless to patients physically, psychologically, and ethically" [53]. To this extent, sharp edges should be avoided favoring soft textures [47]. In addition, the robot body should be *robust* enough to reduce the effects of voluntary or involuntary disruptive actions, considering that children with NDD can be uncontrollably exuberant or impulsive at times.

3.9   Configurability (R9)

Because children with NDD have unique and evolving needs, the value of technology for this target is directly related to its ability to adapt to specific needs and learning requirements of each person or group [13, 50]. The robot should be integrated with the possibility for therapists to configure it (e.g., increasing/decreasing/removing sensory stimuli, or changing visual and sound rewards) to adapt the interactive experience to the specific profile of the current user(s).

3.10   Dyadic Execution Mode (R10)

Involving children in robotic interaction requires a combination of remotely-controlled and autonomous modes. Remote control gives the complete control of the robotic behavior to the caregiver. This is important to manage situations created by children's unexpected actions, to unlock stereotyped behaviors (typical of children with autism), to create new stimuli in response to children's interactions with the robot or movements in the space, or to adapt the stimuli to the specific characteristics of each child. Still, remote control is demanding for the caregiver. She must pay a constant attention to the child and at the same time must operate on the robot, controlling it in a believable and timely way and giving the impression that the robot is behaving autonomously and consistently with the current context. This burden can be alleviated by including some autonomous behaviors in the robot, i.e., programmed <stimuli–user action–stimuli> loops or flows of loops that enable the robot to act in the environment and interact consistently with some a pre-define logic.

3.11   Multiple Roles (R11)

The robot plays different functional roles in the interaction with the children [15]:

(a) *Feedback*: it reacts to an action performed by the child, promoting cause-effect understanding, and plays as rewarding agent, to offer positive reinforcement and promote self-esteem.
(b) *Facilitator*: it suggests what to do and when to do it facilitating task execution.
(c) *Prompt*: it acts as a behavior eliciting agent enhancing attention and engagement.
(d) *Emulator*: it plays as an emulator (acts as the child) or something that is imitated, to trigger the child's imitative reaction and skills.
(e) *Restrictor*: it limits the child's spatial movement possibilities.
(f) *Social Mediator*: it mediates social interaction between the child and others (therapist, peers); it acts as a communication channel through which the child expresses her communication intents as well as a tangible material for shared activities.
(g) *Affective and emotional agent:* it facilitates the creation of affective bond between the robot and the child/children, helping subjects to unlock their emotional rigidity and to feel emotions; it stimulates the children's capability of manifesting their own emotions and interpreting the others' emotional expressions [70].

4   The Design of Puffy

Puffy has been co-designed done in partnership with a team of 2 designers, 4 engineers and 15 therapists (psychologists, neuro-psychiatrists, special educators) from two different rehabilitation centers. In what follows we describe the physical and behavioral characteristics of the robot matching them to the requirements discussed in the previous section.

4.1 Physical Characteristics

General Shape: The visual appearance of Puffy (Fig. 1) meet all requirements stated in *R1*. Its white shape, externally made of a thin, white, opaque plastic textile is inspired by Baymax, the inflatable healthcare robot of the popular Disney animated movie Big Hero 6, and reminds a familiar character that children like and have positively experienced in everyday life. Puffy is approximately 130 cm high (the average height of our target group) and its only facial elements are two black eyes, to help user understanding what the robot is gazing at. Its wide round belly and its curved silhouette confer a fluffy and comfortable warm appearance and contributes to relax children, to promote affections and trust *(R11.g)*, and to give the impression of playing as a gentle "big brother".

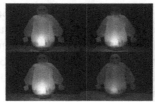

Fig. 1. Puffy

Fig. 2. Light effects in Puffy (Color figure online)

Dynamic Inflatable Structure: Puffy is characterized by an inflatable structure. An embedded fan (that also serves a cooling purpose) is used to blow up Puffy's light plastic "skin" at the beginning of a session and to dynamically transform the shape and size of its inflatable structure in order to convey emotional body signals. Puffy can simulate relaxed breathing (through rhythmic inflating-deflating), manifest satisfaction and confidence (expanding the body through inflation), or express discomfort and sadness (compressing the body by reducing the air inside), enforcing the robot role as Affective and Emotional Agent *(R11.g)*. The resulting body – big, soft, flexible in shape, and humorously rounded – makes Puffy robust, safe and harmless *(R8)*, and pleasurable to touch and hug *(R4)*. These features facilitate the role of Puffy as "Social mediator" *(R11.f)*. For example, Puffy can be manipulated by many children together at the same time (Figs. 3, 4 and 5).

Lights: Inside Puffy there is a commercial smart lamp (a Philips Hue Go) that generates a gamut of luminous feedbacks *(R7)* that, perceived across the white opaque fabric of the robot body, give a sense of magic (Fig. 2). Light stimuli are used not only as an aesthetic medium to attract and create engagement *(R11.c)*. Rhythmic dynamic light can complement the rhythmic expansion/compression of the robot's body, and increase the emotional effect *(R11.g)*. As colors and intensity evoke and convey different emotions, luminous stimuli can be used to enhance emotional interaction *(R6)* and affective bond *(R11.g)*.

Fig. 3. Shared interaction with Puffy (Color figure online)

Fig. 4. A group of children (two of them with NDD) playing together with Puffy at a local school (Color figure online)

Fig. 5. Manifestations of affection towards Puffy (Color figure online)

Music and Voice: Music not only offers stimuli for the sound sensory system *(R7)* but is also known to conveying emotions and affect wellbeing and emotional states *(R6 and R 10.g)*. In some phases of a therapeutic session such as during the introduction and the breaks, Puffy plays soft songs at the frequency of 432 Hz (a frequency that is acknowledged to influence heart rate and improve relaxation), to establish a pleasurable calming atmosphere. While children are engaged in a task, cheerful music offer rewards or is used to re-capture user attention *(R11.c)*. Puffy's cheerful voice (R5) offers vocal instructions and feedbacks during interaction and tasks execution, such as back-channeling expressions ("mm mm, uhmmm, mm mmmm…"), reinforcement or reward phrases.

Vocal interaction capability can range from the production of voice instructions and vocal feedbacks (back-channeling expressions, reinforcement or reward phrases, songs, or rhymes) to the capability of interpreting the users' speech and reacting consistently.

Multimedia On-Body Projections: A compact projector is embedded *inside* Puffy's body and displays visual stimuli (images, videos, or animations) on its belly *(R7)*. These contents – which in rigid socially assistive robots are displayed using a tablet, a PC screen, or a smartphone placed *on* the body – [38] provide instructions, suggestions, or feedbacks *(R11.a-b)* for the tasks in which the children are involved, or are associated to the story Puffy is telling (as discussed later in the paper). Thanks to the white opaque light weighted plastic material and the shape of the inflatable body, projections result curve-rounded and with ambiguous borders that create a pleasant visual effect and enhance the sense of magic of the story being told, contributing to increase the affective bond with the robot *(R11.g)*.

Mobility: Puffy does not walk like Baymax character. Nevertheless, thanks to its holonomic base, our robot has a fluid mobility and is free of moving on the floor in any direction at a speed similar to that of humans in indoor environments *(R3)*, wandering around, chasing the child, or getting close or faraway. Puffy's mobility features, described more precisely in the following section, support the robot's roles as Emulator *(R11.d)* and Restrictor *(R11.e)*. Movements can be also used as prompts, to complement the prompting capability of music, voice, and projected visual contents *(R10.c)*.

4.2   PUFFY: Interaction and Behavior

Puffy-children interaction is multimodal *(R2)*. Puffy supports tangible and vocal interaction *(R4* and *R5)* – enabled by its capability of sensing and interpreting touch, sound, and speech, spatial interaction *(R3)* – enabled by the robot capability of moving and sensing users' movements, distance and position - and emotional interaction *(R6)* – enabled by the capability of recognizing the user facial expressions and voice signals, and to manifest emotional signals. Both tangible and spatial interaction can be combined with emotional interaction, as described below.

Coordinated Spatial + Emotional Interaction: Puffy senses and interprets the physical spatial relationship between itself and the children (e.g., relative position, movement, orientation), which enables various forms of spatial interaction. For example, if an educational session has just started and Puffy locates the child far away, the robot attempts to attract the child's attention: it emits some cheerful sound and turns left and right (as if it were looking around) while its body is illuminated with soft blue light rhythmically changing intensity to increase the sense of movement. Puffy can also combine spatial interaction with emotional interaction, taking into account the psychological and emotional aspects of the spatial relationship between itself and a child. To this end, Puffy exploits an *Interactional Spatial Relationship Model* (Fig. 6) which considers the following elements:

(a) *Interpersonal distance,* measured by an embedded depth sensor and classified according to the Hall's zone system of proxemics interaction (e.g. public, social, personal, intimate [34]); the definition of the parameters for users preferred interpersonal distance can be customized according to various conditions including a child's age and the current task, e.g., as a competitive or cooperative situation [37]).

(b) *Relative (child-robot) bodily orientations* (e.g. face-to-face, side-by-side). Bodily orientation and interpersonal distance are a form of non-verbal communication that implicitly convey a child's current intention how a child wants to manage his/her relationship with Puffy [46].

(c) *Child's and robot's movements in space*, defined by physical parameters such as direction and speed. Depending on the context, the kinematic behavior is interpreted both as "functional" to the current task, or as a psychological and emotional cue (e.g., "escaping from the robot" may be interpreted as an action required by the game or a signal of discomfort).

(d) *Child's emotional state,* which is detected from the analysis of the child's voice tone [42] and facial expressions.

(e) *Child-robot eye contact,* which is again based on the analysis of the child's image; as already mentioned (Sect. 3.1) eye contact is an important nonverbal communication behavior to express interest, attention, and trust towards a conversation partner, and is often missing in children with NDD (especially those with autism).

(f) *Robot's emotional state*: the robot's current emotional state resulting from the Physical Manipulation by the children (see "Tangible") and from movement values.

The current status of the robot-child relationship, defined by the set of the above variables, is used for determining the robot spatial and emotional behavior, as in the following example. Let us assume that there is only one child interacting with Puffy and the model variables have the following values:

(a) {*interpersonal distance* = 140 cm, i.e. located in a point of transition from "social" to "personal" distance},
(b) {*relative bodily orientations*: child = 0, puffy = 0, i.e. "face-to-face"},
(c) {*child's spatial movement* = "standing-still", i.e., no significant movement detected}, {*robot's spatial movement* = "approaching to a child at velocity 0.20 M/sec"},
(d) {*child's emotional state* = "mild", i.e., child's voice detected at medium level of loudness + smile recognized in the face},
(e) {*child-robot eye contact* = "eye-contact by a child detected", i.e., sufficient level of child's interest and attention towards the robot},
(f) {*robot's emotional state* = "quiet"*, i.e., no previous hit; no movement, vibration, or blink}.

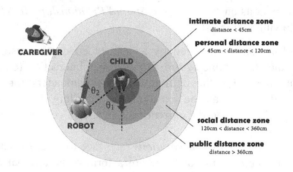

Fig. 6. Model of interactional spatial relationships

Based on the above analysis, Puffy decides that it is the appropriate timing to make a greeting, and sets its voice at medium-high level of loudness (as appropriate at the edge of social zone); then it continues moving towards a child only after it detects the absence of negative emotional response from the child. Approaching the "personal" distance zone around the child, Puffy re-evaluates the current status of the robot-child relationship and adapts its behavior by taking into account the potential risk of its current and next reactions.

For example, Puffy may estimate that it should slow down its speed. The "personal" distance zone around the child is typically reserved to friends and family members who know and trust each other [34], and to avoid the child's feeling of an undesirable intrusion of his personal space of the child), Puffy must be ready to stop. After the robot detects that there is no negative response from the child, it considers that it is the right time to start some form of explicit communication, and for example engages the subject in a conversation adjusting its voice level at medium- loudness (as appropriate at personal distance).

Tangible Interaction: Puffy employs two modes of tangible interaction: Physical Manipulation and Functional Touching. *Physical Manipulation* involves the tactile contact with Puffy (Fig. 4) and involves elements of emotional interaction. The robot's sensorized body can distinguish among caresses, hugs, and two levels of violent punches or slaps, measuring the intensity and dynamics of the body deformation induced by the physical contact. Depending on the evaluation of the manipulation, Puffy produces a specific emotion-based behavior by employing a map of multimodal emotional expressions [41]. Puffy becomes *Happy* when its body is softly caressed or touched. It responds to this pleasurable manipulation by emitting sound expressions of pleasure, vibrating, and rotating itself cheerfully, while internal lights becomes green and blink slowly. Puffy becomes *Angry* when its body is hit with moderate force. It responds to this rude manipulation by moving sharply towards a child, turning light to red, inflating its body and growling (grrr). Puffy becomes *Scared* when its body is brutally hit. It reacts by slowly retreating itself saying "what a fear!" while lights become yellowish and pulse slowly and the body shape shrinks. *Functional Touching* allows a child to make a choice (Fig. 5), express simple instructions to Puffy, or answering a question, by pressing Puffy's body in a specific area. Using the embedded projector, the active areas for functional touching appear dynamically on Puffy's belly, recognizing the position of the child's touch. Digital contents can be personalized by therapists by inserting the tags that are more meaningful for the activity, either realistic images or PCSs (Picture Communication Symbols), commonly used in Augmented Alternative Communication interventions [28].

Voice Interaction: Puffy can react vocally to situations that change its emotional state, as discussed above. Knowing the current state of a task (e.g., "complete"), the robot can use voice to reward the children. In addition, Puffy can interpret at some degree the children's speech, namely, the main sentiment of children's vocalizations and the main concepts expressed, and is programmed to react consistently.

Execution Mode: The execution of Puffy's behaviors is performed in two modalities - *remotely controlled* and *autonomous agent (R10)*. In *remotely controlled mode*, the caregiver triggers the desired stimuli on Puffy's body and drives the robot movements using a remote controller (a joystick). As an *autonomous agent*, Puffy is preprogrammed to act *autonomously* according to the interaction rules defined in Sect. 4.2 and the logic of the activities defined in Sect. 5.

4.3   Configurability

Puffy's behaviors, interaction modalities and sequence or intensity of the stimuli offered are customizable by therapists to address the evolving needs and preferences of each specific child *(R9)*. A simple control panel enables therapists to (1) assign each activity to each child; (2) setup a child's curriculum with a progressive set of levels; (3) add, remove and edit projected elements; (4) choose feedbacks and rewards such as onboard lights colors, voice, and multimedia stimuli.

5 Using Puffy in Educational or Therapeutic Contexts

Puffy can be presented as a new play companion and exploits the potential of *game-based* learning engaging children through two forms of play: free play and structured play. Both free and structured play can be performed by a single child or (preferably) in group, to enhance the social dimension of the experience *(R11.f)*.

Free Play: Free play consists of spontaneous, intrinsically motivated, unstructured tasks and has a fundamental role for the child's physical, cognitive and social development [14]. Free play with Puffy involves all interaction modes but functional touching. The children spontaneously manipulate the robot, try its physical affordances, and explore the physical space together with the robot, and the flow of stimuli is fully under children's control (with possible interplays of stimuli remotely triggered by the caregivers when needed). Free play can be used to facilitate the progressive mental and emotional states of *relaxation* [32], *affection* [2], and *engagement* [36], which are fundamental in any learning process of children with NDD and are a precondition for the execution of structured, goal oriented activities. Initially, the presence of Puffy in the playground could be potentially worrying, as children with NDD are often afraid of the unknown. They should learn that this "object" is predictable and safe, become confident that it is good, harmless, and inoffensive, and progressively achieve a state of *relaxation*, both in the relationship with the robot and towards the other children in the group. As the familiarization with the robot proceeds, children also develop the feeling of strong affective bond towards Puffy, i.e., *affection*, which facilitates a more persistent positive attitude towards the robot. Affection in turn is known to promote *engagement*, the state of active, voluntary involvement in an activity and the willingness to act upon the associated objects maintained for a relatively prolonged time.

Structured Play: Structured play is focused on the development of specific skills by executing activities that follow a predefined flow of tasks and stimuli programmed in the Puffy. The types of activities developed so far are *"Storytelling"*, *"Choice"* and *"Tag"*.

Exploiting the general learning potential of storytelling for all young children [29], stories are widely used in educational and therapeutic practices for children with NDD to stimulate imagination, curiosity, and emotional development [33, 42]. Like other SARs for NDD [23, 42], Puffy is able to narrate stories (Fig. 7). Prior to starting a storytelling, the robot attempts to establish the appropriate spatial relationship with a child by re-adjusting a suitable position that promotes a shared experience, while it continues monitoring the emotional response of a child. Puffy narrates stories by talking and projecting interactive multimedia contents on a curve-rounded screen of its belly. It can also perform movements and activate light and vibration effects to enhance the emotional effect and underline some moments or situations of the narration. In addition, Puffy can engage children during the story, e.g., asking questions (about events, characters, or places in the plot) or prompting interactions or movements, and consider children's actions and interpersonal spatial relationships to determine its own next behavior.

Choice games aim at developing the willingness and capability of making choices as well as memory skills. A game of this types starts with a projection on the robot body where multiple choices are available, then Puffy asks a question and invites children to respond by touching a projected button (Fig. 7).

Tag games aim at fostering children's movement. For example, Puffy invites the children to play together and to move in the room, and then starts chasing them (Fig. 8).

Fig. 7. Puffy telling a story   **Fig. 8.** Choice game **Fig. 9.** Tag   game
(Color figure online)

Caregivers' Role
As in any intervention for subjects with NDD, during both free and structured play with Puffy caregivers - educators or therapists are present to assist and monitor the children, and interact with them striking a balance between giving them autonomy and mediating the experience with the robot. The caregivers act as "facilitator", to suggest what to do and when to do it, as "prompt", to promote attention and concentration, and as "play companion", to share emotions, surprise, and fun. For example, they frequently talks with the children and asks (or explains) what happens to Puffy, and sometime help them also with gestures, e.g., moving a child's head or body in a specific direction when it is evident that (s)he has lost attention. The technological experience becomes an opportunity for social connection between children and caregivers, exposing subjects with NDD to verbal communication and stimulating them to "think aloud" and practice language, which are all important elements to develop appropriate social competences. Depending on children's behaviors and emotional reactions during play, may switch from autonomous to controlled mode, to trigger specific stimuli, suspend-replay a task, or activating a different one (Fig. 9).

6   Technology

An embedded board (Arduino Uno) operates as general control and communication device. The board communicates with a wheeled robotic base (iRobot iCreate) placed on the bottom of the body, six Force Sensing Resistors (FSRs) and the fan. The embedded equipment includes a mini PC, which manages most of the computational aspects of the robot behavior and is connected both with the Arduino Uno and the Microsoft Kinect Sensor placed inside the robot's head. A skeleton sustains a projector, a Philips Hue Go light and the audio speaker (Fig. 10).

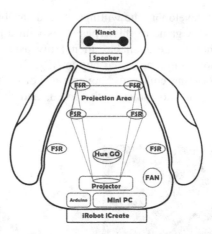

Fig. 10. Puffy technology positioned inside the inflatable structure

The FSRs are used for tangible interaction. Four FSRs enable Functional Touch and are placed at the corners of the projection area, where the user would touch Puffy in order to make choices (Tag games). Two additional FSRs, placed in a lower position (approximately aside the arms, on the left and right side of the body) are used for Physical Manipulation. Using the values coming from these sensors and the time elapsed between one value and the following one (i.e., the duration of a manipulation with the same intensity), we define a set of value ranges associated to different types of Physical Manipulation e.g., caress (low force and low-medium duration time), hug (high force and long duration time), punch or slap (medium force, low duration time), violent punch or slap (high force, low duration time). A caress is recognized as a "soft" deformation of the FSR (force intensity between 400 and 600) that lasts for about 1000 ms. A hug occurs when the deformation is approximately the double and lasts approximately 1500 ms. A slap or a punch is detected when a big deformation of the FSR (force intensity > 900) occurs in a very short time (<1000 ms). Examples of manipulations data along the time are shown in Fig. 11.

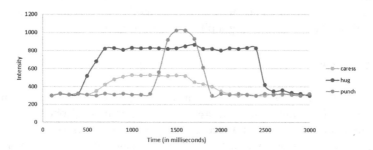

Fig. 11. Examples of children's manipulations (caress vs hug vs punch) showing the force intensity (Y axis) sensed by FSEs along the Time (X axis) in 3 different interactions with Puffy

Differently from other robotic companions employed for the care of NDD children (e.g. Teo [10]), it is Puffy in "first person" that evaluates the parameters needed to execute spatial interaction and determines its own behavior in response to children's movement, position, and orientation in space. The Microsoft Kinect placed in the robot head embeds a depth camera (which look like eyes in Puffy's face), a color camera, and an array of microphones. Depth and color cameras generate body skeleton data that are used to evaluate the following variables along the time, which are calculated for the child who is closest to the robot: relative Puffy-user position; Puffy's and user's body orientation; user's movement and direction. These variable are computed using standard Kinect technology (SDKs) as well as data coming the robot base [71, 72]. Examples of these variables are depicted in Fig. 6 - Sect. 4. In this figure, Theta_1 defines the breadth of the angle between the child's direction and the segment connecting the robot's and the child's position. Theta_2 is the breath of the angle defined by the robot's direction and the same segment. As discussed in Sect. 4.2, the values of these variables, integrated with the results of speech and image processing (see below) are used by a rule-based Behavioral Engine to decide following behavior for the robot to perform. To recognize facial expressions, we use the stream of data generated by the Kinect color and Depth cameras for the child who is closest to the robot. The image processing and facial analysis algorithms use the Kinect SDK and the EmguCV library, a cross platform. Net wrapper to the OpenCV image processing library. OpenCV (Open-source Computer Vision) was selected for its computational efficiency and its strong focus on real time applications. The Kinect microphone array capture user's speech.

The user's speech is interpreted by a Speech Analyzer module, which considers the vocal input of the child who is closest to the robot, and exploits IBM Watson technology and OpenSmile. IBM Speech-to-Text API is used to convert speech into written text. IBM Natural Language Understanding API is used to analyze this text and extract relevant meta-data (concepts, sentiment, and emotions). OpenSmile is an open-source and real-time sound feature extraction tool, which we use to automatically extract the tone and pitch of child's speech. Combining these information with the metadata, a rule-based component of the Behavioral Engine generates the textual answer that is converted in Puffy's voice using IBM Text-to-Speech API. The above process has a number of challenges, which are mainly related to group interaction. Particularly, the issue is the identification of the "closest child" and the need of filtering out his(her) data, permitting separation of this child's vocalizations and images from all other speech and other sounds that are produced within the immediate environment as well as from the images of other persons nearby. We are currently working to improve the level of accuracy reached so far.

7   Comparison

Puffy provides a unique combination of features that are important in robot-enhanced interventions for children with NDD and are seldom supported together in existing robots used in this domain. We have compared Puffy against 21 most relevant robots that, according to the existing literature, have been used in interventions for subjects with NDD: Bobus [47], CHARLIE [7], CPAC [47], DISKCAT [47], FACE [44], Infanoid [15], IROMEC [15], Jumbo [47], KASPAR [57], Keepon [22], Kismet [11], Maestro [47], Nao [30], Paro [66], Roball [47], Robota [5], SAM [19], Tega [38], Teo [10], TREVOR [15], Troy [15]. The source for our analysis has been research publications as well additional public materials e.g., web sites and online videos, which describe the design features of these robots and on-the-field case studies with NDD children. The comparison considers the main requirements discussed in Sect. 3 concerning the roles played by the robot in the interaction with children (Table 1) and the design of the body, the stimuli and the interaction (Table 2). The robots marked with a "*" have been designed since the very beginning for children with NDD (CHARLIE, DISKCAT, IROMEC, Sam, Teo, Puffy) or at least for subjects with neurological impairments (e.g., Paro). For brevity, these robots are hereinafter referred to as "specialized", while the others are called "generic". Besides offering a comparison that highlights the uniqueness of Puffy, our analysis also looks to the current state of the art from a novel perspective, shedding a light on the main design features of existing robots used in interventions for NDD children. Not surprisingly, Puffy – the design of which has been informed by the requirements stated in Sect. 3 - achieves the highest scores in both tables and is the only robot that matches all parameters.

Table 1. Comparison between robots' roles (robot names in alphabetical order)

	Feedback	Facilitator	Prompt	Emulator	Restrictor	Mediator	Affective	Emotional	TOT
Bobus	X					X			2
CHARLIE*	X			X		X	X	X	5
CPAC	X						X		2
DISKCAT*	X			X		X	X		4
FACE	X					X	X		3
Infanoid	X			X		X	X		4
IROMEC*	X	X				X			3
Jumbo	X				X		X		3
KASPAR	X		X	X		X			4
Keepon	X		X				X		3
Kismet	X						X	X	3
Maestro	X				X		X		3
Nao	X	X	X	X		X	X	X	7
Paro*	X						X	X	3
Roball	X						X		2
Robota	X			X		X			3
SAM*	X	X	X			X	X		5
Tega	X	X	X	X		X	X		6
Teo*	X	X	X	X	X	X	X		7
TREVOR	X		X						2
Troy	X					X			2
Puffy*	X	X	X	X	X	X	X	X	8
Total: 22	22	5	8	9	4	15	16	5	
	100%	23%	36%	41%	18%	68%	73%	23%	

Table 2. Comparison between design features (robot names ordered according to their ranking)

	Appearance			Multimodality					Multisensoriality						TOTALS
	Familiarity	Abstract Harmonic.Shape	Neutral Color	Physical Manipulation	Functional Touch	Spatial	Vocal	Emotional	Softness	Light	Sound	Video Anim.	Configurability	Safety and Robustness	
Infanoid								X							1
TREVOR		X													1
FACE							X	X							2
Kismet							X	X							2
Robota				X	X		X				X				4
KASPAR		X					X	X	X				X		5
Troy		X					X				X	X	X		5
Bobus		X		X	X					X	X			X	6
Jumbo	X	X		X	X						X		X		6
CPAC		X		X	X	X				X	X			X	7
Maestro		X		X	X			X		X	X			X	7
Roball		X		X	X	X				X	X			X	7
Nao			X	X	X	X	X				X		X	X	8
CHARLIE*	X	X	X	X	X					X	X			X	8
DISKCAT*	X	X	X	X	X					X	X			X	8
Keepon	X	X	X	X					X	X	X			X	8
Tega		X	X				X	X	X	X	X		X	X	9
IROMEC*		X	X		X	X	X			X	X	X	X	X	10
Paro*	X		X	X	X	X		X	X	X	X			X	10
SAM*	X	X		X	X	X	X		X	X	X	X	X	X	11
Teo*	X		X	X	X	X	X	X	X	X	X		X	X	12
Puffy*	X	X	X	X	X	X	X	X	X	X	X	X	X	X	14
Total: 22	8	14	8	13	16	7	13	12	11	10	13	4	9	13	
	36%	64%	36%	59%	73%	32%	59%	55%	50%	45%	59%	18%	41%	59%	

Concerning Table 1, all robots play as Feedback; it seems to be widely acknowledged the importance not simply of supporting interaction, i.e., providing stimuli in response to user's actions, but also of offering positive reinforcement and rewarding the children. Table 1 also shows an expected dependency between the physical capability of the robot and its roles. For example, 2 robots (Nao and Sam) meet all but one requirements, respectively Space Restrictor (Nao is static) and Emotional Agent (Teo is not equipped with emotion detection functionality). Table 1 also highlights the potential of robots to promote affection: 73% of the robots play as Affective Agent; some robots in this subset (e.g., Paro, Teo, SAM) have been explicitly designed for this role while for others (e.g. [42]) the affection power emerged only during the experimentation with the children. The second most popular role is Social Mediator (68% of the robots). This role is played by all specialized robots and also by 6 generic robots. Specialized robots are typically meant to be used by children under the supervision of the caregiver and all acknowledge that the interaction with the robot promotes also human-human interaction; still, the potential of robotic interaction to develop social skills in children with NDD seems to be achieved also by some generic robots, showing that it might be intrinsic in the robotic interaction paradigm per se.

Concerning Table 2, again the highest total scores (>7) are assigned to all specialized robots, but this top ranked set also includes some generic robots (Nao, Roball, Maestro). The most common physical feature is the abstract non-humanoid shape (64%) and the least common one is the integration with videos and animations (18%). All specialized robots but IROMEC, plus 3 generic robots, are soft, accounting to 50% of the total. The most popular paradigm of interaction is Functional touch (73%) followed by Physical Manipulation and Vocal Interaction (59%). The latter is supported by 4 out of 7 specialized robots. There is some interest in the conversational paradigm in the NDD arena, for improving language and communication skills; still, we should consider that some children with NDD might be nonverbal and could not exploit the benefits of voice-based interaction. A limited number of robots (32%) exploits spatial interaction, an interaction paradigm that is relatively new and deserves further exploration. The values of the various robots resulting from our analysis do not reflect their therapeutic or educational effectives for children with NDD and is therefore not to be interpreted as a "quality" ranking. Certainly, the design and functionalities of the robot have a significant influence in the educational and therapeutic process; still, in general we cannot state that, on the basis of our comparison, some features are more relevant than others. In addition, from our analysis we cannot draw any conclusion on how each specific design feature may influence the benefits (or limitations) for each child's experience with the robot. This is because the profound diversification of the profiles of children with NDD. Due the nature of these disorders, not all children with NDD will react exactly in the same way. Some may show more receptiveness towards some design features but discomfort to others, and with few exceptions we cannot state that some design aspects are more relevant than others. An exception is safety and robustness, which is truly a precondition for this special target and, according to our analysis, and is satisfied only by 59% of the robots (7 specialized robots and 6 generic ones). A rigorous comparative analysis of these aspect can be hardly derived from public material, and would require an in-depth systematic research through controlled empirical studies.

8 Preliminary Evaluation

8.1 Session with NDD Specialists

After the development of the first prototype, we organized a half day workshop with 10 specialists in NDD (therapists, special educators and psychologists) to collect feedbacks on our design solutions. Beside the technical team, participants included 5 caregivers who have been cooperating with our research in the last 3 years and helped us to identify the requirements stated in Sect. 3, and 10 specialists with no limited experience in robotic interaction. The workshop was organized in 3 main phases. We first presented the set of requirements that informed our design; in the focus-group like session that followed we explored participants' agreements or disagreements on each requirement. We collected a general consensus on the requirements and many highlights on the user needs underlying them, as well as examples of how the current practices address such needs, their limitations, and how a robot meeting such requirements would help. In the second phase, we then demonstrated Puffy and participants played freely with Puffy and performed all the activities reported in Sect. 4, alternating remotely controlled (first operated by the technical team, and then by themselves) and autonomous modes. In the final phase, we asked participants to fill an online questionnaire and evaluate Puffy as a whole and on each single feature, on a 4-points Likert scale, and to include comments and justifications of scores. The results were immediately available and were discussed with participants. Figure 12 reports the most salient findings.

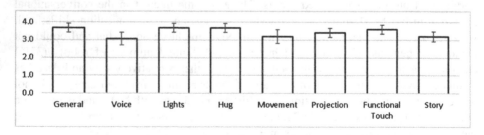

Fig. 12. Preliminary evaluation: key results of specialists' survey

8.2 Session with Children

One of the workshop participants invited us to bring Puffy at her primary school[1] and to try it with 2 children with ASD (medium-functioning, aged 7 and 9). At the school, a big thing like Puffy couldn't go unnoticed and several students enthusiastically asked to play with it. So the robot was used among the entire class of the two ASD children (19

---

[1] There are no "special education" schools in our country; children with disability attend the same school as children without disability, and are assigned to a special educator who assist them during school time.

children, average age 6). They played with the robot for approximately one hour under the supervision of the technical team, the special educator, and the regular teacher. They were initially involved in free play, and then performed one of each type of activities described in the previous sections, interacting with Puffy in turn. The observation of this very informal experimental session indicate that Puffy was perceived as pleasant and fun by the 2 children with NDD. During the experience they showed behaviors that, according to the educator, they had very seldom manifested in the past. For example, they were not afraid by "the new thing" (which would be a typical reaction of subjects with autism) and immediately perceived it as safe, good, harmless: they were invited to be the first ones to play with the robot ("Puffy is here for *you!*") and immediately accepted and started touching it. When it was not their turn of interacting, they did not leave the group as it normally happens, but payed attention to the other peer' action and Puffy's reactions. For all children, Puffy acted as an extraordinary catalyzer of attention and a source of fun. Many children, leaving the session room and saying "Hello" to the robot also asked it to come back again soon.

8.3   Discussion

Concerning the session with specialists, the survey results show a general agreement of the potential of Puffy for children with NDD (as witnesses by the "General" bar in Fig. 12). All participants declared that they would include Puffy in their therapeutic treatment.

Figure 12 shows that the light stimuli are a design feature that specialist consider as particularly promising; many of them declared that the soft lights of Puffy have the power of attracting the children as well as to relax them. The most appreciated interaction mode is tangible interaction, particularly hugging. The unique hugging characteristic of Puffy originate from its big inflatable body, and the above result suggests that inflatable shapes deserves further investigation in the NDD arena. Voice features had the lowest score; according to specialists, Puffy does not hold the capability of automatically creating conversation which are appropriate for children with NDD, who often have a weak vocabulary and make many errors. This comment was somehow expected, as our speech engine use standard speech interpretation mechanisms which are not trained to the characteristics of this target group. Among the qualitative comments reported in the survey, some offered interesting insights on risks. Some specialists observed that that in order to become a reliable element in a therapeutic or educational program, it's important that Puffy has not only attractive features but also enables mechanisms for *avoiding* or *mitigating* the emergence of undesirable situations, e.g., a child's "negative" reaction such as aggressively or stereotypes, supporting not only physical safety (of the robot and the children) but also psychological and social harmless. This problem deserves further multidisciplinary research. Addressing it requires an accurate case analysis, grounded on the current practice and on an extensive experimentation of Puffy, and would lead to the design of adaptation mechanisms in the robot behavior that are beyond the current state of the art in adaptive robotics.

In spite of its brevity and informal nature, also the session at the school supports the hypothesis that Puffy has a good potential for children with NDD. The experience also suggests that this robot might be appropriate not only in the contexts for which it was originally conceived (therapeutic centers) but also in regular schools, and for children with and without disability. This new scenario would require a further analysis to extend the set of activities currently designed for Puffy, in order to address the characteristics of broader targets and contexts. To explore the potential of Puffy also from this perspective, we are currently conducting an exploratory study at a local pre-school involving 79 children (aged 3-5) and their 15 teachers.

A final observation concerns the "fun" nature of Puffy, which at school was enhanced by some unpredictable events during remotely controlled interactions. Caregivers triggered by mistake a number of "crazy" behaviors, which were totally inconsistent with the current interaction context, but particularly funny for all children, including those with ASD. Enforcing behavioral consistency, predictability and repeatability is a fundamental requirement in the design of socially assistive robots for NDD; still, serendipity, unpredictability, and surprise could be design concepts worth to explore in relationship of this target group.

9   Conclusions

Our work offers an original contribution to the design of social robots for children with severe and multiple disability in the cognitive and social sphere. Puffy supports learning through play taking into account the specific characteristics and needs of this target group and is the first example of assistive robot that use inflatable materials.

Puffy exemplifies how different interaction paradigms (spatial, emotional, and tangible interaction), physical features (mobility, inflatable body, from-inside multimedia projections) and multisensory stimuli can be combined and orchestrated to create a novel robotic companion robot for children with NDD. The design of Puffy was informed by a set of requirements that distill the main results of the current state of the art in this field as well, the knowledge of a team of NDD specialists that are collaborating in our research, and the experience gained in the last 10 years in the development of assistive technology for children with NDD. These requirements can be regarded as design guidelines that can benefit researchers and developers in social assistive robotics in this domain. On the basis of these guidelines, we have provided a systematic comparison between Puffy and 21 existing robots that have been used with children in the NDD spectrum. This analysis offers a novel perspective on the current state of the art in assistive robotics for this target group. We performed two preliminary exploratory sessions with Puffy – a focus group with specialists and an activity at a primary school – which offered encouraging results. Still, Puffy has not yet been evaluated in a systematic field study, which is one of the next steps in our research agenda. Additional future actions include the improvement of the design and implementation of Puffy according to the suggestions emerged during the workshop with the specialists, particularly those related to the need of adaptation mechanism to face critical situation of children's distress or misbehavior, and improvements of the vocal interaction capability.

Acknowledgment. Thanks to all teachers, specialists and children from "Via Gallina" and "Munari" kindergarten schools, "Fraternità e Amicizia" and "L'abilità" therapeutic centers.

References

1. American Psychiatric Association: DSM 5. American Psychiatric Association (2013)
2. Bauminger, N.: The facilitation of social-emotional understanding and social interaction in high-functioning children with autism: Intervention outcomes. J. Autism Dev. Disord. **32**(4), 283–298 (2002)
3. Belpaeme, T., Baxter, P.E., Read, R., Wood, R., Cuayáhuitl, H., Kiefer, B., Racioppa, S., Kruijff-Korbayová, I., Athanasopoulos, G., Enescu, V., Looije, R.: Multimodal child-robot interaction: Building social bonds. J. Hum.-Rob. Interact. **1**, 33–53 (2012)
4. Best, C.M., Wilson, J.P., Killpack, M.D.: Control of a pneumatically actuated, fully inflatable, fabric-based, humanoid robot. In: 2015 IEEE-RAS 15th International Conference on Humanoid Robots (Humanoids), pp. 1133–1140. IEEE (2015)
5. Billard, A., Robins, B., Nadel, J., Dautenhahn, K.: Building robota, a mini-humanoid robot for the rehabilitation of children with autism. Assist. Technol. **19**, 37–49 (2007)
6. Bird, G., Leighton, J., Press, C., Heyes, C.: Intact automatic imitation of human and robot actions in autism spectrum disorders. Proc. R. Soc. Lond. B Biol. Sci. **274**(1628), 3027–3031 (2007)
7. Boccanfuso, L., O'Kane, J.M.: CHARLIE: an adaptive robot design with hand and face tracking for use in autism therapy. Int. J. Soc. Rob. **3**, 337–347 (2011)
8. Bonarini, A.: Can my robotic home cleaner be happy? Issues about emotional expression in non-bio-inspired robots. Adapt. Behav. **24**(5), 335–349 (2016)
9. Bonarini, A., Clasadonte, F., Garzotto, F., Gelsomini, M.: Blending robots and full-body interaction with large screens for children with intellectual disability. In: Proceedings of the 14th International Conference on Interaction Design and Children, pp. 351–354. ACM 2015
10. Bonarini, A., Garzotto, F., Gelsomini, M., Romero, M., Clasadonte, F., Yilmaz, A.N.Ç.: A huggable, mobile robot for developmental disorder interventions in a multi-modal interaction space. In: 2016 25th IEEE International Symposium on Robot and Human Interactive Communication (RO-MAN), pp. 823–830. IEEE (2016)
11. Breazeal, C., Scassellati, B.: A context-dependent attention system for a social robot, rn. 255, p. 3 (1999)
12. Breazeal, C.: A motivational system for regulating human-robot interaction. In: AAAI/IAAI, pp. 54–61 (1998)
13. Brodin, J.: Play in children with severe multiple disabilities: play with toys-a review. Int. J. Disabil. Dev. Educ. **46**(1), 25–34 (1999)
14. Bruner, J.S., Jolly, A., Sylva, K.: Play: its role in development and evolution. J. Pers. Assess. (1976)
15. Cabibihan, J.J., Javed, H., Ang, M., Aljunied, S.M.: Why robots? A survey on the roles and benefits of social robots in the therapy of children with autism. Int. J. Soc. Rob. **5**(4), 593–618 (2013)
16. Chella, A., Barone, R.E., Pilato, G., Sorbello, R.: An emotional storyteller robot. In: AAAI Spring Symposium: Emotion, Personality, and Social Behavior, pp. 17–22 (2008)
17. Ciolek, T.M., Kendon, A.: Environment and the spatial arrangement of conversational encounters. Sociol. Inquiry **50**(3–4), 237–271 (1980)
18. Clark, T., Feehan, C., Tinline, C., Vostanis, P.: Autistic symptoms in children with attention deficit-hyperactivity disorder. Eur. Child Adolesc. Psychiatry **8**, 50–55 (1999)
19. Colombo, S., Garzotto, F., Gelsomini, M., Melli, M., Clasadonte, F.: Dolphin sam: a smart pet for children with intellectual disability. In: Proceedings of the International Working Conference on Advanced Visual Interfaces, pp. 352–353. ACM (2016)

20. Dautenhahn, K., Werry, I.: Towards interactive robots in autism therapy: background, motivation and challenges. Pragmat. Cogn. **12**(1), 1–35 (2004)

21. Dautenhahn, K., Werry, I., Salter, T., Boekhorst, R.T.: Towards adaptive autonomous robots in autism therapy: varieties of interactions. In: 2003 IEEE International Symposium on Computational Intelligence in Robotics and Automation, vol. 2, pp. 577–582. IEEE (2003)

22. Den Brok, W.L.J.E., Sterkenburg, P.S.: Self-controlled technologies to support skill attainment in persons with an autism spectrum disorder and/or an intellectual disability: a systematic literature review. Disabil. Rehabil.: Assist. Technol. **10**, 1–10 (2015)

23. Diehl, J.J., Schmitt, L.M., Villano, M., Crowell, C.R.: The clinical use of robots for individuals with autism spectrum disorders: a critical review. Res. Autism Spectr. Disord. **6**(1), 249–262 (2012)

24. Dunst, C.J., Hamby, D.W., Trivette, C.M., Prior, J., Derryberry, G.: Vocal production of young children with disabilities during child-robot interactions. Social Robots Research Reports, Number 5. Orelena Hawks Puckett Institute (2013)

25. Feil-Seifer, D., Matarić, M.J.: Socially assistive robotics. IEEE Rob. Autom. Mag. **18**(1), 24–31 (2011)

26. Ferrara, C., Hill, S.D.: The responsiveness of autistic children to the predictability of social and nonsocial toys. J. Autism Dev. Disord. **10**, 51–57 (1980)

27. Ferrari, E., Robins, B., Dautenhahn, K.: Therapeutic and educational objectives in robot assisted play for children with autism. In: The 18th IEEE International Symposium on Robot and Human Interactive Communication, RO-MAN 2009, pp. 108–114. IEEE (2009)

28. Garzotto, F., Bordogna, M.: Paper-based multimedia interaction as learning tool for disabled children. In: Proceedings of the 9th International Conference on Interaction Design and Children, pp. 79–88. ACM (2010)

29. Garzotto, F.: Interactive storytelling for children: a survey. Int. J. Arts Technol. **7**(1), 5–16 (2014)

30. Gillesen, J.C., Barakova, E.I., Huskens, B.E., Feijs, L.M.: From training to robot behavior: towards custom scenarios for robotics in training programs for ASD. In: 2011 IEEE International Conference on Rehabilitation Robotics (ICORR), pp. 1–7. IEEE (2011)

31. Giullian, N., Ricks, D., Atherton, A., Colton, M., Goodrich, M., Brinton, B.: Detailed requirements for robots in autism therapy. In: 2010 IEEE International Conference on Systems Man and Cybernetics (SMC), pp. 2595–2602. IEEE (2010)

32. Groden, J., Cautela, J., Prince, S., Berryman, J.: The impact of stress and anxiety on individuals with autism and developmental disabilities. In: Schopler, E., Mesibov, G.B. (eds.) Behavioral Issues in Autism, pp. 177–194. Springer, Boston (1994). doi:10.1007/978-1-4757-9400-7_9

33. Grove, N.: Using Storytelling to Support Children and Adults with Special Needs: Transforming Lives Through Telling Tales. Routledge, Abingdon (2012)

34. Hall, E.T.: The Hidden Dimension (1966)

35. Hoa, T.D., Cabibihan, J.J.: Cute and soft: baby steps in designing robots for children with autism. In: Proceedings of the Workshop at SIGGRAPH Asia, pp. 77–79. ACM (2012)

36. Kasari, C., Gulsrud, A.C., Wong, C., Kwon, S., Locke, J.: Randomized controlled caregiver mediated joint engagement intervention for toddlers with autism. J. Autism Dev. Disord. **40**(9), 1045–1056 (2010)

37. Kinoe, Y., Mizuno, N.: Dynamic characteristics of the transformation of interpersonal distance in cooperation. In: Zhou, J., Salvendy, G. (eds.) ITAP 2016. LNCS, vol. 9755, pp. 26–34. Springer, Cham (2016). doi:10.1007/978-3-319-39949-2_3

38. Kory Westlund, J., Lee, J.J., Plummer, L., Faridi, F., Gray, J., Berlin, M., Quintus-Bosz, H., Hartmann, R., Hess, M., Dyer, S., Dos Santos, K.: Tega: a social robot. In: The Eleventh ACM/IEEE International Conference on Human Robot Interaction, p. 561. IEEE Press (2016)
39. Kozima, H., Michalowski, M.P., Nakagawa, C.: Keepon. Int. J. Soc. Rob. 1(1), 3–18 (2009)
40. Kozima, H., Nakagawa, C., Yasuda, Y.: Children–robot interaction: a pilot study in autism therapy. Prog. Brain Res. 164, 385–400 (2007)
41. Kuypers, L.: The Zones of Regulation. Think Social Publishing, San Jose (2011)
42. Park, H.W., Gelsomini, M., Lee, J.J., Breazeal, C.: Telling stories to robots: the effect of backchanneling on a child's storytelling. In: Proceedings of the 2017 ACM/IEEE International Conference on Human-Robot Interaction, pp. 100–108. ACM (2017)
43. Majidi, C.: Soft robotics: a perspective—current trends and prospects for the future. Soft Rob. 1(1), 5–11 (2014)
44. Mazzei, D., Billeci, L., Armato, A., Lazzeri, N., Cisternino, A., Pioggia, G., Igliozzi, R., Muratori, F., Ahluwalia, A., De Rossi, D.: The face of autism. In: RO-MAN, pp. 791–796. IEEE (2010)
45. Mead, R., Matarić, M.J.: Perceptual models of human-robot proxemics. In: Hsieh, M.A., Khatib, O., Kumar, V. (eds.) Experimental Robotics. STAR, vol. 109, pp. 261–276. Springer, Cham (2016). doi:10.1007/978-3-319-23778-7_18
46. Mehrabian, A.: Nonverbal Communication. Transaction Publishers, Piscataway (1972)
47. Michaud, F., Duquette, A., Nadeau, I.: Characteristics of mobile robotic toys for children with pervasive developmental disorders. In: IEEE International Conference on Systems, Man and Cybernetics, vol. 3, pp. 2938–2943. IEEE (2003)
48. Mori, M., MacDorman, K.F., Kageki, N.: The uncanny valley [from the field]. IEEE Rob. Autom. Mag. 19(2), 98–100 (2012)
49. Mumm, J., Mutlu, B.: Human-robot proxemics: physical and psychological distancing in human-robot interaction. In: Proceedings of the 6th International Conference on Human-Robot Interaction, pp. 331–338. ACM (2011)
50. Phillips, B., Zhao, H.: Predictors of assistive technology abandonment. Assist. Technol. 5(1), 36–45 (1993)
51. Pierno, A.C., Mari, M., Lusher, D., Castiello, U.: Robotic movement elicits visuomotor priming in children with autism. Neuropsychologia 46(2), 448–454 (2008)
52. Qi, R., Lam, T.L., Xu, Y.: Mechanical design and implementation of a soft inflatable robot arm for safe human-robot interaction. In: 2014 IEEE International Conference on Robotics and Automation (ICRA), pp. 3490–3495. IEEE (2014)
53. Rabbitt, S.M., Kazdin, A.E., Scassellati, B.: Integrating socially assistive robotics into mental healthcare interventions: applications and recommendations for expanded use. Clin. Psychol. Rev. 35, 35–46 (2015)
54. Ricks, D.J., Colton, M.B.: Trends and considerations in robot-assisted autism therapy. In: 2010 IEEE International Conference on Robotics and Automation (ICRA), pp. 4354–4359. IEEE (2010)
55. Rios-Martinez, J., Spalanzani, A., Laugier, C.: From proxemics theory to socially-aware navigation: A survey. Int. J. Soc. Rob. 7(2), 137–153 (2015)
56. Robins, B., Amirabdollahian, F., Dautenhahn, K.: Investigating child-robot tactile interactions: a taxonomical classification of tactile behaviour of children with autism towards a humanoid robot. In: The Sixth International Conference on Advances in Computer-Human Interactions (ACHI), pp. 89–94 (2013)
57. Robins, B., Dautenhahn, K., Dickerson, P.: From isolation to communication: a case study evaluation of robot assisted play for children with autism with a minimally expressive humanoid robot. In: Second International Conferences on Advances in Computer-Human Interactions, ACHI 2009, pp. 205–211. IEEE (2009)

58. Robins, B., Dautenhahn, K., Dubowski, J.: Does appearance matter in the interaction of children with autism with a humanoid robot? Interact. Stud. **7**(3), 509–542 (2006)

59. Robins, B., Dautenhahn, K., Ferrari, E., Kronreif, G., Prazak-Aram, B., Marti, P., Iacono, I., Gelderblom, G.J., Bernd, T., Caprino, F., Laudanna, E.: Scenarios of robot-assisted play for children with cognitive and physical disabilities. Interact. Stud. **13**, 189–234 (2012)

60. Robins, B., Dautenhahn, K., Te Boekhorst, R., Billard, A.: Robotic assistants in therapy and education of children with autism: can a small humanoid robot help encourage social interaction skills? Univ. Access Inf. Soc. **4**(2), 105–120 (2005)

61. Robins, B., Otero, N., Ferrari, E., Dautenhahn, K.: Eliciting requirements for a robotic toy for children with autism-results from user panels. In: The 16th IEEE International Symposium on Robot and Human Interactive Communication, RO-MAN 2007, pp. 101–106. IEEE (2007)

62. Rommelse, N.N., Franke, B., Geurts, H.M., Hartman, C.A., Buitelaar, J.K.: Shared heritability of attention-deficit/hyperactivity disorder and autism spectrum disorder. Eur. Child Adolesc. Psychiatry **19**(3), 281–295 (2010)

63. Salter, T., Davey, N., Michaud, F.: Designing & developing QueBall, a robotic device for autism therapy. In: 2014 RO-MAN: The 23rd IEEE International Symposium on Robot and Human Interactive Communication, pp. 574–579. IEEE (2014)

64. Scassellati, B., Admoni, H., Matarić, M.: Robots for use in autism research. Ann. Rev. Biomed. Eng. **14**, 275–294 (2012)

65. Shamsuddin, S., Yussof, H., Ismail, L., Hanapiah, F.A., Mohamed, S., Piah, H.A., Zahari, N. I.: Initial response of autistic children in human-robot interaction therapy with humanoid robot NAO. In: 2012 IEEE 8th International Colloquium on Signal Processing and its Applications (CSPA), pp. 188–193. IEEE (2012)

66. Shibata, T., Mitsui, T., Wada, K., Tanie, K.: Subjective evaluation of seal robot: paro-tabulation and analysis of questionnaire results. J. Rob. Mechatron. **14**(1), 13–19 (2002)

67. Short, E., Swift-Spong, K., Greczek, J., Ramachandran, A., Litoiu, A., Grigore, E.C., Feil-Seifer, D., Shuster, S., Lee, J.J., Huang, S., Levonisova, S.: How to train your dragonbot: socially assistive robots for teaching children about nutrition through play. In: 2014 RO-MAN: The 23rd IEEE International Symposium on Robot and Human Interactive Communication, pp. 924–929. IEEE (2014)

68. Stiehl, W.D., Lieberman, J., Breazeal, C., Basel, L., Lalla, L., Wolf, M.: Design of a therapeutic robotic companion for relational, affective touch. In: IEEE International Workshop on Robot and Human Interactive Communication, ROMAN 2005, pp. 408–415. IEEE (2005)

69. Voisembert, S., Riwan, A., Mechbal, N., Barraco, A.: A novel inflatable robot with constant and continuous volume. In: 2011 IEEE International Conference on Robotics and Automation (ICRA), pp. 5843–5848. IEEE (2011)

70. Wilson, M.: Six views of embodied cognition. Psychon. Bull. Rev. **9**, 625–636 (2002)

71. Valoriani, M., Bartoli, L., Garzotto, F., Gelsomini, M., Oliveto, L.: Designing and evaluating touchless playful interaction for ASD children. In: Proceedings of the 2014 Conference on Interaction Design and Children (IDC 2014), pp. 17–26. ACM, New York (2014)

72. Valoriani, M., Bartoli, L., Corradi, C., Garzotto, F.: Motion-based touchless interaction for autistic children's learning. In: Proceedings of the ACM Interaction Design and Children (IDC), pp. 53–44 (2013)

Author Index